Financial Risk Manager
Handbook
Third Edition

Financial Risk Manager
Handbook
Third Edition

Philippe Jorion

GARP

WILEY

John Wiley & Sons, Inc.

Published by John Wiley & Sons, Inc., Hoboken, New Jersey.
Published simultaneously in Canada.

For general information about our other products and services, please contact our Customer Care Department within the United States at 800-762-2974, outside the United States at 317-572-3993 or fax 317-572-4002.

Wiley also publishes its books in a variety of electronic formats. Some content that appears in print may not be available in electronic books. For more information about Wiley products, visit our web site at www.wiley.com.

Library of Congress Cataloging-in-Publication Data:

ISBN-13 978-0-471-70629-8

ISBN-10 0-471-70629-9

Printed in the United States of America

10 9 8 7 6 5 4 3 2 1

About the Author

Philippe Jorion is a Professor of Finance at the Graduate School of Management at the University of California at Irvine. He has also taught at Columbia University, Northwestern University, the University of Chicago, and the University of British Columbia. He holds an M.B.A. and a Ph.D. from the University of Chicago and a degree in engineering from the University of Brussels.

Dr. Jorion has authored more than 80 publications directed at academics and practitioners on the topics of risk management and international finance. Dr. Jorion has also written a number of books, including *Big Bets Gone Bad: Derivatives and Bankruptcy in Orange County*, the first account of the largest municipal failure in U.S. history, and *Value at Risk: The New Benchmark for Managing Financial Risk*, which is aimed at finance practitioners and has become an "industry standard."

Philippe Jorion is a frequent speaker at academic and professional conferences. He is on the editorial board of a number of finance journals and is editor in chief of the *Journal of Risk*.

About GARP

The **Global Association of Risk Professionals** (GARP) was established in 1996. A not-for-profit independent association of financial risk management practitioners, its members represent banks, investment management firms, government regulatory bodies, academic institutions, corporations and other financial organizations.

In just 9 years GARP's global membership has expanded to over 40,000 individuals from over 135 countries around the world.

GARP's mission is to be the leading professional association for financial risk managers, managed by and for its members and dedicated to the advancement of the risk profession through education, training and the promotion of best practices globally.

In fulfillment of its mission, GARP offers the Financial Risk Manager (FRM®) program, the world's leading certification program for a professional financial risk manager. With over 6,500 FRM holders around the world, the FRM designation is considered the benchmark for financial risk managers globally.

In early 2005 GARP organized the GARP Risk Academy™ to deliver a certificate and diploma program in risk-based regulation and other in-depth training courses to its global membership. The Risk Academy's offerings are designed to instill at all levels within an organization a culture of risk awareness.

For further information about GARP, the FRM exam and the GARP Risk Academy, go to GARP's website at *www.garp.com.*

Contents

Part IV: Investment and Risk Management   389

Part V: Credit Risk Management   431

Preface

The FRM Handbook provides the core body of knowledge for financial risk managers. Risk management has rapidly evolved over the last decade and has become an indispensable function in many institutions.

This Handbook was originally written to provide support for candidates taking the FRM examination administered by GARP. As such, it reviews a wide variety of practical topics in a consistent and systematic fashion. It covers quantitative methods and capital markets, as well as market, credit, operational, and integrated risk management. It also discusses regulatory, legal, and accounting issues essential to risk professionals.

This edition has been thoroughly updated. It includes the latest revisions to the Basel Accord, in addition to recent accounting developments. Because risk management has become a pervasive function of investment managers, a new section has been added that deals with investment risk management. Within this section, a new chapter discusses risk management practices for the hedge fund industry, which now exceeds $1 trillion in assets.

Modern risk management systems cut across the entire organization. This breadth is reflected in the subjects covered in this Handbook. This Handbook was designed to be self-contained, but only for readers who already have some exposure to financial markets. To reap maximum benefit from this book, the reader should have taken the equivalent of an MBA-level class on investments.

Finally, I want to acknowledge the help received in the writing of this latest edition. In particular, I would like to thank the numerous readers who shared comments on the previous edition. Any comments and suggestions for improvement are welcome. This feedback will help us to maintain the high quality of the FRM designation.

Philippe Jorion
March 2005

Introduction

GARP's formal mission is to be the leading professional association for financial risk managers, managed by and for its members and dedicated to the advancement of the risk profession through education, training, and the promotion of best practices globally. As a part of delivering on that mission, GARP, along with Philippe Jorion, authors the *Financial Risk Manager Handbook*.

The Handbook follows GARP's FRM Committee's published FRM Study Guide. Over the years the Study Guide has taken on an importance far exceeding its initial intent of providing guidance for FRM candidates. The Study Guide is now being used by universities, educators, and executives around the world to develop graduate-level business and finance courses, as a reference list for purchasing new readings for personal and professional libraries, as an objective and studied outline to assess an employee's or job applicant's risk management qualifications, and as guidance on the important trends currently affecting the financial risk management profession.

Given the expanded and dramatically growing recognition of the financial risk management professional globally, the Handbook has, like the Study Guide, assumed a natural and advanced role beyond its original purpose. It has now become the primary reference manual for risk professionals, academics, and executives around the world.

Professional risk managers must be well versed in any number of risk-related concepts and theories, and must also keep themselves up-to-date with a rapidly changing marketplace. This Handbook is designed to allow them to do just that. It provides a financial risk management practitioner with the latest thinking and approaches to financial risk related issues. It also provides coverage of advanced topics with questions and tutorials to enhance the reader's learning experience.

This Third Edition of the Handbook includes coverage of the newly added section to the FRM examination, Risk Management in Investment Management, and updates the past editions' materials relating to quantitative methods; capital markets; market, credit, and operational risk; and general legal, accounting, and regulatory issues.

The Handbook continues to keep pace with the dynamic financial risk profession while simultaneously offering to serious risk professionals an excellent and cost-effective tool to keep abreast of the latest issues affecting the global risk management community.

Developing credibility and global acceptance for a professional certification program is a lengthy and complicated process. When GARP first administered its FRM exam eight years ago and certified the first of its current 6,500+ FRM holders, the concept of a professional risk manager and a global certification relating to that person's skill set, much less the responsibilities of such an individual within an organization, was more theory than reality. That has now all changed.

The FRM is now the benchmark for a financial risk manager anywhere around the world. Professional risk managers having earned the FRM credential are now globally recognized as having achieved a level of professional competency and a demonstrated ability to dynamically measure and manage financial risk in a real-world setting in accordance with global standards.

GARP is proud to continue to make this Handbook available to financial risk professionals around the world. Philippe Jorion, a preeminent risk professional, has again compiled an exceptional reference book. Supplemented by an interactive test question CD, this Handbook is a requirement for any risk professional's library.

Global Association of Risk Professionals
March 2005

Financial Risk Manager
Handbook
Third Edition

Quantitative Analysis

Chapter 1

Bond Fundamentals

Risk management starts with the pricing of assets. The simplest assets to study are regular, fixed-coupon bonds. Because their cash flows are predetermined, we can translate their stream of cash flows into a present value by discounting at a fixed yield. Thus the valuation of bonds involves understanding compounded interest, discounting, and the relationship between present values and interest rates.

Risk management goes one step further than pricing, however. It examines potential changes in the price of an asset as the interest rate changes. In this chapter, we assume that there is a single interest rate, or yield, that is used to price the bond. This will be our fundamental risk factor. This chapter describes the relationship between bond prices and yield and presents indispensable tools for the management of fixed-income portfolios.

This chapter starts our coverage of quantitative analysis by discussing bond fundamentals. Section 1.1 reviews the concepts of discounting, present values, and future values. Section 1.2 then plunges into the price-yield relationship. It shows how the Taylor expansion rule can be used to relate movements in bond prices to those in yields. The Taylor expansion rule, however, covers much more than bonds. It is a building block of risk measurement methods based on local valuation, as we shall see later. Section 1.3 then presents an economic interpretation of duration and convexity.

The reader should be forewarned that this chapter, like many others in this handbook, is rather compact. This chapter provides a quick review of bond fundamentals with particular attention to risk measurement applications. By the end of this chapter, however, the reader should be able to answer advanced FRM questions on bond mathematics.

1.1 Discounting, Present Value, and Future Value

An investor considers a zero-coupon bond that pays $100 in 10 years. Say that the investment is guaranteed by the U.S. government and has no default risk. Because the payment occurs at a future date, the current value of the investment is surely less than an up-front payment of $100.

To value the payment, we need a **discounting factor**. This is also the **interest rate**, or more simply the **yield**. Define C_t as the cash flow at time t and the discounting factor as y. We define T as the number of periods until maturity (e.g., number of years), also known as the **tenor**. The **present value** (PV) of the bond can be computed as

$$PV = \frac{C_T}{(1 + y)^T} \qquad (1.1)$$

For instance, a payment of $C_T = \$100$ in 10 years discounted at 6% is worth only $55.84 now. So, all else fixed, the market value of a zero-coupon bond decreases with longer maturities. Also, keeping T fixed, the value of the bond decreases as the yield increases.

Conversely, we can compute the **future value** (FV) of the bond as

$$FV = PV \times (1 + y)^T \qquad (1.2)$$

For instance, an investment now worth $PV = \$100$ growing at 6% will have a future value of $FV = \$179.08$ in 10 years.

Here, the yield has a useful interpretation, which is that of an **internal rate of return** on the bond, or annual growth rate. It is easier to deal with rates of returns than with dollar values. Rates of return, when expressed in percentage terms and on an annual basis, are directly comparable across assets. An annualized yield is sometimes defined as the **effective annual rate (EAR)**.

It is important to note that the interest rate should be stated along with the method used for compounding. Annual compounding is very common. Other conventions exist, however. For instance, the U.S. Treasury market uses semiannual compounding. Define in this case y^S as the rate based on semiannual compounding. To maintain comparability, it is expressed in annualized form, that is, after multiplication by 2. The number of periods, or semesters, is now $2T$. The formula for finding y^S is

$$PV = \frac{C_T}{(1 + y^S/2)^{2T}} \qquad (1.3)$$

For instance, a Treasury zero-coupon bond with a maturity of $T = 10$ years would have $2T = 20$ semiannual compounding periods. Comparing with (1.1), we see that

$$(1 + y) = (1 + y^S/2)^2 \qquad (1.4)$$

Continuous compounding is often used in modeling derivatives. It is the limit of the case where the number of compounding periods per year increases to infinity. The continuously compounded interest rate y^C is derived from

$$PV = C_T \times e^{-y^C T} \qquad (1.5)$$

where $e^{(\cdot)}$, sometimes noted as $\exp(\cdot)$, represents the exponential function.

Note that in Equations (1.1), (1.3), and (1.5), the present values and future cash flows are identical. Because of different compounding periods, however, the yields will differ. Hence, the compounding period should always be stated.

Example: Using different discounting methods

Consider a bond that pays $100 in 10 years and has a present value of $55.8395. This corresponds to an annually compounded rate of 6.00% using $PV = C_T/(1 + y)^{10}$, or $(1 + y) = (C_T/PV)^{1/10}$.

This rate can be transformed into a semiannual compounded rate, using $(1 + y^S/2)^2 = (1 + y)$, or $y^S/2 = (1 + y)^{1/2} - 1$, or $y^S = ((1 + 0.06)^{(1/2)} - 1) \times 2 = 0.0591 = 5.91\%$. It can be also transformed into a continuously compounded rate, using $\exp(y^C) = (1 + y)$, or $y^C = \ln(1 + 0.06) = 0.0583 = 5.83\%$.

Note that as we increase the frequency of the compounding, the resulting rate decreases. Intuitively, because our money works harder with more frequent compounding, a lower investment rate will achieve the same payoff at the end.

Key concept:
For fixed present value and cash flows, increasing the frequency of the compounding will decrease the associated yield.

Example 1-1: FRM Exam 2002—Question 48
An investor buys a Treasury bill maturing in 1 month for $987. On the maturity date the investor collects $1,000. Calculate effective annual rate (EAR).
a) 17.0%
b) 15.8%
c) 13.0%
d) 11.6%

Example 1-2: FRM Exam 2002—Question 51

Consider a savings account that pays an annual interest rate of 8%. Calculate the amount of time it would take to double your money. Round to the nearest year.

a) 7 years
b) 8 years
c) 9 years
d) 10 years

Example 1-3: FRM Exam 1999—Question 17

Assume a semiannual compounded rate of 8% per annum. What is the equivalent annually compounded rate?

a) 9.20%
b) 8.16%
c) 7.45%
d) 8.00%

1.2   Price-Yield Relationship

1.2.1   Valuation

The fundamental discounting relationship from Equation (1.1) can be extended to any bond with a fixed cash-flow pattern. We can write the present value of a bond P as the discounted value of future cash flows:

$$P = \sum_{t=1}^{T} \frac{C_t}{(1+y)^t} \tag{1.6}$$

where

C_t = cash flow (coupon or principal) in period t

t = number of periods (e.g., half-years) to each payment

T = number of periods to final maturity

y = discounting factor per period (e.g., $y^S/2$)

A typical cash-flow pattern consists of a fixed coupon payment plus the repayment of the principal, or **face value** at expiration. Define c as the coupon *rate* and F as the face value. We have $C_t = cF$ prior to expiration, and at expiration, we have $C_T = cF + F$. The appendix reviews useful formulas that provide closed-form solutions for such bonds.

When the coupon rate c precisely matches the yield y, using the same compounding frequency, the present value of the bond must be equal to the face value. The bond is said to be a **par bond**.

Equation (1.6) describes the relationship between the yield y and the value of the bond P, given its cash-flow characteristics. In other words, the value P can also be written as a nonlinear function of the yield y:

$$P = f(y) \tag{1.7}$$

Conversely, we can set P to the current market price of the bond, including any accrued interest. From this, we can compute the "implied" yield that will solve this equation.

Figure 1-1 describes the price-yield function for a 10-year bond with a 6% annual coupon. In risk management terms, this is also the relationship between the payoff on the asset and the risk factor. At a yield of 6%, the price is at par, $P = \$100$. Higher yields imply lower prices.

FIGURE 1-1 Price-Yield Relationship

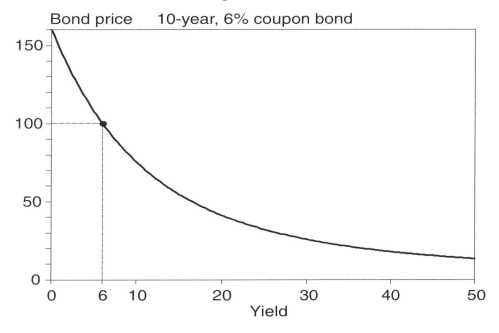

Over a wide range of yield values, this is a highly nonlinear relationship. For instance, when the yield is zero, the value of the bond is simply the sum of cash flows, or $160 in this case. When the yield tends to vary large values, the bond price tends to zero. For small movements around the initial yield of 6%, however, the relationship is quasi-linear.

There is a particularly simple relationship for **consols**, or **perpetual bonds**, which are bonds making regular coupon payments but with no redemption date. For a consol, the maturity is infinite and the cash flows are all equal to a fixed percentage of the face value, $C_t = C = cF$. As a result, the price can be simplified from Equation (1.6) to

$$P = cF \left[\frac{1}{(1+y)} + \frac{1}{(1+y)^2} + \frac{1}{(1+y)^3} + \cdots \right] = \frac{c}{y}F \qquad (1.8)$$

as shown in the appendix. In this case, the price is simply proportional to the inverse of the yield. Higher yields lead to lower bond prices, and vice versa.

Example: Valuing a bond

Consider a bond that pays $100 in 10 years and a 6% annual coupon. Assume that the next coupon payment is in exactly one year. What is the market value if the yield is 6%? If it falls to 5%?

The bond cash flows are $C_1 = \$6, C_2 = \$6, \ldots, C_{10} = \$106$. Using Equation (1.6) and discounting at 6%, this gives the present values of cash flows of $5.66, $5.34, $\ldots$, $59.19, for a total of $100.00. The bond is selling at par. This is logical because the coupon is equal to the yield, which is also annually compounded. Alternatively, discounting at 5% leads to a price of $107.72.

Example 1-4: FRM Exam 1998—Question 12

A fixed-rate bond, currently priced at 102.9, has one year remaining to maturity and is paying an 8% coupon. Assuming the coupon is paid semiannually, what is the yield of the bond?

a) 8%
b) 7%
c) 6%
d) 5%

1.2.2   Taylor Expansion

Let us say that we want to see what happens to the price if the yield changes from its initial value, called y_0, to a new value, $y_1 = y_0 + \Delta y$. Risk management is all about assessing the effect of changes in risk factors such as yields on asset values. Are there shortcuts to help us with this?

We could recompute the new value of the bond as $P_1 = f(y_1)$. If the change is not too large, however, we can apply a very useful shortcut. The nonlinear relationship can be approximated by a **Taylor expansion** around its initial value:[1]

$$P_1 = P_0 + f'(y_0)\Delta y + \frac{1}{2}f''(y_0)(\Delta y)^2 + \cdots \qquad (1.9)$$

where $f'(\cdot) = \frac{dP}{dy}$ is the first derivative and $f''(\cdot) = \frac{d^2 P}{dy^2}$ is the second derivative of the function $f(\cdot)$ valued at the starting point.[2] This expansion can be generalized to situations where the function depends on two or more variables. For bonds, the first derivative is related to the *duration* measure, and the second to *convexity*.

Equation (1.9) represents an infinite expansion with increasing powers of Δy. Only the first two terms (linear and quadratic) are used by finance practitioners. This is because they provide a good approximation to changes in price relative to other assumptions we have to make about pricing assets. If the increment is very small, even the quadratic term will be negligible.

Equation (1.9) is fundamental for risk management. It is used, sometimes in different guises, across a variety of financial markets. We will see later that the Taylor expansion is also used to approximate the movement in the value of a derivatives contract, such as an option on a stock. In this case, Equation (1.9) is

$$\Delta P = f'(S)\Delta S + \frac{1}{2}f''(S)(\Delta S)^2 + \cdots \qquad (1.10)$$

where S is now the price of the underlying asset, such as a stock. Here the first derivative, $f'(S)$, is called *delta*, and the second, $f''(S)$, *gamma*.

The Taylor expansion allows easy aggregation across financial instruments. If we have x_i units (numbers) of bond i and a total of N different bonds in the portfolio, the portfolio derivatives are given by

$$f'(y) = \sum_{i=1}^{N} x_i f_i'(y) \qquad (1.11)$$

---

[1]This is named after the English mathematician Brook Taylor (1685–1731), who published this result in 1715. The full recognition of the importance of this result came in 1755, when Euler applied it to differential calculus.

[2]This first assumes that the function can be written in polynomial form as $P(y + \Delta y) = a_0 + a_1\Delta y + a_2(\Delta y)^2 + \cdots$, with unknown coefficients a_0, a_1, a_2. To solve for the first, we set $\Delta y = 0$. This gives $a_0 = P_0$. Next, we take the derivative of both sides and set $\Delta y = 0$. This gives $a_1 = f'(y_0)$. The next step gives $2a_2 = f''(y_0)$. Note that these are the conventional mathematical derivatives and have nothing to do with *derivatives products* such as options.

We will illustrate this point later for a three-bond portfolio.

Example 1-5: FRM Exam 1999—Question 9

A number of terms in finance are related to the (calculus!) derivative of the price of a security with respect to some other variable. Which pair of terms is defined using second derivatives?

a) Modified duration and volatility
b) Vega and delta
c) Convexity and gamma
d) PV01 and yield to maturity

1.3   Bond Price Derivatives

For fixed-income instruments, the derivatives are so important that they have been given a special name.[3] The negative of the first derivative is the **dollar duration (DD)**:

$$f'(y_0) = \frac{dP}{dy} = -D^* \times P_0 \tag{1.12}$$

where D^* is called the **modified duration**. Thus, dollar duration is

$$\text{DD} = D^* \times P_0 \tag{1.13}$$

where the price P_0 represents the *market* price, including any accrued interest. Sometimes, risk is measured as the **dollar value of a basis point (DVBP)**,

$$\text{DVBP} = [D^* \times P_0] \times 0.0001 \tag{1.14}$$

with 0.0001 representing one basis point (bp) or one-hundredth of a percent. The DVBP, sometimes called the **DV01**, measures can be easily added up across the portfolio.

The second derivative is the **dollar convexity (DC)**:

$$f''(y_0) = \frac{d^2 P}{dy^2} = C \times P_0 \tag{1.15}$$

where C is called the **convexity**.

---

[3]Note that this chapter does not present duration in the traditional textbook order. In line with the advanced focus on risk management, we first analyze the properties of duration as a sensitivity measure. This applies to any type of fixed-income instrument. Later, we will illustrate the usual definition of duration as a weighted-average maturity, which applies for fixed-coupon bonds only.

For fixed-income instruments with known cash flows, the price-yield function is known, and we can compute analytical first and second derivatives. Consider, for example, our simple zero-coupon bond in Equation (1.1), where the only payment is the face value, $C_T = F$. We take the first derivative, which is

$$\frac{dP}{dy} = \frac{d}{dy}\left[\frac{F}{(1+y)^T}\right] = (-T)\frac{F}{(1+y)^{T+1}} = -\frac{T}{(1+y)}P \qquad (1.16)$$

Comparing this with Equation (1.12), we see that the modified duration must be given by $D^* = T/(1+y)$. The conventional measure of **duration** is $D = T$, which does not include division by $(1+y)$ in the denominator. This is also called **Macaulay duration**. Note that duration is expressed in periods, such as T. With annual compounding, duration is in years. With semiannual compounding, duration is in semesters. It then has to be divided by 2 for conversion to years.

Modified duration is the appropriate measure of interest rate exposure. The quantity $(1 + y)$ appears in the denominator because we took the derivative of the present value term with discrete compounding. If we use continuous compounding, modified duration is identical to the conventional duration measure. In practice, the difference between Macaulay and modified duration is usually small.

Let us now go back to Equation (1.16) and consider the second derivative, which is

$$\frac{d^2P}{dy^2} = -(T+1)(-T)\frac{F}{(1+y)^{T+2}} = \frac{(T+1)T}{(1+y)^2} \times P \qquad (1.17)$$

Comparing this with Equation (1.15), we see that the convexity is $C = (T+1)T/(1+y)^2$. Note that its dimension is expressed in periods squared. With semiannual compounding, convexity is measured in semesters squared. It then has to be divided by 4 for conversion to years squared.[4] So convexity must be positive for bonds with fixed coupons.

Putting together all these equations, we get the Taylor expansion for the change in the price of a bond, which is

$$\Delta P = -[D^* \times P](\Delta y) + \frac{1}{2}[C \times P](\Delta y)^2 + \cdots \qquad (1.18)$$

Therefore, duration measures the first-order (linear) effect of changes in yield and convexity measures the second-order (quadratic) term.

---

[4]This is because the conversion to annual terms is obtained by multiplying the semiannual yield Δy by 2. As a result, the duration term must be divided by 2 and the convexity term by 2^2, or 4, for conversion to annual units.

Example: Computing the price approximation

Consider a 10-year zero-coupon Treasury bond trading at a yield of 6%. The present value is obtained as $P = 100/(1 + 6/200)^{20} = 55.368$. As is the practice in the Treasury market, yields are semiannually compounded. Thus all computations should be carried out using semesters, after which final results can be converted to annual units.

Here, Macaulay duration is exactly 10 years, since $D = T$ for a zero-coupon bond. Its modified duration is $D^* = 20/(1 + 6/200) = 19.42$ semesters, which is 9.71 years. Its convexity is $C = 21 \times 20/(1 + 6/200)^2 = 395.89$ semesters squared, which is 98.97 years squared. Dollar duration is $DD = D^* \times P = 9.71 \times \$55.37 = \$537.55$. The DVBP is $DD \times 0.0001 = \$0.0538$.

We want to approximate the change in the value of the bond if the yield goes to 7%. Using Equation (1.18), we have $\Delta P = -[9.71 \times \$55.37](0.01) + 0.5[98.97 \times \$55.37](0.01)^2 = -\$5.375 + \$0.274 = -\$5.101$. Using the linear term only, the new price is $\$55.368 - \$5.375 = \$49.992$. Using the two terms in the expansion, the predicted price is slightly higher, at $\$55.368 - \$5.375 + \$0.274 = \$50.266$.

These numbers can be compared with the exact value, which is $\$50.257$. The linear approximation has a relative pricing error of -0.53%, which is not bad. Adding a quadratic term reduces this to an error of only 0.02%, which is minuscule given typical bid-ask spreads.

More generally, Figure 1-2 compares the quality of the Taylor series approximation. We consider a 10-year bond paying a 6% coupon semiannually. Initially, the yield is also at 6% and, as a result the price of the bond is at par, at $100. The graph compares, for various values of the yield y,

- The actual, exact price $P = f(y_0 + \Delta y)$
- The duration estimate $P = P_0 - D^* P_0 \Delta y$
- The duration and convexity estimate $P = P_0 - D^* P_0 \Delta y + (1/2) C P_0 (\Delta y)^2$

FIGURE 1-2 Price Approximation

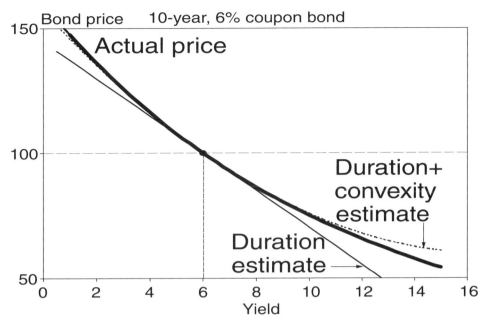

The actual price curve shows an increase in the bond price if the yield falls and, conversely, a depreciation if the yield increases. This effect is captured by the tangent to the true-price curve, which represents the linear approximation based on duration. For small movements in the yield, this linear approximation provides a reasonable fit to the exact price.

> **Key concept:**
> Dollar duration measures the (negative) slope of the tangent to the price-yield curve at the starting point.

For large movements in price, however, the price-yield function becomes more curved and the linear fit deteriorates. Under these conditions, the quadratic approximation is noticeably better.

We should also note that the curvature is away from the origin, which explains the term *convexity* (as opposed to concavity). Figure 1-3 compares curves with different values for convexity. This curvature is beneficial since the second-order effect $0.5[C \times P](\Delta y)^2$ *must* be positive when convexity is positive.

FIGURE 1-3 Effect of Convexity

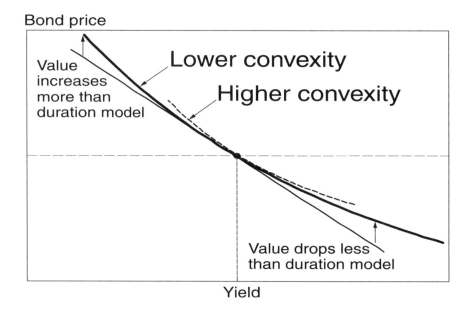

As the figure shows, when the yield rises, the price drops, but less than predicted by the tangent. Conversely, if the yield falls, the price increases faster than along the tangent. In other words, the quadratic term is always beneficial.

> **Key concept:**
> Convexity is always positive for regular coupon-paying bonds. Greater convexity is beneficial for both falling and rising yields.

The bond's modified duration and convexity can also be computed directly from numerical derivatives. Duration and convexity cannot be computed directly for some bonds, such as mortgage-backed securities, because their cash flows are uncertain. Instead, the portfolio manager has access to pricing models that can be used to reprice the securities under various yield environments.

We choose a change in the yield, Δy, and reprice the bond under an up-move scenario, $P_+ = P(y_0 + \Delta y)$, and a down-move scenario, $P_- = P(y_0 - \Delta y)$. **Effective duration** is measured by the numerical derivative. Using $D^* = -(1/P)dP/dy$, it is estimated as

$$D^E = \frac{[P_- - P_+]}{(2P_0 \Delta y)} = \frac{P(y_0 - \Delta y) - P(y_0 + \Delta y)}{(2\Delta y)P_0} \qquad (1.19)$$

Using $C = (1/P)d^2P/dy^2$, **effective convexity** is estimated as

$$C^E = [D_- - D_+]/\Delta y = \left[\frac{P(y_0 - \Delta y) - P_0}{(P_0 \Delta y)} - \frac{P_0 - P(y_0 + \Delta y)}{(P_0 \Delta y)} \right] /\Delta y \quad (1.20)$$

To illustrate, consider a 30-year zero-coupon bond (illustrated in Figure 1-4) with a yield of 6%, semiannually compounded. The initial price is $16.9733. We revalue the bond at 5% and 7%, with prices shown in Table 1-1. The effective duration in Equation (1.19) uses the two extreme points. The effective convexity in Equation (1.20) uses the difference between the dollar durations for the up-move and down-move. Note that convexity is positive if duration increases as yields fall, or if $D_- > D_+$.

FIGURE 1-4 Effective Duration and Convexity

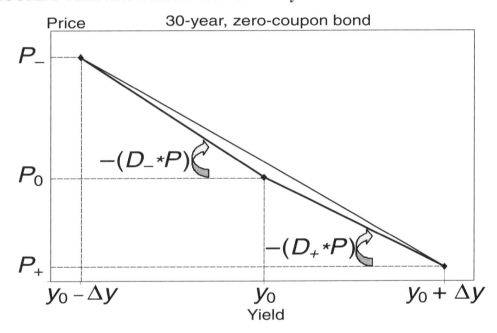

The computations in Table 1-1 show an effective duration of 29.56. This is very close to the true value of 29.13, and it would be even closer if the step Δy were smaller. Similarly, the effective convexity is 869.11, which is close to the true value of 862.48.

TABLE 1-1 Effective Duration and Convexity

State	Yield (%)	Bond Value	Duration Computation	Convexity Computation
Initial y_0	6.00	16.9733		
Up $y_0 + \Delta y$	7.00	12.6934		Duration up: 25.22
Down $y_0 - \Delta y$	5.00	22.7284		Duration down: 33.91
Difference in values			-10.0349	8.69
Difference in yields			0.02	0.01
Effective measure			29.56	869.11
Exact measure			29.13	862.48

Finally, this numerical approach can be applied to estimate the duration of a bond by considering bonds with the same maturity but different coupons. If interest rates decrease by 1%, the market price of a 6% bond should go up to a value close to that of a 7% bond. Thus we replace a drop in yield of Δy by an increase in coupon Δc and use the effective duration method to find the **coupon curve duration**:[5]

$$D^{CC} = \frac{[P_+ - P_-]}{(2P_0 \Delta c)} = \frac{P(y_0; c + \Delta c) - P(y_0; c - \Delta c)}{(2\Delta c)P_0} \tag{1.21}$$

This approach is useful for securities that are difficult to price under various yield scenarios. It requires only the market prices of securities with different coupons.

Example: Computation of coupon curve duration

Consider a 10-year bond that pays a 7% coupon semiannually. In a 7% yield environment, the bond is selling at par and has modified duration of 7.11 years. The prices of 6% and 8% coupon bonds are $92.89 and $107.11, respectively. This gives a coupon curve duration of $(107.11 - 92.89)/(0.02 \times 100) = 7.11$, which in this case is the same as modified duration.

Example 1-6: FRM Exam 1998—Question 22

What is the price impact of a 10-basis-point increase in yield on a 10-year par bond with a modified duration of 7 and convexity of 50?
a) -0.705
b) -0.700
c) -0.698
d) -0.690

---

[5]For an example of a more formal proof, we could take the pricing formula for a consol at par and compute the derivatives with respect to y and c. Apart from the sign, these derivatives are identical when $y = c$.

Example 1-7: FRM Exam 1998—Question 17

A bond is trading at a price of 100 with a yield of 8%. If the yield increases by 1 basis point, the price of the bond will decrease to 99.95. If the yield decreases by 1 basis point, the price of the bond will increase to 100.04. What is the modified duration of the bond?

a) 5.0

b) −5.0

c) 4.5

d) −4.5

Example 1-8: FRM Exam 1998—Question 20

Coupon curve duration is a useful method for estimating duration from market prices of a mortgage-backed security (MBS). Assume the coupon curve of prices for Ginnie Maes in June 2001 is as follows: 6% at 92, 7% at 94, and 8% at 96.5. What is the estimated duration of the 7s?

a) 2.45

b) 2.40

c) 2.33

d) 2.25

Example 1-9: FRM Exam 1998—Question 21

Coupon curve duration is a useful method for estimating convexity from market prices of an MBS. Assume the coupon curve of prices for Ginnie Maes in June 2001 is as follows: 6% at 92, 7% at 94, and 8% at 96.5. What is the estimated convexity of the 7s?

a) 53

b) 26

c) 13

d) −53

1.3.1 Interpreting Duration and Convexity

The preceding section showed how to compute analytical formulas for duration and convexity in the case of a simple zero-coupon bond. We can use the same approach for coupon-paying bonds. Going back to Equation (1.6), we have

$$\frac{dP}{dy} = \sum_{t=1}^{T} \frac{-tC_t}{(1+y)^{t+1}} = -\left[\sum_{t=1}^{T} \frac{tC_t}{(1+y)^t}\right] / P \times \frac{P}{(1+y)} = -\frac{D}{(1+y)}P \quad (1.22)$$

which defines duration as

$$D = \sum_{t=1}^{T} \frac{tC_t}{(1+y)^t} / P \tag{1.23}$$

The economic interpretation of duration is that it represents the average time to wait for each payment, weighted by the present value of the associated cash flow. Indeed, replacing P, we can write

$$D = \sum_{t=1}^{T} t \frac{C_t/(1+y)^t}{\sum C_t/(1+y)^t} = \sum_{t=1}^{T} t \times w_t \tag{1.24}$$

where the weights w represent the ratio of the present value of cash flow C_t relative to the total, and sum to unity. This explains why the duration of a zero-coupon bond is equal to the maturity. There is only one cash flow and its weight is 1.

Figure 1-5 lays out the present value of the cash flows of a 6% coupon, 10-year bond. Given a duration of 7.80 years, this coupon-paying bond is equivalent to a zero-coupon bond maturing in exactly 7.80 years.

FIGURE 1-5 Duration as the Maturity of a Zero-Coupon Bond

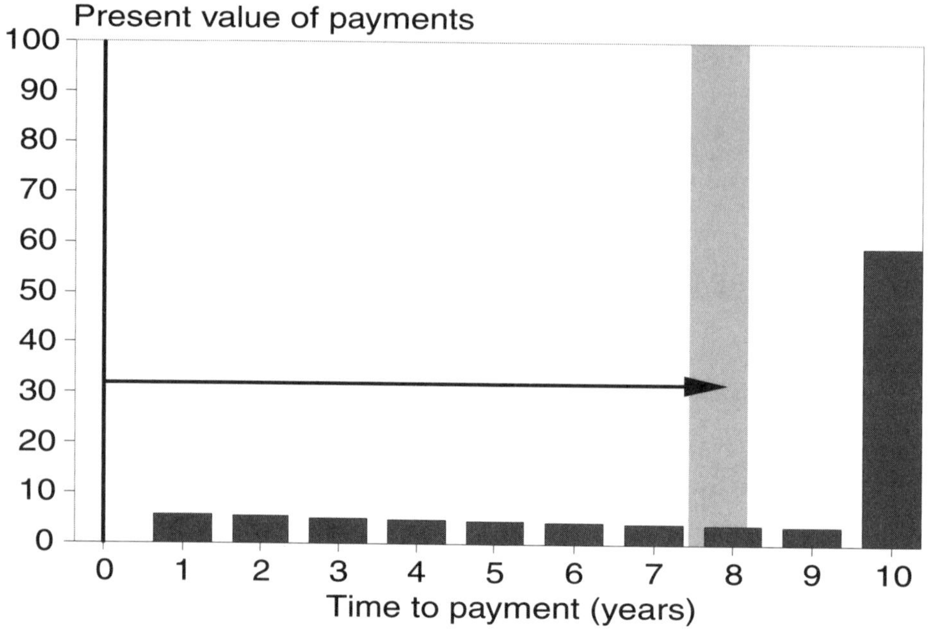

For bonds with fixed coupons, duration is less than maturity. For instance, Figure 1-6 shows how the duration of a 10-year bond varies with its coupon. With a zero coupon, Macaulay duration is equal to maturity. Higher coupons place more weight on prior payments and therefore reduce duration.

Duration can be expressed in a simple form for consols. From Equation (1.8), we have $P = (c/y)F$. Taking the derivative, we find

$$\frac{dP}{dy} = cF\frac{(-1)}{y^2} = (-1)\frac{1}{y}\left[\frac{c}{y}F\right] = (-1)\frac{1}{y}P = -\frac{D_C}{(1+y)}P \qquad (1.25)$$

Hence the Macaulay duration for the consol D_C is

$$D_C = \frac{(1+y)}{y} \qquad (1.26)$$

This shows that the duration of a consol is finite even if its maturity is infinite. Also, it does not depend on the coupon.

FIGURE 1-6 Duration and Coupon

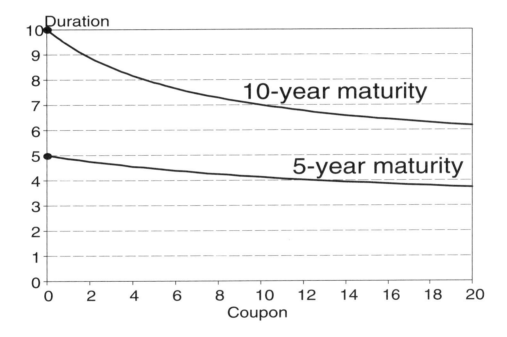

This formula provides a useful rule of thumb. For a long-term coupon-paying bond, duration must be lower than $(1 + y)/y$. For instance, when $y = 6\%$, the upper limit on duration is $D_C = 1.06/0.06$, or 17.7 years. In this environment, the duration of a par 30-year bond is 14.25, which is indeed lower than 17.7 years.

Key concept:
The duration of a long-term bond can be approximated by an upper bound, which is that of a consol with the same yield, $D_C = (1 + y)/y$.

Figure 1-7 describes the relationship between duration, maturity, and coupon for regular bonds in a 6% yield environment. For the zero-coupon bond, $D = T$, which is a straight line going through the origin. For the par 6% bond, duration increases monotonically with maturity until it reaches the asymptote of D_C. The 8% bond has lower duration than the 6% bond for fixed T. Greater coupons, for a fixed maturity, decrease duration, as more of the payments come early.

FIGURE 1-7 Duration and Maturity

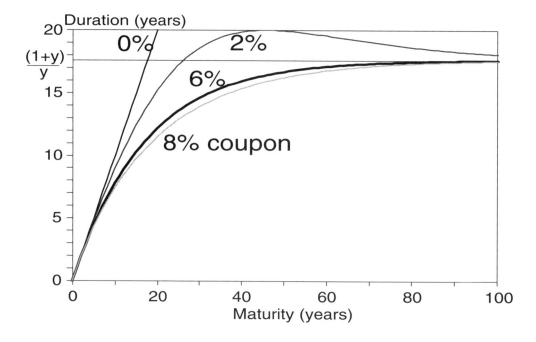

Finally, the 2% bond displays a pattern intermediate between the zero-coupon and 6% bonds. It initially behaves like the zero, exceeding D_C initially and then falling back to the asymptote, which is the same for all coupon-paying bonds.

Now taking the second derivative in Equation (1.22), we have

$$\frac{d^2 P}{dy^2} = \sum_{t=1}^{T} \frac{t(t+1)C_t}{(1+y)^{t+2}} = \left[\sum_{t=1}^{T} \frac{t(t+1)C_t}{(1+y)^{t+2}} \right] \Big/ P \times P \qquad (1.27)$$

which defines convexity as

$$C = \sum_{t=1}^{T} \frac{t(t+1)C_t}{(1+y)^{t+2}} \Big/ P \qquad (1.28)$$

Convexity can also be written as

$$C = \sum_{t=1}^{T} \frac{t(t+1)}{(1+y)^2} \times \frac{C_t/(1+y)^t}{\sum C_t/(1+y)^t} = \sum_{t=1}^{T} \frac{t(t+1)}{(1+y)^2} \times w_t \qquad (1.29)$$

Because the squared t term dominates in the fraction, this basically involves a weighted average of the square of time. Therefore, convexity is much greater for long-maturity bonds because they have payoffs associated with large values of t. The formula also shows that convexity is always positive for such bonds, implying that the curvature effect is beneficial. As we will see later, convexity can be negative for bonds that have uncertain cash flows, such as mortgage-backed securities (MBSs) or callable bonds.

Figure 1-8 displays the behavior of convexity, comparing a zero-coupon bond with a 6% coupon bond with identical maturities. The zero-coupon bond always has greater convexity, because there is only one cash flow at maturity. Its convexity is roughly the square of maturity—for example, about 900 for the 30-year zero. In contrast, the 30-year coupon bond has a convexity of only about 300.

FIGURE 1-8 Convexity and Maturity

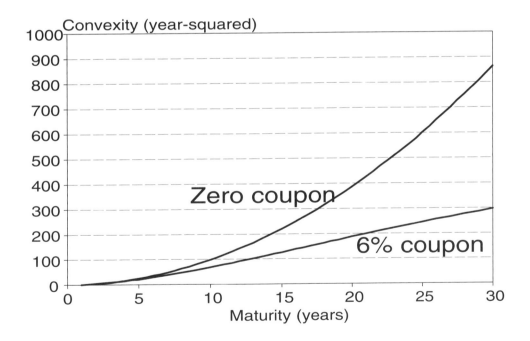

As an illustration, Table 1-2 details the steps of the computation of duration and convexity for a two-year, 6% semiannual coupon-paying bond. We first convert the annual coupon and yield to semiannual equivalents, $3 and 3%. The PV column then reports the present value of each cash flow. We verify that these add up to $100, since the bond must be selling at par.

Next, the Duration Term column multiplies each PV term by time, or more precisely, the number of half-years until payment. This adds up to $382.86, which divided by the price gives $D = 3.83$. This number is measured in half-years, and we need to divide by 2 to convert to years. Macaulay duration is 1.91 years, and modified duration $D^* = 1.91/1.03 = 1.86$ years. Note that, to be consistent, the adjustment in the denominator involves the semiannual yield of 3%.

Finally, the rightmost column shows how to compute the bond's convexity. Each term involves PV_t times $t(t+1)/(1+y)^2$. These terms sum to 1,777.755 or, divided by the price, 17.78. This number is expressed in units of time squared and must be divided by 4 to be converted to annual terms. We find a convexity of $C = 4.44$, in years squared.

TABLE 1-2 Computing Duration and Convexity

Period (half-year) t	Payment C_t	Yield (%) (6 mo)	PV of Payment $C_t/(1+y)^t$	Duration Term tPV_t	Convexity Term] $t(t+1)PV_t$ $\times(1/(1+y)^2)$
1	3	3.00	2.913	2.913	5.491
2	3	3.00	2.828	5.656	15.993
3	3	3.00	2.745	8.236	31.054
4	103	3.00	91.514	366.057	1725.218
Sum:			100.00	382.861	1777.755
(half-years)				3.83	17.78
(years)				1.91	
Modified duration				1.86	
Convexity					4.44

Example 1-10: FRM Exam 2001—Question 71

Calculate the modified duration of a bond with a Macauley duration of 13.083 years. Assume market interest rates are 11.5% and the coupon on the bond is paid semiannually.

a) 13.083
b) 12.732
c) 12.459
d) 12.371

Example 1-11: FRM Exam 2002—Question 118

A Treasury bond has a coupon rate of 6% per annum (the coupons are paid semiannually) and a semiannually compounded yield of 4% per annum. The bond matures in 18 months and the next coupon will be paid 6 months from now. Which number is closest to the bond's Macaulay duration?

a) 1.023 years
b) 1.457 years
c) 1.500 years
d) 2.915 years

Example 1-12: FRM Exam 1998—Question 29

A and B are two perpetual bonds; that is, their maturities are infinite. A has a coupon of 4% and B has a coupon of 8%. Assuming that both are trading at the same yield, what can be said about the duration of these bonds?

a) The duration of A is greater than the duration of B.
b) The duration of A is less than the duration of B.
c) A and B have the same duration.
d) None of the above.

Example 1-13: FRM Exam 1997—Question 24

Which of the following is *not* a property of bond duration?

a) For zero-coupon bonds, Macaulay duration of the bond equals its years to maturity.
b) Duration is usually inversely related to the coupon of a bond.
c) Duration is usually higher for higher yields to maturity.
d) Duration is higher as the number of years to maturity for a bond selling at par or above increases.

Example 1-14: FRM Exam 1999—Question 75

Suppose that your book has an unusually large short position in two investment-grade bonds with similar credit risk. Bond A is priced at par yielding 6.0% with 20 years to maturity. Bond B also matures in 20 years with a coupon of 6.5% and yield of 6%. If risk is defined as a sudden and large drop in interest rate, which bond contributes greater market risk to the portfolio?

a) Bond A.
b) Bond B.
c) Bond A and bond B will have similar market risk.
d) None of the above.

Example 1-15: FRM Exam 2001—Question 104

When the maturity of a plain coupon bond increases, its duration increases:

a) Indefinitely and regularly

b) Up to a certain level

c) Indefinitely and progressively

d) In a way dependent on the bond being priced above or below par

---

Example 1-16: FRM Exam 2000—Question 106

Consider the following bonds:

Bond Number	Maturity (yrs)	Coupon Rate	Frequency	Yield (ABB)
1	10	6%	1	6%
2	10	6%	2	6%
3	10	0%	1	6%
4	10	6%	1	5%
5	9	6%	1	6%

How would you rank the bonds from shortest to longest duration?

a) 5-2-1-4-3

b) 1-2-3-4-5

c) 5-4-3-1-2

d) 2-4-5-1-3

1.3.2   Portfolio Duration and Convexity

Fixed-income portfolios often involve very large numbers of securities. It would be impractical to consider the movements of each security individually. Instead, portfolio managers aggregate the duration and convexity across the portfolio. A manager with a view that rates will increase should shorten the portfolio duration relative to that of the benchmark. Say the benchmark has a duration of five years. The manager shortens the portfolio duration to one year only. If rates increase by 2%, the benchmark will lose approximately $5y \times 2\% = 10\%$. The portfolio, however, will only lose $1y \times 2\% = 2\%$, hence "beating" the benchmark by 8%.

Because the Taylor expansion involves a summation, the portfolio duration is easily obtained from the individual components. Say we have N components indexed by i. Defining D_p^* and P_p as the portfolio modified duration and value, the portfolio dollar duration (DD) is

$$D_p^* P_p = \sum_{i=1}^{N} D_i^* x_i P_i \qquad (1.30)$$

where x_i is the number of units of bond i in the portfolio. A similar relationship holds for the portfolio dollar convexity (DC). If yields are the same for all components, this equation also holds for the Macaulay duration.

Because the portfolio total market value is simply the summation of the component market values,

$$P_p = \sum_{i=1}^{N} x_i P_i \qquad (1.31)$$

we can define the **portfolio weight** as $w_i = x_i P_i / P_p$, provided that the portfolio market value is nonzero. We can then write the portfolio duration as a weighted average of individual durations:

$$D_p^* = \sum_{i=1}^{N} D_i^* w_i \qquad (1.32)$$

Similarly, the portfolio convexity is a weighted average of convexity numbers:

$$C_p = \sum_{i=1}^{N} C_i w_i \qquad (1.33)$$

As an example, consider a portfolio invested in three bonds as described in Table 1-3. The portfolio is long a 10-year and a 1-year bond, and short a 30-year zero-coupon bond. Its market value is $1,301,600. Summing the duration for each component, the portfolio dollar duration is $2,953,800, which translates into a duration of 2.27 years. The portfolio convexity is $-76,918,323/1,301,600 = -59.10$, which is negative due to the short position in the 30-year zero, which has very high convexity.

TABLE 1-3 Portfolio Dollar Duration and Convexity

	Bond 1	Bond 2	Bond 3	Portfolio
Maturity (years)	10	1	30	
Coupon	6%	0%	0%	
Yield	6%	6%	6%	
Price P_i	$100.00	$94.26	$16.97	
Modified duration D_i^*	7.44	0.97	29.13	
Convexity C_i	68.78	1.41	862.48	
Number of bonds x_i	10,000	5,000	$-10,000$	
Dollar amounts $x_i P_i$	$1,000,000	$471,300	$-169,700	$1,301,600
Weight w_i	76.83%	36.21%	-13.04%	100.00%
Dollar duration $D_i^* P_i$	$744.00	$91.43	$494.34	
Portfolio DD: $x_i D_i^* P_i$	$7,440,000	$457,161	$-$4,943,361	$2,953,800
Portfolio DC: $x_i C_i P_i$	68,780,000	664,533	$-146,362,856$	$-76,918,323$

Alternatively, assume the portfolio manager is given a benchmark, which is the first bond. The manager wants to invest in bonds 2 and 3, keeping the portfolio duration equal to that of the target, 7.44 years. To achieve the target value and dollar duration, the manager needs to solve a system of two equations in the numbers x_1 and x_2:

Value:	$100 =	x_1\$94.26 +	x_2\$16.97
Dol. duration:	$7.44 \times \$100 =$	$0.97 \times x_1\$94.26 +$	$29.13 \times x_2\$16.97$

The solution is $x_1 = 0.817$ and $x_2 = 1.354$, which gives a portfolio value of $100 and modified duration of 7.44 years.[6] The portfolio convexity is 199.25, higher than the index. Such a portfolio consisting of very short and very long maturities is called a **barbell portfolio**. In contrast, a portfolio with maturities in the same range is called a **bullet portfolio**. Note that the barbell portfolio has much greater convexity than the bullet because of the payment in 30 years. Such a portfolio would be expected to outperform the bullet portfolio if yields move by a large amount.

In sum, duration and convexity are key measures of fixed-income portfolios. They summarize the linear and quadratic exposure to movements in yields. This explains why they are routinely used by portfolio managers.

Example 1-17: FRM Exam 2002—Question 57

A bond portfolio has the following composition:
1) Portfolio A: price $90,000, modified duration 2.5, long position in 8 bonds
2) Portfolio B: price $110,000, modified duration 3, short position in 6 bonds
3) Portfolio C: price $120,000, modified duration 3.3, long position in 12 bonds
All interest rates are 10%. If the rates rise by 25 basis points, then the bond portfolio value will:
a) Decrease by $11,430
b) Decrease by $21,330
c) Decrease by $12,573
d) Decrease by $23,463

---

[6]This can be obtained by first expressing x_2 in the first equation as a function of x_1 and then substituting back into the second equation. This gives $x_2 = (100 - 94.26x_1)/16.97$, and $744 = 91.43x_1 + 494.34x_2 = 91.43x_1 + 494.34(100 - 94.26x_1)/16.97 = 91.43x_1 + 2913.00 - 2745.79x_1$. Solving, we find $x_1 = (-2169.00)/(-2654.36) = 0.817$ and $x_2 = (100 - 94.26 \times 0.817)/16.97 = 1.354$.

Example 1-18: FRM Exam 2000—Question 110

Which of the following statements are *true*?

I. The convexity of a 10-year zero-coupon bond is higher than the convexity of a 10-year, 6% bond.

II. The convexity of a 10-year zero-coupon bond is higher than the convexity of a 6% bond with a duration of 10 years.

III. Convexity grows proportionately with the maturity of the bond.

IV. Convexity is positive for all types of bonds.

V. Convexity is always positive for "straight" bonds.

a) I only

b) I and II only

c) I and V only

d) II, III, and V only

1.4 Answers to Chapter Examples

Example 1-1: FRM Exam 2002—Question 48

a) The EAR is defined by $FV/PV = (1 + \text{EAR})^T$. So $\text{EAR} = (FV/PV)^{1/T} - 1 = (1,000/987)^{1/12} - 1 = 17.0\%$.

Example 1-2: FRM Exam 2002—Question 51

c) The time T relates the current and future values such that $FV/PV = 2 = (1 + 8\%)^T$. Taking logs of both sides, this gives $T = \ln(2)/\ln(1.08) = 9.006$.

Example 1-3: FRM Exam 1999—Question 17

b) This is derived from $(1 + y^S/2)^2 = (1 + y)$, or $(1 + 0.08/2)^2 = 1.0816$, which gives 8.16%. This makes sense because the annual rate must be higher due to the less frequent compounding.

Example 1-4: FRM Exam 1998—Question 12

d) We need to find y such that $\$4/(1 + y/2) + \$104/(1 + y/2)^2 = \$102.9$. Solving, we find $y = 5\%$. (This can be computed on a HP-12C calculator, for example.) There is another method for finding y. This bond has a duration of about one year, implying that, approximately, $\Delta P = -1 \times \$100 \times \Delta y$. If the yield were 8%, the price would be $100. Instead, the change in price is $\Delta P = \$102.9 - \$100 = \$2.9$. Solving for Δy, the change in yield must be approximately -3%, leading to $8 - 3 = 5\%$.

Example 1-5: FRM Exam 1999—Question 9

c) First derivatives involve modified duration and delta. Second derivatives involve convexity (for bonds) and gamma (for options).

Example 1-6: FRM Exam 1998—Question 22

c) Since this is a par bond, the initial price is $P = \$100$. The price impact is $\Delta P = -D^* P \Delta y + (1/2) C P (\Delta y)^2 = -(7 \times \$100)(0.001) + (1/2)(50 \times \$100)(0.001)^2 = -0.70 + 0.0025 = -0.6975$. The price falls slightly less than predicted by duration alone.

Example 1-7: FRM Exam 1998—Question 17

c) This question deals with effective duration, which is obtained from full repricing of the bond with an increase and a decrease in yield. This gives a modified duration of $D^* = -(\Delta P / \Delta y)/P = -((99.95 - 100.04)/0.0002)/100 = 4.5$.

Example 1-8: FRM Exam 1998—Question 20

b) The initial price of the 7s is 94. The price of the 6s is 92; this lower coupon is roughly equivalent to an up-move of $\Delta y = 0.01$. Similarly, the price of the 8s is 96.5; this higher coupon is roughly equivalent to a down-move of $\Delta y = 0.01$. The effective modified duration is then $D^E = (P_- - P_+)/(2\Delta y P_0) = (96.5 - 92)/(2 \times 0.01 \times 94) = 2.394$.

Example 1-9: FRM Exam 1998—Question 21

a) We compute the modified duration for an equivalent down-move in y as $D_- = (P_- - P_0)/(\Delta y P_0) = (96.5 - 94)/(0.01 \times 94) = 2.6596$. Similarly, the modified duration for an up-move is $D_+ = (P_0 - P_+)/(\Delta y P_0) = (94 - 92)/(0.01 \times 94) = 2.1277$. Convexity is $C^E = (D_- - D_+)/(\Delta y) = (2.6596 - 2.1277)/0.01 = 53.19$. This is positive because modified duration is higher for a down-move than for an up-move in yields.

Example 1-10: FRM Exam 2001—Question 71

d) Modified duration is $D^* = D/(1 + y/200)$ when yields are semiannually compounded. This gives $D^* = 13.083/(1 + 11.5/200) = 12.3716$.

Example 1-11: FRM Exam 2002—Question 118

b) For coupon-paying bonds, Macaulay duration is slightly less than the maturity, which is 1.5 years here. So b) would be a good guess. Otherwise, we can compute duration exactly.

Example 1-12: FRM Exam 1998—Question 29

c) Going back to the duration equation for the consol, Equation (1.26), we see that it does not depend on the coupon but only on the yield. Hence, the durations must be the same. The price of bond A, however, must be half that of bond B.

Example 1-13: FRM Exam 1997—Question 24

c) Duration usually increases as the time to maturity increases (Figure 1-7), so d) is correct. Macaulay duration is also equal to maturity for zero-coupon bonds, so a) is correct. Figure 1-6 shows that duration decreases with the coupon, so b) is correct. As the yield increases, the weight of the payments further into the future decreases, which *decreases* (not increases) the duration. So c) is false.

Example 1-14: FRM Exam 1999—Question 75

a) Bond B has a higher coupon and hence a slightly lower duration than Bond A. Therefore, it will react less strongly than bond A to a given change in yields.

Example 1-15: FRM Exam 2001—Question 104

b) With a fixed coupon, the duration goes up to the level of a consol with the same coupon. See Figure 1-7.

Example 1-16: FRM Exam 2000—Question 106

a) The nine-year bond (number 5) has shorter duration because the maturity is shortest, at nine years, among comparable bonds. Next, we have to decide between bonds 1 and 2, which differ only in the payment frequency. The semiannual bond (number 2) has a first payment in six months and has shorter duration than the annual bond. Next, we have to decide between bonds 1 and 4, which differ only in the yield. With lower yield, the cash flows further in the future have a higher weight, so that bond 4 has greater duration. Finally, the zero-coupon bond has the longest duration. So, the order is 5-2-1-4-3.

Example 1-17: FRM Exam 2002—Question 57

a) The portfolio dollar duration is $D^*P = \sum x_i D_i^* P_i = +8 \times 2.5 \times \$90,000 - 6 \times 3.0 \times \$110,000 + 12 \times 3.3 \times \$120,000 = \$4,572,000$. The change in portfolio value is then $-(D*P)(\Delta y) = -\$4,572,000 \times 0.0025 = -\$11,430$.

Example 1-18: FRM Exam 2000—Question 110

c) Because convexity is proportional to the square of time to payment, the convexity of a bond will be driven by the cash flows far into the future. Answer I is correct because the 10-year zero has only one cash flow, whereas the coupon bond has several others that reduce convexity. Answer II is false because the 6% bond with 10-year duration must have cash flows much further into the future, say 30 years, which will create greater convexity. Answer III is false because convexity grows with the square of time. Answer IV is false because some bonds—for example, MBSs or callable bonds—can have negative convexity. Answer V is correct because convexity must be positive for coupon-paying bonds.

Appendix: Applications of Infinite Series

When bonds have fixed coupons, the bond valuation problem often can be interpreted in terms of combinations of infinite series. The most important infinite series result is for a sum of terms that increase at a geometric rate:

$$1 + a + a^2 + a^3 + \cdots = \frac{1}{1-a} \tag{1.34}$$

This can be proved, for instance, by multiplying both sides by $(1 - a)$ and canceling out terms.

Equally important, consider a geometric series with a finite number of terms, say N. We can write this as the difference between two infinite series:

$$
\begin{aligned}
1 + a + a^2 + a^3 + \cdots + a^{N-1} = {}& (1 + a + a^2 + a^3 + \cdots) \\
& - a^N (1 + a + a^2 + a^3 + \cdots)
\end{aligned}
\tag{1.35}
$$

such that all terms with order N or higher will cancel each other.

We can then write

$$1 + a + a^2 + a^3 + \cdots + a^{N-1} = \frac{1}{1-a} - a^N \frac{1}{1-a} \tag{1.36}$$

These formulas are essential to value bonds. Consider first a consol with an infinite number of coupon payments with a fixed coupon rate c. If the yield is y and the face value F, the value of the bond is

$$
\begin{aligned}
P &= cF \left[\frac{1}{(1+y)} + \frac{1}{(1+y)^2} + \frac{1}{(1+y)^3} + \cdots \right] \\
&= cF \frac{1}{(1+y)} [1 + a^2 + a^3 + \cdots] \\
&= cF \frac{1}{(1+y)} \left[\frac{1}{1-a} \right] \\
&= cF \frac{1}{(1+y)} \left[\frac{1}{(1-1/(1+y))} \right] \\
&= cF \frac{1}{(1+y)} \left[\frac{(1+y)}{y} \right] \\
&= \frac{c}{y} F
\end{aligned}
$$

Similarly, we can value a bond with a *finite* number of coupons over T periods at which time the principal is repaid. This is really a portfolio with three parts:

(1) A long position in a consol with coupon rate c

(2) A short position in a consol with coupon rate c that starts in T periods

(3) A long position in a zero-coupon bond that pays F in T periods.

Note that the combination of (1) and (2) ensures that we have a finite number of coupons. Hence, the bond price should be

$$P = \frac{c}{y}F - \frac{1}{(1+y)^T}\frac{c}{y}F + \frac{1}{(1+y)^T}F = \frac{c}{y}F\left[1 - \frac{1}{(1+y)^T}\right] + \frac{1}{(1+y)^T}F \quad (1.37)$$

where again the formula can be adjusted for different compounding methods.

This is useful for a number of purposes. For instance, when $c = y$, it is immediately obvious that the price must be at par, $P = F$. This formula also can be used to find closed-form solutions for duration and convexity.

Chapter 2

Fundamentals of Probability

The preceding chapter laid out the foundations for understanding how bond prices move in relation to yields. Next we have to characterize movements in bond yields or, more generally, any relevant risk factor in financial markets.

This is done with the tools of probability, a mathematical abstraction that describes the distribution of risk factors. Each risk factor is viewed as a random variable whose properties are described by a probability distribution function. These distributions can be processed with the price-yield relationship to create a distribution of the profit-and-loss profile for the trading portfolio.

This chapter reviews the fundamental tools of probability theory for risk managers. Section 2.1 lays out the foundations, characterizing random variables by their probability density and distribution functions. These functions can be described by their principal moments, mean, variance, skewness, and kurtosis. Distributions with multiple variables are described in Section 2.2. Section 2.3 then turns to functions of random variables. Section 2.4 presents some examples of important distribution functions for risk management, including the uniform, normal, lognormal, Student's, and binomial. Finally, Section 2.5 discusses limit distributions, which can be used to characterize the average and tails of independent random variables.

2.1 Characterizing Random Variables

The classical approach to probability is based on the concept of the **random variable** (rv). This can be viewed as the outcome from throwing a die, for example. Each realization is generated from a fixed process. If the die is perfectly symmetric, we could say that the probability of observing a face with a six in one throw is $p = 1/6$.

Although the event itself is random, we can still make a number of useful statements from a fixed data-generating process.

The same approach can be taken to financial markets, where stock prices, exchange rates, yields, and commodity prices can be viewed as random variables. The assumption of a fixed data-generating process for these variables, however, is more tenuous than for the preceding experiment.

2.1.1 Univariate Distribution Functions

A random variable X is characterized by a **distribution function**,

$$F(x) = P(X \leq x) \tag{2.1}$$

which is the probability that the realization of the random variable X ends up less than or equal to the given number x. This is also called a **cumulative distribution function**.

When the variable X takes discrete values, this distribution is obtained by summing the step values less than or equal to x. That is,

$$F(x) = \sum_{x_j \leq x} f(x_j) \tag{2.2}$$

where the function $f(x)$ is called the **frequency function** or the **probability density function** (p.d.f.). This is the probability of observing x.

When the variable is continuous, the distribution is given by

$$F(x) = \int_{-\infty}^{x} f(u)du \tag{2.3}$$

The density can be obtained from the distribution using

$$f(x) = \frac{dF(x)}{dx} \tag{2.4}$$

Often, the random variable will be described interchangeably by its distribution or its density.

These functions have notable properties. The density $f(u)$ must be positive for all u. As x tends to infinity, the distribution tends to unity because it represents the total probability of any draw for x:

$$\int_{-\infty}^{\infty} f(u)du = 1 \tag{2.5}$$

Figure 2-1 gives an example of a density function $f(x)$ on the top panel, and of a cumulative distribution function $F(x)$ on the bottom panel. $F(x)$ measures the area under the $f(x)$ curve to the left of x, which is represented by the shaded area. Here, this area is 0.24. For small values of x, $F(x)$ is close to zero. Conversely, for large values of x, $F(x)$ is close to unity.

FIGURE 2-1 Density and Distribution Functions

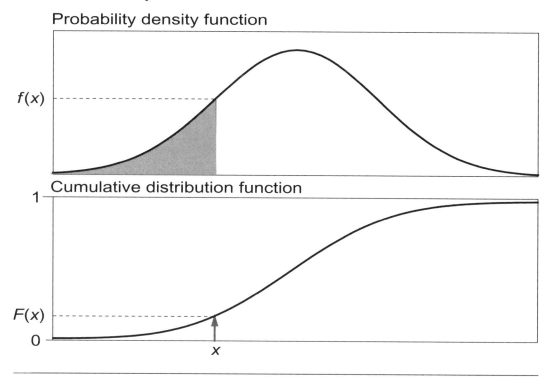

Example: Density functions

A gambler wants to characterize the probability density function of the outcomes from a pair of dice. Because each die has six faces, there are $6^2 = 36$ possible throw combinations. Out of these, there is one occurrence of an outcome of two (each die showing a one), so the frequency of an outcome of two is 1. We can have two occurrences of a three (a one and a two and vice versa), and so on.

The gambler builds the frequency table (Table 2-1) for each value, from 2 to 12. From this, the gambler can compute the probability of each outcome. For instance, the probability of observing three is equal to 2, the frequency $n(x)$, divided by the total number of outcomes, or 36, which gives 0.0556. We can verify that all the probabilities add up to 1, since all occurrences must be accounted for. From the table, we see that the probability of an outcome of three or less is 8.33%.

TABLE 2-1 Probability Density Function

Outcome x_i	Frequency $n(x)$	Probability $f(x)$		Cumulative Probability $F(x)$
2	1	1/36	0.0278	0.0278
3	2	2/36	0.0556	0.0833
4	3	3/36	0.0833	0.1667
5	4	4/36	0.1111	0.2778
6	5	5/36	0.1389	0.4167
7	6	6/36	0.1667	0.5833
8	5	5/36	0.1389	0.7222
9	4	4/36	0.1111	0.8333
10	3	3/36	0.0833	0.9167
11	2	2/36	0.0556	0.9722
12	1	1/36	0.0278	1.0000
Sum	36	1	1.0000	

2.1.2   Moments

A random variable is characterized by its distribution function. Instead of having to report the whole function, it is convenient to summarize it by a few parameters, or **moments**.

For instance, the expected value for x, or **mean**, is given by the integral

$$\mu = E(X) = \int_{-\infty}^{+\infty} xf(x)dx \tag{2.6}$$

which measures the *central tendency* or *center of gravity* of the population.

The distribution can also be described by its **quantile**, which is the cutoff point x with an associated probability c:

$$F(x) = \int_{-\infty}^{x} f(u)du = c \tag{2.7}$$

So there is a probability of c that the random variable will fall *below* x. Because the total probability adds up to 1, there is a probability of $p = 1 - c$ that the random variable will fall *above* x. Define this quantile as $Q(X, c)$. The 50% quantile is known as the **median**.

In fact, value at risk (VAR) can be interpreted as the cutoff point such that a loss will not happen with probability greater than $p = 95\%$, say. If $f(u)$ is the distribution of profits and losses on the portfolio, VAR is defined from

$$F(x) = \int_{-\infty}^{x} f(u)du = (1 - p) \tag{2.8}$$

where p is the right-tail probability, and c the usual left-tail probability. VAR can then be defined as the deviation between the expected value and the quantile,

$$\text{VAR}(c) = E(X) - Q(X, c) \tag{2.9}$$

Figure 2-2 shows an example with $c = 5\%$.

FIGURE 2-2 VAR as a Quantile

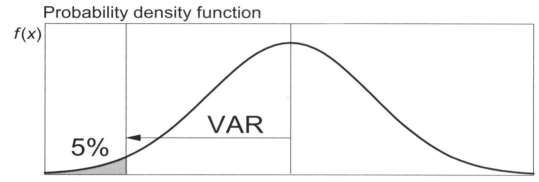

Another useful moment is the squared dispersion around the mean, or **variance**, which is

$$\sigma^2 = V(X) = \int_{-\infty}^{+\infty} [x - E(X)]^2 f(x)dx \tag{2.10}$$

The **standard deviation** is more convenient to use since it has the same units as the original variable X:

$$\text{SD}(X) = \sigma = \sqrt{V(X)} \tag{2.11}$$

Next, the scaled third moment is the **skewness**, which describes departures from symmetry. It is defined as

$$\gamma = \left(\int_{-\infty}^{+\infty} [x - E(X)]^3 f(x)dx \right) \Big/ \sigma^3 \tag{2.12}$$

Negative skewness indicates that the distribution has a long left tail, which indicates a high probability of observing large negative values. If this represents the distribution of profits and losses for a portfolio, this is a dangerous situation. Figure 2-3 displays distributions with various signs for the skewness.

FIGURE 2-3 Effect of Skewness

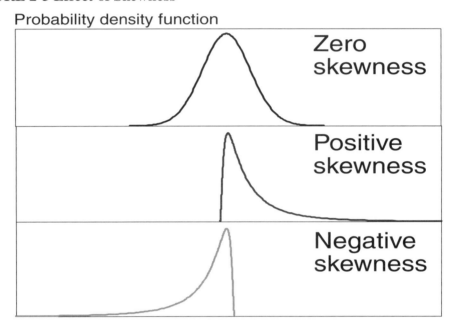

FIGURE 2-4 Effect of Kurtosis

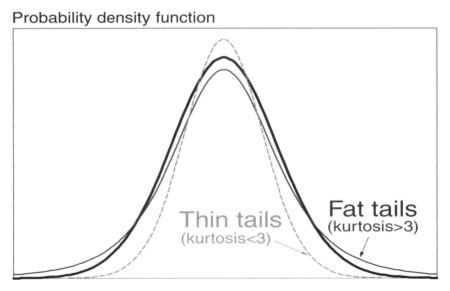

The scaled fourth moment is the **kurtosis**, which describes the degree of "flatness" of a distribution, or the width of its tails. It is defined as

$$\delta = \left(\int_{-\infty}^{+\infty} [x - E(X)]^4 f(x)dx \right) \bigg/ \sigma^4 \qquad (2.13)$$

Because of the fourth power, large observations in the tail will have a large weight and hence create high kurtosis. Such a distribution is called **leptokurtic**, or **fat-tailed**. This parameter is very important for risk measurement. A kurtosis of 3 is considered average. High kurtosis indicates a higher probability of extreme movements. Figure 2-4 displays distributions with various values for the kurtosis.

Example: Computing moments

Our gambler wants to know the expected value of the outcome of throwing two dice. He computes the product of each outcome and the associated probability, as shown in Table 2-2. For instance, the first entry is $xf(x) = 2 \times 0.0278 = 0.0556$. Summing across all events, the mean is $\mu = 7.000$. This is also the median, since the distribution is perfectly symmetric.

TABLE 2-2 Computing Moments of a Distribution

Outcome x_i	Prob. $f(x)$	Mean $xf(x)$	Variance $(x-\mu)^2 f(x)$	Skewness $(x-\mu)^3 f(x)$	Kurtosis $(x-\mu)^4 f(x)$
2	0.0278	0.0556	0.6944	−3.4722	17.3611
3	0.0556	0.1667	0.8889	−3.5556	14.2222
4	0.0833	0.3333	0.7500	−2.2500	6.7500
5	0.1111	0.5556	0.4444	−0.8889	1.7778
6	0.1389	0.8333	0.1389	−0.1389	0.1389
7	0.1667	1.1667	0.0000	0.0000	0.0000
8	0.1389	1.1111	0.1389	0.1389	0.1389
9	0.1111	1.0000	0.4444	0.8889	1.7778
10	0.0833	0.8333	0.7500	2.2500	6.7500
11	0.0556	0.6111	0.8889	3.5556	14.2222
12	0.0278	0.3333	0.6944	3.4722	17.3611
Sum	1.0000	7.0000	$\sigma^2 = 5.8333$	0.0000	80.5000
Denominator				$\sigma^3 = 14.0888$	$\sigma^4 = 34.0278$
		Mean $\mu = 7.00$	StdDev $\sigma = 2.4152$	Skewness $\gamma = 0.0000$	Kurtosis $\delta = 2.3657$

Next, we can use Equation (2.10) to compute the variance. The first term is $(x - \mu)^2 f(x) = (2 - 7)^2 0.0278 = 0.6944$. These terms add up to 5.8333 or, taking the square root, $\sigma = 2.4152$. The skewness terms sum to zero, because for each entry with a positive deviation $(x - \mu)^3$, there is an identical one with a negative sign and with the same probability. Finally, the kurtosis terms $(x - \mu)^4 f(x)$ sum to 80.5. Dividing by $\sigma^4 = 34.0278$ gives a kurtosis of $\delta = 2.3657$.

2.2 Multivariate Distribution Functions

In practice, portfolio payoffs depend on numerous random variables. To simplify, start with two random variables. This could represent two currencies, or two interest rate factors, or default and credit exposure, to give just a few examples.

We can extend Equation (2.1) to

$$F_{12}(x_1, x_2) = P(X_1 \leq x_1, X_2 \leq x_2) \tag{2.14}$$

which defines a joint bivariate distribution function. In the continuous case, this is also

$$F_{12}(x_1, x_2) = \int_{-\infty}^{x_1} \int_{-\infty}^{x_2} f_{12}(u_1, u_2) du_1 du_2 \tag{2.15}$$

where $f(u_1, u_2)$ is now the **joint density**. In general, adding random variables considerably complicates the characterization of the density or distribution functions.

The analysis simplifies considerably if the variables are **independent**. In this case, the joint density separates out into the product of the densities:

$$f_{12}(u_1 u_2) = f_1(u_1) \times f_2(u_2) \tag{2.16}$$

and the integral reduces to

$$F_{12}(x_1, x_2) = F_1(x_1) \times F_2(x_2) \tag{2.17}$$

In other words, the joint probability reduces to the product of the probabilities.

This is very convenient because we only need to know the individual densities to reconstruct the joint density. For example, a credit loss can be viewed as a combination of (1) default, which is a random variable with a value of 1 for default and 0 otherwise, and (2) the exposure, which is a random variable representing the amount at risk—for instance, the positive market value of a swap. If the two variables are independent, we can construct the distribution of the credit loss easily. In the case of the two dice, the events are indeed independent. As a result, the probability of a joint event is simply the product of probabilities. For instance, the probability of throwing two ones is equal to $1/6 \times 1/6 = 1/36$.

It is also useful to characterize the distribution of x_1 abstracting from x_2. By integrating over all values of x_2, we obtain the **marginal density**

$$f_1(x_1) = \int_{-\infty}^{\infty} f_{12}(x_1, u_2) du_2 \tag{2.18}$$

and similarly for x_2. We can then define the **conditional density** as

$$f_{1 \cdot 2}(x_1 \mid x_2) = \frac{f_{12}(x_1, x_2)}{f_2(x_2)} \tag{2.19}$$

Here we keep x_2 fixed and divide the joint density by the marginal probability of observing x_2. This normalization is necessary to ensure that the conditional density is a proper density function that integrates to 1. This relationship is also known as **Bayes' rule**.

When dealing with two random variables, the co-movement can be described by the **covariance**

$$\text{Cov}(X_1, X_2) = \sigma_{12} = \int_1 \int_2 [x_1 - E(X_1)][x_2 - E(X_2)] f_{12}(x_1, x_2) dx_1 dx_2 \tag{2.20}$$

It is often useful to scale the covariance into a unitless number, called the **correlation coefficient**, obtained as

$$\rho(X_1, X_2) = \frac{\text{Cov}(X_1, X_2)}{\sigma_1 \sigma_2} \tag{2.21}$$

The correlation coefficient is a measure of linear dependence. One can show that the correlation coefficient always lies in the interval $[-1, +1]$. A correlation of 1 means that the two variables always move in the same direction. A correlation of -1 means that the two variables always move in opposite directions.

If the variables are independent, the joint density separates out and this becomes

$$\text{Cov}(X_1, X_2) = \left\{ \int_1 [x_1 - E(X_1)] f_1(x_1) dx_1 \right\} \left\{ \int_2 [x_2 - E(X_2)] f_2(x_2) dx_2 \right\} = 0$$

by Equation (2.6), since the average deviation from the mean is zero. In this case, the two variables are said to be **uncorrelated**. Hence independence implies zero correlation (the reverse is not true, however).

Example: Multivariate functions

Consider two variables, such as the Canadian dollar and the euro. Table 2-3a describes the joint density function $f_{12}(x_1, x_2)$, assuming two payoffs only for each variable. Note first that the density indeed sums to $0.30 + 0.20 + 0.15 + 0.35 = 1.00$.

TABLE 2-3a Joint Density Function

	x_1	
x_2	-5	$+5$
-10	0.30	0.15
$+10$	0.20	0.35

From this, we can compute the marginal density for each variable, along with its mean and standard deviation. For instance, the marginal probability of $x_1 = -5$ is given by $f_1(x_1) = f_{12}(x_1, x_2 = -10) + f_{12}(x_1, x_2 = +10) = 0.30 + 0.20 = 0.50$. The marginal probability of $x_1 = +5$ must be 0.50 as well. Table 2-3b shows that the means and standard deviations are, respectively, $\bar{x}_1 = 0.0, \sigma_1 = 5.0$ and $\bar{x}_2 = 1.0, \sigma_2 = 9.95$.

TABLE 2-3b Marginal Density Functions

	Variable 1				Variable 2		
	Prob.	Mean	Variance		Prob.	Mean	Variance
x_1	$f_1(x_1)$	$x_1 f_1(x_1)$	$(x_1 - \bar{x}_1)^2 f_1(x_1)$	x_2	$f_2(x_2)$	$x_2 f_2(x_2)$	$(x_2 - \bar{x}_2)^2 f_2(x_2)$
-5	0.50	-2.5	12.5	-10	0.45	-4.5	54.45
$+5$	0.50	$+2.5$	12.5	$+10$	0.55	$+5.5$	44.55
Sum	1.00	0.0	25.0	Sum	1.00	1.0	99.0
		$\bar{x}_1 = 0.0$	$\sigma_1 = 5.0$			$\bar{x}_2 = 1.0$	$\sigma_2 = 9.95$

Finally, Table 2-3c details the computation of the covariance, which gives Cov $= 15.00$. Dividing by the product of the standard deviations, we get $\rho = \text{Cov}/(\sigma_1 \sigma_2) = 15.00/(5.00 \times 9.95) = 0.30$. The positive correlation indicates that when one variable goes up, the other is more likely to go up than down.

TABLE 2-3c Covariance and Correlation

	$(x_1 - \bar{x}_1)(x_2 - \bar{x}_2) f_{12}(x_1, x_2)$	
	$x_1 = -5$	$x_1 = +5$
$x_2 = -10$	$(-5 - 0)(-10 - 1)0.30 = 16.50$	$(+5 - 0)(-10 - 1)0.15 = -8.25$
$x_2 = +10$	$(-5 - 0)(+10 - 1)0.20 = -9.00$	$(+5 - 0)(+10 - 1)0.35 = 15.75$
Sum	Cov $= 15.00$	

Example 2-1: FRM Exam 1999—Question 21

The covariance between variable A and variable B is 5. The correlation between A and B is 0.5. If the variance of A is 12, what is the variance of B?

a) 10.00

b) 2.89

c) 8.33

d) 14.40

Example 2-2: FRM Exam 2000—Question 81

Which one of the following statements about the correlation coefficient is *false*?

a) It always ranges from -1 to $+1$.

b) A correlation coefficient of zero means that two random variables are independent.

c) It is a measure of linear relationship between two random variables.

d) It can be calculated by scaling the covariance between two random variables.

2.3 Functions of Random Variables

Risk management is about uncovering the distribution of portfolio values. Consider a security that depends on a unique source of risk, such as a bond. The risk manager could model the change in the bond price as a random variable directly. The problem with this choice is that the distribution of the bond price is not stationary, because the price converges to the face value at expiration.

Instead, the practice is to model the change in yields as a random variable because its distribution is better behaved. The next step is to use the relationship between the bond price and the yield to uncover the distribution of the bond price.

This illustrates a general principle of risk management, which is to model the risk factor first, then to derive the distribution of the instrument from information about the function that links the instrument value to the risk factor. This may not be easy to do, unfortunately, if the relationship is highly nonlinear. In what follows, we first focus on the mean and variance of simple transformations of random variables.

2.3.1 Linear Transformation of Random Variables

Consider a transformation that multiplies the original random variable by a constant and adds a fixed amount, $Y = a + bX$. The expectation of Y is

$$E(a + bX) = a + bE(X) \tag{2.22}$$

and its variance is

$$V(a + bX) = b^2 V(X) \tag{2.23}$$

Note that adding a constant never affects the variance since the computation involves the *difference* between the variable and its mean. The standard deviation is

$$SD(a + bX) = b\,SD(X) \tag{2.24}$$

Example: Currency position plus cash

A dollar-based investor has a portfolio consisting of $1 million in cash plus a position in 1,000 million Japanese yen. The distribution of the dollar/yen exchange rate X has a mean of $E(X) = 1/100 = 0.01$ and volatility of $SD(X) = 0.10/100 = 0.001$.

The portfolio value can be written as $Y = a + bX$, with fixed parameters (in millions) $a = \$1$ and $b = \yen 1,000$. Therefore, the portfolio expected value is $E(Y) = \$1 + \yen 1,000 \times 1/100 = \$11$ million, and the standard deviation is $SD(Y) = \yen 1,000 \times 0.001 = \$1$ million.

2.3.2 Sum of Random Variables

Another useful transformation is the summation of two random variables. A portfolio, for instance, could contain one share of Intel plus one share of Microsoft. Each stock price behaves as a random variable.

The expectation of the sum $Y = X_1 + X_2$ can be written as

$$E(X_1 + X_2) = E(X_1) + E(X_2) \tag{2.25}$$

and its variance is

$$V(X_1 + X_2) = V(X_1) + V(X_2) + 2\text{Cov}(X_1, X_2) \tag{2.26}$$

When the variables are uncorrelated, the variance of the sum reduces to the sum of variances. Otherwise, we have to account for the cross-product term.

Key concept:
The expectation of a sum is the sum of expectations. The variance of a sum, however, is the sum of variances only if the variables are uncorrelated.

2.3.3 Portfolios of Random Variables

More generally, consider a linear combination of a number of random variables. This could be a portfolio with fixed weights, for which the rate of return is

$$Y = \sum_{i=1}^{N} w_i X_i \qquad (2.27)$$

where N is the number of assets, X_i is the rate of return on asset i, and w_i is its weight.

This can be written in matrix notation, replacing a string of numbers by a single vector:

$$Y = w_1 X_1 + w_2 X_2 + \cdots + w_N X_N = \begin{bmatrix} w_1 w_2 \cdots w_N \end{bmatrix} \begin{bmatrix} X_1 \\ X_2 \\ \vdots \\ X_N \end{bmatrix} = w'X \qquad (2.28)$$

where w' represents the transposed vector (i.e., horizontal) of weights and X is the vertical vector containing individual asset returns. The appendix for this chapter provides a brief review of matrix multiplication.

The portfolio expected return is now

$$E(Y) = \mu_p = \sum_{i=1}^{N} w_i \mu_i \qquad (2.29)$$

which is a weighted average of the expected returns $\mu_i = E(X_i)$. The variance is

$$V(Y) = \sigma_p^2 = \sum_{i=1}^{N} w_i^2 \sigma_i^2 + \sum_{i=1}^{N} \sum_{j=1, j \neq i}^{N} w_i w_j \sigma_{ij} = \sum_{i=1}^{N} w_i^2 \sigma_i^2 + 2 \sum_{i=1}^{N} \sum_{j<i}^{N} w_i w_j \sigma_{ij} \qquad (2.30)$$

Using matrix notation, the variance can be written as

$$\sigma_p^2 = [w_1 \cdots w_N] \begin{bmatrix} \sigma_{11} & \sigma_{12} & \sigma_{13} & \cdots & \sigma_{1N} \\ \vdots & & & & \vdots \\ \sigma_{N1} & \sigma_{N2} & \sigma_{N3} & \cdots & \sigma_{N} \end{bmatrix} \begin{bmatrix} w_1 \\ \vdots \\ w_N \end{bmatrix}$$

Defining Σ as the covariance matrix, the variance of the portfolio rate of return can be written more compactly as

$$\sigma_p^2 = w' \Sigma w \qquad (2.31)$$

This is a useful expression for describing the risk of the total portfolio.

Example: Computing the risk of a portfolio

Consider a portfolio invested in Canadian dollars and euros. The joint density function is given in Table 2-3a. Here x_1 describes the payoff on the Canadian dollar, with $\mu_1 = 0.00$, $\sigma_1 = 5.00$, and $\sigma_1^2 = 25$. For the euro, $\mu_2 = 1.00$, $\sigma_2 = 9.95$, and $\sigma_2^2 = 99$. The covariance was computed as $\sigma_{12} = 15.00$, with the correlation $\rho = 0.30$. If we have 60% invested in Canadian dollar and 40% in euros, what is the portfolio volatility?

Following Equation (2.31), we write

$$\sigma_p^2 = [0.60 \; 0.40] \begin{bmatrix} 25 & 15 \\ 15 & 99 \end{bmatrix} \begin{bmatrix} 0.60 \\ 0.40 \end{bmatrix} = [0.60 \; 0.40] \begin{bmatrix} 25 \times 0.60 + 15 \times 0.40 \\ 15 \times 0.60 + 99 \times 0.40 \end{bmatrix}$$

$$\sigma_p^2 = [0.60 \; 0.40] \begin{bmatrix} 21.00 \\ 48.60 \end{bmatrix} = 0.60 \times 21.00 + 0.40 \times 48.60 = 32.04$$

Therefore, the portfolio volatility is $\sigma_p = \sqrt{32.04} = 5.66$. Note that this is barely higher than the volatility of the Canadian dollar alone, even though the risk of the euro is much higher. The portfolio risk has been kept low due to a diversification effect, or low correlation between the two assets.

2.3.4 Product of Random Variables

Some risks result from the product of two random variables. A credit loss, for instance, arises from the product of the occurrence of default and the loss given default.

Using Equation (2.20), the expectation of the product $Y = X_1 X_2$ can be written as

$$E(X_1 \, X_2) = E(X_1)E(X_2) + \text{Cov}(X_1, X_2) \tag{2.32}$$

When the variables are independent, this reduces to the product of the means.

The variance is more complex to evaluate. With independence, it reduces to

$$V(X_1 \, X_2) = E(X_1)^2 V(X_2) + V(X_1)E(X_2)^2 + V(X_1)V(X_2) \tag{2.33}$$

2.3.5 Distributions of Transformations of Random Variables

The preceding results focus on the mean and variance of simple transformations only. They do not fully describe the distribution of the transformed variable $Y = g(X)$.

This, unfortunately, is usually complicated for all but the simplest transformations $g(\cdot)$ and densities $f(X)$.

Even if there is no closed-form solution for the density, we can describe the cumulative distribution function of Y when $g(X)$ is a one-to-one transformation from X to Y. This implies that the function can be inverted, or that for a given y we can find x such that $x = g^{-1}(y)$. We can then write

$$P[Y \leq y] = P[g(X) \leq y] = P[X \leq g^{-1}(y)] = F_X(g^{-1}(y)) \qquad (2.34)$$

where $F(\cdot)$ is the cumulative distribution function of X. Here we have assumed the relationship is positive. Otherwise, the right-hand term is changed to $1 - F_X(g^{-1}(y))$.

This allows us to derive the quantile of, say, the bond price from information about the probability distribution of the yield. Suppose we consider a zero-coupon bond, for which the market value V is

$$V = \frac{100}{(1 + r)^T} \qquad (2.35)$$

where r is the yield. This equation describes V as a function of r, or $Y = g(X)$. Using $r = 6\%$ and $T = 30$ years, the current price is $V = \$17.41$. The inverse function $X = g^{-1}(Y)$ is

$$r = (100/V)^{1/T} - 1 \qquad (2.36)$$

We wish to estimate the probability that the bond price could fall below a cutoff price $V = \$15$. We invert the price-yield function and compute the associated yield level, $g^{-1}(y) = (100/\$15)^{1/30} - 1 = 6.528\%$. Lower prices are associated with higher yield levels. Using Equation (2.34), the probability is given by

$$P[V \leq \$15] = P[r \geq 6.528\%]$$

Assuming the yield change is normal with volatility 0.8%, this gives a probability of 25.5%.[1] Even though we do not know the density of the bond price, this method allows us to trace out its cumulative distribution by changing the cutoff price of $15. Taking the derivative, we can recover the density function of the bond price. Figure 2-5 shows that this p.d.f. is skewed to the right.

On the extreme right, if the yield falls to zero, the bond price will go to $100. On the extreme left, if the yield goes to infinity, the bond price will fall to, but not go

---

[1]We shall see later that this is obtained from the standard normal variable $z = (6.528 - 6.000)/0.80 = 0.660$. Using standard normal tables, or the =NORMSDIST(-0.660) Excel function, this gives 25.5%.

below, zero. Relative to the current value of $17.41, there is a greater likelihood of large movements up than down.

This method, unfortunately, cannot be easily extended. For general density functions and transformations, risk managers turn to numerical methods, especially when the number of random variables is large. This is why credit risk models, for instance, all describe the distribution of credit losses through simulations.

FIGURE 2-5 Density Function for the Bond Price

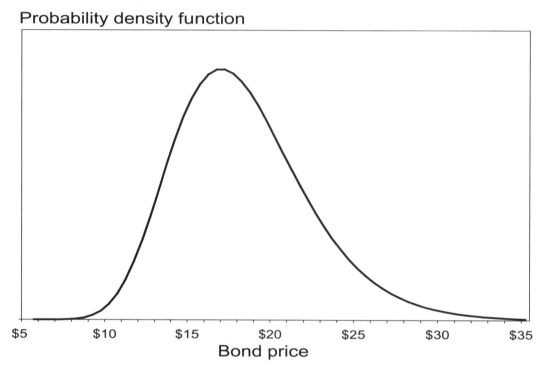

Probability density function

Bond price

Example 2-3: FRM Exam 2002—Question 70

Given that x and y are random variables, and a, b, c, and d are constant, which one of the following definitions is *wrong*?

a) $E(ax + by + c) = aE(x) + bE(y) + c$, if x and y are correlated

b) $V(ax + by + c) = V(ax + by) + c$, if x and y are correlated

c) $\text{Cov}(ax + by, cx + dy) = acV(x) + bdV(y) + (ad + bc)\text{Cov}(x, y)$, if x and y are correlated

d) $V(x - y) = V(x + y) = V(x) + V(y)$, if x and y are uncorrelated

2.4   Important Distribution Functions

2.4.1   Uniform Distribution

The simplest continuous distribution function is the **uniform distribution**. This is defined over a range of values for x, $a \leq x \leq b$. The density function is

$$f(x) = \frac{1}{(b - a)}, \quad a \leq x \leq b \qquad (2.37)$$

which is constant and indeed integrates to unity. This distribution puts the same weight on each observation within the allowable range, as shown in Figure 2-6. We denote this distribution as $U(a, b)$.

Its mean and variance are given by

$$E(X) = \frac{a + b}{2} \qquad (2.38)$$

$$V(X) = \frac{(b - a)^2}{12} \qquad (2.39)$$

The uniform distribution $U(0, 1)$ is widely used as a starting distribution for generating random variables in simulations. We assume that the p.d.f. $f(Y)$ and cumulative distribution $F(Y)$ are known. As any cumulative distribution function ranges from zero to unity, we can draw X from $U(0, 1)$ and then compute $y = F^{-1}(x)$. The random variable Y will then have the desired distribution $f(Y)$.

FIGURE 2-6 Uniform Density Function

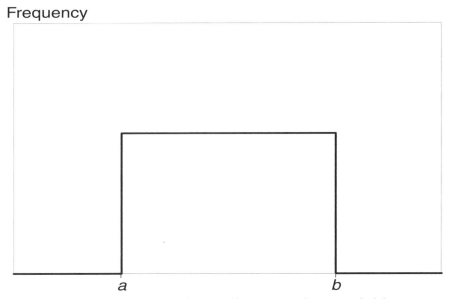

Realization of the uniform random variable

Example 2-4: FRM Exam 2002—Question 119

The random variable X with density function $f(x) = 1/(b-a)$ for
$a < x < b$, and 0 otherwise, is said to have a uniform distribution over (a, b).
Calculate its mean.

a) $(a+b)/2$
b) $a - b/2$
c) $a + b/4$
d) $a - b/4$

2.4.2 Normal Distribution

Perhaps the most important continuous distribution is the **normal distribution**, which adequately represents many random processes. This has a bell-like shape, with more weight in the center and tails tapering off to zero. The daily rate of return in a stock price, for instance, has a distribution similar to the normal p.d.f.

The normal distribution can be characterized by its first two moments only, the mean μ and variance σ^2. The first parameter represents the location and the second the dispersion. The normal density function has the expression

$$f(x) = \frac{1}{\sqrt{2\pi\sigma^2}} \exp\left[-\frac{1}{2\sigma^2}(x-\mu)^2\right] \tag{2.40}$$

Its mean is $E[X] = \mu$ and its variance $V[X] = \sigma^2$. We denote this distribution as $N(\mu, \sigma^2)$. Because the function can be fully specified by these two parameters, it is called a **parametric function**.

Instead of having to deal with different parameters, it is often more convenient to use a **standard normal variable** such as ϵ, which has been standardized, or normalized, so that $E(\epsilon) = 0, V(\epsilon) = \sigma(\epsilon) = 1$. Figure 2-7 plots the **standard normal density**.

First, note that the function is symmetrical around the mean. Its mean of zero is the same as its **mode** (which is the most likely, or highest, point on this curve) and **median** (the value such that the area to the left is a 50% probability). The skewness of a normal distribution is 0, which indicates that it is symmetric around the mean. The kurtosis of a normal distribution is 3. Distributions with fatter tails have a greater kurtosis coefficient.

About 95% of the distribution is contained between the values of $\epsilon_1 = -2$ and $\epsilon_2 = +2$, and 68% of the distribution falls between the values of $\epsilon_1 = -1$ and

$\epsilon_2 = +1$. Table 2-4 gives the values corresponding to right-tail probabilities such that

$$\int_{-\alpha}^{\infty} f(\epsilon)d\epsilon = c \tag{2.41}$$

For instance, the value -1.645 is the quantile that corresponds to a 95% probability.[2]

FIGURE 2-7 Normal Density Function

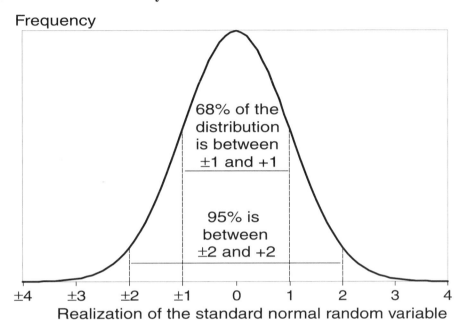

TABLE 2-4 Lower Quantiles of the Standardized Normal Distribution

c	Confidence Level (%)								
	99.99	99.9	99	97.72	97.5	95	90	84.13	50
$-\alpha$	-3.715	-3.090	-2.326	-2.000	-1.960	-1.645	-1.282	-1.000	-0.000

The distribution of any normal variable can be recovered from the standard normal by defining

$$X = \mu + \epsilon\sigma \tag{2.42}$$

Using Equations (2.22) and (2.23), we can show that X indeed has the desired moments, with $E(X) = \mu + E(\epsilon)\sigma = \mu$ and $V(X) = V(\epsilon)\sigma^2 = \sigma^2$.

---

[2]More generally, the cumulative distribution can be found from the Excel function =NORMDIST. For example, we can verify that =NORMSDIST(-1.645) yields 0.04999, or a 5% left-tail probability.

Define, for instance, the random variable as the change in the dollar value of a portfolio. The expected value is $E(X) = \mu$. To find the quantile of X at the specified confidence level c, we replace ϵ by $-\alpha$ in Equation (2.42). This gives $Q(X, c) = \mu - \alpha\sigma$. Using Equation (2.9), we can compute VAR as

$$\text{VAR} = E(X) - Q(X, c) = \mu - (\mu - \alpha\sigma) = \alpha\sigma \qquad (2.43)$$

For example, a portfolio with a standard deviation of $10 million would have a VAR, or potential downside loss, of $16.45 million at the 95% confidence level.

Key concept:
With normal distributions, the VAR of a portfolio is obtained from the product of the portfolio standard deviation and a standard normal deviate factor that reflects the confidence level, for instance, 1.645 at the 95% level.

An important property of the normal distribution is that it is one of the few distributions that is *stable* under addition. In other words, a linear combination of jointly normally distributed random variables has a normal distribution.[3] This is extremely useful because we need to know only the mean and variance of the portfolio to reconstruct its whole distribution.

Key concept:
A linear combination of jointly normal variables has a normal distribution.

Example 2-5: FRM Exam 2000—Question 108
The distribution of one-year returns for a portfolio of securities is normally distributed with an expected value of €45 million and a standard deviation of €16 million. What is the probability that the value of the portfolio one year hence will be between €39 million and €43 million?
a) 8.6%
b) 9.6%
c) 10.6%
d) 11.6%

---

[3]Strictly speaking, this is true only under either of the following conditions: (1) The univariate variables are independently distributed, or (2) the variables are multivariate normally distributed (this invariance property also holds for jointly elliptically distributed variables).

Example 2-6: FRM Exam 1999—Question 12

For a standard normal distribution, what is the approximate area under the cumulative distribution function between the values −1 and 1?

a) 50%

b) 68%

c) 75%

d) 95%

Example 2-7: FRM Exam 1999—Question 13

What is the kurtosis of a normal distribution?

a) 0

b) Cannot be determined, because it depends on the variance of the particular normal distribution considered

c) 2

d) 3

Example 2-8: FRM Exam 1999—Question 16

If a distribution with the same variance as a normal distribution has kurtosis greater than 3, which of the following is *true*?

a) It has fatter tails than the normal distribution.

b) It has thinner tails than the normal distribution.

c) It has the same tail fatness as the normal distribution since the variances are the same.

d) Cannot be determined from the information provided.

2.4.3 Lognormal Distribution

The normal distribution is a good approximation for many financial variables, such as the rate of return on a stock, $r = (P_1 - P_0)/P_0$, where P_0 and P_1 are the stock prices at time 0 and 1.

Strictly speaking, this is inconsistent with reality since a normal variable has infinite tails on both sides. In theory, r could end up below −1, which implies $P_1 < 0$. In reality, due to the limited liability of corporations, stock prices cannot turn negative. In many situations, however, this is an excellent approximation. For instance, with short horizons or small price moves, the probability of having a negative price is so small as to be negligible. If this is not the case, we need to resort to distributions that prevent prices from going negative. One such distribution is the lognormal.

A random variable X is said to have a **lognormal distribution** if its logarithm $Y = \ln(X)$ is normally distributed. Define here $X = (P_1/P_0)$. Because the argument

X in the logarithm function must be positive, the price P_1 can never go below zero.

The lognormal density function has the expression

$$f(x) = \frac{1}{x\sqrt{2\pi\sigma^2}} \exp\left[-\frac{1}{2\sigma^2}(\ln(x) - \mu)^2\right], \quad x > 0 \qquad (2.44)$$

Note that this is more complex than simply plugging $\ln(x)$ in Equation (2.40), because x also appears in the denominator. Its mean is

$$E[X] = \exp\left[\mu + \frac{1}{2}\sigma^2\right] \qquad (2.45)$$

and variance $V[X] = \exp[2\mu + 2\sigma^2] - \exp[2\mu + \sigma^2]$. The parameters were chosen to correspond to those of the normal variable, $E[Y] = E[\ln(X)] = \mu$ and $V[Y] = V[\ln(X)] = \sigma^2$.

Conversely, if we set $E[X] = \exp[r]$, the mean of the associated normal variable is $E[Y] = E[\ln(X)] = (r - \sigma^2/2)$. We will see later that this adjustment is also used in the Black-Scholes option valuation model, where the formula involves a trend in $(r - \sigma^2/2)$ for the log-price ratio.

FIGURE 2-8 Lognormal Density Function

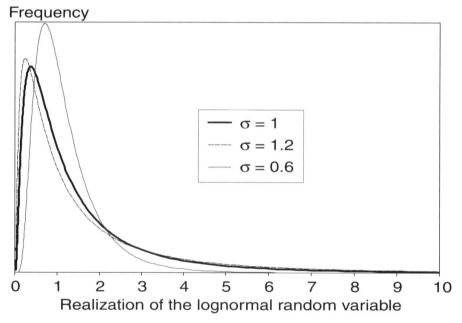

Figure 2-8 depicts the lognormal density function with $\mu = 0$ and $\sigma = 1.0, 1.2, 0.6$. Note that the distribution is skewed to the right. The tail increases for greater values of σ. This explains why as the variance increases, the mean is pulled up in Equation (2.45).

We also note that the distribution of the bond price in our previous example, Equation (2.35), resembles a lognormal distribution. Using continuous compounding instead of annual compounding, the price function is

$$V = 100 \exp(-rT) \tag{2.46}$$

which implies $\ln(V/100) = -rT$. Thus if r is normally distributed, V has a lognormal distribution.

Example 2-9: FRM Exam 2001—Question 72

The lognormal distribution is
a) Positively skewed
b) Negatively skewed
c) Not skewed; that is, its skew equals 2
d) Not skewed; that is, its skew equals 0

Example 2-10: FRM Exam 1999—Question 5

Which of the following statements best characterizes the relationship between the normal and lognormal distributions?
a) The lognormal distribution is the logarithm of the normal distribution.
b) If the natural log of the random variable X is lognormally distributed, then X is normally distributed.
c) If X is lognormally distributed, then the natural log of X is normally distributed.
d) The two distributions have nothing to do with one another.

Example 2-11: FRM Exam 2002—Question 125

Consider a stock with an initial price of $100. Its price one year from now is given by $S = 100 \times \exp(r)$, where the rate of return r is normally distributed with a mean of 0.1 and a standard deviation of 0.2. With 95% confidence, after rounding, S will be between
a) $67.57 and $147.99
b) $70.80 and $149.20
c) $74.68 and $163.56
d) $102.18 and $119.53

Example 2-12: FRM Exam 1998—Question 16

Which of the following statements are *true*?

I. The sum of two random normal variables is also a random normal variable.

II. The product of two random normal variables is also a random normal variable.

III. The sum of two random lognormal variables is also a random lognormal variable.

IV. The product of two random lognormal variables is also a random lognormal variable.

a) I and II only

b) II and III only

c) III and IV only

d) I and IV only

Example 2-13: FRM Exam 2000—Question 128

For a lognormal variable X, we know that $\ln(X)$ has a normal distribution with a mean of zero and a standard deviation of 0.5. What are the expected value and the variance of X?

a) 1.025 and 0.187

b) 1.126 and 0.217

c) 1.133 and 0.365

d) 1.203 and 0.399

2.4.4 Student's t Distribution

Another important distribution is the **Student's t distribution**. This arises in hypothesis testing, because it describes the distribution of the ratio of the estimated coefficient to its standard error.

This distribution is characterized by a parameter k known as the **degrees of freedom**. Its density is

$$f(x) = \frac{\Gamma[(k+1)/2]}{\Gamma(k/2)} \frac{1}{\sqrt{k\pi}} \frac{1}{(1+x^2/k)^{(k+1)/2}} \tag{2.47}$$

where Γ is the gamma function, defined as $\Gamma(k) = \int_0^\infty x^{k-1} e^{-x} dx$. As k increases, this function converges to the normal p.d.f.

The distribution is symmetrical with mean zero and variance

$$V[X] = \frac{k}{k-2} \tag{2.48}$$

provided $k > 2$. Its kurtosis is

$$\delta = 3 + \frac{6}{k - 4} \tag{2.49}$$

provided $k > 4$. Its has fatter tails than the normal, which often allows a better representation of typical financial variables. Typical estimated values of k are around 4 to 6. Figure 2-9 displays the density for $k = 4$ and $k = 50$. The latter is close to the normal. With $k = 4$, however, the p.d.f. has fatter tails. As was done for the normal density, we can use the Student's t to compute VAR as a function of the volatility,

$$\text{VAR} = \alpha_k \sigma \tag{2.50}$$

where the multiplier now depends on the degrees of freedom k.

FIGURE 2-9 Student's t Density Function

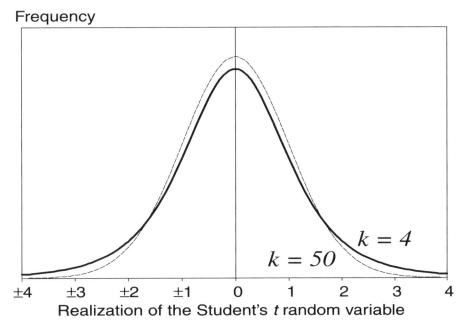

Another distribution derived from the normal is the **chi-square distribution**, which can be viewed as the sum of independent squared standard normal variables:

$$x = \sum_{j=1}^{k} z_j^2 \tag{2.51}$$

where k again represents the degrees of freedom. Its mean is $E[X] = k$ and variance $V[X] = 2k$. For k sufficiently large, $\chi^2(k)$ converges to a normal distribution $N(k, 2k)$. This distribution describes the sample variance.

Another associated distribution is the *F* **distribution**, which can be viewed as the ratio of independent chi-square variables divided by their degrees of freedom:

$$F(a, b) = \frac{\chi^2(a)/a}{\chi^2(b)/b} \tag{2.52}$$

This distribution appears in joint tests of regression coefficients.

Example 2-14: FRM Exam 1999—Question 3

It is often said that distributions of returns from financial instruments are leptokurtic. For such distributions, which of the following comparisons with a normal distribution of the same mean and variance *must* hold?

a) The skew of the leptokurtic distribution is greater.
b) The kurtosis of the leptokurtic distribution is greater.
c) The skew of the leptokurtic distribution is smaller.
d) The kurtosis of the leptokurtic distribution is smaller.

2.4.5 Binomial Distribution

Consider now a random variable that can take discrete values between zero and n. This could be, for instance, the number of times VAR is exceeded over the last year, also called the number of **exceptions**. Thus, the binomial distribution plays an important role in the backtesting of VAR models.

A binomial variable can be viewed as the result of n independent **Bernoulli trials**, where each trial results in an outcome of $y = 0$ or $y = 1$. This applies, for example, to credit risk. In case of default, we have $y = 1$; otherwise $y = 0$. Each Bernoulli variable has expected value $E[Y] = p$ and variance $V[Y] = p(1 - p)$.

A random variable is defined to have a **binomial distribution** if the discrete density function is given by

$$f(x) = \binom{n}{x} p^x (1 - p)^{n-x}, \quad x = 0, 1, \ldots, n \tag{2.53}$$

where $\binom{n}{x}$ is the number of combinations of n things taken x at a time, or

$$\binom{n}{x} = \frac{n!}{x!(n - x)!} \tag{2.54}$$

and the parameter p is between 0 and 1. This distribution also represents the total number of successes in n repeated experiments where each success has a probability of p.

The binomial variable has mean and variance

$$E[X] = pn \tag{2.55}$$

$$V[X] = p(1 - p)n \tag{2.56}$$

It is presented in Figure 2-10 for the case where $p = 0.25$ and $n = 10$. The probability of observing $X = 0, 1, 2 \ldots$ is 5.6%, 18.8%, 28.1%, and so on.

FIGURE 2-10 Binomial Density Function with $p = 0.25, n = 10$

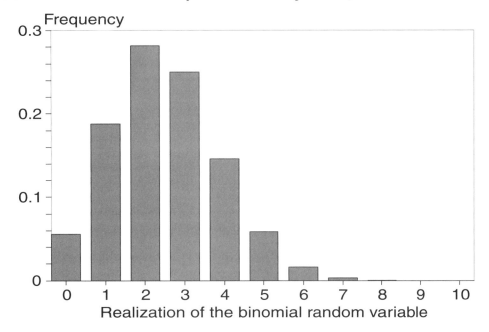

For instance, we want to know the probability of observing $x = 0$ exceptions out of a sample of $n = 250$ observations when the true probability is 1%. We should expect to observe 2.5 exceptions on average across many such samples. There will be, however, some samples with no exceptions at all. This probability is

$$f(X = 0) = \frac{n!}{x!(n - x)!}p^x(1 - p)^{n-x} = \frac{250!}{1 \times 250!}0.01^0 0.99^{250} = 0.081$$

So we would expect to observe 8.1% of samples with zero exceptions, under the null hypothesis. We can repeat this calculation with different values for x. For example, the probability of observing eight exceptions is $f(X = 8) = 0.02\%$ only. We can use this information to test the null hypothesis. Because this probability is so low, observing eight exceptions would make us question whether the true probability is 1%.

2.5 Limit Distributions

2.5.1 Distribution of Averages

The normal distribution is extremely important because of the **central limit theorem** (CLT), which states that the mean of n independent and identically distributed variables converges to a normal distribution as the number of observations n increases. This very powerful result is valid for any underlying distribution, as long as the realizations are independent. For instance, the distribution of total credit losses converges to a normal distribution as the number of loans increases to a large value, assuming defaults are always independent of each other.

Define $\bar{X}$ as the mean $\frac{1}{n}\sum_{i=1}^{n} X_i$, where each variable has mean μ and standard deviation σ. We have

$$\bar{X} \rightarrow N\left(\mu, \frac{\sigma^2}{n}\right) \qquad (2.57)$$

Standardizing the variable, we can write

$$\frac{\bar{X} - \mu}{(\sigma/\sqrt{n})} \rightarrow N(0, 1) \qquad (2.58)$$

If $\bar{X}$ is the sum instead of the mean, this result still holds, but without the $\sqrt{n}$ term in the denominator. Thus, the normal distribution is the limiting distribution of the average, which explains why it has such a prominent place in statistics.

As an example, consider the binomial variable, which is the sum of independent Bernoulli trials. When n is large, we can use the CLT and approximate the binomial distribution by the normal distribution. Using Equation (2.58) for the sum, we have

$$z = \frac{x - pn}{\sqrt{p(1-p)n}} \rightarrow N(0, 1) \qquad (2.59)$$

which is much easier to evaluate than the binomial distribution.

Consider, for example, the issue of whether the number of exceptions x we observe is compatible with a 99% VAR. For our example, the mean and variance of x are $E[X] = 0.01 \times 250 = 2.5$ and $V[X] = 0.01(1 - 0.01) \times 250 = 2.475$. We observe $x = 8$, which gives $z = (8 - 2.5)/\sqrt{2.475} = 3.50$. We can now compare this number to the standard normal distribution. Say we decide to reject the hypothesis that VAR is correct if the statistic falls outside a 95% two-tailed confidence band. This interval is $(-1.96, +1.96)$ for the standardized normal distribution. Here the value of

3.50 is much higher than the cutoff point of $+1.96$. As a result, we would reject the null hypothesis that the true probability of observing an exception is 1% only. In other words, there are simply too many exceptions to be explained by bad luck. It is more likely that the VAR model underestimates risk.

2.5.2 Distribution of Tails

The CLT deals with the mean, or center of the distribution. For risk management purposes, it is also useful to examine the tails of the distribution.

Another powerful theorem is given by **extreme value theory** (EVT). The EVT theorem says that the limit distribution for values x beyond a cutoff point u belongs to the family

$$\begin{aligned} F(y) &= 1 - (1 + \xi y)^{-1/\xi}, & \xi \neq 0 \\ F(y) &= 1 - exp(-y), & \xi = 0 \end{aligned} \tag{2.60}$$

where $y = (x - u)/\beta$. To simplify, we define the loss x as a positive number so that y is also positive. The distribution is characterized by $\beta > 0$, a *scale* parameter, and by ξ, a *shape* parameter that determines the speed at which the tail disappears.

This distribution is called the **generalized Pareto distribution**, because it subsumes other distributions as special cases. For instance, the normal distribution corresponds to $\xi = 0$, in which case the tails disappear at an exponential speed. Typical financial data have $\xi > 0$, which implies *fat tails*, as in the case of the Student's t distribution. This distribution is often used to smooth out the tails of empirical data.

Figure 2-11 illustrates the shape of the density function for U.S. stock market data. The normal density falls off fairly quickly. The EVT density is defined only when the loss x exceeds an arbitrary cutoff point, which is taken as 2 in this case. With $\xi = 0.2$, the EVT density has a fatter tail than the normal density, implying a higher probability of experiencing large losses. This is an important observation for risk management purposes.

Example 2-15: FRM Exam 2001—Question 68

EVT, extreme value theory, helps quantify two key measures of risk:

a) The magnitude of an X-year return in the loss in excess of VAR
b) The magnitude of VAR and the level of risk obtained from scenario analysis
c) The magnitude of market risk and the magnitude of operational risk
d) The magnitude of market risk and the magnitude of credit risk

---

FIGURE 2-11 EVT and Normal Densities

Frequency

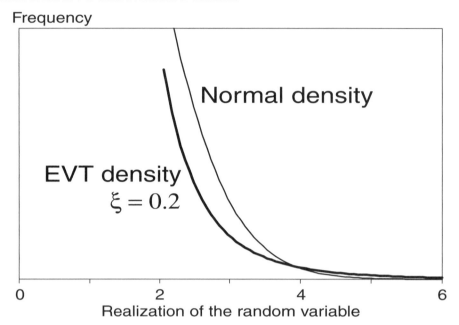

Realization of the random variable

2.6   Answers to Chapter Examples

Example 2-1: FRM Exam 1999—Question 21

c) From Equation (2.21), we have $\sigma_B = \text{Cov}(A, B)/(\rho\sigma_A) = 5/(0.5\sqrt{12}) = 2.89$, for a variance of $\sigma_B^2 = 8.33$.

Example 2-2: FRM Exam 2000—Question 81

b) Correlation is a measure of linear association. Independence implies zero correlation, but the reverse is not always true.

Example 2-3: FRM Exam 2002—Question 70

b) Statement a) is correct, as it is a linear operation. Statement c) is correct, as shown by Equation (2.30). Statement d) is correct, as the covariance term is zero if the variables are uncorrelated. Statement b) is false, as adding a constant c to a variable cannot change the variance. The constant drops out because it is also in the expectation.

Example 2-4: FRM Exam 2002—Question 119

a) The mean is the center of the distribution, which is the average of a and b.

Example 2-5: FRM Exam 2000—Question 108

b) First, we compute the standard variate for each cutoff point: $\epsilon_1 = (43 - 45)/16 =$

-0.125 and $\epsilon_2 = (39 - 45)/16 = -0.375$. Next, we compute the cumulative distribution function for each: $F(\epsilon_1) = 0.450$ and $F(\epsilon_2) = 0.354$. Hence, the difference is a probability of $0.450 - 0.354 = 0.096$.

Example 2-6: FRM Exam 1999—Question 12

b) See Figure 2-7.

Example 2-7: FRM Exam 1999—Question 13

d) Note that b) is not correct because the kurtosis involves σ^4 in the denominator and is hence scale-free.

Example 2-8: FRM Exam 1999—Question 16

a) As in Equation (2.13), the kurtosis adjusts for σ. Greater kurtosis than for the normal implies fatter tails.

Example 2-9: FRM Exam 2001—Question 72

a) The lognormal distribution has a long left tail, as in Figure 2-8. So it is positively skewed.

Example 2-10: FRM Exam 1999—Question 5

c) X is said to be lognormally distributed if its logarithm $Y = \ln(X)$ is normally distributed.

Example 2-11: FRM Exam 2002—Question 125

c) Note that this is a two-tailed confidence band, so $\alpha = 1.96$. We find the extreme values from $\$100 \exp(\mu \pm \alpha\sigma)$. The lower limit is then $V_1 = \$100 \exp(0.10 - 1.96 \times 0.2) = \$100 \exp(-0.292) = \$74.68$. The upper limit is $V_2 = \$100 \exp(0.10 + 1.96 \times 0.2) = \$100 \exp(0.492) = \$163.56$.

Example 2-12: FRM Exam 1998—Question 16

d) Normal variables are stable under addition, so I is true. For lognormal variables X_1 and X_2, we know that their logs, $Y_1 = \ln(X_1)$ and $Y_2 = \ln(X_2)$, are normally distributed. Hence, the sum of their logs, or $\ln(X_1) + \ln(X_2) = \ln(X_1 X_2)$, must also be normally distributed. The product is itself lognormal, so IV is true.

Example 2-13: FRM Exam 2000—Question 128

c) Using Equation (2.45), we have $E[X] = \exp[\mu + 0.5\sigma^2] = \exp[0 + 0.5 \cdot 0.5^2] = 1.1331$. Assuming there is no error in the answers listed for the variance, it is sufficient to find the correct answer for the expected value.

Example 2-14: FRM Exam 1999—Question 3

b) Leptokurtic refers to a distribution with fatter tails than the normal, which implies greater kurtosis.

Example 2-15: FRM Exam 2001—Question 68

a) EVT allows risk managers to approximate distributions in the tails beyond the usual VAR confidence levels. Answers c) and d) are too general. Answer b) is also incorrect, as EVT is based on historical data rather than scenario analyses.

Appendix: Review of Matrix Multiplication

This appendix briefly reviews the mathematics of matrix multiplication. Suppose we have two matrices, A and B, that we wish to multiply to obtain the new matrix $C = AB$. The respective dimensions are $(n \times m)$ for A, that is, n rows and m columns, and $(m \times p)$ for B. The number of columns for A must exactly match (or conform to) the number of rows for B. If so, this will result in a matrix C of dimensions $(n \times p)$.

We can write the matrix A in terms of its individual components a_{ij}, where i denotes the row and j denotes the column:

$$A = \begin{bmatrix} a_{11} & a_{12} & \cdots & a_{1m} \\ \vdots & \vdots & \ddots & \vdots \\ a_{n1} & a_{n2} & \cdots & a_{nm} \end{bmatrix}$$

As an illustration, take a simple example where the matrices are of dimension (2×3) and (3×2).

$$A = \begin{bmatrix} a_{11} & a_{12} & a_{13} \\ a_{21} & a_{22} & a_{23} \end{bmatrix}$$

$$B = \begin{bmatrix} b_{11} & b_{12} \\ b_{21} & b_{22} \\ b_{31} & b_{32} \end{bmatrix}$$

$$C = AB = \begin{bmatrix} c_{11} & c_{12} \\ c_{21} & c_{22} \end{bmatrix}$$

To multiply the matrices, each row of A is multiplied element by element by each column of B. For instance, c_{12} is obtained by taking

$$c_{12} = \begin{bmatrix} a_{11} & a_{12} & a_{13} \end{bmatrix} \begin{bmatrix} b_{12} \\ b_{22} \\ b_{32} \end{bmatrix} = a_{11}b_{12} + a_{12}b_{22} + a_{13}b_{32}$$

The matrix C is then

$$C = \begin{bmatrix} a_{11}b_{11} + a_{12}b_{21} + a_{13}b_{31} & a_{11}b_{12} + a_{12}b_{22} + a_{13}b_{32} \\ a_{21}b_{11} + a_{22}b_{21} + a_{23}b_{31} & a_{21}b_{12} + a_{22}b_{22} + a_{23}b_{32} \end{bmatrix}$$

Matrix multiplication can be easily implemented in Excel using the function =MMULT. First, we highlight the cells representing the output matrix C, say f1:g2. Then we enter the function, for instance =MMULT(a1:c2; d1:e3), where the first range represents the first matrix, A, here 2 by 3, and the second range represents matrix B, here 3 by 2. The final step is to hit the three keys Control-Shift-Return simultaneously.

Chapter 3

Fundamentals of Statistics

The preceding chapter was mainly concerned with the theory of probability, including distribution theory. In practice, researchers have to find methods to choose among distributions and to estimate distribution parameters from real data. The subject of sampling brings us now to the theory of statistics. Whereas probability assumes that the distributions are known, statistics attempts to make inferences from actual data.

Here we sample from the distribution of a population, say the change in the exchange rate, to make inferences about the population. The questions are, what is the best distribution for this random variable, and what are the best parameters for this distribution? Risk measurement typically deals with large numbers of random variables. So we also want to characterize the relationships between the risk factors to which the portfolio is exposed. For example, do we observe that movements in the yen/dollar rate are correlated with movements in the dollar/euro rate? Another type of problem is to develop decision rules to test some hypotheses—for instance, whether the volatility is stable over time.

These examples illustrate two important problems in statistical inference, **estimation** and **tests of hypotheses**. With estimation, we wish to estimate the value of an unknown parameter from sample data. With tests of hypotheses, we wish to verify a conjecture about the data.

This chapter reviews the fundamental tools of statistics theory for risk managers. Section 3.1 discusses the sampling of real data and the construction of returns. The problem of parameter estimation is presented in Section 3.2. Section 3.3 then turns to regression analysis, summarizing important results as well as common pitfalls in their interpretation.

3.1   Real Data

To start with an example, let us say that we observe movements in the daily yen/dollar exchange rate and wish to characterize the distribution of tomorrow's exchange rate.

The risk manager's job is to assess the range of potential gains and losses on a trader's position. He or she observes a sequence of past spot prices, $S_0, S_1, \ldots, S_t$, from which the distribution of tomorrow's price, S_{t+1}, must be inferred.

3.1.1   Measuring Returns

The truly random component in tomorrow's price is not its level, but its change relative to today's price. We measure the *relative rate of change* in the spot price:

$$r_t = (S_t - S_{t-1})/S_{t-1} \tag{3.1}$$

Alternatively, we could construct the logarithm of the price ratio:

$$R_t = \ln[S_t/S_{t-1}] \tag{3.2}$$

which is equivalent to using continuous instead of discrete compounding. This is also expressed as

$$R_t = \ln[1 + (S_t - S_{t-1})/S_{t-1}] = \ln[1 + r_t]$$

Because $\ln(1 + x)$ is close to x if x is small, R_t should be close to r_t provided the return is small. For daily data, there is typically little difference between R_t and r_t.

The return defined so far is the **capital appreciation return**, which ignores the income payment on the asset. Define the dividend or coupon as D_t. In the case of an exchange rate position, this is the interest payment in the foreign currency over the holding period. The **total return** on the asset is

$$r_t^{\text{TOT}} = (S_t + D_t - S_{t-1})/S_{t-1} \tag{3.3}$$

When the horizon is very short, the income return is typically very small compared with the capital appreciation return.

The next question is whether the sequence of variables r_t can be viewed as independent observations. If so, one could hypothesize, for instance, that the random variables are drawn from a normal distribution $N(\mu, \sigma^2)$. We could then proceed to estimate μ and σ^2 from the data and use this information to create a distribution for tomorrow's spot price change.

Independent observations have the very nice property that their joint distributions is the product of their marginal distributions, which considerably simplifies the analysis. The obvious question is whether this assumption is a workable approximation. In fact, there are good economic reasons to believe that rates of change on financial prices are nearly independent.

The hypothesis of **efficient markets** postulates that current prices convey all relevant information about the asset. If so, any change in the asset price must be due to news or events, which are by definition impossible to forecast (otherwise, it would not be news). This implies that changes in prices are unpredictable and hence satisfy our definition of independent random variables.

This hypothesis, also known as the **random walk** theory, implies that the conditional distribution of returns depends only on current prices, and not on the previous history of prices. If so, technical analysis must be a fruitless exercise, because previous patterns in prices cannot help in forecasting price movements.

If in addition the distribution of returns is constant over time, the variables are said to be **independently and identically distributed** (i.i.d.). So we could consider that the observations r_t are independent draws from the same distribution $N(\mu, \sigma^2)$.

Later we will consider deviations from this basic model. Distributions of financial returns typically display fat tails. Also, variances are not constant and display some persistence; expected returns can also slightly vary over time.

3.1.2   Time Aggregation

It is often necessary to translate parameters over a given horizon to another horizon. For example, we may have raw data for daily returns, from which we compute a daily volatility that we want to extend to a monthly volatility.

Returns can be easily related across time when we use the log of the price ratio, because the log of a product is the sum of the logs of the indivual terms. The two-day return, for example, can be decomposed as

$$R_{02} = \ln[S_2/S_0] = \ln[(S_2/S_1) \times (S_1/S_0)] = \ln[S_1/S_0] + \ln[S_2/S_1] = R_{01} + R_{12}$$
(3.4)

This decomposition is only approximate if we use discrete returns, however.

The expected return and variance are then $E(R_{02}) = E(R_{01}) + E(R_{12})$ and $V(R_{02}) = V(R_{01}) + V(R_{12}) + 2\text{Cov}(R_{01}, R_{12})$. Assuming returns are uncorrelated and have identical distributions across days, we have $E(R_{02}) = 2E(R_{01})$ and $V(R_{02}) = 2V(R_{01})$.

Generalizing over T days, we can relate the moments of the T-day returns R_T to those of the one-day returns R_1:

$$E(R_T) = E(R_1)T \tag{3.5}$$

$$V(R_T) = V(R_1)T \tag{3.6}$$

Expressed in terms of volatility, this yields the **square-root-of-time rule**:

$$\text{SD}(R_T) = \text{SD}(R_1)\sqrt{T} \tag{3.7}$$

Key concept:
When successive returns are uncorrelated, the volatility increases as the horizon extends following the square root of time.

It should be emphasized that this holds only if returns have constant parameters across time and are uncorrelated. When there is nonzero correlation across days, the two-day variance is

$$V(R_2) = V(R_1) + V(R_1) + 2\rho V(R_1) = 2V(R_1)(1 + \rho) \tag{3.8}$$

Because we are considering correlations in the time series of the same variable, ρ is called the **autocorrelation coefficient**. A positive value for ρ implies that a movement in one direction in one day is likely to be followed by another movement in the same direction the next day. A positive autocorrelation signals the existence of a **trend**. In this case, Equation (3.8) shows that the two-day variance is greater than that obtained by the square-root-of-time rule.

A negative value for ρ implies that a movement in one direction in one day is likely to be followed by a movement in the other direction the next day. So prices tend to revert back to a mean value. A negative autocorrelation signals **mean reversion**. In this case, the two-day variance is less than that obtained by the square-root-of-time rule.

3.1.3   Portfolio Aggregation

Let us now turn to the aggregation of returns across assets. Consider, for example, an equity portfolio consisting of investments in N shares. Define the number of each share held as q_i with unit price S_i. The portfolio value at time t is then

$$W_t = \sum_{i=1}^{N} q_i S_{i,t} \tag{3.9}$$

We can write the weight assigned to asset i as

$$w_{i,t} = \frac{q_i S_{i,t}}{W_t} \tag{3.10}$$

By construction these weights sum to unity. Using weights, however, rules out situations with zero net investment, $W_t = 0$, such as some derivatives positions. But we could have positive and negative weights if short selling is allowed, or weights greater than 1 if the portfolio can be leveraged.

In the next period, the portfolio value is

$$W_{t+1} = \sum_{i=1}^{N} q_i S_{i,t+1} \tag{3.11}$$

assuming that the unit price incorporates any income payment. The gross, or dollar, return is then

$$W_{t+1} - W_t = \sum_{i=1}^{N} q_i (S_{i,t+1} - S_{i,t}) \tag{3.12}$$

and the *rate* of return is

$$\frac{W_{t+1} - W_t}{W_t} = \sum_{i=1}^{N} \frac{q_i S_{i,t}}{W_t} \frac{(S_{i,t+1} - S_{i,t})}{S_{i,t}} = \sum_{i=1}^{N} w_{i,t} \frac{(S_{i,t+1} - S_{i,t})}{S_{i,t}} \tag{3.13}$$

So the portfolio rate of return is a linear combination of the asset returns:

$$r_{p,t+1} = \sum_{i=1}^{N} w_{i,t} r_{i,t+1} \tag{3.14}$$

The dollar return is then

$$W_{t+1} - W_t = \left[\sum_{i=1}^{N} w_{i,t} r_{i,t+1} \right] W_t \tag{3.15}$$

and has a normal distribution if the individual returns are also normally distributed.

Alternatively, we could express the individual positions in dollar terms,

$$x_{i,t} = w_{i,t} W_t = q_i S_{i,t} \qquad (3.16)$$

The dollar return is also, using dollar amounts,

$$W_{t+1} - W_t = \left[\sum_{i=1}^{N} x_{i,t} r_{i,t+1} \right] \qquad (3.17)$$

As we saw in the previous chapter, the variance of the portfolio dollar return is

$$V[W_{t+1} - W_t] = x' \Sigma x \qquad (3.18)$$

which, along with the expected return, fully characterizes its distribution. The portfolio VAR is then

$$\text{VAR} = \alpha \sqrt{x' \Sigma x} \qquad (3.19)$$

where α depends on the selected density function.

Example 3-1: FRM Exam 2002—Question 46

An investor purchases 100 shares of XYZ at the beginning of the year for $35. The stock pays a cash dividend of $3 per share. The price of the stock at the time of the dividend is $30. The dividend is not reinvested. The stock is sold at the end of the year for $28. Calculate the holding period return for this investment. It is approximately

a) −20.0%

b) −12.6%

c) −11.4%

d) −10.3%

Example 3-2: FRM Exam 1999—Question 4

A fundamental assumption of the random walk hypothesis of market returns is that returns from one time period to the next are statistically independent. This assumption implies

a) Returns from one time period to the next can never be equal.

b) Returns from one time period to the next are uncorrelated.

c) Knowledge of the returns from one time period does not help in predicting returns from the next time period.

d) Both b) and c) are true.

Example 3-3: FRM Exam 2002—Question 3

Consider a stock with daily returns that follow a random walk. The annualized volatility is 34%. Estimate the weekly volatility of this stock assuming that the year has 52 weeks.

a) 6.80%

b) 5.83%

c) 4.85%

d) 4.71%

Example 3-4: FRM Exam 1998—Question 7

Assume an asset price variance increases linearly with time. Suppose the expected asset price volatility for the next two months is 15% (annualized), and for the one month that follows, the expected volatility is 35% (annualized). What is the average expected volatility over the next three months?

a) 22%

b) 24%

c) 25%

d) 35%

Example 3-5: FRM Exam 1997—Question 15

The standard VAR calculation for extension to multiple periods assumes that returns are serially uncorrelated. If prices display trends, the true VAR will be

a) The same as the standard VAR

b) Greater than the standard VAR

c) Less than the standard VAR

d) Unable to be determined

Example 3-6: FRM Exam 2002—Question 2

Assume we calculate a one-week VAR for a natural gas position by rescaling the daily VAR using the square-root rule. Let us now assume that we determine the *true* gas price process to be mean-reverting and recalculate the VAR. Which of the following statements is true?

a) The recalculated VAR will be less than the original VAR.

b) The recalculated VAR will be equal to the original VAR.

c) The recalculated VAR will be greater than the original VAR.

d) There is no necessary relation between the recalculated VAR and the original VAR.

3.2   Parameter Estimation

Armed with our i.i.d. sample of T observations, we can start estimating the parameters of interest, the sample mean, variance, and other moments.

As in the previous chapter, define x_i as the realization of a random sample. The expected return, or mean, $\mu = E(X)$ can be estimated by the sample mean,

$$m = \widehat{\mu} = \frac{1}{T}\sum_{i=1}^{T} x_i \tag{3.20}$$

Intuitively, we assign the same weight of $1/T$ to all observations because they all have the same probability. The variance, $\sigma^2 = E[(X - \mu)^2]$, can be estimated by the sample variance,

$$s^2 = \widehat{\sigma}^2 = \frac{1}{(T-1)}\sum_{i=1}^{T}(x_i - \widehat{\mu})^2 \tag{3.21}$$

Note that we divide by $T - 1$ instead of T. This is because we estimate the variance around an unknown parameter, the mean. So we have fewer degrees of freedom than otherwise. As a result, we need to adjust s^2 to ensure that its expectation equals the true value. In most situations, however, T is large, so that this adjustment is minor.

It is essential to note that these estimated values depend on the particular sample and, hence, have some inherent variability. The sample mean itself is distributed as

$$m = \widehat{\mu} \sim N(\mu, \sigma^2/T) \tag{3.22}$$

If the population distribution is normal, this exactly describes the distribution of the sample mean. Otherwise, the central limit theorem states that this distribution is valid only asymptotically (i.e., for large samples).

For the distribution of the sample variance $\widehat{\sigma}^2$, one can show that when X is normal, the following ratio is distributed as a chi-square with $(T-1)$ degrees of freedom:

$$\frac{(T-1)\widehat{\sigma}^2}{\sigma^2} \sim \chi^2(T-1) \tag{3.23}$$

If the sample size T is large enough, the chi-square distribution converges to a normal distribution:

$$\widehat{\sigma}^2 \sim N\left(\sigma^2, \sigma^4 \frac{2}{(T-1)}\right) \tag{3.24}$$

Using the same approximation, the sample standard deviation has a normal distribution with a standard error of

$$se(\widehat{\sigma}) = \sigma \sqrt{\frac{1}{2T}} \qquad (3.25)$$

We can use this information for **hypothesis testing**. For instance, we would like to detect a constant trend in X. Here, the **null hypothesis** is that $\mu = 0$. To answer the question, we use the distributional assumption in Equation (3.22) and compute a standard normal variable as the ratio of the estimated mean to its standard error, or

$$z = \frac{(m - 0)}{\sigma / \sqrt{T}} \qquad (3.26)$$

Because this is now a standard normal variable, we would not expect to observe values far away from zero. Typically, we would set the confidence level at 95%, which translates into a two-tailed interval for z of $[-1.96, +1.96]$. Roughly, this means that if the absolute value of z is greater than 2, we would reject the hypothesis that m came from a distribution with a mean of zero. We can have some confidence that the true μ is indeed different from zero.

In fact, we do not know the true σ and use the estimated s instead. The distribution is a Student's t with T degrees of freedom:

$$t = \frac{(m - 0)}{s / \sqrt{T}} \qquad (3.27)$$

for which the cutoff values can be found from tables. For large values of T, however, this distribution is close to the normal.

At this point, we need to make an important observation. Equation (3.22) shows that when the sample size increases, the standard error of $\widehat{\mu}$ shrinks at a rate proportional to $1/\sqrt{T}$. The precision of the estimate increases as the number of observations increases.

This result will prove useful in assessing the precision of estimates generated from **numerical simulations**, which are widely used in risk management. Numerical simulations create independent random variables over a fixed number of replications T. If T is too small, the final estimates will be imprecisely measured. If T is very large, the precision will be very good. The precision of the estimates increases at a rate proportional to $1/\sqrt{T}$.

Key concept:

With independent draws, the standard deviation of most statistics is inversely related to the square root of number of observations T. Thus, more observations make for more precise estimates.

Example:

We want to characterize movements in the monthly yen/dollar exchange rate from historical data, taken over 1990 to 1999. Returns are defined in terms of continuously compounded changes, as in Equation (3.2). The sample size is $T = 120$, and estimated parameters are $m = -0.28\%$ and $s = 3.55\%$ (per month).

Using Equation (3.22), the standard error of the mean is approximately $se(m) = s/\sqrt{T} = 0.32\%$. For the null hypothesis of $\mu = 0$, this gives a t-ratio of $t = m/se(m) = -0.28\%/0.32\% = -0.87$. Because this number is less than 2 in absolute value, we cannot reject the hypothesis that the mean is zero at the 95% confidence level. This is a typical result for financial series. The mean is not precisely estimated.

Next, we turn to the precision in the sample standard deviation. By Equation (3.25), its standard error is $se(s) = \sigma\sqrt{\frac{1}{(2T)}} = 0.229\%$. For the null of $\sigma = 0$, this gives a ratio of $z = s/se(s) = 3.55\%/0.229\% = 15.5$, which is very high. So the volatility is not zero.

Therefore, there is much more precision in the measurement of s than in that of m. We can construct 95% confidence intervals around the estimated values. These are

$$[m - 1.96 \times se(m), m + 1.96 \times se(m)] = [-0.92\%, +0.35\%]$$

$$[s - 1.96 \times se(s), s + 1.96 \times se(s)] = [3.10\%, 4.00\%]$$

So we can be reasonably confident that the volatility is between 3% and 4%, but we cannot even be sure that the mean is different from zero.

3.3   Regression Analysis

Regression analysis has particular importance for risk management, because it can be used to explain and forecast financial variables.

3.3.1   Bivariate Regression

In a **linear regression**, the **dependent variable** y is projected on a set of N predetermined **independent variables**, x. In the simplest bivariate case we write

$$y_t = \alpha + \beta x_t + \epsilon_t, \qquad t = 1, \ldots, T \tag{3.28}$$

where α is called the **intercept**, or constant, β is called the **slope**, and ϵ is called the **residual**, or **error term**. This could represent a time series or a cross-section.

The **ordinary least squares** (OLS) assumptions are

- *The errors are independent of x.*
- *The errors have a normal distribution with zero mean and constant variance, conditional on x.*
- *The errors are independent across observations.*

Based on these assumptions, the usual methodology is to estimate the coefficients by minimizing the sum of squared errors. Beta is estimated by

$$\widehat{\beta} = \frac{[1/(T-1)] \sum_t (x_t - \bar{x})(y_t - \bar{y})}{[1/(T-1)] \sum_t (x_t - \bar{x})^2} \tag{3.29}$$

where $\bar{x}$ and $\bar{y}$ correspond to the means of x_t and y_t. Alpha is estimated by

$$\widehat{\alpha} = \bar{y} - \widehat{\beta}\bar{x} \tag{3.30}$$

Note that the numerator in Equation (3.29) is also the sample covariance between two series x_i and x_j, which can be written as

$$\widehat{\sigma_{ij}} = \frac{1}{(T-1)} \sum_{t=1}^{T} (x_{t,i} - \widehat{\mu_i})(x_{t,j} - \widehat{\mu_j}) \tag{3.31}$$

To interpret β, we can take the covariance between y and x, which is

$$\mathrm{Cov}(y, x) = \mathrm{Cov}(\alpha + \beta x + \epsilon, x) = \beta \mathrm{Cov}(x, x) = \beta V(x)$$

because ϵ is conditionally independent of x. This shows that the population β is also

$$\beta(y, x) = \frac{\mathrm{Cov}(y, x)}{V(x)} = \frac{\rho(y, x)\sigma(y)\sigma(x)}{\sigma^2(x)} = \rho(y, x)\frac{\sigma(y)}{\sigma(x)} \tag{3.32}$$

The **regression fit** can be assessed by examining the size of the residuals, obtained by subtracting the fitted values $\widehat{y_t}$ from y_t,

$$\widehat{\epsilon_t} = y_t - \widehat{y_t} = y_t - \widehat{\alpha} - \widehat{\beta}x_t \tag{3.33}$$

and taking the estimated variance as

$$V(\widehat{\epsilon}) = \frac{1}{(T-2)} \sum_{t=1}^{T} \widehat{\epsilon}_t^2 \tag{3.34}$$

We divide by $T-2$ because the estimator uses two unknown quantities, $\widehat{\alpha}$ and $\widehat{\beta}$. Also note that, because the regression includes an intercept, the average value of $\widehat{\epsilon}$ has to be exactly zero.

The quality of the fit can be assessed using a unitless measure called the **regression R-square**. This is defined as

$$R^2 = 1 - \frac{\text{SSE}}{\text{SSY}} = 1 - \frac{\sum_t \widehat{\epsilon}_t^2}{\sum_t (y_t - \bar{y})^2} \tag{3.35}$$

where SSE is the sum of squared errors, and SSY is the sum of squared deviations of y around its mean. If the regression includes a constant, we always have $0 \le R^2 \le 1$. In this case, R-square is also the square of the usual correlation coefficient,

$$R^2 = \rho(y, x)^2 \tag{3.36}$$

R^2 measures the degree to which the size of the errors is smaller than that of the original dependent variables y. To interpret R^2, consider two extreme cases. If the fit is excellent, the errors will all be zero, and the numerator in Equation (3.35) will be zero, which gives $R^2 = 1$. On the other hand, if the fit is poor, SSE will be as large as SSY and the ratio will be 1, giving $R^2 = 0$.

Alternatively, we can interpret R-square by decomposing the variance of $y_t = \alpha + \beta x_t + \epsilon_t$. Because ϵ and x are uncorrelated, this yields

$$V(y) = \beta^2 V(x) + V(\epsilon)$$

Dividing by $V(y)$,

$$1 = \frac{\beta^2 V(x)}{V(y)} + \frac{V(\epsilon)}{V(y)} \tag{3.37}$$

Because R-square is also $R^2 = 1 - V(\epsilon)/V(y)$, it is equal to $= \beta^2 V(x)/V(y)$, which is the contribution in the variation of y due to β and x.

Finally, we can derive the distribution of the estimated coefficients, which is normal and centered around the true values. For the slope coefficient, $\widehat{\beta} \sim N(\beta, V(\widehat{\beta}))$, with variance given by

$$V(\widehat{\beta}) = V(\widehat{\epsilon}) \frac{1}{\sum_t (x_t - \bar{x})^2} \tag{3.38}$$

This can be used to test whether the slope coefficient is significantly different from zero. The associated test statistic

$$t = \widehat{\beta}/\sigma\left(\widehat{\beta}\right) \tag{3.39}$$

has a Student's t distribution. Typically, if the absolute value of the statistic is above 2, we would reject the hypothesis that there is no relationship between y and x.

3.3.2   Autoregression

A particularly useful application is a regression of a variable on a lagged value of itself, called **autoregression**:

$$y_t = \alpha + \beta_k y_{t-k} + \epsilon_t, \qquad t = 1, \ldots, T \tag{3.40}$$

If the coefficient is significant, previous movements in the variable can be used to predict future movements. Here the coefficient β_k is known as the kth-order **autocorrelation coefficient**.

Consider, for instance, a first-order autoregression, where the daily change in the yen/dollar rate is regressed on the previous day's value. A positive coefficient $\widehat{\beta}_1$ indicates a trend. A negative coefficient indicates mean reversion. As an example, assume we find that $\widehat{\beta}_1 = 0.10$, with zero intercept. One day, the yen goes up by 2%. Our best forecast for the next day is another up-move of

$$E[y_{t+1}] = \beta_1 y_t = 0.1 \times 2\% = 0.2\%$$

Autocorrelation changes normal patterns in risk across horizons. When there is no autocorrelation, risk increases with the square root of time. With positive autocorrelation, shocks have a longer-lasting effect and risk increases faster than the square root of time.

3.3.3   Multivariate Regression

More generally, the regression in Equation (3.28) can be written, with N independent variables (perhaps including a constant),

$$\begin{bmatrix} y_1 \\ \vdots \\ y_T \end{bmatrix} = \begin{bmatrix} x_{11} & x_{12} & x_{13} & \ldots & x_{1N} \\ \vdots & & & & \\ x_{T1} & x_{T2} & x_{T3} & \ldots & x_{TN} \end{bmatrix} \begin{bmatrix} \beta_1 \\ \vdots \\ \beta_N \end{bmatrix} + \begin{bmatrix} \epsilon_1 \\ \vdots \\ \epsilon_T \end{bmatrix} \tag{3.41}$$

or in matrix notation,

$$y = X\beta + \epsilon \tag{3.42}$$

The estimated coefficients can be written in matrix notation as

$$\widehat{\beta} = (X'X)^{-1}X'y \tag{3.43}$$

and their covariance matrix as

$$V(\widehat{\beta}) = \sigma^2(\epsilon)(X'X)^{-1} \tag{3.44}$$

We can extend the t-statistic to a multivariate environment. Say we want to test whether the last m coefficients are jointly zero. Define $\widehat{\beta_m}$ as these grouped coefficients and $V_m(\widehat{\beta})$ as their covariance matrix. We set up a statistic

$$F = \frac{\widehat{\beta}'_m V_m(\widehat{\beta})^{-1}\widehat{\beta}_m/m}{\text{SSE}/(T-N)} \tag{3.45}$$

which has an F-distribution with m and $T - N$ degrees of freedom. As before, we would reject the hypothesis if the value of F is too large compared with critical values from tables.

3.3.4 Example

This section gives an example of a regression of a stock return on the market. This is useful in assessing whether movements in the stock can be hedged using stock market index futures, for instance.

We consider 10 years of data for Intel and the S&P 500, using total rates of return over a month. Figure 3-1 plots the 120 combinations of returns, or (y_t, x_t). Apparently, there is a positive relationship between the two variables, as shown by the straight line that represents the regression fit $(\widehat{y_t}, x_t)$.

Table 3-1 displays the regression results. The regression shows a positive relationship between the two variables, with $\widehat{\beta} = 1.349$. This is significantly positive, with a standard error of 0.229 and t-statistic of 5.90. The t-statistic is very high, with an associated probability value (p-value) close to zero. Thus we can be fairly confident of a positive association between the two variables.

FIGURE 3-1 Intel Return vs. S&P Return

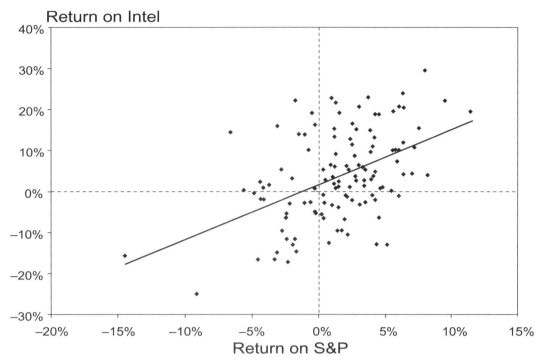

TABLE 3-1 Regression Results

$y = \alpha + \beta x$, $y =$ **Intel return**, $x =$ **S&P return**

R-square	0.228
Standard error of y	10.94%
Standard error of $\widehat{\epsilon}$	9.62%

Coefficient	Estimate	Standard Error	t-statistic	p-value
Intercept $\widehat{\alpha}$	0.0168	0.0094	1.78	0.77
Intercept $\widehat{\beta}$	1.349	0.229	5.90	0.00

This beta coefficient is also called **systematic risk**, or exposure to general market movements. Typically, technology stocks have greater-than-average systematic risk. Indeed, the slope in Intel's regression is greater than unity. To test whether β is significantly different from 1, we can compute a z-score as

$$z = \frac{(\widehat{\beta} - 1)}{s(\widehat{\beta})} = \frac{(1.349 - 1)}{0.229} = 1.53$$

This is less than the usual cutoff value of 2, so we cannot say for certain that Intel's systematic risk is greater than 1.

The R-square of 22.8% can be also interpreted by examining the reduction in dispersion from y to $\widehat{\epsilon}$, which is from 10.94% to 9.62%. The R-square can be written as

$$R^2 = 1 - \frac{(9.62\%^2)}{(10.94\%^2)} = 22.8\%$$

Thus about 23% of the variance of Intel's returns can be attributed to the market.

3.3.5   Pitfalls with Regressions

As with any quantitative method, the usefulness of regression analysis depends on the underlying assumptions being fulfilled for the problem at hand. Potential problems of interpretation are now briefly mentioned.

The original OLS setup assumes that the X variables are predetermined (i.e., exogenous or fixed), as in a controlled experiment. In practice, regressions are performed on actual data that do not satisfy these strict conditions. In the previous regression, returns on the S&P are certainly not predetermined.

If the X variables are stochastic, however, most of the OLS results are still valid as long as the X variables are distributed independently of the errors and their distribution does not involve β and σ^2.

Violations of this assumption are serious because they create biases in the slope coefficients. Biases could lead the researcher to come to the wrong conclusion. For instance, we could have measurement error in the X variables, which causes the measured X to be correlated with ϵ. This so-called **errors in the variables** problem causes a downward bias, or reduces the estimated slope coefficients from their true values. Note that errors in the y variables are not an issue, because they are captured by the error component ϵ.

Another problem is **specification error**. Suppose the true model has N variables, but we use only a subset N_1. If the omitted variables are correlated with the included variables, the estimated coefficients will be biased. This is a very serious problem because it is difficult to identify.

Another class of problem is **multicollinearity**. This arises when the X variables are highly correlated. Some of the variables may be superfluous; for example, the two currencies used may be fixed to each other. As a result, the matrix in Equation (3.43) will be unstable and the estimated β unreliable. This problem will be evident in large standard errors, however. It can be fixed by discarding some of the variables that are highly correlated with others.

The third type of problem has to do with potential biases in the standard errors of the coefficients. This is are especially serious if the standard errors are underestimated, creating a sense of false precision in the regression results and perhaps leading to the wrong conclusions. The OLS approach assumes that the errors are independent across observations. This is generally the case for financial time series, but often not the case in cross-sectional setups. For instance, consider a cross-section of mutual fund returns on some attribute. Mutual fund families often have identical funds, except for the fee structure (e.g., called *A* for a front load, *B* for a deferred load). These funds, however, are invested in the same securities and have the same manager. Thus, their returns are certainly not independent. If we run a standard OLS regression with all funds, the standard errors will be too small. More generally, one has to check that there is no systematic correlation pattern in the residuals. Even with time series, problems can arise with **autocorrelation** in the errors. In addition, the residuals can have different variances across observations, in which case we have **heteroscedasticity**.[1] These problems can be identified by performing diagnostic checks on the residuals. For instance, the variance of residuals should not be related to other variables in the regression. If some relationship is found, then the model must be improved until the residuals are found to be independent.

Finally, even if all the OLS conditions are satisfied, one must be extremely careful about using a regression for forecasting. Unlike physical systems, which are inherently stable, financial markets are dynamic and relationships can change quickly. Indeed, financial anomalies, which show up as strongly significant coefficients in historical regressions, have an uncanny ability to disappear as soon as one tries to exploit them.

Example 3-7: FRM Exam 1999—Question 2

Under what circumstances could the explanatory power of regression analysis be overstated?

a) The explanatory variables are not correlated with one another.

b) The variance of the error term decreases as the value of the dependent variable increases.

c) The error term is normally distributed.

d) An important explanatory variable is omitted that influences the explanatory variables included, and the dependent variable.

---

[1]This is the opposite of the constant-variance case, or homoscedasticity.

Example 3-8: FRM Exam 1999—Question 20

What is the covariance between populations A and B?

A	17	14	12	13
B	22	26	31	29

a) −6.25
b) 6.50
c) −3.61
d) 3.61

Example 3-9: FRM Exam 1999—Question 6

It has been observed that daily returns on spot positions of the euro against the U.S. dollar are highly correlated with returns on spot holdings of the Japanese yen against the dollar. This implies that

a) When the euro strengthens against the dollar, the yen also tends to strengthen against the dollar. The two sets of returns are not necessarily equal.
b) The two sets of returns tend to be almost equal.
c) The two sets of returns tend to be almost equal in magnitude but opposite in sign.
d) None of the above are true.

Example 3-10: FRM Exam 1999—Question 10

An analyst wants to estimate the correlation between stocks on the Frankfurt and Tokyo exchanges. He collects closing prices for select securities on each exchange but notes that Frankfurt closes after Tokyo. How will this time discrepancy bias the computed volatilities for individual stocks and correlations between any pair of stocks, one from each market? There will be

a) Increased volatility with correlation unchanged
b) Lower volatility with lower correlation
c) Volatility unchanged with lower correlation
d) Volatility unchanged with correlation unchanged

Example 3-11: FRM Exam 2000—Question 125

If the F-test shows that the set of X variables explain a significant amount of variation in the Y variable, then

a) Another linear regression model should be tried.
b) A t-test should be used to test which of the individual X variables, if any, should be discarded.
c) A transformation of the Y variable should be made.
d) Another test could be done using an indicator variable to test the significance level of the model.

Example 3-12: FRM Exam 2000—Question 112

Positive autocorrelation in prices can be defined as

a) An upward movement in price is more than likely to be followed by another upward movement in price.

b) A downward movement in price is more than likely to be followed by another downward movement in price.

c) Both a) and b) are correct.

d) Historical prices have no correlation with future prices.

3.4   Answers to Chapter Examples

Example 3-1: FRM Exam 2002—Question 46

c) The return is given by the capital gain plus income, which is $(P_1 + D - P_0)/P_0 = (\$28 + \$3 - \$35)/\$35 = -11.4\%$. This assumes the dividend is not reinvested in the stock or in an interest-bearing account.

Example 3-2: FRM Exam 1999—Question 4

d) An efficient market implies that the distribution of future returns does not depend on past returns. Hence, returns cannot be correlated. It could happen, however, that return distributions are independent but that, just by chance, two successive returns are equal.

Example 3-3: FRM Exam 2002—Question 3

d) Assuming a random walk, we can use the square-root-of-time rule. The weekly volatility is then $34\% \times 1/\sqrt{52} = 4.71\%$.

Example 3-4: FRM Exam 1998—Question 7

b) The methodology is the same as for the time aggregation, except that the variance may not be constant over time. The total (annualized) variance is $0.15^2 \times 2 + 0.35^2 \times 1 = 0.1675$ for three months, or 0.0558 on average. Taking the square root, we get 0.236, or 24%.

Example 3-5: FRM Exam 1997—Question 15

b) This question assumes that VAR is obtained from the volatility using a normal distribution. With trends, or positive correlation between subsequent returns, the two-day variance is greater than that obtained from the square-root-of-time rule. See Equation (3.7).

Example 3-6: FRM Exam 2002—Question 2

a) With mean reversion, the volatility grows more slowly than the square root of time. This is the opposite of the case in the previous question.

Example 3-7: FRM Exam 1999—Question 2

d) If the true regression includes a third variable z that influences both y and x, the error term will not be conditionally independent of x, which violates one of the assumptions of the OLS model. This will artificially increase the explanatory power of the regression. Intuitively, the variable x will appear to explain more of the variation in y simply because it is correlated with z.

Example 3-8: FRM Exam 1999—Question 20

a) First, compute the averages of A and B, which are 14 and 27. Then construct a table as follows.

	A	B	$(A-14)$	$(B-27)$	$(A-14)(B-27)$
	17	22	3	−5	−15
	14	26	0	−1	0
	12	31	−2	4	8
	13	29	−1	2	2
Sum	56	108			−25

Summing the last column gives −25, or an average of −6.25.

Example 3-9: FRM Exam 1999—Question 6

a) Positive correlation means that, on average, a positive movement in one variable is associated with a positive movement in the other variable. Because correlation is scale-free, this has no implication for the actual size of movements.

Example 3-10: FRM Exam 1999—Question 10

c) The nonsynchronicity of prices does not alter the volatility, but will induce some error in the correlation coefficient across series. This is similar to the effect of errors in the variables, which biases downward the slope coefficient and the correlation.

Example 3-11: FRM Exam 2000—Question 125

b) The F-test applies to the group of variables but does not say which one is most significant. To identify which particular variable is significant, we use a t-test and discard the variables that do not appear significant.

Example 3-12: FRM Exam 2000—Question 112

c) Positive autocorrelation means that price movements in one direction are more likely to be followed by price movements in the same direction.

Chapter 4

Monte Carlo Methods

The two preceding chapters dealt with probability and statistics. The former involves the generation of random variables from known distributions. The latter deals with the estimation of distribution parameters from actual data. With estimated distributions in hand, we can proceed to the next step, which is the simulation of random variables for the purpose of risk management. Such simulations, called **Monte Carlo** simulations, are central to financial engineering and risk management. They allow financial engineers to price complex financial instruments. They allow risk managers to build the distribution of portfolios that are too complex to model analytically.

Simulation methods are quite flexible and are becoming easier to implement with technological advances in computing. Their drawbacks should not be underestimated, however. For all their elegance, simulation results depend heavily on the model's assumptions: the shape of the distribution, the parameters, and the pricing functions. Risk managers need to be keenly aware of the effect that errors in these assumptions can have on the results.

This chapter shows how Monte Carlo methods can be used for risk management. Section 4.1 introduces a simple case with just one source of risk. Section 4.2 shows how to apply these methods to construct value at risk (VAR) measures, as well as to price derivatives. Multiple sources of risk are then considered in Section 4.3.

4.1 Simulations with One Random Variable

Simulations involve creating artificial random variables with properties similar to those of the risk factors in the portfolio. These include stock prices, exchange rates, bond yields or prices, and commodity prices.

4.1.1 Simulating Markov Processes

In efficient markets, financial prices should display a random walk pattern. More precisely, prices are assumed to follow a **Markov process**, which is a particular stochastic process where the entire distribution of the future price relies on the current price only. The past history is irrelevant. These processes are built from the following components, described in order of increasing complexity.

■ **The Wiener process.** This describes a variable Δz whose change is measured over the interval Δt such that its mean change is zero and its variance is proportional to Δt:

$$\Delta z \sim N(0, \Delta t) \tag{4.1}$$

If ϵ is a standard normal variable, $N(0, 1)$, this can be written as $\Delta z = \epsilon \sqrt{\Delta t}$. In addition, the increments Δz are independent across time.

■ **The generalized Wiener process.** This describes a variable Δx built up from a Wiener process, that also has a constant trend a per unit time and volatility b:

$$\Delta x = a \Delta t + b \Delta z \tag{4.2}$$

A particular case is the **martingale**, which is a zero-drift stochastic process, $a = 0$. This has the convenient property that the expectation of a future value is the current value,

$$E(x_T) = x_0 \tag{4.3}$$

■ **The Ito process.** This describes a generalized Wiener process whose trend and volatility depend on the *current* value of the underlying variable and time:

$$\Delta x = a(x, t) \Delta t + b(x, t) \Delta z \tag{4.4}$$

This is a Markov process because the distribution depends only on the current value of the random variable x, as well as time. In addition, the innovation in this process has a normal distribution.

4.1.2 The Geometric Brownian Motion

A particular example of an Ito process is the **geometric Brownian motion** (GBM), which is described for the variable S as

$$\Delta S = \mu S \Delta t + \sigma S \Delta z \tag{4.5}$$

The process is geometric because the trend and volatility terms are proportional to the current value of S. This is typically the case for stock prices, for which *rates of return* appear to be more stationary than raw dollar returns, ΔS. It is also used for currencies. Because $\Delta S/S$ represents the capital appreciation only, abstracting from dividend payments, μ represents the expected total rate of return on the asset minus the rate of income payment, or dividend yield in the case of stocks.

Example: A stock price process

Consider a stock that pays no dividends, has an expected return of 10% per annum, and volatility of 20% per annum. If the current price is $100, what is the process for the change in the stock price over the next week? What if the current price is $10?

The process for the stock price is

$$\Delta S = S(\mu \Delta t + \sigma \sqrt{\Delta t} \times \epsilon)$$

where ϵ is a random draw from a standard normal distribution. If the interval is one week, or $\Delta t = 1/52 = 0.01923$, the mean is $\mu \Delta t = 0.10 \times 0.01923 = 0.001923$ and $\sigma \sqrt{\Delta t} = 0.20 \times \sqrt{0.01923} = 0.027735$. The process is $\Delta S = \$100(0.001923 + 0.027735 \times \epsilon)$. With an initial stock price at $100, this gives $\Delta S = 0.1923 + 2.7735\epsilon$. With an initial stock price at $10, this gives $\Delta S = 0.01923 + 0.27735\epsilon$. The trend and volatility are scaled down by a factor of 10.

This model is particularly important because it is the underlying process for the Black-Scholes formula. The key feature of this distribution is the fact that the volatility is proportional to S. This ensures that the stock price will stay positive. Indeed, as the stock price falls, its variance decreases, which makes it unlikely to experience a large down-move that would push the price into negative values. As the limit of this model is a normal distribution for $dS/S = d\ln(S)$, S follows a **lognormal distribution**.

This process implies that, over an interval $T - t = \tau$, the logarithm of the ending price is distributed as

$$\ln(S_T) = \ln(S_t) + (\mu - \sigma^2/2)\tau + \sigma \sqrt{\tau} \, \epsilon \tag{4.6}$$

where ϵ is a standardized normal variable.

Example: A stock price process (continued)

Assume the price in one week is given by $S = \$100 \exp(R)$, where R has annual expected value of 10% and volatility of 20%. Construct a 95% confidence interval for S.

The standard normal deviates that corresponds to a 95% confidence interval are $\alpha_{\text{MIN}} = -1.96$ and $\alpha_{\text{MAX}} = 1.96$. In other words, we have 2.5% in each tail. The 95% confidence band for R is then $R_{\text{MIN}} = \mu \Delta t - 1.96\sigma\sqrt{\Delta t} = 0.001923 - 1.96 \times 0.027735 = -0.0524$ and $R_{\text{MAX}} = \mu \Delta t + 1.96\sigma\sqrt{\Delta t} = 0.001923 + 1.96 \times 0.027735 = 0.0563$. This gives $S_{\text{MIN}} = \$100 \exp(-0.0524) = \$94.89$, and $S_{\text{MAX}} = \$100 \exp(0.0563) = \$105.79$.

Whether a lognormal distribution is much better than the normal distribution depends on the horizon considered. If the horizon is one day only, the choice of the lognormal versus normal assumption does not really matter. It is highly unlikely that the stock price would drop below zero in one day, given typical volatilities. On the other hand, if the horizon is measured in years, the two assumptions do lead to different results. The lognormal distribution is more realistic as it prevents prices from turning negative.

In simulations, this process is approximated by small steps with a normal distribution with mean and variance given by

$$\frac{\Delta S}{S} \sim N(\mu \Delta t, \sigma^2 \Delta t) \tag{4.7}$$

To simulate the future price path for S, we start from the current price S_t and generate a sequence of independent standard normal variables ϵ, for $i = 1, 2, \ldots, n$. The next price, S_{t+1}, is built as $S_{t+1} = S_t + S_t(\mu \Delta t + \sigma \epsilon_1 \sqrt{\Delta t})$. The following price, S_{t+2}, is taken as $S_{t+1} + S_{t+1}(\mu \Delta t + \sigma \epsilon_2 \sqrt{\Delta t})$, and so on until we reach the target horizon, at which point the price $S_{t+n} = S_T$ should have a distribution close to the lognormal.

Table 4-1 illustrates a simulation of a process with a drift (μ) of 0% and volatility (σ) of 20% over the total interval, which is divided into 100 steps.

The initial price is \$100. The local expected return is $\mu \Delta t = 0.0/100 = 0.0$ and the volatility is $0.20 \times \sqrt{1/100} = 0.02$. The second column shows the realization of a uniform $U(0, 1)$ variable, with the corresponding Excel function. The value for the first step is $u_1 = 0.0430$. The next column transforms this variable into a normal variable with mean 0.0 and volatility 0.02, which gives -0.0343, with the Excel function shown. The price increment is then obtained by multiplying the random variable by the previous price, which gives $-\$3.433$. This generates a new value of $S_1 = \$100 - \$3.43 = \$96.57$. The process is repeated until the final price of $\$125.31$ is reached at the 100th step.

TABLE 4-1 Simulating a Price Path

Step i	Random Variable		Price Increment ΔS_i	Price S_{t+i}
	Uniform u_i =RAND()	Normal $\mu \Delta t + \sigma \Delta z$ =NORMINV(u_i,0.0,0.02)		
0				100.00
1	0.0430	-0.0343	-3.433	96.57
2	0.8338	0.0194	1.872	98.44
3	0.6522	0.0078	0.771	99.21
4	0.9219	0.0284	2.813	102.02
$\vdots$				
99				124.95
100	0.5563	0.0028	0.354	125.31

This experiment can be repeated as often as needed. Define K as the number of **replications**, or random trials. Figure 4-1 displays the first three trials. Each leads to a simulated final value S_T^k. This generates a distribution of simulated prices S_T. With just one step, $n = 1$, the distribution must be normal. As the number of steps n grows large, the distribution tends to a lognormal distribution.

While very useful to model stock prices, this model has shortcomings. Price increments are assumed to have a normal distribution. In practice, we observe that price changes have fatter tails than the normal distribution. Returns may also experience changing variances.

In addition, as the time interval Δt shrinks, the volatility shrinks as well. This implies that large discontinuities cannot occur over short intervals. In reality, some assets experience discrete jumps, such as commodities. The stochastic process, therefore, may have to be changed to accommodate these observations.

FIGURE 4-1 Simulating Price Paths

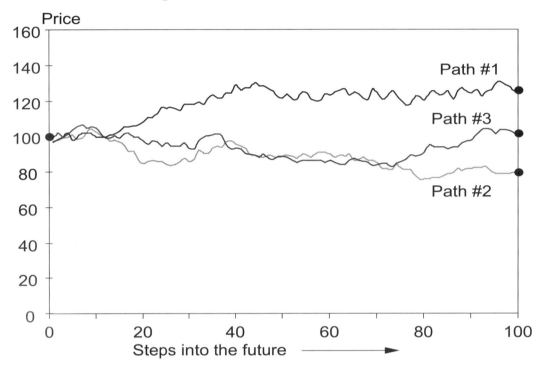

4.1.3   Simulating Yields

The GBM process is widely used for stock prices and currencies. Fixed-income products are another matter, however.

Bond prices display long-term reversion to the face value, which represents the repayment of principal at maturity (assuming there is no default). Such a process is inconsistent with the GBM process, which displays no such mean reversion. The volatility of bond prices also changes in a predictable fashion, as duration shrinks to zero. Similarly, commodities often display mean reversion.

These features can be taken into account by modeling bond yields directly in a first step. In the next step, bond prices are constructed from the value of yields and a pricing function. The dynamics of interest rates r_t can be modeled by

$$\Delta r_t = \kappa(\theta - r_t)\Delta t + \sigma r_t^{\gamma} \Delta z_t \qquad (4.8)$$

where Δz_t is the usual Wiener process. Here, we assume that $0 \leq \kappa < 1, \theta \geq 0, \sigma \geq 0$. Because there is only one stochastic variable for yields, the model is called a **one-factor model**.

This Markov process has a number of interesting features. First, it displays mean reversion to a long-run value of θ. The parameter κ governs the speed of mean reversion. When the current interest rate is high (i.e., $r_t > \theta$), the model creates a negative drift $\kappa(\theta - r_t)$ toward θ. Conversely, low current rates create a positive drift toward θ.

The second feature is the volatility process. This model includes the **Vasicek model** when $\gamma = 0$. Changes in yields are normally distributed because Δr is then a linear function of Δz, which is itself normal. The Vasicek model is particularly convenient because it leads to closed-form solutions for many fixed-income products. The problem, however, is that it could potentially lead to negative interest rates when the initial rate starts from a low value. This is because the volatility of the change in rates does not depend on the level, unlike that in the geometric Brownian motion.

Equation (4.8) is more general, however, because it includes a power of the yield in the variance function. With $\gamma = 1$, this is the **lognormal model**. Ignoring the trend, this gives $\Delta r_t = \sigma r_t \Delta z_t$, or $\Delta r_t / r_t = \sigma \Delta z_t$. This implies that the *rate of change* in the yield dr/r has a fixed variance. Thus, as with the GBM model, smaller yields lead to smaller movements, which makes it unlikely that the yield will drop below zero. This model is more appropriate than the normal model when the initial yield is close to zero.

With $\gamma = 0.5$, this is the **Cox, Ingersoll, and Ross (CIR) model**. Ultimately, the choice of the exponent γ is an empirical issue. Recent research has shown that $\gamma = 0.5$ provides a good fit to the data.

Models in this class are known as **equilibrium models**. They start with some assumptions about economic variables and imply a process for the short-term interest rate r. These models generate a predicted term structure, whose shape depends on the model parameters and the initial short rate. The problem with these models is that they are not flexible enough to provide a good fit to today's term structure. This can be viewed as unsatisfactory, especially by practitioners who argue that they cannot rely on a model that cannot even be trusted to price today's bonds.

In contrast, **no-arbitrage models** are designed to be consistent with today's term structure. In this class of models, the term structure is an input into the parameter estimation. The earliest model of this type was the **Ho and Lee model**,

$$\Delta r_t = \theta(t)\Delta t + \sigma \Delta z_t \tag{4.9}$$

where $\theta(t)$ is a function of time chosen so that the model fits the initial term structure.

This was extended to incorporate mean reversion in the **Hull and White model**,

$$\Delta r_t = [\theta(t) - ar_t]\Delta t + \sigma \Delta z_t \tag{4.10}$$

Finally, the **Heath, Jarrow, and Morton model** goes one step further and allows the volatility to be a function of time.

The downside of these no-arbitrage models is that they impose no consistency between parameters estimated over different dates. The function $\theta(t)$ could be totally different from one day to the next, which is inconsistent because it is supposed to represent the same long-term drift. No-arbitrage models are also more sensitive to outliers, or data errors in bond prices used to fit the term structure.

4.1.4 Binomial Trees

Simulations are very useful for mimicking the uncertainty in risk factors, especially with numerous risk factors. In some situations, however, it is also useful to describe the uncertainty in prices with discrete trees. When the price can take one of two steps, the tree is said to be **binomial**.

The binomial model can be viewed as a discrete equivalent to geometric Brownian motion. As before, we subdivide the horizon T into n intervals $\Delta t = T/n$. At each "node," the price is assumed to go either up with probability p, or down with probability $1 - p$.

The parameters u, d, p are chosen so that, for a small time interval, the expected return and variance equal those of the continuous process. One could choose

$$u = e^{\sigma\sqrt{\Delta t}}, \quad d = (1/u), \quad p = \frac{e^{\mu\Delta t} - d}{u - d} \tag{4.11}$$

This matches the mean, for example,

$$E\left[\frac{S_1}{S_0}\right] = pu + (1-p)d = \frac{e^{\mu\Delta t} - d}{u - d}u + \frac{u - e^{\mu\Delta t}}{u - d}d$$

$$= \frac{e^{\mu\Delta t}(u - d) - du + ud}{u - d} = e^{\mu\Delta t}$$

Table 4-2 shows how a binomial tree is constructed. As the number of steps increases, the discrete distribution of S_T converges to the lognormal distribution. This model will be used in a later chapter to price options.

TABLE 4-2 Binomial Tree

Example 4-1: FRM Exam 2002—Question 126

Consider a stock price S that follows a geometric Brownian motion
$dS = aS\,dt + bS\,dz$, with b strictly positive. Which of the following statements
is *false*?

a) If the drift a is positive, the price one year from now will be above
today's price.

b) The instantaneous rate of return on the stock follows a normal distribution.

c) The stock price S follows a lognormal distribution.

d) This model does not impose mean reversion.

Example 4-2: FRM Exam 1999—Question 19

Considering the one-factor Cox, Ingersoll, and Ross term-structure model and
the Vasicek model:

  I. Drift coefficients are different.

 II. Both include mean reversion.

III. Coefficients of the stochastic term, dz, are different.

IV. CIR is a jump-diffusion model.

a) All of the above are true.

b) I and III are true.

c) II, III, and IV are true.

d) II and III are true.

Example 4-3: FRM Exam 1999—Question 25

The Vasicek model defines a risk-neutral process for r as

$dr = a(b − r)dt + \sigma \, dz$, where a, b, and σ are constants, and r represents the rate of interest. From this equation we can conclude that the model is a

a) Monte Carlo–type model

b) One-factor term-structure model

c) Two-factor term-structure model

d) Decision tree model

Example 4-4: FRM Exam 1999—Question 26

The term $a(b − r)$ in the previous question represents which term?

a) Gamma

b) Stochastic

c) Reversion

d) Vega

Example 4-5: FRM Exam 1998—Question 23

Which of the following interest rate term-structure models tends to capture the mean reversion of interest rates?

a) $dr = a \times (b − r)dt + \sigma \times dz$

b) $dr = a \times dt + \sigma \times dz$

c) $dr = a \times r \times dt + \sigma \times r \times dz$

d) $dr = a \times (r − b) \times dt + \sigma \times dz$

Example 4-6: FRM Exam 1998—Question 24

Which of the following is a shortcoming of modeling a bond option by applying the Black-Scholes formula to bond prices?

a) It fails to capture convexity in a bond.

b) It fails to capture the pull-to-par phenomenon.

c) It fails to maintain put-call parity.

d) It works for zero-coupon bond options only.

Example 4-7: FRM Exam 2000—Question 118

Which group of term-structure models do the Ho-Lee, Hull-White, and Heath-Jarrow-Morton models belong to?

a) No-arbitrage models

b) Two-factor models

c) Lognormal models

d) Deterministic models

Example 4-8: FRM Exam 2000—Question 119

A plausible stochastic process for the short-term rate is often considered to be one where the rate is pulled back to some long-run average level. Which of the following term-structure models does *not* include this characteristic?

a) The Vasicek model

b) The Ho-Lee model

c) The Hull-White model

d) The Cox-Ingersoll-Ross model

Example 4-9: FRM Exam 1999—Question 18

If $S1$ follows a geometric Brownian motion and $S2$ follows a geometric Brownian motion, which of the following is *true*?

a) $\ln(S1 + S2)$ is normally distributed.

b) $S1 \times S2$ is lognormally distributed.

c) $S1 \times S2$ is normally distributed.

d) $S1 + S2$ is normally distributed.

Example 4-10: FRM Exam 2001—Question 76

A martingale is a

a) Zero-drift stochastic process

b) Chaos theory–related process

c) Type of time series

d) Mean-reverting stochastic process

4.2 Implementing Simulations

4.2.1 Simulation for VAR

Implementing Monte Carlo (MC) methods for risk management follows these steps:

1. Choose a stochastic process for the risk factor price S (i.e., its distribution and parameters) starting from the current value S_t.

2. Generate pseudo-random variables representing the risk factor at the target horizon, S_T.

3. Calculate the value of the portfolio at the horizon, $F_T(S_T)$.

4. Repeat steps 2 and 3 as many times as necessary. Call K the number of replications.

These steps create a distribution of values, $F_T^1, \ldots, F_T^K$, which can be sorted to derive the VAR. We measure the cth quantile $Q(F_T, c)$ and the average value $\text{Ave}(F_T)$. If VAR is defined as the deviation from the expected value on the target date, we have

$$\text{VAR}(c) = \text{Ave}(F_T) - Q(F_T, c) \tag{4.12}$$

4.2.2 Simulation for Derivatives

Readers familiar with derivatives pricing will have recognized that this method is similar to the Monte Carlo method for valuing derivatives. In that case, we simply focus on the expected value on the target date discounted to the present:

$$F_t = e^{-r(T-t)} \, \text{Ave}(F_T) \tag{4.13}$$

Thus derivatives valuation focuses on the discounted center of the distribution, while VAR focuses on the quantile on the target date.

Monte Carlo simulations have been long used to price derivatives. As will be seen in a later chapter, pricing derivatives can be done by assuming that the underlying asset grows at the risk-free rate r (assuming no income payment). For instance, pricing an option on a stock with an expected return of 20% is done assuming that (1) the stock grows at the risk-free rate of 10% and (2) we discount at the same risk-free rate. This is called the **risk-neutral approach**.

In contrast, risk measurement deals with actual distributions, sometimes called **physical distributions**. For measuring VAR, the risk manager must simulate asset growth using the actual expected return μ of 20%. Therefore, risk management uses physical distributions, whereas pricing methods use risk-neutral distributions.

It should be noted that simulation methods are not applicable to all types of options. These methods assume that the value of the derivative instrument at expiration can be priced solely as a function of the end-of-period price S_T, and perhaps of its sample path. This is the case, for instance, with an Asian option, where the payoff is a function of the price *averaged* over the sample path. Such an option is said to be **path-dependent**.

Simulation methods, however, cannot be used to price American options, which can be exercised early. The exercise decision should take into account future values of the option. Valuing American options requires modeling such a decision process, which cannot be done in a regular simulation approach because this decision also depends on future values.

Instead, valuing American options requires a **backward recursion**. This method examines whether the option should be exercised starting from the end and working backward in time until the starting time. This can be done using binomial trees.

4.2.3   Accuracy

Finally, we should mention the effect of **sampling variability**. Unless K is extremely large, the empirical distribution of S_T will only be an approximation of the true distribution. There will be some natural variation in statistics measured from Monte Carlo simulations. Since Monte Carlo simulations involve *independent* draws, one can show that the standard error of statistics is inversely related to the square root of K. Thus more simulations will increase precision, but at a slow rate. For example, accuracy is increased by a factor of 10 going from $K = 10$ to $K = 1,000$, but then requires going from $K = 1,000$ to $K = 100,000$ for the same factor of 10.

This accuracy issue is worse for risk management than for pricing, because the quantiles are estimated less precisely than the average. For VAR measures, the precision is also a function of the selected confidence level. Higher confidence levels generate fewer observations in the left tail and hence less precise VAR measures. A 99% VAR using 1,000 replications should be expected to have only 10 observations in the left tail, which is not a large number. The VAR estimate is derived from the 10th and 11th sorted number. In contrast, a 95% VAR is measured from the 50th and 51st sorted number, which will be more precise.

Various methods are available to speed up convergence.

- **Antithetic variable technique.** This technique uses the same sequence twice of random draws from t to T. It takes the original sequence and then changes the sign of all their values. This creates twice the number of points in the final distribution of F_T.

- **Control variate technique.** This technique is used to price options with trees when a similar option has an analytical solution. Say that f_E is a European option with an analytical solution. Going through the tree yields the values of an American and a European option, F_A and F_E. We then assume that the error in F_A is the same as that in F_E, which is known. The adjusted value is $F_A - (F_E - f_E)$.

- **Quasi-random sequences.** These techniques, also called quasi–Monte Carlo (QMC), create draws that are not independent but instead are designed to fill the sample space more uniformly. Simulations have shown that QMC methods converge faster than Monte Carlo methods. In other words, for a fixed number of replications K, QMC values will be on average closer to the true value.

The advantage of traditional MC, however, is that it also provides a standard error, or a measure of precision of the estimate, which is on the order of $1/\sqrt{K}$, because draws are independent. So we have an idea of how far the estimate might be from the true value, which is useful in deciding the number of replications. In contrast, QMC methods give no measure of precision.

Example 4-11: FRM Exam 1999—Question 8

Several different estimates of the VAR of an options portfolio were computed using 1,000 independent, lognormally distributed samples of the underlyings. Because each estimate was made using a different set of random numbers, there was some variability in the answers. In fact, the standard deviation of the distribution of answers was about $100,000. It was then decided to rerun the VAR calculation using 10,000 independent samples per run. The standard deviation of the reruns is most likely to be

a) About $10,000

b) About $30,000

c) About $100,000 (i.e., no change from the previous set of runs)

d) Cannot be determined from the information provided

Example 4-12: FRM Exam 1998—Question 34

A client seeks the value of an Asian option on the short rate. The Asian option gives the holder an amount equal to the average value of the short rate over the period to expiration less the strike rate. To value this option with a one-factor binomial model of interest rates, what method should be used?

a) The backward induction method, since it is the fastest

b) The simulation method using path averages, since the option is path-dependent

c) The simulation method using path averages, since the option is path-independent

d) Either the backward induction method or the simulation method, since both methods return the same value

---

Example 4-13: FRM Exam 1997—Question 17

The measurement error in VAR due to sampling variation should be greater with

a) More observations and a high confidence level (e.g., 99%)

b) Fewer observations and a high confidence level

c) More observations and a low confidence level (e.g., 95%)

d) Fewer observations and a low confidence level

4.3 Multiple Sources of Risk

We now turn to the more general case of simulations with many sources of financial risk. Define N as the number of risk factors. If the factors S_j are independent, the randomization can be performed independently for each variable. For the GBM model,

$$\Delta S_{j,t} = S_{j,t-1}\mu_j \Delta t + S_{j,t-1}\sigma_j \epsilon_{j,t}\sqrt{\Delta t} \tag{4.14}$$

where the standard normal variables ϵ are independent across time and the factor $j = 1, \dots, N$.

In general, however, risk factors are correlated. The simulation can be adapted by first drawing a set of independent variables η and then transforming them into correlated variables ϵ. As an example, with two factors only, we write

$$
\begin{aligned}
\epsilon_1 &= \eta_1 \\
\epsilon_2 &= \rho\eta_1 + (1-\rho^2)^{1/2}\eta_2
\end{aligned}
\tag{4.15}
$$

Here ρ is the coefficient of correlation between the variables ϵ. Because the η's have unit variance and are uncorrelated, we verify that the variance of ϵ_2 is 1, as required:

$$V(\epsilon_2) = \rho^2 V(\eta_1) + [(1-\rho^2)^{1/2}]^2 V(\eta_2) = \rho^2 + (1-\rho^2) = 1$$

Furthermore, the correlation between ϵ_1 and ϵ_2 is given by

$$\text{Cov}(\epsilon_1, \epsilon_2) = \text{Cov}(\eta_1, \rho\eta_1 + (1-\rho^2)^{1/2}\eta_2) = \rho\text{Cov}(\eta_1, \eta_1) = \rho$$

Defining ϵ as the *vector* of values, we verify that the covariance matrix of ϵ is

$$V(\epsilon) = \begin{bmatrix} \sigma^2(\epsilon_1) & \text{Cov}(\epsilon_1, \epsilon_2) \\ \text{Cov}(\epsilon_1, \epsilon_2) & \sigma^2(\epsilon_2) \end{bmatrix} = \begin{bmatrix} 1 & \rho \\ \rho & 1 \end{bmatrix} = R$$

Note that this covariance matrix, which is the expectation of squared deviations from the mean, can also be written as

$$V(\epsilon) = E[(\epsilon - E(\epsilon)) \times (\epsilon - E(\epsilon))'] = E(\epsilon \times \epsilon')$$

because the expectation of ϵ is zero. To generalize this approach to many more risk factors, however, we need a systematic way to derive the transformation in Equation (4.15).

4.3.1   The Cholesky Factorization

We would like to generate N joint values of ϵ that display the correlation structure $V(\epsilon) = E(\epsilon\epsilon') = R$. Because the matrix R is a symmetric real matrix, it can be decomposed into its so-called Cholesky factors,

$$R = TT' \tag{4.16}$$

where T is a lower triangular matrix with zeros on the upper right corners (above the diagonal). This is known as the **Cholesky factorization**.

As in the previous section, we first generate a vector of independent η's. Thus, their covariance matrix is $V(\eta) = I$, where I is the identity matrix with zeros everywhere except on the diagonal.

We then construct the transformed variable $\epsilon = T\eta$. The covariance matrix is now $V(\epsilon) = E(\epsilon\epsilon') = E((T\eta)(T\eta)') = E(T\eta\eta'T') = TE(\eta\eta')T' = TV(\eta)T' = TIT' = TT' = R$. This transformation therefore generates ϵ variables with the desired correlations.

To illustrate, let us go back to our two-variable case. The correlation matrix can be decomposed into its Cholesky factors as

$$\begin{bmatrix} 1 & \rho \\ \rho & 1 \end{bmatrix} = \begin{bmatrix} a_{11} & 0 \\ a_{21} & a_{22} \end{bmatrix} \begin{bmatrix} a_{11} & a_{21} \\ 0 & a_{22} \end{bmatrix} = \begin{bmatrix} a_{11}^2 & a_{11}a_{21} \\ a_{21}a_{11} & a_{21}^2 + a_{22}^2 \end{bmatrix}$$

To find the entries a_{11}, a_{21}, a_{22}, we solve each of the three equations

$$a_{11}^2 = 1$$

$$a_{11}a_{21} = \rho$$

$$a_{21}^2 + a_{22}^2 = 1$$

This gives $a_{11} = 1$, $a_{21} = \rho$, and $a_{22} = (1 - \rho^2)^{1/2}$. The Cholesky factorization is then

$$\begin{bmatrix} 1 & \rho \\ \rho & 1 \end{bmatrix} = \begin{bmatrix} 1 & 0 \\ \rho & (1 - \rho^2)^{1/2} \end{bmatrix} \begin{bmatrix} 1 & \rho \\ 0 & (1 - \rho^2)^{1/2} \end{bmatrix}$$

Note that this conforms to Equation (4.15):

$$\begin{bmatrix} \epsilon_1 \\ \epsilon_2 \end{bmatrix} = \begin{bmatrix} 1 & 0 \\ \rho & (1 - \rho^2)^{1/2} \end{bmatrix} \begin{bmatrix} \eta_1 \\ \eta_2 \end{bmatrix}$$

In practice, this decomposition yields a number of useful insights. The decomposition will fail if the number of independent factors implied in the correlation matrix is less than N. For instance, if $\rho = 1$, the two assets are perfectly correlated, meaning that we have the same factor twice. This could be the case, for instance, of two currencies fixed to each other. The decomposition gives $a_{11} = 1$, $a_{21} = 1$, $a_{22} = 0$. The new variables are then $\epsilon_1 = \eta_1$ and $\epsilon_2 = \eta_1$. The second variable, η_2, is totally superfluous.

4.3.2 The Curse of Dimensionality

Modern risk management is about measuring the risk of large portfolios, which are typically exposed to a large number of risk factors. The problem is that the number of computations increases geometrically with the number of factors N. The covariance matrix, for instance, has dimensions $N(N + 1)/2$. A portfolio with 500 variables requires a matrix with 125,250 entries.

In practice, the risk manager often needs to simplify the number of risk factors, discarding those that do not contribute much to the risk of the portfolio. Simulations based on the full set of variables would be inordinately time-consuming. The art of simulation is to design parsimonious experiments that represent the breadth of movements in risk factors.

This can be done through an economic analysis of the risk factors and portfolio strategies, as done in Part Three of this handbook. Alternatively, the risk manager can perform a statistical decomposition of the covariance matrix. A widely used method for this is **principal-component analysis** (PCA), which finds linear combinations of the risk factors that have maximal explanatory power. This type of analysis, which is as much an art as a science, can be used to reduce the dimensionality of the risk factors.

Example 4-14: FRM Exam 1999—Question 29

(Data-intensive)

Given the covariance matrix

$$\Sigma = \begin{bmatrix} 0.09\% & 0.06\% & 0.03\% \\ 0.06\% & 0.05\% & 0.04\% \\ 0.03\% & 0.04\% & 0.06\% \end{bmatrix}$$

let $\Sigma = XX'$, where X is lower triangular, be a Cholesky decomposition. Then the four elements in the upper left-hand corner of X, $x_{11}, x_{12}, x_{21}, x_{22}$, are, respectively,

a) 3.0%, 0.0%, 4.0%, 2.0%

b) 3.0%, 4.0%, 0.0%, 2.0%

c) 3.0%, 0.0%, 2.0%, 1.0%

d) 2.0%, 0.0%, 3.0%, 1.0%

4.4   Answers to Chapter Examples

Example 4-1: FRM Exam 2002—Question 126

a) All the statements are correct except a), which is too strong. The expected price is higher than today's price, but certainly not the price in all states of the world.

Example 4-2: FRM Exam 1999—Question 19

d) Answers II and III are correct. The two models include mean reversion but have different variance coefficients. Neither includes jumps.

Example 4-3: FRM Exam 1999—Question 25

b) This model postulates only one source of risk in the fixed-income market. This is a one-factor term-structure model.

Example 4-4: FRM Exam 1999—Question 26

c) This represents the expected return with mean reversion.

Example 4-5: FRM Exam 1998—Question 23

a) This is also Equation (4.8), assuming all parameters are positive.

Example 4-6: FRM Exam 1998—Question 24

b) The model assumes that prices follow a random walk with a constant trend, which is not consistent with the fact that the price of a bond will tend to par.

Example 4-7: FRM Exam 2000—Question 118

a) These are no-arbitrage models of the term structure, implemented as either one-factor or two-factor models.

Example 4-8: FRM Exam 2000—Question 119

b) Both the Vasicek and CIR models are one-factor equilibrium models with mean reversion. The Hull-White model is a no-arbitrage model with mean reversion. The Ho-Lee model is an early no-arbitrage model without mean reversion.

Example 4-9: FRM Exam 1999—Question 18

b) Both $S1$ and $S2$ are lognormally distributed since $d\ln(S1)$ and $d\ln(S2)$ are normally distributed. Since the logarithm of $S1 \times S2$ is equal to the sum of the logs, it is also normally distributed. Hence, the variable $S1 \times S2$ is lognormally distributed.

Example 4-10: FRM Exam 2001—Question 76

a) A martingale is a stochastic process with zero drift $dx = \sigma\, dz$, where dz is a Wiener process (i.e., such that $dz \sim N(0, dt)$). The expectation of a future value is the current value, $E[x_T] = x_0$, so it cannot be mean-reverting.

Example 4-11: FRM Exam 1999—Question 8

b) Accuracy with independent draws increases with the square root of K. Thus multiplying the number of replications by a factor of 10 will shrink the standard errors from \$100,000 to $\$100,000/\sqrt{10}$, or to approximately \$30,000.

Example 4-12: FRM Exam 1998—Question 34

b) Asian options create a payoff that depends on the average value of S during the life of the options. Hence, they are "path-dependent" and do not involve early exercise. Such options must be evaluated using simulation methods. *(Requires knowledge of derivative products)*

Example 4-13: FRM Exam 1997—Question 17

b) Sampling variability (or imprecision) increases with (i) fewer observations and (ii) greater confidence levels. To show (i), we can refer to the formula for the precision of the sample mean, which varies inversely with the square root of the number of data points. Similar reasoning applies to (ii). A greater confidence level involves fewer observations in the left tails, from which VAR is computed.

Example 4-14: FRM Exam 1999—Question 29

c) This involves a Cholesky decomposition. We have

$$XX' = \begin{bmatrix} x_{11} & 0 & 0 \\ x_{21} & x_{22} & 0 \\ x_{31} & x_{32} & x_{33} \end{bmatrix} \begin{bmatrix} x_{11} & x_{21} & x_{31} \\ 0 & x_{22} & x_{32} \\ 0 & 0 & x_{33} \end{bmatrix}$$

$$= \begin{bmatrix} x_{11}^2 & x_{11}x_{21} & x_{11}x_{33} \\ x_{21}x_{11} & x_{21}^2 + x_{22}^2 & x_{21}x_{31} + x_{22}x_{32} \\ x_{31}x_{11} & x_{31}x_{21} + x_{32}x_{22} & x_{31}^2 + x_{32}^2 + x_{33}^2 \end{bmatrix}$$

$$\Sigma = \begin{bmatrix} 0.09\% & 0.06\% & 0.03\% \\ 0.06\% & 0.05\% & 0.04\% \\ 0.03\% & 0.04\% & 0.06\% \end{bmatrix}$$

We then laboriously match each term: $x_{11}^2 = 0.0009$, or $x_{11} = 0.03$. Next, $x_{12} = 0$ since this is in the upper right corner, above the diagonal. Next, $x_{11}x_{21} = 0.0006$, or $x_{21} = 0.02$. Next, $x_{21}^2 + x_{22}^2 = 0.0005$, or $x_{22} = 0.01$.

Capital Markets

Chapter 5

Introduction to Derivatives

This chapter provides an overview of derivative instruments. Derivatives are financial contracts traded in private **over-the-counter** (OTC) markets, or on **organized exchanges**. As the term implies, derivatives derive their value from some underlying index, typically the price of an asset. Depending on the type of relationship, they can be broadly classified into two categories: linear and nonlinear instruments.

To the first category belong forward contracts, futures, and swaps. Their value is a linear function of the underlying index. These are *obligations* to exchange payments according to a specified schedule. Forward contracts are relatively simple to evaluate and price. So are futures, which are traded on exchanges. Swaps are more complex but generally can be reduced to portfolios of forward contracts. To the second category belong options, which are traded both OTC and on exchanges. Their value is a nonlinear function of the underlying index. These will be covered in the next chapter.

This chapter describes the general characteristics as well as the pricing of linear derivatives. Pricing is the first step toward risk measurement. The second step consists of combining the valuation formula with the distribution of underlying risk factors to derive the distribution of contract values. This will be done later, in the market risk section.

Section 5.1 provides an overview of the size of the derivatives markets. Section 5.2 presents the valuation and pricing of forwards. Sections 5.3 and 5.4 introduce futures and swap contracts, respectively.

5.1   Overview of Derivatives Markets

A **derivative instrument** can be generally defined as a private contract whose value is derived from some underlying asset price, reference rate, or index—such as a stock, bond, currency, or commodity. In addition, the contract must specify a principal, or **notional** amount, which is defined in terms of currency, shares, bushels, or some other unit. Movements in the value of the derivative depend on the notional amount and the underlying price or index.

In contrast with **securities**, such as stocks and bonds, which are issued to raise capital, derivatives are **contracts**, or private agreements between two parties. Thus the sum of gains and losses on derivatives contracts must be zero. For any gain made by one party, the other party must have suffered a loss of equal magnitude.

At the broadest level, derivatives markets can be classified by the underlying instrument, as well as by type of trading. Table 5-1 describes the size and growth of the global derivatives markets. As of December 2003, the total notional amounts add up to $234 trillion, of which $197 trillion is on OTC markets and $37 trillion is on organized exchanges. These markets have grown exponentially, from $56 trillion in March 1995.

The table shows that interest rate contracts are the most widespread type of derivatives, especially swaps. On the OTC market, currency contracts are also widely used, especially outright forwards and **forex swaps**, which are a combination of spot and short-term forward transactions. Among exchange-traded instruments, interest rate futures and options are the most common.

The magnitude of the notional amount total of $234 trillion is difficult to grasp. This number is several times the world **gross domestic product (GDP)**, which amounts to approximately $30 trillion. It is also greater than the total outstanding value of stocks, which is $31 trillion, and of debt securities, which is $51 trillion.

Notional amounts give an indication of equivalent positions in cash markets. For example, a long futures contract on a stock index with a notional of $1 million is equivalent to a cash position in the stock market of the same magnitude.

Notional amounts, however, do not give much information about the risks of the positions. The liquidation value of OTC derivatives contracts, for instance, is estimated at $7 trillion, which is only 3.5% of the notional. For futures contracts, which are marked to market daily, market values are close to zero. The risk of these derivatives is best measured by the potential change in mark-to-market values over the horizon, or their value at risk.

TABLE 5-1 Global Derivatives Markets 1995–2003
(Billions of U.S. Dollars)

	Notional Amounts	
	March 1995	Dec. 2003
OTC instruments	**47,530**	**197,177**
Interest rate contracts	**26,645**	**141,991**
Forwards (FRAs)	4,597	10,769
Swaps	18,283	111,209
Options	3,548	20,012
Foreign exchange contracts	**13,095**	**24,484**
Forwards and forex swaps	8,699	12,387
Swaps	1,957	6,371
Options	2,379	5,726
Equity-linked contracts	**579**	**3,787**
Forwards and swaps	52	601
Options	527	3,186
Commodity contracts	**318**	**1,406**
Others	**6,893**	**25,510**
Exchange-traded instruments	**8,838**	**36,736**
Interest rate contracts	**8,380**	**33,917**
Futures	5,757	13,123
Options	2,623	20,794
Foreign exchange contracts	**88**	**120**
Futures	33	80
Options	55	40
Stock-index contracts	**370**	**2,699**
Futures	128	502
Options	242	2,197
Total	**55,910**	**233,913**

Source: Bank for International Settlements

5.2 Forward Contracts

5.2.1 Definition

The most common transactions in financial instruments are **spot transactions**, that is, transactions for physical delivery as soon as is practical (perhaps in two business days or in a week). Historically, grain farmers went to a centralized location to meet buyers for their product. As markets developed, the farmers realized that it would be beneficial to trade for delivery at some future date. This allowed them to hedge out price fluctuations for the sale of their anticipated production.

This gave rise to **forward contracts**, which are private agreements to exchange a given asset against cash (or sometimes another asset) at a fixed point in the future. The terms of the contract include the quantity (number of units or shares), date, and price at which the exchange will be done.

A position that implies buying the asset is said to be **long**. A position to sell is said to be **short**. Note that, since this instrument is a private contract, any gain to one party must be offset by a loss to the other.

These instruments represent contractual obligations, as the exchange must occur no matter what happens to the intervening price, unless default occurs. Unlike an option contract, there is no choice of whether to take delivery or not.

To avoid the possibility of losses, the farmer could enter a forward sale of grain for dollars. By so doing, he locks up a price now for delivery in the future. We then say that the farmer is **hedged** against movements in the price.

We use the notations

$$t = \text{current time}$$

$$T = \text{time of delivery}$$

$$\tau = T - t = \text{time to maturity}$$

$$S_t = \text{current spot price of the asset in dollars}$$

$$F_t(T) = \text{current forward price of the asset for delivery at } T$$

$$\text{(also written as } F_t \text{ or } F \text{ to avoid clutter)}$$

$$V_t = \text{current value of contract}$$

$$r = \text{current domestic risk-free rate for delivery at } T$$

$$n = \text{quantity, or number of units in contract}$$

The **face amount** or **principal value** of the contract is defined as the amount nF to pay at maturity, like a bond. This is also called the notional amount. We will assume that interest rates are continuously compounded so that the present value of a dollar paid at expiration is $\text{PV}(\$1) = e^{-r\tau}$.

Say the initial forward price is $F_t = \$100$. A speculator agrees to buy $n = 500$ units for F_t at T. At expiration, the payoff on the forward contract is determined as follows:

(1) The speculator pays $nF = \$50,000$ in cash and receives 500 units of the underlying.

(2) The speculator could then sell the underlying at the prevailing spot price S_T, for a profit of $n(S_T - F)$. For example, if the spot price is $S_T = \$120$, the profit is $500 \times (\$120 - \$100) = \$10,000$. This is also the mark-to-market value of the contract at expiration.

In summary, the value of the forward contract at expiration, for one unit of the underlying asset, is

$$V_T = S_T - F \tag{5.1}$$

Here the value of the contract at expiration is derived from the purchase and **physical delivery** of the underlying asset. There is a payment of cash in exchange for the actual asset.

Another mode of settlement is **cash settlement**. This involves simply measuring the market value of the asset upon maturity, S_T, and agreeing for the "long" to receive $nV_T = n(S_T - F)$. This amount can be positive or negative, involving a profit or loss.

Figures 5-1 and 5-2 present the payoff patterns on long and short positions in a forward contract, respectively. It is important to note that the payoffs are *linear* in the underlying spot price. Also, the positions in the two figures are symmetrical around the horizontal axis. For a given spot price, the sum of the profit or loss for the long and the short is zero. This reflects the fact that forwards are private contracts between two parties.

5.2.2 Valuing Forward Contracts

In the evaluation of forward contracts, two important questions arise. First, how is the current forward price F_t determined? Second, what is the current value V_t of an outstanding forward contract?

Initially, we assume that the underlying asset pays no income. This will be generalized in the next section. We also assume no transaction costs, that is, zero bid-ask spread on spot and forward quotations as well as the ability to lend and borrow at the same risk-free rate.

FIGURE 5-1 Payoff of Profits on Long Forward Contract

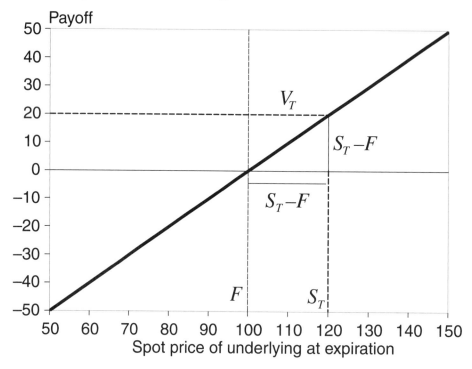

FIGURE 5-2 Payoff of Profits on Short Forward Contract

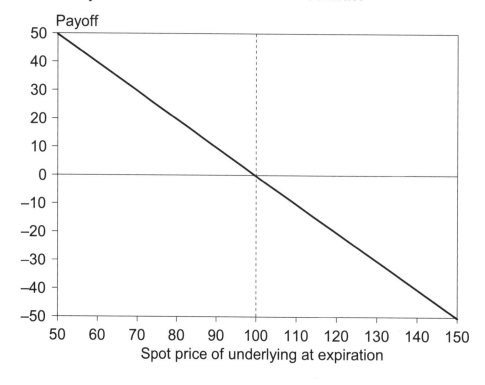

Generally, forward contracts are established so that their initial value is zero. This is achieved by setting the forward price F_t appropriately by a **no-arbitrage relationship** between the cash and forward markets. No-arbitrage is a situation where positions with the same payoff have the same price. This rules out situations where **arbitrage profits** can exist. Arbitrage is a zero-risk, zero-net investment strategy that still generates profits.

Consider these strategies:

- Buy one share/unit of the underlying asset at the spot price S_t and hold it until time T.

- Enter a forward contract to buy one share/unit of same underlying asset at the forward price F_t. In order to have sufficient funds at maturity to pay F_t, we invest the present value of F_t in an interest-bearing account. This is the present value $F_t e^{-r\tau}$. The forward price F_t is set so that the initial cost of the forward contract, V_t, is zero.

The two portfolios are economically equivalent because they will be identical at maturity. Each will contain one share of the asset. Hence their up-front cost must be the same. To avoid arbitrage, we must have

$$S_t = F_t e^{-r\tau} \tag{5.2}$$

This equation defines the fair forward price F_t such that the initial value of the contract is zero. For instance, assuming $S_t = \$100, r = 5\%$, and $\tau = 1$, we have $F_t = S_t e^{r\tau} = \$100 \times \exp(0.05 \times 1) = \$105.13$. More generally, the term multiplying F_t is the present value factor for maturity τ, or PV($\$1$).

We see that the forward rate is higher than the spot rate. This reflects the fact that there is no down payment to enter the forward contract, unlike the case for the cash position. As a result, the forward price must be higher than the spot price to reflect the time value of money.

Abstracting from transaction costs, any deviation creates an arbitrage opportunity. This can be taken advantage of by buying the cheap asset and selling the expensive one. Assume, for instance, that $F = \$110$. We determined that the fair value is $S_t e^{r\tau} = \$105.13$, based on the cash price. We apply the principle of buying low at $\$105.13$ and selling high at $\$110$. We can lock in a sure profit by

(1) Buying now the asset spot at $\$100$

(2) Selling now the asset forward at $\$110$

This can be done by borrowing the $\$100$ to buy the asset now. At expiration, we will owe principal plus interest, or $105.13, but will receive $110, for a profit of $4.87. This would be a blatant arbitrage opportunity, or "money machine."

Now consider a mispricing where $F = \$102$. We apply the principle of buying low at $102 and selling high at $105.13. We can lock in a sure profit by

(1) Short-selling now the asset spot at $100

(2) Buying now the asset forward at $102

From the short sale, we invest the cash, which will grow to $105.13. At expiration, we will have to deliver the stock, but this will be acquired through the forward purchase. We pay $102 for this and are left with a profit of $3.13.

This transaction involves the **short sale** of the asset, which is more involved than an outright purchase. When purchasing, we pay $100 and receive one share of the asset. When short-selling, we borrow one share of the asset and promise to give it back at a future date; in the meantime, we sell it at $100.[1]

5.2.3 Valuing an Off-Market Forward Contract

We can use the same reasoning to evaluate an outstanding forward contract with a locked-in delivery price of K. In general, such a contract will have nonzero value because K differs from the prevailing forward rate. Such a contract is said to be **off-market**.

Consider these strategies:

(1) Buy one share/unit of the underlying asset at the spot price S_t and hold until time T.

(2) Enter a forward contract to buy one share/unit of same underlying asset at price K; in order to have sufficient funds at maturity to pay K, we invest the present value of K in an interest-bearing account. This present value is $Ke^{-r\tau}$. In addition, we have to pay the market value of the forward contract, or V_t.

The up-front cost of the two portfolios must be identical. Hence, we must have $V_t + Ke^{-r\tau} = S_t$, or

$$V_t = S_t - Ke^{-r\tau} \tag{5.3}$$

which defines the market value of an outstanding long position.[2] This gains value when the underlying increases in value. A short position would have the reverse sign.

---

[1]In practice, we may not get full access to the proceeds of the sale when it involves individual stocks. The broker will typically allow us to withdraw only 50% of the cash. The rest is kept as a performance bond should the transaction lose money.

[2]Note that V_t is not the same as the forward price F_t. The former is the value of the contract; the latter refers to a specification of the contract.

Later, we will extend this relationship to the measurement of risk by considering the distribution of the underlying risk factors, S_t and r.

For instance, assume we still hold the previous forward contract with $F_t = \$105.13$, and after one month the spot price moves to $S_t = \$110$. The fixed rate is $K = \$105.13$ throughout the life of the contract. The interest has not changed at $r = 5\%$, but the maturity is now shorter by one month, $\tau = 11/12$. The new value of the contract is $V_t = S_t - Ke^{-r\tau} = \$110 - \$105.13\exp(-0.05 \times 11/12) = \$110 - \$100.42 = \$9.58$. The contract is now more valuable than before because the spot price has moved up.

5.2.4   Valuing Forward Contracts with Income Payments

We previously considered a situation where the asset produces no income payment. In practice, the asset may be

- A stock that pays a regular dividend
- A bond that pays a regular coupon
- A stock index that pays a dividend stream approximated by a continuous yield
- A foreign currency that pays a foreign currency–denominated interest rate

Whichever income is paid on the asset, we can usefully classify the payment as **discrete**, that is, with fixed dollar amounts at regular points in time, or on a **continuous** basis, that is, accrued in proportion to the time the asset is held. We must assume that the income payment is fixed or is certain. More generally, a storage cost is equivalent to a negative dividend.

We use these definitions:

$$D = \text{discrete (dollar) dividend or coupon payment}$$

$$r_t^*(T) = \text{foreign risk-free rate for delivery at } T$$

$$q_t(T) = \text{dividend yield}$$

Whether the payment is a dividend or a foreign interest rate, the principle is the same. We can afford to invest less in the asset up front to get one unit at expiration. This is because the income payment can be reinvested into the asset. Alternatively, we can borrow against the value of the income payment to increase our holding of the asset.

Continuing our example, consider a stock priced at $100 that pays a dividend of $D = \$1$ in three months. The present value of this payment discounted over three months is $De^{-r\tau} = \$1 \exp(-0.05 \times 3/12) = \$0.99$. We need to put up only $S_t - PV(D) = \$100.00 - 0.99 = \$99.01$ to get one share in one year. Put differently, we buy 0.9901 fractional shares now and borrow against the (sure) dividend payment of \$1 to buy an additional 0.0099 fractional share, for a total of 1 share.

The pricing formula in Equation (5.2) is extended to

$$F_t e^{-r\tau} = S_t - PV(D) \tag{5.4}$$

where $PV(D)$ is the present value of the dividend/coupon payments. If there is more than one payment, $PV(D)$ represents the sum of the present values of the individual payments, discounted at the appropriate risk-free rate. With storage costs, we need to *add* the present value of storage costs $PV(C)$ to the right side of Equation (5.4).

The approach is similar for an asset that pays a continuous income, defined per unit time, instead of discrete amounts. Holding a foreign currency, for instance, should be done through an interest-bearing account paying interest that accrues with time. Over the horizon τ, we can afford to invest less up front, $S_t e^{-r^*\tau}$, in order to receive one unit at maturity. Equation (5.4) is now

$$F_t e^{-r\tau} = S_t e^{-r^*\tau} \tag{5.5}$$

Hence the forward price should be

$$F_t = S_t e^{-r^*\tau} / e^{-r\tau} \tag{5.6}$$

If instead interest rates are annually compounded, this gives

$$F_t = S_t (1 + r)^\tau / (1 + r^*)^\tau \tag{5.7}$$

If $r^* < r$, we have $F_t > S_t$ and the asset trades at a **forward premium**. Conversely, if $r^* > r$, $F_t < S_t$ and the asset trades at a **forward discount**. Thus the forward price is higher or lower than the spot price, depending on whether the yield on the asset is lower than or higher than the domestic risk-free interest rate.

Equation (5.6) represents **interest rate parity** in dealing with currencies. Note that both the spot and forward prices must be expressed in dollars per unit of the foreign currency when the domestic currency interest rate is r. This is the case, for example, for the dollar/euro or dollar/pound exchange rate. If, on the other hand, the exchange rate is expressed in units of foreign currency per dollar, then r must be the rate on the foreign currency. For the yen/dollar rate, for example, S is in yen per dollar, r is the yen interest rate, and r^* is the dollar interest rate.

Key concept:
The forward price differs from the spot price to reflect the time value of money and the income yield on the underlying asset. It is higher than the spot price if the yield on the asset is lower than the domestic risk-free interest rate, and vice versa.

With income payments, the value of an outstanding forward contract is

$$V_t = S_t e^{-r^* \tau} - K e^{-r\tau} \qquad (5.8)$$

If F_t is the new, current forward price, we can also write

$$V_t = F_t e^{-r\tau} - K e^{-r\tau} = (F - K)e^{-r\tau} \qquad (5.9)$$

This provides a useful alternative formula for the valuation of a forward contract. The intuition here is that we could liquidate the outstanding forward contract by entering a reverse position at the current forward rate. The payoff at expiration is $(F - K)$, which, discounted back to the present, gives Equation (5.9).

Key concept:
The current value of an outstanding forward contract can be found by entering an offsetting forward position and discounting the net cash flow at expiration.

Example 5-1: FRM Exam 2002—Question 56
Consider a forward contract on a stock market index. Identify the false statement. Everything else being constant,
a) The forward price depends directly on the level of the stock market index.
b) The forward price will fall if underlying stocks increase the level of dividend payments over the life of the contract.
c) The forward price will rise if time to maturity is increased.
d) The forward price will fall if the interest rate is raised.

Example 5-2: FRM Exam 1999—Question 31

Consider an eight-month forward contract on a stock with a price of $98/share. The delivery date is eight months hence. The firm is expected to pay a $1.80 per share dividend in four months. Riskless zero-coupon interest rates (continuously compounded) for different maturities are for less than/equal to 4% for six months, and for eight months, 4.5%. The theoretical forward price (to the nearest cent) is

a) 99.15
b) 99.18
c) 100.98
d) 96.20

Example 5-3: FRM Exam 2001—Question 93

Calculate the price of a one-year forward contract on gold. Assume the storage cost for gold is $5.00 per ounce, with payment made at the end of the year. Spot gold is $290 per ounce and the risk-free rate is 5%.

a) $304.86
b) $309.87
c) $310.12
d) $313.17

Example 5-4: FRM Exam 1999—Question 41

Assume a dollar asset provides no income for the holder and an investor can borrow money at risk-free interest rate r; then the forward price F for time T and spot price S at time t of the asset are related. If the investor observes that $F > S \exp[r(T - t)]$, then in order to take a profit the investor can

a) Borrow S dollars for a period of $(T - t)$ at the rate of r, buy the asset, and short the forward contract.
b) Borrow S dollars for a period of $(T - t)$ at the rate of r, buy the asset, and long the forward contract.
c) Sell short the asset and invest the proceeds of S dollars for a period of $(T - t)$ at the rate of r, and short the forward contract.
d) Sell short the asset and invest the proceeds of S dollars for a period of $(T - t)$ at the rate of r, and long the forward contract.

Example 5-5: FRM Exam 2002—Question 5

A commodity forward contract for delivery in four months is written with a forward price of $38. The underlying asset's spot price is $40. The continuously compounded interest rate is 5%. In present value terms, how much is the potential arbitrage profit, assuming there are no transaction or storage costs and the commodity pays no dividends?

a) $0 (the forward price is fair)

b) $1.67

c) $2.63

d) $2.88

5.3 Futures Contracts

5.3.1 Definitions of Futures

Forward contracts allow users to take positions that are economically equivalent to those in the underlying cash markets. Unlike cash markets, however, they do not involve substantial up-front payments. Thus, forward contracts can be interpreted as having *leverage*. Leverage is efficient, as it makes our money work harder.

Leverage creates credit risk for the counterparty, however. For a cash trade, there is no leverage. When a speculator buys a stock at the price of $100, the counterparty receives the cash and has no credit risk. In contrast, when a speculator enters a forward contract to buy an asset at the price of $105, there is no up-front payment. In effect the speculator borrows from the counterparty to invest in the asset. There is a risk of default should the value of the contract to the speculator fall sufficiently. In response, futures contracts have been structured to minimize the credit risk for all counterparties. Otherwise, from a market risk standpoint, futures contracts are basically identical to forward contracts.

Futures contracts are standardized, negotiable, and exchange-traded contracts to buy or sell an underlying asset. They differ from forward contracts as follows.

- **Trading on organized exchanges.** In contrast to forwards, which are OTC contracts tailored to customers' needs, futures are traded on organized exchanges (either with a physical location or electronic).

- **Standardization.** Futures contracts are offered with a limited choice of expiration dates. They trade in fixed contract sizes. This standardization ensures an active secondary market for many futures contracts, which can be easily traded, purchased or resold. In other words, most futures contracts have good liquidity. The trade-off is that futures are less precisely suited to the need of some hedgers, which creates basis risk (to be defined later).

■ **Clearinghouse.** Futures contracts are also standardized in terms of the counterparty. After each transaction is confirmed, the clearinghouse basically interposes itself between the buyer and the seller, ensuring the performance of the contract. Thus, unlike forward contracts, counterparties do not have to worry about the credit risk of the other side of the trade. Instead, the credit risk is that of the clearinghouse (or the broker), which is generally excellent.

■ **Marking to market.** Because the clearinghouse has to deal with the credit risk of the two original counterparties, it has to monitor credit risk closely. This is achieved by daily marking to market, which involves settlement of the gains and losses on the contract every day. This will avoid the accumulation of large losses over time, potentially leading to an expensive default.

■ **Margins.** Although daily settlement accounts for past losses, it does not provide a buffer against future losses. This is the goal of **margins**, which represent the up-front posting of collateral that can be seized should the other party default.

Example: Margins for a futures contract

Consider a futures contract on 1,000 units of an asset worth $100. A long futures position is economically equivalent to holding $100,000 worth of the asset directly. To enter the futures position, a speculator has to post only $5,000 in margin, for example. This amount is placed in an equity account with the broker.

The next day, the futures price moves down by $3, leading to a loss of $3,000 for the speculator. The profit or loss is added to the equity account, bringing it down to $5,000 − $3,000 = $2,000. The speculator would then receive a **margin call** from the broker, asking to have an additional $3,000 of capital posted to the account. In case he or she fails to meet the margin call, the broker has the right to liquidate the position.

Since futures trading is centralized on an exchange, it is easy to collect and report aggregate trading data. **Volume** is the number of contracts traded during the day, which is a flow item. **Open interest** represents the number of outstanding contracts at the close of the day, which is a stock item.

5.3.2   Valuing Futures Contracts

Valuation principles for futures contracts are very similar to those for forward contracts. The main difference between the two types of contracts is that any profit or loss accrues *during* the life of the futures contract instead of all at once, at expiration.

When interest rates are assumed constant or deterministic, forward and futures prices must be equal. With stochastic interest rates, there may be a small difference, depending on the correlation between the value of the asset and interest rates.

If the correlation is zero, then it makes no difference whether payments are received earlier or later. The futures price must be the same as the forward price. In contrast, consider a contract whose price is positively correlated with the interest rate. If the value of the contract goes up, it is more likely that interest rates will go up as well. This implies that profits can be withdrawn and reinvested at a higher rate. Relative to forward contracts, this marking-to-market feature is beneficial to a long futures position. As a result, the futures price must be higher in equilibrium.

In practice, this effect is observable only for interest-rate futures contracts, whose value is *negatively* correlated with interest rates. Because this feature is unattractive for the long position, the futures price must be *lower* than the forward price. Chapter 8 will explain how to compute the adjustment, called the **convexity effect**.

Example 5-6: FRM Exam 2000—Question 7

For an asset that is strongly positively correlated with interest rates, which one of the following is *true*?
a) Long-dated forward contracts will have higher prices than long-dated futures contracts.
b) Long-dated futures contracts will have higher prices than long-dated forward contracts.
c) Long-dated forward and long-dated futures prices are always the same.
d) The "convexity effect" can be ignored for long-dated futures contracts on that asset.

5.4   Swap Contracts

Swap contracts are OTC agreements to exchange a *series* of cash flows according to prespecified terms. The underlying asset can be an interest rate, an exchange rate, an equity, a commodity price, or any other index. Typically, swaps are established for longer periods than forwards and futures.

For example, a 10-year currency swap could involve an agreement to exchange every year 5 million dollars against 3 million pounds over the next 10 years, in addition to a principal amount of 100 million dollars against 50 million pounds at expiration. The principal is also called **notional principal**.

Another example is a 5-year interest rate swap in which one party pays 8% of the principal amount of 100 million dollars in exchange for receiving an interest payment indexed to a floating interest rate. In this case, since both payments are the same amount in the same currency, there is no need to exchange principal at maturity.

Swaps can be viewed as a portfolio of forward contracts. They can be priced using valuation formulas for forwards. Our currency swap, for instance, can be viewed as a combination of 10 forward contracts with various face values, maturity dates, and rates of exchange. We will give detailed examples in later chapters.

5.5   Answers to Chapter Examples

Example 5-1: FRM Exam 2002—Question 56

d) Defining the dividend yield as q, the forward price depends on the cash price according to $F \exp(-rT) = S \exp(-qT)$. This can also be written as $F = S \exp[+(r-q)T]$. Generally, $r > q$. Statement a) is correct: F depends directly on S. Statement b) is also correct, as higher q decreases the term between brackets and hence F. Statement c) is correct because the term $r - q$ is positive, leading to a larger term in brackets as the time to maturity T increases. Statement d) is false, as increasing r makes the forward contract more attractive, or increases F.

Example 5-2: FRM Exam 1999—Question 31

a) We need first to compute the PV of the dividend payment, which is $PV(D) = \$1.8 \exp(-0.04 \times 4/12) = \$1.776$. By Equation (5.4), $F = [S - PV(D)] \exp(r\tau)$. Hence, $F = (\$98 - \$1.776) \exp(0.045 \times 8/12) = \$99.15$.

Example 5-3: FRM Exam 2001—Question 93

b) Assuming continuous compounding, the present value factor is $PV = \exp(-0.05) = 0.951$. Here, the storage cost C is equivalent to a negative dividend and must be evaluated as of now. This gives $PV(C) = \$5 \times 0.951 = \$4.756$. Generalizing Equation (5.4), we have $F = (S + PV(C))/PV(\$1) = (\$290 + \$4.756)/0.951 = \$309.87$. Assuming discrete compounding gives $\$309.5$, which is close.

Example 5-4: FRM Exam 1999—Question 41

a) The forward price is too high relative to the fair rate, so we need to sell the forward contract. In exchange, we need to buy the asset. To ensure a zero initial cash flow, we need to borrow the present value of the asset.

Example 5-5: FRM Exam 2002—Question 5

c) The present value of the forward price is given by $F \times \text{PV}(\$1) = \$38 \times \exp(-5\% \times 4/12) = \$37.37$. Normally, this should be equal to the spot price if there is no income or transaction or storage costs. So one could enter a long position in a forward contract and at the same time sell the asset spot. The current profit is $S - F \times \text{PV}(\$1) = \$40 - \$37.37 = \$2.63$.

Example 5-6: FRM Exam 2000—Question 7

b) The convexity effect is important for long-dated contracts, so d) is wrong. This positive correlation makes it more beneficial to have a long futures position since profits can be reinvested at higher rates. Hence the futures price must be higher than the forward price. Note that the relationship assumed here is the opposite of that of Eurodollar futures contracts, where the value of the asset is *negatively* correlated with interest rates.

Chapter 6

Options

This chapter turns to nonlinear derivatives, or options. As described in Table 5-1, options account for a large part of the derivatives markets. On organized exchanges, options represent $23 trillion in derivatives outstanding. Over-the-counter options add up to more than $29 trillion in notional amounts.

Although the concept behind these instruments is not new, option markets have blossomed since the early 1970s because of a breakthrough in pricing options, the Black-Scholes formula, and advances in computing power. We start with plain, **vanilla** options, calls and puts. These are the basic building blocks of many financial instruments. They are also more common than complicated, **exotic** options.

The purpose of this chapter is to present a compact overview of important concepts for options, including their pricing. We will cover option sensitivities (the "Greeks") in a future chapter. Section 6.1 presents the payoff functions on basic options and combinations thereof. We then discuss option premiums in Section 6.2. The Black-Scholes pricing approach is presented in Section 6.3. Next, Section 6.4 briefly summarizes more complex options. Finally, Section 6.5 shows how to value options using a numerical, binomial tree model.

6.1   Option Payoffs

6.1.1   Basic Options

Options are instruments that give their holder the *right* to buy or sell an asset at a specified price until a specified expiration date. The specified delivery price is known as the **delivery price**, **exercise price**, or **strike price** and is denoted by K.

Options to buy are **call options**. Options to sell are **put options**. As options confer a right to the purchaser of the option, but not an obligation, they will be exercised only if they generate profits. In contrast, forwards involve an obligation to either buy or sell and can generate profits or losses. Like forward contracts, options can be purchased or sold. In the latter case, the seller is said to **write** the option.

Depending on the timing of exercise, options can be classified into European or American options. **European options** can be exercised at maturity only. **American options** can be exercised at any time, before or at maturity. Because American options include the right to exercise at maturity, they must be at least as valuable as European options. In practice, however, the value of this early exercise feature is small, as an investor can generally receive better value by reselling the option on the open market instead of exercising it.

We use these notations, in addition to those in the previous chapter:

K = exercise price

c = value of European call option

C = value of American call option

p = value of European put option

P = value of American put option

To illustrate, take an option on an asset that currently trades at \$85 with a delivery price of \$100 in one year. If the spot price stays at \$85 at expiration, the holder of the call will not **exercise** the option, because the option is not profitable with a stock price less than \$100. In contrast, if the price goes to \$120, the holder will exercise the right to buy at \$100, will acquire the stock now worth \$120, and will enjoy a "paper" profit of \$20. This profit can be realized by selling the stock. For put options, a profit accrues if the spot price falls below the exercise price $K = \$100$.

Thus the payoff profile of a long position in the call option at expiration is

$$C_T = \text{Max}(S_T - K, 0) \qquad (6.1)$$

The payoff profile of a long position in a put option is

$$P_T = \text{Max}(K - S_T, 0) \qquad (6.2)$$

If the current asset price S_t is close to the strike price K, the option is said to be **at-the-money**. If the current asset price S_t is such that the option could be exercised now at a profit, the option is said to be **in-the-money**. In the remaining situation, the option is said to be **out-of-the-money**. A call will be in-the-money if $S_t > K$. A put will be in-the-money if $S_t < K$.

As in the case of forward contracts, the payoff at expiration can be cash settled. Instead of actually buying the asset, the contract could simply pay $20 if the price of the asset is $120.

Because buying options can generate only profits (at worst zero) at expiration, an option contract must be a valuable asset (or at worst have zero value). This means that a payment is needed to acquire the contract. This up-front payment, which is much like an insurance premium, is called the option "premium." This premium cannot be negative. An option becomes more expensive as it moves in-the-money.

Thus the payoffs on options must take into account this cost (for long positions) or benefit (for short positions). To compute the total payoff, we should translate all option payoffs by the *future* value of the premium, that is, $ce^{r\tau}$ for European call options.

Figure 6-1 displays the total profit payoff on a call option as a function of the asset price at expiration. Assuming that $S_T = \$120$, the proceeds from exercise are $\$120 - \$100 = \$20$, from which we have to subtract the future value of the premium, say $10. In the graphs that follow, we always take into account the cost of the option.

FIGURE 6-1 Profit Payoffs on Long Call

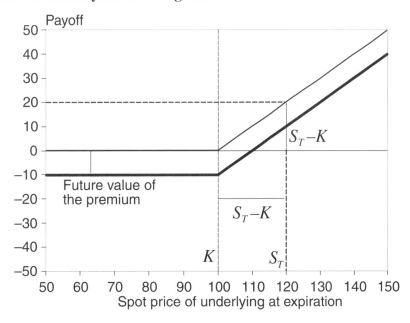

Figure 6-2 summarizes the payoff patterns on long and short positions in a call and a put contract. Sometimes they are referred to as "hockey stick" diagrams. Unlike those of forwards, these payoffs are **nonlinear** in the underlying spot price. This is because forwards are obligations, whereas options are rights. Note that the positions for the same contract are symmetrical around the horizontal axis. For a given spot price, the sum of the profit or loss for the long and for the short is zero.

FIGURE 6-2 Profit Payoffs on Long and Short Calls and Puts

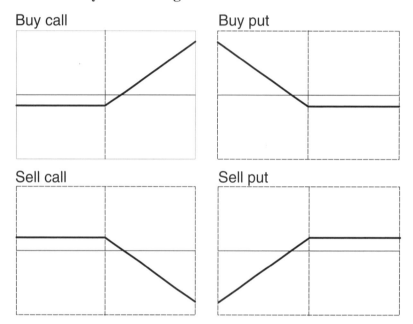

So far, we have covered options on cash instruments. Options can also be struck on futures. When exercising a call, the investor becomes long the futures contract at a price set to the strike price. Conversely, exercising a put creates a short position in the futures contract. Because positions in futures are equivalent to leveraged positions in the underlying cash instrument, options on cash instruments and on futures are equivalent.

6.1.2 Put-Call Parity

Option payoffs can be used as the basic building blocks for more complex positions. A long position in the underlying asset can be decomposed into a long call plus a short put, as shown in Figure 6-3.

FIGURE 6-3 Decomposing a Long Position in the Asset

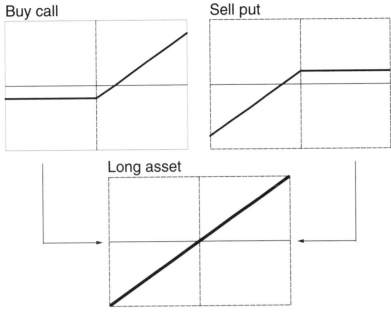

The figure shows that the long call provides the equivalent of the upside while the short put generates the same downside risk as holding the asset. This link creates a relationship between the value of the call and that of the put, known as **put-call parity**. The relationship is illustrated in Table 6-1, which examines the payoff at initiation and at expiration under the two possible states of the world. We consider only European options with the same maturity and exercise price. Also, we assume no income payment on the underlying asset.

TABLE 6-1 Put-Call Parity

Portfolio	Position:	Initial Payoff	FinalPayoff	
			$S_T < K$	$S_T \geq K$
(1)	Buy call	$-c$	0	$S_T - K$
	Sell put	$+p$	$-(K - S_T)$	0
	Invest	$-Ke^{-r\tau}$	K	K
	Total	$-c + p - Ke^{-r\tau}$	S_T	S_T
(2)	Buy asset	$-S$	S_T	S_T

The portfolio consists of a long position in the call, a short position in the put, and an investment to ensure that we will be able to pay the exercise price at maturity. Long positions are represented by negative values as they are outflows.

The table shows that the final payoffs to portfolio (1) add up to S_T in the two states of the world, which is the same as a long position in the asset itself. Hence, to avoid arbitrage, the initial payoff must be equal to the current cost of the asset, which is S_t. So we must have $-c + p - Ke^{-r\tau} = -S$. More generally, with income paid at the rate of r^*, put-call parity can be written as

$$c - p = Se^{-r^*\tau} - Ke^{-r\tau} = (F - K)e^{-r\tau} \tag{6.3}$$

Because $c \geq 0$ and $p \geq 0$, this relationship can be also used to determine lower bounds for European calls and puts. Note that the relationship does not hold exactly for American options since there is a likelihood of early exercise, which could lead to mismatched payoffs.

Key concept:
A long position in an asset is equivalent to a long position in a European call with a short position in an otherwise identical put, combined with a risk-free position.

Example 6-1: FRM Exam 1999—Question 35

According to put-call parity, writing a put is like
a) Buying a call, buying stock, and lending
b) Writing a call, buying stock, and borrowing
c) Writing a call, buying stock, and lending
d) Writing a call, selling stock, and borrowing

Example 6-2: FRM Exam 2002—Question 47

A two-year European call option has a market price of $50 with a strike price of $140. The underlying stock price is $100 with a two-year annualized interest rate of 5% and a dividend yield of 2% (annualized). What is the number closest to the market price of a two-year European put struck at $140?
a) $77
b) $10
c) $90
d) $81

Example 6-3: FRM Exam 2002—Question 25

The price of a non–dividend-paying stock is $20. A six-month European call option with a strike price of $18 sells for $4. A European put option on the same stock, with the same strike price and maturity, sells for $1.47. The continuously compounded risk-free interest rate is 6% per annum. Are these three securities (the stock and the two options) consistently priced?

a) No, there is an arbitrage opportunity worth $2.00.

b) No, there is an arbitrage opportunity worth $2.53.

c) No, there is an arbitrage opportunity worth $14.00.

d) Yes.

6.1.3 Combination of Options

Options can be combined in different ways, either with each other or with the underlying asset. Consider first combinations of the underlying asset and an option. A long position in the stock can be accompanied by a short sale of a call to collect the option premium. This operation, called a **covered call**, is described in Figure 6-4. Likewise, a long position in the stock can be accompanied by a purchase of a put to protect the downside. This operation is called a **protective put**.

FIGURE 6-4 Creating a Covered Call

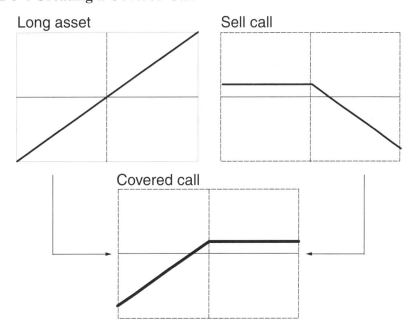

We can also combine a call and a put with the same or different strike prices and maturities. When the strike prices of the call and the put and their maturities are the same, the combination is referred to as a **straddle**. Figure 6-5 shows how to construct a long straddle, buying a call and a put with the same maturity and strike price. This position is expected to benefit from a large price move, whether up or down. The reverse position is a short straddle.

When the strike prices are different, the combination is referred to as a **strangle**. Since strangles are out-of-the-money, they are cheaper to buy than straddles.

FIGURE 6-5 Creating a Long Straddle

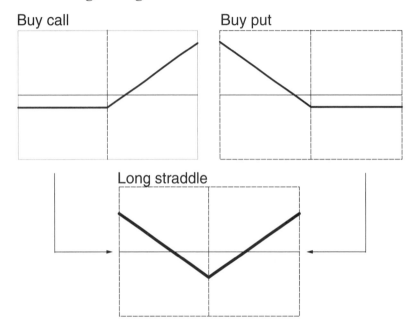

Thus far, we have concentrated on positions involving two classes of options. One can, however, establish positions with one class of options, called **spreads**. Calendar or **horizontal spreads** correspond to different maturities. **Vertical spreads** correspond to different strike prices. The names of the spreads are derived from the manner in which they are listed in newspapers: time is listed horizontally and strike prices are listed vertically.

For instance, a **bull spread** is positioned to take advantage of an increase in the price of the underlying asset. Conversely, a **bear spread** represents a bet on a falling price. Figure 6-6 shows how to construct a bull(ish) vertical spread with two calls with the same maturity. This could also be constructed with puts, however. Here, the spread is formed by buying a call option with a low exercise price K_1 and selling another call with a higher exercise price K_2. Note that the cost of the first call $c(S, K_1)$ must exceed the cost of the second call $c(S, K_2)$, because the first option is more in-the-money than the second. Hence, the sum of the two premiums represents a net cost. At expiration, when $S_T > K_2$, the payoff is $\text{Max}(S_T - K_1, 0) - \text{Max}(S_T - K_2, 0) = (S_T - K_1) - (S_T - K_2) = K_2 - K_1$, which is positive. Thus this position is expected to benefit from an up-move while incurring only limited downside risk.

FIGURE 6-6 Creating a Bull Spread

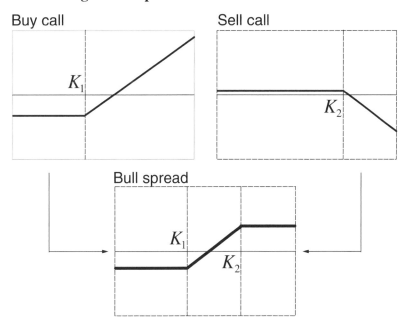

Spreads involving more than two positions are referred to as butterfly or sandwich spreads. The latter is the opposite of the former. A **butterfly spread** involves three types of options with the same maturity: a long call at a strike price K_1, two short calls at a higher strike price K_2, and a long call position at an even higher strike price K_3. We can verify that this position is expected to benefit when the underlying asset price stays stable, close to K_2.

Example 6-4: FRM Exam 2001—Question 90

Which of the following is the riskiest form of speculation using option contracts?

a) Setting up a spread using call options
b) Buying put options
c) Writing naked call options
d) Writing naked put options

Example 6-5: FRM Exam 1999—Question 50

A covered call writing position is equivalent to

a) A long position in the stock and a long position in the call option

b) A short put position

c) A short position in the stock and a long position in the call option

d) A short call position

Example 6-6: FRM Exam 1999—Question 33

Which of the following will create a bull spread?

a) Buy a put with a strike price of $X = 50$, and sell a put with $K = 55$.

b) Buy a put with a strike price of $X = 55$, and sell a put with $K = 50$.

c) Buy a call with a premium of 5, and sell a call with a premium of 7.

d) Buy a call with a strike price of $X = 50$, and sell a put with $K = 55$.

Example 6-7: FRM Exam 2000—Question 5

Consider a bullish spread option strategy of buying one call option with a $30 exercise price at a premium of $3 and writing a call option with a $40 exercise price at a premium of $1.50. If the price of the stock increases to $42 at expiration and the option is exercised on the expiration date, the net profit per share at expiration (ignoring transaction costs) will be

a) $8.50

b) $9.00

c) $9.50

d) $12.50

Example 6-8: FRM Exam 2002—Question 42

Consider a bearish option strategy of buying one $50 strike put for $7, selling two $42 strike puts for $4 each, and buying one $37 put for $2. All options have the same maturity. Calculate the final profit (P/L) per share of the strategy if the underlying is trading at $33 at expiration.

a) $1 per share

b) $2 per share

c) $3 per share

d) $4 per share

6.2 Option Premiums

6.2.1 General Relationships

So far, we have examined the payoffs at expiration only. Also important is the instantaneous relationship between the option value and the current price S, which is displayed in Figures 6-7 and 6-8.

FIGURE 6-7 Relationship between Call Value and Spot Price

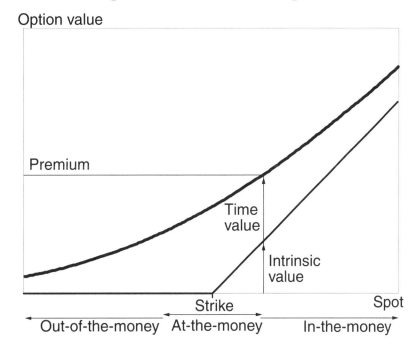

For a call, a higher price S increases the current value of the option, but in a nonlinear, convex fashion. For a put, lower values for S increase the value of the option, also in a convex fashion. As time goes by, the curved line approaches the hockey stick line.

Figures 6-6 and 6-7 decompose the current premium into

- An **intrinsic value**, which basically consists of the value of the option if exercised today, or $\text{Max}(S_t - K, 0)$ for a call, and $\text{Max}(K - S_t, 0)$ for a put
- A **time value**, which consists of the remainder, reflecting the possibility that the option will create further gains in the future

Consider, for example, a one-year call with strike $K = \$100$. The current price is $S = \$120$ and interest rate $r = 5\%$. The asset pays no dividend. Say the call premium is \$26.17. This can be decomposed into an intrinsic value of $\$120 - \$100 = \$20$ and time value of \$6.17. The time value increases with the volatility of the underlying asset. It also generally increases with the maturity of the option.

FIGURE 6-8 Relationship between Put Value and Spot Price

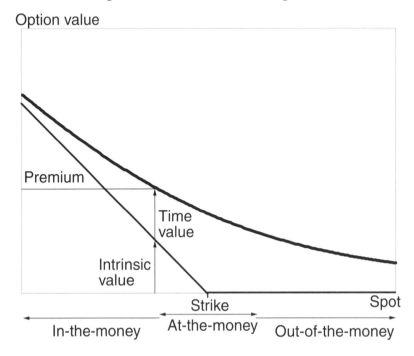

As shown in the figures, options are also classified into

- **At-the-money**, when the current spot price is close to the strike price
- **In-the-money**, when the intrinsic value is large
- **Out-of-the-money**, when the spot price is much below the strike price for calls and conversely for puts (out-of-the-money options have zero intrinsic value)

We can also identify some general bounds for European options that should always be satisfied; otherwise there would be an arbitrage opportunity (a money machine). For simplicity, assume no dividend. We know that a European option is worth less than an American option. First, the current value of a call must be less than or equal to the asset price:

$$c_t \leq C_t \leq S_t \tag{6.4}$$

This is because, in the limit, an option with zero exercise price is equivalent to holding the stock. We are sure to exercise.

Second, the value of a European call must be greater than or equal to the price of the asset minus the present value of the strike price:

$$c_t \geq S_t - Ke^{-r\tau} \tag{6.5}$$

To prove this, Table 6-2 considers the final payoffs for two portfolios: (1) a long call and (2) a long stock with a loan of K. In each case, an outflow, or payment, is represented with a negative sign. A receipt has a positive sign.

We consider the two states of the world, $S_T < K$ and $S_T \geq K$. In the state $S_T \geq K$, the call is exercised and the two portfolios have exactly the same value, which is $S_T - K$. In the state $S_T < K$, however, the second portfolio has a negative value and is worth less than the value of the call, which is zero.

Since the payoffs on the call dominate those on the second portfolio, buying the call must be more expensive. Hence the initial cost of the call c must be greater than, or at worst equal to, the up-front cost of the portfolio, which is $S_t - Ke^{-r\tau}$. Alternatively, this can be derived from put-call parity, or Equation (6.3), with $p \geq 0$.

TABLE 6-2 Lower Option Bound for a Call

Portfolio	Position	Initial Payoff	Final Payoff $S_T < K$	$S_T \geq K$
(1)	Buy call	$-c$	0	$S_T - K$
(2)	Buy asset	$-S_t$	S_T	S_T
	Borrow	$+Ke^{-r\tau}$	$-K$	$-K$
	Total	$-S + Ke^{-r\tau}$	$S_T - K < 0$	$S_T - K$

Note that since $e^{-r\tau} < 1$, we must have $S_t - Ke^{-r\tau} > S_t - K$ before expiration. Thus $S_t - Ke^{-r\tau}$ is a more informative lower bound than $S_t - K$. As an example, continue with our call option. The lower bound is $S_t - Ke^{-r\tau} = \$120 - \$100 \exp(-5\% \times 1) = \$24.88$. This is more informative than $S - K = \$20$.

We can also describe upper and lower bounds for put options. The value of a put cannot be worth more than K,

$$p_t \leq P_t \leq K \tag{6.6}$$

which is the upper bound if the price falls to zero. Using an argument similar to that in Table 6-2, we can show that the value of a European put must satisfy the following lower bound:

$$p_t \geq Ke^{-r\tau} - S_t \tag{6.7}$$

6.2.2   Early Exercise of Options

These relationships can be used to assess the value of early exercise for American options. The basic trade-off is between the value of the American option **dead**, that is, exercised, or **alive**, that is, nonexercised. Thus, the choice is between exercising the option and selling it on the open market.

Consider an American call on a non–dividend-paying stock. By exercising early, the holder gets exactly $S_t - K$. The value of the option alive, however, must be worth more than that of the equivalent European call. From Equation (6.5), this must satisfy $c_t \geq S_t - Ke^{-r\tau}$, which is strictly greater than $S_t - K$. Hence, an American call on a non–dividend-paying stock *should never* be exercised early.

In our example, the lower bound on the European call is \$24.88. If we exercise the American call, we get only $S - K = \$120 - \$100 = \$20$. Because this is less than the minimum value of the European call, the American call should not be exercised. As a result, the value of the American feature is zero and we always have $c_t = C_t$.

The only reason to exercise a call early is to capture a dividend payment. Intuitively, a high income payment makes holding the asset more attractive than holding the option. Thus American options on income-paying assets may be exercised early. Note that this applies also to options on futures, since the implied income stream on the underlying is the risk-free rate.

> **Key concept:**
> An American call option on a non–dividend-paying stock (or asset with no income) should never be exercised early. If the asset pays income, early exercise may occur, with a probability that increases with the size of the income payment.

For an American put, we must have

$$P_t \geq K - S_t \tag{6.8}$$

because it could be exercised now. Unlike the relationship for calls, this lower bound, $K - S_t$, is strictly greater than the lower bound for European puts, $Ke^{-r\tau} - S_t$. So we could have early exercise.

To decide whether to exercise early or not, the holder of the option has to balance the benefit of exercising, which is to receive K now instead of later, against the loss of killing the time value of the option. Because it is better to receive money now than later, it may be worth exercising the put option early.

Thus, American puts on non–income-paying assets *could* be exercised early, unlike calls. The probability of early exercise decreases for lower interest rates and with higher income payments on the asset. In each case, it becomes less attractive to sell the asset.

> **Key concept:**
> An American put option on a non–dividend-paying stock (or asset with no income) may be exercised early. If the asset pays income, the possibility of early exercise decreases with the size of the income payments.

Example 6-9: FRM Exam 2002—Question 50

Given strictly positive interest rates, the best way to close out a long American call option position early (option written on a stock that pays no dividends) would be to

a) Exercise the call

b) Sell the call

c) Deliver the call

d) Do none of the above

Example 6-10: FRM Exam 1998—Question 58

Which of the following statements about options on futures is *true*?

a) An American call is equal in value to a European call.

b) An American put is equal in value to a European put.

c) Put-call parity holds for both American and European options.

d) None of the above statements are true.

Example 6-11: FRM Exam 1999—Question 34

What is the lower pricing bound for a European call option with a strike price of 80 and one year until expiration? The price of the underlying asset is 90, and the one-year interest rate is 5% per annum. Assume continuous compounding of interest.

a) 14.61

b) 13.90

c) 10.00

d) 5.90

6.3   Valuing Options

6.3.1   Pricing by Replication

We now turn to the pricing of options. The philosophy of pricing models consists of replicating the payoff on the instrument. To avoid arbitrage then, the price of the instrument must equal the price of the replicating portfolio.

Consider a call option on a stock whose price is represented by a binomial process. The initial price of $S_0 = \$100$ can move only up or down, to two values (hence the name "binomial"), $S_1 = \$150$ or $S_2 = \$50$. The option is a call with $K = \$100$, and therefore it can take only a value of $c_1 = \$50$ or $c_2 = \$0$. We assume that the rate of interest is $r = 25\%$, so that a dollar invested now grows to $\$1.25$ at maturity.

$$
\begin{array}{ll}
& S_1 = \$150 \quad c_1 = \$50 \\
& \nearrow \\
S_0 = \$100 & \\
& \searrow \\
& S_2 = \$50 \quad c_2 = \$0
\end{array}
$$

The key idea of derivatives pricing is **replication**. In other words, we exactly replicate the payoff on the option by a suitable portfolio of the underlying asset plus a position, long or short, in a risk-free bill. This is feasible in this simple setup because we have two states of the world and two instruments, the stock and the bond. To prevent arbitrage, the current value of the derivative must be the same as that of the portfolio.

The portfolio consists of n shares and a risk-free investment currently valued at B (a negative value implies borrowing). We set $c_1 = nS_1 + B$, or $\$50 = n\$150 + B$, and $c_2 = nS_2 + B$, or $\$0 = n\$50 + B$, and solve the 2 by 2 system, which gives $n = 0.5$ and $B = -\$25$. At time $t = 0$, the value of the loan is $B_0 = \$25/1.25 = \$20$. The current value of the portfolio is $nS_0 + B_0 = 0.5 \times \$100 - \$20 = \$30$. Hence the current value of the option must be $c_0 = \$30$. This derivation shows the essence of option pricing methods.

Note that we did not need the actual probability of an up-move. Define this as p. To see how this can be derived, we write the current value of the stock as the discounted expected payoff assuming investors were risk-neutral:

$$
S_0 = [p \times S_1 + (1 - p) \times S_2]/(1 + r) \tag{6.9}
$$

where the term in brackets is the expectation of the future spot price, given by the probability times its value for each state. Solving for $100 = [p \times 150 + (1 - p) \times 50]/1.25$, we find a risk-neutral probability of $p = 0.75$. We now value the option in the same fashion:

$$
c_0 = [p \times c_1 + (1 - p) \times c_2]/(1 + r) \tag{6.10}
$$

which gives

$$
c_0 = [0.75 \times \$50 + 0.25 \times \$0]/1.25 = \$30
$$

This simple example illustrates a very important concept, which is **risk-neutral pricing**.

6.3.2   Black-Scholes Valuation

The Black-Scholes (BS) model is an application of these ideas that provides an elegant closed-form solution to the pricing of European calls. The derivation of the model is based on four assumptions:

Black-Scholes Model Assumptions
- *The price of the underlying asset moves in a continuous fashion.*
- *Interest rates are known and constant.*
- *The variance of underlying asset returns is constant.*
- *Capital markets are perfect* (i.e., short sales are allowed, there are no transaction costs or taxes, and markets operate continuously).

The most important assumption behind the model is that prices are continuous. This rules out discontinuities in the sample path, such as jumps, which cannot be hedged in this model.

The statistical process for the asset price is modeled by a geometric Brownian motion: Over a very short time interval, dt, the logarithmic return has a normal distribution with mean $= \mu\, dt$ and variance $= \sigma^2\, dt$. The total return can be modeled as

$$dS/S = \mu\, dt + \sigma\, dz \tag{6.11}$$

where the first term represents the drift component and the second is the stochastic component, with dz distributed normally with mean zero and variance dt.

This process implies that the logarithm of the ending price is distributed as

$$\ln(S_T) = \ln(S_0) + (\mu - \sigma^2/2)\tau + \sigma\sqrt{\tau}\,\epsilon \tag{6.12}$$

where ϵ is a $N(0, 1)$ random variable.

Based on these assumptions, Black and Scholes (1972) derived a closed-form formula for European options on a non–dividend-paying stock, called the **Black-Scholes model**. The key point of the analysis is that a position in the option can be replicated by a "delta" position in the underlying asset. Hence, a portfolio combining the asset and the option in appropriate proportions is "locally" risk-free, that is, for small movements in prices. To avoid arbitrage, this portfolio must return the risk-free rate.

As a result, we can directly compute the present value of the derivative as the discounted expected payoff

$$f_t = E_{\mathrm{RN}}[e^{-r\tau}F(S_T)] \tag{6.13}$$

where the underlying asset is assumed to grow at the risk-free rate, and the discounting is also done at the risk-free rate. Here the subscript RN refers to the fact that the analysis assumes **risk neutrality**. In a risk-neutral world, the expected return on all securities must be the risk-free rate of interest, r. The reason is that risk-neutral investors do not require a risk premium to induce them to take risks. The BS model value can be computed assuming that all payoffs grow at the risk-free rate and are discounted at the same risk-free rate.

This risk-neutral valuation approach is without a doubt the most important tool in derivatives pricing. Before the Black-Scholes breakthrough, Samuelson had derived a very similar model in 1965, but with the asset growing at the rate μ and discounting as some other rate μ^*.[1] Because μ and μ^* are unknown, the Samuelson model was not practical. The risk-neutral valuation is merely an artificial method to obtain the correct solution, however. It does not imply that investors are in fact risk-neutral.

Furthermore, this approach has limited uses for risk management. The BS model can be used to derive the **risk-neutral probability** of exercising the option. For risk management, however, what matters is the actual probability of exercise, also called the **physical probability**. This can differ from the BS probability.

In the case of a European call, the final payoff is $F(S_T) = \text{Max}(S_T - K, 0)$. Initially, we assume no dividend payment on the asset. The current value of the call is given by

$$c = SN(d_1) - Ke^{-r\tau}N(d_2) \tag{6.14}$$

where $N(d)$ is the cumulative distribution function for the standard normal distribution:

$$N(d) = \int_{-\infty}^{d} \Phi(x)dx = \frac{1}{\sqrt{2\pi}} \int_{-\infty}^{d} e^{-1/2x^2} dx$$

with Φ defined as the standard normal density function. $N(d)$ is also the area to the left of a standard normal variable with value equal to d, as shown in Figure 6-9. Note that since the normal density is symmetrical, $N(d) = 1 - N(-d)$, or the area to the left of d is the same as the area to the right of $-d$.

---

[1] Samuelson, Paul (1965), Rational Theory of Warrant Price, *Industrial Management Review* 6, 13–39.

FIGURE 6-9 Cumulative Distribution Function

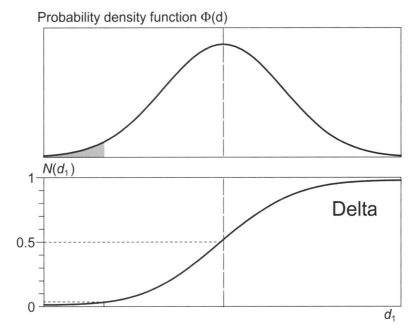

The values of d_1 and d_2 are

$$d_1 = \frac{\ln(S/Ke^{-r\tau})}{\sigma\sqrt{\tau}} + \frac{\sigma\sqrt{\tau}}{2}, \quad d_2 = d_1 - \sigma\sqrt{\tau}$$

By put-call parity, the European put option value is

$$p = S[N(d_1) - 1] - Ke^{-r\tau}[N(d_2) - 1] \tag{6.15}$$

Example: Computing the Black-Scholes value

Consider an at-the-money call on a stock worth $S = \$100$, with a strike price of $K = \$100$ and maturity of six months. The stock has annual volatility of $\sigma = 20\%$ and pays no dividend. The risk-free rate is $r = 5\%$.

First, we compute the present value factor, which is $e^{-r\tau} = \exp(-0.05 \times 6/12) = 0.9753$. We then compute the value of $d_1 = \ln[S/Ke^{-r\tau}]/\sigma\sqrt{\tau} + \sigma\sqrt{\tau}/2 = 0.2475$ and $d_2 = d_1 - \sigma\sqrt{\tau} = 0.1061$. Using standard normal tables or the =NORMSDIST Excel function, we find $N(d_1) = 0.5977$ and $N(d_2) = 0.5422$. Note that both values are greater than 0.5 since d_1 and d_2 are both positive. The option is at-the-money. As S is close to K, d_1 is close to zero and $N(d_1)$ close to 0.5.

The value of the call is $c = SN(d_1) - Ke^{-r\tau}N(d_2) = \$6.89$.

The value of the call can also be viewed as an equivalent position of $N(d_1) = 59.77\%$ in the stock and some borrowing: $c = \$59.77 - \$52.88 = \$6.89$. Thus this is a leveraged position in the stock.

The value of the put is \$4.42. Buying the call and selling the put costs $\$6.89 - \$4.42 = \$2.47$. This indeed equals $S - Ke^{-r\tau} = \$100 - \$97.53 = \$2.47$, which confirms put-call parity.

We should note that Equation (6.14) can be reinterpreted in view of the discounting formula in a risk-neutral world, Equation (6.13)

$$c = E_{RN}[e^{-r\tau}\text{Max}(S_T - K, 0)] = e^{-r\tau}\left[\int_K^\infty Sf(S)\,dS\right] - Ke^{-r\tau}\left[\int_K^\infty f(S)\,dS\right] \tag{6.16}$$

We see that the integral term multiplying K is the risk-neutral probability of exercising the call, or the probability that the option will end up in-the-money, $S > K$. Matching this up with (6.14), this gives

$$\text{Risk-neutral probability of exercise} = \left[\int_K^\infty f(S)\,dS\right] = N(d_2) \tag{6.17}$$

6.3.3   Extensions

Merton (1973) expanded the BS model to the case of a stock paying a continuous dividend yield q. Garman and Kohlhagen (1983) extended the formula to foreign currencies, reinterpreting the yield as the foreign rate of interest $q = r^*$, in what is called the **Garman-Kohlhagen model**.

The Merton model then replaces all occurrences of S by $Se^{-r^*\tau}$. The call is worth

$$c = Se^{-r^*\tau}N(d_1) - Ke^{-r\tau}N(d_2) \tag{6.18}$$

It is interesting to take the limit of Equation (6.14) as the option moves more in-the-money, that is, when the spot price S is much greater than K. In this case, d_1 and d_2 become very large and the functions $N(d_1)$ and $N(d_2)$ tend to unity. The value of the call then tends to

$$c(S \gg K) = Se^{-r^*\tau} - Ke^{-r\tau} \tag{6.19}$$

which is the valuation formula for a forward contract. A call that is deep in-the-money is equivalent to a long forward contract, because we are almost certain to exercise.

The **Black model** (1976) applies the same formula to options on futures. The only conceptual difference lies in the income payment to the underlying instrument. With an option on cash, the income is the dividend or interest on the cash instrument. In contrast, with a futures contract, the economically equivalent stream of income is the riskless interest rate. The intuition is that a futures can be viewed as equivalent to a position in the underlying asset with the investor setting aside an amount of cash equivalent to the present value of F.

> **Key concept:**
> With an option on futures, the implicit income is the risk-free rate of interest.

For the Black model, we simply replace S by F, the current futures quote, and replace r^* by r, the domestic risk-free rate. The Black model for the valuation of options on futures is

$$c = [FN(d_1) - KN(d_2)]e^{-r\tau} \tag{6.20}$$

Finally, we should note that standard options involve a choice to exchange cash for the asset. This is a special case of an **exchange option**, which involves the surrender of an asset (call it B) in exchange for acquiring another (call it A). The payoff on such a call is

$$c_T = \text{Max}(S_T^A - S_T^B, 0) \tag{6.21}$$

where S^A and S^B are the respective spot prices. Some financial instruments involve the maximum of the value of two assets, which is equivalent to a position in one asset plus an exchange option:

$$\text{Max}(S_t^A, S_t^B) = S_T^B + \text{Max}(S_T^A - S_T^B, 0) \tag{6.22}$$

Margrabe (1978) has shown that the valuation formula is similar to the usual model, except that K is replaced by the price of asset B (S_B), and the risk-free rate by the yield on asset B (q_B).[2] The volatility σ is now that of the difference between the two assets, which is

$$\sigma_{AB}^2 = \sigma_A^2 + \sigma_B^2 - 2\rho_{AB}\sigma_A\sigma_B \tag{6.23}$$

---

[2]Margrabe, W. (1978), The Value of an Option to Exchange One Asset for Another, *Journal of Finance* 33, 177–186. See also Stulz, R. (1982), Options on the Minimum or the Maximum of Two Risky Assets: Analysis and Applications, *Journal of Financial Economics* 10, 161–185.

These options also involve the correlation coefficient. So if we have a triplet of options, involving A, B, and the option to exchange B into A, we can compute σ_A, σ_B, and σ_{AB}. This allows us to infer the correlation coefficient. The pricing formula is called the **Margrabe model**.

6.3.4 Market versus Model Prices

In practice, the BS model is widely used to price options. All of the parameters are observable, except for the volatility. If we observe a market price, however, we can solve for the volatility parameter that sets the model price equal to the market price. This is called the **implied standard deviation** (ISD).

If the model is correct, the ISD should be constant across strike prices. In fact, this is not what we observe. Plots of the ISD against the strike price display what is called a **volatility smile** pattern, meaning that ISDs increase for low and high values of K. This effect has been observed in a variety of markets, and can even change over time. Before the stock market crash of October 1987, for instance, the effect was minor. Since then, it has become more pronounced.

Example 6-12: FRM Exam 2001—Question 91
Using the Black-Scholes model, calculate the value of a European call option given the following information: spot rate = 100; strike price = 110; risk-free rate = 10%; time to expiry = 0.5 years; $N(d_1) = 0.457185$; $N(d_2) = 0.374163$.
a) $10.90
b) $9.51
c) $6.57
d) $4.92

Example 6-13: FRM Exam 1999—Question 55
If the Garman-Kohlhagen formula is used for valuing options on a dividend-paying stock, then to be consistent with its assumptions, upon receipt of the dividend, the dividend should be
a) Placed into a non–interest-bearing account
b) Placed into an interest-bearing account at the risk-free rate assumed in the G-K model
c) Used to purchase more stock of the same company
d) Placed into an interest-bearing account, paying interest equal to the dividend yield of the stock

---

Example 6-14: FRM Exam 1998—Question 2

In the Black-Scholes expression for a European call option the term used to compute option probability of exercise is

a) d_1

b) d_2

c) $N(d_1)$

d) $N(d_2)$

6.4   Other Option Contracts

The options described so far are standard, plain-vanilla options. Many other types of options, however, have been developed.

Binary options, also called **digital options**, pay a fixed amount, say Q, if the asset price ends up above the strike price:

$$c_T = Q \times I(S_T - K) \tag{6.24}$$

where $I(x)$ is an indicator variable that takes the value of 1 if $x \geq 0$ and 0 otherwise. The payofff function is illustrated in Figure 6-10 when $K = \$100$.

FIGURE 6-10 Payoff on a Binary Option

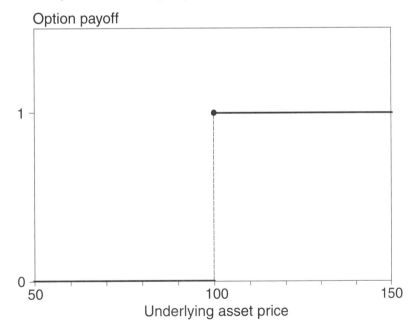

Because the probability of ending in-the-money in a risk-neutral world is $N(d_2)$, the initial value of this option is simply

$$c = Qe^{-r\tau} N(d_2) \tag{6.25}$$

These options involve a sharp discontinuity around the strike price. Just below K, their value is zero. Just above, the value is the notional Q. Due to this discontinuity, these options are very difficult to hedge.

Another important class of options are barrier options. **Barrier options** are options where the payoff depends on the value of the asset hitting a barrier during a certain period of time. A **knock-out option** disappears if the price hits a certain barrier. A **knock-in option** comes into existence when the price hits a certain barrier.

An example of a knock-out option is the **down-and-out call**. This disappears if S hits a specified level H during its life. In this case, the knock-out price H must be lower than the initial price S_0. The option that appears at H is the **down-and-in call**. With identical parameters, the two options are perfectly complementary. When one disappears, the other appears. As a result, these two options must add up to a regular call option. Similarly, an **up-and-out call** ceases to exist when S reaches $H > S_0$. The complementary option is the **up-and-in call**.

Figure 6-11 compares price paths for the four possible combinations of calls. In all figures, the dark line describes the relevant price path during which the option is alive; the grey line describes the remaining path.

The graphs illustrates that the down-and-out call and down-and-in call add up to the regular price path of a regular European call option. Thus at initiation, the value of these two options must add up to

$$c = c_{DO} + c_{DI} \tag{6.26}$$

Because all these values are positive (or at worst zero), the value of each premium c_{DO} and c_{DI} must be no greater than that of c. A similar reasoning applies to the two options in the right panels.

Similar combinations exist for put options. An **up-and-out put** ceases to exist when S reaches $H > S_0$. A **down-and-out put** ceases to exist when S reaches $H < S_0$. The only difference with respect to Figure 6-11 is that the option is exercised at maturity if $S < K$.

FIGURE 6-11 Paths for Knock-out and Knock-in Call Options

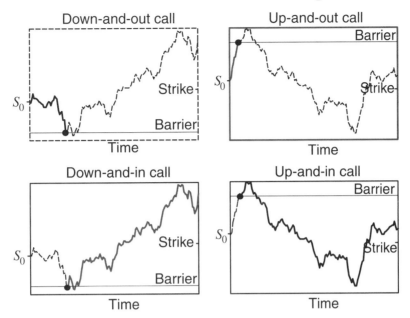

Barrier options are attractive because they are "cheaper" than the equivalent European options. This, of course, reflects the fact that they are less likely to be exercised than other options. These options are also difficult to hedge due to the fact that a discontinuity arises as the spot price get closer to the barrier. Just above the barrier, the option has positive value. For a very small movement in the asset price, going below the barrier, this value disappears.

Finally, another widely used class of options are Asian options. **Asian options**, or **average rate options**, generate payoffs that depend on the average value of the underlying spot price during the life of the option, instead of the ending value. Define this as $S_{AVE}(t, T)$. The final payoff for a call is

$$c_T = \text{Max}(S_{AVE}(t, T) - K, 0) \tag{6.27}$$

Because an average over a period is less variable than the final value at the end of the same period, such options are "cheaper" than regular options due to lower volatility. In fact, the price of the option can be treated like that of an ordinary option with the volatility set equal to $\sigma / \sqrt{3}$ and an adjustment made to the dividend yield.[3] As a result of the averaging process, such options are easier to hedge than ordinary options.

---

[3] This is strictly true only when the averaging is a geometric average. In practice, average options involve an arithmetic average, for which there is no analytic solution; the lower volatility adjustment is just an approximation.

Example 6-15: FRM Exam 1997—Question 10

Knock-out options are often used instead of regular options because

a) Knock-outs have a lower volatility.

b) Knock-outs have a lower premium.

c) Knock-outs have a shorter maturity on average.

d) Knock-outs have a smaller gamma.

Example 6-16: FRM Exam 2002—Question 19

Of the following options, which one does *not* benefit from an increase in the stock price when the current stock price is $100 and the barrier has not yet been crossed:

a) A down-and-out call with out barrier at $90 and strike at $110

b) A down-an-in call with in barrier at $90 and strike at $110

c) An up-and-in put with barrier at $110 and strike at $100

d) An up-and-in call with barrier at $110 and strike at $100

6.5   Valuing Options by Numerical Methods

Some options have analytical solutions, such as the Black-Scholes models for European vanilla options. For more general options, however, we need to use numerical methods.

The basic valuation formula for derivatives is Equation (6.13), which states that the current value is the discounted present value of expected cash flows, where all assets grow at the risk-free rate and are discounted at the same risk-free rate.

We can use the Monte Carlo simulation methods presented in Chapter 4 to generate sample paths and final option values, and discount them into the present. Such simulation methods can be used for European or even path-dependent options, such as Asian options.

Simulation methods, however, cannot account for the possibility of early exercise. Instead, binomial trees must be used to value American options. As explained previously, the method consists of chopping up the time horizon into n intervals Δt and setting up the tree so that the characteristics of price movements fit the lognormal distribution.

At each node, the initial price S can go up to uS with probability p or down to dS with probability $(1 - p)$. The parameters u, d, p are chosen so that, for a small time interval, the expected return and variance equal those of the continuous process. One could choose, for instance,

$$u = e^{\sigma\sqrt{\Delta t}}, \quad d = (1/u), \quad p = \frac{e^{\mu\Delta t} - d}{u - d} \tag{6.28}$$

Since this a risk-neutral process, the total expected return must be equal to the risk-free rate r. Allowing for an income payment of r^*, this gives $\mu = r - r^*$.

The tree is built starting from the current time to maturity, from the left to the right. Next, the derivative is valued by starting at the end of the tree and working backward to the initial time, from the right to the left.

Consider first a European call option. At time T (maturity) and node j, the call option is worth $\text{Max}(S_{Tj} - K, 0)$. At time $T - 1$ and node j, the call option is the discounted expected value of the option at time T and nodes j and $j + 1$:

$$c_{T-1,j} = e^{-r\Delta t}[pc_{T,j+1} + (1 - p)c_{T,j}] \tag{6.29}$$

We then work backward through the tree until the current time.

For American options, the procedure is slightly different. At each point in time, the holder compares the values of the option *alive* and *dead* (i.e., exercised). The American call option value at node $T - 1, j$ is

$$C_{T-1,j} = \text{Max}[(S_{T-1,j} - K), c_{T-1,j}] \tag{6.30}$$

Example: Computing an American option value

Consider an at-the-money call on a foreign currency with a spot price of \$100, a strike price of $K = \$100$, and a maturity of six months. The annualized volatility is $\sigma = 20\%$. The domestic interest rate is $r = 5\%$; the foreign rate is $r^* = 8\%$. Note that we require an income payment for the American feature to be valuable. If $r^* = 0$, we know that the American option is worth the same as a European option, which can be priced with the Black-Scholes model. There would be no point in using a numerical method.

First, we divide the period into four intervals, for instance, so that $\Delta t = 0.50/4 = 0.125$. The discounting factor over one interval is $e^{-r\Delta t} = 0.9938$. We then compute:

$$u = e^{\sigma\sqrt{\Delta t}} e^{0.20\sqrt{0.125}} = 1.0733$$

$$d = (1/u)0.9317$$

$$a = e^{(r-r^*)\Delta t} e^{(-0.03)0.125} = 0.9963$$

$$p = \frac{a - d}{u - d}(0.9963 - 0.9317)/(1.0733 - 0.9317) = 0.4559$$

The procedure for pricing the option is detailed in Table 6-3. First we lay out the tree for the spot price, starting with $S = 100$ at time $t = 0$, then $uS = 107.33$ and $dS = 93.17$ at time $t = 1$, and so on.

This allows us to value the European call. We start from the end, at time $t = 4$, and set the call price to $c = S - K = 132.69 - 100.00 = 32.69$ for the highest spot price, 15.19 for the next price and so on, down to $c = 0$ if the spot price is below $K = 100.00$. At the previous step and highest node, the value of the call is

$$c = 0.9938[0.4559 \times 32.69 + (1 - 0.4559) \times 15.19] = 23.02$$

Continuing through the tree to time 0 yields a European call value of \$4.43. The Black-Scholes formula gives an exact value of \$4.76. Note how close the binomial approximation is, with just four steps. A finer partition would quickly improve the approximation.

TABLE 6-3 Computation of American Option Value

	0	1	2	3	4
Spot price S_t	→	→	→	→	→
					132.69
				123.63	115.19
			115.19	107.33	100.00
		107.33	100.00	93.17	86.81
	100.00	93.17	86.81	80.89	75.36
European call c_t	←	←	←	←	←
					32.69
				23.02	15.19
			14.15	6.88	0.00
		8.10	3.12	0.00	0.00
	4.43	1.41	0.00	0.00	0.00
Exercised call $S_t - K$					
					32.69
				23.63	15.19
			15.19	7.33	0.00
		7.33	0.00	0.00	0.00
	0.00	0.00	0.00	0.00	0.00
American call C_t	←	←	←	←	←
					32.69
				23.63	15.19
			15.19	7.33	0.00
		8.68	3.32	0.00	0.00
	4.74	1.50	0.00	0.00	0.00

Next, we examine the American call. At time $t = 4$, the values are the same as above since the call expires. At time $t = 3$ and node $j = 4$, the option holder can either keep the call, in which case the value is still $23.02, or exercise. When exercised, the option payoff is $S - K = 123.63 - 100.00 = 23.63$. Since this is greater than the value of the option alive, the holder should optimally exercise the option. We replace the European option value by $23.63 at that node. Continuing through the tree in the same fashion, we find a starting value of $4.74. The value of the American call is slightly greater than the European call price, as expected.

6.6 Answers to Chapter Examples

Example 6-1: FRM Exam 1999—Question 35

b) A short put position is equivalent to a long asset position plus shorting a call. To fund the purchase of the asset, we need to borrow. This is because the value of the call or put is small relative to the value of the asset.

Example 6-2: FRM Exam 2002—Question 47

d) Because this is a European call, we can use put-call parity, or $c - p = S \exp(-qT) - K \exp(-rT)$. The put should be worth $p = \$50 - \$100 \exp(-2\% \times 2) + \$140 \times \exp(-5\% \times 2) = \$50 - \$96.12 + \$126.98 = \$80.87$.

Example 6-3: FRM Exam 2002—Question 25

d) Put-call parity applies to these European options. With no dividend, the relationship is $c - p = S - K \exp(-r\tau)$. The first term is $c - p = \$4 - \$1.47 = \$2.53$. The second term is $S - K \exp(-r\tau) = \$20 - \$18 \exp[-6\%(6/12)] = \$2.53$. Because the two numbers are the same, there is no arbitrage opportunity.

Example 6-4: FRM Exam 2001—Question 90

c) Long positions in options can lose at worst the premium, so b) is wrong. Spreads involve long and short positions in options and have limited downside loss, so a) is wrong. Writing options exposes the seller to very large losses. In the case of puts, the worst loss is the strike price K, if the asset price goes to zero. In the case of calls, however, the worst loss is in theory unlimited because there is a small probability of a huge increase in S. Between c) and d), c) is the best answer.

Example 6-5: FRM Exam 1999—Question 50

b) A covered call is long the asset plus a short call. This preserves the downside but eliminates the upside, which is equivalent to a short put.

Example 6-6: FRM Exam 1999—Question 33

a) The purpose of a bull spread is to create a profit when the underlying price increases. The strategy involves the same options but with different strike prices. It can be achieved with calls or puts. Answer c) is incorrect, as a bull spread based on calls involves buying a call with high premium and selling another with lower premium. Answer d) is incorrect as it mixes a call and a put. Among the two puts $p(K = \$55)$ must have higher value than $p(K = \$50)$. If the spot price ends up above 55, none of the puts is exercised. The profit must be positive, which implies selling the put with $K = 55$ and buying a put with $K = 50$.

Example 6-7: FRM Exam 2000—Question 5

a) The proceeds from exercise are $(\$42 - \$30) - (\$42 - \$40) = \$10$. From this should be deducted the net cost of the options, which is $\$3 - \$1.5 = \$1.5$, ignoring the time value of money. This adds up to a net profit of $\$8.50$.

Example 6-8: FRM Exam 2002—Question 42

b) Because the final price is below the lowest of the three strike prices, all the puts will be exercised. The final payoff is $(\$50 - \$33) - 2(\$42 - \$33) + (\$37 - \$33) = \$17 - \$18 + \$4 = \$3$. From this, we have to deduct the up-front cost, which is $-\$7 + 2(\$4) - \$2 = -\$1$. The total profit then, ignoring the time value of money, is $\$3 - \$1 = \$2$ per share.

Example 6-9: FRM Exam 2002—Question 50

b) When there is no dividend, there is never any reason to exercise an American call early. Instead, the option should be sold to another party.

Example 6-10: FRM Exam 1998—Question 58

d) Futures have an "implied" income stream equal to the risk-free rate. As a result, an American call may be exercised early. Similarly, the American put may be exercised early. Also, the put-call parity works only when there is no possibility of early exercise, or with European options.

Example 6-11: FRM Exam 1999—Question 34

b) The call lower bound, when there is no income, is $S_t - Ke^{-r\tau} = \$90 - \$80 \exp(-0.05 \times 1) = \$90 - \$76.10 = \$13.90$.

Example 6-12: FRM Exam 2001—Question 91

c) We use Equation (6.14) assuming there is no income payment on the asset. This gives $c = SN(d_1) - K \exp(-r\tau)N(d_2) = 100 \times 0.457185 - 110 \exp(-0.1 \times 0.5) \times 0.374163 = \$6.568$.

Example 6-13: FRM Exam 1999—Question 55

c) The GK formula assumes that income payments are reinvested in the stock itself. Answers a) and b) assume reinvestment at a zero and risk-free rate, which is incorrect. Answer d) is not feasible.

Example 6-14: FRM Exam 1998—Question 2

d) This is the term multiplying the present value of the strike price, by Equation (6.15).

Example 6-15: FRM Exam 1997—Question 10

b) Knock-outs are no different from regular options in terms of maturity or underlying volatility, but are cheaper than the equivalent European option since they involve a lower probability of final exercise.

Example 6-16: FRM Exam 2002—Question 19

b) A down-and-out call where the barrier has not been touched is still alive and hence benefits from an increase in S, so a) is incorrect. A down-and-in call comes alive only when the barrier is touched; so an increase in S brings it away from the barrier. This is not favorable, so b) is correct. An up-and-in put would benefit from an increase in S as this brings it closer to the barrier of $110, so c) is not correct. Finally, an up-and-in call would also benefit if S gets closer to the barrier.

Chapter 7

Fixed-Income Securities

The next two chapters provide an overview of fixed-income markets, and securities and their derivatives. Originally, **fixed-income securities** referred to bonds that promise fixed coupon payments. Over time, this narrow definition has evolved to include any security that obligates the borrower to make specific payments to the bondholder on specified dates. Thus, a **bond** is a security that is issued in connection with a borrowing arrangement. In exchange for receiving cash, the borrower becomes obligated to make a series of payments to the bondholder.

Fixed-income derivatives are instruments whose value derives from some bond price, interest rate, or other bond market variable. Due to their complexity, these instruments are analyzed in the next chapter.

Section 7.1 provides an overview of the different segments of the bond market. Section 7.2 then introduces the various types of fixed-income securities. Section 7.3 reviews the basic tools for analyzing fixed-income securities, including the determination of cash flows, the measurement of duration, and the term structure of interest rates and forward rates. Because of their importance, mortgage-backed securities (MBSs) are analyzed separately in Section 7.4. That section also discusses collateralized mortgage obligations (CMOs), which illustrate the creativity of financial engineering.

7.1   Overview of Debt Markets

Fixed-income markets are truly global. To help sort the various categories of the bond markets, Table 7-1 provides a broad classification of bonds by borrower and currency type. Bonds issued by resident entities and denominated in the domestic currency are called **domestic bonds**. In contrast, **foreign bonds** are those floated by a foreign issuer in the domestic currency and subject to domestic country regulations (e.g., by the government of Sweden in dollars in the United States). **Eurobonds** are mainly placed outside the country of the currency in which they are denominated and are sold by an international syndicate of financial institutions (e.g., a dollar-denominated bond issued by IBM and marketed in London).[1] Foreign bonds and Eurobonds constitute the **international bond market**. Finally, **global bonds** are placed at the same time in the Eurobond and one or more domestic markets with securities fungible between these markets.

TABLE 7-1 Classification of Bond Markets

	By Resident	By Nonresident
In domestic currency	Domestic bond	Foreign bond
In foreign currency	Eurobond	Eurobond

The domestic bond market can be further decomposed into these categories:

■ **Government bonds**, issued by central governments, also called **sovereign bonds** (e.g., by the United States in dollars)

■ **Government agency and guaranteed bonds**, issued by agencies or guaranteed by the central government (e.g., by Fannie Mae, a U.S. government agency), which are public financial institutions

■ **State and local bonds**, issued by local governments, other than the central government, also known as **municipal bonds** (e.g., by the state of California)

■ Bonds issued by private **financial institutions**, including banks, insurance companies, or issuers of asset-backed securities (e.g., by Citibank in the U.S. market)

■ **Corporate bonds**, issued by private nonfinancial corporations, including industrials and utilities (e.g., by IBM in the U.S. market)

Table 7-2 breaks down the world debt securities market, which was worth $51 trillion at the end of 2003. This includes the **bond markets**, traditionally defined as

---

[1] These should not be confused with bonds denominated in the euro, which can be of any type.

fixed-income securities with remaining maturities beyond one year, and the shorter-term **money markets**, with maturities below one year. The table includes all publicly tradable debt securities sorted by country of issuer and issuer type as of 2003.

The table shows that U.S. entities have issued a total of $17.6 trillion in domestic debt and $3.1 trillion in international debt, for a total amount of $20.7 trillion, which is by far the biggest debt securities market. Next comes the Eurozone market, with a size of $12.5 trillion, and the Japanese market, with $7.9 trillion.

TABLE 7-2 Global Debt Securities Markets 2003 (Billions of U.S. Dollars)

Country of Issuer	Domestic	Of Which			Int'l	Total
		Government	Financials	Corporates		
United States	17,635	5,021	10,130	2,484	3,108	20,743
Japan	7,818	5,831	1,217	770	121	7,939
Germany	2,091	1,024	958	109	1,335	3,426
Italy	2,088	1,354	538	196	385	2,473
France	1,847	1,030	581	236	748	2,595
United Kingdom	1,275	510	382	382	1,304	2,578
Canada	709	516	104	89	290	999
Spain	663	406	143	115	232	896
Netherlands	585	256	264	65	956	1,541
South Korea	446	124	164	157	56	502
Belgium	444	318	89	36	103	547
China	440	287	141	12	13	453
Denmark	387	105	263	20	52	440
Australia	305	89	129	87	227	532
Brazil	300	247	51	3	73	373
Sweden	279	142	113	24	125	404
Switzerland	223	97	98	28	18	242
Austria	203	99	89	15	178	381
Subtotal	37,739	17,458	15,454	4,828	9,324	47,063
Others	1,893	1,404	238	251	2,349	4,242
Subtotal, Eurozone	8,223	4,667	2,723	833	4,275	12,498
Total	39,631	18,861	15,692	5,079	11,673	51,305

Source: Bank for International Settlements

As Table 7-2 shows, the largest sector is for domestic government debt. This sector includes sovereign debt issued by emerging countries in their own currencies (e.g., Mexican peso–denominated debt issued by the Mexican government). Few of these markets have long-term issues, because of their history of high inflation, which renders long-term bonds very risky. In Mexico, for instance, the market consists mainly of **cetes**, which are peso-denominated, short-term Treasury bills.

Among international debt, the emerging market sector also includes debt denominated in U.S. dollars, such as **Brady bonds**, which are sovereign bonds issued in exchange for bank loans, and the **tesebonos**, which are dollar-denominated bills issued by the Mexican government. Brady bonds are hybrid securities whose principal is collateralized by U.S. Treasury zero-coupon bonds. As a result, there is no risk of default on the principal, unlike the case for coupon payments.

The domestic financial market is also important, especially for mortgage-backed securities. **Mortgage-backed securities** (MBSs), or mortgage **pass-throughs**, are securities issued in conjunction with mortgage loans, either residential or commercial. Payments on MBSs are repackaged cash flows supported by mortgage payments made by property owners. MBSs can be issued by government agencies as well as by private financial corporations. More generally, **asset-backed securities** (ABSs) are securities whose cash flows are supported by assets such as credit card receivables or car loan payments.

Finally, the remainder of the domestic market represents bonds raised by private, nonfinancial corporations. This sector, by far the largest in the United States, is growing rather quickly as corporations recognize that bond issuances are a lower-cost source of funds than bank debt. The advent of the common currency, the euro, is also leading to a growing, more liquid and efficient corporate bond market in Europe.

7.2 Fixed-Income Securities

7.2.1 Instrument Types

Bonds pay interest on a regular basis—semiannually for U.S. Treasury and corporate bonds, annually for others such as Eurobonds, or quarterly for others. The most common types of bonds are

- **Fixed-coupon bonds**, which pay a fixed percentage of the principal every period and the principal as a **balloon**, one-time, payment at maturity

- **Zero-coupon bonds**, which pay no coupons but only the principal; their return is derived from price appreciation only

■ **Annuities**, which pay a constant amount over time that includes interest plus amortization, or gradual repayment, of the principal

■ **Perpetual bonds or consols**, which have no set redemption date and whose value derives from interest payments only

■ **Floating-coupon bonds**, which pay interest equal to a reference rate plus a margin, reset on a regular basis—usually called **floating-rate notes** (FRN)

■ **Structured notes**, which have more complex coupon patterns to satisfy the investor's needs

■ **Inflation-protected notes**, whose principal is indexed to the **Consumer Price Index** (CPI), providing protection against an increasing rate of inflation[2]

There are many variations on these themes. For instance, **step-up bonds** have fixed coupons that start at a low rate and increase over time.

It is useful to consider floating-rate notes in more detail. Take, for instance, a 10-year $100 million FRN paying semiannually six-month LIBOR in arrears.[3] **LIBOR** is the London Interbank Offer Rate, a benchmark cost of borrowing for highly rated (AA) credits. Every semester, on the **reset date**, the value of six-month LIBOR is recorded. Say LIBOR is initially at 6%. At the next coupon date, the payment will be $(\frac{1}{2}) \times \$100 \times 6\% = \$3$ million. Simultaneously, we record a new value for LIBOR, say 8%. The next payment will then increase to $4 million, and so on. At maturity, the issuer pays the last coupon plus the principal. Like a cork at the end of a fishing line, the coupon payment "floats" with the current interest rate.

Among structured notes, we should mention **inverse floaters**, also known as reverse floaters, which have coupon payments that vary inversely with the level of interest rates. A typical formula for the coupon is $c = 12\% - $ LIBOR, if positive, payable semiannually. Assume the principal is $100 million. If LIBOR starts at 6%, the first

---

[2]In the United States, these government bonds are called **Treasury inflation-protected securities** (TIPS). The coupon payment is fixed in real terms, say 3%. If after six months the cumulative inflation is 2%, the principal value of the bond increases from $100 to $100 \times (1 + 2\%) = \$102$. The first semi-annual coupon payment is then $(3\%/2) \times \$102 = \$1.53$.

[3]Note that the index could be defined differently. The floating payment could be tied to a Treasury rate, or LIBOR with a different maturity—say three-month LIBOR. The pricing of the FRN will depend on the index. Also, the coupon will typically be set to LIBOR plus some spread that depends on the creditworthiness of the issuer.

coupon will be $(1/2) \times \$100 \times (12\% - 6\%) = \$3$ million. If after six months LIBOR moves to 8%, the second coupon will be $(1/2) \times \$100 \times (12\% - 8\%) = \$2$ million. The coupon will go to zero if LIBOR moves above 12%. Conversely, the coupon will increase if LIBOR drops. Hence, inverse floaters do best in a falling-interest-rate environment.

Bonds can also be issued with option features. The most important are

- **Callable bonds**, where the issuer has the right to "call" back the bond at fixed prices on fixed dates, the purpose being to call back the bond when the cost of issuing new debt is lower than the current coupon paid on the bond

- **Puttable bonds**, where the investor has the right to "put" the bond back to the issuer at fixed prices on fixed dates, the purpose being to dispose of the bond should its price deteriorate

- **Convertible bonds**, where the bond can be converted into the common stock of the issuing company at a fixed price on a fixed date, the purpose being to partake in the good fortunes of the company (these will be covered in the chapter on equities)

The key to analyzing these bonds is to identify and price the option feature. For instance, a callable bond can be decomposed into a long position in a straight bond minus a call option on the bond price. The call feature is unfavorable for investors who will demand a lower price to purchase the bond, thereby increasing its yield. Conversely, a put feature will make the bond more attractive, increasing its price and lowering its yield. Similarly, the convertible feature allows companies to issue bonds at a lower yield than otherwise.

Example 7-1: FRM Exam 1998—Question 3

The price of an inverse floater
a) Increases as interest rates increase
b) Decreases as interest rates increase
c) Remains constant as interest rates change
d) Behaves like none of the above

Example 7-2: FRM Exam 2000—Question 9

An investment in a callable bond can be analytically decomposed into a

a) Long position in a noncallable bond and a short position in a put option

b) Short position in a noncallable bond and a long position in a call option

c) Long position in a noncallable bond and a long position in a call option

d) Long position in a noncallable bond and a short position in a call option

---

7.2.2 Methods of Quotation

Most bonds are quoted on a **clean price** basis, that is, without accounting for the accrued income from the last coupon. For U.S. bonds, this clean price is expressed as a percentage of the face value of the bond with fractions in thirty-seconds—for instance, as 104-12, which means $104 + 12/32$, for the 6.25% May 2030 Treasury bond. Transactions are expressed in number of units (e.g., $20 million face value).

Actual payments, however, must account for the accrual of interest. This is factored into the **gross price**, also known as the **dirty price**, which is equal to the clean price plus accrued interest. In the U.S. Treasury market, accrued interest (AI) is computed on an *actual/actual* basis:

$$\text{AI} = \text{Coupon} \times \frac{\text{Actual number of days since last coupon}}{\text{Actual number of days between last and next coupon}} \qquad (7.1)$$

The fraction involves the actual number of days in both the numerator and denominator. For instance, say the 6.25% May 2030 paid the last coupon on November 15 and will pay the next coupon on May 15. The denominator is, counting the number of days in each month, $15 + 31 + 31 + 29 + 31 + 30 + 15 = 182$. If the trade settles on April 26, there are $15 + 31 + 31 + 29 + 31 + 26 = 163$ days in the period. The accrued is computed from the $3.125 coupon as

$$\$3.125 \times \frac{163}{182} = \$2.798763$$

The total, gross price for this transaction is

$$(\$20,000,000/100) \times [(104 + 12/32) + 2.798763] = \$21,434,753$$

Different markets have different day count conventions. A 30/360 convention, for example, considers that all months count as 30 days exactly. The computation of the accrued interest is tedious but must be performed precisely to settle the trades.

We should note that the accrued interest in the LIBOR market is based on *actual/360*. For instance, the interest accrued on a 6% $1 million loan over 92 days is

$$\$1,000,000 \times 0.06 \times \frac{92}{360} = \$15,333.33$$

Another notable pricing convention is the discount basis for Treasury bills. These bills are quoted in terms of an annualized discount rate (DR) to the face value, defined as

$$DR = (\text{Face} - P)/\text{Face} \times (360/t) \tag{7.2}$$

where P is the price and t is the actual number of days. The dollar price can be recovered from

$$P = \text{Face} \times [1 - DR \times (t/360)] \tag{7.3}$$

For instance, a bill quoted at 5.19% discount with 91 days to maturity could be purchased for

$$\$100 \times [1 - 5.19\% \times (91/360)] = \$98.6881$$

This price can be transformed into a conventional yield to maturity, using

$$F/P = (1 + y \times t/365) \tag{7.4}$$

which gives 5.33% in this case. Note that the yield is greater than the discount rate because it is a rate of return based on the initial price. Because the price is lower than the face value, the yield must be greater than the discount rate.

Example 7-3: FRM Exam 1998—Question 13

A U.S. Treasury bill selling for $97,569 with 100 days to maturity and a face value of $100,000 should be quoted on a bank discount basis at
a) 8.75%
b) 8.87%
c) 8.97%
d) 9.09%

7.3   Analysis of Fixed-Income Securities

7.3.1   The NPV Approach

Fixed-income securities can be valued by, first, laying out their cash flows and, second, computing their net present value using the appropriate discount rate. Let us write the market value of a bond P as the present value of future cash flows:

$$P = \sum_{t=1}^{T} \frac{C_t}{(1+y)^t} \tag{7.5}$$

where

C_t = cash flow (coupon and/or principal repayment) in period t

t = number of periods (e.g., half-years) to each payment

T = number of periods to final maturity

y = yield to maturity for this particular bond

P = price of the bond, including accrued interest

For a fixed-rate bond with face value F, the cash flow C_t is cF each period, where c is the coupon rate, plus F upon maturity. Other cash flow patterns are possible, however. Figure 7-1 illustrates the time profile of the cash flows C_t for three bonds with initial market value of $100, 10-year maturity, and 6% annual interest. The figure describes a straight coupon-paying bond, an annuity, and a zero-coupon bond. As long as the cash flows are predetermined, the valuation is straightforward.

FIGURE 7-1 Time Profile of Cash Flows

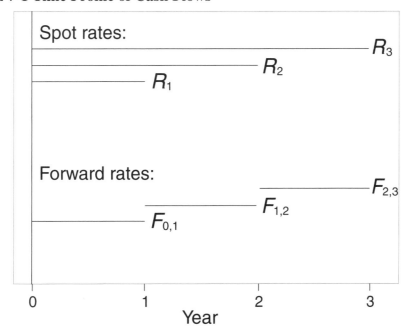

Given the market price, solving for y gives the yield to maturity. This yield is another way to express the price of the bond and is more convenient for comparing various bonds. The yield is also the *expected* rate of return on the bond, provided all coupons are reinvested at the same rate. This interpretation fails, however, when the cash flows are random or when the life of the bond can change due to option-like features.

7.3.2 Pricing

We can also use information from the fixed-income market to assess the fair value of the bond. Say we observe that the yield to maturity for comparable bonds is y_T. We can then discount the cash flows using the same, market-determined yield. This gives a fair value for the bond:

$$\hat{P} = \sum_{t=1}^{T} \frac{C_t}{(1 + y_T)^t} \qquad (7.6)$$

Note that the discount rate y_T does not depend on t, but is fixed for all payments for this bond.

This approach, however, ignores the shape of the term structure of interest rates. Short maturities, for example, could have much lower rates, in which case it is inappropriate to use the same yield. We should really be discounting each cash flow at the zero-coupon rate that corresponds to each time period. Define R_t as the **spot interest rate** for maturity t and this risk class (i.e., same currency and credit risk). The fair value of the bond is then

$$\hat{P} = \sum_{t=1}^{T} \frac{C_t}{(1 + R_t)^t} \qquad (7.7)$$

We can then check whether the market price is greater or lower. If the term structure is flat, the two approaches will be identical.

Alternatively, to assess whether a bond is rich or cheap, we can add a fixed amount SS, called the **static spread**, to the spot rates so that the NPV equals the current price:

$$P = \sum_{t=1}^{T} \frac{C_t}{(1 + R_t + \text{SS})^t} \qquad (7.8)$$

All else equal, a bond with a large static spread is preferable to another with a lower spread. It means the bond is cheaper, or has a higher expected rate of return.

It is simpler, but less accurate, to compute a **yield spread**, YS, using yield to maturity:

$$P = \sum_{t=1}^{T} \frac{C_t}{(1 + y_T + \text{YS})^t} \tag{7.9}$$

Table 7-3 gives an example of a 7% coupon, two-year bond. The term structure environment, consisting of spot rates and par yields, is described on the left side. The right side lays out the present value of the cash flows (PVCF). Discounting the two cash flows at the spot rates gives a fair value of $\hat{P} = \$101.9604$. In fact, the bond is selling at a price of $P = \$101.5000$, so the bond is cheap.

We can convert the difference in prices to annual yields. The yield to maturity on this bond is 6.1798%, which implies a yield spread of $\text{YS} = 6.1798 - 5.9412 = 0.2386\%$. Using the static spread approach, we find that adding $\text{SS} = 0.2482\%$ to the spot rates gives the current price. The second measure is more accurate than the first.

TABLE 7-3 Bond Price and Term Structure

Maturity (Year) i	Term Structure Spot Rate R_i	Par Yield y_i	7% Bond PVCF Discounted at: Spot SS = 0	Yield+YS $\Delta y = 0.2386$	Spot+SS SS(s) = 0.2482
1	4.0000	4.0000	6.7308	6.5926	6.7147
2	6.0000	5.9412	95.2296	94.9074	94.7853
Sum			101.9604	101.5000	101.5000
Price			101.5000	101.5000	101.5000

Cash flows with different credit risks need to be discounted with different rates. For example, the principal on Brady bonds is collateralized by U.S. Treasury securities and carries no default risk, in contrast to the coupons. As a result, it has become common to separate the discounting of the principal from that of the coupons. Valuation is done in two steps. First, the principal is discounted to a present value using the appropriate Treasury yield. The present value of the principal is subtracted from the market value. Next, the coupons are discounted at what is called the **stripped yield**, which accounts for the credit risk of the issuer.

7.3.3 Duration

Armed with a cash flow profile, we can proceed to compute duration. As we have seen in Chapter 1, **duration** is a measure of the exposure, or sensitivity, of the bond price to movements in yields. When cash flows are fixed, duration is measured as the weighted maturity of each payment, where the weights are proportional to the present value of the cash flows. Using the same notations as in Equation (7.5), recall that **Macaulay duration** is

$$D = \sum_{t=1}^{T} t \times w_t = \sum_{t=1}^{T} t \times \frac{C_t/(1+y)^t}{\sum C_t/(1+y)^t}. \tag{7.10}$$

Key concept:
Duration can be viewed as the weighted average time to wait for each payment only when the cash flows are predetermined.

More generally, duration is a measure of interest rate exposure:

$$\frac{dP}{dy} = -\frac{D}{(1+y)}P = -D^*P \tag{7.11}$$

where D^* is **modified duration**. The second term, D^*P, is also known as the **dollar duration**. Sometimes this sensitivity is expressed as the **dollar value of a basis point** (also known as DV01), defined as

$$\frac{dP}{0.01\%} = \text{DVBP} \tag{7.12}$$

For fixed cash flows, duration can be computed using Equation (7.10). Otherwise, we can infer duration from an economic analysis of the security. Consider a **floating-rate note** (FRN) with no credit risk. Just before the reset date, we know that the coupon will be set to the prevailing interest rate. The FRN is then similar to cash, or a money market instrument, that has no interest rate risk and hence is selling at par with zero duration. Just after the reset date, the investor is locked into a fixed coupon over the accrual period. The FRN is then economically equivalent to a zero-coupon bond with maturity equal to the time to the next reset date.

Key concept:
The duration of a floating-rate note is the time to wait until the next reset period, at which time the FRN should be at par.

Example 7-4: FRM Exam 1999—Question 53

Consider a 9% annual coupon 20-year bond trading at 6% with a price of 134.41.
When rates rise 10 bps, the price reduces to 132.99, and when rates decrease
by 10 bps, the price goes up to 135.85. What is the modified duration of the bond?

a) 11.25

b) 10.61

c) 10.50

d) 10.73

Example 7-5: FRM Exam 1998—Question 31

A 10-year zero-coupon bond is callable annually at par (its face value) starting
at the beginning of year 6. Assume a flat yield curve of 10%. What is the
bond duration?

a) 5 years

b) 7.5 years

c) 10 years

d) Cannot be determined based on the data given

Example 7-6: FRM Exam 1999—Question 91

The modified duration of a fixed-rate bond, in the case of flat yield curve, can be
interpreted as (where B is the bond price and y is the yield to maturity)

a) $-[1/B]\,[\partial B/\partial y]$

b) $[1/B]\,[\partial B/\partial y]$

c) $-[y/B]\,[\partial B/\partial y]$

d) $[(1+y)/B]\,[\partial B/\partial y]$

Example 7-7: FRM Exam 1997—Question 49

A money markets desk holds a floating-rate note with an eight-year maturity. The
interest rate is floating at the three-month LIBOR rate, reset quarterly. The next
reset is in one week. What is the approximate duration of the floating-rate note?

a) Eight years

b) Four years

c) Three months

d) One week

7.4   Spot and Forward Rates

In addition to the cash flows, we need detailed information on the term structure of
interest rates to value fixed-income securities and their derivatives. This information
is provided by **spot rates**, which are zero-coupon investment rates that start at the

current time. From spot rates, we can infer **forward rates**, which are rates that start at a future date. Both are essential building blocks for the pricing of bonds.

Consider, for instance, a one-year rate that starts in one year. This forward rate is defined as $F_{1,2}$ and can be inferred from the one-year and two-year spot rates, R_1 and R_2. The forward rate is the breakeven future rate that equalizes the return on investments of different maturities. An investor has the choice to lock in a two-year investment at the two-year rate, or to invest for a term of one year and roll over at the one-to-two-year forward rate.

The two portfolios will have the same payoff when the future rate $F_{1,2}$ is such that

$$(1 + R_2)^2 = (1 + R_1)(1 + F_{1,2}) \tag{7.13}$$

For instance, if $R_1 = 4.00\%$ and $R_2 = 4.62\%$, we have $F_{1,2} = 5.24\%$.

More generally, the T-period spot rate can be written as a geometric average of the spot and forward rates:

$$(1 + R_T)^T = (1 + R_1)(1 + F_{1,2}) \cdots (1 + F_{T-1,T}) \tag{7.14}$$

where $F_{i,i+1}$ is the forward rate of interest prevailing now (at time t) over a horizon of i to $i + 1$. This sequence is shown in Figure 7-2. Table 7-4 displays a sequence of spot rates, forward rates, and par yields, using annual compounding.

FIGURE 7-2 Spot and Forward Rates

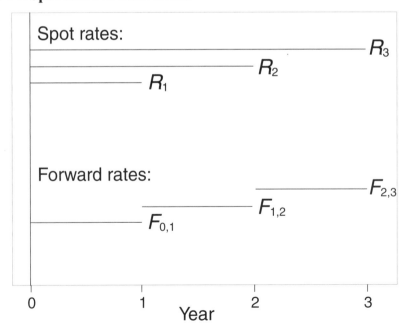

TABLE 7-4 Spot Rates, Forward Rates, and Par Yields

Maturity (Year) i	Spot Rate R_i	Forward Rate $F_{i-1,i}$	Par Yield y_i	Discount Function $D(t_i)$
1	4.000	4.000	4.000	0.9615
2	4.618	5.240	4.604	0.9136
3	5.192	6.350	5.153	0.8591
4	5.716	7.303	5.640	0.8006
5	6.112	7.712	6.000	0.7433
6	6.396	7.830	6.254	0.6893
7	6.621	7.980	6.451	0.6383
8	6.808	8.130	6.611	0.5903
9	6.970	8.270	6.745	0.5452
10	7.112	8.400	6.860	0.5030

Forward rates allow us to project future cash flows that depend on future rates. The $F_{1,2}$ forward rate, for example, can be taken as the market's expectation of the second coupon payment on an FRN with annual payments and resets. We will show later that positions in forward rates can be taken easily with derivative instruments.

Forward rates have to be positive; otherwise there would be an arbitrage opportunity. We abstract from transaction costs and assume we can invest and borrow at the same rate. For instance, $R_1 = 11.00\%$ and $R_2 = 4.62\%$ gives $F_{1,2} = -1.4\%$. This means that $(1 + R_1) = 1.11$ is greater than $(1 + R_2)^2 = 1.094534$. To take advantage of this discrepancy, we could borrow \$1 million for two years and invest it for one year. After the first year, the proceeds are kept in cash, or under the proverbial mattress, for the second period. The investment gives \$1,110,000 and we have to pay back \$1,094,534 only. This would create a profit of \$15,466 out of thin air, which is highly unlikely in practice. Interest rates must be positive for the same reason.

The forward rate can be interpreted as a measure of the slope of the term structure. We can, for instance, expand both sides of Equation (7.12). After neglecting cross-product terms, we have

$$F_{1,2} \approx R_2 + (R_2 - R_1) \tag{7.15}$$

Thus, with an upward-sloping term structure, R_2 is above R_1, and $F_{1,2}$ will also be above R_2.

We can also show that in this situation, the spot rate curve is above the par yield curve. Consider a bond with two payments. The two-year par yield y_2 is implicitly defined from

$$P = \frac{cF}{(1 + y_2)} + \frac{(cF + F)}{(1 + y_2)^2} = \frac{cF}{(1 + R_1)} + \frac{(cF + F)}{(1 + R_2)^2}$$

where P is set to par $P = F$. The par yield can be viewed as a weighted average of spot rates. In an upward-sloping environment, par yield curves involve coupons that are discounted at shorter and thus lower rates than the final payment. As a result, the par yield curve lies below the spot rate curve.[4] When the spot rate curve is flat, the spot curve is identical to the par yield curve and to the forward curve. In general, the curves differ. Figure 7-3 displays the case of an upward-sloping term structure. It shows that the yield curve is below the spot curve while the forward curve is above the spot curve. With a downward-sloping term structure, as shown in Figure 7-4, the yield curve is above the spot curve, which is above the forward curve.

FIGURE 7-3 Upward-Sloping Term Structure

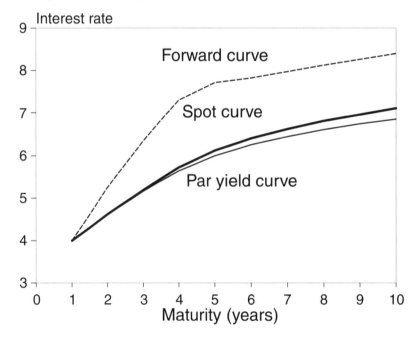

In practice, spot curves are fitted to actual bond prices. To ensure some continuity in the spot rates, practitioners assume a particular functional form for the **discount function**, which is simply the current price of a dollar paid at t. For instance, a cubic polynomial would be

---

[4]For a formal proof, consider a two-period par bond with a face value of $1 and coupon of y_2. We can write the price of this bond as $1 = y_2/(1 + R_1) + (1 + y_2)/(1 + R_2)^2$. After simplification, this gives $y_2 = R_2(2 + R_2)/(2 + F_{1,2})$. In an upward-sloping environment, $F_{1,2} > R_2$ and thus $y_2 < R_2$.

$$D(t) = \frac{1}{(1+R_t)^t} = a_0 + a_1 + a_2 t^2 + a_3 t^3 \qquad (7.16)$$

Clearly, $a_0 = 1$. We then have three remaining parameters to estimate. Using a sample of bonds, this can be done by minimizing the errors between the market prices and their theoretical prices,

$$\hat{P} = \sum_{t=1}^{T} C_t \times D(t) = f(a_1, a_2, a_3) \qquad (7.17)$$

which are a function of the three unknown parameters. To allow for more realistic shapes, this function can have different parameters over various intervals—up to one year, from one to five years, and so on. The parameters then have to be chosen so that the functions below and above each **knot point**, (e.g., one year in our example) have the same value and first derivative.

FIGURE 7-4 Downward-Sloping Term Structure

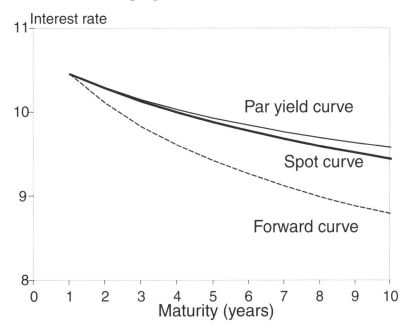

Example 7-8: FRM Exam 2002—Question 52

A seven-year zero-coupon bond carries an annual yield of 6.75%, and a six-year zero-coupon bond carries an annual yield of 5.87%. Calculate the one-year forward rate six years from now. Assume annual compounding.

a) 6.31%

b) 12.03%

c) 12.19%

d) 12.62%

Example 7-9: FRM Exam 1997—Question 1

Suppose a risk manager has made the mistake of valuing a zero-coupon bond using a swap (par) rate rather than a zero-coupon rate. Assume the par curve is upward sloping. The risk manager is therefore

a) Indifferent to the rate used
b) Overestimating the value of the bond
c) Underestimating the value of the bond
d) Lacking sufficient information

Example 7-10: FRM Exam 1999—Question 1

Suppose that the yield curve is upward sloping. Which of the following statements is *true*?

a) The forward rate yield curve is above the zero-coupon yield curve, which is above the coupon-bearing bond yield curve.
b) The forward rate yield curve is above the coupon-bearing bond yield curve, which is above the zero-coupon yield curve.
c) The coupon-bearing bond yield curve is above the zero-coupon yield curve, which is above the forward rate yield curve.
d) The coupon-bearing bond yield curve is above the forward rate yield curve, which is above the zero-coupon yield curve.

7.5 Mortgage-Backed Securities

7.5.1 Description

Mortgage-backed securities (MBSs) represent claims on repackaged mortgage loans. Their basic cash-flow patterns start from an annuity, where the homeowner makes a monthly fixed payment that covers principal and interest.

Whereas mortgage loans are subject to credit risk, due to the possibility of default by the homeowner, most traded securities have third-party guarantees against credit risk. For instance, MBSs issued by Fannie Mae, an agency that is sponsored by the U.S. government, carry a guarantee of full interest and principal payment, even if the original borrower defaults.

Even so, MBSs are complex securities due to the uncertainty in their cash flows. Consider the traditional fixed-rate mortgage. Homeowners have the possibility of making early payments of principal. This represents a long position in an option. In some cases, these prepayments are random—for instance, when the homeowner sells the home due to changing job or family conditions. In other cases, these prepayments are more predictable. When interest rates fall, prepayments increase as homeowners can refinance at a lower cost. This is similar to the rational early exercise of American call options.

Generally, these factors affect refinancing patterns:

■ *Age of the loan*: Prepayment rates are generally low just after the mortgage loan has been issued and gradually increase over time until they reach a stable, or "seasoned," level. This effect is known as **seasoning**.

■ *Spread between the mortgage rate and current rates*: Increases in the spread increase prepayments. Like a callable bond, there is a greater benefit to refinancing if it achieves a significant cost saving.

■ *Refinancing incentives*: The smaller the costs of refinancing, the more likely homeowners will refinance often.

■ *Previous path of interest rates*: Refinancing is more likely to occur if rates have been high in the past but have recently dropped. In this scenario, past prepayments have been low but should rise sharply. In contrast, if rates are low but have been so for a while, most of the principal will already have been prepaid. This path dependence is usually referred to as **burnout**.

■ *Level of mortgage rates*: Lower rates increase affordability and turnover.

■ *Economic activity*: An economic environment where more workers change job location creates greater job turnover, which is more likely to lead to prepayments.

■ *Seasonal effects*: There is typically more home buying in the spring, leading to increased prepayments in early fall.

The prepayment rate is summarized into what is called the **conditional prepayment rate (CPR)**, which is expressed in annual terms. This number can be translated into a monthly number, known as the **single monthly mortality (SMM) rate**, using the adjustment

$$(1 - \text{SMM})^{12} = (1 - \text{CPR}) \tag{7.18}$$

For instance, if CPR $= 6\%$ annually, the monthly proportion of principal paid early will be SMM $= 1 - (1 - 0.06)^{1/12} = 0.005143$, or 0.514% monthly. For a loan with a beginning monthly balance (BMB) of \$50,525 and a scheduled principal payment of SP = \$67, the prepayment will be 0.005143 × (\$50,525 − \$67) = \$260.

To price the MBS, the portfolio manager should describe the schedule of projected prepayments during the remaining life of the bond. This depends on many factors, including the age of the loan.

Prepayments can be described using an industry standard, known as the **Public Securities Association (PSA)** prepayment model. The PSA model assumes a CPR of 0.2% for the first month, which goes up by 0.2% per month for the next 30 months and remains at 6% thereafter. Formally, this is

$$CPR = Min[6\% \times (t/30), 6\%] \tag{7.19}$$

This pattern is shown in Figure 7-5 as the 100% PSA speed. By convention, prepayment patterns are expressed as a percentage of the PSA speed—for example, 165% PSA for a faster pattern and 70% PSA for a slower pattern.

Example: Computing the CPR

Consider an MBS issued 20 months ago with a speed of 150% PSA. What are the CPR and SMM?

The PSA speed is $Min[6\% \times (20/30), 6\%] = 0.04$. Applying the 150 factor, we have CPR = 150% × 0.04 = 0.06. This implies SMM = 0.514%.

The next step is to project cash flows based on the prepayment speed pattern. Figure 7-6 displays cash-flow patterns for a 30-year MBS with a face amount of \$100 million and a 7.5% interest rate, three months into its life. The horizontal, "0% PSA" line describes the annuity pattern without any prepayment. The "100% PSA" line describes an increasing pattern of cash flows, peaking in 27 months and decreasing thereafter. This point corresponds to the stabilization of the CPR at 6%. This pattern is more marked for the "165% PSA" line, which assumes a faster prepayment speed.

FIGURE 7-5 Prepayment Pattern

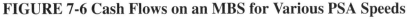

Early prepayments lead to fewer payments later, which explains why the 100% PSA line is initially higher than the 0% line and becomes lower as the principal is paid off more quickly.

FIGURE 7-6 Cash Flows on an MBS for Various PSA Speeds

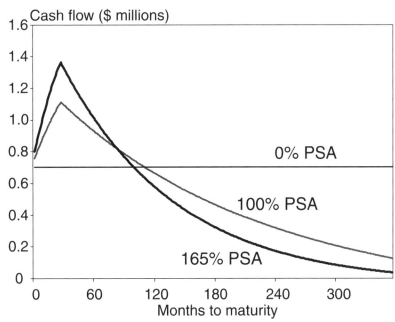

Example 7-11: FRM Exam 1999—Question 51

Suppose the CPR for a mortgage-backed security is 6%. What is the corresponding SMM rate?

a) 0.514%

b) 0.334%

c) 0.5%

d) 1.355%

Example 7-12: FRM Exam 1999—Question 87

A CMO bond class with a duration of 50 means that

a) It has a discounted cash-flow weighted average life of 50 years.

b) For a 100-bp change in yield, the bond's price will change by roughly 50%.

c) For a 1-bp change in yield, the bond's price will change by roughly 5%.

d) None of the above is correct.

Example 7-13: FRM Exam 1998—Question 14

In analyzing the monthly prepayment risk of mortgage-backed securities, an annual prepayment rate (CPR) is converted to a monthly prepayment rate (SMM). Which of the following formulas should be used for the conversion?

a) $SMM = (1 - CPR)^{1/12}$

b) $SMM = 1 - (1 - CPR)^{1/12}$

c) $SMM = 1 - (CPR)^{1/12}$

d) $SMM = 1 + (1 - CPR)^{1/12}$

7.5.2 Prepayment Risk

Like other bonds, mortgage-backed securities are subject to market risk, due to fluctuations in interest rates. They are also, however, subject to **prepayment risk**, which is the risk that the principal will be repaid early.

Consider, for instance, an 8% MBS, which is illustrated in Figure 7-7. If rates drop to 6%, homeowners will rationally prepay early to refinance the loan. Because the average life of the loan is shortened, this is called **contraction risk**. Conversely, if rates increase to 10%, homeowners will be less likely to refinance early, and prepayments will slow down. Because the average life of the loan is extended, this is called **extension risk**.

FIGURE 7-7 Negative Convexity of MBSs

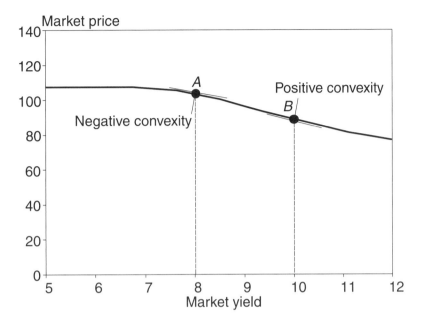

As shown in Figure 7-7, this feature creates "negative convexity" at point *A*. This reflects the fact that the investor in an MBS is short an option. At point *B*, interest rates are very high and there is little likelihood that the homeowner will refinance early. The option is nearly worthless and the MBS behaves like a regular bond, with positive convexity.

This changing cash-flow pattern makes standard duration measures unreliable. Instead, sensitivity measures are computed using **effective duration** and **effective convexity**, as explained in Chapter 1. The measures are based on the estimated price of the MBS for three yield values, with suitable assumptions about how changes in rates should affect prepayments.

Table 7-5 shows an example. In each case, we consider an up-move and down-move of 25 bp. In the first, "unchanged" panel, the PSA speed is assumed to be constant at 165% PSA. In the second, "changed" panel, we assume a higher PSA speed if rates drop and a lower speed if rates increase. When rates drop, the MBS value goes up, but not as much as if the prepayment speed had not changed, which reflects contraction risk. When rates increase, the MBS value drops by more than if the prepayment speed had not changed, which reflects extension risk.

TABLE 7-5 Computing Effective Duration and Convexity

	Initial	Unchanged PSA		Changed PSA	
Yield	7.50%	+25 bp	−25 bp	+25 bp	−25 bp
PSA		165% PSA	165% PSA	150% PSA	200% PSA
Price	100.125	98.75	101.50	98.7188	101.3438
Duration		5.49 years		5.24 years	
Convexity		0		−299	

As we saw in Chapter 1, **effective duration** is measured as

$$D^E = \frac{P(y_0 - \Delta y) - P(y_0 + \Delta y)}{(2 P_0 \Delta y)} \tag{7.20}$$

Effective convexity is measured as

$$C^E = \left[\frac{P(y_0 - \Delta y) - P_0}{(P_0 \Delta y)} - \frac{P_0 - P(y_0 + \Delta y)}{(P_0 \Delta y)} \right] \Big/ \Delta y \tag{7.21}$$

In the first, "unchanged" panel, the effective duration is 5.49 years and convexity close to zero. In the second, "changed" panel, the effective duration is 5.24 years and convexity is negative, as expected, and quite large.

Key concept:

Mortgage-backed securities have negative convexity, which reflects the short position in an option granted to the homeowner to repay early. This creates extension risk when rates increase or contraction risk when rates fall.

The option feature in MBSs increases their yield. To ascertain whether the securities represent good value, portfolio managers need to model the option component. The approach most commonly used is the **option-adjusted spread (OAS)**.

Starting from the **static spread**, the OAS method involves running simulations of various interest rate scenarios and prepayments to establish the option cost. The OAS is then

$$OAS = \text{Static spread} - \text{Option cost} \tag{7.22}$$

which represents the net richness or cheapness of the MBS. Within the same risk class, a security trading at a high OAS is preferable to others.

The OAS is more stable over time than the spread, because the latter is affected by the option component. This explains why during market rallies (i.e., when long-term Treasury yields fall) yield spreads on current coupon mortgages often widen. These mortgages are more likely to be prepaid early, which makes them less attractive. Their option cost increases, pushing up the yield spread.

Example 7-14: FRM Exam 1998—Question 18

Which of the following risks are common to mortgage-backed securities and emerging market Brady bonds?

  I. Interest rate risk

 II. Prepayment risk

III. Default risk

IV. Political risk

a) I only

b) II and III only

c) I and III only

d) III and IV only

Example 7-15: FRM Exam 1999—Question 44

The following are reasons that a prepayment model will not accurately predict future mortgage prepayments. Which of these will have the greatest effect on the convexity of mortgage pass-throughs?

a) Refinancing incentive

b) Seasoning

c) Refinancing burnout

d) Seasonality

Example 7-16: FRM Exam 2001—Question 95

The option-adjusted duration of a callable bond will be close to the duration of a similar noncallable bond when

a) The bond trades above the call price.

b) The bond has a high volatility.

c) The bond trades much lower than the call price.

d) The bond trades above parity.

7.5.3 Financial Engineering and CMOs

The MBS market has grown enormously in the last twenty years in the United States and is growing fast in other markets. MBSs allow capital to flow from investors to borrowers in an efficient fashion.

One major drawback of MBSs, however, is their negative convexity. This makes it difficult for investors, such as pension funds, to invest in MBSs because the life of these instruments is uncertain, making it more difficult to match the duration of pension assets to the horizon of pension liabilities.

In response, the finance industry has developed new classes of securities based on MBSs with more appealing characteristics. These are the **collateralized mortgage obligations (CMOs)**, which are new securities that redirect the cash flows of an MBS pool to various segments.

Figure 7-8 illustrates the process. The cash flows from the MBS pool go into a **special-purpose vehicle (SPV)**, which is a legal entity that issues different claims, or **tranches**, with various characteristics, like slices in a pie. These are structured so that the cash flow from the first tranche, for instance, is more predictable than the original cash flows. The uncertainty is then pushed into the other tranches.

FIGURE 7-8 Creating CMO Tranches

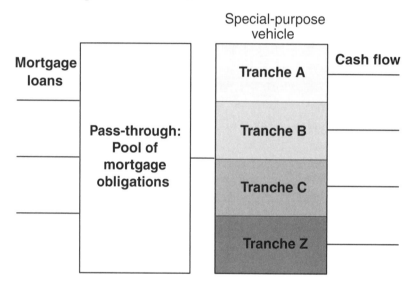

Starting from an MBS pool, financial engineering creates securities that are better tailored to investors' needs. It is important to realize, however, that the cash flows and risks are fully preserved; they are only redistributed across tranches. Whatever transformation is brought about, the resulting package must obey basic laws of conservation for the underlying securities and the package of resulting securities.[5]

At every single point in time, we must have the same cash flows going into and coming out of the SPV. As a result, we must have the same market value and the same risk profile. In particular, the weighted duration and convexity of the portfolio

---

[5] As Lavoisier, the French chemist who was executed during the French revolution, said, *Rien ne se perd, rien ne se crée* (nothing is lost, nothing is created).

of tranches must add up to the original duration and convexity. If tranche A has less convexity than the underlying securities, the other tranches must have more convexity.

Similar structures apply to **collateralized bond obligations** (CBOs), **collateralized loan obligations** (CLOs), and **collateralized debt obligations** (CDOs), which are a set of tradable bonds backed by bonds, loans, or debt (bonds and loans), respectively. These structures rearrange credit risk and will be explained in more detail later.

As an example of a two-tranche structure, consider an SPV with collateral consisting of a regular 5-year, 6% coupon $100 million note. This can be split up into a floater that pays LIBOR on a notional of $50 million, and an **inverse floater** that pays $12\% - $ LIBOR on a notional of $50 million. Because the coupon C_{IF} on the inverse floater cannot go below zero, this imposes another condition on the floater coupon C_F. The exact formulas are:

$$C_F = \text{Min(LIBOR, 12\%)} \qquad C_{IF} = \text{Max(12\% - LIBOR, 0)}$$

We verify that the outgoing cash flows exactly add up to the incoming flows. For each coupon payment, we have, in millions

$$\$50 \times \text{LIBOR} + \$50 \times (12\% - \text{LIBOR}) = \$100 \times 6\% = \$6$$

so this is a perfect match. At maturity, the total payments of twice $50 million add up to $100 million, so this matches as well.

We can also decompose the risk of the original structure into that of the two components. Assume a flat term structure and say the duration of the original 5-year note is $D = 4.5$ years. The portfolio dollar duration is

$$\$50,000,000 \times D_F + \$50,000,000 \times D_{IF} = \$100,000,000 \times D$$

Just before a reset, the duration of the floater is close to zero ($D_F = 0$). Hence, the duration of the inverse floater must be $D_{IF} = (\$100,000,000/\$50,000,000) \times D = 2 \times D$, or 9 years, which is twice that of the original note. Note that the duration of the inverse floater is much greater than its maturity. This illustrates the point that duration is an interest rate sensitivity measure. When cash flows are uncertain, duration is not necessarily related to maturity. Intuitively, the first tranche, the floater, has zero risk, so all of the risk must be absorbed into the second tranche. The total risk of the portfolio is conserved.

This analysis can be easily extended to inverse floaters with greater leverage. Suppose the coupon is tied to twice LIBOR—for example, $18\% - 2 \times$ LIBOR. The principal must be allocated in the amount x, in millions, for the floater and $100 - x$ for the inverse floater so that the coupon payment is preserved. We set

$$x \times \text{LIBOR} + (100 - x) \times (18\% - 2 \times \text{LIBOR}) = \$6$$

$$[x - 2(100 - x)] \times \text{LIBOR} + (100 - x) \times 18\% = \$6$$

Because LIBOR will change over time, this can be satisfied only if the term between brackets is always zero. This implies $3x - 200 = 0$, or $x = \$66.67$ million. Thus, two-thirds of the notional must be allocated to the floater, and one-third to the inverse floater. The inverse floater now has three times the duration of the original note.

> **Key concept:**
> Collateralized mortgage obligations (CMOs) rearrange the total cash flows, total value, and total risk of the underlying securities. At all times, the total cash flows, value, and risk of the tranches must equal those of the collateral. If some tranches are less risky than the collateral, others must be more risky.

When the collateral is a mortgage-backed security, CMOs can be referred to by prioritizing the payment of principal into different tranches. This is referred to as **sequential-pay tranches**. Tranche A, for instance, will receive the principal payment on the whole underlying mortgage first. This creates more certainty in the cash flows accruing to tranche A, which makes it more appealing to some investors. Of course, this is to the detriment of others. After principal payments to tranche A are exhausted, tranche B receives all principal payments on the underlying MBS. And so on for other tranches.

Another popular construction is the **IO/PO** structure. An **interest-only (IO)** tranche receives only the interest payments on the underlying MBS. The **principal-only (PO)** tranche then receives only the principal payments. As before, the market value of the IO and PO must exactly add up to that of the MBS. Figure 7-9 describes the price behavior of the IO and PO. Note that the vertical addition of the two components always equals the value of the MBS.

To analyze the PO, it is useful to note that the sum of all principal payments is constant (because we have no default risk). Only the timing is uncertain. In contrast, the sum of all interest payments depends on the timing of principal payments. Later principal payments create greater total interest payments.

If interest rates fall, principal payments will come early, which reflects contraction risk. Because the principal is paid earlier and the discount rate decreases, the PO should appreciate sharply in value. On the other hand, the faster prepayments mean fewer interest payments over the life of the MBS, which is unfavorable to the IO. The IO should depreciate.

Conversely, if interest rates rise, prepayments will slow down, which reflects extension risk. Because the principal is paid later and the discount rate increases, the PO should lose value. On the other hand, the slower prepayments mean more interest payments over the life of the MBS, which is favorable to the IO. The IO appreciates in value, up to the point where the higher discount rate effect dominates. Thus, IOs are bullish securities with negative duration, as shown in Figure 7-9.

FIGURE 7-9 Creating an IO and PO from an MBS

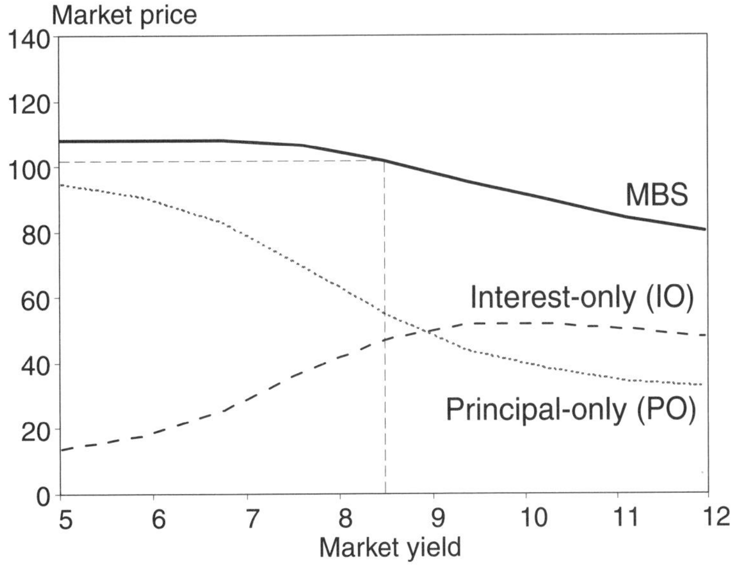

Example 7-17: FRM Exam 2000—Question 13

A CLO is generally

a) A set of loans that can be traded individually in the market

b) A pass-through

c) A set of bonds backed by a loan portfolio

d) None of the above

Example 7-18: FRM Exam 2002—Question 34

Suppose you have a position of $100 million in the instruments below. Each one has a maturity of 10 years. Which instrument is most likely to have a DV01 that exceeds the DV01 of a Treasury strip with 10-year maturity?

a) Perpetual floating-rate notes

b) Convertibles

c) Inverse floating-rate securities

d) Corporate zero-coupon notes

Example 7-19: FRM Exam 1998—Question 32

A 10-year reverse floater pays a semiannual coupon of 8% minus 6-month LIBOR. Assume the yield curve is 8% flat, the current 10-year note has a duration of 7 years, and the interest rate on the note was just reset. What is the duration of the note?

a) 6 months

b) Shorter than 7 years

c) Longer than 7 years

d) 7 years

Example 7-20: FRM Exam 1999—Question 79

Suppose the coupon and the modified duration of a 10-year bond priced to par are 6.0% and 7.5, respectively. What is the approximate modified duration of a 10-year inverse floater priced to par with a coupon of $18\% - 2 \times LIBOR$?

a) 7.5

b) 15.0

c) 22.5

d) 0.0

Example 7-21: FRM Exam 2000—Question 3

How would you describe the typical price behavior of a low-premium mortgage pass-through security?

a) It is similar to a U.S. Treasury bond.

b) It is similar to a plain-vanilla corporate bond.

c) When interest rates fall, its price increase will exceed that of a comparable-duration U.S. Treasury bond.

d) When interest rates fall, its price increase will lag that of a comparable-duration U.S. Treasury bond.

7.6   Answers to Chapter Examples

Example 7-1: FRM Exam 1998—Question 3

b) As interest rates increase, the coupon decreases. In addition, the discount factor increases. Hence, the value of the note must decrease even more than a regular fixed-coupon bond.

Example 7-2: FRM Exam 2000—Question 9

d) With a callable bond the issuer has the option to call the bond early if its price would otherwise go up. Hence, the investor is short an option. A long position in a callable bond is equivalent to a long position in a noncallable bond plus a short position in a call option.

Example 7-3: FRM Exam 1998—Question 13

a) $DR = (Face - Price)/Face \times (360/t) = (\$100,000 - \$97,569)/\$100,000 \times (360/100) = 8.75\%$. Note that the yield is 9.09%, which is higher.

Example 7-4: FRM Exam 1999—Question 53

b) Using Equation (7.8), we have $D^* = -(dP/P)/dy = [(135.85 - 132.99)/134.41] /[0.001 \times 2] = 10.63$. This is also a measure of effective duration.

Example 7-5: FRM Exam 1998—Question 31

c) Because this is a zero-coupon bond, it will always trade below par, and the call should never be exercised. Hence its duration is the maturity, 10 years.

Example 7-6: FRM Exam 1999—Question 91

a) By Equation (7.8).

Example 7-7: FRM Exam 1997—Question 49

d) Duration is not related to maturity when coupons are not fixed over the life of the investment. We know that at the next reset, the coupon on the FRN will be set at the prevailing rate. Hence, the market value of the note will be equal to par at that time. The duration or price risk is related only to the time to the next reset, which is one week here.

Example 7-8: FRM Exam 2002—Question 52

c) This is obtained from $(1 + R_7)^7 = (1 + R_6)^6 (1 + F_{67})$. Solving, we find $F_{67} = [(1 + 6.75\%)^7/(1 + 5.87\%)^6] - 1 = 12.19\%$.

Example 7-9: FRM Exam 1997—Question 1

b) If the par curve is rising, it must be below the spot curve. As a result, the discounting will use rates that are too low, overestimating the bond value.

Example 7-10: FRM Exam 1999—Question 1

a) See Figures 7-3 and 7-4. The coupon yield curve is an average of the spot, zero-coupon curve, and hence has to lie below the spot curve when it is upward sloping. The forward curve can be interpreted as the spot curve plus the slope of the spot curve. If the latter is upward sloping, the forward curve has to be above the spot curve.

Example 7-11: FRM Exam 1999—Question 51

a) Using $(1 - 6\%) = (1 - SMM)^{12}$, we find SMM $= 0.51\%$.

Example 7-12: FRM Exam 1999—Question 87

b) Discounted cash flows are not useful for CMOs because they are uncertain. So duration is a measure of interest rate sensitivity. We have $(dP/P) = D^* dy = 50 \times 1\% = 50\%$.

Example 7-13: FRM Exam 1998—Question 14

b) As $(1 - SMM)^{12} = (1 - CPR)$.

Example 7-14: FRM Exam 1998—Question 18

c) MBSs are subject to I, II, III (either homeowner or agency default). Brady bonds are subject to I, III, IV. Neither is exposed to currency risk.

Example 7-15: FRM Exam 1999—Question 44

a) The question is which factor has the greatest effect on the interest rate convexity, or increases the prepayment rate when rates fall. Seasoning and seasonality are not related to interest rates. Burnout lowers the prepayment rate. So refinancing incentives is the remaining factor that most affects the option feature.

Example 7-16: FRM Exam 2001—Question 95

c) This question is applicable to MBSs as well as callable bonds. From Figure 7-7, we see that the callable bond behaves like a straight bond when market yields are high or when the bond price is low. So c) is correct and a) and d) must be wrong.

Example 7-17: FRM Exam 2000—Question 13

c) Like a CMO, a CLO represents a set of tradable securities backed by some collateral, in this case a loan portfolio.

Example 7-18: FRM Exam 2002—Question 34

c) Treasury strips have Macaulay duration equal to 10 years. Floating-rate notes have duration close to zero. Inverse floaters (with a leverage of 1), have twice the duration of the equivalent coupon bond, so this must be very high. Corporate notes and convertibles have duration close to 10 years but are also exposed to other risk factors.

Example 7-19: FRM Exam 1998—Question 32

c) The duration is normally about 14 years. Note that if the current coupon is zero, the inverse floater behaves like a zero-coupon bond with a duration of 10 years.

Example 7-20: FRM Exam 1999—Question 79

c) Following the same reasoning as above, we must divide the fixed-rate bonds into two-thirds FRN and one-third inverse floater. This will ensure that the inverse floater payment is related to twice LIBOR. As a result, the duration of the inverse floater must be three times that of the bond.

Example 7-21: FRM Exam 2000—Question 3

d) MBSs are unlike regular bonds, Treasuries, or corporates because of their negative convexity. When rates fall, homeowners prepay early, which means that the price appreciation is less than that of comparable-duration regular bonds.

Chapter 8

Fixed-Income Derivatives

This chapter turns to the analysis of fixed-income derivatives. These are instruments whose value derives from a bond price, interest rate, or other bond market variable. As discussed in Chapter 5, fixed-income derivatives account for the largest proportion of the global derivatives markets. Understanding fixed-income derivatives is also important because many fixed-income securities have derivative-like characteristics.

This chapter focuses on the use of fixed-income derivatives, as well as their pricing. Pricing involves finding the fair market value of the contract. For risk management purposes, however, we also need to assess the range of possible movements in contract values. This will be examined in the chapters on market risk and credit exposure.

This chapter presents the most important interest rate derivatives and discusses fundamentals of pricing. Due to the nature of the topic, this chapter is rather technical in nature. Section 8.1 discusses interest rate forward contracts, also known as forward rate agreements. Section 8.2 turns to the discussion of interest rate futures, covering Eurodollar and Treasury bond futures. Although these products are dollar-based, similar products exist on other capital markets. Swaps are analyzed in Section 8.3. Swaps are very important instruments due to their widespread use. Finally, interest rate options are covered in Section 8.4, including caps and floors, swaptions, and exchange-traded options.

8.1   Forward Contracts

Forward rate agreements (FRAs) are over-the-counter financial contracts that allow counterparties to lock in an interest rate starting at a future time. The buyer of an FRA locks in a borrowing rate, and the seller locks in a lending rate. In other words, the "long" benefits from an increase in rates and the "short" benefits from a fall in rates.

As an example, consider an FRA that settles in one month on three-month LIBOR. Such an FRA is called 1×4. The first number corresponds to the first settlement date, and the second to the time to final maturity. Call τ the period to which LIBOR applies, three months in this case. On the settlement date, in one month, the payment to the long involves the net value of the difference between the spot rate S_T (the prevailing three-month LIBOR rate) and the locked-in forward rate F. The payoff is $S_T - F$, as with other forward contracts, present-valued to the first settlement date. This gives

$$V_T = (S_T - F) \times \tau \times \text{Notional} \times \text{PV}(\$1) \tag{8.1}$$

where $\text{PV}(\$1) = \$1/(1 + S_T\tau)$. The amount is cash settled.

Figure 8-1 shows that a *short* position in an FRA is equivalent to borrowing short-term to finance a long-term investment. In both cases, there is no up-front investment. The duration is equal to the difference between the durations of the two legs, and can be found by taking the derivative of Equation (8.1). The duration of a short FRA is τ. Its dollar duration is $\text{DD} = \tau \times \text{Notional} \times \text{PV}(\$1)$.

FIGURE 8-1 Decomposition of a Short FRA Position

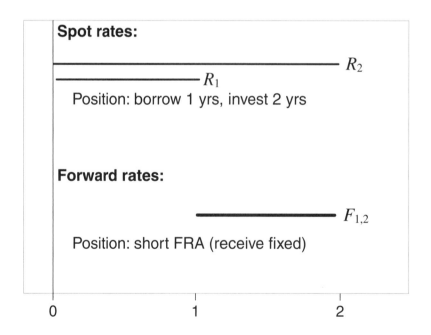

Example: Using an FRA

A company will receive $100 million in six months to be invested for a six-month period. The treasurer is afraid rates will fall, in which case the investment return will be lower. The company needs to take a position that will offset this loss by generating a gain when rates fall. Because a short FRA gains when rates fall, the treasurer needs to *sell* a 6 × 12 FRA on $100 million at the rate of, say, $F = 5\%$. This locks in an investment rate of 5% starting in six months.

When the FRA expires in six months, assume that the prevailing six-month spot rate is $S_T = 3\%$. This will lower the investment return on the cash received, which is the scenario the treasurer feared. Using Equation (8.1), the FRA has a payoff of $V_T = -(3\% - 5\%) \times (6/12) \times \$100$ million = $1,000,000, which multiplied by the present value factor gives $980,392. In effect, this payment offsets the lower return that the company received on a floating investment, guaranteeing a return equal to the forward rate. This contract is equivalent to borrowing the present value of $100 million for 6 months and investing the proceeds for 12 months.

Key concept:
A long FRA position benefits from an increase in rates. A short FRA position is similar to a long position in a bond. Its duration is positive and equal to the difference between the two maturities.

Example 8-1: FRM Exam 2002—Question 27
A long position in a FRA 2 × 5 is equivalent to the following positions in the spot market:
a) Borrowing in two months to finance a five-month investment
b) Borrowing in five months to finance a two-month investment
c) Borrowing half a loan amount at two months and the remainder at five months
d) Borrowing in two months to finance a three-month investment

---

Example 8-2: FRM Exam 2001—Question 70
Consider the buyer of a 6 × 9 FRA. The contract rate is 6.35% on a notional amount of $10 million. Calculate the settlement amount of the *seller* if the settlement rate is 6.85%. Assume a 30/360 day count basis.
a) $-12,500$
b) $-12,290$
c) $+12,500$
d) $+12,290$

Example 8-3: FRM Exam 2001—Question 73

The following instruments are traded on an ACT/360 basis:

three-month deposit (91 days), at 4.5%; 3×6 FRA (92 days), at 4.6%;

6×9 FRA (90 days), at 4.8%; 9×12 FRA (92 days), at 6%.

What is the one-year interest rate on an ACT/360 basis?

a) 5.19%

b) 5.12%

c) 5.07%

d) 4.98%

8.2 Futures

Whereas FRAs are over-the-counter contracts, futures are traded on organized exchanges. We will cover the most important types of futures contracts, Eurodollar and T-bond futures.

8.2.1 Eurodollar Futures

Eurodollar futures are futures contracts tied to a forward LIBOR rate. Since their creation on the Chicago Mercantile Exchange, Eurodollar futures have spawned equivalent contracts such as Euribor futures (denominated in euros),[1] Euroswiss futures (denominated in Swiss francs), and Euroyen futures (denominated in Japanese yen). These contracts are akin to FRAs involving three-month forward rates starting on a wide range of dates, up to 10 years into the future.

The formula for calculating the value of one contract is

$$P_t = 10,000 \times [100 - 0.25(100 - \mathrm{FQ}_t)] = 10,000 \times [100 - 0.25 F_t] \qquad (8.2)$$

where FQ_t is the quoted Eurodollar futures price. This is quoted as 100.00 minus the interest rate F_t, expressed as a percentage, that is, $\mathrm{FQ}_t = 100 - F_t$. The 0.25 factor represents the three-month maturity, or 0.25 years. For instance, if the market quotes $\mathrm{FQ}_t = 94.47$, we have $F_t = 100 - 94.47 = 5.53$, and the contract value is $P = 10,000[100 - 0.25 \times 5.53] = \$986,175$. At expiration, the contract value settles to

$$P_T = 10,000 \times [100 - 0.25 S_T] \qquad (8.3)$$

---

[1]Euribor futures are based on the European Bankers Federation's Euribor Offered Rate (EBF Euribor). The contracts differ from Euro LIBOR futures, which are based on the British Bankers' Association London Interbank Offer Rate (BBA LIBOR) but are much less active.

where S_T is the three-month Eurodollar spot rate prevailing at T. Payments are cash settled.

As a result, F_t can be viewed as a three-month forward rate that starts at the maturity of the futures contract. The formula for the contract price may look complicated but in fact is structured so that an increase in the interest rate leads to a decrease in the price of the contract, as is usual for fixed-income instruments. Also, because the change in the price is related to the interest rate by a factor of 0.25, this contract has a constant duration of three months. The DV01 is $\$10,000 \times 0.25 \times 0.01 = \$25$.

Example: Using Eurodollar futures

As in the previous section, the treasurer wants to hedge a future investment of $100 million in six months for a six-month period. The company needs to take a position that will offset the earnings loss by generating a gain when rates fall. Because a long Eurodollar futures position gains when rates fall, the treasurer should *buy* Eurodollar futures.

If the futures contract trades at $FQ_t = 95.00$, the dollar value of one contract is $P = 10,000 \times [100 - 0.25(100 - 95)] = \$987,500$. The treasurer needs to buy a suitable number of contracts that will provide the best hedge against the loss of earnings. The computation of this number will be detailed in a future chapter.

Chapter 5 explained that the pricing of forwards is similar to that of futures, except when the value of the futures contract is strongly correlated with the reinvestment rate. This is the case with Eurodollar futures.

Interest rate futures contracts are designed to move like a bond, that is, to lose value when interest rates increase. The correlation is negative. This implies that when interest rates rise, the futures contract loses value and, in addition, funds have to be provided precisely when the borrowing cost or reinvestment rate is higher. Conversely, when rates drop, the contract gains value and the profits can be withdrawn but are now reinvested at a lower rate. Relative to forward contracts, this marking-to-market feature is *disadvantageous* to long futures positions. This has to be offset by a *lower* futures contract value. Given that the value is negatively related to the futures rate, by $P_t = 10,000 \times [100 - 0.25 \times F_t]$, this implies a *higher* Eurodollar futures rate F_t.

The difference is called the **convexity adjustment** and can be described as[2]

$$\text{Futures rate} = \text{Forward rate} + (1/2)\sigma^2 t_1 t_2 \qquad (8.4)$$

where σ is the volatility of the change in the short-term rate, t_1 is the time to maturity of the futures contract, and t_2 is the maturity of the rate underlying the futures contract.

Example: Convexity adjustment

Consider a 10-year Eurodollar contract, for which $t_1 = 10$ and $t_2 = 10.25$. The maturity of the futures contract itself is 10 years and that of the underlying rate is 10 years plus three months.

Typically, $\sigma = 1\%$, so the adjustment is $(1/2)0.01^2 \times 10 \times 10.25 = 0.51\%$. So, if the forward price is 6%, the equivalent futures rate would be 6.51%. Note that the effect is significant for long maturities only. Changing t_1 to one year and t_2 to 1.25, for instance, reduces the adjustment to 0.006%, which is negligible.

Example 8-4: FRM Exam 1998—Question 7

What are the differences between forward rate agreements (FRAs) and Eurodollar futures?

  I. FRAs are traded on an exchange, whereas Eurodollar futures are not.
 II. FRAs have better liquidity than Eurodollar futures.
III. FRAs have standard contract sizes, whereas Eurodollar futures do not.

a) I only
b) I and II only
c) II and III only
d) None of the above

8.2.2   T-Bond Futures

T-bond futures are futures contracts tied to a pool of Treasury bonds that consists of all bonds with a remaining maturity greater than 15 years (and noncallable within 15 years). Similar contracts exist on shorter rates, including 2-, 5-, and 10-year Treasury notes. Government bond futures also exist in other markets, including Canada, the United Kingdom, the Eurozone, and Japan.

Futures contracts are quoted similarly to T-Bonds—for example, 97-02—in percent plus thirty-seconds, with a notional of $100,000. Thus the price of the contract

---

[2]This formula is derived from the Ho-Lee model. See, for instance, Hull (2000), *Options, Futures, and Other Derivatives,* Upper Saddle River, NJ: Prentice-Hall.

is $P = \$100,000 \times (97 + 2/32)/100 = \$97,062.50$. The next day, if yields go up and the quoted price falls to 96-0, the new price is $96,000, and the loss on the long position is $P_2 - P_1 = -\$1,062.50$.

It is important to note that the T-bond futures contract is settled by physical delivery. To ensure interchangeability between the deliverable bonds, the futures contract uses a **conversion factor** (CF) for delivery. This factor multiplies the futures price for payment to the short. The goal of the CF is to attempt to equalize the net cost of delivering the various eligible bonds.

The conversion factor is needed due to the fact that bonds trade at widely different prices. High-coupon bonds trade at a premium, low-coupon bonds at a discount. Without this adjustment, the party with the short position (the"short") would always deliver the same, cheap bond and there would be little exchangeability between bonds. Exchangeability is an important feature, as it minimizes the possibility of market squeezes. A **squeeze** occurs when holders of the short position cannot acquire or borrow the securities required for delivery under the terms of the contract.

So the "short" buys a bond, delivers it, and receives the quoted futures price times a CF that is specific to the delivered bond (plus accrued interest). The short should rationally pick the bond that minimizes the net cost,

$$\text{Cost} = \text{Price} - \text{Futures quote} \times \text{CF} \tag{8.5}$$

The bond with the lowest net cost is called **cheapest to deliver** (CTD).

In practice, the CF is set by the exchange at initiation of the contract for each bond. It is computed by discounting the bond's cash flows at a notional 6% rate, assuming a flat term structure. Take, for instance, the 10 5/8% of 2015. The CF is computed as

$$\text{CF} = \frac{(10.675\%/2)}{(1 + 6\%/2)^1} + \cdots + \frac{(1 + 10.675\%/2)}{(1 + 6\%/2)^T} \tag{8.6}$$

which gives CF = 1.4533. High-coupon bonds have higher CFs. Also, because the coupon is greater than 6%, the CF is greater than 1.

The net cost calculations are illustrated in Table 8-1 for three bonds. The net cost for the first bond in the table is $\$141.938 - 97.0625 \times 1.4533 = \$0.877$. The net cost for the second bond in the table is $0.544. Because this is the lowest entry, this bond is the CTD. Note how the CF adjustment brings the cost of all bonds much closer to each other compared with the original prices.

TABLE 8-1 Calculation of CTD

Bond	Price	Futures	CF	Cost
10 5/8% Aug 2015	141.938	97.0625	1.4533	0.877
8 7/8% Aug 2017	127.094	97.0625	1.3038	0.544
5 1/2% Nov 2028	91.359	97.0625	0.9326	0.839

The adjustment is not perfect when current yields are far from 6%, or when the term structure is not flat, or when bonds do not trade at their theoretical prices. When rates are below 6%, discounting cash flows at 6% creates an downside bias for CF that increases for longer-term bonds. A 30-year bond priced at 5%, for example, will be worth much more than a 15-year bond. This tends to favor short-term bonds for delivery. When the term structure is upward sloping, the opposite occurs, and there is a tendency for long-term bonds to be delivered.

As a first approximation, this CTD bond drives the characteristics of the futures contract. As before, the equilibrium futures price is given by

$$F_t e^{-r\tau} = S_t - \text{PV}(D) \tag{8.7}$$

where S_t is the gross price of the CTD and $\text{PV}(D)$ is the present value of the coupon payments. This has to be further divided by the conversion factor for this bond. The duration of the futures contract is also given by that of the CTD. In fact, this relationship is only approximate because the short has an *option* to deliver the cheapest of a group of bonds. The value of this delivery option should depress the futures price since the party who is long the futures is also short the option, which is unfavorable. Unfortunately, this complex option is not easy to evaluate.

Example 8-5: FRM Exam 2000—Question 11

The Chicago Board of Trade has reduced the notional coupon of its Treasury futures contracts from 8% to 6%. Which of the following statements are likely to be *true* as a result of the change?

a) The cheapest-to-deliver status will become more unstable if yields hover near the 6% range.

b) When yields fall below 6%, higher-duration bonds will become cheapest to deliver, whereas lower-duration bonds will become cheapest to deliver when yields range above 6%.

c) The 6% coupon would decrease the duration of the contract, making it a more effective hedge for the long end of the yield curve.

d) There will be no impact at all by the change.

8.3   Swaps

Swaps are agreements by two parties to exchange cash flows in the future according to a prearranged formula. Interest rate swaps have payments tied to an interest rate. The most common type of swap is the **fixed-for-floating** swap, where one party commits to pay a fixed percentage of notional against a receipt that is indexed to a floating rate, typically LIBOR. The risk is that of a change in the level of rates.

Other types of swaps are **basis swaps**, where both payments are indexed to a floating rate. For instance, the swap can involve exchanging payments tied to three-month LIBOR against a three-month Treasury bill rate. The risk is that of a change in the spread between the reference rates.

8.3.1   Instruments

Consider two counterparties, A and B, that can raise funds, either at fixed or floating rates, of $100 million over 10 years. A wants to raise floating, and B wants to raise fixed.

Table 8-2a displays capital costs. Company A has an **absolute advantage** in the two markets as it can raise funds at rates systematically lower compared with B. Company A, however, has a **comparative advantage** in raising fixed as the cost is 1.2% lower than for B. In contrast, the cost of raising floating is only 0.70% lower than for B. Conversely, company B must have a comparative advantage in raising floating.

This provides a rationale for a swap that will be to the mutual advantage of the two parties. If both companies directly issue funds in their final desired market, the total cost will be LIBOR + 0.30% (for A) and 11.20% (for B), for a total of LIBOR + 11.50%. In contrast, the total cost of raising capital where each has a comparative advantage is 10.00% (for A) and LIBOR + 1.00% (for B), for a total of LIBOR + 11.00%. The gain to both parties from entering a swap is 11.50% − 11.00% = 0.50%. For instance, the swap described in Tables 8-2b and 8-2c splits the benefit equally between the two parties.

TABLE 8-2a Cost of Capital Comparison

Company	Fixed	Floating
A	10.00%	LIBOR + 0.30%
B	11.20%	LIBOR + 1.00%

TABLE 8-2b Swap to Company A

Operation	Fixed	Floating
Issue debt	Pay 10.00%	
Enter swap	Receive 10.00%	Pay LIBOR + 0.05%
Net		Pay LIBOR + 0.05%
Direct cost		Pay LIBOR + 0.30%
Savings		0.25%

Company A issues fixed debt at 10.00%, and then enters a swap whereby it promises to pay LIBOR + 0.05% in exchange for receiving 10.00% fixed payments. Its net, effective funding cost is therefore LIBOR + 0.05%, which is less than the direct cost by 25 bp.

TABLE 8-2c Swap to Company B

Operation	Floating	Fixed
Issue debt	Pay LIBOR + 1.00%	
Enter swap	Receive LIBOR + 0.05%	Pay 10.00%
Net		Pay 10.95%
Direct cost		Pay 11.20%
Savings		0.25%

Similarly, Company B issues floating debt at LIBOR + 1.00%, and then enters a swap whereby it receives LIBOR + 0.05% in exchange for paying 10.00% fixed. Its net, effective funding cost is therefore $11.00\% - 0.05\% = 10.95\%$, which is less than the direct cost by 25 bp. Both parties benefit from the swap.

In terms of actual cash flows, swap payments are typically *netted* against each other. For instance, if the first LIBOR rate is at 9% assuming annual payments, Company A would be owed $10\% \times \$100 = \$1$ million, and would have to pay LIBOR + 0.05%, or $9.05\% \times \$100 = \$0.905$ million. This gives a net receipt of $95,000. There is no need to exchange principals since both involve the same amount.

Swaps are often quoted in terms of spreads relative to the yield of similar-maturity Treasury notes. For instance, a dealer may quote 10-year swap spreads as 31/34bp against LIBOR. If the current note yield is 6.72, this means that the dealer is willing to pay $6.72 + 0.31 = 7.03\%$ against receiving LIBOR, or is willing to receive $6.72 + 0.34 = 7.06\%$ against paying LIBOR. Of course, the dealer makes a profit from the spread, which is rather small, at 3 bp. Swap rates are quoted for AA-rated counterparties. For lower-rated counterparties the spread would be higher.

8.3.2   Pricing

We now discuss the pricing of interest rate swaps. Consider, for instance, a three-year $100 million swap where we receive a fixed coupon of 5.50% against LIBOR. Payments are annual and we ignore credit spreads. We can price the swap using either of two approaches, taking the difference between two bond prices or valuing a sequence of forward contracts. This is illustrated in Figure 8-2.

FIGURE 8-2 Alternative Decompositions for Swap Cash Flows

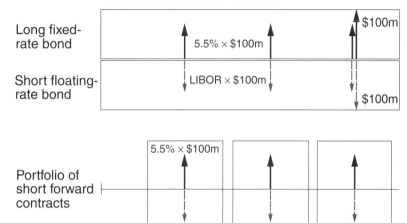

The top part of the figure shows that this swap is equivalent to a long position in a fixed-rate, 5.5% three-year bond and a short position in a three-year floating-rate note (FRN). If B_F is the value of the fixed-rate bond and B_f is the value of the FRN, the value of the swap is $V = B_F - B_f$.

The value of the FRN should be close to par. Just before a reset, B_f will behave exactly like a cash investment, as the coupon for the next period will be set to the prevailing interest rate. Therefore, its market value should be close to the face value. Just after a reset, the FRN will behave like a bond with a six-month maturity. But overall, fluctuations in the market value of B_f should be small.

Consider now the swap value. If at initiation the swap coupon is set to the prevailing par yield, B_F is equal to the face value, $B_F = 100$. Because $B_f = 100$ just before the reset on the floating leg, the value of the swap is zero, $V = B_F - B_f = 0$. This is like a forward contract at initiation.

After the swap is consummated, its value will be affected by interest rates. If rates fall, the swap will move in-the-money, since it receives higher coupons than prevailing market yields. B_F will increase whereas B_f will barely change.

Thus the duration of a receive-fixed swap is similar to that of a fixed-rate bond, including the fixed coupons and principal at maturity. This is because the duration of the floating leg is close to zero. The fact that the principals are not exchanged does not mean that the duration computation should not include the principal. Duration should be viewed as an interest rate sensitivity.

Key concept:
A position in a receive-fixed swap is equivalent to a long position in a bond with similar coupon characteristics and maturity offset by a short position in a floating-rate note. Its duration is close to that of the fixed-rate note.

We now value the three-year swap using term structure data from the preceding chapter. The time is just before a reset, so $B_f = \$100$ million. We compute B_F (in millions) as

$$B_F = \frac{\$5.5}{(1 + 4.000\%)} + \frac{\$5.5}{(1 + 4.618\%)^2} + \frac{\$105.5}{(1 + 5.192\%)^3} = \$100.95$$

The outstanding value of the swap is therefore $V = \$100.95 - \$100 = \$0.95$ million.

Alternatively, the swap can be valued as a sequence of forward contracts, as shown in the bottom part of Figure 8-2. Recall from Chapter 5 that the value of a unit position in a long forward contract is given by

$$V_i = (F_i - K)\exp(-r_i \tau_i) \tag{8.8}$$

where F_i is the current forward rate, K the prespecified rate, and r_i the spot rate for time τ_i. Extending this to multiple maturities, and to discrete compounding using R_i, the swap can be valued as

$$V = \sum_i n_i (F_i - K)/(1 + R_i)^{\tau_i} \tag{8.9}$$

where n_i is the notional amount for maturity i.

A long forward rate agreement benefits if rates go up. Indeed, Equation (8.8) shows that the value increases if F_i goes up. In the case of our swap, we *receive* a fixed rate K. So the position loses money if rates go up, as we could have received a higher rate. Hence, the sign on Equation (8.9) must be reversed.

Using the forward rates listed in Table 7-4, we find

$$V = -\frac{\$100(4.000\% - 5.50\%)}{(1 + 4.000\%)} - \frac{\$100(5.240\% - 5.50\%)}{(1 + 4.618\%)^2} - \frac{\$100(6.350\% - 5.50\%)}{(1 + 5.192\%)^3}$$

$$V = +1.4423 + 0.2376 - 0.7302 = \$0.95 \text{ million}$$

This is identical to the previous result, as it should be. The swap is in-the-money primarily because of the first payment, which pays a rate of 5.5% whereas the forward rate is only 4.00%.

Thus, interest rate swaps can be priced and hedged using a sequence of forward rates, such as those implicit in Eurodollar contracts. In practice, the practice of daily marking to market futures induces a slight convexity bias in futures rates, which have to be adjusted downward to get forward rates.

Figure 8-3 compares a sequence of quarterly forward rates with the five-year swap rate prevailing at the same time. Because short-term forward rates are less than the swap rate, the near payments are in-the-money. In contrast, the more distant payments are out-of-the-money. The current market value of this swap is zero, which implies that all the near-term positive values must be offset by distant negative values.

FIGURE 8-3 Sequence of Forward Rates and Swap Rate

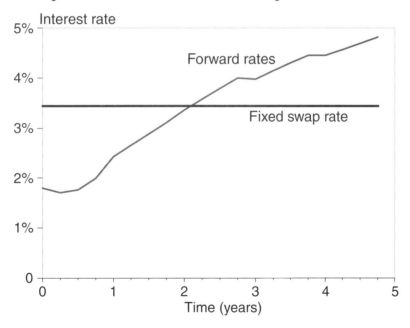

Example 8-6: FRM Exam 1998—Question 46

Which of the following positions has the same exposure to interest rates as the receiver of the floating rate on a standard interest rate swap?

a) Long a floating-rate note with the same maturity

b) Long a fixed-rate note with the same maturity

c) Short a floating-rate note with the same maturity

d) Short a fixed-rate note with the same maturity

Example 8-7: FRM Exam 2002—Question 30

Consider the following plain-vanilla swap. Party A pays a fixed rate of 8.29% per annum on a semiannual basis (180/360) and receives from party B LIBOR + 30 basis points. The current six-month LIBOR rate is 7.35% per annum.
The notional principal is $25 million. What is the net swap payment of party A?

a) $20,000

b) $40,000

c) $80,000

d) $110,000

Example 8-8: FRM Exam 2000—Question 55

Bank One enters into a five-year swap contract with Mervin Co. to pay LIBOR in return for a fixed 8% rate on a principal of $100 million. Two years from now, the market rate on three-year swaps at LIBOR is 7%. At this time Mervin Co. declares bankruptcy and defaults on its swap obligation. Assume that the net payment is made only at the end of each year for the swap contract period. What is the market value of the loss incurred by Bank One as a result of the default?

a) $1.927 million

b) $2.245 million

c) $2.624 million

d) $3.011 million

Example 8-9: FRM Exam 1999—Question 42

A multinational corporation is considering issuing a fixed-rate bond. However, by using interest rate swaps and floating-rate notes, the issuer can achieve the same objective. To do so, the issuer should consider

a) Issuing a floating-rate note of the same maturity and entering into an interest rate swap paying fixed and receiving float

b) Issuing a floating-rate note of the same maturity and entering into an interest rate swap paying float and receiving fixed

c) Buying a floating-rate note of the same maturity and entering into an interest rate swap paying fixed and receiving float

d) Buying a floating-rate note of the same maturity and entering into an interest rate swap paying float and receiving fixed

---

8.4   Options

There is a large variety of fixed-income options. We briefly describe here caps and floors, swaptions, and exchange-traded options. In addition to these stand-alone instruments, fixed-income options are embedded in many securities. For instance, a callable bond can be viewed as a regular bond plus a short position in an option.

In considering fixed-income options, the underlying can be a yield or a price. Due to the negative price-yield relationship, a call option on a bond can also be viewed as a put option on the underlying yield.

8.4.1   Caps and Floors

A **cap** is a call option on interest rates with unit value

$$C_T = \text{Max}[i_T - K, 0] \tag{8.10}$$

where $K = i_C$ is the cap rate and i_T is the rate prevailing at maturity.

In practice, caps are purchased jointly with the issuance of floating-rate notes that pay LIBOR plus a spread on a periodic basis for the term of the note. By purchasing the cap, the issuer ensures that the cost of capital will not exceed the capped rate. Such caps are really a combination of individual options, called **caplets**.

The payment on each caplet is determined by C_T, the notional, and an accrual factor. Payments are made in **arrears**, that is, at the end of the period. For instance, take a one-year cap on a notional of $1 million and a six-month LIBOR cap rate of 5%. The agreement period is from January 15 to the next January with a reset on July 15. Suppose that on July 15, LIBOR is at 5.5%. On the following January, the payment is

$$\$1 \text{ million} \times (0.055 - 0.05)(184/360) = \$2,555.56$$

using actual/360 interest accrual. If the cap is used to hedge an FRN, this would help to offset the higher coupon payment, which is now 5.5%.

A **floor** is a put option on interest rates with value

$$P_T = \text{Max}[K - i_T, 0] \tag{8.11}$$

where $K = i_F$ is the floor rate. A **collar** is a combination of buying a cap and selling a floor. This combination decreases the net cost of purchasing the cap protection. Figure

8-4 shows an example of a price path, with a cap rate of 3.5% and a floor rate of 2%. There are three instances where the cap is exercised, leading to a receipt of payment. There is one instance where the rate is below the floor, requiring a payment.

FIGURE 8-4 Exercise of Cap and Floor

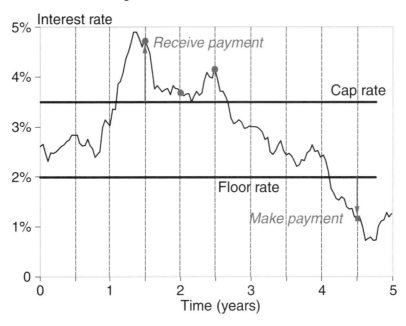

When the cap and floor rates converge to the same value, $K = i_C = i_F$, the overall debt cost becomes fixed instead of floating. The collar is then the same as a pay-fixed swap, which is the equivalent of put-call parity,

$$\text{Long cap } (i_C = K) + \text{Short floor } (i_F = K) = \text{Long pay-fixed swap} \qquad (8.12)$$

Caps are typically priced using a variant of the Black model, assuming that interest rate changes are lognormal. The value of the cap is set equal to a portfolio of N caplets, which are European-style individual options on different interest rates with regularly spaced maturities,

$$c = \sum_{j=1}^{N} c_j \qquad (8.13)$$

For each caplet, the unit price is

$$c_j = [F N(d_1) - K N(d_2)] \text{PV}(\$1) \qquad (8.14)$$

where F is the current forward rate for the period t_j to t_{j+1}, K is the cap rate, and PV($\$1$) is the discount factor to time t_{j+1}. To obtain a dollar amount, we must adjust for the notional amount as well as the length of the accrual period.

The volatility entering the pricing model, σ, is that of the forward rate between now and the expiration of the option contract, that is, at t_j. Generally, volatilities are quoted as one number for all caplets within a cap, called **flat volatilities**:

$$\sigma_j = \sigma$$

Alternatively, volatilities can be quoted separately for each forward rate in the caplet, called **spot volatilities**.

Example: Computing the value of a cap

Consider the previous cap on $1 million at the capped rate of 5%. Assume a flat term structure at 5.5% and a volatility of 20% pa. The reset is on July 15, in 181 days. The accrual period is 184 days.

Since the term structure is flat, the six-month forward rate starting in six months is also 5.5%. First, we compute the present value factor, which is PV($1) $= 1/(1 + 0.055 \times 365/360) = 0.9472$, and the volatility, which is $\sigma\sqrt{\tau} = 0.20\sqrt{181/360} = 0.1418$.

We then compute the value of $d_1 = \ln[F/K]/\sigma\sqrt{\tau} + \sigma\sqrt{\tau}/2 = \ln[0.055/0.05]/0.1418 + 0.1418/2 = 0.7430$ and $d_2 = d_1 - \sigma\sqrt{\tau} = 0.7430 - 0.1418 = 0.6012$. We find $N(d_1) = 0.7713$ and $N(d_2) = 0.7261$. The unit value of the call is $c = [FN(d_1) - KN(d_2)]$PV(1)$= 0.5789\%$. Finally, the total price of the call is $1 million $\times 0.5789\% \times (184/360) = \$2,959$.

Figure 8-3 can be taken as an illustration of the sequence of forward rates. If the cap rate is the same as the prevailing swap rate, the cap is said to be *at-the-money*. In the figure, the near caplets are out-of-the-money because $F_i < K$. The distant caplets, however, are in-the-money.

Example 8-10: FRM Exam 1999—Question 54

The cap-floor parity can be stated as
a) Short cap + Long floor = Fixed-rate bond
b) Long cap + Short floor = Fixed swap
c) Long cap + Short floor = Floating-rate bond
d) Short cap + Short floor = Interest rate collar

Example 8-11: FRM Exam 2002—Question 22

An interest rate cap runs for 12 months based on 3-month LIBOR with a strike price of 4%. Which of the following is generally *true*?

a) The cap consists of three caplet options with maturities of 3 months, the first one starting today based on 3-month LIBOR set in advance and paid in arrears.

b) The cap consists of four caplets starting today, based on LIBOR set in advance and paid in arrears.

c) The implied volatility of each caplet will be identical no matter how the yield curve moves.

d) Rate caps have only a single option based on the maturity of the structure.

Example 8-12: FRM Exam 1999—Question 60

For a five-year ATM cap on the three-month LIBOR, what can be said about the individual caplets, in a downward-sloping term structure environment?

a) The short-maturity caplets are ITM; long-maturity caplets are OTM.

b) The short-maturity caplets are OTM; long-maturity caplets are ITM.

c) All the caplets are ATM.

d) The moneyness of the individual caplets also depends on the volatility term structure.

8.4.2 Swaptions

Swaptions are OTC options that give the buyer the right to enter a swap at a fixed point in time at specified terms, including a fixed coupon rate.

These contracts take many forms. A **European swaption** is exercisable on a single date at some point in the future. On that date, the owner has the right to enter a swap with a specific rate and term. Consider, for example, a "1Y × 5Y" swaption. This gives the owner the right to enter in one year a long or short position in a five-year swap.

A fixed-term **American swaption** is exercisable on any date during the exercise period. In our example, this would be during the next year. If, for instance, exercise occurs after six months, the swap would terminate in five years and six months from now. So, the termination date of the swap depends on the exercise date. In contrast, a **contingent American swaption** has a prespecified termination date—for instance, exactly six years from now. Finally, a **Bermudan option** gives the holder the right to exercise on a specific set of dates during the life of the option.

As an example, consider a company that, in one year, will issue five-year floating-rate debt. The company wishes to swap the floating payments into fixed payments.

The company can purchase a swaption that will give it the right to create a five-year pay-fixed swap at the rate of 8%. If the prevailing swap rate in one year is higher than 8%, the company will exercise the swaption; otherwise it will not. The value of the option at expiration will be

$$P_T = \text{Max}[V(i_T) - V(K), 0] \tag{8.15}$$

where $V(i)$ is the value of a swap to pay a fixed rate i, i_T is the prevailing swap rate at swap maturity, and K is the locked-in swap rate. This contract is called a European 6/1 put swaption, or 1 into 5-year payer option.

Such a swap is equivalent to an option on a bond. Because this swaption creates a profit if rates rise, it is akin to a one-year put option on a six-year bond. A put option benefits when the bond value falls, which happens when rates rise. Conversely, a swaption that gives the right to receive fixed is akin to a call option on a bond. Table 8-3 summarizes the terminology for swaps, caps and floors, and swaptions.

Swaptions are typically priced using a variant of the Black model, assuming that interest rates are lognormal. The value of the swaption is then equal to a portfolio of options on different interest rates, all with the same maturity. In practice, swaptions are traded in terms of volatilities instead of option premiums.

TABLE 8-3 Summary of Terminology for OTC Swaps and Options

Product	Buy (Long)	Sell (Short)
Fixed/floating swap	Pay fixed Receive floating	Pay floating Receive fixed
Cap	Pay premium Receive Max$(i - i_C, 0)$	Receive premium Pay Max$(i - i_C, 0)$
Floor	Pay premium Receive Max$(i_F - i, 0)$	Receive premium Pay Max$(i_F - i, 0)$
Put swaption (payer option)	Pay premium Option to pay fixed and receive floating	Receive premium If exercised, receive fixed and pay floating
Call swaption (receiver option)	Pay premium Option to pay floating and receive fixed	Receive premium If exercised, receive floating and pay fixed

---

Example 8-13: FRM Exam 1997—Question 18

The price of an option that gives you the right to receive fixed on a swap will decrease as

a) Time to expiry of the option increases.

b) Time to expiry of the swap increases.

c) The swap rate increases.

d) Volatility increases.

Example 8-14: FRM Exam 2000—Question 10

Consider a 2 into 3-year Bermudan swaption (i.e., an option to obtain a swap that starts in 2 years and matures in 5 years). Consider the following statements:

  I. A lower bound on the Bermudan price is a 2 into 3-year European swaption.

 II. An upper bound on the Bermudan price is a cap that starts in 2 years and matures in 5 years.

III. A lower bound on the Bermudan price is a 2 into 5-year European option.

Which of the preceding statements is (are) *true*?

a) I only

b) II only

c) I and II

d) III only

8.4.3 Exchange-Traded Options

Among exchange-traded fixed-income options, we describe options on Eurodollar futures and on T-bond futures.

Options on Eurodollar futures give the owner the right to enter a long or short position in Eurodollar futures at a fixed price. The payoff on a put option, for example, is

$$P_T = \text{Notional} \times \text{Max}[K - \text{FQ}_T, 0] \times (90/360) \qquad (8.16)$$

where K is the strike price and FQ_T the prevailing futures price quote at maturity. In addition to the cash payoff, the option holder enters a position in the underlying futures. Since this is a put, it creates a short position after exercise, with the counterparty taking the opposing position. Note that since futures are settled daily, the value of the contract is zero.

Since the futures price can also be written as $\text{FQ}_T = 100 - i_T$ and the strike price as $K = 100 - i_C$, the payoff is also

$$P_T = \text{Notional} \times \text{Max}[i_T - i_C, 0] \times (90/360) \qquad (8.17)$$

which is equivalent to that of a cap on rates. Thus a put on Eurodollar futures is equivalent to a caplet on LIBOR.

In practice, there are minor differences in the contracts. Options on Eurodollar futures are American style instead of European style. Also, payments are made at the expiration date of Eurodollar futures options instead of in arrears.

Options on T-bond futures give the owner the right to enter a long or short position in futures at a fixed price. The payoff on a call option, for example, is

$$C_T = \text{Notional} \times \text{Max}[F_T - K, 0] \tag{8.18}$$

An investor who thinks that rates will fall, or that the bond market will rally, could buy a call on T-bond futures. In this manner, he or she will participate in the upside, without downside risk.

8.5   Answers to Chapter Examples

Example 8-1: FRM Exam 2002—Question 27

b) An FRA defined as $t_1 \times t_2$ involves a forward rate starting at time t_1 and ending at time t_2. The buyer of this FRA locks in a borrowing rate for months 3 to 5. This is equivalent to borrowing for five months and reinvesting the funds for the first two months.

Example 8-2: FRM Exam 2001—Question 70

b) The seller of an FRA agrees to receive fixed. Since rates are now higher than the contract rate, this contract must show a loss for the seller. The loss is $10,000,000 \times (6.85\% - 6.35\%) \times (90/360) = \$12,500$ when paid in arrears (i.e., in nine months). On the settlement date (i.e., brought forward by three months), the loss is $\$12,500/(1 + 6.85\% \times 0.25) = \$12,290$.

Example 8-3: FRM Exam 2001—Question 73

c) The one-year spot rate can be inferred from the sequence of three-month spot and consecutive three-month forward rates. We can compute the future value factor for each leg:

For 3-mo., $(1 + 4.5\% \times 91/360) = 1.011375$

For 3×6, $(1 + 4.6\% \times 92/360) = 1.011756$

For 6×9, $(1 + 4.8\% \times 90/360) = 1.01200$

For 9×12, $(1 + 6.0\% \times 92/360) = 1.01533$

The product is $1.05142 = (1 + r \times 365/360)$, which gives $r = 5.0717\%$.

Example 8-4: FRM Exam 1998—Question 7

d) FRAs are OTC contracts, so I is wrong. Since Eurodollar futures are the most active contracts in the world, liquidity is excellent and II is wrong. Eurodollar contracts have fixed contract sizes, $1 million, so III is wrong.

Example 8-5: FRM Exam 2000—Question 11

a) The goal of the CF is to equalize differences between various deliverable bonds. In the extreme, if we discounted all bonds using the current term structure, the CF would provide an exact offset to all bond prices, making all of the deliverable bonds equivalent. This reduction from 8% to 6% notional more closely reflects recent interest rates. It will lead to more instability in the CTD, which is exactly the effect intended. b) is not correct, as yields lower than 6% imply that the CF for long-term bonds is lower than otherwise. This will tend to favor bonds with high conversion factors, or shorter bonds. Also, a lower coupon increases the duration of the contract, so c) is not correct.

Example 8-6: FRM Exam 1998—Question 46

d) Paying fixed on the swap is the same as being short a fixed-rate note.

Example 8-7: FRM Exam 2002—Question 30

c) The net rate is $8.29\% - \text{LIBOR} - 0.30\% = 8.29\% - 7.65\% = 0.64\%$. Applied to the notional of $25 million, this gives $(180/360) \times 0.64\% \times \$25,000,000 = \$80,000$.

Example 8-8: FRM Exam 2000—Question 55

c) Using Equation (8.9) for three remaining periods, we have the discounted value of the net interest payment, or $(8\% - 7\%)\$100m = \$1m$, discounted at 7%, which is $\$934,579 + \$873,439 + \$816,298 = \$2,624,316$.

Example 8-9: FRM Exam 1999—Question 42

a) Receiving a floating rate on the swap will offset the payment on the note, leaving a net obligation at a fixed rate.

Example 8-10: FRM Exam 1999—Question 54

a) With the same strike price, a short cap/long floor loses money if rates increase, which is equivalent to a long position in a fixed-rate bond.

Example 8-11: FRM Exam 2002—Question 22

a) Interest rate caps involve multiple options, or caplets. The first one has terms that are set in three months. It locks in $\text{Max}[R(t+3)-4\%,0]$. Payment occurs in arrears in six months. The second one is a function of $\text{Max}[R(t+6)-4\%,0]$. The third is a function of $\text{Max}[R(t+9)-4\%,0]$ and is paid at $t+12$. The sequence then stops because the cap has a term of 12 months only. This means there are three caplets.

Example 8-12: FRM Exam 1999—Question 60

a) In a downward-sloping rate environment, forward rates are higher for short maturities. Caplets involve the right to buy at the same fixed rate for all caplets. Hence short maturities are ITM.

Example 8-13: FRM Exam 1997—Question 18

c) The value of a call increases with the maturity of the call and the volatility of the underlying asset value (which here also increases with the maturity of the swap contract). So a) and d) are wrong. In contrast, the value of the right to receive an asset at K decreases as K increases.

Example 8-14: FRM Exam 2000—Question 10

c) A swaption is a one-time option that can be exercised either at one point in time (European), at any point during the exercise period (American), or on a discrete set of dates during the exercise period (Bermudan). All of these dates are before the start of the swap. As such the Bermudan option must be more valuable than the European option, *ceteris paribus*, because it covers the same period and gives more choice. Also, a cap is a series of options that start on the swap date and can be exercised continuously during the life of the swap. As such, it must be more valuable than any option that is exercisable only once. Statements I and II match the exercise date of the option and the final maturity. Statement III, in contrast, describes an option that matures in seven years, and so cannot be compared with the original swaption.

Chapter 9

Equity, Currency, and Commodity Markets

Having covered fixed-income instruments, we now turn to equity, currency, and commodity markets. Equities, or common stocks, represent ownership shares in a corporation. Due to the uncertainty in their cash flows, as well as in the appropriate discount rate, equities are much more difficult to value than fixed-income securities. They are also less amenable to the quantitative analysis that is used in fixed-income markets. Equity derivatives, however, can be priced reasonably precisely in relation to underlying stock prices.

The foreign currency markets include spot, forward, options, futures, and swap markets. The foreign exchange markets are by far the largest financial markets in the world, with daily turnover estimated at $1,880 billion in 2004.

Commodity markets consist of agricultural products, metals, energy, and other products. Commodities differ from financial assets as their holding provides an implied benefit known as convenience yield but also incurs storage costs.

Section 9.1 introduces equity markets and presents valuation methods. Section 9.2 briefly discusses convertible bonds and warrants. These differ from the usual equity options in that exercising them creates new shares. Section 9.3 then provides an overview of important equity derivatives, including stock index futures, stock options, stock index options, and equity swaps. Section 9.4 presents a brief introduction to currency markets. Contracts such as futures, forwards, and options have been developed in previous chapters and do not require special treatment here. In contrast, currency swaps are analyzed in some detail in Section 9.5 due to their unique features and importance. Finally, Section 9.6 discusses commodity markets.

9.1 Equities

9.1.1 Overview

Common stocks, also called **equities**, are securities that represent ownership in a corporation. Bonds are senior to equities, that is, have a prior claim on the firm's assets in case of bankruptcy. Hence equities represent **residual claims** to what is left of the value of the firm after bonds, loans, and other contractual obligations have been paid off.

Another important feature of common stocks is their **limited liability**, which means that the most shareholders can lose is their original investment. This is unlike owners of unincorporated businesses, whose creditors have a claim on the personal assets of the owner should the business turn bad.

Table 9-1 describes the global equity markets. The total market value of common stocks was approximately $31 trillion at the end of 2003. The United States accounts for the largest proportion, followed by the Eurozone, Japan, and the United Kingdom.

TABLE 9-1 Global Equity Markets, 2003
(Billions of U.S. Dollars)

United States	14,266
Eurozone	4,949
Japan	2,953
United Kingdom	2,460
Other Europe	1,234
Other Pacific	1,482
Canada	889
Developed	28,233
Emerging	2,969
World	31,202

Source: World Federation of Exchanges

Preferred stocks differ from common stock because they promise to pay a specific stream of dividends. So they behave like a perpetual bond, or consol. Unlike bonds, however, failure to pay these dividends does not result in default. Instead, the corporation must withhold dividends to common stock holders until the preferred dividends have been paid out. In other words, preferred stocks are junior to bonds, but senior to common stocks.

With **cumulative preferred dividends**, all current and previously postponed dividends must be paid before any dividends on common stock shares can be paid. Preferred stocks usually have no voting rights.

Unlike interest payments, preferred stock dividends are not tax-deductible expenses. Preferred stocks, however, have an offsetting tax advantage. Corporations that receive preferred dividends pay taxes on only 30% of the amount received, which lowers their income tax burden. As a result, most preferred stocks are held by corporations. The market capitalization of preferred stocks is much lower than that of common stocks, as can be seen from the IBM example below. Trading volumes are also much lower.

Example: IBM preferred stock

IBM issued 11.25 million preferred shares in June 1993. These are traded as 45 million "depositary" shares, each representing one-fourth of the preferred, under the ticker "IBM-A" on the NYSE. Dividends accrue at the rate of $7.50 per annum, or $1.875 per depositary share.

As of April 2001, the depositary shares were trading at $25.4, within a narrow 52-week trading range of [$25.00, $26.25]. Using the valuation formula for a consol, the shares trade at an implied yield of 7.38%. The total market capitalization of the IBM-A shares amounts to approximately $260 million. In comparison, the market value of the common stock is $214,602 million, which is more than 800 times larger.

9.1.2 Valuation

Common stocks are extremely difficult to value. Like any other asset, their value derives from their future benefits, that is, from their stream of future cash flows (i.e., dividend payments) or future stock price.

We have seen that valuing Treasury bonds is relatively straightforward, as the stream of cash flows, coupon and principal payments, can be easily laid out and discounted to the present.

This is an entirely different affair from common stocks. Consider, for illustration, a "simple" case where a firm pays out a dividend D over the next year that grows at the constant rate of g. We ignore the final stock value and discount at the constant rate of r, such that $r > g$. The firm's value, P, can be assessed using the net present value formula, as for a bond:

$$P = \sum_{t=1}^{\infty} C_t/(1+r)^t$$
$$= \sum_{t=1}^{\infty} D(1+g)^{(t-1)}/(1+r)^t$$
$$= [D/(1+r)] \sum_{t=0}^{\infty} [(1+g)/(1+r)]^t$$
$$= [D/(1+r)] \times \left[\frac{1}{1-(1+g)/(1+r)} \right]$$
$$= [D/(1+r)] \times [(1+r)/(r-g)]$$

This is the so-called Gordon-growth model,

$$P = \frac{D}{r-g} \tag{9.1}$$

as long as the discount rate exceeds the growth rate of dividends, $r > g$.

The problem with equities is that the growth rate of dividends is uncertain and, in addition, it is not clear what the required discount rate should be. To make things even harder, some companies simply do not pay any dividends, and instead create value from the appreciation of their share price.

Still, this valuation formula indicates that large variations in equity prices can arise from small changes in the discount rate or in the growth rate of dividends, explaining the large volatility of equities. More generally, the risk and expected return of the equity depends on the underlying business fundamentals as well as on the amount of leverage, or debt in the capital structure.

For financial intermediaries for which the value of underlying assets can be measured precisely, we can value the equity from the underlying assets and the cost of borrowing. This situation, however, is more akin to the pricing of a derivative from the price of the underlying than to pricing the asset directly.

Example 9-1: FRM Exam 1998—Question 50

A hedge fund leverages its $100 million of investor capital by a factor of 3 and invests it into a portfolio of junk bonds yielding 14%. If its borrowing costs are 8%, what is the yield on investor capital?

a) 14%
b) 18%
c) 26%
d) 42%

9.2 Convertible Bonds and Warrants

9.2.1 Definitions

We now turn to convertible bonds and warrants. While these instruments have option-like features, they differ from regular options. When a call option is exercised, for instance, the "long" purchases an outstanding share from the "short." There is no net creation of shares. In contrast, the exercise of convertible bonds and of warrants (and of executive stock options) entails the creation of new shares, as the option is sold by the corporation itself. Because the number of shares goes up, the existing shares are said to be **diluted** by the creation of new shares.

Warrants are long-term call options issued by a corporation on its own stock. They are typically created at the time of a bond issue, but they trade separately from the bond to which they were originally attached. When a warrant is exercised, it results in a cash inflow to the firm, which issues more shares.

Convertible bonds are bonds issued by a corporation that can be converted to equity at certain times using a predetermined exchange ratio. They are equivalent to a regular bond plus a warrant. This allows the company to issue debt with a lower coupon than otherwise would be possible.

For example, a bond with a **conversion ratio** of 10 allows its holder to convert one bond with par value of $1,000 into 10 shares of the common stock. The **conversion price**, which is really the strike price of the option, is $1,000/10 = $100. The corporation will typically issue the convertible deep out of the money, for example, when the stock price is at $50. When the stock price moves—for instance, to $120—the bond can be converted to stock for an immediate option profit of ($120 − $100) × 10 = $200.

Figure 9-1 describes the relationship between the value of the convertible bond and the **conversion value**, defined as the current stock price times the conversion ratio. The convertible bond value must be greater than the price of an otherwise identical straight bond and the conversion value.

For high values of the stock price, the firm is unlikely to default and the straight bond price is constant, reflecting the discounting of cash flows at the risk-free rate. In this situation, it is almost certain that the option will be exercised, and the convertible value is close to the conversion value. For low values of the stock price, the firm is likely to default and the straight bond price drops, reflecting the likely loss upon default. In this situation, it is almost certain the option will not be exercised, and the convertible value is close to the straight bond value. In the intermediate region, the convertible value depends on both the conversion and straight bond values. The convertible is also sensitive to interest rate risk.

FIGURE 9-1 Convertible Bond Price and Conversion Value

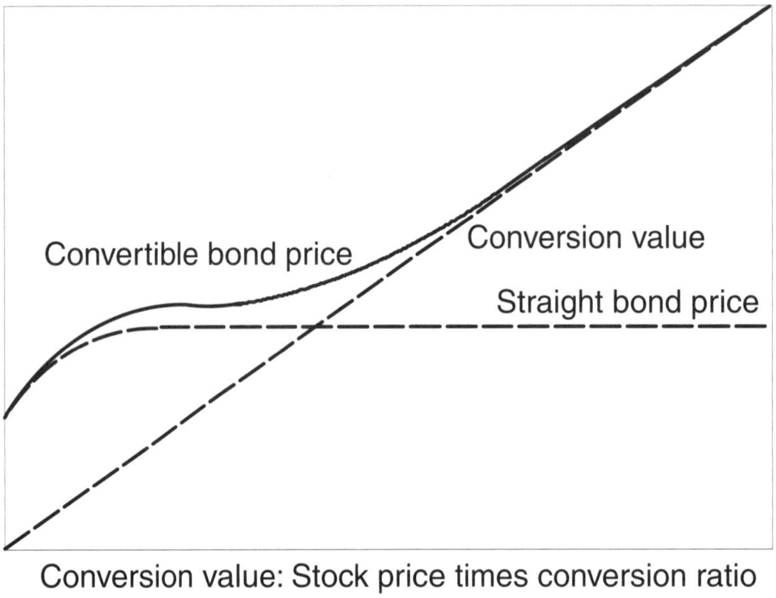

Conversion value: Stock price times conversion ratio

Example: A convertible bond

Consider an 8% annual coupon, 10-year convertible bond with a face value of $1,000. The yield on similar-maturity straight debt issued by the company is currently 8.50%, which gives a current value of straight debt of $967. The bond can be converted to common stock at a ratio of 10 to 1.

Assume first that the stock price is $50. The conversion value is then $500, much less than the straight debt value of $967. This corresponds to the left area in Figure 9-1. If the convertible trades at $972, its promised yield is 8.42%. This is close to the yield of straight debt, as the option has little value.

Assume next that the stock price is $150. The conversion value is then $1,500, much higher than the straight debt value of $967. This corresponds to the right area in Figure 9-1. If the convertible trades at $1,505, its promised yield is 2.29%. In this case, the conversion option is in-the-money, which explains why the yield is so low.

9.2.2 Valuation

Warrants can be valued by adapting standard option pricing models to the dilution effect of new shares. Consider a company with N outstanding shares and M outstanding warrants, each allowing the holder to purchase γ shares at the fixed price of K. At origination, the value of the firm includes the warrant, or

$$V_0 = N S_0 + M W_0 \tag{9.2}$$

where S_0 is the initial stock price just before issuing of the warrant, and W_0 is the up-front value of the warrant.

After dilution, the total value of the firm includes the value of the firm before exercise (including the original value of the warrants) plus the proceeds from exercise (i.e., $V_T + M\gamma K$). The number of shares then increases to $N + \gamma M$. The total payoff to the warrant holder is

$$W_T = \gamma \, \mathrm{Max}(S_T - K, 0) = \gamma \, (S_T - K) = \gamma \left(\frac{V_T + M\gamma K}{N + \gamma M} - K \right) \tag{9.3}$$

which must be positive. After simplification, this is

$$W_T = \gamma \left(\frac{V_T - NK}{N + \gamma M} \right) = \frac{\gamma}{N + \gamma M} (V_T - NK) = \frac{\gamma N}{N + \gamma M} \left(\frac{V_T}{N} - K \right) \tag{9.4}$$

which is equivalent to $n = \gamma N / (N + \gamma M)$ options on the stock price. The warrant can be valued using standard option models, with the asset value equal to the stock price plus the warrant proceeds, multiplied by the factor n,

$$W_0 = n \times c\left(S_0 + \frac{M}{N} W_0, K, \tau, \sigma, r, d \right) \tag{9.5}$$

with the usual parameters. Here the unit asset value is $\frac{V_0}{N} = S_0 + \frac{M}{N} W_0$. This must be solved iteratively since W_0 appears on both sides of the equation. If, however, M is small relative to the current float, or number of outstanding shares N, the formula reduces to a simple call option in the amount γ:

$$W_0 = \gamma \, c(S_0, K, \tau, \sigma, r, d) \tag{9.6}$$

Example: Pricing a convertible bond

Consider a zero-coupon, 10-year convertible bond with face value of $1,000. The yield on similar-maturity straight debt issued by the company is currently 8.158%, using continuous compounding, which gives a straight debt value of $442.29.

The bond can be converted to common stock at a ratio of 10 to 1 at expiration only. This gives a strike price of $K = 100. The current stock price is $60. The stock pays no dividend and has annual volatility of 30%. The risk-free rate is 5%, also continuously compounded.

Ignoring dilution effects, the Black-Scholes model gives an option value of $216.79. So the theoretical value for the convertible bond is $P = $442.29+$216.79 = 659.08. If the market price is lower than $659, the convertible is said to be cheap. This, of course, assumes that the pricing model and input assumptions are correct.

One complication is that most convertibles are also callable at the discretion of the firm. Convertible securities can be called for several reasons. First, an issue can be called to force conversion to common stock when the stock price is high enough. Bondholders typically have a month during which they can still convert, in which case this is a **forced conversion**. This call feature gives the corporation more control over conversion. It also allows the company to raise equity capital by forcing the bondholders to pay the exercise price.

Second, the call may be exercised when the option value is worthless and the firm can refinance its debt at a lower coupon. This is similar to the call of a nonconvertible bond, except that the convertible must be *busted*, which occurs when the stock price is much lower than the conversion price.

Example 9-2: FRM Exam 1997—Question 52

A convertible bond trader has purchased a long-dated convertible bond with a call provision. Assuming there is a 50% chance that this bond will be converted to stock, which combination of stock price and interest rate level would constitute the *worst*-case scenario?
a) Decreasing rates and decreasing stock prices
b) Decreasing rates and increasing stock prices
c) Increasing rates and decreasing stock prices
d) Increasing rates and increasing stock prices

Example 9-3: FRM Exam 2001—Question 119

A corporate bond with face value of $100 is convertible at $40, and the corporation has called it for redemption at $106. The bond is currently selling at $115, and the stock's current market price is $45. Which of the following would a bondholder most likely do?

a) Sell the bond

b) Convert the bond to common stock

c) Allow the corporation to call the bond at 106

d) None of the above

Example 9-4: FRM Exam 2001—Question 117

What is the main reason convertible bonds are generally issued with a call?

a) To make their analysis less easy for investors

b) To protect against unwanted takeover bids

c) To reduce duration

d) To force conversion if in-the-money

9.3   Equity Derivatives

Equity derivatives can be traded on over-the-counter markets as well as organized exchanges. We consider only the most popular instruments.

9.3.1   Stock Index Futures

Stock index futures are actively traded all over the world. In fact, the turnover corresponding to the notional amount is often greater than the total amount of trading in physical stocks in the same market. The success of these contracts can be explained by their versatility for risk management. Stock index futures allow investors to manage efficiently their exposure to broad stock market movements. Speculators can easily take directional bets with futures, on the upside or downside. Hedgers also find that futures provide a cost-efficient method to protect against price risk.

Perhaps the most active contract is the S&P 500 futures contract on the Chicago Mercantile Exchange (CME). The contract notional is defined as $250 times the index level. Table 9-2 displays quotations as of December 31, 1999.

The table shows that most of the volume was concentrated in the "near" contract, March in this case. Translating the trading volume in number of contracts into a dollar equivalent, we have $250 \times 1484.2 \times 34,897$, which gives $13 billion. So these markets are very liquid. As a comparison, the average daily volume was \$35 billion in 2001. This was close to the trading volume of \$42 billion for stocks on the New York Stock Exchange (NYSE).

TABLE 9-2 Sample S&P Futures Quotations

Maturity	Open	Settle	Change	Volume	Open Interest
March	1480.80	1484.20	+3.40	34,897	356,791
June	1498.00	1503.10	+3.60	410	8,431

We can also compute the daily profit on a long position, which would have been \$250 × (+3.40), or \$850 on that day. In relative terms, this daily move was +3.4/1480.8, which is only 0.23%. The typical daily standard deviation is about 1%, which gives a typical profit or loss of \$3,710.50.

These contracts are cash settled. They do not involve delivery of the underlying stocks at expiration. In terms of valuation, the futures contract is priced according to the usual cash-and-carry relationship,

$$F_t e^{-r\tau} = S_t e^{-y\tau} \tag{9.7}$$

where y is now the dividend yield defined per unit time. For instance, the yield on the S&P was $y = 0.94\%$ per annum on that day.

Here, we assume that the dividend yield is known in advance and paid on a continuous basis. In general, this is not necessarily the case but can be viewed as a good approximation. With a large number of firms in the index, dividends will be spread reasonably evenly over the quarter.

To check if the futures contract was fairly valued, we need the spot price, $S = 1469.25$; the short-term interest rate, $r = 5.3\%$; and the number of days to maturity, which was 76 (to March 16). Note that rates are not continuously compounded. The present value factor is $\text{PV}(\$1) = 1/(1 + r\tau) = 1/(1 + 5.3\%(76/365)) = 0.9891$. Similarly, the present value of the dividend stream is $1/(1 + y\tau) = 1/(1 + 0.94\%(76/365)) = 0.9980$. The fair price is then

$$F = [S/(1 + y\tau)] (1 + r\tau) = [1469.25 \times 0.9980]/0.9891 = 1482.6$$

This is rather close to the settlement value of $F = 1484.2$. The discrepancy is probably due to the fact that the quotes were not measured simultaneously. Because the yield is less than the interest rate, the forward price is greater than the spot price.

Figure 9-2 displays the convergence of futures and cash prices for the December 1999 S&P 500 futures contract traded on the CME. The futures price is always above the spot price. The correlation between the two prices is very high, reflecting the cash-and-carry relationship in Equation (9.7).

FIGURE 9-2 Futures and Cash Prices for S&P 500 Futures

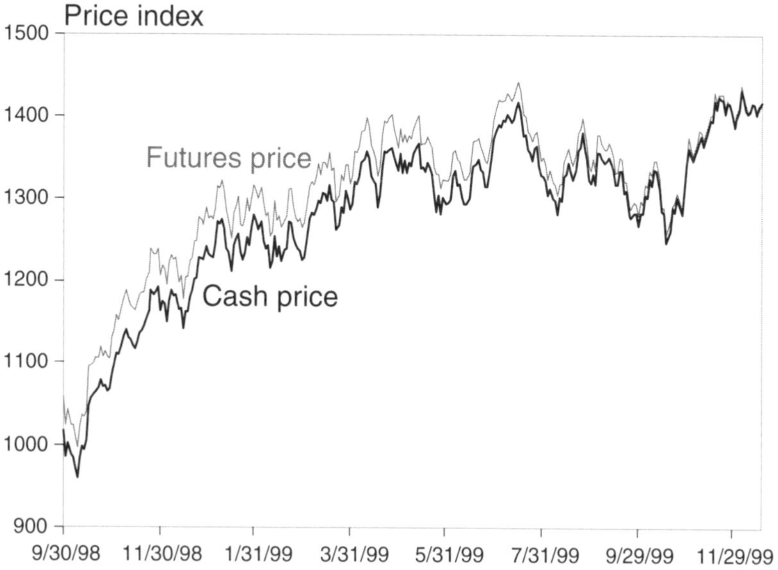

Because financial institutions engage in stock index arbitrage, we would expect the cash-and-carry relationship to hold very well. One notable exception was during the market crash of October 19, 1987. The market lost more than 20% in a single day. Throughout the day, however, futures prices were more up to date than cash prices because of execution delays in cash markets. As a result, the S&P stock index futures value was very cheap compared with the underlying cash market. Arbitrage, however, was made difficult due to chaotic market conditions.

Example 9-5: FRM Exam 2000—Question 12

Suppose the price for a six-month S&P index futures contract is 552.3. If the risk-free interest rate is 7.5% per year and the dividend yield on the stock index is 4.2% per year, and the market is complete and there is no arbitrage, what is the price of the index today?

a) 543.26
b) 552.11
c) 555.78
d) 560.02

Example 9-6: FRM Exam 1998—Question 9

To prevent arbitrage profits, the theoretical future price of a stock index should be fully determined by which of the following?

  I. Cash market price
 II. Financing cost
III. Inflation
 IV. Dividend yield

a) I and II only
b) II and III only
c) I, II, and IV only
d) All of the above

9.3.2   Single Stock Futures

In late 2000, the United States passed legislation authorizing trading in **single stock futures**, which are futures contracts on individual stocks. Such contracts were already trading in Europe and elsewhere. In the United States, electronic trading started in November 2002 and now takes place on "OneChicago," a joint venture of Chicago exchanges.

Each contract gives the obligation to buy or sell 100 shares of the underlying stock. Settlement usually involves physical delivery, that is, exchange of the underlying stock. Relative to trading in the underlying stocks, single stock futures have many advantages. Positions can be established more efficiently due to their low margin requirements, which are generally 20% of the cash value. In contrast, margins for stocks are higher. Also, short selling eliminates the costs and inefficiencies associated with the stock loan process. Other than physical settlement, these contracts trade like stock index futures.

9.3.3   Equity Options

Options can be traded on individual stocks, on stock indices, or on stock index futures. In the United States, stock options trade, for example, on the Chicago Board Options Exchange (CBOE). Each option gives the right to buy or sell a round lot of 100 shares. Settlement involves physical delivery.

Traded options are typically American style, so their valuation should include the possibility of early exercise. In practice, however, their values do not differ much from those of European options, which can be priced by the Black-Scholes model. When the stock pays no dividend, the values are the same. For more precision, we can use numerical models such as binomial trees to take into account dividend payments.

The most active *index* options in the United States are options on the S&P 100 and S&P 500 index traded on the CBOE. The former are American style, while the latter are European style. These options are cash settled, as it would be too complicated to deliver a basket of 100 or 500 underlying stocks. Each contract is for $100 times the value of the index. European options on stock indices can be priced with the Black-Scholes formula, using y as the dividend yield on the index as we did in the previous section for stock index futures.

Finally, options on S&P 500 stock index futures are also popular. These give the right to enter a long or short futures position at a fixed price. Exercise is cash settled.

9.3.4 Equity Swaps

Equity swaps are agreements to exchange cash flows tied to the return on a stock market index for a fixed or floating rate of interest. An example is a swap that provides the return on the S&P 500 index every six months in exchange for payment of LIBOR plus a spread. The swap will typically be priced to have zero value at initiation. Equity swaps can be valued as portfolios of forward contracts, as in the case of interest rate swaps. We will see later how to price currency swaps. The same method can be used for equity swaps.

These swaps are used by investment managers to acquire exposure to, for example, an emerging market without having to invest in the market itself. In some cases, these swaps can also be used to skirt restrictions on foreign investments.

9.4 Currency Markets

The **forex**, or currency markets, have enormous trading activity, with daily turnover estimated at $1,880 billion in 2004. Their size and growth are indicated in Table 9-2. This trading activity dwarfs that of bond or stock markets. In comparison, the daily trading volume on the New York Stock Exchange (NYSE) is approximately $50 billion.

Even though the largest share of these transactions is between dealers, or with other financial institutions, the volume of trading with nonfinancial institutions is still quite large, at $267 billion daily.

TABLE 9-2 Average Daily Trading Volume in Currency Markets
(Billions of U.S. Dollars)

Year	Spot	Forwards and Forex Swaps	Total
1989	350	240	590
1992	416	404	820
1995	517	673	1,190
1998	592	898	1,490
2001	399	811	1,210
2004	656	1,224	1,880
Of which, between:			
Dealers			993
Financials			620
Others			267

Source: Bank for International Settlements surveys.

Spot transactions are exchanges of two currencies for settlement as soon as is practical, typically in two business days. They account for about 35% of trading volume. Other transactions are outright forward contracts and forex swaps. **Outright forward contracts** are agreements to exchange two currencies at a future date, and account for about 12% of the total market. **Forex swaps** involve two transactions, an exchange of currencies on a given date and a reversal at a later date, and account for 53% of the total market.[1]

In addition to these contracts, the market includes OTC forex options ($117 billion daily) and exchange-traded derivatives ($22 billion daily). The most active currency futures are traded on the Chicago Mercantile Exchange (CME) and settled by physical delivery. The CME also trades options on currency futures.

As we have seen, currency forwards, futures, and options can be priced according to standard valuation models, with the income payment specified to be a continuous flow defined by the foreign interest rate, r^*.

Currencies are generally quoted in **European terms**, that is, in units of the foreign currency per dollar. The yen, for example, may be quoted as 120 yen per U.S. dollar. Two notable exceptions are the British pound (sterling) and the euro, which are quoted in **American terms**, that is, in dollars per unit of the foreign currency. The pound, for example, may be quoted as 1.6 dollars per pound.

---

[1] Forex swaps are typically of a short-term nature and should not be confused with long-term currency swaps, which involve a stream of payments over longer horizons.

Example 9-7: FRM Exam 2002—Question 63

The one-year U.S. dollar (USD) interest rate is 3% and the one-year Canadian dollar (CAD) interest rate is 4.5%. The current USD/CAD spot exchange rate is CAD 1.5000 per USD. Calculate the one-year forward rate.

a) 1.5225

b) 1.5218

c) 1.5207

d) 1.5199

9.5   Currency Swaps

Currency swaps are agreements by two parties to exchange a stream of cash flows in different currencies according to a prearranged formula.

9.5.1   Instruments

Consider two counterparties, company A and company B, that can raise funds either in dollars or in yen, $100 million or ¥10 billion, at the current rate of 100¥/$, over 10 years. Company A wants to raise dollars, and company B wants to raise yen. Table 9-4a displays the borrowing costs. This example is similar to that of interest rate swaps, except that rates are now in different currencies.

Company A has an **absolute advantage** in the two markets as it can raise funds at rates systematically lower than company B. Company B, however, has a **comparative advantage** in raising dollars, as the cost is only 0.50% higher than for company A, compared with the cost difference of 1.50% in yen. Conversely, company A must have a comparative advantage in raising yen.

TABLE 9-4a Cost of Capital Comparison

Company	Yen	Dollar
A	5.00%	9.50%
B	6.50%	10.00%

This provides the basis for a swap that will be to the mutual advantage of both parties. If both institutions directly issue funds in their final desired market, the total cost will be 9.50% (for A) and 6.50% (for B), for a total of 16.00%. In contrast, the total cost of raising capital where each has a comparative advantage is 5.00% (for A) and 10.00% (for B), for a total of 15.00%. The gain to both parties from entering a swap is $16.00 - 15.00 = 1.00\%$. For instance, the swap described in Tables 9-4b and 9-4c splits the benefit equally between the two parties.

TABLE 9-4b Swap to Company A

Operation	Yen	Dollar
Issue debt	Pay yen 5.00%	
Enter swap	Receive yen 5.00%	Pay dollar 9.00%
Net		Pay dollar 9.00%
Direct cost		Pay dollar 9.50%
Savings		0.50%

Company A issues yen debt at 5.00% and then enters a swap whereby it promises to pay 9.00% in dollar in exchange for receiving 5.00% yen payments. Its effective funding cost is therefore 9.00%, which is less than the direct cost by 50 bp.

Similarly, company B issues dollar debt at 10.00% and then enters a swap whereby it receives 9.00% dollars in exchange for paying 5.00% yen. If we add the difference in dollar funding costs of 1.00% to the 5.00% yen funding cost, the effective funding cost is 6.00%, which is less than the direct cost by 50 bp.[2] Both parties benefit from the swap.

TABLE 9-4c Swap to Company B

Operation	Dollar	Yen
Issue debt	Pay dollar 10.00%	
Enter swap	Receive dollar 9.00%	Pay yen 5.00%
Net		Pay yen 6.00%
Direct cost		Pay yen 6.50%
Savings		0.50%

While payments are typically netted for an interest rate swap, because they are in the same currency, this is not the case for currency swaps. Full interest payments are made in different currencies. In addition, at initiation and termination, there is exchange of principal in different currencies. For instance, assuming annual payments, company A will receive 5.0% on a notional of ¥10 billion, which is ¥500 million in exchange for paying 9.0% on a notional of $100 million, or $9 million every year.

---

[2]Note that company B is somewhat exposed to currency risk, as funding costs cannot be simply added when they are denominated in different currencies. The error, however, is of second-order magnitude.

9.5.2   Pricing

Consider now the pricing of the swap to company A. This involves receiving 5.00% yen in exchange for paying 9.00% dollars. As with interest rate swaps, we can price the swap using either of two approaches, taking the difference between two bond prices or valuing a sequence of forward contracts.

This swap is equivalent to a long position in a fixed-rate, 5%, 10-year yen-denominated bond and a short position in a 10-year, 9% dollar-denominated bond. The value of the swap is that of a long yen bond minus a dollar bond. Defining S as the dollar price of the yen and P and P^* as the values of the dollar and yen bond, we have

$$V = S(\$/¥)P^*(¥) - P(\$) \tag{9.8}$$

Here we indicate the value of the yen bond by an asterisk, P^*.

In general, the bond value can be written as $P(c, r, F)$ where the coupon is c, the yield is r, and the face value is F. Our swap is initially worth (in millions)

$$V = \frac{1}{100}P(5\%, 5\%, ¥10{,}000) - P(9\%, 9\%, \$100) = \frac{\$1}{¥100}¥10{,}000 - \$100 = \$0$$

Thus, the initial value of the swap is zero, assuming a flat term structure for both countries and no credit risk.

We can identify three conditions under which the swap will be in-the-money. This will happen if the dollar value of the yen S appreciates, or if the yen interest rate r^* falls, or if the dollar interest rate r goes up.

Thus the swap is exposed to three risk factors, the spot rate and two interest rates. The latter exposures are given by the duration of the equivalent bond.

Key concept:
A position in a receive–foreign currency swap is equivalent to a long position in a foreign currency bond offset by a short position in a dollar bond.

The swap can be alternatively valued as a sequence of forward contracts. Recall that the valuation of a forward contract on one yen is given by

$$V_i = (F_i - K)\exp(-r_i \tau_i) \tag{9.9}$$

using continuous compounding. Here, r_i is the dollar interest rate, F_i is the prevailing forward rate (in $/¥), and K is the locked-in rate of exchange defined as the ratio of the dollar to yen payment on this maturity. Extending this to multiple maturities, the swap is valued as

$$V = \sum_i n_i (F_i - K) \exp(-r_i \tau_i) \tag{9.10}$$

where $n_i F_i$ is the dollar value of the yen payments translated at the forward rate, and the other term, $n_i K$, is the dollar payment in exchange.

Table 9-5 compares the two approaches for a three-year swap with annual payments. Market rates have now changed and are $r = 8\%$ for U.S. yields, and $r^* = 4\%$ for yen yields. We assume annual compounding. The spot exchange rate has moved from 100¥/\$ to 95¥/\$, reflecting a depreciation of the dollar (or appreciation of the yen).

TABLE 9-5 Pricing a Currency Swap

	Specifications		Market Data
	Notional Amount (millions)	Contract Rates	Market Rates
Dollar	\$100	9%	8%
Yen	¥10,000	5%	4%
Exchange rate		100¥/\$	95¥/\$

Valuation Using Bond Approach (millions)						
	Dollar Bond			Yen Bond		
Time (year)	Dollar Payment	PV(\$1)	PV(CF)	Yen Payment	PV(¥1)	PV(CF)
1	9	0.9259	8.333	500	0.9615	480.769
2	9	0.8573	7.716	500	0.9246	462.278
3	109	0.7938	86.528	10,500	0.8890	9,334.462
Total			\$102.58			¥10,277.51
Swap (\$)			−\$102.58			\$108.18
Value						\$5.61

Valuation Using Forward Contract Approach (millions)						
Time (year)	Forward Rate (¥/\$)	Yen Receipt (¥)	Yen Receipt (\$)	Dollar Payment (\$)	Difference CF (\$)	PV(CF) (\$)
1	91.48	500	5.47	−9.00	−3.534	−3.273
2	88.09	500	5.68	−9.00	−3.324	−2.850
3	84.83	10,500	123.78	−109.00	14.776	11.730
Value						\$5.61

The middle panel shows the valuation using the difference between the two bonds.

First, we discount the cash flows in each currency at the newly prevailing yield. This gives $P = \$102.58$ for the dollar bond and ¥10,277.51 for the yen bond. Translating the latter at the new spot rate of ¥95, we get \$108.18. The swap is now valued at $\$108.18 - \$102.58$, which is a positive value of $V = \$5.61$ million. The appreciation of the swap is principally driven by the appreciation of the yen.

The bottom panel of the table shows how the swap can be valued by a sequence of forward contracts. First, we compute the forward rates for the three maturities. For example, the one-year rate is $95 \times (1 + 4\%)/(1 + 8\%) = 91.48$ ¥/\$, by interest rate parity. Next, we convert each yen receipt to dollars at the forward rate—for example, ¥500 million in one year, which is \$5.47 million. This is offset against a payment of \$9 million, for a net planned cash outflow of $-\$3.53$ million. Discounting and adding up the planned cash flows, we get $V = \$5.61$ million, which must be exactly equal to the value found using the alternative approach.

Example 9-8: FRM Exam 1999—Question 37

The table below shows quoted fixed borrowing rates (adjusted for taxes) in two different currencies for two different firms.

	Yen	Pounds
Company A	2%	4%
Company B	3%	6%

Which of the following is *true*?
a) Company A has a comparative advantage borrowing in both yen and pounds.
b) Company A has a comparative advantage borrowing in pounds.
c) Company A has a comparative advantage borrowing in yen.
d) Company A can arbitrage by borrowing in yen and lending in pounds.

Example 9-9: FRM Exam 2001—Question 67

Consider the following currency swap: Counterparty A swaps 3% on \$25 million for 7.5% on 20 million sterling. There are now 18 months remaining in the swap, and the term structures of interest rates are flat in both countries with dollar rates currently at 4.25% and sterling rates currently at 7.75%. The current \$/sterling exchange rate is \$1.65. Calculate the value of the swap. Use continuous compounding. Assume six months until the next annual coupon, and use current market rates to discount.
a) $-\$1,237,500$
b) $-\$4,893,963$
c) $-\$9,068,742$
d) $-\$8,250,000$

9.6 Commodities

9.6.1 Products

Commodities are typically traded on exchanges. Contracts include spot, futures, and options on futures. There is also an OTC market for long-term commodity swaps, where payments are tied to the price of a commodity against a fixed or floating rate.

Commodity contracts can be classified as:

- **Agricultural products**, including grains and oilseeds (corn, wheat, soybean), food and fiber (cocoa, coffee, sugar, orange juice)
- **Livestock and meat** (cattle, hogs)
- **Base metals** (aluminum, copper, nickel, zinc)
- **Precious metals** (gold, silver, platinum)
- **Energy products** (natural gas, heating oil, unleaded gasoline, crude oil)

The **Goldman Sachs Commodity Index** (GSCI) is a broad index of commodity price performance, containing 49% energy products, 9% industrial/base metals, 3% precious metals, 28% agricultural products, and 12% livestock products. The CME trades futures and options contracts on the GSCI.

In the last five years, active markets have developed for **electricity products**, that is, electricity futures for delivery at specific locations—California/Oregon border (COB), Palo Verde, and so on. These markets have mushroomed following the deregulation of electricity prices, which has led to more variability in electricity prices.

More recently, OTC markets and exchanges have introduced **weather derivatives**, where the payout is indexed to temperature or precipitation. On the CME, for instance, contract payouts are based on the "Degree Day Index" over a calendar month. This index measures the extent to which the daily temperature deviates from the average. These contracts allow users to hedge situations where their income is negatively affected by extreme weather. Markets are also evolving in newer products, such as indices of consumer bankruptcy and catastrophe insurance contracts.

Such commodity markets allow participants to exchange risks. Farmers, for instance, can sell their crops at a fixed price on a future date, insuring themselves against variations in crop prices. Likewise, consumers can buy these crops at a fixed price.

9.6.2   Pricing of Futures

Commodities differ from financial assets in two notable respects: they may be expensive, or even impossible, to store, and they may generate a flow of benefits that are not directly measurable.

The first dimension involves the cost of carrying a physical inventory of commodities. For most financial instruments, this cost is negligible. For bulky commodities, this cost may be high. Other commodities, such as electricity, cannot be stored easily.

The second dimension involves the benefit from holding the physical commodity. For instance, a company that manufactures copper pipes benefits from an inventory of copper, which is used up in its production process. This flow is called **convenience yield** for the holder. For a financial asset, this flow would be a monetary income payment for the investor.

Consider the first factor, storage cost only. The cash-and-carry relationship should be modified as follows. We compare two positions. In the first, we buy the commodity spot plus pay up front the present value of storage costs $PV(C)$. In the second, we enter a forward contract and invest the present value of the forward price. Since the two positions are identical at expiration, they must have the same initial value:

$$F_t e^{-r\tau} = S_t + PV(C) \tag{9.11}$$

where $e^{-r\tau}$ is the present value factor. Alternatively, if storage costs are incurred per unit time and defined as c, we can restate this relationship as

$$F_t e^{-r\tau} = S_t e^{c\tau} \tag{9.12}$$

Due to these costs, the forward rate should be much greater than the spot rate, as the holder of a forward contract benefits not only from the time value of money but also from avoiding storage costs.

Example: Computing the forward price of gold

This example uses data from December 1999. The spot price of gold is $S = \$288$, the one-year interest rate is $r = 5.73\%$ (continuously compounded), and storage costs are $\$2$ per ounce per year, paid up front. The fair price for a one-year forward contract should be $F = [S + PV(C)]e^{r\tau} = [\$288 + \$2]e^{5.73\%} = \$307.1$.

Let us now turn to the convenience yield, which can be expressed as y per unit time. In fact, y represents the net benefit from holding the commodity, after storage costs. Following the same reasoning as before, the forward price on a commodity should be given by

$$F_t e^{-r\tau} = S_t e^{-y\tau} \tag{9.13}$$

where $e^{-y\tau}$ is an actualization factor. This factor may have an economically identifiable meaning, reflecting demand and supply conditions in the cash and futures markets. Alternatively, it can be viewed as a *plug-in* that, given F, S, and $e^{-r\tau}$, will make Equation (9.13) balance.

Figure 9-3 displays the shape of the term structure of spot and futures prices for the New York Mercantile Exchange (NYMEX) crude oil contract. On December 1997, the term structure is relatively flat. On December 1998, the term structure becomes strongly upward sloping. Part of this slope can be explained by the time value of money (the term $e^{-r\tau}$ in the equation). In contrast, the term structure is downward sloping on December 1999. This can be interpreted in terms of a large convenience yield from holding the physical asset (in other words, the term $e^{-y\tau}$ in the equation dominates).

FIGURE 9-3 Spot and Futures Prices for Crude Oil

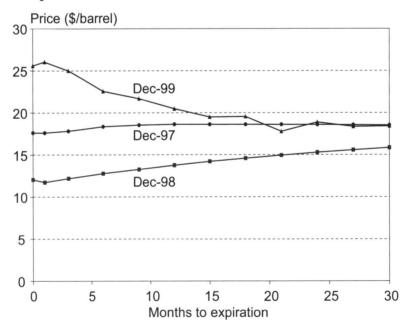

Let us focus on the one-year contract. Using $S = \$25.60$, $F = \$20.47$, $r = 5.73\%$, and solving for y,

$$y = r - \frac{1}{\tau}\ln(F/S) \tag{9.14}$$

we find $y = 28.10\%$, which is quite large. In fact, variations in y can be substantial. Just one year before, a similar calculation would have given $y = -9\%$, which implies a negative convenience yield, or a storage cost.

Table 9-6 displays futures prices for selected contracts. Futures prices are generally increasing with maturity, reflecting the time value of money, storage cost, and low convenience yields. There are some irregularities, however, reflecting anticipated imbalances between demand and supply. For instance, gasoline futures prices increase in the summer due to increased automobile driving. Natural gas displays the opposite pattern, where prices increase during the winter due to the demand for heating. Agricultural products can also be highly seasonal. In contrast, futures prices for gold are increasing monotonically with time, since this is a perfectly storable good.

TABLE 9-6 Futures Prices as of December 30, 1999

Maturity	Corn	Sugar	Copper	Gold	Nat. Gas	Gasoline
Jan			85.25	288.5		0.6910
Mar	204.5	18.24	86.30	290.6	2.328	0.6750
July	218.0	19.00	87.10	294.9	2.377	0.6675
Sept	224.0	19.85	87.90	297.0	2.418	0.6245
Dec	233.8	18.91	88.45	300.1	2.689	
Mar01	241.5	18.90	88.75	303.2	2.494	
⋮						
Dec01	253.5			312.9	2.688	

9.6.3 Futures and Expected Spot Prices

An interesting issue is whether today's futures price gives the best forecast of the future spot price. If so, it satisfies the **expectations hypothesis**, which can be written as

$$F_t = E_t[S_T] \tag{9.15}$$

The reason this relationship may hold is as follows. Say the one-year oil futures price is $F = \$20.47$. If the market forecasts that oil prices in one year will be at $25, one could make a profit by going long a futures contract at the cheap futures price of $F = \$20.47$, waiting a year, then buying oil at $20.47, and reselling it at the higher price of $25. In other words, deviations from this relationship imply **speculative profits**.

To be sure, these profits are not risk-free. Hence, they may represent some compensation for risk. For instance, if the market is dominated by producers who want to hedge by selling oil futures, F will be abnormally low compared with expectations. Thus the relationship between futures prices and expected spot prices can be complex.

For financial assets for which the arbitrage between cash and futures is easy, the futures or forward rate is solely determined by the cash-and-carry relationship, (i.e., the interest rate and income on the asset). For commodities, however, the arbitrage may not be so easy. As a result, the futures price may deviate from the cash-and-carry relationship through this convenience yield factor. Such prices may reflect expectations of future spot prices, as well as speculative and hedging pressures.

A market is said to be in **contango** when the futures price trades at a premium relative to the spot price, as shown in Figure 9-4. Using Equation (9.14), this implies that the convenience yield is smaller than the interest rate, $y < r$.

FIGURE 9-4 Patterns of Contango and Backwardation

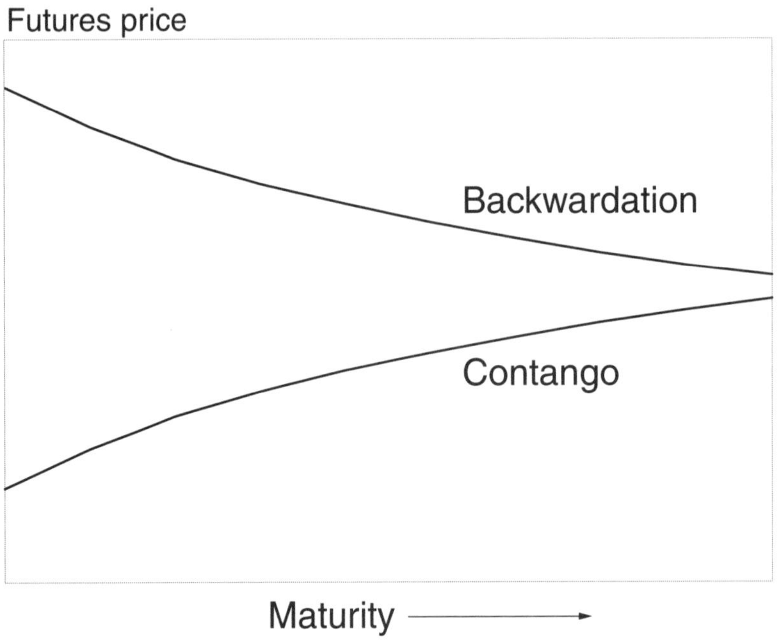

Futures price

Backwardation

Contango

Maturity ───────▶

A market is said to be in **backwardation** (or inverted) when forward prices trade at a discount relative to spot prices. This implies that the convenience yield is greater than the interest rate, $y > r$. In other words, a high convenience yield puts a higher price on the cash market, as there is great demand for immediate consumption of the commodity.

With backwardation, the futures price tends to increase as the contract nears maturity. In such a situation, a **rollover strategy** should be profitable, provided prices do not move too much. This involves buying a long maturity contract, waiting, and then selling it at a higher price in exchange for buying a cheaper, longer-term contract.

This strategy is comparable to **riding the yield curve** when it is positively sloped. This involves buying long maturities and waiting to have yields fall due to the passage of time. If the shape of the yield curve does not change too much, this will generate a capital gain from bond price appreciation.

This was basically the strategy followed by Metallgesellschaft Refining & Marketing (MGRM), the U.S. subsidiary of Metallgesellschaft, which rolled over purchases of WTI crude oil futures as a hedge against OTC sales to customers. The problem was that the basis, $S - F$, which had been generally positive, turned negative, creating losses for the company. In addition, these losses caused cash-flow or liquidity problems. MGRM ended up liquidating the positions, which led to a realized loss of $1.3 billion.

Key concept:
Markets are in contango if spot prices are lower than forward prices. Markets are in backwardation if spot prices are higher than forward prices. Backwardation occurs when there is high current demand for the commodity, which implies high convenience yields.

Example 9-10: FRM Exam 1999—Question 32
The spot price of corn on April 10 is 207 cents/bushel. The futures price of the September contract is 241.5 cents/bushel. If hedgers are net short, which of the following statements is *most* accurate concerning the expected spot price of corn in September?
a) The expected spot price of corn is higher than 207.
b) The expected spot price of corn is lower than 207.
c) The expected spot price of corn is higher than 241.5.
d) The expected spot price of corn is lower than 241.5.

Example 9-11: FRM Exam 1998—Question 24

In commodity markets, the complex relationships between spot and forward prices are embodied in the commodity price curve. Which of the following statements is *true*?

a) In a backwardation market, the discount in forward prices relative to the spot price represents a positive yield for the commodity supplier.

b) In a backwardation market, the discount in forward prices relative to the spot price represents a positive yield for the commodity consumer.

c) In a contango market, the discount in forward prices relative to the spot price represents a positive yield for the commodity supplier.

d) In a contango market, the discount in forward prices relative to the spot price represents a positive yield for the commodity consumer.

Example 9-12: FRM Exam 1998—Question 48

If a commodity is more expensive for immediate delivery than for future delivery, the commodity curve is said to be in

a) Contango

b) Backwardation

c) Reversal

d) None of the above

Example 9-13: FRM Exam 1997—Question 45

In the commodity markets, being long the future and short the cash exposes you to which of the following risks?

a) Increasing backwardation

b) Increasing contango

c) Change in volatility of the commodity

d) Decreasing convexity

Example 9-14: FRM Exam 1998—Question 27

Metallgesellschaft AG's oil hedging program used a *stack-and-roll* strategy that eventually led to large losses. What can be said about this strategy? The strategy involved

a) Buying short-dated futures or forward contracts to hedge long-term exposure, with the expectation that the short-term oil price would not decline

b) Buying short-dated futures or forward contracts to hedge long-term exposure, with the expectation that the short-term oil price would decline

c) Selling short-dated futures or forward contracts to hedge long-term exposure, with the expectation that the short-term oil price would not decline

d) Selling short-dated futures or forward contracts to hedge long-term exposure, with the expectation that the short-term oil price would decline

---

9.7 Answers to Chapter Examples

Example 9-1: FRM Exam 1998—Question 50

c) The fund borrows $200 million and invests $300 million, which creates a yield of $300 × 14% = $42 million. Borrowing costs are $200 × 8% = $16 million, for a difference of $26 million on equity of $100 million, or 26%. Note that this is a yield, not an expected rate of return, if we expect some losses from default. This higher yield also implies higher risk.

Example 9-2: FRM Exam 1997—Question 52

c) Abstracting from the convertible feature, the value of the fixed-coupon bond will fall if rates increase; also, the value of the convertible feature falls as the stock price decreases.

Example 9-3: FRM Exam 2001—Question 119

a) The conversion rate is expressed here in terms of the conversion price. The conversion rate for this bond is $100 into $40, or 1 bond into 2.5 shares. Immediate conversion will yield 2.5 × $45 = $112.5. The call price is $106. Since the market price is higher than the call price and the conversion value, and the bond is being called, the best value is achieved by selling the bond.

Example 9-4: FRM Exam 2001—Question 117

d) Companies issue convertible bonds because the coupon is lower than for regular bonds. In addition, these bonds are callable in order to force conversion to the stock at a favorable ratio. In the previous question, for instance, conversion would provide equity capital to the firm at the price of $40, while the market price is at $45.

Example 9-5: FRM Exam 2000—Question 12

a) This is the cash-and-carry relationship, solved for S. We have $Se^{-y\tau} = Fe^{-r\tau}$, or $S = 552.3 \times \exp(-7.5/200)/\exp(-4.2/200) = 543.26$. We verify that the forward price is greater than the spot price since the dividend yield is less than the risk-free rate.

Example 9-6: FRM Exam 1998—Question 9

c) The futures price depends on S, r, y, and time to maturity. The rate of inflation is not in the cash-and-carry formula, although it is embedded in the nominal interest rate.

Example 9-7: FRM Exam 2002—Question 63

b) Assuming annual compounding, Equation (9.7) shows that the forward price is set from $F/(1 + r\tau) = S/(1 + r^*\tau)$, where r is the domestic interest rate, r^* the foreign rate, and S the spot rate expressed in domestic currency. Note that S is 1.5 CAD per USD, so the domestic currency is the Canadian dollar. The forward price is $F = 1.500(1 + 4.5\%)/(1 + 3\%) = 1.5218$ in CAD. So, the U.S. dollar is more expensive forward than spot, which is logical because it has a lower interest rate than the Canadian dollar.

Example 9-8: FRM Exam 1999—Question 37

b) A company can have a comparative advantage in only one currency, that with the greatest difference in capital cost, 2% for pounds versus 1% for yen.

Example 9-9: FRM Exam 2001—Question 67

c) We use the bond valuation approach. The receive-dollar swap is equivalent to a long position in the dollar bond and a short position in the sterling bond.

Time	Dollar Bond			Sterling Bond		
	Dollar	PV($1)	PV(CF)	Sterling	PV(GBP1)	PV(CF)
(year)	Payment	(4.25%)	(dollars)	Payment	(7.75%)	(sterling)
1	750,000	0.97897	734,231	1,500,000	0.96199	1,442,987
2	25,750,000	0.93824	24,159,668	21,500,000	0.89025	19,140,432
Total			24,893,899			20,583,418
Dollars			+$24,893,899			−$33,962,640
Value						−$9,068,742

Example 9-10: FRM Exam 1999—Question 32

c) If hedgers are net short, they are selling corn futures even if it involves a risk premium such that the selling price is lower than the expected future spot price. Thus the expected spot price of corn is higher than the futures price. Note that the current spot price is irrelevant.

Example 9-11: FRM Exam 1998—Question 24

b) First, forward prices are at a discount versus spot prices only in a backwardation market. The high spot price represents a convenience yield to the consumer of the product, who holds the physical asset.

Example 9-12: FRM Exam 1998—Question 48

b) Backwardation means that the spot price is greater than the futures price.

Example 9-13: FRM Exam 1997—Question 45

a) Shorting the cash exposes the position to increasing cash prices, assuming, for instance, fixed futures prices, hence increasing backwardation.

Example 9-14: FRM Exam 1998—Question 27

a) Because MG was selling oil forward to clients, it had to hedge by buying short-dated future oil contracts. In theory, price declines in one market were to be offset by gains in another. In futures markets, however, losses are realized immediately, which may lead to liquidity problems (and did so). Thus, the expectation was that oil prices would stay constant.

Market Risk Management

Chapter 10

Introduction to Market Risk Measurement

This chapter provides an introduction to the measurement of market risk. Market risk is primarily measured using **value at risk** (VAR). VAR is a statistical measure of downside risk that is simple to explain. VAR measures the *total* portfolio risk, taking into account portfolio diversification and leverage.

In theory, risk managers should consider the entire distribution of profits and losses over the specified horizon. In practice, this distribution is summarized by one number: the worst loss at a specified confidence level, such as 99%. VAR, however, is only one of the measures that risk managers focus on. It should be complemented by **stress testing**, which identifies potential losses under extreme market conditions, which are associated with much higher confidence levels.

Section 10.1 gives a brief overview of financial market risks and the history of risk measurement systems. Section 10.2 defines VAR and shows how to compute VAR for a very simple portfolio. It also discusses caveats, or pitfalls to be aware of, in interpreting VAR numbers. This section shows how VAR methods, developed primarily for financial institutions, are now applied to measures of cash flow at risk. Section 10.3 turns to the choice of VAR parameters, that is, the confidence level and horizon. Next, Section 10.4 describes the broad components of a VAR system. Section 10.5 shows to complement VAR with stress tests. Finally, Section 10.6 covers liquidity risk, which can take the form of asset liquidity risk or funding risk. Liquidity can be an important source of financial risk, but is typically only loosely accounted for in risk measurement systems.

10.1 Introduction to Financial Market Risks

10.1.1 Types of Financial Risks

Financial risks include market risk, credit risk, and operational risk. **Market risk** is the risk of losses due to movements in financial market prices or volatilities. **Credit risk** is the risk of losses due to the fact that counterparties may be unwilling or unable to fulfill their contractual obligations. **Operational risk** is the risk of loss resulting from failed or inadequate internal processes, systems, and people, or from external events. Often, however, these three categories interact, so that any classification is to some extent arbitrary.

For example, credit risk can interact with other types of risk. At the most basic level, it involves the risk of default on the asset, such as a loan or bond. When the asset is traded, however, market risk also reflects credit risk. Take a corporate bond, for example. Some of the price movement may be due to movements in risk-free interest rates, which is pure market risk. The remainder will reflect the market's changing perception of the likelihood of default. Thus, for traded assets, there is no clear-cut delineation of market and credit risk. Some arbitrary classification must take place. Furthermore, operational risk is often involved as well.

Consider a simple transaction in which a trader purchases 1 million British pounds (BP) spot from bank A. The current rate is $1.5/BP, for settlement in two business days. So our bank will have to deliver $1.5 million in two days in exchange for receiving BP 1 million. This simple transaction involves a series of risks.

- *Market risk:* During the day, the spot rate could change. Suppose that after a few hours the rate moves to $1.4/BP. The trader cuts the position and enters a spot sale with another bank, bank B. The million pounds is now worth only $1.4 million, for a loss of $100,000 to be realized in two days. The loss is the change in the market value of the investment.

- *Credit risk:* The next day, bank B goes bankrupt. The trader must now enter a new, replacement trade with bank C. If the spot rate has dropped further from $1.4/BP to $1.35/BP, the gain of $50,000 on the spot sale with bank B is now at risk. The loss is the change in the market value of the investment, if positive. Thus there is interaction between market and credit risk.

■ *Settlement risk:* The next day, our bank wires the $1.5 million to bank A in the morning, which defaults at noon and does not deliver the promised BP 1 million. This is also known as **Herstatt risk**, named after the German bank that defaulted on such obligations in 1974, potentially destabilizing the whole financial system. The loss is now potentially the whole principal in dollars.

■ *Operational risk:* Suppose that our bank wired the $1.5 million to the wrong bank, bank D. After two days, our back office gets the money back, which is then wired to bank A along with compensatory interest. The loss is the interest on the amount due.

10.1.2 Risk Management Tools

In the past, risks were measured using a variety of ad hoc tools, none of which was satisfactory. These included **notional amounts**, **sensitivity measures**, and **scenarios**. While these measures provide some intuition of risk, they do not measure what matters, that is, the downside risk for the total portfolio. They fail to take into account differences in volatilities across markets, correlations across risk factors, and the probability of adverse moves in the risk factors.

Consider, for instance, a five-year **inverse floater**, which pays a coupon equal to 16% minus twice current LIBOR, if positive, on a notional principal of $100 million. The initial market value of the note is $100 million. This investment is extremely sensitive to movements in interest rates. If rates go up, the present value of the cash flows will drop sharply. In addition, the discount rate also increases. The combination of a decrease in the numerator terms and an increase in the denominator terms will push the price down sharply.

The question is, how much could an investor lose on this investment over a specified horizon? The *notional amount* provides only an indication of the potential loss. The worst-case scenario is one where interest rates rise above 8%. In this situation, the coupon will drop to $16 - 2 \times 8 =$ zero. The bond becomes a zero-coupon bond, whose value is $68 million, discounted at 8%. This gives a loss of $100 - $68 = $32 million. While sizable, this is still less than the notional.

A *sensitivity measure* such as duration is more helpful. As we saw in Chapter 7, the bond has three times the duration of a similar 5-year note. Assume the latter is 4.5 years. This gives a modified duration of $D = 3 \times 4.5 = 13.5$ years. This duration measure reveals the extreme sensitivity of the bond to interest rates but does not answer the question of whether such a disastrous movement in interest rates is likely. It also ignores the nonlinearity between the note price and yields.

Scenario analysis provides some improvement, as it allows the investor to investigate nonlinear, extreme effects in price. But again, the method does not associate the loss with a probability.

Another general problem is that these sensitivity or scenario measures do not allow the investor to aggregate risk across different markets. Say this investor also holds a position in a bond denominated in another currency, the euro. Do the risks add up, or do they diversify each other?

The great beauty of value at risk is that it provides a neat answer to all these questions. One number aggregates the risks across the whole portfolio, taking into account leverage and diversification, and providing a risk measure with an associated probability.

If the worst increase in yield at the 95% level is 1.65%, we can compute VAR as

$$VAR = \text{Market value} \times \text{Modified duration} \times \text{Worst yield increase} \qquad (10.1)$$

This gives VAR = $100 × 13.5 × 0.0165 = $22 million. The investor can now make a statement such as *the worst loss at the 95% confidence level is approximately $22 million*, with appropriate caveats. This is a huge improvement over traditional risk measurement methods, as it expresses risk in an intuitive fashion, bringing risk transparency to the masses.

The VAR revolution started in 1993, when it was endorsed by the Group of Thirty (G-30) as part of "best practices" for dealing with derivatives. The methodology behind VAR, however, is not new. It results from a merging of finance theory, which focuses on the pricing and sensitivity of financial instruments, and statistics, which studies the behavior of the risk factors. The idea behind VAR, or total portfolio risk, can be traced to the pioneering work of Markowitz in 1952.

10.2   VAR as a Downside Risk Measure

10.2.1   VAR: Definition

VAR is a summary measure of downside risk expressed in dollars, or in the reference currency. A general definition is

> *VAR is the maximum loss over a target horizon such that there is a low,*
> *prespecified probability that the actual loss will be larger.*

Consider, for instance, a position of $4 billion short the yen, long the dollar. This position corresponds to a well-known hedge fund that took a bet that the yen would fall in value against the dollar. How much could this position lose over a day?

To answer this question, we could use 10 years of historical daily data on the yen/dollar rate and simulate a daily return. The simulated daily return in dollars is then

$$R_t(\$) = Q_0(\$)[S_t - S_{t-1}]/S_{t-1} \tag{10.2}$$

where Q_0 is the current dollar value of the position and S is the spot rate in yen per dollar measured over two consecutive days.

For instance, for two hypothetical days $S_1 = 112.0$ and $S_2 = 111.8$. The simulated return is

$$R_2(\$) = \$4,000 \text{ million} \times [111.8 - 112.0]/112.0 = -\$7.2 \text{ million}$$

Repeating this operation over the whole sample, or 2,527 trading days, creates a time series of fictitious returns, which is plotted in Figure 10-1.

We can now construct a frequency distribution of daily returns. For instance, there are four losses below $160 million, three losses between $160 million and $120 million, and so on. The histogram, or frequency distribution, is graphed in Figure 10-2. We can also order the losses from worst to best return.

We now wish to summarize the distribution by one number. We could describe the quantile, that is, the level of loss that will not be exceeded at some high **confidence level**. Select, for instance, this confidence level as $c = 95\%$. This corresponds to a **right-tail probability**. We could also define VAR in terms of a **left-tail probability**, which we write as $p = 1 - c$.

Define x as the dollar profit or loss. VAR is typically reported as a positive number, even if it is a loss. It is defined implicitly as

$$c = \int_{-\text{VAR}}^{\infty} f(x)dx \tag{10.3}$$

When the outcomes are discrete, VAR is the smallest loss such that the right-tail probability is at least c.

FIGURE 10-1 Simulated Daily Returns

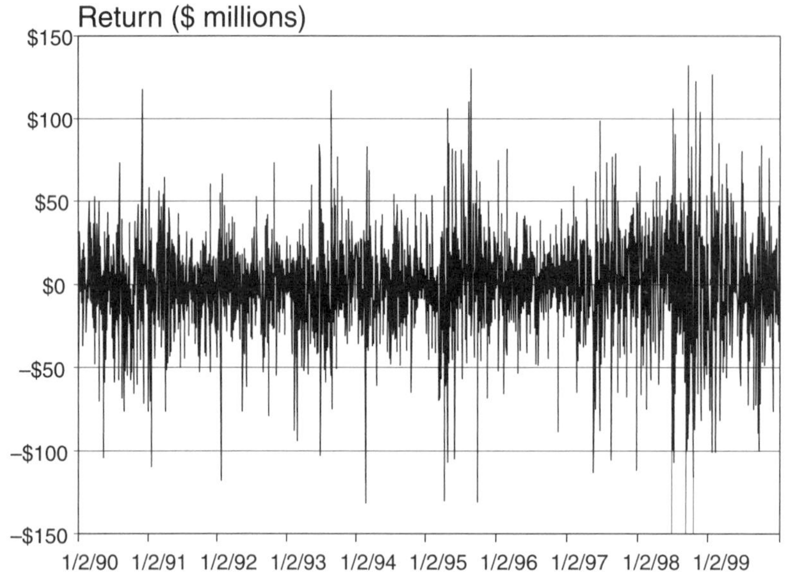

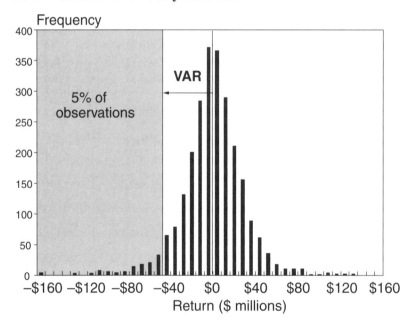

FIGURE 10-2 Distribution of Daily Returns

Sometimes, VAR is reported as the deviation between the mean and the quantile. This second definition is more consistent than the usual one. Because it considers the deviation between two values on the target date, it takes into account the time value of money. In most applications, however, the time horizon is very short, in which case the average return on financial series is close to zero. As a result, the two definitions usually give similar values.

In this hedge fund example, we want to find the cutoff value R^* such that the probability of a loss worse than $-R^*$ is $p = 1 - c = 5\%$. With a total of $T = 2,527$ observations, this corresponds to a total of $pT = 0.05 \times 2,527 = 126$ observations in the left tail. We pick from the ordered distribution the cutoff value, which is $R^* = \$47.1$ million. We can now make a statement such as

> *The maximum loss over one day is about \$47 million at the 95% confidence level.*

This describes risk in a way that notional amounts or exposures cannot convey.

Finally, from the confidence level, we can determine the number of expected exceedances n over a period of N days:

$$n = p \times N \tag{10.4}$$

Example 10-1: FRM Exam 1999—Question 89

What is the correct interpretation of a \$3 million overnight VAR figure with 99% confidence level? The institution

a) Can be expected to lose at most \$3 million in 1 out of next 100 days
b) Can be expected to lose at least \$3 million in 95 out of next 100 days
c) Can be expected to lose at least \$3 million in 1 out of next 100 days
d) Can be expected to lose at most \$6 million in 2 out of next 100 days

---

10.2.2 VAR: Caveats

VAR is a useful summary measure of risk, subject to some caveats.

- *VAR does not describe the worst loss.* This is not what VAR is designed to measure. Indeed, we would expect the VAR number to be exceeded with a frequency of p, that is, 5 days out of 100, for a 95% confidence level. This is perfectly normal. In fact, backtesting procedures are designed to check whether the frequency of exceedances is in line with p.

- *VAR does not describe the losses in the left tail.* VAR does not say anything about the distribution of losses in its left tail. It just indicates the probability of such a value occurring. For the same VAR number, however, we can have very different distribution shapes. In the case of Figure 10-2, the average value of the losses worse than $47 million is around $74 million, which is 60% worse than the VAR. So it would be unusual to sustain many losses beyond $200 million.

Other distributions are possible, however, with the same VAR. Figure 10-3 illustrates a distribution with 125 occurrences of large losses of $160 million. Because there is still one observation left at $47 million, the VAR is unchanged at $47 million. Yet this distribution implies a high probability of sustaining very large losses, unlike the original one.

This can create other strange results. For instance, one can construct examples, albeit stretched, where the VAR of a portfolio is greater than the sum of the VARs for its components. As a result, VAR fails to qualify as a *subadditive* risk measure, which is one of the desirable properties listed in the appendix. Subadditivity implies that the risk of a portfolio must be less than the sum of risks of the portfolio components.

FIGURE 10-3 Altered Distribution with the Same VAR

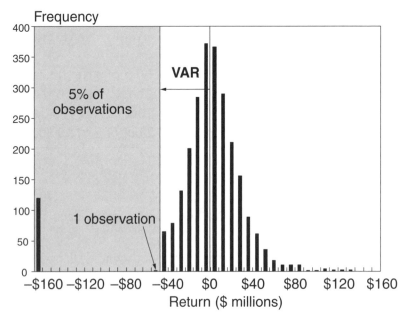

■ *VAR is measured with some error.* The VAR number itself is subject to normal sampling variation. In our example, we used 10 years of daily data. Another sample period, or a period of different length, will lead to a different VAR number. Different statistical methodologies or simplifications can also lead to different

VAR numbers. One can experiment with sample periods and methodologies to get a sense of the precision in VAR. Hence, it is useful to remember that there is limited precision in VAR numbers. What matters is the first-order magnitude.

10.2.3   Alternative Measures of Risk

The conventional VAR measure is the *quantile* of the distribution, measured in dollars. This single number is a convenient summary, but its very simplicity may be dangerous. Figure 10-3 shows that the same VAR can apply to very different distribution patterns. The appendix reviews desirable properties for risk measures and shows that VAR may display undesirable properties under some conditions. In particular, the VAR of a portfolio can be greater than the sum of subportfolio VARs. If so, merging portfolios can increase risk, which is a strange result. Alternative measures of risk are described below.

The Entire Distribution

In our example, VAR is simply one quantile in the distribution. The risk manager, however, has access to the whole distribution and could report a range of VAR numbers for increasing confidence levels.

The Conditional VAR

A related concept is the expected value of the loss when it exceeds VAR. This measures the average of the loss conditional on the fact that it is greater than VAR. Define the VAR number as $-q$. Formally, the **conditional VAR** (CVAR) is the negative of

$$E[X \mid X < q] = \int_{-\infty}^{q} x f(x) dx \Big/ \int_{-\infty}^{q} f(x) dx \qquad (10.5)$$

Note that the denominator represents the probability of a loss exceeding VAR, which is also $p = 1 - c$. This ratio is also called **expected shortfall**, **tail conditional expectation**, **conditional loss**, or **expected tail loss**. It tells us how much we could lose if we are "hit" beyond VAR. Because CVAR is an average of the tail loss, one can show that it qualifies as a *subadditive* risk measure. For our yen position, the average loss beyond the $47 million VAR is

$$CVAR = \$74 \text{ million}$$

The Standard Deviation

A simple summary measure of the distribution is the usual standard deviation (SD),

$$\mathrm{SD}(X) = \sqrt{\frac{1}{(N-1)} \sum_{i=1}^{N} [x_i - E(X)]^2} \tag{10.6}$$

The advantage of this measure is that it takes into account all observations, not just the few around the quantile. Any large negative value, for example, will affect the computation of the variance, increasing $\mathrm{SD}(X)$. If we are willing to take a stand on the shape of the distribution, say normal or Student's t, we do know that the standard deviation is the most efficient measure of dispersion. For example, for our yen position, this value is

$$\mathrm{SD} = \$29.7 \text{ million}$$

Using a normal approximation and $\alpha = 1.645$, we get a VAR estimate of $49 million, which is not far from the empirical quantile of $47 million. Under these conditions, VAR inherits all properties of the standard deviation. In particular, the SD of a portfolio must be smaller than the sum of the SDs of subportfolios, so it is subadditive.

The disadvantage of the standard deviation is that it is symmetrical and cannot distinguish between large losses or gains. Also, computing VAR from SD requires a distributional assumption, which may not be valid.

The Semi–Standard Deviation

This is a simple extension of the usual standard deviation that considers only data points that represent a loss. Define N_L as the number of such points. The measure is

$$\mathrm{SD}_L(X) = \sqrt{\frac{1}{(N_L)} \sum_{i=1}^{N} [\mathrm{Min}(x_i, 0)]^2} \tag{10.7}$$

The advantage of this measure is that it accounts for asymmetries in the distribution, such as negative skewness, which is especially dangerous. The semi–standard deviation is sometimes used to report downside risk, but is much less intuitive, and less popular, than VAR.

The Drawdown

Drawdown is the decline from a peak over a fixed time interval. Define x^{MAX} as the local maximum over the period $[0, T]$, which occurs at time $t_{MAX} \in [0, T]$. Relative to this value, the drawdown at time t is

$$\text{DD}(X) = \frac{(x^{MAX} - x_t)}{x^{MAX}} \tag{10.8}$$

The maximum drawdown is the largest such value over the period, or decline from peak to trough (local maximum to local minimum).

This measure is useful if returns are not independent from period to period. When a market trends, for example, the cumulative loss over a longer period is greater than the loss extrapolated from a shorter period. Alternatively, drawdowns are useful measures of risk if the portfolio is actively managed. A portfolio insurance program, for example, should have lower drawdowns relative to a fixed position in the risky asset because it cuts the position as losses accumulate.

The disadvantage of this measure is that it is backward looking. It cannot be constructed from the current position, as in the case of VAR. In addition, the maximum drawdown corresponds to different time intervals (i.e., $t_{MAX} - t_{MIN}$). As a result, maximum drawdown measures are not directly comparable across portfolios, in contrast with VAR or the standard deviation, which is defined over a fixed horizon or in annual terms.

Example 10-2: FRM Exam 1998—Question 22

Considering arbitrary portfolios A and B, and their combined portfolio C, which of the following relationships *always* holds for VARs of A, B, and C?
a) $\text{VAR}_A + \text{VAR}_B = \text{VAR}_C$
b) $\text{VAR}_A + \text{VAR}_B \geq \text{VAR}_C$
c) $\text{VAR}_A + \text{VAR}_B \leq \text{VAR}_C$
d) None of the above

10.2.4   Cash Flow at Risk

VAR methods have been developed to measure the mark-to-market risk of commercial bank portfolios. By now, these methods have spread to other financial institutions (e.g., investment banks, savings and loans) and the investment management industry.

In each case, the objective function is the market value of the portfolio, assuming fixed positions. VAR methods, however, are now also spreading to other sectors (e.g., nonfinancial corporations), where the emphasis is on periodic earnings. **Cash flow at risk** (CFAR) measures the worst shortfall in cash flows due to unfavorable movements in market risk factors. This involves quantities, Q, unit revenues, P, and unit costs, C. Simplifying, we can write

$$\text{CF} = Q \times (P - C) \tag{10.9}$$

Suppose we focus on the exchange rate, S, as the market risk factor. Each of these variables can be affected by S. Revenues and costs can be denominated in the foreign currency, partially or wholly. Quantities can also be affected by the exchange rate through foreign competition effects. Because quantities are random, this creates **quantity uncertainty**. The risk manager needs to model the relationship between quantities and risk factors. Once this is done, simulations can be used to project the cash-flow distribution and identify the worst loss at some confidence level. Next, the firm can decide whether to hedge and if so, the best instrument to use.

A classic example is the value of a farmer's harvest, say corn. At the beginning of the year, costs are fixed and do not contribute to risk. The price of corn and the size of the harvest in the fall, however, are unknown. Suppose price movements are primarily driven by supply shocks, such as the weather. If there is a drought during the summer, quantities will fall and prices will increase, and conversely if there is an exceptionally abundant harvest. Because of the negative correlation between Q and P, total revenues will fluctuate less than if quantities were fixed. Such relationships need to be factored into the risk measurement system because they will affect the hedging program.

10.3   VAR Parameters

To measure VAR, we first need to define two quantitative parameters, the confidence level and the horizon.

10.3.1   Confidence Level

The higher the confidence level c, the greater the VAR measure. Varying the confidence level provides useful information about the return distribution and potential extreme losses. It is not clear, however, whether one should stop at 99%, 99.9%, 99.99%, and so on. Each of these values will create an increasingly larger, but less likely, loss.

Another problem is that, as c increases, the number of occurrences below VAR shrinks, leading to poor measures of high quantiles. With 1,000 observations, for example, VAR can be taken as the 10th lowest observation for a 99% confidence level.

If the confidence level increases to 99.9%, VAR is taken from the lowest observation only. Finally, there is no simple way to estimate a 99.99% VAR from this sample because it has too few observations.

The choice of confidence level depends on the use of VAR. For most applications, VAR is simply a benchmark measure of downside risk. If so, what really matters is *consistency* of the VAR confidence level across trading desks or time.

In contrast, if the VAR number is being used to decide how much capital to set aside to avoid bankruptcy, then a high confidence level is advisable. Obviously, institutions would prefer to go bankrupt very infrequently. This **capital adequacy** use, however, applies to the overall institution and not to trading desks.

Another important point is that VAR models are useful only insofar as they can be verified. This is the purpose of backtesting, which systematically checks whether the frequency of losses exceeding VAR is in line with $p = 1 - c$. For this purpose, the risk manager should choose a value of c that is not too high. Picking, for instance, $c = 99.99\%$ should lead, on average, to one exceedance out of 10,000 trading days, or 40 years. In other words, it is going to be impossible to verify that the true probability associated with VAR is indeed 99.99%. For all these reasons, the usual recommendation is to pick a confidence level that is not too high, such as 95% to 99%.

10.3.2   Horizon

The longer the horizon T, the greater the VAR measure. This extrapolation is driven by two factors, the behavior of the risk factors and the portfolio positions.

To extrapolate from a one-day horizon to a longer horizon, we need to assume that returns are independently and identically distributed. This allows us to transform a daily volatility to a multiple-day volatility by multiplication by the square root of time. We also need to assume that the distribution of daily returns is unchanged for longer horizons, which restricts the class of distribution to the so-called stable family, of which the normal distribution is a member. If so, we have

$$\text{VAR}(T \text{ days}) = \text{VAR}(1 \text{ day}) \times \sqrt{T} \qquad (10.10)$$

This requires (1) the distribution to be invariant to the horizon (i.e., the same α as for the normal), (2) the distribution to be the same for various horizons (i.e., no time decay in variances), and (3) innovations to be independent across days.

> **Key concept:**
> VAR can be extended from a one-day horizon to T days by multiplication by the square root of time. This adjustment is valid with i.i.d. returns that have a normal distribution.

The choice of the horizon also depends on the characteristics of the portfolio. If the positions change quickly, or if exposures (e.g., option deltas) change as underlying prices change, increasing the horizon will create "slippage" in the VAR measure.

Again, the choice of the horizon depends on the use of VAR. If the purpose is to provide an accurate benchmark measure of downside risk, the horizon should be relatively short—ideally, less than the average period for major portfolio rebalancing.

In contrast, if the VAR number is being used to decide how much capital to set aside to avoid bankruptcy, then a long horizon is advisable. Institutions will want to have enough time for corrective action as problems start to develop.

In practice, the horizon cannot be less than the frequency of reporting of profits and losses. Typically, banks measure P&L on a daily basis, and corporates use a longer interval (ranging from daily to monthly). This interval is the minimum horizon for VAR.

Another criterion relates to the backtesting issue. Shorter time intervals create more data points matching the forecast VAR with the actual, subsequent P&L. As the power of the statistical tests increases with the number of observations, it is advisable to have a horizon as short as possible.

For all these reasons, the usual recommendation is to pick a horizon that is as short as feasible, for instance, one day for trading desks. The horizon needs to be appropriate to the asset classes and the purpose of risk management. For institutions such as pension funds, for instance, a one-month horizon may be more appropriate.

For **capital adequacy purposes**, institutions should select a high confidence level and a long horizon. There is a trade-off, however, between these two parameters. Increasing one *or* the other will increase VAR.

Example 10-3: FRM Exam 1997—Question 7

To convert VAR from a 1-day holding period to a 10-day holding period, the VAR number is generally multiplied by

a) 2.33
b) 3.16
c) 7.25
d) 10.00

10.3.3 Application: The Basel Rules

The Basel market risk charge requires VAR to be computed with the following parameters:

- A horizon of 10 trading days, or two calendar weeks
- A 99% confidence interval
- An observation period based on at least a year of historical data and updated at least once a quarter

Under the **internal models approach** (IMA), the **market risk charge** (MRC) is measured as follows:

$$\text{MRC}_t^{IMA} = \text{Max}\left(k\frac{1}{60}\sum_{i=1}^{60}\text{VAR}_{t-i}, \ \text{VAR}_{t-1}\right) + SRC_t \qquad (10.11)$$

which involves the average of the trading VAR over the last 60 days, times a supervisor-determined multiplier k (with a minimum value of 3), as well as yesterday's VAR, and a specific risk charge SRC.

The specific risk charge is designed to provide a buffer against losses due to idiosyncratic factors related to the individual issuer of the security. It includes the risk that an individual debt or equity moves by more or less than the general market, as well as event risk. Consider, for instance, a corporate bond issued by Ford Motor, a company with a credit rating of BBB. The market risk component should capture the effect of movements in yields for an index of BBB-rated corporate bonds. In contrast, SRC should capture the effect of credit downgrades for Ford. SRC can be computed from the VAR of subportfolios of debt and equity positions that contain specific risk.

The Basel Committee allows the 10-day VAR to be obtained from an extrapolation of 1-day VAR figures. Thus VAR is really

$$\text{VAR}_t(10, 99\%) = \sqrt{10} \times \text{VAR}_t(1, 99\%)$$

Presumably, the 10-day period corresponds to the time required for corrective action by bank regulators should an institution start to run into trouble. Presumably as well, the 99% confidence level corresponds to a low probability of bank failure due to market risk. Even so, one occurrence every 100 periods implies a high frequency of failure. There are $52/2 = 26$ two-week periods in one year. Thus, one failure should be expected to happen every $100/26 = 3.8$ years, which is still much too frequent.

This explains why the Basel Committee has applied a multiplier factor, $k \geq 3$, to guarantee further safety.

Example 10-4: FRM Exam 1997—Question 16

Which of the following quantitative standards is *not* required by the Amendment to the Capital Accord to Incorporate Market Risk?
a) Minimum holding period of 10 days
b) 99th percentile, one-tailed confidence interval
c) Minimum historical observation period of two years
d) Update of data sets at least quarterly

Example 10-5: FRM Exam 2002—Question 62

Specific risk capital charge is designed
a) To protect against credit risk related to the individual issuer of a security
b) To protect against a five–standard deviation adverse movement in the price of an individual security
c) To protect against an upward scenario shift in the price of an individual security owing to factors related to the individual issues
d) To protect against credit and liquidity risk related to the individual issuer of a security

---

10.4 Elements of VAR Systems

We now turn to the analysis of elements of a VAR system. As described in Figure 10-4, a VAR system combines the following steps:

1. From market data, construct the distribution of risk factors (e.g., normal, empirical, or other).

2. Collect the portfolio positions and map them to the risk factors.

3. Based on a VAR method (delta-normal, historical, Monte Carlo), construct the portfolio VAR. These methods will be explained in a subsequent chapter.

10.4.1 Portfolio Positions

We start with portfolio positions. The assumption is that all positions are constant over the horizon. This, of course, cannot be true in an environment where traders turn over their portfolio actively. Rather, it is a simplification.

FIGURE 10-4 Elements of a VAR System

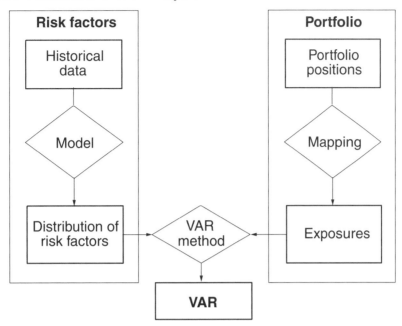

The true risk can be greater or lower than the VAR measure. It can be greater if VAR is based on close-to-close positions that reflect lower trader limits. If traders take more risks during the day, the true risk will be greater than indicated by VAR. Conversely, the true risk can be lower if management enforces loss limits, in other words, cuts down the risk that traders can take if losses develop.

10.4.2   Risk Factors

The **risk factors** represent a subset of all market variables that adequately span the risks of the current, or allowed, portfolio. There are literally tens of thousands of securities available, but a much more restricted set of useful risk factors.

The key is to choose market factors that are adequate for the portfolio. For a simple fixed-income portfolio, one bond market risk factor may be enough. In contrast, for a highly leveraged portfolio, multiple risk factors are needed. For an option portfolio, volatilities should be added as risk factors. In general, the more complex the strategies, the greater the number of risk factors that should be used.

10.4.3   VAR Methods

Similarly, the choice of the VAR method depends on the nature of the portfolio. A simple method may be sufficient for simple portfolios. For a fixed-income portfolio, a linear method may be adequate. In contrast, if the portfolio contains options, we need to include nonlinear effects. For simple, plain-vanilla options, we may be able to approximate their price behavior with a first and second derivative (delta and gamma). For more complex options, such as digital or barrier options, this may not be sufficient.

This is why risk management is as much an art as a science. Risk managers need to make reasonable approximations to come up with a cost-efficient measure of risk. They also need to be aware of the fact that traders could be induced to find "holes" in the risk management system.

A VAR system alone will not provide effective protection against market risk. It needs to be used in combination with limits on notionals and on exposures and, in addition, should be supplemented by stress tests.

Example 10-6: FRM Exam 1997—Question 23

The standard VAR calculation for extension to multiple periods also assumes that positions are fixed. If risk management enforces loss limits, the true VAR will be
a) The same
b) Greater than calculated
c) Less than calculated
d) Unable to be determined

Example 10-7: FRM Exam 1997—Question 9

A trading desk has limits only in outright foreign exchange and outright interest rate risk. Which of the following products cannot be traded within the current limit structure?
a) Vanilla interest rate swaps, bonds, and interest rate futures
b) Interest rate futures, vanilla interest rate swaps, and callable interest rate swaps
c) Repos and bonds
d) Foreign exchange swaps, and back-to-back exotic foreign exchange options

---

10.5   Stress Testing

As shown in the yen example in Figure 10-2, VAR does not purport to account for extreme losses. This is why VAR should be complemented by **stress testing**, which aims at identifying situations that could create extraordinary losses for the institution.

Stress testing is a key risk management process that includes (1) scenario analysis; (2) stressing models, volatilities, and correlations; and (3) policy response development. **Scenario analysis** submits the portfolio to large movements in financial market variables. These scenarios can be created using a number of methods.

■ *Moving key variables one at a time*, which is a simple and intuitive method. Unfortunately, it is difficult to assess realistic co-movements in financial variables. It is unlikely that all variables will move in the worst possible direction at the same time.

■ *Using historical scenarios*, for instance, the 1987 stock market crash, the devaluation of the British pound in 1992, the bond market debacle of 1984, and so on.

■ *Creating prospective scenarios*, for instance, working through the effects, direct and indirect, of a U.S. stock market crash. Ideally, the scenario should be tailored to the portfolio at hand, assessing the worst thing that could happen to current positions.

Stress testing is useful in guarding against **event risk**, which is the risk of loss due to an observable political or economic event. The problem (from the viewpoint of stress testing) is that such events are relatively rare and may be difficult to anticipate. They include

■ *Changes in government* leading to changes in economic policies

■ *Changes in economic policies*, such as default, capital controls, inconvertibility, changes in tax laws, expropriations, and so on

■ *Coups, civil wars, invasions*, or other signs of political instability

■ *Currency devaluations*, which are usually accompanied by other drastic changes in market variables

These risks often arise in **emerging markets**,[1] perhaps due to their lack of relative political stability. To guard against event risk, risk managers should construct prospective events and analyze their impact on portfolio values. However, this is not an easy matter. Recent events have demonstrated that markets seem to be systematically taken by surprise. Precious few seem to have anticipated the Russian default, for instance. The Argentinian default was also unique in many respects.

---

[1]The term *emerging stock market* was coined by the International Finance Corporation (IFC) in 1981. IFC defines an emerging stock market as one located in a developing country. Using the World Bank's definition, this includes all countries with a GNP per capita less than $8,625 in 1993.

Example: Turmoil in Argentina

Argentina is a good example of political risk in emerging markets. Up to 2001, the Argentine peso was fixed to the U.S. dollar at a one-to-one exchange rate. The government had promised to defend the currency at all costs. Argentina, however, suffered from the worst economic crisis in decades, compounded by the cost of excessive borrowing.

In December 2001, Argentina announced it would stop paying interest on its $135 billion foreign debt. This was the largest sovereign default recorded so far. Economy Minister Cavallo also announced sweeping restrictions on withdrawals from bank accounts to avoid capital flight. On December 20, President Fernando de la Rua resigned after 25 people died in street protests and rioting. President Duhalde took office on January 2 and devalued the currency on January 6. The exchange rate promptly moved from 1 peso to more than 3 pesos per dollar.

Such moves could have been factored into risk management systems by scenario analysis. What was totally unexpected, however, was the government's announcement that it would treat bank loans and deposits differentially. Dollar-denominated bank deposits were converted to devalued pesos, but dollar-denominated bank loans were converted to pesos at a one-to-one rate. This mismatch rendered much of the banking system technically insolvent, because loans (bank assets) overnight became less valuable than deposits (bank liabilities). Whereas risk managers had contemplated the market risk effect of a devaluation, few had considered the possibility of such political actions.

By 2005, the Argentinian government proposed to pay back about 30% of the face value of its debt. This recovery rate was very low by historical standards.

The goal of stress testing is to identify areas of potential vulnerability. This is not to say that the institution should be totally protected against every possible contingency, as this would make it impossible to take any risk. Rather, the objective of stress testing and management response should be to ensure that the institution can withstand likely scenarios without going bankrupt. Stress testing can be easily implemented once the VAR structure is in place. In Figure 10-4, all that is needed is to enter the scenario values into the risk factor inputs.

Example 10-8: FRM Exam 1998—Question 20

VAR measures should be supplemented by portfolio stress testing because

a) VAR measures indicate that the minimum loss will be the VAR; they don't indicate how large the losses can be.

b) Stress testing provides a precise maximum-loss level.

c) VAR measures are correct only 95% of the time.

d) Stress testing scenarios incorporate reasonably probable events.

Example 10-9: FRM Exam 2000—Question 105

Value-at-risk analysis should be complemented by stress testing because stress testing

a) Provides a maximum loss, expressed in dollars

b) Summarizes the expected loss over a target horizon within a minimum confidence interval

c) Assesses the behavior of portfolio at a 99% confidence level

d) Identifies losses that go beyond the normal losses measured by VAR

10.6 Liquidity Risk

Liquidity risk is usually viewed as a component of market risk. Lack of liquidity can cause the failure of an institution, even when it is technically solvent. We will see in the chapters on regulation that commercial banks have an inherent liquidity imbalance between their assets (long-term loans) and their liabilities (bank deposits) that provides a rationale for deposit insurance.

The problem with liquidity risk is that it is less amenable to formal analysis than traditional market risk. The industry is still struggling with the measurement of liquidity risk. Often, liquidity risk is loosely factored into VAR measures—for instance, by selectively increasing volatilities. These adjustments, however, are mainly ad hoc. Some useful lessons have been learned from the near failure of LTCM. These are discussed in a report by the Counterparty Risk Management Policy Group (CRMPG), which is described in a later chapter.

Liquidity risk consists of both asset liquidity risk and funding liquidity risk.

■ **Asset liquidity risk**, also called **market/product liquidity risk**, arises when transactions cannot be conducted at quoted market prices due to the size of the required trade relative to normal trading lots.

■ **Funding liquidity risk**, also called **cash-flow risk**, arises when the institution cannot meet payment obligations.

These two types of risk interact with each other if the portfolio contains illiquid assets that must be sold at distressed prices. Funding liquidity needs can be met from (1) sales of cash, (2) sales of other assets, and (3) borrowings.

Asset liquidity risk can be managed by setting limits on certain markets or products and by means of diversification. Funding liquidity risk can be managed by proper planning of cash-flow needs, by setting limits on cash-flow gaps, and by having a robust plan in place for raising fresh funds should the need arise.

Asset liquidity can be measured by a price-quantity function, which describes how the price is affected by the quantity transacted. Highly liquid assets, such as major currencies or Treasury bonds, are characterized by

■ **Tightness**, which is a measure of the divergence between actual transaction prices and quoted mid-market prices

■ **Depth**, which is a measure of the volume of trades that can be made without affecting prices too much (e.g., the bid/offer prices) and is in contrast to **thinness**

■ **Resiliency**, which is a measure of the speed at which price fluctuations from trades are dissipated

In contrast, illiquid markets are those where transactions can quickly affect prices. These include assets such as exotic OTC derivatives or emerging-market equities, which have low trading volumes. All else equal, illiquid assets are more affected by current demand and supply conditions and are usually more volatile than liquid assets.

Illiquidity is both asset-specific and marketwide. Large-scale changes in market liquidity seem to occur on a regular basis, most recently during the bond market rout of 1994 and the credit crisis of 1998. Such crises are characterized by a **flight to quality**, which occurs when there is a shift in demand away from low-grade securities toward high-grade securities. The low-grade market then becomes illiquid with depressed prices. This is reflected in an increase in the yield spread between corporate and government issues.

Even government securities can be affected differentially. The yield spread can widen between off-the-run securities and corresponding on-the-run securities. **On-the-run** securities are those issued most recently and hence are more active and liquid.

Other securities are called **off-the-run**. Consider, for instance, the latest-issued 30-year U.S. Treasury bond. This **benchmark** bond is called on-the-run until another 30-year bond is issued, at which time it becomes off-the-run. Because these securities are very similar in terms of market and credit risk, the yield spread is a measure of the **liquidity premium**.

Example 10-10: FRM Exam 2002—Question 36

The following statements compare a highly liquid asset against an (otherwise similar) illiquid asset. Which statement is most likely to be *false*?

a) It is possible to trade a larger quantity of the liquid asset without affecting the price.

b) The liquid asset has a smaller bid-ask spread.

c) The liquid asset has higher price volatility since it trades more often.

d) The liquid asset has higher trading volume.

Example 10-11: FRM Exam 1997—Question 54

"Illiquid" describes an instrument that

a) Does not trade in an active market

b) Does not trade on any exchange

c) Cannot be easily hedged

d) Is an over-the-counter (OTC) product

Example 10-12: FRM Exam 1998—Question 7

(*Requires some knowledge of markets*) Which of the following products has the least liquidity?

a) U.S. on-the-run Treasuries

b) U.S. off-the-run Treasuries

c) Floating-rate notes

d) High-grade corporate bonds

Example 10-13: FRM Exam 2000—Question 74

In a market crash, which of the following are usually *true*?

  I. Fixed-income portfolios hedged with short U.S. government bonds and futures lose less than those hedged with interest rate swaps given equivalent durations.

 II. Bid offer spreads widen because of lower liquidity.

III. The spreads between off-the-run bonds and benchmark issues widen.

a) I, II and III

b) II and III

c) I and III

d) None of the above

Example 10-14: FRM Exam 2000—Question 83

Which one of the following statements about liquidity risk in derivatives instruments is *not true*?

a) Liquidity risk is the risk that an institution may not be able to, or cannot easily, unwind or offset a particular position at or near the previous market price because of inadequate market depth or disruptions in the marketplace.

b) Liquidity risk is the risk that the institution will be unable to meet its payment obligations on settlement dates or in the event of margin calls.

c) Early termination agreements can adversely impact liquidity because an institution may be required to deliver collateral or settle a contract early, possibly at a time when the institution may face other funding and liquidity pressures.

d) An institution that participates in the exchange-traded derivatives markets has potential liquidity risks associated with the early termination of derivatives contracts.

10.7   Answers to Chapter Examples

Example 10-1: FRM Exam 1999—Question 89

c) There will be a loss worse than VAR in, on average, $n = 1\% \times 100 = 1$ day out of 100.

Example 10-2: FRM Exam 1998—Question 22

d) This is the correct answer given the "always" requirement and the fact that VAR is not always subadditive. Otherwise, b) is not a bad answer, but it requires some additional distributional assumptions.

Example 10-3: FRM Exam 1997—Question 7

b) The square root of 10 is 3.16.

Example 10-4: FRM Exam 1997—Question 16

c) The Capital Accord requires a minimum historical observation period of one year.

Example 10-5: FRM Exam 2002—Question 62

a) Specific risk capital is supposed to provide a cushion against idiosyncratic risk, such as a bond default or event risk, in the trading book. It does not cover liquidity risk, which is difficult to ascertain anyway.

Example 10-6: FRM Exam 1997—Question 23

c) Less than calculated. Loss limits cut down the positions as losses accumulate. This is similar to a long position in an option, where the delta increases as the price increases, and vice versa. Long positions in options have shortened left tails, and hence involve less risk than an unprotected position.

Example 10-7: FRM Exam 1997—Question 9

b) Callable interest rate swaps involve options, for which there is no limit. Also note that back-to-back options are perfectly hedged and have no market risk.

Example 10-8: FRM Exam 1998—Question 20

a) The goal of stress testing is to identify losses that go beyond the "normal" losses measured by VAR.

Example 10-9: FRM Exam 2000—Question 105

d) Stress testing identifies low-probability losses beyond the usual VAR measures. It does not, however, provide a maximum loss.

Example 10-10: FRM Exam 2002—Question 36

c) Compare two stocks. The liquid stock typically has higher trading volumes and lower bid-ask spreads, so b) and d) are true. It also has greater depth, meaning that large quantities can be traded without affecting prices too much, so a) is true. As a result, the remaining answer, c), must be wrong. There is no necessary relationship between trading activity and volatility.

Example 10-11: FRM Exam 1997—Question 54

a) Illiquid instruments are ones that do not trade actively. Answers b) and d) are not correct, as OTC products, which do not trade on exchanges, such as Treasuries, can be quite liquid. The lack of easy hedging alternatives does not imply that the instrument itself is illiquid.

Example 10-12: FRM Exam 1998—Question 7

c) Ranking these assets in decreasing order of asset liquidity, we have a), b), d), and c). Floating-rate notes are typically issued in smaller amounts and have customized payment schedules. As a result, they are typically less liquid than the other securities.

Example 10-13: FRM Exam 2000—Question 74

b) In a crash, bid offer spreads widen, as do liquidity spreads. Answer I is incorrect because Treasuries usually rally more than swaps, which leads to *greater* losses for a portfolio short Treasuries than swaps.

Example 10-14: FRM Exam 2000—Question 83

d) Answer a) refers to asset liquidity risk, answers b) and c) to funding liquidity risk. Answer d) is incorrect since exchange-traded derivatives are marked to market daily and hence can be terminated at any time without additional cash-flow needs.

Appendix: Desirable Properties for Risk Measures

The purpose of a risk measure is to summarize the entire distribution of dollar returns X by one number, $\rho(X)$. Artzner et al. (1999) list four desirable properties of risk measures for capital adequacy purposes.[2]

■ **Monotonicity:** If $X_1 \leq X_2, \rho(X_1) \geq \rho(X_2)$.

  In other words, if a portfolio has systematically lower values than another (in each state of the world), it must have greater risk.

■ **Translation Invariance:** $\rho(X + k) = \rho(X) - k$.

  In other words, adding cash k to a portfolio should reduce its risk by k. This reduces the lowest portfolio value. As with X, k is measured in dollars.

■ **Homogeneity:** $\rho(bX) = b\rho(X)$.

  In other words, increasing the size of a portfolio by a factor b should scale its risk measure by the same factor b. This property applies to the standard deviation.[3]

■ **Subadditivity:** $\rho(X_1 + X_2) \leq \rho(X_1) + \rho(X_2)$.

  In other words, the risk of a portfolio must be less than the sum of separate risks. Merging portfolios cannot increase risk.

The usefulness of these criteria is that they force us to think about ideal properties and, more important, potential problems with simplified risk measures. Indeed, Artzner et al. show that the quantile-based VAR measure fails to satisfy the last property. They give some pathological examples of positions that combine to create portfo-

---

[2]See Artzner, P., F. Delbaen, J.-M. Eber, and D. Heath (1999), Coherent Measures of Risk, *Mathematical Finance* 9 (July), 203–228.

[3]This assumption, however, may be questionable in the case of huge portfolios that could not be liquidated without substantial market impact. Thus, it ignores liquidity risk.

lios with larger VAR. They also show that the conditional VAR, $E[-X \mid X \leq -\text{VAR}]$, satisfies all these desirable coherence properties.

Assuming a normal distribution, however, the standard deviation–based VAR satisfies the subadditivity property. This is because the volatility of a portfolio is less than the sum of volatilities: $\sigma(X_1 + X_2) \leq \sigma(X_1) + \sigma(X_2)$. We only have a strict equality when the correlation is perfect (positive for long positions). More generally, this property holds for **elliptical distributions**, for which contours of equal density are ellipsoids.

Example: Why VAR is not necessarily subadditive

Consider a trader with an investment in a corporate bond with face value of $100,000 and default probability of 0.5%. Over the next period, we can either have no default, with a return of zero, or default with a loss of $100,000. The payoffs are thus −$100,000 with probability of 0.5% and +$0 with probability 99.5%. Since the probability of getting $0 is greater than 99%, the VAR at the 99% confidence level is $0, without taking the mean into account. This is consistent with the definition of VAR as the smallest loss such that the right-tail probability is at least 99%.

Now consider a portfolio invested in three bonds (A, B, C) with the same characteristics and independent payoffs. The VAR numbers add up to $\sum_i \text{VAR}_i = \$0$. To compute the portfolio VAR, we tabulate the payoffs and probabilities:

State	Bonds	Probability	Payoff
No default		$0.995 \times 0.995 \times 0.995 = 0.9850749$	$0
1 default	A, B, C	$3 \times 0.005 \times 0.995 \times 0.995 = 0.0148504$	−$100,000
2 defaults	AB, AC, BC	$3 \times 0.005 \times 0.005 \times 0.995 = 0.0000746$	−$200,000
3 defaults	ABC	$0.005 \times 0.005 \times 0.005 = 0.0000001$	−$300,000

Here the probability of zero or one default is $0.9851 + 0.0148 = 99.99\%$. The portfolio VAR is therefore $100,000, which is the lowest number such that the probability exceeds 99%. Thus the portfolio VAR is greater than the sum of individual VARs. In this example, VAR is not subadditive. This is an undesirable property because it creates disincentives to aggregate the portfolio, since it appears to have higher risk.

Admittedly, this example is a bit contrived. Nevertheless, it illustrates the danger of focusing on VAR as a sole measure of risk. The portfolio may be structured to display a low VAR. When a loss occurs, however, this may be a huge loss. This is an issue with asymmetrical positions, such as short positions in options or undiversified portfolios exposed to credit risk.

Chapter 11

Sources of Market Risk

We now turn to a systematic analysis of the major financial market risk factors. Section 11.1 presents a general overview of financial market risks. Downside risk can be decomposed into two types of drivers, exposures and risk factors. This decomposition is useful because it separates risk into a component over which the risk manager has control (exposure) and another component that is exogenous (the risk factors). We illustrate this decomposition in the context of a simple asset, a fixed-coupon bond.

The next four sections then turn to the major categories of market risk. Currency, fixed-income, equity, and commodities risk are analyzed in Sections 11.2, 11.3, 11.4, and 11.5, respectively. Currency risk refers to the volatility of floating exchange rates and devaluation risk, for fixed currencies. Fixed-income risk relates to term structure risk, global interest rate risk, real yield risk, credit spread risk, and prepayment risk. Equity risk can be described in terms of country risk, industry risk, and stock-specific risk. Commodity risk includes volatility risk, convenience yield risk, and delivery and liquidity risk. This chapter focuses primarily on volatility and correlation measures as drivers of risk. Also important is the shape of the distribution, however.

Finally, Section 11.6 discusses simplifications in risk models. We explain how the multitude of risk factors can be summarized into a few essential drivers. Such factor models include the diagonal model, which decomposes returns into a marketwide factor and residual risk.

11.1 Sources of Loss: A Decomposition

To examine sources of losses, consider a plain fixed-coupon bond. The potential for loss can be decomposed into the effect of dollar *duration* D^*P and the changes in the yield dy. The bond's value change is given by

$$dP = -(D^*P) \times dy \qquad (11.1)$$

This illustrates the general principle that losses can occur because of a combination of two factors:

- The exposure to the factor, or dollar duration (a choice variable)

- The movement in the factor itself (which is external to the portfolio)

This linear characterization also applies to *systematic risk* and option *delta*. We can, for instance, decompose the return on stock i, R_i, into a component due to the market R_M and some residual risk, which we ignore for now because its effect washes out in a large portfolio:

$$R_i = \alpha_i + \beta_i \times R_M + \epsilon_i \approx \beta_i \times R_M \qquad (11.2)$$

We ignore the constant α_i because it does not contribute to risk, as well as the residual ϵ_i, which is diversified. **Specific risk** can be defined as risk that is due to issuer-specific price movements, after accounting for general market factors.

Note that R_i is expressed here in terms of **rate of return** and, hence, has no dimension. To get a change in a dollar price, we write

$$dP_i = R_i P_i \approx (\beta P_i) \times R_M \qquad (11.3)$$

Similarly, the change in the value of a derivative f can be expressed in terms of the change in the price of the underlying asset S,

$$df = \Delta \times dS \qquad (11.4)$$

To avoid confusion, we use the conventional notations of Δ for the first partial derivative of the option. Changes are expressed in infinitesimal amounts df and dS.

Equations (11.1), (11.2), and (11.4) all reveal that the change in value is linked to an **exposure** coefficient and a change in market variable:

Market loss = Exposure × Adverse movement in financial variable

To have a loss, we need to have some exposure *and* an unfavorable move in the risk factor. This decomposition is also useful to understand the drivers of discontinuities in the portfolio value. These can come from either discontinuous payoffs or from jumps in the risk factors. Discontinuous payoffs arise with some instruments, such as binary options, that pay a fixed amount if the option ends up in the money and nothing otherwise. Discontinuities can also arise if there are jumps in the risk factors, such as the 1987 stock market crash, or as a result of event risk.

Example 11-1: FRM Exam 1997—Question 16

The risk of a stock or bond that is *not* correlated with the market (and thus can be diversified) is known as

a) Interest rate risk

b) FX risk

c) Model risk

d) Specific risk

11.2 Currency Risk

Currency risk arises from potential movements in the value of foreign currencies. This includes currency-specific volatility, correlations across currencies, and devaluation risk. Currency risk arises in the following environments.

- In a *pure currency float*, the external value of a currency is free to move, to depreciate or appreciate, as pushed by market forces. An example is the dollar/euro exchange rate.

- In a *fixed currency system*, a currency's external value is fixed (or pegged) to another currency. An example is the Hong Kong dollar, which is fixed against the U.S. dollar. This does not mean there is no risk, however, due to possible readjustments in the **parity value**, called devaluations or revaluations.

- In a *change in currency regime*, a currency that was previously fixed becomes flexible, or vice versa. For instance, the Argentinian peso was fixed against the dollar until 2001, and floated thereafter. Changes in regime can also lower currency risk, as in the recent case of the euro.[1]

---

[1] As of 2005, the Eurozone includes a block of 12 countries, Austria, Belgium/Luxembourg, Finland, France, Germany, Ireland, Italy, the Netherlands, Portugal, and Spain. Greece joined on January 1, 2001. Currency risk has not been totally eliminated, however, as there is always a possibility that the currency union could dissolve.

11.2.1 Currency Volatility

Table 11-1 compares the RiskMetrics volatility forecasts for a group of 21 currencies.[2] Ten of these correspond to "industrial countries," the others to "emerging" markets.

TABLE 11-1 Currency Volatility against U.S. Dollar (Percent)

Country	Currency Code	End 2002			End 1996
		Daily	Monthly	Annual	Annual
Argentina	ARS	0.663	3.746	12.98	0.42
Australia	AUD	0.405	2.310	8.00	8.50
Canada	CAD	0.403	1.863	6.45	3.60
Switzerland	CHF	0.495	2.664	9.23	10.16
Denmark	DKK	0.421	2.275	7.88	7.78
Britain	GBP	0.398	2.165	7.50	9.14
Hong Kong	HKD	0.004	0.016	0.05	0.26
Indonesia	IDR	0.356	2.344	8.12	1.61
Japan	JPY	0.613	3.051	10.57	6.63
Korea	KRW	0.434	2.279	7.89	4.49
Mexico	MXN	0.511	2.615	9.06	6.94
Malaysia	MYR	0.000	0.001	0.01	1.60
Norway	NOK	0.477	2.608	9.03	7.60
New Zealand	NZD	0.631	3.140	10.88	7.89
Philippines	PHP	0.303	1.423	4.93	0.57
Sweden	SEK	0.431	2.366	8.20	6.38
Singapore	SGD	0.230	1.304	4.52	1.79
Thailand	THB	0.286	1.544	5.35	1.23
Taiwan	TWD	0.166	0.981	3.40	0.94
South Africa	ZAR	1.050	4.915	17.03	8.37
Euro	EUR	0.422	2.284	7.91	8.26

These numbers are standard deviations, adapted from value-at-risk (VAR) forecasts at the 95% confidence level divided by 1.645. The table reports daily, monthly, and annualized standard deviations at the end of 2002 and 1996. Annual volatilities are obtained from monthly volatilities multiplied by the square root of 12.

Across developed markets, volatility typically ranges from 6% to 11% per annum. The Canadian dollar is notably lower at 4% to 6% volatility. Some currencies, such as the Hong Kong dollar, have very low volatility, reflecting their pegging to the U.S. dollar. This does not mean that they have low risk, however. They are subject to **devaluation risk**, which is the risk that the currency peg could fail. This has happened

---

[2]For updates, see www.riskmetrics.com.

to Thailand and Indonesia, which in 1996 had low volatility but converted to a floating exchange rate regime, with much higher volatility in the latter period.

The typical impact of a currency devaluation is illustrated in Figure 11-1. Each currency has been scaled to a unit value at the end of the month just before the devaluation. In previous months, we observe only small variations in exchange rates. In contrast, the devaluation itself leads to a dramatic drop in value ranging from 20% to an extreme of 80% in the case of the rupiah.

Currency risk is also related to other financial risks, in particular interest rate risk. Often, interest rates are raised in an effort to stem the depreciation of a currency, resulting in a positive correlation between the currency and the bond market. These interactions should be taken into account in designing scenarios for stress tests.

FIGURE 11-1 Effect of Currency Devaluation

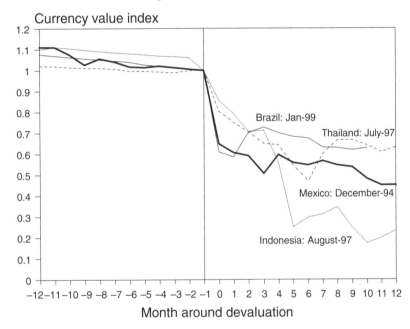

11.2.2   Correlations

Next we briefly describe the correlations between these currencies against the U.S. dollar. Generally, correlations are low, mostly in the range of −0.10 to 0.20. This indicates substantial benefits from holding a well-diversified currency portfolio.

There are, however, blocks of currencies with very high correlations. European currencies, such as the DKK, SEK, NOK, and CHF, have high correlations with each other and the euro, on the order of 0.90. The GBP also has high correlations with

European currencies, around 0.60–0.70. As a result, investing across European currencies does little to diversify risk, from the viewpoint of a U.S. dollar–based investor.

11.2.3 Cross-Rate Volatility

Exchange rates are expressed relative to a base currency, usually the dollar. The **cross rate** is the exchange rate between two currencies other than the reference currency. For instance, say S_1 represents the dollar/pound rate and that S_2 represents the dollar/euro (EUR) rate. Then the euro/pound rate is given by the ratio

$$S_3(\text{EUR}/\text{BP}) = \frac{S_1(\$/\text{BP})}{S_2(\$/\text{EUR})} \tag{11.5}$$

Using logs, we can write

$$\ln[S_3] = \ln[S_1] - \ln[S_2] \tag{11.6}$$

The volatility of the cross rate is

$$\sigma_3^2 = \sigma_1^2 + \sigma_2^2 - 2\rho_{12}\sigma_1\sigma_2 \tag{11.7}$$

Alternatively, this shows that we could infer the correlation coefficient ρ_{12} from the triplet of variances. Note that this assumes that both the numerator and denominator are in the same currency. Otherwise, the log of the cross rate is the sum of the logs, and the negative sign in Equation (11.7) must be changed to a positive sign.

Example 11-2: FRM Exam 1997—Question 10

Which currency pair would you expect to have the lowest volatility?
a) USD/EUR
b) USD/CAD
c) USD/JPY
d) USD/MXN

Example 11-3: FRM Exam 1997—Question 14

What is the implied correlation between JPY/EUR and EUR/USD given the following volatilities for foreign exchange rates?
JPY/USD at 8%
JPY/EUR at 10%
EUR/USD at 6%
a) 60%
b) 30%
c) −30%
d) −60%

11.3   Fixed-Income Risk

Fixed-income risk arises from potential movements in the level and volatility of bond yields. Figure 11-2 plots the U.S. Treasury yield curve at monthly intervals since 1986. The lower right scale shows maturities ranging from three months to 10 years. The graph demonstrates that yield curves move in complicated fashion. For the risk manager, this will create **yield curve risk** for fixed-income portfolios.

FIGURE 11-2 Movements in the U.S. Yield Curve

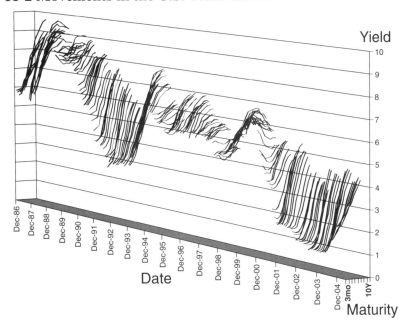

11.3.1   Factors Affecting Yields

Movements in yields reflect economic fundamentals. The primary determinant of movements in interest rates is **inflationary expectations**. Any perceived increase in the forecast rate of inflation will make bonds with fixed nominal coupons less attractive, thereby increasing their yield.

Figure 11-3 compares the level of short-term U.S. interest rates with the concurrent level of inflation. The graphs show that most of the movements in nominal rates can be explained by inflation. In more recent years, however, inflation has been subdued. Rates have fallen accordingly.

The **real interest rate** is defined as the nominal rate minus the rate of inflation over the same period. This is generally positive but in recent years has been negative as the Federal Reserve has kept nominal rates to very low levels in order to stimulate economic activity.

FIGURE 11-3 Inflation and Interest Rates

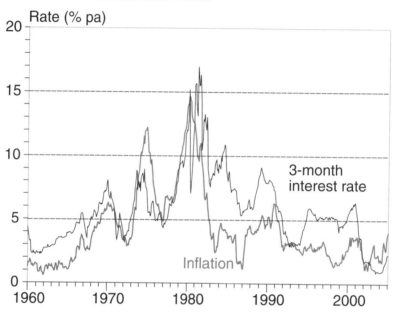

These figures display complex movements in the term structure of interest rates. It would be convenient if these movements could be summarized by a small number of variables. In practice, market observers focus on a long-term rate (say the yield on the 10-year note) and a short-term rate (say the yield on a three-month bill). These two rates usefully summarize movements in the term structure, which are displayed in Figure 11-4. Shaded areas indicate periods of U.S. economic recession.

Generally, the two rates move in tandem, although the short-term rate displays more variability. The **term spread** is defined as the difference between the long rate and the short rate. Figure 11-5 relates the term spread to economic activity. As the graph shows, periods of recession usually witness an increase in the term spread. Slow economic activity decreases the demand for capital, which in turn decreases short-term rates and increases the term spread.

FIGURE 11-4 Movements in the Term Structure

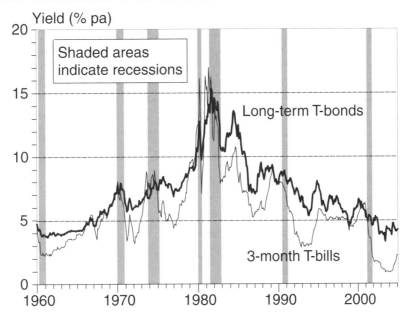

FIGURE 11-5 Term Structure Spread

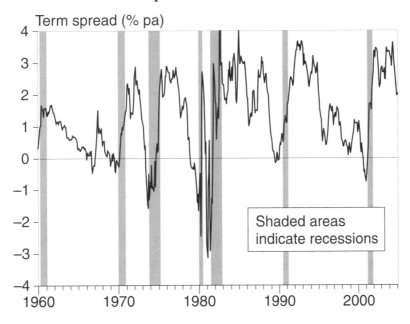

11.3.2   Bond Price and Yield Volatility

Table 11-2 compares the RiskMetrics volatility forecasts for U.S. bond prices as of 2002 and 1996. The table includes Eurodeposits, fixed swap rates, and zero-coupon Treasury rates, for maturities ranging from 30 days to 30 years.

TABLE 11-2 U.S. Fixed-Income Price Volatility (Percent)

Type/ Maturity	Code	Yield Level	End 2002			End 1996
			Daily	Mty	Annual	Annual
Euro-30d	R030	1.360	0.002	0.012	0.04	0.05
Euro-90d	R090	1.353	0.005	0.030	0.10	0.08
Euro-180d	R180	1.348	0.009	0.064	0.22	0.19
Euro-360d	R360	1.429	0.030	0.188	0.65	0.58
Swap-2Y	S02	1.895	0.110	0.634	2.20	1.57
Swap-3Y	S03	2.428	0.184	1.027	3.56	2.59
Swap-4Y	S04	2.865	0.257	1.429	4.95	3.59
Swap-5Y	S05	3.224	0.329	1.836	6.36	4.70
Swap-7Y	S07	3.815	0.454	2.535	8.78	6.69
Swap-10Y	S10	4.434	0.643	3.613	12.52	9.82
Zero-2Y	Z02	1.593	0.107	0.631	2.18	1.64
Zero-3Y	Z03	1.980	0.172	0.999	3.46	2.64
Zero-4Y	Z04	2.372	0.248	1.428	4.95	3.69
Zero-5Y	Z05	2.773	0.339	1.935	6.70	4.67
Zero-7Y	Z07	3.238	0.458	2.603	9.02	6.81
Zero-9Y	Z09	3.752	0.576	3.259	11.29	8.64
Zero-10Y	Z10	3.989	0.637	3.600	12.47	9.31
Zero-15Y	Z15	4.247	0.894	5.018	17.38	13.82
Zero-20Y	Z20	4.565	1.132	6.292	21.80	17.48
Zero-30Y	Z30	5.450	1.692	9.170	31.77	23.53

Risk can be measured as either return volatility or yield volatility. Using the duration approximation, the volatility of the rate of return in the bond price is

$$\sigma\left(\frac{dP}{P}\right) = |D^*| \times \sigma(dy) \qquad (11.8)$$

Table 11.2 shows that short-term deposits have very little price risk, as expected, due to their short maturity and duration. The price risk of 10-year bonds is around 10% annually, which is similar to that of floating currencies. The risk of 30-year bonds is higher, at 20% to 30%, which is similar to that of equities.

Instead of measuring price volatilities, it is more intuitive to consider yield volatilities, $\sigma(dy)$. These are displayed in Table 11-3. Yield volatility is relatively stable across maturities, around 1% per annum for swaps and zeros, and 0.5% for Eurodeposits.

TABLE 11-3 U.S. Fixed-Income Yield Volatility, 2002 (Percent)

Type/ Maturity	Code	Yield Level	$\sigma(dy)$ Daily	$\sigma(dy)$ Mty	$\sigma(dy)$ Annual
Euro-30d	R030	1.360	0.021	0.130	0.45
Euro-90d	R090	1.353	0.017	0.106	0.37
Euro-180d	R180	1.348	0.017	0.112	0.39
Euro-360d	R360	1.429	0.027	0.160	0.55
Swap-2Y	S02	1.895	0.048	0.265	0.92
Swap-3Y	S03	2.428	0.055	0.297	1.03
Swap-4Y	S04	2.865	0.059	0.320	1.11
Swap-5Y	S05	3.224	0.061	0.334	1.16
Swap-7Y	S07	3.815	0.062	0.339	1.17
Swap-10Y	S10	4.434	0.062	0.347	1.20
Zero-2Y	Z02	1.593	0.046	0.264	0.91
Zero-3Y	Z03	1.980	0.051	0.291	1.01
Zero-4Y	Z04	2.372	0.057	0.321	1.11
Zero-5Y	Z05	2.773	0.063	0.356	1.23
Zero-7Y	Z07	3.238	0.062	0.351	1.21
Zero-9Y	Z09	3.752	0.062	0.349	1.21
Zero-10Y	Z10	3.989	0.062	0.350	1.21
Zero-15Y	Z15	4.247	0.058	0.327	1.13
Zero-20Y	Z20	4.565	0.056	0.309	1.07
Zero-30Y	Z30	5.450	0.057	0.305	1.06

Example 11-4: FRM Exam 1999—Question 86

For purposes of computing the market risk of a U.S. Treasury bond portfolio, it is easiest to measure

a) Yield volatility because yields have positive skewness

b) Price volatility because bond prices are positively correlated

c) Yield volatility for bonds sold at a discount and price volatility for bonds sold at a premium to par

d) Yield volatility because it remains more constant over time than price volatility, which must approach zero as the bond approaches maturity

---

Example 11-5: FRM Exam 2002—Question 31

Consider the following single bond position of $10 million, a modified duration of 3.6 years, and an annualized yield volatility of 2%. Using the duration method and assuming that the daily return on the bond position is independently identically normally distributed, calculate the 10-day holding period VAR of the position with a 99% confidence interval assuming there are 252 business days in a year.

a) $409,339
b) $396,742
c) $345,297
d) $334,186

11.3.3 Correlations

Table 11-4 displays correlation coefficients for all maturity pairs at a one-day horizon. Correlations are generally very high, suggesting that yields are affected by a common factor.

If the yield curve were to move in strict parallel fashion, all correlations should be equal to 1. In practice, the yield curve displays more complex patterns but still obeys some smoothness conditions. This implies that movements in adjoining maturities are highly correlated. For instance, the correlation between the 9-year zero and 10-year zero is 0.997, which is very high. Correlations are the lowest for maturities further apart, for instance 0.601 between the 2-year zero and 30-year zero.

TABLE 11-4 U.S. Fixed-Income Price Correlations, 2002 (Daily)

	Z02	Z03	Z04	Z05	Z07	Z09	Z10	Z15	Z20	Z30
Z02	1.000									
Z03	0.992	1.000								
Z04	0.972	0.994	1.000							
Z05	0.943	0.977	0.995	1.000						
Z07	0.933	0.969	0.988	0.995	1.000					
Z09	0.912	0.949	0.970	0.979	0.994	1.000				
Z10	0.890	0.928	0.950	0.959	0.982	0.997	1.000			
Z15	0.863	0.906	0.933	0.946	0.973	0.991	0.996	1.000		
Z20	0.817	0.865	0.898	0.916	0.948	0.971	0.980	0.994	1.000	
Z30	0.601	0.663	0.709	0.743	0.789	0.827	0.848	0.889	0.935	1.000

These high correlations give risk managers an opportunity to simplify the number of risk factors they have to deal with. Suppose, for instance, that the portfolio consists of global bonds in 17 different currencies. Initially, the risk manager decides to keep 14 risk factors in each market. This leads to a very large number of correlations within but also across all markets. With 17 currencies and 14 maturities, the total number of risk factors is $N = 17 \times 14 = 238$. The correlation matrix has $N \times (N - 1) = 238 \times 237 = 56,406$ elements off the diagonal. Surely some of this information is superfluous.

The matrix in Table 11-4 can be simplified using principal components. **Principal components** is a statistical technique that extracts linear combinations of the original variables that explain the highest proportion of diagonal components of the matrix. For this matrix, the first principal component explains 94% of the total variance and has similar weights on all maturities. Hence, it could be called a **level risk factor**. The second principal component explains 4% of the total variance. As it is associated with opposite positions on short and long maturities, it could be called a **slope risk factor** (or twist). Sometimes a third factor is found that represents a **curvature risk factor** or a **bend risk factor** (also called a butterfly).

Previous research has indeed found that, in the United States and other fixed-income markets, movements in yields could be usefully summarized by two to three factors that typically explain over 95% of the total variance.

Example 11-6: FRM Exam 2000—Question 96

Which one of the following statements about the historical U.S. Treasury yield curve changes is *true*?

a) Changes in long-term yields tend to be larger than changes in short-term yields.

b) Changes in long-term yields tend to be of approximately the same size as changes in short-term yields.

c) The same size yield change in both long-term and short-term rates tends to produce a larger price change in short-term instruments when all securities are trading near par.

d) The largest part of total return variability of spot rates is due to parallel changes, with a smaller portion due to slope changes and the residual due to curvature changes.

11.3.4   Global Interest Rate Risk

Different fixed-income markets are exposed to their own sources of risk. The Japanese government bond market, for example, is exposed to yen interest rates. Yet in all markets, we observe similar patterns. To illustrate, Table 11-5 shows price and yield volatilities for 17 different fixed-income markets, focusing only on 10-year zeros.

The level of yields falls within a remarkably narrow range, 4% to 6%. This reflects the fact that yields are primarily driven by **inflationary expectations**, which have become similar across all these markets. Indeed, central banks across all these countries have proved their common determination to keep inflation in check. Two notable exceptions are South Africa, where yields are at 10.7%, and Japan, where yields are at 0.9%. These two countries are experiencing much higher and lower inflation, respectively, than the rest of the group.

TABLE 11-5 Global Fixed-Income Volatility, 2002 (Percent)

Country	Code	Yield Level	Price Vol. Daily	Price Vol. Mty	Price Vol. Annual	Yield Vol. $\sigma(dy)$ Daily	Yield Vol. $\sigma(dy)$ Mty	Yield Vol. $\sigma(dy)$ Annual
Austrl.	AUD	5.236	0.676	3.660	12.68	0.066	0.353	1.22
Belgium	BEF	4.453	0.352	1.995	6.91	0.035	0.196	0.68
Canada	CAD	4.950	0.426	2.438	8.45	0.042	0.237	0.82
Germany	DEM	4.306	0.349	1.967	6.81	0.035	0.194	0.67
Denmark	DKK	4.563	0.307	1.765	6.12	0.031	0.174	0.60
Spain	ESP	4.399	0.359	2.024	7.01	0.036	0.198	0.69
France	FRF	4.383	0.351	1.952	6.76	0.035	0.192	0.67
Britain	GBP	4.415	0.333	1.848	6.40	0.033	0.181	0.63
Ireland	IEP	4.456	0.353	1.950	6.75	0.035	0.191	0.66
Italy	ITL	4.582	0.348	1.999	6.93	0.034	0.194	0.67
Japan	JPY	0.918	0.171	1.153	3.99	0.015	0.096	0.33
Nether.	NLG	4.335	0.356	1.985	6.88	0.035	0.194	0.67
New Zl.	NZD	6.148	0.477	2.741	9.49	0.047	0.272	0.94
Sweden	SEK	4.812	0.361	2.055	7.12	0.036	0.204	0.71
U.S.	USD	3.989	0.637	3.600	12.47	0.062	0.350	1.21
S.Afr.	ZAR	10.650	0.535	3.358	11.63	0.055	0.337	1.17
Euro	EUR	4.306	0.352	1.978	6.85	0.035	0.195	0.68

The table also shows that most countries have an annual volatility of yield changes around 0.6% to 1.2%. Again, Japan is an exception, which suggests that the volatility of yields is not independent of the level of yields.

In fact, we would expect this volatility to decrease as yields drop toward zero and to be higher when yields are higher. This can be modeled by relating the volatility of yield changes to a function of the yield level, as explained in Chapter 4. One such function is the Cox, Ingersoll, and Ross (1985) model, which posits that movements in yields should be proportional to the square root of the yield level:

$$\sigma\left(\frac{\Delta y}{\sqrt{y}}\right) = \text{Constant} \qquad (11.9)$$

Thus neither the normal nor the lognormal model is totally appropriate.

Finally, correlations are very high across continental European bond markets that are part of the euro. For example, the correlation between French and German bonds is above 0.975. These markets are now moving in synchronization, as monetary policy is dictated by the **European Central Bank** (ECB). Eurozone bonds differ only in terms of credit risk.

11.3.5 Real Yield Risk

So far, the analysis has considered only **nominal interest rate risk**, as most bonds represent obligations in nominal terms (i.e., in dollars for the coupon and principal payment). Recently, however, many countries have issued inflation-protected bonds, which make payments that are fixed in real terms but indexed to the rate of inflation.

In this case, the source of risk is **real interest rate risk**. This real yield can be viewed as the internal rate of return that will make the discounted value of promised real bond payments equal to the current real price. This is a new source of risk, as movements in real interest rates may not correlate perfectly with movements in nominal yields.

Example: Real and nominal yields

Consider, for example, the 10-year Treasury Inflation Protected (TIP) note paying a 3% coupon in real terms. The actual coupon and principal payments are indexed to increases in the Consumer Price Index (CPI).

The TIP is now trading at a clean real price of 108–23+. Discounting the coupon payments and the principal gives a real yield of $r = 1.98\%$. Note that since the bond is trading at a premium, the real yield must be lower than the coupon.

Projecting the rate of inflation at $\pi = 2\%$, semiannually compounded, we infer the projected nominal yield as $(1 + y/200) = (1 + r/200)(1 + \pi/200)$, which gives 4.00%. This is the same order of magnitude as the current nominal yield on the 10-year Treasury note, which is 3.95%. The two bonds have a very different risk profile, however. If the rate of inflation moves to 5%, payments on the TIP will grow at 5% plus 2%, while the coupon on the regular note will stay fixed.

Example 11-7: FRM Exam 1997—Question 42

What is the relationship between yield on the current inflation-proof bond issued by the U.S. Treasury and a standard Treasury bond with similar terms?

a) The yields should be about the same.

b) The yield of the inflation-proof bond should approximately equal the yield on the Treasury minus the real interest.

c) The yield of the inflation-proof bond should approximately equal the yield on the Treasury plus the real interest.

d) None of the above is correct.

11.3.6 Credit Spread Risk

Credit spread risk is the risk that yields on duration-matched credit-sensitive bonds and Treasury bonds could move differently. Credit risk will be analyzed in more detail in the section of the book devoted to that topic. Suffice to say that the credit spread represents a compensation for the loss due to default, plus perhaps a risk premium that reflects investor risk aversion.

A position in a credit spread can be established by investing in credit-sensitive bonds, such as corporates, agencies, and mortgage-backed securities (MBSs), and shorting Treasuries with the appropriate duration. This type of position benefits from a stable or shrinking credit spread, but loses from a widening of spreads. Because credit spreads cannot turn negative, their distribution is asymmetric, however. When spreads are tight, large moves imply increases in spreads rather than decreases. Thus positions in credit spreads can be exposed to large losses.

Figure 11-6 displays the time series of credit spreads since 1960. The graph shows that credit spreads display cyclical patterns, increasing during a recession and decreasing during economic expansions. Greater spreads during recessions reflect the greater number of defaults during difficult times.

11.3.7 Prepayment Risk

Prepayment risk arises in the context of home mortgages when there is uncertainty about whether the homeowner will refinance his or her loan early. It is a prominent feature of **mortgage-backed securities**, where the investor has granted the borrower an option to repay the debt early.

FIGURE 11-6 Credit Spreads

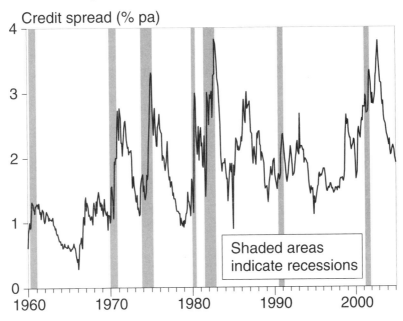

This option, however, is much more complex than an ordinary option, due to the multiplicity of factors involved. We saw in Chapter 7 that it depends on the age of the loan (seasoning), the current level of interest rates, the previous path of interest rates (burnout), economic activity, and seasonal patterns. Assuming that the prepayment model adequately captures all these features, investors can evaluate the attractiveness of MBSs by calculating their **option-adjusted spread** (OAS). This represents the spread over the equivalent Treasury minus the cost of the option component.

Example 11-8: FRM Exam 2002—Question 128

During 2002, an Argentinean pension fund with 80% of its assets in dollar-denominated debt lost more than 40% of its value. Which of the following reasons could explain all of the 40% loss?

a) The assets were invested in a diversified portfolio of AAA firms in the United States.

b) The assets invested in local currency in Argentina lost all their value, and the value of the dollar-denominated assets stayed constant.

c) The dollar-denominated assets were invested in U.S. Treasury debt, but the fund had bought credit protection on sovereign debt from Argentina.

d) The fund had invested 80% of its funds in dollar-denominated sovereign debt from Argentina.

Example 11-9: FRM Exam 1999—Question 71

An investor holds mortgage interest-only strips (IO) backed by a Fannie Mae 7% coupon. She wants to hedge this position by shorting Treasury interest strips off the 10-year on-the-run. The curve steepens as the one-month rate drops, while the six-month to 10-year rates remain stable. What will be the effect on the value of this portfolio?

a) Both the IO and the hedge will appreciate in value.

b) The IO and the hedge value will be almost unchanged (a very small appreciation is possible).

c) The change in value of both the IO and hedge cannot be determined without additional details.

d) The IO will depreciate, but the hedge will appreciate.

11.4 Equity Risk

Equity risk arises from potential movements in the value of stock prices. We will show that we can usefully decompose the total risk into marketwide risk and stock-specific risk.

11.4.1 Stock Market Volatility

Table 11-6 compares the RiskMetrics volatility forecasts for a group of 31 stock markets. The selected indices are those most recognized in each market—for example, the S&P 500 in the United States, Nikkei 225 in Japan, and FTSE-100 in Britain. Most of these have an associated futures contract, so positions can be taken or hedged in futures. Nearly all of these indices are weighted by market capitalization, although there is now a trend toward weighting by **market float**, which is the market value of freely traded shares. For some companies, a large fraction of outstanding shares may be kept by strategic investors (company management or a government, for example).

We immediately note that risk is much greater than for currencies, typically ranging from 12% to 40%. Markets that are less diversified or are exposed to greater fluctuations in economic fundamentals are more volatile. **Concentration** refers to the proportion of the index due to the biggest stocks. In Finland, for instance, half of the index represents one firm only, Nokia. This lack of diversification creates more volatility in the index.

TABLE 11-6 Equity Volatility (Percent)

Stock Market Country	Code	End 2002			End 1996
		Daily	Monthly	Annual	Annual
Argentina	ARS	1.921	10.06	34.8	22.1
Austria	ATS	0.771	4.17	14.4	11.7
Australia	AUD	0.662	3.58	12.4	13.4
Belgium	BEF	1.453	8.41	29.1	9.3
Canada	CAD	0.841	5.09	17.6	13.8
Switzerland	CHF	1.401	8.34	28.9	11.1
Germany	DEM	2.576	13.89	48.1	18.6
Denmark	DKK	1.062	6.77	23.5	12.5
Spain	ESP	1.497	8.81	30.5	15.0
Finland	FIM	1.790	10.65	36.9	14.5
France	FRF	1.691	10.59	36.7	16.1
Britain	GBP	1.498	8.41	29.1	11.1
Hong Kong	HKD	1.007	5.57	19.3	17.3
Indonesia	IDR	1.218	7.45	25.8	14.4
Ireland	IEP	1.081	6.53	22.6	10.0
Italy	ITL	1.575	9.07	31.4	17.0
Japan	JPY	1.299	7.18	24.9	19.9
Korea	KRW	1.861	9.40	32.6	25.5
Mexico	MXN	0.925	5.87	20.3	17.5
Malaysia	MYR	0.709	3.81	13.2	12.7
Netherlands	NLG	1.911	11.55	40.0	14.8
Norway	NOK	1.160	6.80	23.5	13.3
New Zealand	NZD	0.480	2.79	9.7	10.1
Philippines	PHP	0.807	4.49	15.6	16.2
Portugal	PTE	0.879	5.82	20.2	6.9
Sweden	SEK	1.612	9.91	34.3	16.9
Singapore	SGD	0.817	4.72	16.4	11.9
Thailand	THB	0.680	4.39	15.2	29.7
Taiwan	TWD	1.317	7.72	26.7	15.3
U.S.	USD	1.214	7.42	25.7	12.9
South Africa	ZAR	0.023	0.72	2.5	11.9

Example 11-10: FRM Exam 1997—Question 43

Which of the following statements about the S&P 500 index is *true*?

I. The index is calculated using market prices as weights.

II. The implied volatilities of options of the same maturity on the index are different.

III. The stocks used in calculating the index remain the same for each year.

IV. The S&P 500 represents only the 500 largest U.S. corporations.

a) II only

b) I and II only

c) II and III only

d) III and IV only

11.5   Commodity Risk

Commodity risk arises from potential movements in the value of commodity contracts, which include agricultural products, metals, and energy products.

11.5.1   Commodity Volatility

Table 11-7 displays the volatility of the commodity contracts currently covered by the RiskMetrics system. These can be grouped into *precious metals* (gold, platinum, silver), *base metals* (aluminum, copper, nickel, zinc), and *energy products* (natural gas, heating oil, unleaded gasoline, crude oil–West Texas Intermediate).

Precious metals have an annual volatility around 15% to 17%, on the same order of magnitude as equity markets. Among base metals, spot volatility is similar. Energy products, in contrast, are much more volatile, with numbers ranging from 35% to a high of 53% per annum in 2002. This is due to the fact that energy products are less storable than metals and, as a result, are much more affected by variations in demand and supply.

11.5.2   Futures Risk

The forward or futures price on a commodity can be expressed as

$$F_t e^{-r\tau} = S_t e^{-y\tau} \tag{11.10}$$

where $e^{-r\tau}$ is the present-value factor in the base currency and $e^{-y\tau}$ includes a **convenience yield** y (net of storage cost). This represents an implicit flow benefit from

TABLE 11-7 Commodity Volatility (Percent)

Commodity Term	Code	End 2002			End 1996
		Daily	Monthly	Annual	Annual
Gold, spot	GLD.C00	0.969	4.41	15.3	5.5
Platinum, spot	PLA.C00	0.811	4.54	15.7	6.5
Silver, spot	SLV.C00	1.095	5.12	17.7	18.1
Aluminium, spot	ALU.C00	0.702	3.85	13.3	16.8
3-month	ALU.C03	0.621	3.46	12.0	15.8
15-month	ALU.C15	0.528	2.99	10.3	13.9
27-month	ALU.C27	0.493	2.72	9.4	13.5
Copper, spot	COP.C00	0.850	4.45	15.4	35.4
3-month	COP.C03	0.824	4.30	14.9	24.9
15-month	COP.C15	0.788	4.04	14.0	21.5
27-month	COP.C27	0.736	3.84	13.3	22.7
Nickel, spot	NIC.C00	1.451	8.11	28.1	22.7
3-month	NIC.C03	1.392	7.78	27.0	22.1
15-month	NIC.C15	1.202	7.07	24.5	22.7
Zinc, spot	ZNC.C00	1.118	5.56	19.3	12.4
3-month	ZNC.C03	1.060	5.22	18.1	11.5
15-month	ZNC.C15	0.895	4.41	15.3	11.6
27-month	ZNC.C27	0.841	4.11	14.2	13.1
Natural gas, 1m	GAS.C01	2.882	15.66	54.3	95.8
3-month	GAS.C03	2.846	13.56	47.0	55.2
15-month	GAS.C06	1.343	7.62	26.4	34.4
27-month	GAS.C12	1.145	6.48	22.5	25.7
Heating oil, 1m	HTO.C01	2.196	10.39	36.0	34.4
3-month	HTO.C03	1.905	9.24	32.0	26.2
6-month	HTO.C06	1.489	7.46	25.9	23.5
12-month	HTO.C12	1.284	6.07	21.0	22.7
Unleaded gas, 1m	UNL.C01	2.859	14.08	48.8	31.0
3-month	UNL.C03	2.132	9.85	34.1	26.2
6-month	UNL.C06	1.665	8.01	27.7	23.5
Crude oil, 1m	WTI.C01	2.147	10.11	35.0	32.8
3-month	WTI.C03	1.885	8.87	30.7	29.6
5-month	WTI.C06	1.621	7.54	26.1	28.1
12-month	WTI.C12	1.296	6.02	20.8	28.9

holding the commodity, as explained in Chapter 9. For precious metals, this convenience yield is close to zero.

While this convenience yield is conceptually similar to that of a dividend yield on a stock index, it cannot be measured as regular income. Rather, it should be viewed as a "plug-in" that, given F, S, and $e^{-r\tau}$, will make Equation (11.10) balance. Further, it can be quite volatile.

As Table 11-7 shows, futures prices are less volatile for longer maturities. This decreasing term structure of volatility is more marked for energy products and less so for base metals. In addition, movements in futures prices are much less tightly related to spot prices than for financial contracts.

This is illustrated in Table 11-8, which displays correlations for copper contracts (spot, 3-, 15-, and 27-month) as well as for natural gas and crude oil contracts (1-, 3-, 6-, and 12-month). For copper, the cash/15-month correlation is 0.995. For natural gas and oil, the 1-month/12-month correlations are 0.575 and 0.787, respectively. These are much lower numbers. Thus, variations in the basis are much more important for energy products than for financial products, or even metals.

TABLE 11-8 Correlations across Maturities, 2002 (Daily)

Copper	COP.C00	COP.C03	COP.C15	COP.C27
COP.C00	1			
COP.C03	.999	1		
COP.C15	.995	.995	1	
COP.C27	.992	.993	.998	1
Nat. gas	GAS.C01	GAS.C03	GAS.C06	GAS.C12
GAS.C01	1			
GAS.C03	.860	1		
GAS.C06	.718	.734	1	
GAS.C12	.575	.445	.852	1
Crude oil	WTI.C01	WTI.C03	WTI.C06	WTI.C12
WTI.C01	1			
WTI.C03	.960	1		
WTI.C06	.904	.973	1	
WTI.C12	.787	.871	.954	1

This is confirmed in Figure 11-7, which compares the spot and futures prices for crude oil. There is much more variation in the basis between the spot and futures prices for crude oil. The market switches from backwardation ($S > F$) to contango ($S < F$). As a result, the futures contract represents a separate risk factor. Energy risk measurement systems require separate risk factors for each maturity.

FIGURE 11-7 Futures and Spot for Crude Oil

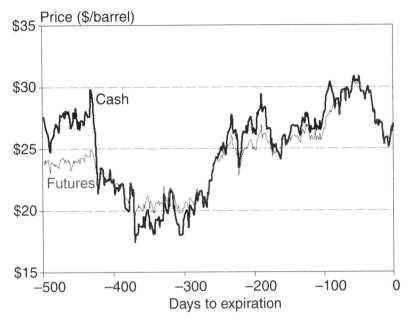

In addition to traditional market sources of risk, positions in commodity futures are also exposed to delivery and liquidity risks. Asset liquidity risk is due to the low volume in some of these markets, relative to other financial products.

Also, taking delivery or having to deliver on a futures contract that is carried to expiration is costly. Transportation, storage, and insurance costs can be quite high. Futures delivery also requires complying with the type and location of the commodity that is to be delivered.

Example 11-11: FRM Exam 1997—Question 23

Identify the *major* risks of being short $50 million of gold two weeks forward and being long $50 million of gold one year forward.

  I. Gold liquidity squeeze

 II. Spot risk

III. Gold lease rate risk

IV. USD interest rate risk

a) II only

b) I, II, and III only

c) I, III, and IV only

d) I, II, III, and IV

Example 11-12: FRM Exam 1997—Question 12

Which of the following products should have the highest expected volatility?

a) Crude oil

b) Gold

c) Japanese Treasury bills

d) EUR/CHF

11.6   Risk Simplification

The fundamental idea behind modern risk measurement methods is to aggregate the portfolio risk at the highest level. In practice, it would be too complex to model each risk factor individually. Instead, some simplification is required. We have seen, for example, that movements in the term structure of interest rates could be simplified to a few major risk factors. This approach expands on the **diagonal model** proposed by Professor William Sharpe. This was initially applied to stocks, but the methodology can be used in any market.

11.6.1   Diagonal Model

The diagonal model starts with a statistical decomposition of the return on stock i into a marketwide return and an idiosyncratic risk. The diagonal model adds the assumption that all specific risks are uncorrelated. Hence, any correlation across two stocks must come from the joint effect of the market.

We decompose the return on stock i, R_i, into a constant, a component due to the market, R_M, and some residual risk:

$$R_i = \alpha_i + \beta_i \times R_M + \epsilon_i \tag{11.11}$$

where β_i is called the systematic risk of stock i. It is also the regression slope ratio:

$$\beta_i = \frac{\text{Cov}[R_i, R_M]}{V[R_M]} = \rho_{iM} \frac{\sigma(R_i)}{\sigma(R_M)} \tag{11.12}$$

Note that the residual is uncorrelated with R_M by assumption. The contribution of William Sharpe was to show that equilibrium in capital markets imposes restrictions on the α_i. For risk managers, who focus primarily on risk, however, the diagonal model allows considerable simplifications in the risk model, so we ignore the intercept in what follows.

Consider a portfolio that consists of positions w_i on the various assets. We have

$$R_p = \sum_{i=1}^{N} w_i R_i \tag{11.13}$$

Using Equation (11.11), the portfolio return is also

$$R_p = \sum_{i=1}^{N} (w_i \beta_i R_M + w_i \epsilon_i) = \beta_p R_M + \sum_{i=1}^{N} (w_i \epsilon_i) \tag{11.14}$$

The portfolio variance is

$$V[R_p] = \beta_p^2 V[R_M] + \sum_{i=1}^{N} \left(w_i^2 V[\epsilon_i] \right) \tag{11.15}$$

since all the residual terms are uncorrelated. Suppose that, for simplicity, the portfolio is equally weighted and that the residual variances are all the same, $V[\epsilon_i] = V$. This implies $w_i = w = 1/N$. As the number of assets, N, increases, the second term will tend to

$$\sum_{i=1}^{N} \left(w_i^2 V[\epsilon_i] \right) \rightarrow N \times [(1/N)^2 V] = (V/N)$$

which should vanish as N increases. In this situation, the only remaining risk is the general market risk, consisting of β^2 times the variance of the market:

$$V[R_p] \rightarrow \beta_p^2 V[R_M]$$

So this justifies ignoring specific risk in large, well-diversified portfolios. The appendix shows how this approach can be used to build a covariance matrix from general market factors.

11.6.2 Fixed-Income Portfolio Risk

As an example of portfolio simplification, we turn to the analysis of a corporate bond portfolio with N individual bonds. Each "name" is potentially a source of risk. Instead of modeling all securities, the risk manager should attempt to simplify the risk profile of the portfolio. Potential major risk factors are movements in a set of J Treasury zero-coupon rates, z_j, and in K credit spreads, s_k, sorted by credit rating. The goal is to provide a good approximation to the risk of the portfolio.

In addition, it is not practical to model the risk of all bonds. The bonds may not have a sufficient history. Even if they do, the history may not be relevant if it does not account for the probability of default.

We model the movement in each corporate bond yield y_i by a movement in the Treasury factor z_j at the closest maturity and in the credit rating class s_k to which it belongs. The remaining component is ϵ_i, which is assumed to be independent across i. We have $y_i = z_j + s_k + \epsilon_i$. This decomposition is illustrated in Figure 11-8 for a corporate bond rated BBB with a 20-year maturity.

FIGURE 11-8 Yield Decomposition

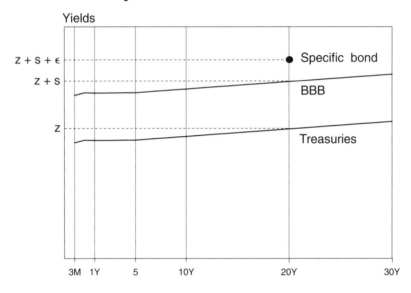

The movement in the bond price is

$$\Delta P_i = -\text{DVBP}_i \Delta y_i = -\text{DVBP}_i \Delta z_j - \text{DVBP}_i \Delta s_k - \text{DVBP}_i \Delta \epsilon_i \qquad (11.16)$$

where DVBP is the total dollar value of a basis point for the associated risk factor. We hold n_i units of this bond, so its value is

$$P = \sum_{i=1}^{N} n_i P_i \qquad (11.17)$$

Expanding the portfolio into its components, we have

$$\Delta P = -\sum_{i=1}^{N} n_i \Delta P_i = -\sum_{i=1}^{N} n_i \text{DVBP}_i \Delta y_i \qquad (11.18)$$

Using the risk factor decomposition, the portfolio price movement is

$$\Delta P = -\sum_{j=1}^{J} \text{DVBP}_j^z \Delta z_j - \sum_{k=1}^{K} \text{DVBP}_k^s \Delta s_k - \sum_{i=1}^{N} n_i \text{DVBP}_i \Delta \epsilon_i \qquad (11.19)$$

where DVBP_j^z results from the summation of $n_i \text{DVBP}_i$ for all bonds that are exposed to the jth maturity. As in Equation (11.15), The total variance can be decomposed into

$$V[\Delta P] = \text{General risk} + \sum_{i=1}^{N} n_i^2 \text{DVBP}_i^2 \, V[\Delta \epsilon_i] \qquad (11.20)$$

If the portfolio is well diversified, the general risk term should dominate. So we could simply ignore the second term. Ignoring specific risk, a portfolio composed of thousands of securities can be characterized by its exposure to just a few government maturities and credit spreads. This is a considerable simplification.

Example 11-13: FRM Exam 2002—Question 44

The historical simulation (HS) approach is based on the empirical distributions and a large number of risk factors. The RiskMetrics approach assumes normal distributions and uses mapping on equity indices. The HS approach is more likely to provide an accurate estimate of VAR than the RiskMetrics approach for a portfolio that consists of

a) A small number of emerging-market securities
b) A small number of broad-market indexes
c) A large number of emerging-market securities
d) A large number of broad-market indexes

11.7   Answers to Chapter Examples

Example 11-1: FRM Exam 1997—Question 16

d) Specific risk represents the risk that is not correlated with marketwide movements.

Example 11-2: FRM Exam 1997—Question 10

b) From the table. Among floating exchange rates, the USD/CAD has low volatility.

Example 11-3: FRM Exam 1997—Question 14

d) The logs of JPY/EUR and EUR/USD add up to that of JPY/USD:
ln[JPY/USD] = ln[JPY/EUR] + ln[EUR/USD]. So $\sigma^2(\text{JPY/USD}) =$
$\sigma^2(\text{JPY/EUR}) + \sigma^2(\text{EUR/USD}) + 2\rho\sigma(\text{JPY/EUR})\sigma(\text{EUR/USD})$, or
$8^2 = 10^2 + 6^2 + 2\rho 10 \times 6$, or $2\rho 10 \times 6 = -72$, or $\rho = -0.60$.

Example 11-4: FRM Exam 1999—Question 86

d) Historical yield volatility is more stable than price risk for a specific bond.

Example 11-5: FRM Exam 2002—Question 31

d) The VAR is given by $\alpha\sigma(dP)\sqrt{T}$, where $\sigma(dP) = (PD^*)\sigma(dy)$. The dollar duration is $(PD^*) = \$36$ million. The worst daily movement in yields is $\alpha\sigma(dy)\sqrt{T} = 2.33 \times 0.02\sqrt{(10/252)} = 0.009283$. The VAR is then $\$36,000,000 \times 0.009283 = \$334,186$.

Example 11-6: FRM Exam 2000—Question 96

d) Most of the movements in yields can be explained by a single-factor model, or parallel moves. Once this effect is taken into account, short-term yields move more than long-term yields, so a) and b) are wrong.

Example 11-7: FRM Exam 1997—Question 42

d) The yield on the inflation-protected bond is a real yield, or nominal yield minus expected inflation.

Example 11-8: FRM Exam 2002—Question 128

d) In 2001, Argentina defaulted on its debt, both in the local currency and in dollars. Answer a) is wrong because a diversified portfolio could not have lost so much. The funds were invested at 80% in dollar-denominated assets, so b) is wrong. Even a total wipeout of the local-currency portion could not explain a loss of 40% on the portfolio. If the fund had bought credit protection, it would not have lost as much, so c) is wrong. The fund must have had credit exposure to Argentina, so answer d) is correct.

Example 11-9: FRM Exam 1999—Question 71

b) If most of the term structure is unaffected, the hedge will not change in value given that it is driven by 10-year yields. Also, there will be little change in refinancing. For the IO, the slight decrease in the short-term discount rate will increase the present value of short-term cash flows, but the effect is small.

Example 11-10: FRM Exam 1997—Question 43

a) The "smile" effect represents different implied volatilities for the same maturity, so II is correct. Otherwise, the index is computed using market values, number of shares times price, so I is wrong. The stocks are selected by Standard & Poor's but are not always the largest ones. Finally, the stocks in the index are regularly changed.

Example 11-11: FRM Exam 1997—Question 23

c) There is no spot risk since the two contracts have offsetting exposure to the spot rate. There is, however, basis risk (lease rate and interest rate) and liquidity risk.

Example 11-12: FRM Exam 1997—Question 12

a) From comparing the tables on currencies, fixed-income, and commodities, the volatility of crude oil, at around 35% per annum, is the highest.

Example 11-13: FRM Exam 2002—Question 44

a) The question deals with the distribution of the assets and the effect of diversification. Emerging-market securities are more volatile and less likely to be normally distributed than broad-market indices. In addition, a small portfolio is less likely to be well represented by a mapping approach, and is less likely to be normal. The RiskMetrics approach assumes that the conditional distribution is normal and simplifies risk by mapping. This will be acceptable with a large number of securities with distributions close to the normal, which is answer d). Answer a) describes the least diversified portfolio, for which the HS method is best.

Appendix: Simplification of the Covariance Matrix

This appendix shows how the diagonal model can be used to construct a simplified covariance matrix, which is useful for some VAR approaches. Say we have $N = 100$ assets, which implies a covariance matrix with $N(N + 1)/2 = 5,050$ entries.

First, we derive the covariance between any two stocks under the one-factor model

$$\text{Cov}[R_i, R_j] = \text{Cov}[\beta_i R_M + \epsilon_i, \beta_j R_M + \epsilon_j] = \beta_i \beta_j \sigma_M^2 \qquad (11.21)$$

using the assumption that the residual components are uncorrelated with each other and with the market. Also, the variance of a stock is

$$\text{Cov}[R_i, R_i] = \beta_i^2 \sigma_M^2 + \sigma_{\epsilon,i}^2 \qquad (11.22)$$

The covariance matrix is then

$$\Sigma = \begin{bmatrix} \beta_1^2 \sigma_M^2 + \sigma_{\epsilon,1}^2 & \beta_1 \beta_2 \sigma_M^2 & \cdots & \beta_1 \beta_N \sigma_M^2 \\ \vdots & & & \\ \beta_N \beta_1 \sigma_M^2 & \beta_N \beta_2 \sigma_M^2 & \cdots & \beta_N^2 \sigma_M^2 + \sigma_{\epsilon,N}^2 \end{bmatrix}$$

which can also be written as

$$
\Sigma = \begin{bmatrix} \beta_1 \\ \vdots \\ \beta_N \end{bmatrix} [\beta_1 \cdots \beta_N] \sigma_M^2 + \begin{bmatrix} \sigma_{\epsilon,1}^2 & \cdots & 0 \\ \vdots & & \vdots \\ 0 & \cdots & \sigma_{\epsilon,N}^2 \end{bmatrix}
$$

Using matrix notation, we have

$$
\Sigma = \beta\beta'\sigma_M^2 + D_\epsilon \tag{11.23}
$$

This consists of N elements in the vector β, N elements on the diagonal of the matrix D_ϵ, plus the variance of the market itself. The diagonal model reduces the number of parameters from $N \times (N+1)/2$ to $2N+1$, a considerable improvement. For example, with 100 assets the number is reduced from 5,050 to 201.

In summary, this diagonal model substantially simplifies the risk structure of an equity portfolio. Risk managers can proceed in two steps: first, managing the overall market risk of the portfolios, and second, managing the concentration risk of individual securities.

Still, this one-factor model could miss common effects among groups of stocks, such as industry effects. To account for these, Equation (11.11) can be generalized to K factors:

$$
R_i = \alpha_i + \beta_{i1}y_1 + \cdots + \beta_{iK}y_K + \epsilon_i \tag{11.24}
$$

where $y_1, \ldots, y_K$ are the factors, which are assumed independent of each other for simplification. The covariance matrix generalizes Equation (11.23) to

$$
\Sigma = \beta_1\beta_1'\sigma_1^2 + \cdots + \beta_K\beta_K'\sigma_K^2 + D_\epsilon \tag{11.25}
$$

The number of parameters is now $(N \times K + K + N)$. For example, with 100 assets and five factors, this number is 605, which is still much lower than 5,050 for the unrestricted model.

Chapter 12

Hedging Linear Risk

Risk that has been measured can be managed. This chapter turns to the active management of market risks.

The traditional approach to market risk management includes **hedging**. Hedging consists of taking positions that lower the risk profile of the portfolio. The techniques for hedging have been developed in the futures markets, where farmers, for instance, use financial instruments to hedge the price risk of their products.

This implementation of hedging is quite narrow, however. Its objective is to find the optimal position in a futures contract that minimizes the variance, or more generally the VAR, of the total position. The portfolio consists of two positions, a fixed inventory to be hedged and a "hedging" instrument. In this chapter, the value of the hedging instrument is linearly related to the underlying risk factor.

More generally, we can distinguish between

- **Static hedging**, which consists of putting on, and leaving, a position until the hedging horizon, and

- **Dynamic hedging**, which consists of continuously rebalancing the portfolio to the horizon. This can create a risk profile similar to positions in options.

Dynamic hedging is associated with options, which will be examined in the next chapter. Since options have nonlinear payoffs in the underlying asset, the hedge ratio, which can be viewed as the slope of the tangent to the payoff function, must be readjusted as the price moves.

Even with static hedging, hedging will create **hedge slippage**, or **basis risk**. Basis risk arises when changes in payoffs on the hedging instrument do not perfectly offset changes in the value of the inventory position.

307

A final note on hedging is in order. Obviously, if the objective of hedging is to lower volatility, hedging will eliminate downside risk but also any upside in the position. The objective of hedging is to lower risk, not to make profits, so this is a double-edged sword. Whether hedging is beneficial should be examined in the context of the trade-off between risk and return.

This chapter discusses linear hedging. A particularly important application is hedging with futures. Section 12.1 presents an introduction to futures hedging with a unit hedge ratio. Section 12.2 then turns to a general method for finding the optimal hedge ratio. This method is applied in Section 12.3 for hedging bonds and equities.

12.1   Introduction to Futures Hedging

12.1.1   Unitary Hedging

Consider the situation of a U.S. exporter who has been promised a payment of 125 million Japanese yen in seven months. This is a cash position, or anticipated inventory. The perfect hedge would be to enter a seven-month forward contract over-the-counter (OTC). Assume for this illustration that this OTC contract is not convenient. Instead, the exporter decides to turn to an exchange-traded futures contract, which can be bought or sold easily.

The Chicago Mercantile Exchange (CME) lists yen contracts with a face amount of ¥12,500,000 that expire in nine months. The exporter places an order to sell 10 contracts, with the intention of reversing the position in seven months, when the contract will still have two months to maturity.[1] Because the amount sold is the same as the underlying, this is called a **unitary hedge**.

Table 12-1 describes the initial and final conditions for the contract. At each date, the futures price is determined by interest parity. Suppose that the yen depreciates sharply, or that the dollar goes up from ¥125 to ¥150. This leads to a loss on the anticipated cash position of ¥125,000,000 × (0.006667 − 0.00800) = −$166,667. This loss, however, is offset by a gain on the futures, which is (−10) × ¥125,000,000 ×

---

[1]In practice, if the liquidity of long-dated contracts is not adequate, the exporter could use nearby contracts and roll them over prior to expiration into the next contracts. When there are multiple exposures, this practice is known as a **stack hedge**. Another type of hedge is the **strip hedge**, which involves hedging the exposures with a number of different contracts. While a stack hedge has superior liquidity, it also entails greater basis risk than a strip hedge. Hedgers must decide whether the greater liquidity of a stack hedge is worth the additional basis risk.

$(0.006711 - 0.00806) = \$168,621$. The net is a small gain of \$1,954. Overall, the exporter has been hedged.

TABLE 12-1 A Futures Hedge

Item	Initial Time	Exit Time	Gain or Loss
Market Data			
Maturity (months)	9	2	
U.S. interest rate	6%	6%	
Yen interest rate	5%	2%	
Spot (¥/$)	¥125.00	¥150.00	
Futures (¥/$)	¥124.07	¥149.00	
Contract Data			
Spot ($/¥)	0.008000	0.006667	$-\$166,667$
Futures ($/¥)	0.008060	0.006711	\$168,621
Basis ($/¥)	-0.000060	-0.000045	\$1,954

This example shows that futures hedging can be quite effective, removing the effect of fluctuations in the risk factor. Define Q as the amount of yen transacted and S and F as the spot and futures rates, indexed by 1 at the initial time and by 2 at the exit time. The P&L on the unhedged transaction is

$$Q[S_2 - S_1] \tag{12.1}$$

The hedged profit is

$$Q[(S_2 - S_1) - (F_2 - F_1)] = Q[(S_2 - F_2) - (S_1 - F_1)] = Q[b_2 - b_1] \tag{12.2}$$

where $b = S - F$ is the **basis**. The hedged profit depends only on the movement in the basis. Hence the effect of hedging is to transform price risk into basis risk. A short hedge position is said to be *long the basis*, since it benefits from an increase in the basis.

In this case, the basis risk is minimal for a number of reasons. First, the cash and futures correspond to the same asset. Second, the cash-and-carry relationship holds very well for currencies. Third, the remaining maturity at exit is rather short. This is not always the case, however.

12.1.2 Basis Risk

Basis risk arises when the characteristics of the futures contract differ from those of the underlying position. Futures contracts are standardized to a particular grade, such as West Texas Intermediate (WTI) for oil futures traded on the NYMEX. This defines the grade of crude oil deliverable against the contract. A hedger, however, may have a position in a different grade, which may not be perfectly correlated with WTI. Thus basis risk is the uncertainty whether the cash-futures spread will widen or narrow during the hedging period. Hedging can be effective, however, if movements in the basis are dominated by movements in cash markets.

For most commodities, basis risk is inevitable. Organized exchanges strive to create enough trading and liquidity in their listed contracts, which requires standardization. Speculators also help to increase trading volumes and provide market liquidity. Thus there is a trade-off between liquidity and basis risk.

Basis risk is higher with **cross-hedging**, which involves using a futures contract on a totally different asset or commodity than the cash position. For instance, a U.S. exporter who is due to receive a payment in Norwegian kroner (NK) could hedge using a futures contract on the $/euro exchange rate. Relative to the dollar, the euro and the NK should behave similarly, but there is still some basis risk.

Basis risk is lowest when the underlying position and the futures contract correspond to the same asset. Even so, some basis risk remains because of differing maturities. As we saw in the yen hedging example, the maturity of the futures contract is nine rather than seven months. As a result, the liquidation price of the futures is uncertain.

Figure 12-1 describes the various time components for a hedge using T-bond futures. The first component is the *maturity of the underlying bond*, say 20 years. The second component is the *time to futures expiration*, say nine months. The third component is the *hedge horizon*, say seven months. Basis risk occurs when the hedge horizon does not match the time to futures expiration.

Example 12-1: FRM Exam 2000—Question 78

What feature of cash and futures prices tends to make hedging possible?

a) They always move together in the same direction and by the same amount.

b) They move in opposite directions by the same amount.

c) They tend to move together generally in the same direction and by the same amount.

d) They move in the same direction by different amounts.

FIGURE 12-1 Hedging Horizon and Contract Maturity

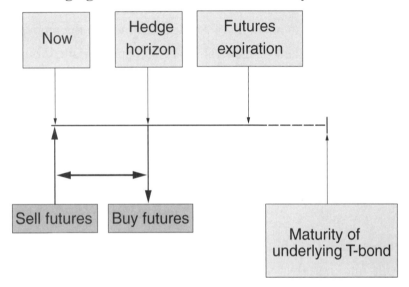

Example 12-2: FRM Exam 2000—Question 17

Which one of the following statements is *most* correct?

a) For a portfolio of stocks, the portfolio's value can be fully hedged by purchasing a stock index futures contract.

b) Speculators play an important role in the futures market by providing the liquidity that makes hedging possible and assuming the risk that hedgers are trying to eliminate.

c) Someone generally using futures contracts for hedging does not bear the basis risk.

d) Cross-hedging involves an additional source of basis risk because the asset being hedged is exactly the same as the asset underlying the futures.

Example 12-3: FRM Exam 2000—Question 79

Under which scenario is basis risk likely to exist?

a) A hedge (which was initially matched to the maturity of the underlying) is lifted before expiration.

b) The correlation of the underlying and the hedge vehicle is less than 1 and their volatilities are unequal.

c) The underlying instrument and the hedge vehicle are dissimilar.

d) All of the above are correct.

12.2 Optimal Hedging

The previous section gave an example of a unit hedge, where the amounts transacted are identical in the two markets. In general, this is not appropriate. We have to decide how much of the hedging instrument to transact.

Consider a situation where a portfolio manager has an inventory of carefully selected corporate bonds that should do better than their benchmark. The manager wants to guard against interest rate increases, however, over the next three months. In this situation, it would be too costly to sell the entire portfolio only to buy it back later. Instead, the manager can implement a temporary hedge using derivative contracts, for instance, T-bond futures.

Here, we note that the only risk is **price risk**, as the quantity of the inventory is known. This may not always be the case, however. Farmers, for instance, have uncertainty over both prices and the size of their crops. Thus, the hedging problem is substantially more complex, as it involves hedging *revenues*, which involves analyzing demand and supply conditions.

12.2.1 The Optimal Hedge Ratio

Define ΔS as the change in the dollar value of the inventory and ΔF as the change in the dollar value of one futures contract. The inventory, or position to be hedged, can be existing or **anticipatory**, that is, to be received in the future with a great degree of certainty. The manager is worried about potential movements in the value of the inventory ΔS.

If the manager goes long N futures contracts, the total change in the value of the portfolio is

$$\Delta V = \Delta S + N \Delta F \tag{12.3}$$

One should try to find the hedge that reduces risk to the minimum level. The variance of total profits is equal to

$$\sigma^2_{\Delta V} = \sigma^2_{\Delta S} + N^2 \sigma^2_{\Delta F} + 2N \sigma_{\Delta S, \Delta F} \tag{12.4}$$

Note that volatilities are initially expressed in dollars, not in rates of return, as we attempt to stabilize dollar values.

Taking the derivative with respect to N,

$$\frac{\partial \sigma^2_{\Delta V}}{\partial N} = 2N \sigma^2_{\Delta F} + 2 \sigma_{\Delta S, \Delta F} \tag{12.5}$$

For simplicity, drop the Δ in the subscripts. Setting Equation (12.5) equal to zero and solving for N, we get

$$N^* = -\frac{\sigma_{\Delta S, \Delta F}}{\sigma^2_{\Delta F}} = -\frac{\sigma_{SF}}{\sigma^2_F} = -\rho_{SF} \frac{\sigma_S}{\sigma_F} \tag{12.6}$$

where σ_{SF} is the covariance between futures and spot price changes. Here N^* is the **minimum-variance hedge ratio**.

In practice, there is often confusion about the definition of the portfolio value and unit prices. Here S consists of the number of units (shares, bonds, bushels, gallons) times the unit price (stock price, bond price, wheat price, fuel price).

It is sometimes easier to deal with unit prices and to express volatilities in terms of *rates of changes in unit prices*, which are unitless. Defining quantities Q and unit prices s, we have $S = Qs$. Similarly, the notional amount of one futures contract is $F = Q_f f$. We can then write

$$\sigma_{\Delta S} = Q\sigma(\Delta s) = Qs\sigma(\Delta s/s)$$

$$\sigma_{\Delta F} = Q_f\sigma(\Delta f) = Q_f f\sigma(\Delta f/f)$$

$$\sigma_{\Delta S, \Delta F} = \rho_{sf}[Qs\sigma(\Delta s/s)][Q_f f\sigma(\Delta f/f)]$$

Using Equation (12.6), the optimal hedge ratio N^* can also be expressed as

$$N^* = -\rho_{SF}\frac{Qs\sigma(\Delta s/s)}{Q_f f\sigma(\Delta f/f)} = -\rho_{SF}\frac{\sigma(\Delta s/s)}{\sigma(\Delta f/f)}\frac{Qs}{Q_f f} = -\beta_{sf}\frac{Q \times s}{Q_f \times f} \tag{12.7}$$

where β_{sf} is the coefficient in the regression of $\Delta s/s$ on $\Delta f/f$. The second term represents an adjustment factor for the size of the cash position and of the futures contract.

The optimal amount N^* can be derived from the slope coefficient of a regression of $\Delta s / s$ on $\Delta f / f$:

$$\frac{\Delta s}{s} = \alpha + \beta_{sf} \frac{\Delta f}{f} + \epsilon \tag{12.8}$$

As seen in Chapter 3, standard regression theory shows that

$$\beta_{sf} = \frac{\sigma_{sf}}{\sigma_f^2} = \rho_{sf} \frac{\sigma_s}{\sigma_f} \tag{12.9}$$

Thus the **best hedge** is obtained from a regression of the (change in the) value of the inventory on the value of the hedge instrument.

Key concept:
The optimal hedge is given by the negative of the beta coefficient of a regression of changes in the cash value on changes in the payoff on the hedging instrument.

We can do more than this, though. At the optimum, we can find the variance of profits by replacing N in Equation (12.4) by N^*, which gives

$$\sigma_V^{*2} = \sigma_S^2 + \left(\frac{\sigma_{SF}}{\sigma_F^2}\right)^2 \sigma_F^2 + 2\left(\frac{-\sigma_{SF}}{\sigma_F^2}\right) \sigma_{SF} = \sigma_S^2 + \frac{\sigma_{SF}^2}{\sigma_F^2} + 2\frac{-\sigma_{SF}^2}{\sigma_F^2} = \sigma_S^2 - \frac{\sigma_{SF}^2}{\sigma_F^2} \tag{12.10}$$

We can measure the quality of the optimal hedge ratio in terms of the amount by which we decreased the variance of the original portfolio:

$$R^2 = \frac{\sigma_S^2 - \sigma_V^{*2}}{\sigma_S^2} \tag{12.11}$$

After substitution of Equation (12.10), we find that $R^2 = (\sigma_S^2 - \sigma_S^2 + \sigma_{SF}^2/\sigma_F^2)/\sigma_S^2 = \sigma_{SF}^2/(\sigma_F^2 \sigma_S^2) = \rho_{SF}^2$. This unitless number is also the coefficient of determination, or the percentage of variance in $\Delta s / s$ explained by the independent variable $\Delta f / f$. Thus this regression also gives us the **effectiveness** of the hedge, which is measured by the proportion of variance eliminated.

We can also express the volatility of the hedged position from Equation (12.10) using R^2 as

$$\sigma_V^* = \sigma_S \sqrt{(1 - R^2)} \tag{12.12}$$

This shows that if $R^2 = 1$, the regression fit is perfect, and the resulting portfolio has zero risk. In this situation, the portfolio has no basis risk. However, if R^2 is very low, the hedge is not effective.

Example 12-4: FRM Exam 2001—Question 86

If two securities have the same volatility and a correlation equal to -0.5, their minimum-variance hedge ratio is

a) 1:1

b) 2:1

c) 4:1

d) 16:1

Example 12-5: FRM Exam 1999—Question 66

The hedge ratio is the ratio of the size of the position taken in the futures contract to the size of the exposure. Assuming the standard deviation of the change in spot price is σ_1 and the standard deviation of the change in futures price is σ_2, the correlation between the changes in spot price and future price is ρ. What is the optimal hedge ratio?

a) $1/\rho \times \sigma_1/\sigma_2$

b) $1/\rho \times \sigma_2/\sigma_1$

c) $\rho \times \sigma_1/\sigma_2$

d) $\rho \times \sigma_2/\sigma_1$

Example 12-6: FRM Exam 2002—Question 35

A company expects to buy 1 million barrels of West Texas Intermediate crude oil in one year. The annualized volatility of the price of a barrel of WTI is calculated at 12%. The company chooses to hedge by buying a futures contract on Brent crude. The annualized volatility of the Brent futures is 17% and the correlation coefficient is 0.68. Calculate the variance-minimizing hedge ratio.

a) 0.62

b) 0.53

c) 0.48

d) 0.42

12.2.2   Example

An airline knows that it will need to purchase 10,000 metric tons of jet fuel in three months. It wants some protection against an upturn in prices using futures contracts.

The company can hedge using heating oil futures contracts traded on NYMEX. The notional for one contract is 42,000 gallons. As there is no futures contract on jet fuel, the risk manager wants to check if heating oil could provide an efficient hedge instead. The current price of jet fuel is $277/metric ton. The futures price of heating oil is \$0.6903/gallon. The standard deviation of the rate of change in jet fuel prices over three months is 21.17%, that of futures is 18.59%, and the correlation is 0.8243.

Compute

a) The notional and the standard deviation of the unhedged fuel cost in dollars

b) The optimal number of futures contract to buy/sell, rounded to the closest integer

c) The standard deviation of the hedged fuel cost in dollars

Answer

a) The position notional is $Qs = \$2,770,000$. The standard deviation in dollars is

$$\sigma(\Delta s/s)sQ = 0.2117 \times \$277 \times 10,000 = \$586,409$$

For reference, that of one futures contract is

$$\sigma(\Delta f/f)fQ_f = 0.1859 \times \$0.6903 \times 42,000 = \$5,389.72$$

with a futures notional of $fQ_f = \$0.6903 \times 42,000 = \$28,992.60$.

b) The cash position corresponds to a payment, or liability. Hence, the company will have to *buy* futures as protection. First, we compute beta, which is $\beta_{sf} = 0.8243$ (0.2117/0.1859) = 0.9387. The corresponding covariance term is $\sigma_{sf} = 0.8243 \times 0.2117 \times 0.1859 = 0.03244$. Adjusting for the notionals, this is $\sigma_{SF} = 0.03244 \times \$2,770,000 \times \$28,993 = 2,605,268,452$. The optimal hedge ratio is, using Equation (12.7),

$$N^* = \beta_{sf}\frac{Q \times s}{Q_f \times f} = 0.9387\frac{10,000 \times \$277}{42,000 \times \$0.69} = 89.7$$

or 90 contracts after rounding (which we ignore in what follows).

c) To find the risk of the hedged position, we use Equation (12.10). The volatility of the unhedged position is $\sigma_S = \$586,409$. The variance of the hedged position is

$$
\begin{aligned}
\sigma_S^2 &= (\$586,409)^2 & &= +343,875,515,281 \\
-\sigma_{SF}^2/\sigma_F^2 &= -(2,605,268,452/5,390)^2 & &= -233,653,264,867 \\
\hline
V \text{ (hedged)} & & &= +110,222,250,414
\end{aligned}
$$

Taking the square root, the volatility of the hedged position is $\sigma_V^* = \$331,997$. Thus the hedge has reduced the risk from \$586,409 to \$331,997. Computing R^2, we find that 1 minus the ratio of the hedged and unhedged variances is (1 − 110,222,250,414/

343,875,515,281) = 67.95%. This is exactly the square of the correlation coefficient, $0.8243^2 = 0.6795$, or effectiveness of the hedge.

Figure 12-2 displays the relationship between the risk of the hedged position and the number of contracts. With no hedging, the volatility is \$586,409. As N increases, the risk decreases, reaching a minimum for $N^* = 90$ contracts. The graph also shows that the quadratic relationship is relatively flat for a range of values around the minimum. Choosing anywhere between 80 and 100 contracts will have little effect on the total risk. Given the substantial reduction in risk, the risk manager could choose to implement the hedge.

FIGURE 12-2 Risk of Hedged Position and Number of Contracts

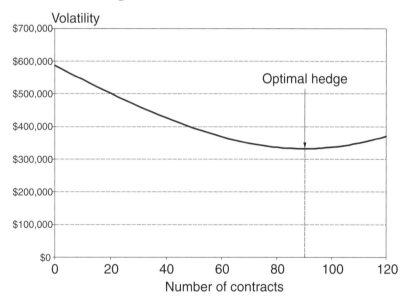

12.2.3 Liquidity Issues

Although futures hedging can be successful in mitigating market risk, it can create other risks. Futures contracts are marked to market daily. Hence they can involve large cash inflows or outflows. Cash outflows, in particular, can create liquidity problems, especially when they are not offset by cash inflows from the underlying position.

Example 12-7: FRM Exam 1999—Question 67

In the early 1990s, Metallgesellchaft, a German oil company, suffered a loss of $1.33 billion in their hedging program. They rolled over short-dated futures to hedge long-term exposure created through their long-term fixed-price contracts to sell heating oil and gasoline to their customers. After a time, they abandoned the hedge because of a large negative cash flow. The cash-flow pressure was due to the fact that MG had to hedge its exposure by

a) Short futures and there was a decline in oil price
b) Long futures and there was a decline in oil price
c) Short futures and there was an increase in oil price
d) Long futures and there was an increase in oil price

12.3   Applications of Optimal Hedging

The linear framework presented so far is completely general. We now specialize it to two important cases, duration and beta hedging. The first applies to the bond market, the second to the stock market.

12.3.1   Duration Hedging

Modified duration can be viewed as a measure of the exposure of relative changes in prices to movements in yields. Using the definitions in Chapter 1, we can write

$$\Delta P = (-D^* P) \Delta y \tag{12.13}$$

where D^* is the modified duration. The **dollar duration** is defined as $(D^* P)$.

Assuming the duration model holds, which implies that the change in yield Δy does not depend on maturity, we can rewrite this expression for the cash and futures positions as

$$\Delta S = (-D_S^* S) \Delta y \qquad \Delta F = (-D_F^* F) \Delta y$$

where D_S^* and D_F^* are the modified durations of S and F, respectively. Note that these relationships are supposed to be perfect, without an error term. The variances and covariance are then

$$\sigma_S^2 = (D_S^* S)^2 \sigma^2(\Delta y) \qquad \sigma_F^2 = (D_F^* F)^2 \sigma^2(\Delta y) \qquad \sigma_{SF} = (D_F^* F)(D_S^* S)\sigma^2(\Delta y)$$

We can replace these in Equation (12.6):

$$N^* = -\frac{\sigma_{SF}}{\sigma_F^2} = -\frac{(D_F^* F)(D_S^* S)}{(D_F^* F)^2} = -\frac{(D_S^* S)}{(D_F^* F)} \tag{12.14}$$

Alternatively, this can be derived as follows. Write the total portfolio payoff as

$$\Delta V = \Delta S + N \Delta F$$
$$= (-D_S^* S)\Delta y + N(-D_F^* F)\Delta y$$
$$= -[(D_S^* S) + N(D_F^* F)] \times \Delta y$$

which is zero when the net exposure, represented by the term in brackets, is zero. In other words, the optimal hedge ratio is simply the negative of the ratio of the dollar duration of cash relative to the dollar duration of the hedge. This ratio can also be expressed in terms of the dollar value of a basis point (DVBP).

More generally, we can use N as a tool to modify the total duration of the portfolio. If we have a target duration of D_V, this can be achieved by setting $[(D_S^* S) + N(D_F^* F)] = D_V^* V$, or

$$N = \frac{(D_V^* V - D_S^* S)}{(D_F^* F)} \qquad (12.15)$$

of which Equation (12.14) is a special case.

> **Key concept:**
> The optimal duration hedge is given by the ratio of the dollar duration of the position to that of the hedging instrument.

Example 1

A portfolio manager holds a bond portfolio worth $10 million with a modified duration of 6.8 years, to be hedged for three months. The current futures price is 93-02, with a notional of $100,000. We assume that its duration can be measured by that of the cheapest-to-deliver, which is 9.2 years.

Compute

a) The notional of the futures contract

b) The number of contracts to buy/sell for optimal protection

Answer

a) The notional is $[93 + (2/32)]/100 \times \$100,000 = \$93,062.5$.

b) The optimal number to *sell* is, from Equation (12.14),

$$N^* = -\frac{(D_S^* S)}{(D_F^* F)} = -\frac{6.8 \times \$10,000,000}{9.2 \times \$93,062.5} = -79.4$$

or 79 contracts after rounding. Note that the DVBP of the futures is about $9.2 \times$ $\$93,000 \times 0.01\% = \$85$.

Example 2

On February 2, a corporate treasurer wants to hedge a July 17 issue of \$5 million of commercial paper with a maturity of 180 days, leading to anticipated proceeds of \$4.52 million. The September Eurodollar futures trades at 92 and has a notional amount of \$1 million.

Compute

a) The current dollar value of the futures contract

b) The number of contracts to buy/sell for optimal protection

Answer

a) The current dollar price is given by $\$10,000[100 - 0.25(100 - 92)] = \$980,000$. Note that the duration of the futures is always three months (90 days), since the contract refers to three-month LIBOR.

b) If rates increase, the cost of borrowing will be higher. We need to offset this by a gain, or a short position in the futures. The optimal number is, from Equation (12.14),

$$N^* = -\frac{(D_S^* S)}{(D_F^* F)} = -\frac{180 \times \$4,520,000}{90 \times \$980,000} = -9.2$$

or 9 contracts after rounding. Note that the DVBP of the futures is about $0.25 \times$ $\$1,000,000 \times 0.01\% = \$25$.

> **Example 12-8: FRM Exam 2000—Question 73**
> What assumptions does a duration-based hedging scheme make about the way in which interest rates move?
> a) All interest rates change by the same amount.
> b) A small parallel shift occurs in the yield curve.
> c) Any parallel shift occurs in the term structure.
> d) Interest rates movements are highly correlated.

Example 12-9: FRM Exam 1999—Question 61

If all spot interest rates are increased by one basis point, a value of a portfolio of swaps will increase by $1,100. How many Eurodollar futures contracts are needed to hedge the portfolio?

a) 44

b) 22

c) 11

d) 1,100

Example 12-10: FRM Exam 1999—Question 109

Roughly how many three-month LIBOR Eurodollar futures contracts are needed to hedge a position in a $200 million, five-year receive-fixed swap?

a) Short 250

b) Short 3,200

c) Short 40,000

d) Long 250

12.3.2   Beta Hedging

We now turn to equity hedging using stock index futures. **Beta**, or **systematic risk**, can be viewed as a measure of the exposure of the rate of return on a portfolio i to movements in the "market" m:

$$R_{it} = \alpha_i + \beta_i R_{mt} + \epsilon_{it} \tag{12.16}$$

where β represents the systematic risk, α the intercept (which is not a source of risk and therefore is ignored for risk management purposes), and ϵ the residual component, which is uncorrelated with the market. We can also write, in line with the previous sections and ignoring the residual and intercept,

$$(\Delta S/S) \approx \beta(\Delta M/M) \tag{12.17}$$

Now, assume that we have at our disposal a stock index futures contract, which has a beta of unity $(\Delta F/F) = 1(\Delta M/M)$. For options, the beta is replaced by the net delta, $(\Delta C) = \delta(\Delta M)$.

As in the case of bond duration, we can write the total portfolio payoff as

$$\Delta V = \Delta S + N\Delta F$$

$$= (\beta S)(\Delta M/M) + NF(\Delta M/M)$$

$$= [(\beta S) + NF] \times (\Delta M/M)$$

which is set to zero when the net exposure, represented by the term in brackets, is zero. The optimal number of contracts to short is

$$N^* = -\frac{\beta S}{F} \qquad\qquad (12.18)$$

Key concept:
The optimal hedge with stock index futures is given by the the beta of the cash position times its value divided by the notional of the futures contract.

Example

A portfolio manager holds a stock portfolio worth $10 million with a beta of 1.5 relative to the S&P 500. The current futures price is 1,400, with a multiplier of $250.

Compute

a) The notional of the futures contract

b) The number of contracts to sell short for optimal protection

Answer

a) The notional amount of the futures contract is $250 × 1,400 = $350,000.

b) The optimal number of contract to short is, from Equation (12.18),

$$N^* = -\frac{\beta S}{F} = -\frac{1.5 \times \$10,000,000}{1 \times \$350,000} = -42.9$$

or 43 contracts after rounding.

The quality of the hedge will depend on the size of the residual risk in the market model of Equation (12.16). For large portfolios, the approximation may be good. In contrast, hedging an individual stock with stock index futures may give poor results.

For instance, the correlation of a typical U.S. stock with the S&P 500 is 0.50. For an industry index, it is typically 0.75. Using the regression effectiveness in Equation (12.12), we find that the volatility of the hedged portfolio is still about $\sqrt{1 - 0.5^2} = 87\%$ of the unhedged volatility for a typical stock and about 66% of the unhedged volatility for a typical industry. The lower number shows that hedging with general stock index futures is more effective for large portfolios. To obtain finer coverage of equity risks, hedgers could use futures contracts on industrial sectors, or even single stock futures.

Example 12-11: FRM Exam 2000—Question 93

Assume Global Funds manages an equity portfolio worth $50,000,000 with a beta of 1.8. Further, assume that there exists an index call option contract with a delta of 0.623 and a value of $500,000. How many options contracts are needed to hedge the portfolio?

a) 169

b) 289

c) 306

d) 321

12.4   Answers to Chapter Examples

Example 12-1: FRM Exam 2000—Question 78

c) Hedging is made possible by the fact that cash and futures prices usually move in the same direction and by the same amount.

Example 12-2: FRM Exam 2000—Question 17

b) Answer a) is wrong because we need to hedge by *selling* futures. Answer c) is wrong because futures hedging creates some basis risk. Answer d) is wrong because cross-hedging involves *different* assets. Speculators do serve some social function, which is to create liquidity for others.

Example 12-3: FRM Exam 2000—Question 79

d) Basis risk occurs if movements in the value of the cash and hedged positions do not offset each other perfectly. This can happen if the instruments are dissimilar or if the correlation is not unity. Even with similar instruments, if the hedge is lifted before the maturity of the underlying, there is some basis risk.

Example 12-4: FRM Exam 2001—Question 86

b) Set x as the amount to invest in the second security, relative to that in the first (or the hedge ratio). The variance is then proportional to $1 + x^2 + 2x\rho$. Taking the derivative and setting to zero, we have $x = -\rho = 0.5$. Thus one security must have twice the amount in the other. Alternatively, the hedge ratio is given by $N^* = -\rho\frac{\sigma_S}{\sigma_F}$, which gives 0.5. Answer b) is the only one that is consistent with this number or its inverse.

Example 12-5: FRM Exam 1999—Question 66

c) See Equation (12.6).

Example 12-6: FRM Exam 2002—Question 35

c) The hedge ratio is given by $\rho_{sf}(\sigma_s/\sigma_f) = 0.68 \times (12\%/17\%) = 0.48$.

Example 12-7: FRM Exam 1999—Question 67

b) MG was long futures to offset the promised forward sales to clients. It lost money as oil futures prices fell.

Example 12-8: FRM Exam 2000—Question 73

b) The assumption is that of (1) parallel and (2) small moves in the yield curve. Answers a) and c) are the same, and omit the size of the move. Answer d) would require perfect, not high, correlation plus small moves.

Example 12-9: FRM Exam 1999—Question 61

a) The DVBP of the portfolio is $1,100. That of the futures is $25. Hence the ratio is $1,100/25 = 44$.

Example 12-10: FRM Exam 1999—Question 109

b) The dollar duration of a 5-year 6% par bond is about 4.3 years. Hence the DVBP of the position is about $200,000,000 \times 4.3 \times 0.0001 = \$86,000$. That of the futures is $25. Hence the ratio is $86,000/25 = 3,440$.

Example 12-11: FRM Exam 2000—Question 93

b) The hedging instrument has a market beta that is not unity, but 0.623. The optimal hedge ratio is $N = -(1.8 \times \$50,000,000)/(0.623 \times \$500,000) = 288.9$.

Chapter 13

Nonlinear Risk: Options

The previous chapter focused on "linear" hedging, using contracts such as forwards and futures, whose values are linearly related to the underlying risk factors. Positions in these contracts are fixed over the hedge horizon. Because linear combinations of normal random variables are also normally distributed, linear hedging maintains normal distributions, albeit with lower variances.

Hedging nonlinear risks, however, is much more complex. Because options have nonlinear payoffs, the distribution of option values can be sharply asymmetrical. Due to the ubiquitous nature of options, risk managers need to be able to evaluate the risk of positions with options. Since options can be replicated by dynamic trading of the underlying instruments, this also provides insights into the risks of active trading strategies.

In a previous chapter, we saw that market losses can be ascribed to the combination of two factors: exposure and adverse movements in the risk factor. Thus, a large loss could occur because of the risk factor, which is bad luck. Too often, however, losses occur because the exposure profile is similar to a short option position. This is less forgivable, because exposure is under the control of the portfolio manager.

The challenge is to develop measures that provide an intuitive understanding of the exposure profile. Section 13.1 introduces option pricing and the Taylor approximation.[1] It starts from the Black-Scholes formula presented in Chapter 6. Partial derivatives, also known as "Greeks," are analyzed in Section 13.2. Section 13.3 then turns to the interpretation of dynamic hedging and discusses the distribution profile of option positions.

---

[1] The reader should be forewarned that this chapter is more technical than others. It presupposes some exposure to option pricing and hedging.

13.1 Evaluating Options

13.1.1 Definitions

We consider a **derivative** instrument whose value depends on an underlying asset, which can be a price, an index, or a rate. As an example, consider a call option where the underlying asset is a foreign currency. We use these definitions:

$$S_t = \text{current spot price of the asset in dollars}$$

$$F_t = \text{current forward price of the asset}$$

$$K = \text{exercise price of option contract}$$

$$f_t = \text{current value of derivative instrument}$$

$$r_t = \text{domestic risk-free rate}$$

$$r_t^* = \text{foreign risk-free rate (also written as } y)$$

$$\sigma_t = \text{annual volatility of the rate of change in } S$$

$$\tau = \text{time to maturity}$$

More generally, r^* represents the income payment on the asset, which represents the *annual rate* of dividend or coupon payments on a stock index or bond.

For most options, we can write the value of the derivative as the function

$$f_t = f(S_t, r_t, r_t^*, \sigma_t, K, \tau) \tag{13.1}$$

The contract specifications are represented by K and the time to maturity τ. The other factors are affected by market movements, creating volatility in the value of the derivative. For simplicity, we drop the time subscripts in what follows.

Derivatives pricing is all about finding the value of f, given the characteristics of the option at expiration and some assumptions about the behavior of markets. For a forward contract, for instance, the expression is very simple. It reduces to

$$f = Se^{-r^*\tau} - Ke^{-r\tau} \tag{13.2}$$

More generally, we may be unable to derive an analytical expression for the functional form of the derivative, requiring numerical methods.

13.1.2   Taylor Expansion

We are interested in describing the movements in f. The exposure profile of the derivative can be described *locally* by taking a Taylor expansion,

$$df = \frac{\partial f}{\partial S}dS + \frac{1}{2}\frac{\partial^2 f}{\partial S^2}dS^2 + \frac{\partial f}{\partial r}dr + \frac{\partial f}{\partial r^*}dr^* + \frac{\partial f}{\partial \sigma}d\sigma + \frac{\partial f}{\partial \tau}d\tau + \cdots \quad (13.3)$$

Because the value depends on S in a nonlinear fashion, we added a quadratic term for S. The terms in Equation (13.3) approximate a nonlinear function by linear and quadratic polynomials.

Option pricing is about finding f. **Option hedging** uses the partial derivatives. **Risk management** is about combining those with the movements in the risk factors.

Figure 13-1 describes the relationship between the value of a European call and the underlying asset. The actual price is the solid line. The straight thin line is the linear (delta) estimate, which is the tangent at the initial point. The other line is the quadratic (delta plus gamma) estimate, which gives a much better fit because it has more parameters.

Note that, because we are dealing with sums of local price movements, we can aggregate the sensitivities at the portfolio level. This is similar to computing the portfolio duration from the sum of durations of individual securities, appropriately weighted.

FIGURE 13-1 Delta-Gamma Approximation for a Long Call

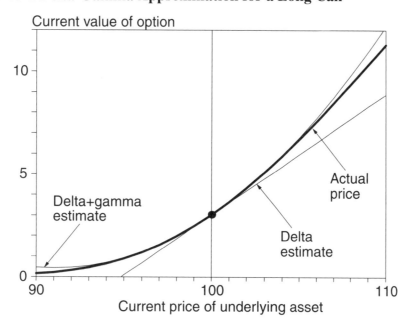

Defining $\Delta = \frac{\partial f}{\partial S}$, for example, we can summarize the portfolio or "book" Δ_P in terms of the total sensitivity,

$$\Delta_P = \sum_{i=1}^{N} x_i \Delta_i \qquad (13.4)$$

where x_i is the number of options of type i in the portfolio. To hedge against first-order price risk, it is sufficient to hedge the *net* portfolio delta. This is more efficient than trying to hedge every instrument individually.

The Taylor approximation may fail for a number of reasons:

■ *Large movements in the underlying risk factor*

■ *Highly nonlinear exposures*, such as options near expiry or exotic options

■ *Cross-partials effect*, such as σ changing in relation to S

If this is the case, we need to turn to a **full revaluation** of the instrument. Using the subscripts 0 and 1 as the initial and final values, the change in the option value is

$$f_1 - f_0 = f(S_1, r_1, r_1^*, \sigma_1, \ K, \tau_1) - f(S_0, r_0, r_0^*, \sigma_0, \ K, \tau_0) \qquad (13.5)$$

13.1.3   Option Pricing

We now present the various partial derivatives for conventional European call and put options. As seen in Chapter 6, the **Black-Scholes** (BS) model provides a closed-form solution from which these derivatives can be computed analytically.

The key point of the BS derivation is that a position in the option can be replicated by a "delta" position in the underlying asset. Hence, a portfolio combining the asset and the option in appropriate proportions is risk-free "locally," that is, for small movements in prices. To avoid arbitrage, this portfolio must return the risk-free rate. The option value is the discounted expected payoff,

$$f_t = E_{\mathrm{RN}}[e^{-r\tau} F(S_T)] \qquad (13.6)$$

where E_{RN} represents the expectation of the future payoff in a "risk-neutral" world, that is, assuming the underlying asset grows at the risk-free rate and the discounting also employs the risk-free rate.

In the case of a European call, the final payoff is $F(S_T) = \text{Max}(S_T - K, 0)$, and the current value of the call is given by

$$c = Se^{-r^*\tau}N(d_1) - Ke^{-r\tau}N(d_2) \qquad (13.7)$$

where $N(d)$ is the cumulative distribution function for the standard normal distribution:

$$N(d) = \int_{-\infty}^{d} \Phi(x)dx = \frac{1}{\sqrt{2\pi}} \int_{-\infty}^{d} e^{(-1/2x^2)}dx$$

with Φ defined as the standard normal density function. $N(d)$ is also the area to the left of a standard normal variable with value equal to d. The values of d_1 and d_2 are

$$d_1 = \frac{\ln(Se^{-r^*\tau}/Ke^{-r\tau})}{\sigma\sqrt{\tau}} + \frac{\sigma\sqrt{\tau}}{2}, \quad d_2 = d_1 - \sigma\sqrt{\tau}$$

By put-call parity, the European put option value is

$$p = Se^{-r^*\tau}[N(d_1) - 1] - Ke^{-r\tau}[N(d_2) - 1] \qquad (13.8)$$

Example 13-1: FRM Exam 1999—Question 65

It is often possible to estimate the value at risk of a vanilla European options portfolio by using a delta-gamma methodology rather than exact valuation formulas because

a) Delta and gamma are the first two terms in the Taylor series expansion of the change in option price as a function of the change in the underlying, and the remaining terms are often insignificant.

b) It is only delta and gamma risk that can be hedged.

c) Unlike the price, delta and gamma for a European option can be computed in closed form.

d) Both a) and c), but not b), are correct.

Example 13-2: FRM Exam 1999—Question 88

Why is the delta normal approach not suitable for measuring options portfolio risk?

a) There is a lack of data to compute the variance/covariance matrix.

b) Options are generally short-dated instruments.

c) There are nonlinearities in option payoff.

d) Black-Scholes pricing assumptions are violated in the real world.

13.2   Option "Greeks"

13.2.1   Option Sensitivities: Delta and Gamma

Given the closed-form solutions for European options, we can derive all partial derivatives. The most important sensitivity is the **delta**, which is the first partial derivative
with respect to the price. For a call option, this can be written explicitly as:

$$\Delta_c = \frac{\partial c}{\partial S} = e^{-r^*\tau} N(d_1) \tag{13.9}$$

which is always positive and below unity.

Figure 13-2 relates delta to the current value of S, for various maturities. The
essential feature of this figure is that Δ varies substantially with the spot price and
with time. As the spot price increases, d_1 and d_2 become very large and Δ tends
toward $e^{-r^*\tau}$, close to 1 for short maturities. In this situation, the option behaves
like an outright position in the asset. Indeed, the limit of Equation (13.7) is $c =
Se^{-r^*\tau} - Ke^{-r\tau}$, which is exactly the value of our forward contract, Equation (13.2).

FIGURE 13-2 Option Delta

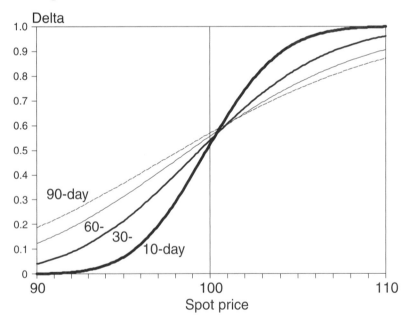

At the other extreme, if S is very low, Δ is close to zero and the option is not very
sensitive to S. When S is close to the strike price K, Δ is close to 0.5 and the option
behaves like a position of 0.5 in the underlying asset.

> **Key concept:**
> The delta of an at-the-money call option is close to 0.5. Delta moves to 1 as the call goes deep in-the-money. It moves to 0 as the call goes deep out-of-the-money.

The delta of a put option is

$$\Delta_p = \frac{\partial p}{\partial S} = e^{-r^*\tau}[N(d_1) - 1] \tag{13.10}$$

which is always negative. It behaves similarly to the call Δ, except for the sign. The delta of an at-the-money put is about -0.5.

> **Key concept:**
> The delta of an at-the-money put option is close to -0.5. Delta moves to 1 as the put goes deep in-the-money. It moves to 0 as the put goes deep out-of-the-money.

The figure also shows that as the option nears maturity, the Δ function becomes more curved. The function converges to a step function—0 when $S < K$, and 1 otherwise. Close-to-maturity options have unstable deltas.

For a European call or put, gamma (Γ) is the second-order term,

$$\Gamma = \frac{\partial^2 c}{\partial S^2} = \frac{e^{-r^*\tau}\Phi(d_1)}{S\sigma\sqrt{\tau}} \tag{13.11}$$

which is driven by the "bell shape" of the normal density function Φ. This is also the derivative of Δ with respect to S. Thus Γ measures the "instability" in Δ. Note that gamma is identical for a call and put with identical characteristics.

Figure 13-3 plots the call option gamma. At-the-money options have the highest gamma, which indicates that Δ changes very fast as S changes. In contrast, both in-the-money options and out-of-the-money options have low gammas because their delta is constant, close to 1 or 0, respectively. The figure also shows that as the maturity nears, the option gamma increases. This leads to a useful rule:

> **Key concept:**
> For vanilla options, nonlinearities are most pronounced for short-term at-the-money options.

Thus, gamma is similar to the concept of convexity developed for bonds. Fixed-coupon bonds, however, always have positive convexity, whereas options can create positive or negative convexity. Positive convexity or gamma is beneficial, as it implies that the value of the asset drops more slowly and increases more quickly than otherwise. In contrast, negative convexity can be dangerous because it implies faster price falls and slower price increases.

FIGURE 13-3 Option Gamma

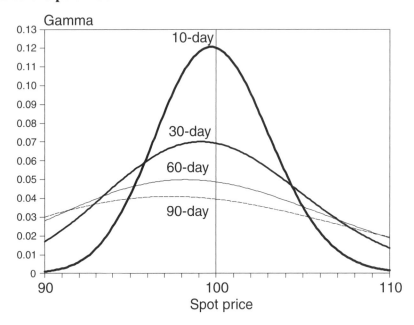

Figure 13-4 summarizes the delta and gamma exposures of positions in options. Long positions in options, whether calls or puts, create positive convexity. Short positions create negative convexity. In exchange for assuming the harmful effect of this negative convexity, option sellers receive the premium.

Example 13-3: FRM Exam 2001—Question 79

A bank has sold USD 300,000 of call options on 100,000 equities. The equities trade at 50, the option strike price is 49, the maturity is in three months, volatility is 20%, and the interest rate is 5%. How does the bank delta hedge? (Round to the nearest thousand shares.)
a) Buy 65,000 shares
b) Buy 100,000 shares
c) Buy 21,000 shares
d) Sell 100,000 shares

FIGURE 13-4 Delta and Gamma of Option Positions

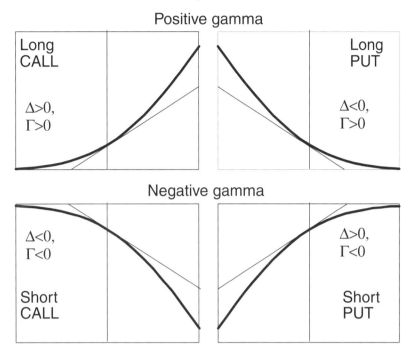

Example 13-4: FRM Exam 1999—Question 69

A portfolio is long a call that is delta hedged by trading in the underlying security. Assuming that the call is fairly valued and the market is in equilibrium, which of the following formulas indicates the standard deviation of the expected profit or loss from holding the hedged position until option expiry? (In the following, N is the frequency of hedging (52 = weekly), T is the time to expiry, and σ is the annualized volatility. K is a constant.)

a) $K\sigma/\sqrt{N}$

b) $K\sqrt{N}/\sigma^2$

c) $K\sigma^2/N$

d) KN/σ

13.2.2   Option Sensitivities: Vega

Unlike linear contracts, options are exposed not only to movements in the direction of the spot price, but also to its volatility. Options therefore can be viewed as "volatility bets."

The sensitivity of an option to volatility is called the option **vega** (sometimes also called lambda or kappa). For European calls and puts, this is

$$\Lambda = \frac{\partial c}{\partial \sigma} = Se^{-r^*\tau}\sqrt{\tau}\ \Phi(d_1) \tag{13.12}$$

which also has the "bell shape" of the normal density function Φ. As with gamma, vega is identical for similar call and put positions. Λ must be positive for long option positions.

Figure 13-5 plots the call option vega. The graph shows that at-the-money options are the most sensitive to volatility. The time effect, however, is different from that for gamma, because the term $\sqrt{\tau}$ appears in the numerator instead of the denominator. This implies that vega decreases with maturity, unlike gamma, which increases with maturity.

FIGURE 13-5 Option Vega

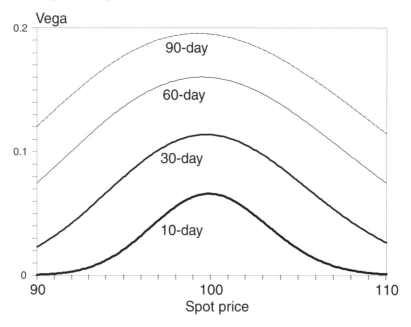

Changes in the volatility parameter can be a substantial source of risk. Figure 13-6 illustrates the time variation in the option-σ for options on the dollar/mark exchange rate. Here, the average value is about 11%, with a typical daily volatility in σ of 1.5%.[2]

---

[2]There is strong mean reversion in these data, so daily volatilities cannot be extrapolated to annual data.

FIGURE 13-6 Movements in Implied Volatility

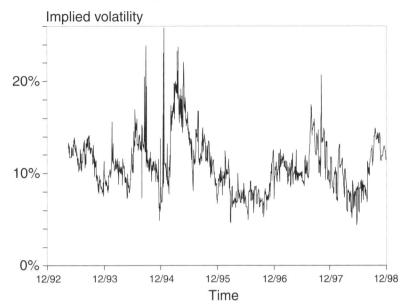

13.2.3   Option Sensitivities: Rho

The sensitivity to the domestic interest rate, also called **rho**, is

$$\rho_c = \frac{\partial c}{\partial r} = K e^{-r\tau} \tau N(d_2) \tag{13.13}$$

For a put,

$$\rho_p = \frac{\partial p}{\partial r} = -K e^{-r\tau} \tau N(-d_2) \tag{13.14}$$

An increase in the rate of interest increases the value of the call, as the underlying asset grows at a higher rate, which increases the probability of exercising the call, with a fixed strike price K. In the limit, for an infinite interest rate, the probability of exercise is 1 and the call option is equivalent to the stock itself. The reasoning is opposite for a put option.

The exposure to the yield on the asset is, for calls and puts, respectively,

$$\rho_C^* = \frac{\partial c}{\partial r^*} = -S e^{-r^*\tau} \tau N(d_1) \tag{13.15}$$

$$\rho_P^* = \frac{\partial p}{\partial r^*} = S e^{-r^*\tau} \tau N(-d_1) \tag{13.16}$$

An increase in the dividend yield decreases the growth rate of the underlying asset, which is harmful to the value of the call. Again, the reasoning is opposite for a put option.

13.2.4 Option Sensitivities: Theta

Finally, the variation in option value due to the passage of time is called **theta**. This is also the **time decay**. Unlike other factors, however, the movement in remaining maturity is perfectly predictable. Time is not a risk factor.

For a European call, this is

$$\Theta_c = \frac{\partial c}{\partial t} = -\frac{\partial c}{\partial \tau} = -\frac{Se^{-r^*\tau}\sigma\,\Phi(d_1)}{2\sqrt{\tau}} + r^*Se^{-r^*\tau}N(d_1) - rKe^{-r\tau}N(d_2) \quad (13.17)$$

For a European put, this is

$$\Theta_p = \frac{\partial p}{\partial t} = -\frac{\partial p}{\partial \tau} = -\frac{Se^{-r^*\tau}\sigma\,\Phi(d_1)}{2\sqrt{\tau}} - r^*Se^{-r^*\tau}N(-d_1) + rKe^{-r\tau}N(-d_2)$$
$$(13.18)$$

Theta is generally negative for long positions in both calls and puts. This means that the option loses value as time goes by.

For American options, however, Θ is *always* negative. Because they give their holder the choice to exercise early, shorter-term American options are unambiguously less valuable than longer-term options.

Figure 13-7 displays the behavior of a call option theta for various prices of the underlying asset and maturities. For long positions in options, theta is negative, which reflects the fact that the option is a wasting asset. Like gamma, theta is greatest for short-term at-the-money options, when measured in absolute value. At-the-money options lose a lot of value when the maturity is near.

13.2.5 Option Pricing and the "Greeks"

Having defined the option sensitivities, we can illustrate an alternative approach to the derivation of the Black-Scholes formula. Recall that the underlying process for the asset follows a stochastic process known as a **geometric Brownian motion** (GBM),

$$dS = \mu S\,dt + \sigma S\,dz \quad (13.19)$$

where dz has a normal distribution with mean zero and variance dt.

FIGURE 13-7 Option Theta

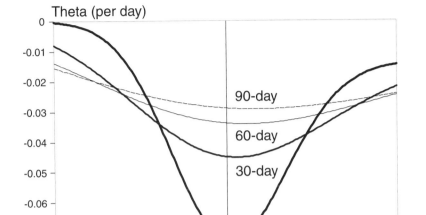

Considering only this *single* source of risk, we can return to the Taylor expansion in Equation (13.3). The value of the derivative is a function of S and time, which we can write as $f(S, t)$. The question is, how does f evolve over time?

We can relate the stochastic process of f to that of S using **Ito's lemma**, named after its creator. This can be viewed as an extension of the Taylor approximation to a stochastic environment. Applied to the GBM, this gives

$$df = \left(\frac{\partial f}{\partial S}\mu S + \frac{1}{2}\frac{\partial^2 f}{\partial S^2}\sigma^2 S^2 + \frac{\partial f}{\partial \tau}\right)dt + \left(\frac{\partial f}{\partial S}\sigma S\right)dz \qquad (13.20)$$

This is also

$$df = (\Delta \mu S + \tfrac{1}{2}\Gamma \sigma^2 S^2 + \Theta)dt + (\Delta \sigma S)dz \qquad (13.21)$$

The first term, including dt, is the trend. The second, including dz, is the stochastic component.

Next, we construct a portfolio delicately balanced between S and f that has no exposure to dz. Define this portfolio as

$$\Pi = f - \Delta S \qquad (13.22)$$

Using (13.19) and (13.21), its stochastic process is

$$
\begin{aligned}
d\Pi &= [\Delta\mu S + \tfrac{1}{2}\Gamma\sigma^2 S^2 + \Theta)dt + (\Delta\sigma S)dz] - \Delta[\mu S dt + \sigma S dz] \\
&= (\Delta\mu S)dt + (\tfrac{1}{2}\Gamma\sigma^2 S^2)dt + \Theta\, dt + (\Delta\sigma S)dz - (\Delta\mu S)dt - (\Delta\sigma S)dz \\
&= (\tfrac{1}{2}\Gamma\sigma^2 S^2 + \Theta)dt
\end{aligned}
$$

(13.23)

This simplification is extremely important. Note how the terms involving dz cancel each other out. The portfolio has been immunized against this source of risk. At the same time, the terms in μS also happened to cancel each other out. The fact that μ disappears from the trend in the portfolio is important, as it explains why the trend of the underlying asset does not appear in the Black-Scholes formula.

Continuing, we note that the portfolio Π has no risk. To avoid arbitrage, it must return the risk-free rate:

$$
d\Pi = [r\Pi]dt = r(f - \Delta S)dt
$$

(13.24)

If the underlying asset has a dividend yield of y, this must be adjusted to

$$
d\Pi = (r\Pi)dt + y\Delta S\, dt = r(f - \Delta S)dt + y\Delta S\, dt
$$

(13.25)

Setting the trends in Equations (13.23) and (13.24) equal to each other, we must have

$$
(r - y)\Delta S + \tfrac{1}{2}\Gamma\sigma^2 S^2 + \Theta = rf
$$

(13.26)

This is the Black-Scholes **partial differential equation (PDE)**, which applies to any contract, or portfolio, that derives its value from S. The solution of this equation, with appropriate boundary conditions, leads to the BS formula for a European call, Equation (13.7).

We can use this relationship to understand how the sensitivities relate to each other. Consider a portfolio of derivatives, all on the same underlying asset, that is delta hedged. Setting $\Delta = 0$ in Equation (13.26), we have

$$
\tfrac{1}{2}\Gamma\sigma^2 S^2 + \Theta = rf
$$

(13.27)

This shows that, for such a portfolio, when Γ is large and positive, Θ must be negative if rf is small. In other words, a delta-hedged position with positive gamma, which is beneficial in terms of price risk, must have negative theta, or time decay. An example is the long straddle examined in Chapter 6. Such a position is delta-neutral and has large gamma or convexity. It would benefit from a large move in S, whether up or down. This portfolio, however, involves buying options whose value decays very quickly with time. Thus, there is an intrinsic trade-off between Γ and Θ.

> **Key concept:**
> For delta-hedged portfolios, Γ and Θ must have opposite signs. Portfolios with positive convexity, for example, must experience time decay.

13.2.6 Option Sensitivities: Summary

We summarize the sensitivities of option positions with some illustrative data in Table 13-1. Three strike prices are considered, $K = 90$, 100, and 110. We verify that the Γ, Λ, Θ measures are all highest when the option is at-the-money ($K = 100$). Such options have the most nonlinear patterns.

TABLE 13-1 Derivatives for a European Call

Parameters: $S = \$100, \sigma = 20\%, r = 5\%, y = 3\%, \tau = 3$ months

	Variable	Unit	Strike $K = 90$	$K = 100$	$K = 110$	Worst Loss Variable	Loss
c		Dollars	$11.02	$4.22	$1.05		
		Change per:					
Δ	Spot price	dollar	0.868	0.536	0.197	−$2.08	−$1.114
Γ	Spot price	dollar	0.020	0.039	0.028	4.33	$0.084
Λ	Volatility	(% pa)	0.103	0.198	0.139	−2.5	−$0.495
ρ	Interest rate	(% pa)	0.191	0.124	0.047	−0.10	−$0.013
ρ^*	Asset yield	(% pa)	−0.220	−0.135	−0.049	0.10	−$0.014
Θ	Time	day	−0.014	−0.024	−0.016		

The table also shows the loss for the worst daily movement in each risk factor at the 95% confidence level. For S, this is $dS = -1.645 \times 20\% \times \$100/\sqrt{252} = -\$2.08$. We combine this with delta, which gives a potential loss of $\Delta \times dS = -\$1.114$, or about a fourth of the option value.

Next, we examine the second-order term, S^2. The worst squared daily movement is $dS^2 = 2.08^2 = 4.33$ in the risk factor at the 95% confidence level. We combine this with gamma, which gives a potential gain of $\frac{1}{2}\Gamma \times dS^2 = 0.5 \times 0.039 \times 4.33 = \$0.084$.

Note that this is a gain because gamma is positive, but much smaller than the first-order effect. Thus the worst loss due to S would be $-\$1.114 + \$0.084 = -\$1.030$ using the linear and quadratic effects.

For σ, we observe a volatility on the order of 1.5%. The worst daily move is therefore $-1.645 \times 1.5 = -2.5$, expressed as a percentage, which gives a worst loss of $-\$0.495$. Finally, for r, we assume an annual volatility of changes in rates of 1%. The worst daily move is then $-1.645 \times 1/\sqrt{252} = -0.10$, as a percentage, which gives a worst loss of $-\$0.013$. So most of the risk originates from S. In this case, a linear approximation using Δ would only capture most of the downside risk. For near-term at-the-money options, however, the quadratic effect will be more important.

Example 13-5: FRM Exam 2001—Question 123

Which of the following "Greeks" contributes most to the risk of an option that is close to expiration and deep in-the-money?
a) Vega
b) Rho
c) Gamma
d) Delta

Example 13-6: FRM Exam 1998—Question 43

If risk is defined as the potential for unexpected loss, which factors contribute to the risk of a long put option position?
a) Delta, vega, rho
b) Vega, rho
c) Delta, vega, gamma, rho
d) Delta, vega, gamma, theta, rho

Example 13-7: FRM Exam 1998—Question 44

Same as Example 13-6 for a short call position.

Example 13-8: FRM Exam 1998—Question 45

Same as Example 13-6 for a long straddle position.

Example 13-9: FRM Exam 1999—Question 39

Which type of option experiences accelerating time decay as expiration approaches in an unchanged market?
a) In-the-money
b) Out-of-the-money
c) At-the-money
d) None of the above

Example 13-10: FRM Exam 1999—Question 38

Which of the following statements about option time value is *true*?

a) Deeply out-of-the-money options have more time value than at-the-money options with the same remaining time to expiration.

b) Deeply in-the-money options have more time value than at-the-money options with the same amount of time to expiration.

c) At-the-money options have higher time value than either out-of-the money or in-the-money options with the same remaining time to expiration.

d) At-the-money options have no time value.

Example 13-11: FRM Exam 1999—Question 56

According to the Black-Scholes model for evaluating European options on non–dividend-paying stock, which option sensitivity (Greek) would be identical for a call and a put option, given that the implied volatility, time to maturity, strike price, and risk-free interest rate are the same?

  I. Gamma

 II. Vega

III. Theta

IV. Rho

a) II only

b) I and II

c) All the above

d) III and IV

Example 13-12: FRM Exam 1998—Question 36

An investor bought a short-term at-the-money swaption straddle from a derivative dealer two days ago. Which of the following risk factors could lead to a loss to the investor?

  I. Interest rate delta risk

 II. Gamma risk

III. Vega risk

 IV. Theta (time decay) risk

  V. Counterparty credit risk

a) I and II only

b) I, II, and III only

c) I, III, IV, and V

d) I, II, III, IV, and V

Example 13-13: FRM Exam 1998—Question 37

An investor sold a short-term at-the-money swaption straddle to a derivative dealer two days ago. The option premium was paid up-front. Which of the following risk factors could lead to a loss to the investor?

  I. Interest rate delta risk

 II. Gamma risk

III. Vega risk

IV. Theta (time decay) risk

 V. Counterparty credit risk

a) I and II only

b) I, II, and III only

c) I, III, IV, and V only

d) I, II, III, IV, and V

Example 13-14: FRM Exam 2000—Question 76

How can a trader produce a short vega, long gamma position?

a) Buy short-maturity options, and sell long-maturity options.

b) Buy long-maturity options, and sell short-maturity options.

c) Buy and sell options of long maturity.

d) Buy and sell options of short maturity.

Example 13-15: FRM Exam 2001—Question 113

An option portfolio exhibits high unfavorable sensitivity to increases in implied volatility while experiencing significant daily losses with the passage of time. Which strategy would the trader most likely employ to hedge this portfolio?

a) Sell short-dated options and buy long-dated options

b) Buy short-dated options and sell long-dated options

c) Sell short-dated options and sell long-dated options

d) Buy short-dated options and buy long-dated options

13.3   Dynamic Hedging

The BS derivation showed how to price and hedge options. Perhaps even more important, it showed that holding a call option is equivalent to holding a fraction of the underlying asset, where the fraction changes dynamically over time.

13.3.1   Delta and Dynamic Hedging

This equivalence is illustrated in Figure 13-8, which displays the current value of a call as a function of the current spot price. The long position in one call is replicated by a partial position in the underlying asset. For an at-the-money position, the initial delta is about 0.5.

As the stock price increases from P_1 to P_2, the slope of the option curve, or delta, increases from Δ_1 to Δ_2. As a result, the option can be replicated by a larger position in the underlying asset. Conversely, when the stock price decreases, the size of the position is cut, as in a graduated stop-loss order. Thus the dynamic adjustment buys more of the asset as its price goes up and, conversely, sells it after a fall.

FIGURE 13-8 Dynamic Replication of a Call Option

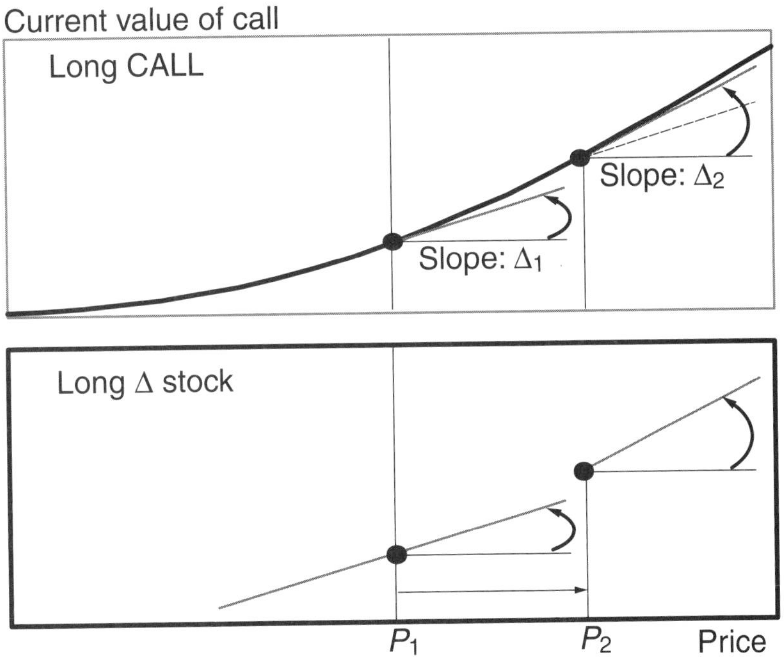

Figure 13-9 shows the dynamic replication of a put. We start at-the-money with Δ close to -0.5. As the price S goes up, Δ increases toward 0. Note that this is an increase since the initial delta was negative. As with the long call position, we *buy* more of the asset *after* its price has gone up. In contrast, short positions in calls and puts imply the opposite pattern. Dynamic hedging implies selling more of the asset after its price has gone up.

FIGURE 13-9 Dynamic Replication of a Put Option

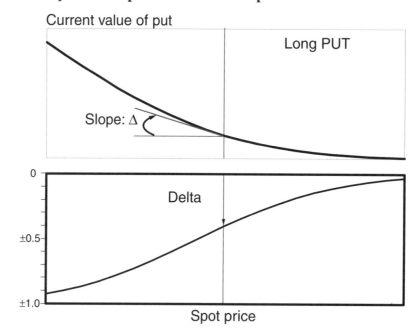

13.3.2   Implications

For risk managers, these patterns are extremely important for a number of reasons. First, a dynamic replication of a long option position is bound to lose money. This is because it buys the asset *after* the price has gone up—in other words, too late. Each transaction loses a small amount of money, which will accumulate precisely to the option premium.

A second point is that these automatic trading systems, if applied on large scale, have the potential to be destabilizing. Selling on a downturn in price can exacerbate the downside move. Some have argued that the crash of 1987 was due to the large-scale selling of portfolio insurers in a falling market. These portfolio insurers were in effect replicating a long position in puts, blindly selling when the market was falling.[3]

A third point is that this pattern of selling an asset after its price has gone down is similar to prudent risk management practices. Typically, traders must cut down their positions after they incur large losses. This is similar to decreasing Δ when S drops. Thus, loss-limit policies bear some resemblance to a long position in an option.

---

[3]The exact role of portfolio insurance, however, is still hotly debated. Others have argued that the crash was aggravated by a breakdown in market structures, that is, the additional uncertainty due to the inability of the stock exchanges to handle abnormal trading volumes.

Finally, the success of this replication strategy critically hinges on the assumption of a continuous GBM price process. This makes it theoretically possible to rebalance the portfolio as often as needed. In practice, the replication may fail if prices experience drastic jumps.

13.3.3   Distribution of Option Payoffs

Unlike linear derivatives such as forwards and futures, payoffs on options are intrinsically asymmetric. This is not necessarily because of the distribution of the underlying factor, which is often symmetric, but rather is due to the exposure profile. Long positions in options, whether calls or puts, have positive gamma, positive skewness, or long right tails. In contrast, short positions in options are short gamma and hence have negative skewness or long left tails. This is illustrated in Figure 13-10.

FIGURE 13-10 Distributions of Payoffs on Long and Short Options

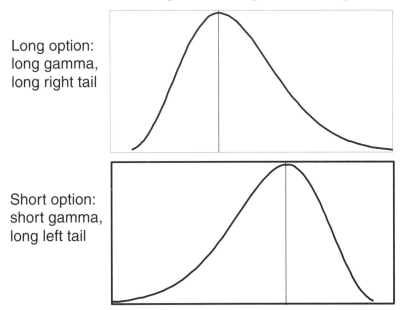

We now summarize VAR formulas for simple option positions. Assuming a normal distribution, the VAR of the underlying asset is

$$\text{VAR}(dS) = \alpha S \sigma (dS/S) \qquad (13.28)$$

where α corresponds to the desired confidence level (e.g., $\alpha = 1.645$ for a 95% confidence level). The linear VAR for an option is

$$\text{VAR}_1(dc) = \Delta \text{VAR}(dS) \qquad (13.29)$$

The quadratic VAR for an option is

$$\text{VAR}_2(dc) = \Delta\,\text{VAR}(dS) - \frac{1}{2}\Gamma\,\text{VAR}(dS)^2 \qquad (13.30)$$

Long option positions have positive gammas and hence lower risk compared with the use of a linear model. Conversely, negative gammas translate into quadratic VARs that exceed linear VARs.

Lest we think that such options require sophisticated risk management methods, what matters is the *extent* of nonlinearity. Figure 13-11 illustrates the risk of a call option with a maturity of three months. It shows that the degree of nonlinearity also depends on the horizon. With a VAR horizon of two weeks, the range of possible values for S is quite narrow. If S follows a normal distribution, the option value will be approximately normal. However, if the VAR horizon is set at two months, the nonlinearities in the exposure combine with the greater range of price movements to create a heavily skewed distribution.

So for plain-vanilla options, the linear approximation may be adequate as long as the VAR horizon is kept short. For more exotic options, or longer VAR horizons, the risk manager needs to account for nonlinearities.

FIGURE 13-11 Skewness and VAR Horizon

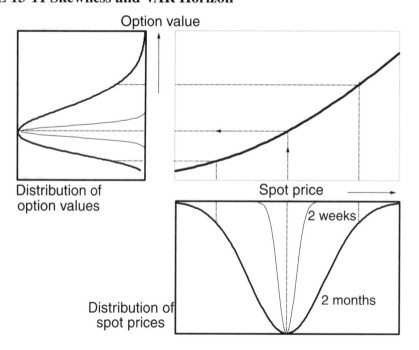

Example 13-16: FRM Exam 2001—Question 80

Which position is most risky?

a) Gamma-negative, delta-neutral

b) Gamma-positive, delta-positive

c) Gamma-negative, delta-positive

d) Gamma-positive, delta-neutral

Example 13-17: FRM Exam 1997—Question 28

Consider the risk of a long call on an asset with a notional amount of $1 million. The VAR of the underlying asset is 7.8%. If the option is a short-term at-the-money option, the VAR of the option position is slightly

a) Less than $39,000 when second-order terms are considered

b) More than $39,000 when second-order terms are considered

c) Less than $78,000 when second-order terms are considered

d) More than $78,000 when second-order terms are considered

Example 13-18: FRM Exam 1998—Question 27

A trader has an option position in crude oil with a delta of 100,000 barrels and gamma of minus 50,000 barrels per dollar move in price. Using the delta-gamma methodology, compute the VAR on this position, assuming the extreme move on crude oil is $2.00 per barrel.

a) $100,000

b) $200,000

c) $300,000

d) $400,000

Example 13-19: FRM Exam 1999—Question 94

A commodities trading firm has an options portfolio with a two-day VAR of $1.6 million. What would be an appropriate translation of this VAR to a 10-day horizon?

a) $8.0 million

b) $3.2 million

c) $5.6 million

d) Cannot be determined from the information provided

Example 13-20: FRM Exam 2000—Question 97

A trader buys an at-the-money call option with the intention of delta-hedging it to maturity. Which one of the following is likely to be the most profitable over the life of the option?

a) An increase in implied volatility

b) The underlying price steadily rising over the life of the option

c) The underlying price steadily decreasing over the life of the option

d) The underlying price drifting back and forth around the strike over the life of the option

---

13.4   Answers to Chapter Examples

Example 13-1: FRM Exam 1999—Question 65

a) The delta-gamma approximation is reasonably good for vanilla options (especially ones not too close to maturity).

Example 13-2: FRM Exam 1999—Question 88

c) Nonlinearities cause distributions to be nonnormal. Note that for long-term vanilla options, the delta-normal method may be appropriate.

Example 13-3: FRM Exam 2001—Question 79

a) This is an at-the-money option with a delta of about 0.5. Since the bank sold calls, it needs to delta-hedge by buying the shares. With a delta of 0.54, it would need to buy approximately 50,000 shares. Answer a) is the closest. Note that most other information is superfluous.

Example 13-4: FRM Exam 1999—Question 69

a) The volatility of the hedged portfolio must be proportional to the volatility of the underlying asset, σ. The volatility of the hedged position increases as the rebalancing horizon increases. If we have continuous rebalancing (N very large), there should be no risk. Otherwise, it must be inversely related to the number of rebalancings N.

Example 13-5: FRM Exam 2001—Question 123

d) A short-dated in-the-money option behaves essentially like a position of delta in the underlying asset. The gamma and vega are low.

Example 13-6: FRM Exam 1998—Question 43

a) Theta is not a risk factor since time movements are deterministic. Gamma is positive for a long position and therefore lowers risk. The remaining exposures are delta, vega, and rho.

Example 13-7: FRM Exam 1998—Question 44

c) Gamma now creates risk.

Example 13-8: FRM Exam 1998—Question 45

b) The position is now delta-neutral and has positive gamma. The remaining exposures are vega and rho.

Example 13-9: FRM Exam 1999—Question 39

c) Time decay describes the loss of option value, which is greatest for at-the-money options with short maturities.

Example 13-10: FRM Exam 1999—Question 38

c) See Figure 13-7, describing the option theta.

Example 13-11: FRM Exam 1999—Question 56

b) An otherwise identical call and put have the same gamma and vega. Theta is different, even though the formula contains the same first term, due to the differential effect of time on r and y. Rho is totally different, positive for the call and negative for the put.

Example 13-12: FRM Exam 1998—Question 36

c) The investor is long the option and has already paid the premium. Therefore, there is credit risk, as the counterparty could default when the contracts have positive value. The position is also exposed to decreases in volatility (vega risk) and the passage of time (theta risk). There is no gamma risk, as the position has positive gamma.

Example 13-13: FRM Exam 1998—Question 37

b) This is the reverse of the previous position. There is no credit risk, as only the investor can lose money, not the dealer. Now there is gamma risk. The position is also exposed to increases in volatility (vega risk).

Example 13-14: FRM Exam 2000—Question 76

a) Long positions in options have positive gamma and vega. Gamma (or instability in delta) increases near maturity; vega decreases near maturity. So to obtain positive gamma and negative vega, we need to buy short-maturity options and sell long-maturity options.

Example 13-15: FRM Exam 2001—Question 113

a) Such a portfolio is short vega (volatility) and short theta (time). We need to implement a hedge that is delta-neutral and involves buying and selling options with different maturities. Long positions in short-dated options have high negative theta and low positive vega. Hedging can be achieved by selling short-term options and buying long-term options.

Example 13-16: FRM Exam 2001—Question 80

c) The worst combination involves some directional risk plus some negative gamma. Directional risk, delta-positive, could lead to a large loss if the underlying price falls.

Example 13-17: FRM Exam 1997—Question 28

a) An ATM option has a delta of about 50% delta and is long gamma. Its linear VAR is $0.50 \times 0.078 \times \$1,000,000 = \$39,000$. Because the gamma is positive, the risk is slightly lower than the linear VAR.

Example 13-18: FRM Exam 1998—Question 27

c) Note that gamma is negative. Using the Taylor approximation, the worst loss is obtained as the price move of $df = \Delta(-dS) + \frac{1}{2}\Gamma(dS)^2 = 100,000 \times -\$2 + \frac{1}{2}(-50,000)(\$2)^2 = -\$200,000 - \$100,000 = -\$300,000$.

Example 13-19: FRM Exam 1999—Question 94

d) As Figure 13-11 shows, the distribution profile of an option changes as the horizon changes. This makes it difficult to extrapolate short-horizon VAR to longer horizons without knowing more information on gamma, for instance.

Example 13-20: FRM Exam 2000—Question 97

d) An important aspect of the question is the fact that the option is held to maturity. Answer a) is incorrect because changes in the implied volatility would change the value of the option, but this has no effect when holding to maturity. The profit from the dynamic portfolio will depend on whether the actual volatility differs from the initial implied volatility. It does not depend on whether the option ends up in-the-money or not, so answers b) and c) are incorrect. The portfolio will be profitable if the actual volatility is small, which implies small moves around the strike price.

Chapter 14

Modeling Risk Factors

We now turn to an analysis of the distribution of risk factors used in risk measurement. A previous chapter described the major risk factors, including fixed-income, equity, currency, and commodity price risk. The emphasis was on volatility as a measure of dispersion. More generally, risk managers need to consider the whole shape of the distribution, which is not necessarily normal, as well as potential time variation in this distribution.

Most financial time series are characterized by fatter tails than the normal distribution. In addition, there is ample empirical evidence that, over short horizons, risk changes in a predictable fashion. This time variation could potentially explain the observed high frequency of extreme observations. These could be generated from distributions with temporarily higher volatility.

Section 14.1 starts by describing the normal distribution. We compare the normal and lognormal distributions and explain why this choice is so popular. A major failing of this distribution, however, is its inability to represent the frequency of large observations found in financial data. Section 14.2 discusses distributions that have fatter tails than the normal.

Section 14.3 turns to time variation in risk. We summarize the generalized autoregressive conditional heteroscedastic (GARCH) model and a special case, which is RiskMetrics' exponentially weighted moving average (EWMA).

351

14.1 Normal and Lognormal Distributions

14.1.1 Why the Normal?

The normal, or Gaussian, distribution is usually the first choice for modeling asset returns. This distribution plays a special role in statistics, as it is easy to handle and is stable under addition, meaning that a sum of normal variables is itself normal. It also provides the limiting distribution of the average of *independent* random variables (through the Central Limit Theorem).

Empirically, the normal distribution provides a rough, first-order approximation to the distribution of many random variables: rates of changes in currency prices, rates of changes in stock prices, rates of changes in bond prices, changes in yields, and rates of changes in commodity prices. All of these are characterized by greater frequencies of small moves than large moves, reflected in a greater weight in the center of the distribution.

14.1.2 Computing Returns

In what follows, the random variable is the new price P_1, given the current price P_0. Defining $r = (P_1 - P_0)/P_0$ as the rate of return in the price, we can start with the assumption is that this random variable is drawn from a normal distribution,

$$r \sim \Phi(\mu, \sigma) \tag{14.1}$$

with some mean μ and standard deviation σ. Turning to prices, we have $P_1 = P_0(1 + r)$ and

$$P_1 \sim P_0 + \Phi(P_0\mu, P_0\sigma) \tag{14.2}$$

For instance, starting from a stock price of \$100, if $\mu = 0\%$ and $\sigma = 15\%$, we have $P_1 \sim \$100 + \Phi(\$0, \$15)$.

For many of these variables, however, the normal distribution cannot even be theoretically correct. Because of limited liability, stock prices cannot go below zero. Similarly, commodity prices and yields cannot turn negative. This is why another popular distribution is the **lognormal distribution**, which is such that

$$R = \ln(P_1/P_0) \sim \Phi(\mu, \sigma) \tag{14.3}$$

By taking the logarithm, the price is given by $P_1 = P_0 \exp(R)$, which precludes prices from turning negative, as the exponential function is always positive. Figure 14-1 compares the normal and lognormal distributions over a one-year horizon with $\sigma = 15\%$ annually. The distributions are very similar, except for the tails. The lognormal is skewed to the right.

FIGURE 14-1 Normal and Lognormal Distributions: Annual Horizon

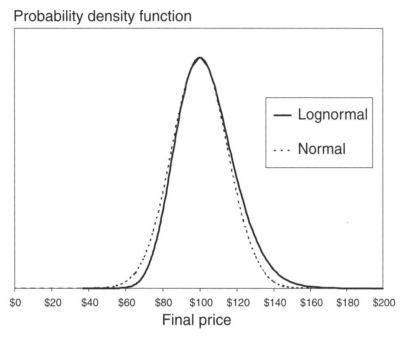

The difference between the two distributions is driven by the size of the volatility parameter over the horizon. Small values of this parameter imply that the distributions are virtually identical. This can happen either when the asset is not very risky, that is, when the annual volatility is small, or when the horizon is very short. In this situation, there is very little chance of prices turning negative. The limited-liability constraint is not important.

> **Key concept:**
> The normal and lognormal distributions are very similar for short horizons or low volatilities.

As an example, Table 14-1 compares the computations of returns over a one-day and one-year horizon. The one-day returns are 1.000% and 0.995% for discrete and log returns, respectively, which translates into a relative difference of 0.5%, which is minor. The difference is more significant over longer horizons.

TABLE 14-1 Comparison between Discrete and Log Returns

	Daily	Annual
Initial price	100	100
Ending price	101	115
Discrete return	1.0000	15.0000
Log return	0.9950	13.9762
Relative difference	0.50%	7.33%

14.1.3 Time Aggregation

Longer horizons can be accommodated assuming a constant lognormal distribution across horizons. Over two periods, for instance, the price movement can be described as the sum of the price movements over each day:

$$R_{t,2} = \ln(P_t/P_{t-2}) = \ln(P_t/P_{t-1}) + \ln(P_{t-1}/P_{t-2}) = R_{t-1} + R_t \qquad (14.4)$$

If returns are identically and independently distributed (i.i.d.), the variance of multiple-period returns is, defining T as the number of steps,

$$V[R(0, T)] = V[R(0, 1)] + V[R(1, 2)] + \cdots + V[R(T - 1, T)] = V[R(0, 1)]T \qquad (14.5)$$

since the variances are all the same and all the covariance terms are zero because of the independence assumption. Similarly, the mean of multiple-period returns is

$$E[R(0, T)] = E[R(0, 1)] + E[R(1, 2)] + \cdots + E[R(T - 1, T)] = E[R(0, 1)]T \qquad (14.6)$$

assuming expected returns are the same for each day.

Thus the multiple-period volatility is

$$\sigma_T = \sigma\sqrt{T} \qquad (14.7)$$

If the distribution is stable under addition, that is, we can use the same multiplier for a one-period and a T-period return, we have a multiple-period VAR of

$$\text{VAR} = \alpha(\sigma\sqrt{T})W \qquad (14.8)$$

In other words, extension to multiple periods follows a square-root-of-time rule. Figure 14-2 shows how VAR grows with the length of the horizon and for various confidence levels. This is scaled to an annual standard deviation of 1, which is an 84.1%

VAR. The figure shows that VAR increases more slowly than time. The one-month 99% VAR is 0.67, increasing only to 2.33 at a one-year horizon.

In summary, the square-root-of-time rule applies under the following conditions:

- The distribution is the same at each period, that is, there is no predictable time variation in expected return or in risk.

- Returns are uncorrelated/independent across periods, so that all covariance terms disappear.

- The distribution is the same for one- and T-period returns, or is stable under addition, such as the normal.

FIGURE 14-2 VAR at Increasing Horizons

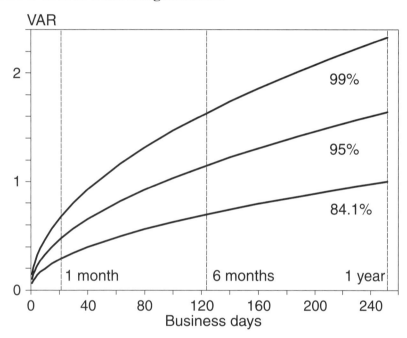

If returns are not independent, we may be able to characterize the risk in some cases. For instance, when returns follow a first-order autoregressive process,

$$R_t = \rho R_{t-1} + u_t \tag{14.9}$$

we can write the variance of two-day returns as

$$V[R_t + R_{t-1}] = V[R_t] + V[R_{t-1}] + 2\operatorname{Cov}[R_t, R_{t-1}] = \sigma^2 + \sigma^2 + 2\rho\sigma^2 \tag{14.10}$$

or

$$V[R_t + R_{t-1}] = \sigma^2 \times 2[1 + \rho] \tag{14.11}$$

A positive value for ρ describes a situation where a movement in one direction is likely to be followed by another in the same direction. This implies that markets are trending. In this case, the longer-term volatility increases faster than with the usual square-root-of-time rule. On the other hand, a negative value for ρ describes a situation where a movement in one direction is likely to be reversed later. In this mean-reversion case, the longer-term volatility increases more slowly than with the usual square-root-of-time rule.

Example 14-1: FRM Exam 1999—Question 64

Under what circumstances is it appropriate to scale up a VAR estimate from a shorter holding period to a longer holding period using the square-root-of-time rule?

a) It is never appropriate.

b) It is always appropriate.

c) When either mean reversion or trend is present in the historical data series.

d) When neither mean reversion nor trend is present in the historical data series.

Example 14-2: FRM Exam 1998—Question 5

Consider a portfolio with a one-day VAR of $1 million. Assume that the market is trending with an autocorrelation of 0.1. Under this scenario, what would you expect the two-day VAR to be?

a) $2 million

b) $1.414 million

c) $1.483 million

d) $1.449 million

14.2 Fat Tails

Perhaps the most serious problem with the normal distribution is the fact that its tails "disappear" too fast, at least faster than what is empirically observed in financial data. We typically observe that every market experiences one or more daily moves of four standard deviations or more per year. Such frequency is incompatible with a normal distribution. With a normal distribution, the probability of this happening is 0.0032% for one day, which implies a frequency of once every 125 years.

Key rule of thumb:

Every financial market experiences one or more daily price moves of 4 standard deviations or more each year. And in any year, there is usually at least one market that has a daily move greater than 10 standard deviations.

This empirical observation can be explained in a number of ways: (1) The true distribution has fatter tails (e.g., Student's t), or (2) the observations are drawn from a mix of distributions (e.g., a mix of two normals, one with low risk and the other with high risk), or (3) the distribution is nonstationary.

The first explanation is certainly a possibility. Figure 14-3 displays the density function of the normal and Student's t distributions, with 4 and 6 degrees of freedom (df). The Student density has fatter tails, which better reflect the occurrences of extreme observations in empirical financial data.

FIGURE 14-3 Normal and Student Distributions

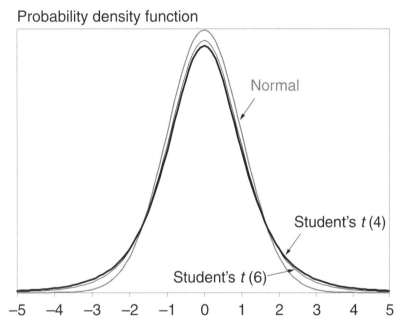

This information is further detailed in Table 14-2. The left panel reports the tail probability of an observation lower than the deviate. For instance, the probability of observing a draw less than -3 is 0.001, or 0.1%, for the normal, 0.012 for the Student's t with 6 degrees of freedom, and 0.020 for the Student's t with 4 degrees of freedom.

TABLE 14-2 Comparison of the Normal and Student's t Distributions

Deviate	Tail Probability			Expected Number in 250 Days		
	Normal	t df $= 6$	t df $= 4$	Normal	t df $= 6$	t df $= 4$
-5	0.00000	0.00123	0.00375	0.00	0.31	0.94
-4	0.00003	0.00356	0.00807	0.01	0.89	2.02
-3	0.00135	0.01200	0.01997	0.34	3.00	4.99
-2	0.02275	0.04621	0.05806	5.69	11.55	14.51
-1	0.15866	0.17796	0.18695	39.66	44.49	46.74
				Deviate (alpha)		
Probability $= 1\%$				2.33	3.14	3.75
Ratio to normal				1.00	1.35	1.61

We can transform these into an expected number of occurrences in one year, or 250 business days. The right panel shows that the corresponding numbers are 0.34, 3.00, and 4.99 for the respective distributions. In other words, the normal distribution projects only 0.3 days of movements below $z = -3$. With a Student's t with df $= 4$, the expected number is five in a year, which is closer to reality.

The bottom panel reports the deviate corresponding to a 99% right-tail confidence level, or a 1% left tail. For the normal distribution, this is the usual 2.33. For the Student's t with df $= 4$, α is 3.75, much higher. The ratio of the two is 1.61. Thus a rule of thumb would be to correct the VAR measure from a normal distribution by a ratio of 1.61 to achieve the desired coverage in the presence of fat tails. More generally, this explains why "safety factors" are used to multiply VAR measures, such as the Basel multiplicative factor of 3.

Example 14-3: FRM Exam 1999—Question 83

In the presence of fat tails in the distribution of returns, VAR based on the delta-normal method would (for a linear portfolio)
a) Underestimate the true VAR
b) Be the same as the true VAR
c) Overestimate the true VAR
d) Cannot be determined from the information provided

14.3   Time Variation in Risk

An alternative explanation is that empirical data can be viewed as drawn from a normal distribution with time-varying parameters. This is useful only if this time variation has some structure, or predictability.

14.3.1   GARCH

A specification that has proved quite successful in practice is the **generalized autoregressive conditional heteroscedastic (GARCH)** model, developed by Engle (1982) and Bollerslev (1986).

This class of models assumes that the return at time t has a normal distribution, for example, conditional on parameters μ_t and σ_t:

$$r_t \sim \Phi(\mu_t, \sigma_t) \tag{14.12}$$

The important point is that σ is indexed by time. In this context, we define the **conditional variance** as that conditional on current information. This may differ from the **unconditional variance**, which is the same for the whole sample. Thus the average variance is unconditional, whereas a time-varying variance is conditional.

There is substantial empirical evidence that conditional volatility models successfully forecast risk. The general assumption is that the conditional returns have a normal distribution, although this could be extended to other distributions such as Student's t.

The GARCH model assumes that the conditional variance depends on the latest innovation and on the previous conditional variance. Define $h_t = \sigma_t^2$ as the conditional variance, using information up to time $t - 1$, and r_{t-1} as the previous day's return. The simplest such model is the GARCH(1, 1) process,

$$h_t = \alpha_0 + \alpha_1 r_{t-1}^2 + \beta h_{t-1} \tag{14.13}$$

which involves one lag of the innovation and one lag of the previous forecast. The β term is important because it allows persistence in the shocks, which is a realistic feature of the data.

The average, unconditional variance is found by setting $E[r_{t-1}^2] = h_t = h_{t-1} = h$. Solving for h, we find

$$h = \frac{\alpha_0}{1 - \alpha_1 - \beta} \tag{14.14}$$

This model will be stationary when the sum of parameters $\alpha_1 + \beta$ is less than unity. This sum is also called the **persistence**, as it defines the speed at which shocks to the variance revert to their long-run values.

To understand how the process works, consider Table 14-3. The parameters are $\alpha_0 = 0.01$, $\alpha_1 = 0.03$, $\beta = 0.95$. The unconditional variance is $0.01/(1 - 0.03 -$

0.95) = 0.7 daily, which is typical of a currency series, as it translates into an annualized volatility of 11%. The process is stable since $\alpha_1 + \beta = 0.98 < 1$.

At time 0, we start with variance $h_0 = 1.1$ (expressed in percent squared). The conditional volatility is $\sqrt{h_0} = 1.05\%$. The next day, there is a large return of 3%. The new variance forecast is then $h_1 = 0.01 + 0.03 \times 3^2 + 0.95 \times 1.1 = 1.32$. The conditional volatility has gone up to 1.15%. If nothing happens in the following days, the next variance forecast is $h_2 = 0.01 + 0.03 \times 0^2 + 0.95 \times 1.32 = 1.27$, and so on.

TABLE 14-3 Building a GARCH Forecast

Time $t-1$	Return r_{t-1}	Conditional Variance h_t	Conditional Risk $\sqrt{h_t}$	Conditional 95% Limit $2\sqrt{h_t}$
0	0.0	1.10	1.05	±2.10
1	3.0	1.32	1.15	±2.30
2	0.0	1.27	1.13	±2.25
3	0.0	1.22	1.10	±2.20

Figure 14-4 illustrates the dynamics of shocks to a GARCH process for various values of the persistence parameter. As the conditional variance deviates from the starting value, it slowly reverts to the long-run value at a speed determined by $\alpha_1 + \beta$.

FIGURE 14-4 Shocks to a GARCH Process

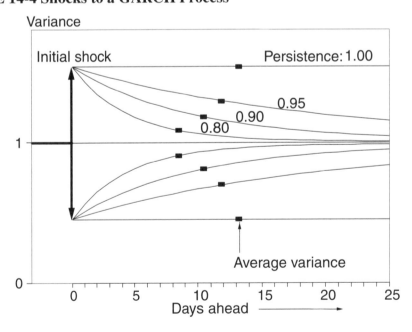

Note that these are forecasts of one-day variances. If the horizon is longer, say 25 days, what matters is the *average* variance over the horizon, whose value is marked on the graph.

The graph also shows why the square-root-of-time rule for extrapolating returns does not apply when risk is time-varying. If the initial value of the variance is greater than the long-run average, simply extrapolating the one-day variance to a longer horizon will overstate the average variance. Conversely, starting from a lower value and applying the square-root-of-time rule will understate risk.

> **Key concept:**
> Use of the square-root-of-time rule to scale one-day returns to longer horizons is generally inappropriate when risk is time-varying.

14.3.2   EWMA

The RiskMetrics approach is a particular, convenient case of the GARCH process. Variances are modeled using an **exponentially weighted moving-average (EWMA)** forecast. The forecast is a weighted average of the previous forecast, with weight λ, and of the latest squared innovation, with weight $(1 - \lambda)$:

$$h_t = \lambda h_{t-1} + (1 - \lambda)r_{t-1}^2 \tag{14.15}$$

The λ parameter, also called the **decay factor**, determines the relative weights placed on previous observations. The EWMA model places geometrically declining weights on past observations, assigning greater importance to recent observations. By recursively replacing h_{t-1} in Equation (14.15), we have

$$h_t = (1 - \lambda)[r_{t-1}^2 + \lambda r_{t-2}^2 + \lambda^2 r_{t-3}^2 + \cdots] \tag{14.16}$$

The weights thus decrease at a geometric rate. The lower λ, the more quickly older observations are forgotten. RiskMetrics has chosen $\lambda = 0.94$ for daily data and $\lambda = 0.97$ for monthly data.

Table 14-4 shows how to build the EWMA forecast using a parameter of $\lambda = 0.95$, which is consistent with the previous GARCH example. At time 0, we start with variance $h_0 = 1.1$, as before. The next day we have a return of 3%. The new variance forecast is then $h_1 = 0.05 \times 3^2 + 0.95 \times 1.1 = 1.50$. The next day this moves to $h_2 = 0.05 \times 0^2 + 0.95 \times 1.50 = 1.42$, and so on.

TABLE 14-4 Building an EWMA Forecast

Time $t-1$	Return r_{t-1}	Conditional Variance h_t	Conditional Risk $\sqrt{h_t}$	Conditional 95% Limit $2\sqrt{h_t}$
0	0.0	1.10	1.05	± 2.1
1	3.0	1.50	1.22	± 2.4
2	0.0	1.42	1.19	± 2.4
3	0.0	1.35	1.16	± 2.3

This model is a special case of the GARCH process, where α_0 is set to 0, and α_1 and β sum to unity. The model therefore has permanent persistence. Shocks to the volatility do not decay, as shown in Figure 14-4, when the persistence is 1.00. Thus longer-term extrapolation from the GARCH and EWMA models may give quite different forecasts. Over a one-day horizon, however, the two models are quite similar and are often indistinguishable from each other.

Figure 14-5 displays the pattern of weights for previous observations. With $\lambda = 0.94$, the weights decay rather quickly. The weight on the last day is $(1 - \lambda) = (1 - 0.94) = 0.06$. The weight on the previous day is $(1 - \lambda)\lambda = 0.0564$, and so on. The weight drops below 0.00012 for data more than 100 days old. With $\lambda = 0.97$, the weights start at a lower level but decay more slowly. In comparison, moving-average models have a fixed window, with weights equal within the window but otherwise zero.

Example 14-4: FRM Exam 2002—Question 13

The GARCH model is useful for simulating asset returns. Which of the following statements about this model is *false*?

a) The exponentially weighted moving-average (EWMA) approach of RiskMetrics is a particular case of a GARCH process.

b) GARCH allows for time-varying volatility.

c) GARCH can produce fat tails in the return distribution.

d) GARCH imposes a positive conditional mean return.

FIGURE 14-5 Weights on Past Observations

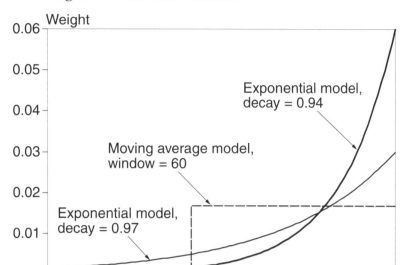

Example 14-5: FRM Exam 1999—Question 103

The current estimate of daily volatility is 1.5%. The closing price of an asset yesterday was $30.00. The closing price of the asset today is $30.50. Using the EWMA model with $\lambda = 0.94$, the updated estimate of volatility is

a) 1.5096
b) 1.5085
c) 1.5092
d) 1.5083

Example 14-6: FRM Exam 1999—Question 72

Until January 1999 the historical volatility for the Brazilian real versus the U.S. dollar had been very low for several years. On January 13, 1999, Brazil abandoned its defense of the currency peg. Using the data from the close of business on January 13, which of the following methods for calculating volatility would have shown the greatest jump in measured historical volatility?

a) 250-day equal weight
b) Exponentially weighted with a daily decay factor of 0.94
c) 60-day equal weight
d) All of the above

14.3.3 Option Data

All the previous forecasts were based on historical data. While conditional volatility models are a substantial improvement over models that assume constant risk, they are always, by definition, one step too late.

These models start to react *after* a big shock has occurred. In many situations, this may be too late. Hence, the quest for forward-looking risk measures.

Such forward-looking measures are contained in option implied standard deviations (ISDs). ISDs are obtained by first assuming an option pricing model and then inverting the model, that is, solving for the parameter that will make the model price equal to the observed market price.

Define $f()$ as an option pricing function, such as the Black-Scholes model for European options. Normally, we input σ into f along with other parameters and then solve for the option price. However, if the market trades these options and if all the other inputs are observable, we can recover σ_{ISD} by setting the model price equal to the market price:

$$c_{MARKET} = f(\sigma_{ISD}) \tag{14.17}$$

This assumes that the model fits the data perfectly, which may not be the case for out-of-the-money options. Hence, this method works best for short-term (two weeks to three months) at-the-money options.

This approach can even be generalized to implied correlations. For this, we need triplets of options (e.g., \$/yen, \$/euro, yen/euro). The first one can be used to recover σ_1, the second σ_2, and the third the covariance σ_{12}, from which the implied correlation ρ_{12} can be recovered.

There is much empirical evidence that ISDs provide superior forecasts of future risk. This is to be expected, as the essence of option trading is to place volatility bets.

Key concept:
Whenever possible, use the information in option ISDs to forecast risk.

The main drawback of this method is that, while historical time series models can be applied systematically to all series for which we have data, we do not have actively traded options for all risk factors. In addition, we have even fewer combinations of options that permit us to compute implied correlations. This makes it difficult to integrate ISDs with time series models.

14.3.4   Implied Distributions

Options can be used to derive much more than the volatility. Recently, option watchers have observed some inconsistencies in the pricing of options, especially for stock index options. In particular, options that differ only in their strike prices are characterized by different ISDs. Options that are out-of-the-money have higher ISDs than at-the-money options. This has become known as the **smile effect** in ISDs, shown in Figure 14-6, which plots equity ISDs against the ratio of the strike price over the current spot price. In this case, the smile is totally asymmetric (more like a smirk).

FIGURE 14-6 Smile Effect

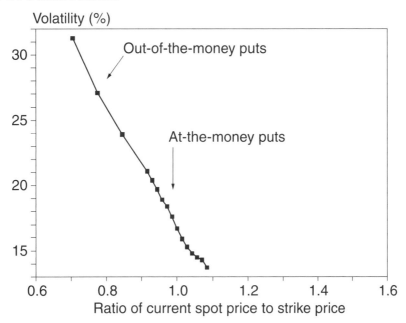

Low values of the ratio, describing out-of-the-money puts, are associated with high ISDs. In other words, out-of-the-money puts appear overpriced relative to others. Here the effect is asymmetric, or most pronounced for the left side.

Different ISDs are clearly inconsistent with the joint assumption of a lognormal distribution for prices and efficient markets. Perhaps the data are trying to tell a story. This effect was pronounced after the stock market crash of 1987, raising the possibility that the market expected another crash, although with low probability.

Recently, Rubinstein (1994) has extended the concept of ISD to the whole **implied distribution** of future prices. By judiciously choosing options with sufficiently spaced strike prices, one can recover the entire implied distribution that is consistent with option prices. This distribution, shown in Figure 14-7, displays a hump for values of the future price 30% below the current price. This hump is nowhere apparent in the usual lognormal distribution.

FIGURE 14-7 Implied Distribution

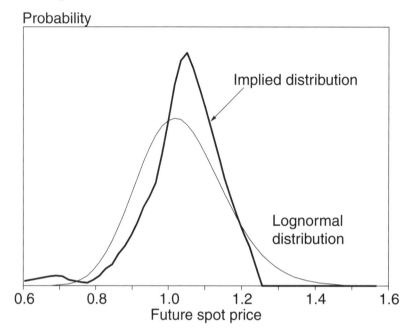

This puzzling result can be given two interpretations. The first is that the market indeed predicts a small probability of a future crash. The second has to do with the fact that this distribution derived from option prices assumes risk-neutrality, since the Black-Scholes approach values options assuming investors are risk-neutral. Thus this distribution may differ from the true, objective distribution due to a **risk premium**. Intuitively, investors may be very averse to a situation where they have to suffer a large fall in the value of their stock portfolios. As a result, they will bid up the price of put options, which is reflected in a higher-than-otherwise implied volatility.

This is currently an area of active research. The consensus, however, is that options should contain valuable information about future distributions since, after all, option traders bet good money on their forecasts.

14.4   Answers to Chapter Examples

Example 14-1: FRM Exam 1999—Question 64

d) The presence of either mean reversion or trend (or time variation in risk) implies a different distribution of returns for different holding periods.

Example 14-2: FRM Exam 1998—Question 5

c) Knowing that the variance is $V(\text{2-day}) = V(\text{1-day})[2 + 2\rho]$, we find VAR(2-day) $= \text{VAR(1-day)}\sqrt{2 + 2\rho} = \$1\sqrt{2 + 0.2} = \$1.483$, assuming the same distribution for the different horizons.

Example 14-3: FRM Exam 1999—Question 83

a) With fat tails, the normal VAR would underestimate the true VAR.

Example 14-4: FRM Exam 2002—Question 13

d) The GARCH model allows for time variation in volatility and includes the EWMA model as a special case. It can also induce fat tails in the return distribution, but it says nothing about the mean, so d) is false.

Example 14-5: FRM Exam 1999—Question 103

a) The updated volatility is, from Equation (14.15), the square root of

$$h_t = \lambda(\text{current volatility})^2 + (1 - \lambda)(\text{current return})^2$$

Using log returns, we find $R = 1.653\%$ and $\sigma_t = 1.5096\%$. With discrete returns, we find $R = 1.667\%$ and $\sigma_t = 1.5105\%$.

Example 14-6: FRM Exam 1999—Question 72

b) The EWMA puts a weight of 0.06 on the latest observation, which is higher than the weight of 0.0167 for the 60-day MA and 0.004 for the 250-day MA.

Chapter 15

VAR Methods

So far, we have considered sources of risk in isolation. This approach reflects the state of the art up to the beginning of the 1990s. Until then, risk was measured and managed at the level of a desk or business unit. Similarly, courses in finance dealt separately with equity risk, interest rate risk, and currency risk. The profession of finance was basically compartmentalized. This approach, however, fails to take advantage of portfolio theory, which has taught us that risk should be measured at the level of the portfolio.

This chapter turns to firm-wide VAR methods. These can be separated into local valuation and full valuation methods. **Local valuation methods** make use of the valuation of the instruments at the current point, along with the first and perhaps the second partial derivatives. **Full valuation methods**, in contrast, reprice the instruments over a broad range of values for the risk factors.

These methods are discussed in Section 15.1. Section 15.2 presents an overview of the three main VAR methods. Section 15.3 works through a detailed example, a forward currency contract.

Movements in the value of this contract depend on three risk factors, the spot exchange rate, the local interest rate, and the foreign interest rate. This illustrates the process of **mapping**, which consists of replacing each instrument by its exposures on the selected risk factors.

Even with many more forward contracts, we could still use the same three fundamental risk factors. It would be infeasible to model all instruments individually, because there are too many. The art of risk management consists of choosing a set of limited risk factors that will adequately cover the spectrum of risks for the portfolio at hand. Thus, risk management is truly the art of approximation.

15.1   VAR: Local versus Full Valuation

The various approaches to VAR described in Figure 15-1. The left branch describes local valuation methods, also known as **analytical methods**. These include linear models and nonlinear models. Linear models are based on the covariance matrix approach. This matrix can be simplified using factor models, or even a diagonal model, which is a one-factor model.

Nonlinear models take into account the first and second partial derivatives. The latter are called gamma or convexity. The right branch describes full valuation methods, including historical or Monte Carlo simulations.

FIGURE 15-1 VAR Methods

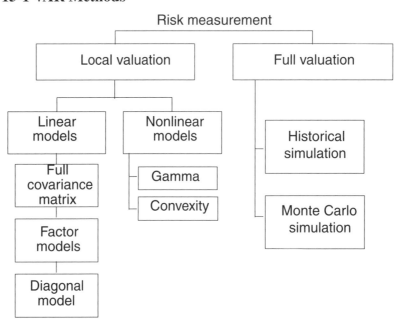

15.1.1   Local Valuation

VAR was born from the recognition that we need an estimate that accounts for various sources of risk and expresses loss in terms of probability. Extending the duration equation to the worst change in yield at some confidence level dy, we have

$$(\text{Worst } dP) = (-D^* P) \times (\text{Worst } dy) \qquad (15.1)$$

where D^* is modified duration. For a long position in the bond, the worst movement in yield is an increase at, say, the 95% confidence level. This will lead to a fall in the bond value at the same confidence level. We call this approach **local valuation**, because it uses information about the initial price and the exposure at the initial point. As a result, VAR for the bond is given by

$$\text{VAR}(dP) = (D^*P) \times \text{VAR}(dy) \qquad (15.2)$$

The main advantage of this approach is its simplicity: The distribution of the price is the same as that of the change in yield. This is particularly convenient for portfolios with numerous sources of risks, because linear combinations of normal distributions are normally distributed. Figure 15-2, for example, shows how the linear exposure combined with the normal density (in the right panel) combines to create a normal density.

FIGURE 15-2 Distribution with Linear Exposures

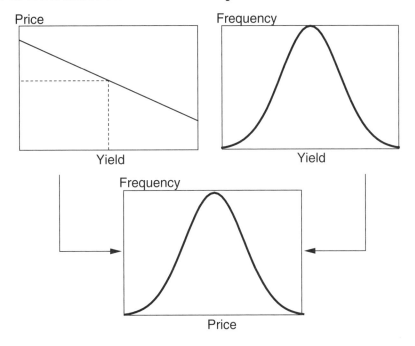

15.1.2   Full Valuation

More generally, to take into account nonlinear relationships, we would have to reprice the bond under different scenarios for the yield. Defining y_0 as the initial yield,

$$(\text{Worst } dP) = P[y_0 + (\text{Worst } dy)] - P[y_0] \qquad (15.3)$$

We call this approach **full valuation**, because it requires repricing the asset.

This approach is illustrated in Figure 15-3, where the nonlinear exposure combined with the normal density creates a distribution that is no longer symmetrical, but skewed to the right. This is more precise but, unfortunately, more complex than a simple, linear valuation method.

FIGURE 15-3 Distribution with Nonlinear Exposures

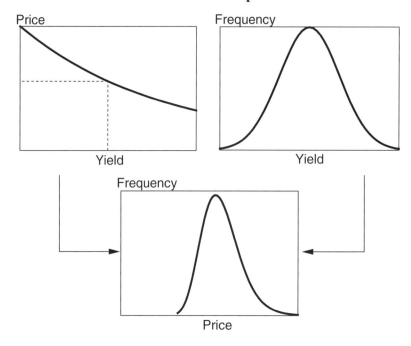

15.1.3 Delta-Gamma Method

Ideally, we would like to keep the simplicity of the local valuation while accounting for nonlinearities in the payoffs patterns. Using the Taylor expansion,

$$dP \approx \frac{\partial P}{\partial y}dy + (1/2)\frac{\partial^2 P}{\partial y^2}(dy)^2 = -D^*P\,dy + (1/2)CP(dy)^2 \qquad (15.4)$$

where the second-order term involves convexity C. Note that the valuation is still local because we value the bond only once, at the original point. The first and second derivatives are also evaluated at the local point.

Because the price is a monotonous function of the underlying yield, we can use the Taylor expansion to find the worst down-move in the bond price from the worst move in the yield. Calling this $dy^* = \text{VAR}(dy)$, we have

$$(\text{Worst } dP) = P(y_0 + dy^*) - P(y_0) \approx (-D^*P)(dy^*) + (1/2)(C\,P)(dy^*)^2 \ (15.5)$$

This leads to a simple adjustment for VAR:

$$\text{VAR}(dP) = (D^*P) \times \text{VAR}(dy) - (1/2)(C\ P) \times \text{VAR}(dy)^2 \qquad (15.6)$$

More generally, this method can be applied to derivatives, for which we write the Taylor approximation as

$$df \approx \frac{\partial f}{\partial S}dS + (1/2)\frac{\partial^2 f}{\partial S^2}dS^2 = \Delta dS + (1/2)\Gamma\ dS^2 \qquad (15.7)$$

where Γ is now the second derivative, or gamma, as for convexity.

For a long call option, the worst value is achieved as the underlying price moves down by VAR(dS). With $\Delta > 0$ and $\Gamma > 0$, the VAR for the derivative is now

$$\text{VAR}(df) = \Delta \times \text{VAR}(dS) - (1/2)\Gamma \times \text{VAR}(dS)^2 \qquad (15.8)$$

This method is called **delta-gamma** because it provides an analytical, second-order correction to the delta-normal VAR. This explains why long positions in options, with positive gamma, have less risk than with a linear model. Conversely, short positions in options have greater risk than implied by a linear model.

This simple adjustment, unfortunately, works only when the payoff function is monotonous, that is, involves a one-to-one relationship between the option value f and S. More generally, the **delta-gamma-delta** VAR method involves, first, computing the moments of df using Equation (15.7) and, second, choosing the normal distribution that provides the best fit to these moments.

The improvement brought about by this method depends on the size of the second-order coefficient, as well as the size of the worst move in the risk factor. For forward contracts, for instance, $\Gamma = 0$, and there is no point in adding second-order terms. Similarly, for most fixed-income instruments over a short horizon, the convexity effect is relatively small and can be ignored.

Example 15-1: FRM Exam 2002—Question 38

If you use delta-VAR for a portfolio of options, which of the following statements is *always* correct?

a) It necessarily understates the VAR because it uses a linear approximation.

b) It can sometimes overstate the VAR.

c) It performs most poorly for a portfolio of deep in-the money options.

d) It performs most poorly for a portfolio of deep out-of-the money options.

15.2   VAR Methods: Overview

15.2.1   Mapping

This section provides an introduction to the three VAR methods. The portfolio could consist of a large number of instruments, say M. Because it would be too complex to model each instrument separately, the first step is **mapping**, which consists of replacing the instruments by positions on a limited number of risk factors. Say we have N risk factors. The positions are then aggregated across instruments, which yields dollar exposures x_i.

For instance, we could reduce the large spectrum of maturities in the U.S. fixed-income market by 14 maturities. We then replace the positions in every bond by exposures on these 14 risk factors. Perhaps this can be reduced further. For some portfolios, one interest rate risk factor may be sufficient.

Figure 15-4 displays the mapping process. We have six instruments, say different forward contracts on the same currency but with different maturities. These can be replaced by positions on three risk factors only. In the next section, we provide a fully worked-out example.

FIGURE 15-4 Mapping Approach

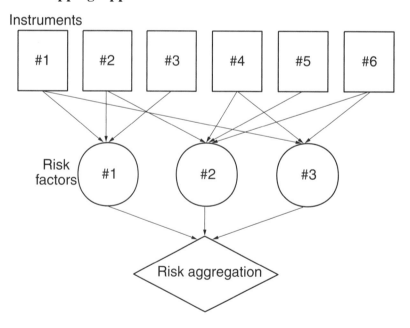

The distribution of the portfolio return $R_{p,t+1}$ is then derived from the exposures and movements in risk factors, Δf. Some care has to be taken defining the risk factors (in gross return, change in yield, rate of return, and so on); the exposures x have to be consistently defined. Here, R_p must be measured as the change in *dollar* value of the portfolio (or whichever base currency is used).

15.2.2   Delta-Normal Method

The **delta-normal method** is the simplest VAR approach. It assumes that the portfolio exposures are linear and that the risk factors are jointly normally distributed. As such, it is a local valuation method.

Because the portfolio return is a linear combination of normal variables, it is normally distributed. Using matrix notations, the portfolio variance is given by

$$\sigma^2(R_{p,t+1}) = x_t' \Sigma_{t+1} x_t \qquad (15.9)$$

where Σ_{t+1} is the forecast of the covariance matrix over the horizon.

If the portfolio volatility is measured in dollars, VAR is obtained directly from the standard normal deviate α that corresponds to the confidence level c:

$$\text{VAR} = \alpha \sigma(R_{p,t+1}) \qquad (15.10)$$

This is called the **diversified VAR**, because it accounts for diversification effects. In contrast, the **undiversified VAR** is simply the sum of the individual VARs for each risk factor. It assumes that all prices will move in the worst direction simultaneously, which is unrealistic.

The RiskMetrics approach is basically similar to the delta-normal approach. The only difference is that the risk factor returns are measured as logarithms of the price ratios, instead of rates of returns.

The main benefit of this approach is its appealing simplicity. This is also its drawback. The delta-normal method cannot account for nonlinear effects such as those encountered with options. It may also underestimate the occurrence of large observations because of its reliance on a normal distribution.

15.2.3   Historical-Simulation Method

The **historical-simulation** (HS) method is a full valuation method. It consists of going back in time (e.g., over the last 250 days) and applying current weights to a time series of historical asset returns. It replays a "tape" of history with current weights.

Define the current time as t; we observe data from 1 to t. The current portfolio value is P_t, which is a function of the current risk factors:

$$P_t = P[f_{1,t}, f_{2,t}, \ldots, f_{N,t}] \qquad (15.11)$$

We sample the factor movements from the historical distribution, without replacement:

$$\Delta f_i^k = \{\Delta f_{i,1}, \Delta f_{i,2}, \ldots, \Delta f_{i,t}\} \qquad (15.12)$$

From this we can construct hypothetical factor values, starting from the current one,

$$f_i^k = f_{i,t} + \Delta f_i^k \qquad (15.13)$$

which are used to construct a hypothetical value of the current portfolio under the new scenario, using Equation (15.11):

$$P^k = P\left[f_1^k, f_2^k, \ldots, f_N^k\right] \qquad (15.14)$$

We can now compute changes in portfolio values from the current position $R^k = (P^k - P_t)/P_t$.

We sort the t returns and pick the one that corresponds to the cth quantile, $R_p(c)$. VAR is obtained from the difference between the average and the quantile,

$$\text{VAR} = \text{AVE}[R_p] - R_p(c) \qquad (15.15)$$

The advantage of this method is that it makes no distributional assumption about the return distribution, which may include fat tails. The main drawback of the method is its reliance on a short historical moving window to infer movements in market prices. If this window does not contain some market moves that are likely, it may miss some risks.

15.2.4 Monte Carlo Simulation Method

The **Monte Carlo simulation method** is basically similar to historical simulation, except that the movements in risk factors are generated by drawings from some distribution. Instead of Equation (15.12), we have

$$\Delta f^k \sim g(\theta), \quad k = 1, \ldots, K \qquad (15.16)$$

where g is the joint distribution (e.g., normal or Student's t) and θ the required parameters. The risk manager samples **pseudo-random numbers** from this distribution and then generates pseudo-dollar returns as before. Finally, the returns are sorted to produce the desired VAR.

This method is the most flexible, but also carries an enormous computational burden. It requires users to make assumptions about the stochastic process and to understand the sensitivity of the results to these assumptions. Thus, it is subject to **model risk**.

Monte Carlo methods also create inherent sampling variability because of the randomization. Different random numbers will lead to different results. It may take a large number of iterations to converge to a stable VAR measure. It should be noted that when all risk factors have a normal distribution and exposures are linear, the method should converge to the VAR produced by the delta-normal VAR.

15.2.5 Comparison of Methods

Table 15-1 provides a summary comparison of the three mainstream VAR methods. Among these methods, delta-normal is by far the easiest to implement and communicate. For simple portfolios with little optionality, this may be perfectly appropriate. In contrast, the presence of options may require a full valuation method.

TABLE 15-1 Comparison of Approaches to VAR

Feature	Delta-Normal	Historical Simulation	Monte Carlo Simulation
Valuation	Linear	Full	Full
Distribution			
Shape	Normal	Actual	General
Extreme events	Low probability	In recent data	Possible
Implementation			
Ease of computation	Yes	Intermediate	No
Communicability	Easy	Easy	Difficult
VAR precision	Excellent	Poor with short window	Good with many iterations
Major pitfalls	Nonlinearities, fat tails	Time variation in risk, unusual events	Model risk

---

Example 15-2: FRM Exam 2001—Question 92

Under usually accepted rules of market behavior, the relationship between parametric delta-normal VAR and historical VAR tends to be

a) Parametric VaR will be higher.

b) Parametric VaR will be lower.

c) It depends on the correlations.

d) None of the above are correct.

Example 15-3: FRM Exam 1997—Question 12

Delta-normal, historical simulation, and Monte Carlo are various methods available to compute VAR. If underlying returns are normally distributed, then

a) Delta-normal VAR will be identical to historical-simulation VAR.

b) Delta-normal VAR will be identical to Monte Carlo VAR.

c) Monte Carlo VAR will approach delta-normal VAR as the number of replications ("draws") increases.

d) Monte Carlo VAR will be identical to historical-simulation VAR.

Example 15-4: FRM Exam 1998—Question 6

Which VAR methodology is least effective for measuring options risks?

a) Variance-covariance approach

b) Delta-gamma

c) Historical simulation

d) Monte Carlo

Example 15-5: FRM Exam 1999—Question 82

BankLondon, with a substantial position in five-year AA-grade Eurobonds, has recently launched an initiative to calculate 10-day spread VAR. As a risk manager for the Eurobond trading desk, you have been asked to provide an estimate for the AA-spread VAR. The extreme move used for the gilts yield is 40 bp and for the Eurobond yield is 50 bp. These are based on the standard deviation of absolute (not proportional) changes in yields. The correlation between changes in the two is 89%. What is the extreme move for the spread?

a) 19.35 bp

b) 14.95 bp

c) 10 bp

d) 23.24 bp

Example 15-6: FRM Exam 1999—Questions 15 and 90

The VAR of one asset is 300 and the VAR of another one is 500. If the correlation between changes in asset prices is 1/15, what is the combined VAR (assuming normal distributions)?

a) 525

b) 775

c) 600

d) 700

15.3 Example

15.3.1 Mark-to-Market

We now illustrate the computation of VAR for a simple example. The problem at hand is to evaluate the one-day downside risk of a currency forward contract. We will show that to compute VAR we need to first value the portfolio, mapping the value of the portfolio on fundamental risk factors, then generate movements in these risk factors, and finally combine the risk factors with the valuation model to simulate movements in the contract value.

Assume that on December 31, 1998, we have a forward contract to buy £10 million in exchange for delivering \$16.5 million in three months.

As before, we use these definitions:

S_t = current spot price of the pound in dollars

F_t = current forward price

K = purchase price set in contract

f_t = current value of contract

r_t = domestic risk-free rate

r_t^* = foreign risk-free rate

τ = time to maturity

To be consistent with conventions in the foreign exchange market, we define the present value factors using discrete compounding:

$$P_t = \mathrm{PV}(\$1) = \frac{1}{1 + r_t \tau}, \qquad P_t^* = \mathrm{PV}(\pounds 1) = \frac{1}{1 + r_t^* \tau} \qquad (15.17)$$

The current market value of a forward contract to buy one pound is given by

$$f_t = S_t \frac{1}{1 + r_t^* \tau} - K \frac{1}{1 + r_t \tau} = S_t P_t^* - K P_t \qquad (15.18)$$

which is exposed to three risk factors, the spot rate and the two interest rates. In addition, we can use this equation to derive the exposures on the risk factors. After differentiation, we have

$$df = \frac{\partial f}{\partial S} dS + \frac{\partial f}{\partial P^*} dP^* + \frac{\partial f}{\partial P} dP = P^* \, dS + S \, dP^* - K \, dP \qquad (15.19)$$

Alternatively,

$$df = (SP^*) \frac{dS}{S} + (SP^*) \frac{dP^*}{P^*} - (KP) \frac{dP}{P} \qquad (15.20)$$

Intuitively, the forward contract is equivalent to

- A long position of (SP^*) on the spot rate
- A long position of (SP^*) in the foreign bill
- A short position of (KP) in the domestic bill (borrowing)

We can now mark to market our contract. If Q represents our quantity, £10 million, the current market value of our contract is

$$V_t = Q f_t = £10,000,000 S_t \frac{1}{1 + r_t^* \tau} - \$16,500,000 \frac{1}{1 + r_t \tau} \qquad (15.21)$$

On the valuation date, we have $S_t = 1.6637, r_t = 4.9375\%$, and $r_t^* = 5.9688\%$. Hence

$$P_t = \frac{1}{1 + r_t \tau} = \frac{1}{(1 + 4.9375\% \times 90/360)} = 0.9879$$

and similarly, $P_t^* = 0.9854$. The current market value of our contract is

$$V_t = £10,000,000 \times 1.6637 \times 0.9854 - \$16,500,000 \times 0.9879 = \$93,581$$

which is slightly in the money. We are going to use this formula to derive the distribution of contract values under different scenarios for the risk factors.

15.3.2 Risk Factors

Assume now that we consider only the last 100 days to be representative of movements in market prices. Table 15-2 displays quotations on the spot and three-month rates for the last 100 business days, starting on August 10.

TABLE 15-2 Historical Market Factors

	Market Factors			
Date	$ Eurorate (3mo-%pa)	£ Eurorate (3mo-%pa)	Spot Rate $S($/£)$	Number
8/10/98	5.5938	7.4375	1.6341	
8/11/98	5.5625	7.5938	1.6315	1
8/12/98	6.0000	7.5625	1.6287	2
8/13/98	5.5625	7.4688	1.6267	3
8/14/98	5.5625	7.6562	1.6191	4
8/17/98	5.5625	7.6562	1.6177	5
8/18/98	5.5625	7.6562	1.6165	6
8/19/98	5.5625	7.5625	1.6239	7
8/20/98	5.5625	7.6562	1.6277	8
8/21/98	5.5625	7.6562	1.6387	9
8/24/98	5.5625	7.6562	1.6407	10
⋮				
12/15/98	5.1875	6.3125	1.6849	90
12/16/98	5.1250	6.2188	1.6759	91
12/17/98	5.0938	6.3438	1.6755	92
12/18/98	5.1250	6.1250	1.6801	93
12/21/98	5.1250	6.2812	1.6807	94
12/22/98	5.2500	6.1875	1.6789	95
12/23/98	5.2500	6.1875	1.6769	96
12/24/98	5.1562	6.1875	1.6737	97
12/29/98	5.1875	6.1250	1.6835	98
12/30/98	4.9688	6.0000	1.6667	99
12/31/98	**4.9375**	**5.9688**	**1.6637**	100

TABLE 15-3 Movements in Market Factors

	Movements in Market Factors			
Number	$dr($1)$	$dr(£1)$	$dP/P($1)$	$dP/P(£1)$	$dS($/£)/S$
1	−0.0313	0.1563	0.00000	−0.00046	−0.0016
2	0.4375	−0.0313	−0.00116	0.00000	−0.0017
3	−0.4375	−0.0937	0.00100	0.00015	−0.0012
4	0.0000	0.1874	−0.00008	−0.00054	−0.0047
5	0.0000	0.0000	−0.00008	−0.00008	−0.0009
6	0.0000	0.0000	−0.00008	−0.00008	−0.0007
7	0.0000	−0.0937	−0.00008	0.00015	0.0046
8	0.0000	0.0937	−0.00008	−0.00031	0.0023
9	0.0000	0.0000	−0.00008	−0.00008	0.0068
10	0.0000	0.0000	−0.00008	−0.00008	0.0012
⋮					
90	0.0937	0.0625	−0.00031	−0.00023	−0.0044
91	−0.0625	−0.0937	0.00008	0.00015	−0.0053
92	−0.0312	0.1250	0.00000	−0.00038	−0.0002
93	0.0312	−0.2188	−0.00015	0.00046	0.0027
94	0.0000	0.1562	−0.00008	−0.00046	0.0004
95	0.1250	−0.0937	−0.00039	0.00015	−0.0011
96	0.0000	0.0000	−0.00008	−0.00008	−0.0012
97	−0.0938	0.0000	0.00015	−0.00008	−0.0019
98	0.0313	−0.0625	−0.00015	0.00008	0.0059
99	−0.2187	−0.1250	0.00046	0.00023	−0.0100
100	−0.0313	−0.0312	0.00000	0.00000	−0.0018

We first need to convert these quotes to true random variables, that is, with zero mean and constant dispersion. Table 15-3 displays the one-day changes in interest rates dr, as well as the relative changes in the associated present value factors dP/P and in spot rates dS/S. For instance, for the first day,

$$dr_1 = 5.5625 - 5.5938 = -0.0313$$

$$dS/S_1 = (1.6315 - 1.6341)/1.6341 = -0.0016$$

This information is now used to construct the distribution of risk factors.

15.3.3   VAR: Historical Simulation

The **historical-simulation method** takes historical movements in the risk factors to simulate potential future movements. For instance, one possible scenario for the U.S. interest rate is that, starting from the current value $r_0 = 4.9375$, the movement the next day could be similar to that observed on August 11, which is a decrease of $dr_1 = -0.0313$. The new value is $r(1) = 4.9062$. We compute the simulated values of other variables as

$$r^*(1) = 5.9688 + 0.1563 = 6.1251$$

$$S(1) = 1.6637 \times (1 - 0.0016) = 1.6611.$$

Armed with these new values, we can reprice the forward contract, which is now worth

$$V_t = £10,000,000 \times 1.6611 \times 0.9849 - \$16,500,000 \times 0.9879 = \$59,941$$

Note that, because the contract is long the pound that fell in value, the current value of the contract has decreased relative to the initial value of $93,581.

We record the new contract value and repeat this process for all the movements from day 1 to day 100. This creates a distribution of contract values, which is reported in the last column of Table 15-4.

The final step consists of sorting the contract values, as shown in Table 15-5. Suppose we want to report VAR relative to the initial value (instead of relative to the average on the target date.) The last column in the table reports the *change* in the portfolio value, $V(k) - V_0$. These range from a loss of $200,752 to a gain of $280,074.

TABLE 15-4 Simulated Market Factors

Number	Simulated Market Factors					Hypothetical MTM Contract
	$r(\$1)$	$r(£1)$	$S(\$/£)$	PV($)	PV(£)	
1	4.9062	6.1251	1.6611	0.9879	0.9849	$59,941
2	5.3750	5.9375	1.6608	0.9867	0.9854	$84,301
3	4.5000	5.8751	1.6617	0.9889	0.9855	$59,603
4	4.9375	6.1562	1.6559	0.9878	0.9848	$9,467
5	4.9375	5.9688	1.6623	0.9878	0.9853	$79,407
6	4.9375	5.9688	1.6625	0.9878	0.9853	$81,421
7	4.9375	5.8751	1.6713	0.9878	0.9855	$172,424
8	4.9375	6.0625	1.6676	0.9878	0.9851	$128,149
9	4.9375	5.9688	1.6749	0.9878	0.9853	$204,361
10	4.9375	5.9688	1.6657	0.9878	0.9853	$113,588
⋮						
90	5.0312	6.0313	1.6564	0.9876	0.9851	$23,160
91	4.8750	5.8751	1.6548	0.9880	0.9855	$7,268
92	4.9063	6.0938	1.6633	0.9879	0.9850	$83,368
93	4.9687	5.7500	1.6683	0.9877	0.9858	$148,705
94	4.9375	6.1250	1.6643	0.9878	0.9849	$93,128
95	5.0625	5.8751	1.6619	0.9875	0.9855	$84,835
96	4.9375	5.9688	1.6617	0.9878	0.9853	$74,054
97	4.8437	5.9688	1.6605	0.9880	0.9853	$58,524
98	4.9688	5.9063	1.6734	0.9877	0.9854	$193,362
99	4.7188	5.8438	1.6471	0.9883	0.9856	−$73,811
100	4.9062	5.9376	1.6607	0.9879	0.9854	$64,073
	4.9375	**5.9688**	**1.6637**	**0.9879**	**0.9854**	**$93,581**

TABLE 15-5 Distribution of Portfolio Values

Number	Sorted Values	
	Hypothetical MTM	Change in MTM
1	−$107,171	−$200,752
2	−$73,811	−$167,392
3	−$46,294	−$139,875
4	−$37,357	−$130,938
5	−$33,651	−$127,232
6	−$22,304	−$115,885
7	−$11,694	−$105,275
8	$7,268	−$86,313
9	$9,467	−$84,114
10	$13,744	−$79,837
⋮		
90	$193,362	$99,781
91	$194,405	$100,824
92	$204,361	$110,780
93	$221,097	$127,515
94	$225,101	$131,520
95	$228,272	$134,691
96	$233,479	$139,897
97	$241,007	$147,426
98	$279,672	$186,091
99	$297,028	$203,447
100	$373,655	$280,074

FIGURE 15-5 Empirical Distribution of Value Changes

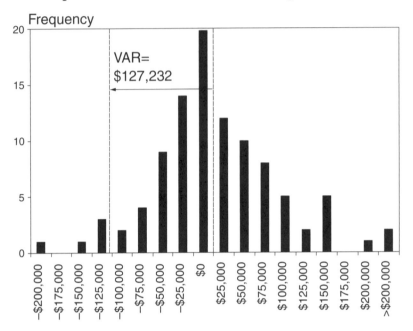

We can now characterize the risk of the forward contract by its entire distribution, which is shown in Figure 15-5. The purpose of VAR is to report a single number as a downside risk measure. Let us take, for instance, the 95% lower quantile. From Table 15-5, we identify the fifth lowest value out of a hundred, which is $127,232. Ignoring the mean, the 95% VAR is $VAR_{HS} = \$127,232$.

15.3.4   VAR: Delta-Normal Method

The **delta-normal** method takes a different approach to constructing the distribution of the portfolio value. We assume that the three risk factors (dS/S), (dP/P), (dP^*/P^*) are jointly normally distributed. We can write Equation (15.20) as

$$df = (SP^*)\frac{dS}{S} + (SP^*)\frac{dP^*}{P^*} - (KP)\frac{dP}{P} = x_1\,dz_1 + x_2\,dz_2 + x_3\,dz_3 \quad (15.22)$$

where the dz are normal variables and x are exposures.

Define Σ as the (3 by 3) covariance matrix of the dz, and x as the vector of exposures. We compute VAR from $\sigma^2(df) = x'\Sigma x$. Table 15-6 details the steps. First, we compute the covariance matrix of the three risk factors. The top of the table shows the standard deviation of daily returns as well as correlations. From these, we construct the covariance matrix.

Next, the table shows the vector of exposures, x'. The matrix multiplication Σx is shown on the following lines. After that, we compute $x'(\Sigma x)$, which yields the variance. Taking the square root, we have $\sigma(df) = \$77,306$. Finally, we transform this into a 95% quantile by multiplying by 1.645, which gives $\text{VAR}_{\text{DN}} = \$127,169$.

Note how close this number is to the VAR_{HS} of \$127,232 found previously. This suggests that the distribution of these variables is close to normal. Indeed, the empirical distribution in Figure 15-5 roughly looks like a normal distribution. The fitted distribution is shown in Figure 15-6.

TABLE 15-6 Covariance Matrix Approach

Covariance Matrix of Market Factors

	dP/P($1)	dP/P(£1)	dS($/£)/S
Standard deviation:	0.022%	0.026%	0.473%

Correlation matrix:	dP/P($1)	dP/P(£1)	dS($/£)/S
dP/P($1)	1.000	0.137	0.040
dP/P(£1)	0.137	1.000	−0.063
dS($/£)/S	0.040	−0.063	1.000

Covariance matrix:	dP/P($1)	dP/P(£1)	dS($/£)/S
Σ dP/P($1)	4.839E-08	7.809E-09	4.155E-08
dP/P(£1)	7.809E-09	6.720E-08	−7.688E-08
dS($/£)/S	4.155E-08	−7.688E-08	2.237E-05

Exposures:

x' −\$16,300,071 \$16,393,653 \$16,393,653

Σx

4.839E-08	7.809E-09	4.155E-08		−$16,300,071		$0.020
7.809E-09	6.720E-08	−7.688E-08	×	$16,393,653	=	−$0.286
4.155E-08	−7.688E-08	2.237E-05		$16,393,653		$364.852

$\sigma^2 = x'(\Sigma x)$ Variance:

−$16,300,071	$16,393,653	$16,393,653	×	$0.020 −$0.286 $364.852	=	$5,976,242,188

σ Standard deviation..**\$77,306**

FIGURE 15-6 Normal Distribution of Value Changes

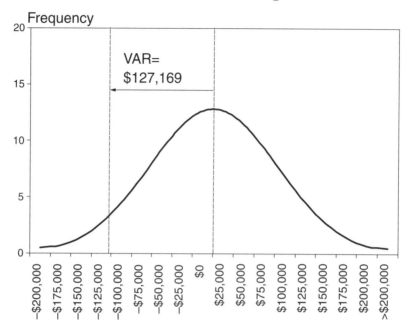

15.4   Answers to Chapter Examples

Example 15-1: FRM Exam 2002—Question 38

b) This question has to be read very carefully in view of the "always" characterization. Delta-VAR could understate or overstate the true VAR, depending on whether the position is net long or short options, so a) is incorrect. Delta-VAR is generally better for in-the-money options, because these have low gamma, so c) is false. For out-of-the-money options, delta is close to zero, so the delta-VAR method would predict zero risk. The risk could indeed be very small, so d) is incorrect. So b) is the most generally correct statement.

Example 15-2: FRM Exam 2001—Question 92

b) Parametric VAR usually assumes a normal distribution. Given that actual distributions of financial variables have fatter tails than the normal distribution, parametric VAR at high confidence levels will generally underestimate VAR.

Example 15-3: FRM Exam 1997—Question 12

c) In finite samples, the simulation methods will in general be different from the delta-normal method, and from each other. As the sample size increases, however,

Monte Carlo VAR should converge to delta-normal VAR when returns are normally distributed.

Example 15-4: FRM Exam 1998—Question 6

a) The variance-covariance approach does not take into account second-order curvature effects.

Example 15-5: FRM Exam 1999—Question 82

d) $\text{VAR} = \sqrt{40^2 + 50^2 - 2 \times 40 \times 50 \times 0.89} = 23.24$

Example 15-6: FRM Exam 1999—Questions 15 and 90

c) $\text{VAR} = \sqrt{300^2 + 500^2 + 2 \times 300 \times 500 \times 1/15} = \$600$

Investment and Risk Management

Chapter 16

Portfolio Management

Value-at-risk techniques were developed in the early 1990s to control the risk of proprietary trading desks of commercial banks. The advent of these methods was spurred by commercial bank regulation but quickly spread to investment banks, which also have large trading operations. These techniques have been incorporated in the panoply of risk measurement tools used in the investment management industry. Institutional investors pay particular attention to the control of risk in their investment portfolios.

Risk that can be measured can be managed better. Even so, **risk management** accounts for only one facet of the investment process, which is risk. Investors assume risk only because they expect to be compensated for it in the form of higher returns. The real issue is how to balance risk against expected return.

This trade-off is the subject of **portfolio management**, which is much broader than risk management. Once a portfolio reflecting the best trade-off between risk and expected return is selected, the total fund risk can be allocated to various managers using a process called **risk budgeting**.

At the end of the investment process, it is important to assess whether realized returns were in line with the risks assumed. The purpose of **performance attribution** methods is to decompose the investment performance into various factors, some of which are due to general market factors, with the remainder specific to the fund manager.

The purpose of this chapter is to present risk and performance measurement tools in the investment management industry. Section 16.1 gives a brief introduction to institutional investors. Risk and performance measurement techniques are developed in Section 16.2. Finally, Section 16.3 discusses risk budgeting. Hedge funds, because of their importance, will be covered in the next chapter.

16.1 Institutional Investors

Institutional investors are entities that have large amounts of funds to invest for an organization, or on behalf of others. This is in contrast with *private* investors.[1] As shown in Table 16-1, institutional investors can be classified into investment companies, pension funds, insurance funds, and others. The latter category includes endowment funds, bank-managed funds, and private partnerships, also known as hedge funds. **Hedge funds** are private partnership funds that can take long and short positions in various markets and are accessible only to large investors.

TABLE 16-1 Classification of Institutional Investors

Investment companies	Open-end funds
	Closed-end funds
Pension funds	Defined-benefit
	Defined-contribution
Insurance funds	Life
	Non-life
Others	Foundations and endowment funds
	Non-pension funds managed by banks
	Private partnerships

Even though institutional investors and bank proprietary desks are generally exposed to similar risk factors, their philosophies are quite different. Bank trading desks employ high leverage and are aggressive investors. They typically have short horizons and engage in active trading in generally liquid markets. Financial institutions, such as commercial banks, investment banks, and broker-dealers, are sometimes called the **sell side** because they are primarily geared toward selling financial services.

On the other hand, institutional investors are part of the **buy side** because they are buying financial services from the sell side, or Wall Street in the United States. In contrast to the sell side, institutional investors have little or no leverage and are more conservative investors. Most have longer time horizons and can invest in less liquid markets. Many hedge funds, however, have greater leverage and trade very actively, like bank trading desks.

---

[1]The SEC has formal definitions of, for example, "qualified institutional buyers" under Rule 144a.

16.2 Portfolio Management

Value at risk provides an estimate of downside risk measured as a dollar loss over the horizon. Assuming a parametric distribution for the gains and losses, this can be converted to a standard deviation measure. One question, however, is the choice of whether risk should be measured in absolute terms or relative to some **benchmark**. This section starts with the issue of risk measurement, then turns to performance measurement and attribution, and finally shows how risk budgeting can be used to manage risk actively.

16.2.1 Risk Measurement

■ **Absolute risk** is measured in terms of shortfall relative to the initial value of the investment, or perhaps an alternative investment in cash. It should be expressed in dollar terms (or in the relevant base currency). Let us use the standard deviation as the risk measure and define P as the initial portfolio value and R_P as the rate of return. Absolute risk in dollar terms is

$$\sigma(\Delta P) = \sigma(\Delta P/P) \times P = \sigma(R_P) \times P \qquad (16.1)$$

■ **Relative risk** is measured relative to a benchmark index and represents active management risk. Defining B as the benchmark, the deviation is $e = R_P - R_B$, which is also known as the **tracking error**. In dollar terms, this is $e \times P$. The risk is

$$\sigma(e)P = [\sigma(R_P - R_B)] \times P = [\sigma(\Delta P/P - \Delta B/B)] \times P = \omega \times P \quad (16.2)$$

where ω is called the **tracking error volatility** (TEV). Defining σ_P and σ_B as the volatility of the portfolio and of the benchmark and ρ as their correlation, the variance of the difference is

$$\omega^2 = \sigma_P^2 - 2\rho\sigma_P\sigma_B + \sigma_B^2 \qquad (16.3)$$

For instance, if $\sigma_P = 25\%$, $\sigma_B = 20\%$, and $\rho = 0.961$, we have $\omega^2 = 25\%^2 - 2 \times 0.961 \times 25\% \times 20\% + 20\%^2 = 0.0064$, giving $\omega = 8\%$.

To compare these two approaches, take the case of an active equity portfolio manager who is given the task of beating a benchmark, perhaps the S&P 500 index for large U.S. stocks or the MSCI world index for global stock.[2] If the active portfolio return is -6% over the year but the benchmark dropped by -10%, the excess return is positive: $e = -6\% - (-10\%) = 4\%$. So, in relative terms, the portfolio has done well even though the absolute performance is negative. On the other hand, a portfolio could return $+6\%$, which is good using absolute measures, but not so good if the benchmark went up by $+10\%$.

Using absolute or relative risk depends on how the trading or investment operation is judged. For a bank trading portfolios or hedge funds, market risk is measured in absolute terms. These are sometimes called **total return funds**. Institutional portfolio managers that are given the task of beating a benchmark or peer group measure market risk in relative terms.

As is sometimes said, "risk is in the eye of the beholder." For investors with fixed future liabilities, the risk is not being able to perform on these liabilities. For pension funds with **defined benefits**, these liabilities consist of promised payments to current and future pensioners and are called **defined-benefit obligations**. For life insurance companies, these liabilities represent the likely pattern of future claim payments. These liabilities can be represented by their net present value. In general, the present value of long-term fixed payments behaves very much like a *short position in a fixed-rate bond*. If the payments are indexed to inflation, the analogous instrument is an inflation-protected bond.

The difference between the current values of assets and liabilities is called the **surplus**. Risk should then be measured as the potential shortfall in surplus over the horizon. This is sometimes called **surplus at risk**. This VAR-type measure is an application of relative risk, where the benchmark is the present value of liabilities. **Immunization** occurs when the asset portfolio is perfectly hedged against changes in the value of the liabilities.

Example 16-1: Absolute and Relative Risk

An investment manager is given the task of beating a benchmark. Hence the risk should be measured

a) In terms of loss relative to the initial investment
b) In terms of loss relative to the expected portfolio value
c) In terms of loss relative to the benchmark
d) In terms of loss attributed to the benchmark

---

[2]This refers to the *Morgan Stanley Capital International* index. MSCI provides a battery of country, industry, and global stock indices that are widely used as benchmarks.

Example 16-2: Pension Liabilities

The AT&T pension plan reports a projected benefit obligation of $17.4 billion.
If the discount rate decreases by 0.5%, this liability will increase by $0.8 billion.
Based on this information, the liabilities behave like a
a) Short position in the stock market
b) Short position in cash
c) Short position in a bond with maturity of about nine years
d) Short position in a bond with duration of about nine years

---

Example 16-3: Pension Immunization

A pension plan reports $12 billion in assets and $10 billion in present value of
the benefit obligations. Future pension benefits are indexed to the rate of inflation.
To immunize its liabilities, the plan should
a) Invest $12 billion of assets in fixed-coupon long-term bonds
b) Invest $10 billion of assets in fixed-coupon long-term bonds
c) Invest $10 billion of assets in cash
d) Invest $10 billion of assets in Treasury Inflation-Protected Securities

---

16.2.2   Performance Measurement

This dichotomy, absolute versus relative returns, carries through performance measurement, which evaluates the risk-adjusted performance of the fund. The **Sharpe ratio** (SR) measures the ratio of the average rate of return, $\mu(R_P)$, in excess of the risk-free rate R_F, to the absolute risk:

$$\text{SR} = \frac{\mu(R_P) - R_F}{\sigma(R_P)} \tag{16.4}$$

This approach can be extended to include VAR, or the quantile of returns, in the denominator instead of the volatility of returns. Here, risk is taken in absolute terms.

A related measure is the **Sortino ratio** (SOR). This replaces the standard deviation in the denominator by the semi–standard deviation, $\sigma_L(R_P)$, which considers only data points that represent a loss. The ratio is

$$\text{SOR} = \frac{\mu(R_P) - R_F}{\sigma_L(R_P)} \tag{16.5}$$

where $\sigma_L(R_P) = \sqrt{\frac{1}{(N_L)} \sum_{i=1}^{N}[\text{Min}(R_{P,i}, 0)]^2}$, and N_L is the number of observed losses. The Sortino ratio is more relevant than the Sharpe ratio when the return distribution is skewed to the left. It is much less widely used, however.

In contrast, the **information ratio** (IR) measures the ratio of the average rate of return in excess of the benchmark to the TEV:

$$IR = \frac{\mu(R_P) - \mu(R_B)}{\omega} \tag{16.6}$$

Table 16-2 presents an illustration. The risk-free interest rate is $R_F = 3\%$ and the portfolio average return is -6%, with volatility of 25%. Hence, the Sharpe ratio of the portfolio is SR $= [(-6\%) - (3\%)]/25\% = -0.36$. Because this is negative, the absolute performance is poor.

TABLE 16-2 Absolute and Relative Performance

	Average	Volatility	Performance
Cash	3%	0%	
Portfolio P	−6%	25%	$SR = -0.36$
Benchmark B	−10%	20%	$SR = -0.65$
Deviation e	4%	8%	$IR = 0.50$

Assume now that the benchmark returned -10% over the same period and that the tracking error volatility was 8%. Hence, the information ratio is IR $= [(-6\%) - (-10\%)]/8\% = 0.50$, which is positive. The relative performance is good even though the absolute performance is poor. Note that this information ratio of 0.50 is typical of the performance of the top 25th percentile of money managers and is considered "good."[3]

Example 16-4: Sharpe and Information Ratios

A portfolio manager returns 10% with a volatility of 20%. The benchmark returns 8% with risk of 14%. The correlation between the two is 0.98. The risk-free rate is 3%. Which of the following statements is *correct*?
a) The portfolio has higher SR than the benchmark.
b) The portfolio has negative IR.
c) The IR is 0.35.
d) The IR is 0.29.

16.2.3 Performance Attribution

So far, we have implemented a simple adjustment for risk that takes into account a volatility measure. To evaluate the performance of investment managers, however, it is

---

[3]See Grinold and Kahn (2000), *Active Portfolio Management*, McGraw-Hill, New York.

crucial to decompose the total return into a component due to market risk premia and to other factors. Exposure to the stock market is widely believed to reward investors with a long-term premium, called the **equity premium**. Assume that this premium is EP = 4% annually. This is the expected return in excess of the risk-free rate. For simplicity, we assume that the same rate applies to lending and borrowing.

Now take the example of an investment fund of $1 million. A long position of $1.5 million, or 150% in passive equities financed by 50% borrowing, should have an *excess return* composed of the total return on the 150% equity position, minus the cost of borrowing 50%, minus the risk-free rate. This gives

$$[150\% \times (\text{EP} + R_F) - 50\% R_F] - R_F = 1.5 \times \text{EP} = 6\%$$

This could also be achieved by taking a notional position of $1.5 million in stock index futures and parking the investment in cash, including the margin. So an investment manager who returns 6% in excess of the risk-free rate in this way is not really delivering any value added because this extra amount is simply due to exposure to the market. Therefore, it is crucial to account for factors that are known to generate risk premia.

Define $R_{m,t}$ as the rate of return in period t on the stock market, say the S&P 500 for U.S. equities, $R_{F,t}$ as the risk-free rate, and $R_{P,t}$ as the return on the portfolio. The general specification for this adjustment consists of estimating the regression

$$R_{P,t} - R_{F,t} = \alpha_P + \beta_P[R_{m,t} - R_{F,t}] + \epsilon_{P,t}, \quad t = 1, \ldots, T \qquad (16.7)$$

where β_P is the exposure of portfolio P to the market factor, or **systematic risk**, and α_P is the abnormal performance after taking into account the exposure to the market.

"Abnormal" can only be defined in terms of "normal" performance. One such definition is the **capital asset pricing model** (CAPM). Under some conditions, William Sharpe demonstrated that equilibrium in capital markets requires a linear relationship between expected excess returns and systematic risk. For stock or portfolio i, we must have

$$E(R_i) - R_F = 0 + \beta_i[E(R_M) - R_F] \qquad (16.8)$$

Comparing with Equation (16.7), this requires all α's to be zero in equilibrium.[4]

---

[4]The CAPM is based on equilibrium in capital markets, which requires that the demand for securities from risk-averse investors match the available supply. It also assumes that asset returns have a normal distribution. A major problem with this theory is that it may not be testable unless the "market" is exactly identified.

This equation can be generalized to multiple factors. Assume we believe that in addition to the market premium, a premium is earned for *value* (or for low–price-to-book companies) and *size* (of for small firms). We need to take this information into account in evaluating the manager: otherwise he or she may load up on factors that are priced but not recorded in the performance attribution system.

With K factors, Equation (16.7) is

$$R_i = \alpha_i + \beta_{i1} y_1 + \cdots + \beta_{iK} y_K + \epsilon_i \tag{16.9}$$

As in the case of the CAPM, the **arbitrage pricing theory** (APT), developed by Professor Stephen Ross, shows that there is a relationship between α_i and the factor exposures.[5]

Whether Equation (16.7) or (16.9) is used, the alpha term is also known as **Jensen's alpha**. This term is widely used in the investment management industry to describe the performance adjusted for market factors.

This decomposition is also useful for detecting **timing ability**, which consists of adding value by changing exposures on risk factors and **security selection ability**, which adds value from the careful selection of securities, after accounting for exposures on major risk factors.

Return to the estimation of Equation (16.7). Denoting $\overline{R} = (1/T) \sum_{t=1}^{T} (R_t - R_{F,t})$ as the average over the sample period, the estimated alpha is

$$\widehat{\alpha} = \overline{R} - \widehat{\beta} \overline{R}_m \tag{16.10}$$

If there is no exposure to the market ($\beta = 0$), Equation (16.10) shows that alpha is the sample average of the investment returns. More generally, Equation (16.10) properly accounts for the exposure to the systematic risk factor. In the case of our investment fund, we have $\overline{R} = 6\%$ and $\beta = 1.5\%$. So the alpha is

$$\widehat{\alpha} = 6\% - 1.5 \times 4\% = 0$$

which correctly indicates that there is no value added.

---

[5]The theory does not rely on equilibrium but simply on the assumption that there should be no arbitrage opportunities in capital markets, a much weaker requirement. It does not even need the factor model to hold strictly; instead, it requires only that the residual risk be very small. This must be the case if a sufficient number of common factors is identified and in a well-diversified portfolio. The APT model does not require the market to be identified, which is an advantage. Like the CAPM, however, tests of this model are ambiguous since the theory provides no guidance as to what the factors should be.

> **Key concept:**
> Performance evaluation must take into account the component of returns that can be attributed to exposures on general market factors (or risk premia). An investment manager adds value only if the residual return, called alpha, is positive.

> **Example 16-5: Performance Evaluation**
> Assume that a hedge fund provides a large positive alpha. The fund can take leveraged long and short positions in stocks. The market went up over the period. Based on this information,
> a) If the fund has net positive beta, all of the alpha must come from the market.
> b) If the fund has net negative beta, part of the alpha comes from the market.
> c) If the fund has net positive beta, part of the alpha comes from the market.
> d) If the fund has net negative beta, all of the alpha must come from the market.

16.2.4 Performance Evaluation and Survivorship

Another key issue in evaluating the performance of a group of investment managers is survivorship. This occurs when funds are dropped from the investment universe for reasons related to poor performance and "survivors" only are considered. Commercial databases often give information on funds that are "alive," because clients are no longer interested in "dead" funds.

The problem is that the average performance of the group of funds under examination becomes subject to **survivorship bias**. In other words, the apparent performance of the existing funds is too high, or biased upward relative to the true performance of the underlying population, due to the omission of some poorly performing funds.

The extent of this bias depends on the attrition rate of the funds and can be very severe. Mutual fund studies, for example, report an **attrition rate** of 3.6% per year. This represents the fraction of funds existing at the beginning of the year that become "dead" during the year. In this sample, the survivorship bias is estimated at approximately 0.70% per annum.[6] This represents the difference between the performance of the surviving sample and that of the true population. This is a significant number because it is on the order of management fees, which are around 1% of assets per annum. Samples with higher attrition rates have larger biases. For example, **Commodity Trading Advisors** (CTA), a category of hedge funds, are reported to have an attrition

---

[6]Carhart, Mark, Jennifer Carpenter, Anthony Lynch, and David Musto (2002), Mutual Fund Survivorship, *Review of Financial Studies* 15, 1355–1381.

rate of 16% per year, leading to survivorship biases on the order of 5.2% per annum, which is very high.[7]

Other sources of bias can be introduced due to the inclusion criteria and the voluntary reporting of returns. A fund with excellent performance is more likely to be chosen for inclusion by the database vendor. Or the investment manager of such a fund may be more inclined to submit the fund returns to the database. Consequently, there is a bias toward adding funds with better returns. Or a fund may decide to stop reporting returns if its performance drops. This is called **selection bias**. This bias differs from survivorship bias because it also exists when dead funds are included in the sample.

Finally, another subtle bias arises when firms "incubate" different types of funds before making them available to outsiders. Say 10 different funds are started by the same company over a two-year period. Some will do well and others will not, partly due to chance. The best-performing fund is then open to the public, with its performance instantly backfilled for the previous two years. The other funds are ignored or disbanded. As a result, the performance of the public fund is not representative of what should be expected. This is called **instant-history bias**. The difference between it and selection bias is that the fund was not open to investors during the reported period.

Key concept:
Performance evaluation can be overly optimistic if based on a sample of funds affected by survivorship, selection, or instant-history bias. The extent of survivorship bias increases with the attrition rate.

Example 16-6: Mutual Fund Performance
Every year *Business Week* reports the performance of a group of existing equity mutual funds, selected for their popularity. Taking the average performance of this group of funds will create
a) Survivorship bias only
b) Selection bias only
c) Both survivorship and selection bias
d) Instant-history bias only

---

[7]CTAs are investment managers who trade futures and options. In the United States, they are regulated by the Commodity Futures Trading Commission (CTFC).

16.3   Risk Budgeting

The revolution in risk management reflects the recognition that risk should be measured at the highest level, that is, firm-wide or portfolio-wide. This ability to measure total risk has led to a top-down allocation of risk, called **risk budgeting**. Risk budgeting is the process of parceling out the total risk of the fund, or risk budget, to various asset classes and managers.

This concept is being implemented by institutional investors as a follow-up to their **asset allocation process**. Asset allocation consists of finding the optimal allocation into major asset classes, the one that provides the best risk/return trade-off for the investor. This choice defines the total risk profile of the portfolio.

Consider, for instance, an investor having to decide how much to invest in U.S. stocks, in U.S. bonds, and in non-U.S. bonds. Risk is measured in absolute terms, assuming returns have a joint normal distribution. More generally, this could be extended to other distributions or to a historical simulation method. The allocation will depend on the expected return and volatility of each asset class, as well as their correlations. Table 16-3 illustrates these data, which are based on historical dollar returns measured over the period 1978 to 2003.

TABLE 16-3 Risk Budgeting

Asset		Expected Return	Volatility	Correlations 1	2	3	Percentage Allocation	VAR
U.S. stocks	1	13.80%	15.50%	1.00			60.0	$15.3
U.S. bonds	2	8.40%	7.40%	0.20	1.00		7.7	$0.9
Non-U.S. bonds	3	9.60%	11.10%	0.04	0.40	1.00	32.3	$5.9
Portfolio		12.00%	10.30%				100.0	$16.9

Say the investor decides that the portfolio with the best risk/return trade-off has an expected return of 12.0% with total risk of 10.3%. Table 16-3 shows a portfolio allocation of 60.0%, 7.7%, and 32.3% to U.S. stocks, U.S. bonds, and non-U.S. bonds, respectively.

The volatility can be measured in terms of a 95% annual VAR. This defines a total risk budget of VAR $= \alpha \sigma W = 1.645 \times 10.3\% \times \$100 = \$16.9$ million. This VAR budget can then be parceled out to various asset classes and active managers within asset classes.

Risk budgeting is the process by which these efficient portfolio allocations are transformed into VAR assignments. At the asset class level, the individual VARs are

$15.3, $0.9, and $5.9 million, respectively. For instance, the VAR budget for U.S. stocks is 60.0% × (1.645 × 15.50% × $100) = $15.3 million. Note that the sum of individual VARs is $22.1 million, which is more than the portfolio VAR of $16.9 million due to diversification effects.

The process can be repeated at the next level. The fund has a risk budget of $15.3 million devoted to U.S. equities, with an allocation of $60 million. This allocation could be split equally between two active equity managers. Assume that the two managers are equally good, with a correlation of returns of 0.5. The optimal risk budget for each is then $8.83 million. We can verify that the total risk budget is

$$\sqrt{8.83^2 + 8.83^2 + 2 \times 0.5 \times 8.83 \times 8.83} = \sqrt{233.91} = \$15.3$$

Note that, as in the previous step, the sum of the risk budgets, which is $8.83 + $8.83 = $17.66 million, is greater than the total risk budget of $15.3 million. This is because the latter takes into account diversification effects. If the two managers were perfectly correlated with each other, the risk budget would have to be $15.3/2 = $7.65 million for each. This higher risk budget is useful because it allows full advantage to be taken of the manager's positive alpha.

The risk budgeting process highlights the importance of correlations across managers. To control their risk better, institutional investors often choose equity managers that follow different market segments or strategies. For example, the first manager could invest in small-growth stocks, the second in medium-size value stocks. Or the investor could pick a first manager that follows momentum-based strategies and a second manager that follows value-based strategies. The first type tends to buy more of a stock after its price has gone up, and the second after the price has become more attractive (i.e., low). Different styles lead to low correlations across managers. For a given total risk budget, low correlations mean that each manager can be assigned a higher risk budget, leading to a greater value added for the fund.

These low correlations explain why investors must watch for **style drift**, which refers to the situation where an investment manager changes investment style. This is a problem for the investor because it can change the total portfolio risk. If all the managers, for instance, drift into the small-growth category, the total risk of the fund will increase. Style drift is controlled by choosing benchmarks with different characteristics, such as small-growth and medium-value indices, and by controls on the tracking error volatility for each manager.[8]

In conclusion, this risk budgeting approach is spreading rapidly to the field of investment management. Such an approach has all the benefits of VAR. It provides a consistent measure of risk across all subportfolios. It forces managers and investors to confront squarely the amount of risk they are willing to assume. It gives them tools to monitor their risk in real time.

Example 16-7: Pension Fund Risk

The AT&T pension fund reports total assets worth $19.6 billion and liabilities of $17.4 billion. Assume the surplus has a normal distribution and volatility of 10% per annum. The 95% surplus at risk over the next year is
a) $360 million
b) $513 million
c) $2,860 million
d) $3,220 million

Example 16-8: Risk Budgeting

The AT&T pension fund has 68%, or about $13 billion, invested in equities. Assume a normal distribution and volatility of 15% per annum. The fund measures absolute risk with a 95%, one-year VAR, which gives $3.2 billion. The pension plan wants to allocate this risk to two equity managers, each with the same VAR budget. Given that the correlation between managers is 0.5, the VAR budget for each should be
a) $3.2 billion
b) $2.4 billion
c) $1.9 billion
d) $1.6 billion

16.4   Answers to Chapter Examples

Example 16-1: Absolute and Relative Risk

c) This is an example of risk measured in terms of deviations of the active portfolio relative to the benchmark. Answers a) and b) are incorrect because they refer to absolute risk. Answer d) is incorrect because it refers to the absolute risk of the benchmark.

---

[8]For more details on the effect of TEV constraints, see Jorion (2003), Portfolio Optimization with Constraints on Tracking Error, *Financial Analysts Journal* (September), 70–82.

Example 16-2: Pension Liabilities

d) We can compute the modified duration of the liabilities as $D^* = -(\Delta P/P)/\Delta y = -(0.8/17.4)/0.0005 = 9.2$ years. So, the liabilities behave like a short position in a bond with a duration of around nine years. Answers a) and b) are incorrect because the liabilities have fixed future payoffs, which do not resemble cash flow patterns on equities or cash. Answer c) is incorrect because the duration of a bond with a nine-year maturity is less than nine years. For example, the duration of a 6% coupon par bond with nine-year maturity is only seven years.

Example 16-3: Pension Immunization

d) Immunization occurs when assets are invested so as to perfectly hedge changes in liabilities. So the amount to invest is $10 billion, which is the value of liabilities. In this case, we are told that the pension payments are indexed to the rate of inflation. Because the liabilities are tied to inflation, immunization requires that the assets should react in a similar way to inflation. This can be achieved with Treasury Inflation-Protected Securities (TIPS).

Example 16-4: Sharpe and Information Ratios

d) The Sharpe ratios of the portfolio and benchmark are $(10\% - 3\%)/20\% = 0.35$, and $(8\% - 3\%)/14\% = 0.36$, respectively. So, the SR of the portfolio is lower than that of the benchmark. Answer a) is incorrect. The TEV is the square root of $20\%^2 + 14\%^2 - 2 \times 0.98 \times 20\% \times 14\%$, which is $\sqrt{0.00472} = 6.87\%$. So the IR of the portfolio is $(10\% - 8\%)/6.87\% = 0.29$. This is positive, so answer b) is incorrect. Answer c) is the SR of the portfolio, not the IR, so it is incorrect.

Example 16-5: Performance Evaluation

c) Because the market went up, a portfolio with positive beta will have part of its positive performance due to the market effect. A portfolio with negative beta will have in part a negative performance due to the market. Answer a) is incorrect because the fund manager could still have generated some of its alpha through judicious stock picking. Answers b) and d) are incorrect because a negative beta combined with a rising market should lead to a decrease, not an increase, in the alpha.

Example 16-6: Mutual Fund Performance

c) The publication lists existing funds, so it must be subject to survivorship bias, because dead funds are not considered. In addition, there is selection bias because the publication focuses on just the popular funds, which are large and likely to have done well. Answers a) and b) are incomplete. Answer d) is also incomplete.

Example 16-7: Pension Fund Risk

a) The fund's surplus is the excess of assets over liabilities, which is $19.6 - $17.4 = $2.2 billion. The surplus at risk at the 95% level over one year is, assuming a normal distribution, $1.645 \times 10\% \times \$2,200 = \$360$ million. Answer b) is incorrect because it uses a 99% confidence level. Answers c) and d) are incorrect because they apply the risk to the liabilities and assets instead of the surplus.

Example 16-8: Risk Budgeting

c) Call x the risk budget allocation to each manager. This should be such that $x^2 + x^2 + 2\rho xx = \$3.2^2$. Solving for $x\sqrt{1 + 1 + 2\rho} = x\sqrt{3} = \$3.2$, we find $x = \$1.85$ billion. Answer a) is incorrect because it refers to the total VAR. Answer b) is incorrect because it assumes a correlation of zero. Answer d) is incorrect because it simply divides the $3.2 billion VAR by 2, which ignores diversification effects.

Chapter 17

Hedge Fund Risk Management

The first hedge fund was started by A.W. Jones in 1949. Unlike the typical equity mutual fund, the fund took long *and* short positions in equities. This style still represents the largest fraction of hedge funds, about 40%.

Since then, the hedge fund industry has undergone exponential growth. Hedge funds now account for close to $1 trillion in equity capital. **Hedge funds** are private partnership funds that have very few limitations on investment strategy. As a result, they can take long and short positions in various markets and also allow leverage. Due to this leverage, the assets they control are greater than $1 trillion. Hedge funds have become an important force in financial markets, accounting for the bulk of trading in some markets.

Unlike mutual funds, who are open to any investor, hedge funds are accessible only to large investors. This is because of their perceived risk, which can be traced to their use of leverage and short positions. To control their risk, most hedge funds have adopted strict risk controls based on VAR techniques. Because some types of hedge fund strategies are very similar to those of proprietary trading desks of commercial banks, it was only natural for hedge funds to adopt similar risk management tools.

The purpose of this chapter is to provide an overview of risk management for the hedge fund industry. Section 17.1 gives an introduction to the hedge fund industry. Section 17.2 discusses leverage measurement for hedge funds, which can take both long and short positions. Section 17.3 then analyzes commonly used strategies for hedge funds and shows how to identify and measure their risk. Finally, Section 17.4 discusses transparency issues for hedge funds.

17.1   The Hedge Fund Industry

The growth of the hedge fund industry is described in Figure 17-1. By now, there are more than 8,000 hedge fund managers controlling close to $1 trillion in assets, up from only $35 billion in 1991. This represents an annualized rate of growth of 29%. In comparison, U.S. mutual funds currently manage $8 trillion, up from $1.4 trillion in 1991. This represents an annualized rate of growth of 15%. So hedge funds have grown at twice the rate of mutual funds over the same period.

FIGURE 17-1 Growth of Hedge Fund Industry

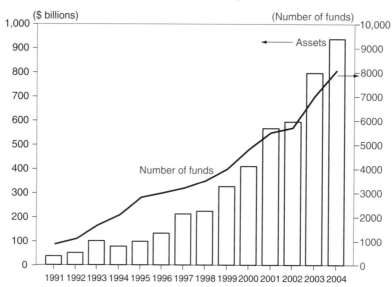

Source: Hennessee Group. Data as of December of each year.

The growth of this industry is due to a number of factors. On the investor side, the performance of hedge funds has been attractive, especially compared with the poor record of stock markets during the 2000–2002 period. Hedge funds also claim to have low beta, which makes them useful as diversifiers. On the manager side, hedge funds provide greater remuneration than traditional investment funds. Typical investment management fees for mutual funds range from a fixed 0.5% to 2% of asset value. In contrast, hedge funds commonly charge a fixed 2% of assets plus 20% of the performance above cash. Hedge funds also typically have fewer restrictions on their investment strategy, often allowing style drift.

17.2 Leverage, and Long and Short Positions

To understand the mechanics of this type of fund, and the limits to leverage, we need to describe the use of margins and stock borrowing.

In typical corporate balance sheet analysis, **balance sheet leverage** is defined as the ratio of balance sheet assets over equity. This simplistic measure, however, assumes that all the risk is coming from the assets, or that the future value of liabilities is known. Such a definition is not adequate for hedge funds, or most financial institutions, for that matter. In these cases, both assets and liabilities, long and short positions, are risky.

In what follows, we illustrate the use of long and short positions in stocks. This analysis, however, can be extended to any asset that can be shorted, subject to its own specific margin requirements.

17.2.1 Long Position

Let us start with the simplest case, which is a long position in a risky asset. Consider a speculator with $100 (say, millions) invested in one stock. This can be achieved with $100 of investor equity. Or the investor can borrow. Suppose the broker requires a 50% margin deposit, so that the investor needs to invest only $50. The remainder is provided by the broker, which gives a $50 loan. The balance sheet of the position is described below, with the risky entry in bold. Defining leverage as the ratio of assets over equity, the leverage of this position is 2 to 1.

Assets	Liabilities
$100 **Long stock**	$50 Broker loan
	$50 Equity

The risk is that of a *decrease* in the value of the stock. In the worst scenario, the stock price falls to zero, in which case the value of the equity will fall from $50 to −$50, or by $100. Because the stock price cannot go below zero, this is the absolute worst loss on the position.

Note that leverage can also be obtained by using derivatives instead of cash instruments. This includes single stock futures, contracts for differences, or equity swaps. If a stock futures position can be entered with a margin of only 10%, the economically equivalent liabilities would consist of a loan of $90 plus equity of $10. The risk of dollar loss is still the same, $100 at worst, but the leverage is now much higher than before, at 10 to 1.

17.2.2   Short Position

Consider next a situation where the speculator wants to short the stock instead. Under a stock loan agreement, the owner of a stock sells the stock to our speculator in exchange for cash and a future demand to get the stock back. In the meantime, the speculator must pass along any cash flow on the stock, such as dividends, to the original owner.[1] When the operation is reversed, the stock lender returns the cash plus the short-term interest rate minus a **stock loan fee**. This is typically 20 basis points (bp) for most stocks but can reach 400 bp for stocks that are hard to borrow (said to be "on special"). In the meantime, the stock lender will have invested the cash, earning a net fee of 20 bp. From the viewpoint of the stock lender, this is an easy way to increase the return on the stock by a modest amount.

The stock borrower will now sell the stock in anticipation of a fall in the price. The sale, however, will go through a broker, who will not allow the seller to have full access to the sales proceeds. In the United States, under Regulation T, the broker keeps 50% of the sales proceeds. This margin, which can be posted as any security owned clear by the speculator, will impose a limit on the leverage of the speculator.

So the speculator receives $100 worth of stocks, sells them, and keeps at least $50 as margin with the broker. The hope is for a fall in the stock price so that the stock can be repurchased later at a lower price.

All of the cash flows are arranged at the same time. The speculator needs to send $100 to the stock lender, half of which will come from the remaining proceeds and the other half from the equity invested, or own funds. The balance sheet for the short position is described below, with the risky entry in bold. Here, leverage can be defined as the ratio of the absolute value of the short position to the equity, which is 2 to 1. As in the previous long-only case, we have a position of $50 in equity leveraged into a position of $100 in stocks. Regulation T imposes a maximum leverage ratio of 2, which is the inverse of the 50% of the short-sales proceeds kept by the broker.

---

[1]Stock loans are made on a day-to-day basis. The lender can demand the return of the stock at any time, with a three-day period for delivery.

Assets	Liabilities
$100 Cash lent to stock owner	$100 **Short stock**
$50 Margin at the broker	$50 Equity

Here, the risk is that of an *increase* in the value of the stock. If the stock goes up by $50, the equity will be wiped out. If the stock goes up by $100, the equity will become negative, −$50. Unlike the long position, however, there is theoretically no limit on how large the loss could be. The stock price could go to $1,000, for instance, in which case the loss would also be $1,000, which is much more than the initial value of the stock. Thus the distribution of losses on long and short positions is asymmetrical. This is because the distribution of prices itself is asymmetrical. It is limited to zero from below but has unlimited upper values, albeit with decreasing probabilities for increasingly high values.

17.2.3   Long and Short Positions

Consider now a typical hedge fund, which has both long and short positions. Say the initial capital is $100. This is the equity, or **net asset value** (NAV). The fund could buy $100 worth of stocks, and short $100 worth of stocks, as above. Part of the long stock position can be used to satisfy the broker's minimum margin requirement of $50 for shorting the stock. The balance sheet for the long and short positions is described below, with the risky entries in bold.

Assets	Liabilities
$100 **Long stock**	
$100 Cash lent to stock owner	$100 **Short stock**
	$100 Equity

Let us now turn to traditional risk measures. Define V_L, V_S, and V_E as the (absolute) dollar values of the long stock positions, short stock positions, and equity, respectively. V_A is the value of total assets. If β_L and β_S are the betas of the long and short stock positions, the total dollar beta is

$$(\beta_L V_L - \beta_S V_S) = \beta_E V_E \qquad (17.1)$$

which defines the net beta of equity, or β_E. This measure, however, ignores idiosyncratic risk.

Traditional **leverage** is commonly used as a risk measure:

$$\text{Leverage} = \frac{V_A}{V_E} = \frac{\text{Long stock positions plus cash}}{\text{Equity}} \tag{17.2}$$

In our example, this is ($100+$100)/($100) = 2. This, however, ignores the hedging effect of short stock positions, so it is inadequate.

Using gross amounts, **gross leverage** is

$$\text{Gross leverage} = \frac{V_L + V_S}{V_E} = \frac{\text{Long positions plus absolute value of short positions}}{\text{Equity}} \tag{17.3}$$

In our example, this is ($100 + $100)/($100) = 2.

Gross leverage is often used as a rough measure of hedge fund risk. This measure, however, fails to capture the systematic risk of the equity position adequately. If the long and short positions have the same value and market beta, the net beta is zero, so there is really no directional market risk. In the limit (even though there would be no reason to do so), if the long and short positions are invested in the same stock, there is no risk. Yet gross leverage is high.

Another definition sometimes used is **net leverage**, which is

$$\text{Net leverage} = \frac{V_L - V_S}{V_E} = \frac{\text{Long positions minus absolute value of short positions}}{\text{Equity}} \tag{17.4}$$

In our example, this is ($100 − $100)/($100) = 0.

Net leverage is also inadequate as a risk measure. Although it roughly accounts for systematic risk, it fails to take into account potential divergences in the value of the long and short positions. It is appropriate only under restrictive assumptions. For example, if the betas of the long and short positions are the same, then the equity beta is

$$\beta_E = \frac{\beta_L(V_L - V_S)}{V_E} = \beta_L \times \text{Net leverage} \tag{17.5}$$

so this net leverage term measures the multiplier applied to the beta of the long position. This totally ignores idiosyncratic risk, however, which is precisely the type of risk that the hedge fund manager should take views on. In conclusion, neither of these leverage measures seems adequate as a risk indicator.

This is why the industry has moved to risk measures based on value at risk. The dollar VAR of the position accounts for the size of positions, volatilities, and correlations between assets and liabilities. As such, it is a superior measure of the risk of loss to equity.

Example 17-1: Leverage and Hedge Funds

A hedge fund with $100 million in equity is long $200 million in some stocks and short $150 million in other stocks. The gross leverage and net leverage are, respectively,

a) 2.0 and 0.5

b) 2.0 and 1.5

c) 3.5 and 0.5

d) 3.5 and 1.5

Example 17-2: Hedging and Returns

Continuing Example 17-1, assume the stock market went up by 20% last year. Ignore the risk-free rate and idiosyncratic risk, and assume the average beta of both long and short positions is 1. Over the same period, the return on the fund should be

a) 20%

b) 15%

c) 10%

d) 5%

17.3 Hedge Fund Risk Management

17.3.1 Types of Market Risk

Hedge funds are a much more heterogeneous group of investment managers than others. They follow a great variety of strategies, which can be classified into different styles. More generally, their market risk can be categorized as directional and nondirectional risks.

■ **Directional risks** involve exposures to the direction of movements in major financial market variables. These directional exposures are measured by first-order or linear approximations such as

—**Beta** for exposure to general stock market movements

—**Duration** for exposure to the level of interest rates

—**Delta** for exposure of options to the price of the underlying asset

■ **Nondirectional risks** involve other, remaining exposures, such as nonlinear exposures, exposures to hedged positions, and exposures to volatilities. These nondirectional exposures are measured by exposures to differences in price movements, or quadratic exposures, such as

—**Basis risk** in dealing with differences in prices or in interest rates

—**Residual risk** in dealing with equity portfolios

—**Convexity** in dealing with second-order effects for interest rates

—**Gamma** in dealing with second-order effects for options

—**Volatility risk** in dealing with volatility effects

Directional trades can take long or short positions on the major risk factors, such as equities, currencies, fixed-income, and commodities. Directional risks are greater than nondirectional risks. For funds that take directional risks, total portfolio risk is controlled through diversification across sources of risk, trading strategies, and risk limits.

Many categories of hedge funds are hedged against directional risks. As a result, they are exposed to nondirectional risks. Such strategies need to take long *and* short positions in directional trades, thereby leaving exposure to remaining, nondirectional risks. The example we gave in the previous section was long $100 in a stock offset by a short position worth $100 in another stock. Such a strategy has little directional risk to the stock market but is exposed to a change in the relative value of the two stocks. Limiting risk also limits rewards, however. As a result, nondirectional strategies are often highly leveraged in order to multiply gains from taking nondirectional bets.

17.3.2 Hedge Fund Styles

Hedge funds can be classified into various styles, reflecting the type of trading and markets they are exposed to. Table 17-1 lists various hedge fund styles. To some extent, this classification is arbitrary. Definitions of categories vary within the industry. Different hedge fund index providers, for example, use different classifications, even though the underlying pool of hedge funds is similar. Classifications can also lose meaning if hedge funds managers change strategies over time.

The table also reports the number of existing funds in each group, as well as the risk, measured as the annual standard deviation of equity.[2] Styles are listed in order of decreasing risk.

---

[2]Note that the risk measures are for live funds only. Hence, the data are subject to survivorship bias. The risk of existing funds is less than that of dead funds.

TABLE 17-1 Hedge Fund Styles

Type	Number	Risk	Description
Directional strategies			
Long/short equity	360	20.7%	Positions in equity markets that include short sales but are not market neutral (includes emerging markets)
Global macros	40	12.6%	Long or short positions in global markets to implement views across all asset classes (includes global tactical asset allocation)
Nondirectional strategies			
Relative value			
Equity market neutral	36	8.6%	Simultaneous long and short positions in equities with net beta close to zero
Fixed-income arbitrage	32	6.3%	Offsetting long and short positions to exploit anomalies in fixed-income securities (includes mortgage arbitrage)
Convertible arbitrage	59	5.4%	Long or short positions in convertible bonds hedged for interest rate and stock risk
Event driven			
Merger arbitrage	107	6.4%	Positions driven by corporate events such as
Distressed securities			mergers, takeovers, reorganizations, and bankruptcy proceedings
Fund structure			
Managed futures	94	19.7%	Positions in futures and option contracts (includes CTAs)
Funds of funds	185	8.0%	Portfolio diversified across various types of hedge funds

Source: TASS database, sample of live funds as of March 2003. Adapted from Gupta and Liang (2005), Do Hedge Funds Have Enough Capital? A VAR Approach, *Journal of Financial Economics*. Risk is annualized volatility, measured from the monthly standard deviation, multiplied by the square root of 12.

Long/Short Equity

The first category consists of directional strategies. These include **long/short equity funds**, which as the table shows, is the most prevalent strategy. These funds are not market neutral. Most have a long bias, for example, 160% of NAV in long positions and 50% in short positions. Others are net short.

These funds are exposed to the general market risk factor, in addition to sector and idiosyncratic risks. Because of leverage, the volatility is high, at 20.7% on average across all such funds. This is on the order of the volatility of an unleveraged position in the S&P 500.

Global Macros

Next are **global macros funds**, which take directional, leveraged bets on global asset classes, equities, fixed-income, currencies, and commodities. Because they span so many markets, these funds do not have a homogeneous risk profile. An example is the Soros fund that shorted the British pound against the German mark just before its devaluation, leading to a reported gain of $1 billion for the hedge fund. This group is close to **global tactical asset allocation** (GTAA), which is a traditional investment manager category. GTAA managers take positions across national stock markets, fixed-income markets, and currencies to take advantage of short-term views, often through derivatives.

These funds are exposed to a number of general market risk factors, in addition to sector and idiosyncratic risks. The average volatility is 12.6%. This is less than the previous category because these funds also invest in other markets, which are less volatile than equities.

We now turn to nondirectional strategies. The first three categories are sometimes called **relative value funds**, because they rely on comparisons of securities with similar characteristics, buying the cheap ones while selling the expensive ones in the hope of future convergence.

Equity Market Neutral

The first group is **equity market neutral funds**, which attempt to maintain zero beta through balanced long and short positions in equity markets. These funds may or may not be neutral across other risk factors, including industries, styles, and countries.

So these funds are exposed to these other risk factors (industries, styles, countries) in addition to idiosyncratic, stock-specific risks. Balance sheet leverage is moderate, no more than three times. The average volatility is 8.6%, which is much less than that of equity indices, due to the hedging effect of the short positions.

Fixed-Income Arbitrage

The next group is **fixed-income arbitrage funds**. This is a generic term for a number of strategies that involve fixed-income securities and derivatives. The hedge fund manager assesses the relative value of various fixed-income instruments. For instance, if the on-the-run bond is expensive relative to the off-the-run bond, the fund would buy the undervalued security and sell the expensive one. This position has a net duration close to zero but is exposed to the spread between the two securities. Other examples include taking positions in swap spreads, or in asset-backed securities when their option-adjusted spread is high. This group includes mortgage arbitrage.

These funds avoid directional exposures to interest rates but are exposed to other nondirectional risks, such as spread risk. Due to the small expected profit of each trade, fixed-income arbitrage funds are highly leveraged, with leverage ratios ranging from 10 to 25.

Example: LTCM's bet

Long-Term Capital Management (LTCM) started as a fixed-income arbitrage fund, taking positions in relative value trades, such as duration-matched positions in long swap, short Treasuries. It started the year 1998 with $4.7 billion in equity capital.

On August 21, 1998, the 10-year Treasury yield dropped from 5.38% to 5.32%. The swap rate, in contrast, increased from 6.01% to 6.05%. This divergence was highly unusual. Assuming a notional position of $50,000 million and modified duration of 8 years, this translates to a value change of $-8 \times (5.32 - 5.38)/100 \times \$50,000 = +\$240$ million on a long Treasury position and $-8 \times (6.05 - 6.01)/100 \times \$50,000 = -\$160$ million on a long swap position. As the spread position is long the swap and short Treasury, this leads to a total loss of $400 million.

LTCM also took positions in option markets, selling options when they were considered expensive and dynamically hedging to maintain a net delta of zero. Implied volatilities went up sharply on August 21, leading to further losses on the option positions. On that day, LTCM's reported loss was $550 million.

The average volatility of this group is 6.3%. The distribution of payoffs is typically asymmetric, however. Swap spreads, for example, cannot narrow below zero but can increase to very large values, and have done so. This asymmetry in the distribution of spreads is reflected in that of profits.

Convertible Arbitrage

The last group in the relative value category is **convertible arbitrage funds**. The hedge fund manager assesses the relative value of convertible bonds using proprietary option pricing models. If the convertible bond is cheap, the hedge fund buys the bond and at the same time hedges the interest rate risk by shorting Treasury bonds, or T-bond futures. Because a convertible bond has positive delta with respect to the underlying stock, the hedge fund also needs to short the stock so that the net delta of the position is close to zero. Hedging can also use credit default swaps to protect against company default.

These funds avoid directional exposures to interest rates but are exposed to other nondirectional risks, such as spread risk. Being typically long convertible bonds, the long option position creates positive gamma and vega (long implied volatility). The bond position creates positive convexity unless the bond is callable. This strategy is also exposed to corporate event risk, such as default (if not hedged) and takeover. Convertible bonds are also exposed to liquidity risk because they trade infrequently. Leverage is moderate, no more than six times. The average volatility of this group is 5.4%. This appears low but, as discussed later, may be an inaccurate measure of risk.

Event Driven

The next group includes **event-driven funds**, which attempt to capitalize on the occurrence of specific corporate events. This group includes **merger arbitrage funds** and **distressed securities funds**.

Let us focus first on merger arbitrage funds, also known as **risk arbitrage funds**. **Mergers and acquisitions** are transactions that combine two firms into one new firm.[3] The parties can be classified as the **acquiring firm**, or bidder, which initiates the offer, and the **target firm**, or acquired firm, which receives the offer. The bidder offers to buy the target at a **takeover premium**, which is the difference between the offer price and the target's stock price before the bid. This premium is typically high, averaging 50% of the initial share price.

Upon the announcement of the merger, the price of the target firm reacts strongly, increasing by, say, 40%. This still falls short of the takeover price, due to uncertainty as to whether the transaction will occur. The completion rate is 83% on average, so there is always a possibility the transaction could fail.

Offers can take the form of cash or stock of the bidding company. For a cash deal, the risk arbitrage position simply consists of buying the target's stock and hoping the price will eventually move to the takeover price. For a stock deal, the bidder offers to exchange each target share for Δ shares of the bidder. The risk arbitrage position then consists of a long position in the target offset by a short position of Δ in the bidder's

---

[3]These are sometimes called takeovers. Takeovers can take the form of mergers or tender offers. Mergers are negotiated directly with the target managers, and approved by the board of directors and then by shareholder vote. Tender offers are offers to buy shares made directly to target shareholders.

stock. These positions generate an average of 10% pa in risk-adjusted excess returns.[4]

Example: Exxon-Mobil merger

On December 1, 1998, Exxon confirmed that it had agreed to buy Mobil, another major oil company, in a transaction valued at $85 billion, which was the biggest acquisition ever. The deal created the world's largest traded oil company, with a market value of $250 billion. Under the terms of the agreement, each shareholder of Mobil would receive $\Delta = 1.32015$ shares of Exxon in exchange.

Before the announcement, the initial prices of Mobil and Exxon were $78.4 and $72.7, respectively, which implies a modest premium of $(1.32016 \times \$72.7)/\$78.4 - 1 = 22\%$. Over the three days around the announcement, Mobil's stock price went up by $+6.9\%$ to $84.2 and Exxon's price went down by $-1/5\%$ to $71.6. This stock price reaction is typical of acquisition announcements.

The exchange was consummated on November 30, 1999, after regulatory and shareholder approval. On that day, the respective stock prices for Mobil and Exxon were $104.4 and $79.3. Multiplying the latter by 1.32015, we get $104.7, which is close to the final stock price for Mobil. So, the two prices converged to the same converted value. The profit from the risk arbitrage trade was $(\$104.4 - \$84.2) - 1.32016(\$79.3 - \$71.6) = \$10.0$ per share.

Event-driven funds also include **distressed securities funds**, which take positions in securities, debt or equity, of firms in financial difficulty. In such situations, the hedge fund manager needs to assess the effect of restructuring or the bankruptcy process on the market price of the securities. This requires an evaluation of the financial situation of the firm, as well as a good understanding of legal issues involved. If, for instance, the debt of a bankrupt company trades at 40 cents on the dollar, the hedge fund would benefit if the payment after reorganization is 50 cents.

These funds are exposed to event risk, that is, that the takeover or reorganization fails. They may also be exposed to equity market risk and interest rate risk if these exposures are not hedged. Because distressed securities do not trade actively, there is also liquidity risk. Leverage for event-driven funds is low to moderate, no more than two times.

---

[4]These profits, however, seem to be related to limits to arbitrage, as they are lower for firms that are large and have low idiosyncratic risk. See Baker, Malcolm, and Serkan Savasoglu (2002), Limited Arbitrage in Mergers and Acquisitions, *Journal of Financial Economics* 64, 91–115.

The average volatility for event-driven funds is 6.4%, which is fairly low. This, however, hides the fact that the distribution of payoffs is asymmetric. Typically, the upside is more limited than the downside should the takeover or reorganization fail. So these funds are short volatility, or exposed to rare events.

Managed Futures Funds

The next category of hedge funds differs from others on the basis of the fund structure. **Managed futures funds** consist of managers who use commodity and financial futures and options traded on organized exchanges. Trading strategies often involve **technical trading**, where positions depend on patterns in price histories. Leverage is high, leading to high volatility.

These funds have directional exposures to all the markets that have listed futures contracts. Their risk factors overlap with global macro funds. GTAA strategies, for instance, often involve stock index and currency futures. The average volatility of this group is 19.7%, which is fairly high.

Funds of Funds

Finally, **funds of funds** are diversified portfolios of hedge funds that try to achieve diversification by careful selection of styles and investment managers. Funds of funds can also take views on strategies, increasing allocation to strategies that are expected to perform better. They can also be leveraged, with borrowings ranging from one to four times equity. This amplifies both returns and risks. Funds of funds charge additional management fees on top of those levied by the underlying funds.

A related category is **hedge fund indices**. These are unmanaged, passive baskets of hedge funds. They provide diversification benefits at low direct management costs.

Also relatively new are **collateralized fund obligations** (CFOs), which are pools of hedge funds whose total payoff is sliced into various tranches, much like CMOs. From the viewpoint of the hedge fund manager, this structure offers the advantage that investor money is locked in until the maturity of the bonds.

The average volatility for this group is 8.0%. This low number reflects the diversification across managers and styles.

This list makes it clear that hedge funds are a very heterogeneous group. They are exposed to a wide variety of risk factors, follow different trading rules, and have varying levels of leverage and risk. The measurement of risk, however, can be a difficult issue for some hedge funds.

Example 17-3: Risks in Fixed-Income Arbitrage

Identify the risks in a fixed-income arbitrage strategy that takes long positions in interest rate swaps hedged with short positions in Treasuries.

a) The strategy could lose from decreases in the swap-Treasury spread.

b) The strategy could lose from increases in the Treasury rate, all else fixed.

c) The payoff in the strategy has negative skewness.

d) The payoff in the strategy has positive skewness.

Example 17-4: Risks in Convertible Arbitrage

Identify the risks in a convertible arbitrage strategy that takes long positions in convertible bonds hedged with short positions in Treasuries and the underlying stock.

a) Short implied volatility

b) Long duration

c) Long stock delta

d) Positive gamma

Example 17-5: Risks in Merger Arbitrage—I

A major acquisition has just been announced, targeting company B. The bid from Company A is an exchange offer with a ratio of 2. Just after the announcement, the prices of A and B are $50 and $90, respectively. A hedge fund takes a long position in company B hedged with A's stock. After the acquisition goes through, the prices move to $120 and $60. For each share of B, the gain is

a) $30

b) $20

c) $10

d) $0 since the acquisition is successful

Example 17-6: Risks in Merger Arbitrage—II

Suppose the payoff from a merger arbitrage operation is $5 million if successful, −$20 million if not. The probability of success is 83%. The expected payoff on the operation is

a) $5 million

b) $0.75 million

c) $0 since markets are efficient

d) Symmetrically distributed

17.3.3 Liquidity and Model Risk

Hedge funds take leveraged positions to increase returns, especially with nondirectional trades such as fixed-income arbitrage, where the expected return on each trade is generally low.

Perversely, this creates other types of risks, including **liquidity risk**. This strategy indeed failed for Long-Term Capital Management (LTCM), a highly leveraged hedge fund that purported to avoid directional risks. LTCM had a leverage ratio of 25 to 1. It had grown to $125 billion in assets, four times the asset size of the next largest hedge fund. Once the fund started to accumulate losses, it became difficult to maneuver the portfolio and to raise more funds from investors. LTCM also lost funding from brokers. The fund ended up losing $4.4 billion, or 92% of its equity.

Table 17-2 links sources of liquidity risk to a hedge fund balance sheet. Liquidity risk arises on the asset side and is a function of the size of the positions as well as of the price impact of a trade of a given size on the instrument. On the liabilities side, funding risk arises when the hedge fund cannot renew funding from its broker, or when losses in marked-to-market positions or increases in haircuts lead to cash outflows. Funding risk also arises when the fund faces investor redemptions.

TABLE 17-2 Sources of Liquidity Risk

Assets	**Liabilities**
Size of position	Funding
Price impact for unit trade	Mark-to-market, haircuts
	Equity
	Investor redemptions

The price impact function is instrument-specific. For example, major currencies, large stocks, Treasury bills, and bonds are extremely liquid, meaning that large amounts can be transacted without too much effect on the price. Other markets are by nature less liquid. For instance, minor currencies, small stocks, and most corporate bonds are generally illiquid.

LTCM dealt with mostly liquid instruments but was exposed to liquidity risk due to the sheer size of its positions. This is why hedge funds often say they have a **maximum capacity**. Beyond that optimal size, trading becomes difficult due to market impact.

Some categories of hedge funds have intrinsic liquidity risk because the instruments are thinly traded, implying a large price impact for most trades. This is the case with convertible bonds and especially with distressed securities. Because these funds invest in thinly traded bonds, liquidity risk arises even for small funds.

Typically, funds with greater liquidity risk impose a longer **lockup period** and **redemption notice period**. The former refers to the minimum time period during which investor money is to be held in the fund. The latter refers to the period required for notifying the fund of an intended redemption. Lockup periods average three months, and can extend to five years. The advance notice period averages 30 days.

Instrument liquidity risk creates another problem, which is stale prices. Assume that the reporting period is one month. The hedge fund reports a **net asset value** at the end of each month. If transaction prices are not observed at the end of the month, the valuation may be using a price from a trade that occurred in the middle of the month. This price is called a **stale price** because it is "old" and does not reflect a market-clearing trade on the day of reporting. Unfortunately, this will distort the reported NAVs as well as the risk measures.

The first effect is that the reported monthly volatility will be less than the true volatility. This is because prices are based on trades during the month, which is similar to an averaging process. Averages are less volatile than end-of-period values.

The second effect is that monthly changes will display positive autocorrelation. A movement in one direction will be only partially captured using prices measured during the month. The following month, part of the same movement will show up in the return. This positive autocorrelation substantially increases the risk over longer horizons. Consider, for instance, the extrapolation of a one-month volatility or VAR to two months. The usual adjustment factor is $\sqrt{T} = \sqrt{2} = 1.41$. With autocorrelation of $\rho = 0.5$, this adjustment factor is instead $\sqrt{(1+1+2\rho)} = \sqrt{2(1+0.5)} = 1.73$. So the true risk is understated by $(1.73-1.41)/1.73 = 18\%$. This effect increases with the length of the horizon. As a result, the annualized volatility presented in Table 17-1, which extrapolates monthly volatility using the square root of time, may understate the true annual risk. Long-term measures of risk must specifically account for the observed autocorrelation.

A third, related effect is that measures of systematic risk will be systematically biased downward. If the market goes up during a month, only a fraction of this increase will be reflected in the NAV, leading to beta measures that are too low.[5] Corrections to the beta involve measuring the portfolio's beta with the contemporaneous market return plus the beta with respect to the one-month lagged return plus the beta with respect to the one-month future return. With thin trading, the sum of these three betas should be higher than the contemporaneous beta, and also closer to the true systematic risk.[6]

Another type of risk that is exacerbated by leverage is **model risk**. This occurs when the investment strategy relies on valuation or risk models that are flawed. Due to leverage, small errors in the model can create big errors in the risk measure. Indeed, LTCM's risk measurement system was deficient, leading to a fatal underestimation of the amount of capital required to support its positions.

Example 17-7: Liquidity Risks

Asset liquidity risk is most pronounced for
a) A $10 million position in distressed securities
b) A $10 million position in Treasury bonds
c) A $100 million position in distressed securities
d) A $100 million position in Treasury bonds

Example 17-8: Risk and Illiquidity

Illiquid positions will create
a) Negative autocorrelation in returns
b) Positive autocorrelation in returns
c) Zero autocorrelation in returns
d) An overstatement of the systematic risk measure

17.4   Hedge Fund Transparency

Because hedge funds follow proprietary trading strategies, they are generally reluctant to reveal information about their trading ideas or positions. This lack of transparency has serious disadvantages for investors.

Disclosure allows *risk monitoring* of the hedge fund, which is especially useful with active trading. This can help to avoid situations where the hedge fund manager

---

[5]See Asness, C., R. Krial, and J. Liew (2001), Do Hedge Funds Hedge?, *Journal of Portfolio Management* 28:6–19.

[6]This correction is called the *Dimson beta*. See Dimson, E., (1979), Risk Measurement When Shares are Subject to Infrequent Trading, *Journal of Financial Economics* 7:197–226.

unexpectedly increases leverage or changes style. Closer monitoring of the fund can also decrease the probability of fraud.

Disclosure is also important for *risk aggregation*. The investor should know how the hedge fund interacts with other assets in the portfolio. Whether the hedge fund has a positive or negative correlation with the rest of the portfolio will have an effect on the total portfolio risk.

Greater disclosure is often resisted on the grounds that it would disclose *proprietary positions*, leading to the possibility of a third party trading against the hedge fund. This threat, however, comes from the broker-dealer community, not the investors.

If this is an issue, confidentiality agreements should prevent leakages of sensitive information.

One party has access to the full details of the positions. This is the **prime broker**, who provides custodian services, clearing and execution of trades, brokerage, and reporting to hedge fund managers. Brokers also provide credit lines for financing leverage and short selling capabilities.

Another argument sometimes advanced is *lack of investor sophistication*. In other words, disclosing positions would dump too much information on investors who might not able to use it. Indeed, a simple listing of the positions would provide limited information in the absence of a rationale for the trading strategy. Some investors, however, are fairly sophisticated. In recent years, funds of funds have developed advanced methods to measure their total portfolio risk based on the complete positions of the hedge funds they allocate assets to.

These last two arguments can be addressed with external risk measurement services. These firms have access to the individual positions of hedge funds, with the proper confidentiality agreements, and provide aggregate risk measures to investors. They release only exposures to major risk factors, such as net duration, net systematic risk, and so on. This solution neatly solves the problems of risk aggregation and managers' widespread reluctance to disclose detailed information about their positions.

A last issue, especially with complex or illiquid assets, is **improper valuation of assets**. This problem arises when assets do not have market-clearing prices at the end of the reporting period. In the United States, hedge fund managers typically calculate the NAV themselves. As a result, some unscrupulous hedge fund managers have succumbed to the temptation to misreport the pricing of the fund's assets in order to hide their trading losses.[7]

Indeed, a recent study has shown that valuation problems played a role in 35% of hedge fund failures and that 57% of those valuation problems were caused by fraud or misrepresentation.[8] The growth of the hedge fund industry, along with the increasing occurrence of fraud, explains why the Securities and Exchange Commission (SEC) issued a new rule in December 2004 that requires hedge funds to *register* as investment advisors.[9] Registration gives the SEC the authority to conduct examinations of hedge fund activities. Hopefully, these will help to identify compliance problems at an early stage and will provide a deterrent to fraud. Registration also requires the hedge fund to designate a **chief compliance officer**. Although this new rule has been very controversial, in practice about half of all U.S.-based hedge funds are already registered as investment advisers.

As will be seen in the section on operational risk, sound risk management relies heavily on the principle of independence. Some hedge funds are now using external companies that provide independent valuation services. Figure 17-2 describes a best-practices architecture for valuation and risk measurement in hedge funds.

FIGURE 17-2 Architecture of Hedge Fund Risk Systems

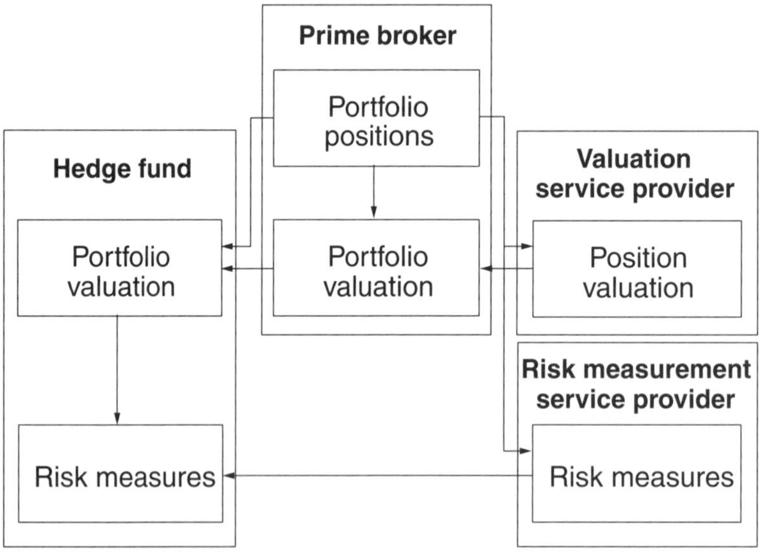

---

[7]A 2003 report by the SEC, however, notes that there is no evidence that hedge fund advisors engage *disproportionately* in fraudulent activities.

[8]See Kundro, C., and S. Feffer (2003), Valuation Issues and Operational Risk in Hedge Funds, *Capco White Paper.*

[9]This rule applies to U.S.-based hedge funds, and to non-U.S. funds that have at least 14 U.S. investors. Funds with less than $25 million under management do not have to comply.

Portfolio positions are recorded by the prime broker, who can provide portfolio valuation. The hedge fund, however, may also use external service providers for valuation and risk measurement, both of which are based on the portfolio positions. All of this information is then fed into the portfolio and risk measurement system for the hedge fund manager.

Hedge funds play a very important role in financial markets. Like any other speculator trading in the expectation of making profits, hedge funds enhance market liquidity by creating higher levels of trading, which leads to tighter bid-ask spreads for everybody. For example, recent statistics indicate that hedge funds make up about 80% of the trading volume in U.S. distressed debt. This trading activity creates market-clearing prices, which provide useful price information to market observers. In addition, funds such as those using relative value strategies help to push prices to their equilibrium values faster. Overall, hedge funds help to improve market liquidity and move prices closer to their fair values. Thus, as Adam Smith suggested a long time ago in *An Inquiry into the Nature and Causes of the Wealth of Nations*, by performing their "greedy" speculative function, hedge funds play a socially beneficial role.

Example 17-9: Transparency

Investors should insist on learning about the positions of hedge funds because
a) They want to trade ahead of the hedge fund.
b) They do not understand the trading strategies behind the positions.
c) They want to aggregate the risk of hedge funds with the rest of their portfolio.
d) They receive the information from the prime broker anyway.

Example 17-10: Fraud

The term *Ponzi scheme* is attributed to Carlo Ponzi, who in 1919 established an inventive pyramid scheme using new investor funds to repay earlier investors. The investment was based on a relative-value trade, in which postal coupons were bought overseas for the equivalent of one U.S. cent and resold for six American one-cent stamps. After transaction costs were factored in, however, the trade was unprofitable. Nevertheless, thousands of people invested with him, lured by a promise of 50% return in 90 days. Ultimately, he lost $140 million in investor funds, in today's dollars, and was jailed for fraud. This scheme
a) Has never been used by a hedge fund
b) Is not exposed to currency risk
c) Can be attributed to misrepresentation of asset values
d) Today would not be subject to SEC registration requirements

---

17.5   Answers to Chapter Examples

Example 17-1: Leverage and Hedge Funds

c) The gross leverage is $(200 + 150)/100 = 3.5$. The net leverage is $(200 - 150)/100 = 0.5$.

Example 17-2: Hedging and Returns

c) The net return on the stock portfolio is $(\beta_L\$200 - \beta_S\$150) \times 20\%$. With betas of 1, this is $10 million. Given that the equity is $100 million, the rate of return is 10%. The rate of return is less than the market because most of the exposure to the market is hedged.

Example 17-3: Risks in Fixed-Income Arbitrage

c) The strategy has no exposure to the level of rates but is exposed to a widening of the swap-Treasury spread. Assume, for instance, that the swap and Treasury rates are initially 5.5% and 5%. If these rates change to 5.3% and 4.5%, for example, values for the swap and the Treasury bond would increase. Because the drop in the Treasury rate is larger, however, the price of the Treasury bond would fall more than the swap, leading to a net loss on the position. The strategy should *gain* from decreases in the swap-Treasury spread, so a) is wrong. The strategy should *gain* from increases in the Treasury rate, all else equal, so b) is wrong. Finally, the distribution of the payoff depends on the distribution of the swap-Treasury spread. Because this cannot go below zero, there is a limit on the upside. The position has negative skewness, so c) is correct.

Example 17-4: Risks in Convertible Arbitrage

d) This position is hedged against interest rate risk, so b) is wrong. It is also hedged against directional movements in the stock, so c) is wrong. The position is long an option (the option to convert the bond into the stock) and so is long implied volatility, so a) is wrong. Long options positions have positive gamma.

Example 17-5: Risks in Merger Arbitrage—I

c) The position is long one share of company B offset by a short position in two shares of company A. The payoff is $(\$120 - \$90) - 2(\$60 - \$50) = \$30 - \$20 = \$10$.

Example 17-6: Risks in Merger Arbitrage—II

b) The expected payoff is the sum of probabilities times the payoff in each state of the world, or $83\% \times \$5 + 17\% \times (-\$20) = \$4.15 - \$3.40 = \$0.75$. Note that the distribution is highly asymmetric, with a small probability of a large loss.

Example 17-7: Liquidity Risks

c) Asset liquidity risk is a function of the size of the position and the intrinsic liquidity of the instrument. Distressed securities trade much less than Treasury bonds, and so have more intrinsic liquidity. A $100 million position is more illiquid than a $10 million position in the same instrument.

Example 17-8: Risk and Illiquidity

b) Illiquidity will create trends in returns, as market shocks during a month will be partially recorded in two consecutive months. This is positive autocorrelation. Also, illiquidity creates an *understatement* of the systematic risk measure.

Example 17-9: Transparency

c) Risk aggregation is an important reason for investors to learn about the positions of their investment in hedge funds. Answer a) is incorrect because front-running the hedge fund would be a reason *not* to disclose position information. Answer b) is incorrect because not understanding the trading strategies would be a reason *not* to require position information. Answer d) is incorrect because investors do not receive position information from the prime broker.

Example 17-10: Fraud

c) Ponzi schemes are widely used by all kinds of people to defraud investors. Similar schemes have been used by hedge funds, most recently Tradewinds LLC, a hedge fund whose manager was arrested for fraud. So a) is incorrect. Answer b) is also incorrect because the strategy involves buying coupons in a foreign currency, and so is exposed to currency risk. Nowadays this type of hedge fund would be subject to SEC registration requirement, because it is based in the United States, so d) is wrong. Carlo Ponzi was able to attract new capital because he misrepresented the return on his fund, which can occur only if there is misrepresentation of NAV.

PART five

Credit Risk Management

Chapter 18

Introduction to Credit Risk

Credit risk is the risk of an economic loss from the failure of a counterparty to fulfill its contractual obligations. Its effect is measured by the cost of replacing cash flows if the other party defaults.

This chapter provides an introduction to the measurement of credit risk. The study of credit risk has undergone tremendous developments in the last few years. Fueled by advances in the measurement of market risk, institutions are now, for the first time, attempting to quantify credit risk on a portfolio basis.

Credit risk, however, offers unique challenges. It requires constructing the distribution of default probabilities, of loss given default, and of credit exposures, all of which contribute to credit losses and should be measured in a portfolio context. In comparison, the measurement of market risk using value at risk is a simple affair.

For most institutions, however, market risk pales in significance compared with credit risk. Indeed, the amount of risk-based capital for the banking system reserved for credit risk is vastly greater than that for market risk. The history of financial institutions has also shown that the biggest banking failures were due to credit risk.

Credit risk involves the possibility of nonpayment, either on a future obligation or during a transaction. Section 18.1 introduces **settlement risk**, which arises from the exchange of principals in different currencies during a short window. We discuss exposure to settlement risk and methods to deal with it.

Traditionally, however, credit risk is viewed as presettlement risk. Section 18.2 analyzes the components of a credit risk system and the evolution of credit risk measurement systems. Section 18.3 then shows how to construct the distribution of credit losses for a portfolio given default probabilities for the various credits in the portfolio.

The key drivers of portfolio credit risk are the correlations between defaults.

Section 18.4 takes a fixed $100 million portfolio with an increasing number of obligors and shows how the distribution of losses is dramatically affected by correlations.

18.1 Settlement Risk

18.1.1 Presettlement versus Settlement Risk

Counterparty credit risk consists of both presettlement and settlement risk. **Presettlement risk** is the risk of loss due to the counterparty's failure to perform on an obligation during the life of the transaction. This includes default on a loan or bond or failure to make the required payment on a derivative transaction. Presettlement risk exists over long periods—years—starting from the time it is contracted until settlement.

In contrast, **settlement risk** is due to the *exchange* of cash flows and is of a much shorter-term nature. This risk arises as soon as an institution makes the required payment and exists until the offsetting payment is received. This risk is greatest when payments occur in different time zones, especially for foreign exchange transactions where notionals are exchanged in different currencies. Failure to perform on settlement can be caused by counterparty default, liquidity constraints, or operational problems.

Most of the time, settlement failure due to operational problems leads to minor economic losses, such as additional interest payments. In some cases, however, the loss can be quite large, extending to the full amount of the transferred payment. An example of major settlement risk is the 1974 failure of Herstatt Bank. The day it went bankrupt, Herstatt had received payments from a number of counterparties but defaulted before payments were made on the other legs of the transactions.

18.1.2 Handling Settlement Risk

In March 1996, the Bank for International Settlements (BIS) issued a report warning that the private sector should find ways to reduce settlement risk in the $1.2 trillion/day global foreign exchange market.[1] The report noted that central banks had "significant concerns regarding the risk stemming from the current arrangements for settling FX

---

[1]Committee on Payment and Settlement Systems (1996), *Settlement Risk in Foreign Exchange Transactions*, BIS (online), available at http://www.bis.org/publ/cpss17.pdf.

trades." It explained that "the amount at risk to even a single counterparty could exceed a bank's capital," which creates **systemic risk**. The threat of regulatory action led to a reexamination of settlement risk.

The status of a trade can be classified into five categories:

- *Revocable:* When the institution can still cancel the transfer without the consent of the counterparty
- *Irrevocable:* After the payment has been sent and before payment from the other party is due
- *Uncertain:* After the payment from the other party is due but before it is actually received
- *Settled:* After the counterparty payment has been received
- *Failed:* After it has been established that the counterparty has not made the payment

Settlement risk occurs during the periods of irrevocable and uncertain status, which can take from one to three days.

While this type of credit risk can lead to substantial economic losses, the short-term nature of settlement risk makes it fundamentally different from presettlement risk. Managing settlement risk requires unique tools, such as **real-time gross settlement** (RTGS) systems. These systems aim at reducing the interval between the time an institution can no longer stop a payment and the receipt of the funds from the counterparty.

Settlement risk can be further managed with netting agreements. One such arrangement is **bilateral netting**, which involves two banks. Instead of making payments of gross amounts to each other, the banks tot up the balance and settle only the net balance outstanding in each currency. At the level of instruments, netting also occurs with **contracts for differences** (CFD). Instead of exchanging principals in different currencies, the contracts are settled in dollars at the end of the contract term.[2]

The next step up is a **multilateral netting system**, also called **continuous-linked settlements**, where payments are netted for a group of banks that belong to the system. This idea became reality when the **CLS Bank**, established in 1998 with 60 bank participants, became operational on September 9, 2002. Every evening, CLS Bank provides a schedule of payments for the member banks to follow during the next day.

---

[2]These are similar to **nondeliverable forwards**, which are used to trade emerging-market currencies outside the jurisdiction of the emerging-market regime and are also settled in dollars.

Payments are not released until funds are received and all transactions confirmed. The risk now has been reduced to that of the netting institution. In addition to reducing settlement risk, the netting system has the advantage of reducing the number of trades between participants by up to 90%, which lowers transaction costs.

Example 18-1: FRM Exam 2000—Question 36

Settlement risk in foreign exchange is generally due to
a) Notionals being exchanged
b) Net value being exchanged
c) Multiple currencies and countries involved
d) High volatility of exchange rates

Example 18-2: FRM Exam 2000—Question 85

Which one of the following statements about multilateral netting systems is *not* accurate?
a) Systemic risks can actually increase because they concentrate risks on the central counterparty, the failure of which exposes all participants to risk.
b) The concentration of risks on the central counterparty eliminates risk because of the high quality of the central counterparty.
c) By altering settlement costs and credit exposures, multilateral netting systems for foreign exchange contracts could alter the structure of credit relations and affect competition in the foreign exchange markets.
d) In payment netting systems, participants with net debit positions will be obligated to make a net settlement payment to the central counterparty, which, in turn, is obligated to pay those participants with net credit positions.

18.2   Overview of Credit Risk

18.2.1   Drivers of Credit Risk

We now examine the drivers of credit risk, traditionally defined as presettlement risk. Credit risk measurement systems attempt to quantify the risk of losses due to counterparty default. The distribution of credit risk can be viewed as a compound process driven by these variables:

- **Default**, which is a discrete state for the counterparty—either the counterparty is in default or not. This occurs with some **probability of default** (PD).
- **Credit exposure** (CE), also known as **exposure at default** (EAD), which is the economic value of the claim on the counterparty at the time of default.

■ **Loss given default** (LGD), which represents the fractional loss due to default. As an example, take a situation where default results in a **fractional recovery rate** of 30% only. LGD is then 70% of the exposure.

Traditionally, credit risk has been measured in the context of loans or bonds for which the exposure, or economic value, of the asset is close to its notional, or face value. This is an acceptable approximation for bonds but certainly not for derivatives, which can have positive or negative value. Credit exposure is defined as the positive value of the asset:

$$(\text{Credit exposure})_t = \text{Max}(V_t, 0) \qquad (18.1)$$

This is so because if the counterparty defaults with money owed to it, the full amount has to be paid.[3] In contrast, if it owes money, only a fraction may be recovered. Thus, presettlement risk arises only when the contract's replacement cost has a positive value to the institution (i.e., is "in-the-money").

18.2.2 Measurement of Credit Risk

The evolution of credit risk management tools has gone through these steps:

■ Notional amounts
■ Risk-weighted amounts
■ External/internal credit ratings
■ Internal portfolio credit models

Initially, risk was measured by the total notional amount. A multiplier, say 8%, was applied to this amount to establish the amount of required capital to hold as a reserve against credit risk.

The problem with this approach is that it ignores variations in the probability of default. In 1988, the Basel Committee instituted a rough categorization of credit risk by *risk class*, providing risk weights to multiply notional amounts. This was the first attempt to force banks to carry capital in relation to the risks they were taking.

These risk weights proved to be too simplistic, however, creating incentives for banks to alter their portfolios in order to maximize their shareholder returns subject to the Basel capital requirements. This had the perverse effect of introducing more risk into the balance sheets of commercial banks, which was certainly not the intended

---

[3]This is because there are *no walk-away clauses*, explained in Chapter 28.

purpose of the 1988 rules. As an example, there was no differentiation between AAA-rated and C-rated corporate credits. Since loans to C-credits are more profitable than those to AAA-credits, given the same amount of regulatory capital, the banking sector responded by shifting its loan mix toward lower-rated credits.

This led to the 2001 proposal by the Basel Committee to allow banks to use their own internal or external credit ratings. These credit ratings provide a better representation of credit risk, where *better* is defined as more in line with economic measures. The new proposals will be described in more detail in a following chapter.

Even with these improvements, credit risk is still measured on a stand-alone basis. This harks back to the days of finance before the benefits of diversification were formalized by Markowitz. One has to hope that eventually the banking system will be given proper incentives to diversify its credit risk.

18.2.3   Credit Risk versus Market Risk

The tools recently developed to measure market risk have proved invaluable in assessing credit risk. Even so, there are a number of major differences between market and credit risk, which are listed in Table 18-1.

TABLE 18-1 Comparison of Market Risk and Credit Risk

Item	Market Risk	Credit Risk
Sources of risk	Market risk only	Default risk, recovery risk, market risk
Distributions	Mainly symmetric, perhaps fat tails	Skewed to the left
Time horizon	Short term (days)	Long term (years)
Aggregation	Business/trading unit	Whole firm vs. counterparty
Legal issues	Not applicable	Very important

As mentioned previously, credit risk results from a compound process with three sources of risk. The nature of this risk creates a distribution that is strongly skewed to the left, unlike most market risk factors. This is because credit risk is akin to short positions in options. At best, the counterparty makes the required payment and there is no loss. At worst, the entire amount due is lost.

The time horizon is also different. Whereas the time required for corrective action is relatively short in the case of market risk, it is much longer for credit risk. Positions also turn over much more slowly for credit risk than for market risk, although the advent of credit derivatives has made it easier to hedge credit risk.

Finally, the level of aggregation is different. Limits on market risk may apply at the level of a trading desk, business units, and eventually the whole firm. In contrast, limits on credit risk must be defined at the counterparty level, for all positions taken by the institution.

Credit risk can also mix with market risk. Movements in corporate bond prices indeed reflect changing expectations of credit losses. In this case, it is not so clear whether this volatility should be classified as market risk or credit risk.

18.3   Measuring Credit Risk

18.3.1   Credit Losses

To simplify, consider credit risk due to the effect of defaults only. This is what is called **default mode**. The distribution of credit losses from a portfolio of N instruments can be described as

$$\text{Credit loss} = \sum_{i=1}^{N} b_i \times \text{CE}_i \times (1 - f_i) \tag{18.2}$$

where
- b_i is a (Bernoulli) random variable that takes the value of 1 if default occurs and 0 otherwise, with probability p_i, such that $E[b_i] = p_i$
- CE_i is the credit exposure at the time of default
- f_i is the recovery rate, or $(1 - f_i)$ the loss given default

In theory, all of these could be random variables. For what follows, we will assume that the only random variable is the default event b.

18.3.2   Joint Events

Equation (18.2) then shows that the expected credit loss is

$$E[\text{CL}] = \sum_{i=1}^{N} E[b_i] \times \text{CE}_i \times (1 - f_i) = \sum_{i=1}^{N} p_i \times \text{CE}_i \times (1 - f_i) \tag{18.3}$$

The dispersion in credit losses, however, critically depends on the correlations between the default events.

It is often convenient, although not necessarily justified, to assume that the events are statistically independent. This simplifies the analysis considerably, as the probability of any joint event is simply the product of the individual event probabilities:

$$p(A \text{ and } B) = p(A) \times p(B) \qquad (18.4)$$

At the other extreme, if the two events are perfectly correlated, that is, if B always default when A defaults, we have

$$p(A \text{ and } B) = p(B \mid A) \times p(A) = 1 \times p(A) = p(A) \qquad (18.5)$$

When the marginal probabilities are equal, $p(A) = p(B)$.

Suppose, for instance, that the marginal probabilities are $p(A) = p(B) = 1\%$. Then the probability of the joint event is 0.01% in the independence case and 1% in the perfect-correlation case.

More generally, one can show that the probability of a joint default depends on the marginal probabilities and the correlations. As we have seen in Chapter 2, the expectation of the product can be related to the covariance:

$$E[b_A \times b_B] = \text{Cov}[b_A, b_B] + E[b_A]E[b_B] = \rho \sigma_A \sigma_B + p(A)p(B) \qquad (18.6)$$

Given that b_A is a Bernoulli variable, its standard deviation is $\sigma_A = \sqrt{p(A)[1 - p(A)]}$, and similarly for b_B. We then have

$$p(A \text{ and } B) = \text{Corr}(A, B)\sqrt{p(A)[1 - p(A)]}\sqrt{p(B)[1 - p(B)]} + p(A)p(B) \qquad (18.7)$$

For example, if the correlation is unity and $p(A) = p(B) = p$, we have

$$p(A \text{ and } B) = 1 \times [p(1 - p)]^{1/2} \times [p(1 - p)]^{1/2} + p^2 = [p(1 - p)] + p^2 = p$$

as shown in Equation (18.5).

If the correlation is 0.5 and $p(A) = p(B) = 0.01$, however, we have $p(A \text{ and } B) = 0.00505$, which is only half of each of the marginal probabilities. This example is illustrated in Table 18-2, which lays out the full joint distribution. Note how the probabilities in each row and column sum to the marginal probability. From this information, we can infer all remaining probabilities. For example, the probability of B not defaulting when A is in default is $0.01 - 0.00505 = 0.00495$.

TABLE 18-2 Joint Probabilities

A	B Default	B No Default	Marginal
Default	0.00505	0.00495	0.01
No default	0.00495	0.98505	0.99
Marginal	0.01	0.99	

18.3.3   An Example

As an example of credit loss distribution, consider a portfolio of $100 million with three bonds, A, B, and C, with various probabilities of default. To simplify, we assume (1) that the exposures are constant, (2) that the recovery in case of default is zero, and (3) that default events are independent across issuers.

Table 18-3 displays the exposures and default probabilities. The second panel lists all possible states. In state 1, there is no default, which has a probability of $(1 - p_1)(1 - p_2)(1 - p_3) = (1 - 0.05)(1 - 0.10)(1 - 0.20) = 0.684$, given independence. In state 2, bond A defaults and the others do not, with probability $p_1(1 - p_2)(1 - p_3) = 0.05(1 - 0.10)(1 - 0.20) = 0.036$. And so on for the other states.

TABLE 18-3 Portfolio Exposures, Default Risk, and Credit Losses

Issuer	Exposure	Probability
A	$25	0.05
B	$30	0.10
C	$45	0.20

Default i	Loss L_i	Probability $p(L_i)$	Cumulative Probability	Expected $L_i p(L_i)$	Variance $(L_i - EL_i)^2 p(L_i)$
None	$0	0.6840	0.6840	0.000	120.08
A	$25	0.0360	0.7200	0.900	4.97
B	$30	0.0760	0.7960	2.280	21.32
C	$45	0.1710	0.9670	7.695	172.38
A, B	$55	0.0040	0.9710	0.220	6.97
A, C	$70	0.0090	0.9800	0.630	28.99
B, C	$75	0.0190	0.9990	1.425	72.45
A, B, C	$100	0.0010	1.0000	0.100	7.53
Sum				$13.25	434.7

Figure 18-1 plots the frequency distribution of credit losses. From the table, we can compute an expected loss of $13.25 million, which is also $E[\text{CL}] = \sum p_i \times \text{CE}_i =$

$0.05 \times 25 + 0.10 \times 30 + 0.20 \times 45$. This is the average credit loss over many repeated, hypothetical "samples." The table also shows how to compute the variance as

$$V[\mathrm{CL}] = \sum_{i=1}^{N} (L_i - E[\mathrm{CL}_i])^2 p(L_i)$$

which gives a standard deviation of $\sigma(\mathrm{CL}) = \sqrt{434.7} = \$20.9$ million.

FIGURE 18-1 Distribution of Credit Losses

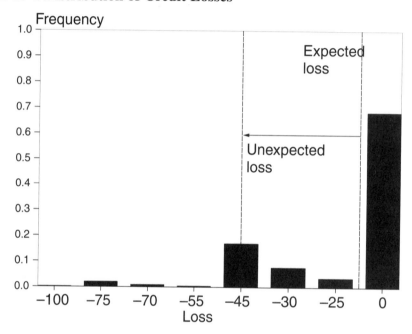

Alternatively, we can express the range of losses with a 95% quantile, which is the lowest number CL_i such that

$$P(\mathrm{CL} \le \mathrm{CL}_i) \ge 95\% \tag{18.8}$$

From Table 18-3, this is $45 million. Figure 18-2 plots the cumulative distribution function and shows that the 95% quantile is $45 million. In terms of deviations from the mean, this gives an unexpected loss of $45 - 13.2 = \$32$ million. This is a measure of **credit VAR**.

This very simple three-bond portfolio provides a useful example of the measurement of the distribution of credit risk. It shows that the distribution is skewed to the left. In addition, the distribution has irregular "bumps" that correspond to the default events. The chapter on managing credit risk will elaborate on this point.

FIGURE 18-2 Cumulative Distribution of Credit Losses

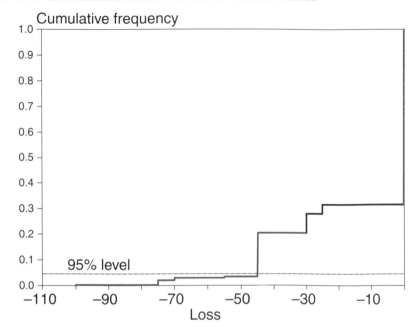

Example 18-3: FRM Exam 2002—Question 130

You have granted an unsecured loan to a company. This loan will be paid off by a single payment of $50 million. The company has a 3% chance of defaulting over the life of the transaction, and your calculations indicate that if they default you would recover 70% of your loan from the bankruptcy courts. If you are required to hold a credit reserve equal to your expected credit loss, how great a reserve should you hold?

a) $450,000

b) $750,000

c) $1,050,000

d) $1,500,000

Example 18-4: FRM Exam 2000—Question 46

An investor holds a portfolio of $50 million. This portfolio consists of A-rated bonds ($20 million) and BBB-rated bonds ($30 million). Assume that the one-year probabilities of default for A-rated and BBB-rated bonds are 2% and 4%, respectively, and that they are independent. If the recovery value for A-rated bonds in the event of default is 60% and the recovery value for BBB-rated bonds is 40%, what is the one-year expected credit loss from this portfolio?

a) $672,000

b) $742,000

c) $880,000

d) $923,000

Example 18-5: FRM Exam 1998—Question 38

Calculate the probability of a subsidiary and parent company both defaulting over the next year. Assume that the subsidiary will default if the parent defaults, but the parent will not necessarily default if the subsidiary defaults. Also assume that the parent has a one-year probability of default of 0.50% and the subsidiary has a one-year probability of default of 0.90%.

a) 0.450%
b) 0.500%
c) 0.545%
d) 0.550%

Example 18-6: FRM Exam 1998—Question 16

A portfolio manager has been asked to take the risk related to the default of two securities A and B. She has to make a large payment if, and only if, both A and B default. For taking this risk, she will be compensated by receiving a fee. What can be said about this fee?

a) The fee will be larger if the default of A and of B are highly correlated.
b) The fee will be smaller if the default of A and of B are highly correlated.
c) The fee is independent of the correlation between the default of A and of B.
d) None of the above is correct.

Example 18-7: FRM Exam 1998—Question 42

A German bank lends €100 million to a Russian bank for one year and receives €120 million worth of Russian government securities as collateral. Assuming that the one-year 99% VAR on the Russian government securities is €20 million and the Russian bank's one-year probability of default is 5%, what is the German bank's probability of losing money on this trade over the next year?

a) Less than 0.05%
b) Approximately 0.05%
c) Between 0.05% and 5%
d) Greater than 5%

Example 18-8: FRM Exam 2000—Question 51

A portfolio consists of two (long) assets of £100 million each. The probability of default over the next year is 10% for the first asset and 20% for the second asset, and the joint probability of default is 3%. Estimate the expected loss on this portfolio due to credit defaults over the next year assuming a 40% recovery rate for both assets.

a) £18 million
b) £22 million
c) £30 million
d) None of the above

18.4   Credit Risk Diversification

Modern banking was built on the sensible notion that a portfolio of loans is less risky than are single loans. As with market risk, the most important feature of credit risk management is the ability to diversify across defaults.

To illustrate this point, Figure 18-3 presents the distribution of losses for a $100 million loan portfolio. The probability of default is fixed at 1%. If default occurs, recovery is zero.

In the first panel, there is one loan only. We can either have no default, with probability 99%, or a loss of $100 million, with probability 1%. The expected loss is

$$EL = 0.01 \times \$100 + 0.99 \times 0 = \$1 \text{ million}$$

The problem, of course, is that if default occurs, it will be a big hit to the bottom line, possibly bankrupting the lending bank.

Basically, this is what happened to Peregrine Investments Holdings, one of Hong Kong's leading investment banks which failed due to the Asian crisis of 1997. The bank failed in large part from a single loan to PT Steady Safe, an Indonesian taxicab operator, that amounted to $235 million, a quarter of the bank's equity capital.

In the case of our single loan, the spread of the distribution is quite large, with a variance of 99, which implies a standard deviation (SD) of about $10 million. Simply focusing on the standard deviation, however, is not adequately informative given the severe skewness in the distribution.

In the second panel, we consider 10 loans, each for $10 million. The total notional is the same as before. We assume that defaults are independent. The expected loss is still $1 million, or $10 \times 0.01 \times \$10$ million. The SD, however, is now $3 million, much less than before.

The third panel considers one hundred loans of $1 million each. The expected loss is still $1 million, but the SD is now $1 million, even lower. Finally, the fourth panel considers a thousand loans of $100,000, which create a SD of $0.3 million.

For comparability, all these graphs use the same vertical and horizontal scale. This, however, does not reveal the distributions fully. This is why the fifth panel expands the distribution with 1,000 counterparties, which looks similar to a normal distribution. This reflects the **central limit theorem**, which states that the distribution of the sum of *independent* variables tends to a normal distribution. Remarkably, even starting from a highly skewed distribution, we end up with a normal distribution due to diversification effects.

In addition, the spread of the distribution becomes very small. This explains why portfolios of consumer loans, which are spread over a large number of credits, are less risky than typical portfolios of corporate loans.

With N events that occur with the same probability p, define the variable $X = \sum_{i=1}^{N} b_i$ as the number of defaults (where $b_i = 1$ when default occurs). The expected credit loss on our portfolio is then

$$E[\text{CL}] = E[X] \times \$100/N = pN \times \$100/N = p \times \$100 \qquad (18.9)$$

which depends not on N but rather on the average probability of default and total exposure, \$100 million. When the events are independent, the variance of this variable is, using the results from a binomial distribution,

$$V[\text{CL}] = V[X] \times (\$100/N)^2 = p(1 - p)N \times (\$100/N)^2 \qquad (18.10)$$

which gives a standard deviation of

$$\text{SD}[\text{CL}] = \sqrt{p(1 - p)} \times \$100/\sqrt{N}. \qquad (18.11)$$

For a constant total notional, this shrinks to zero as N increases.

We should note the crucial assumption that the credits are independent. When this is not the case, the distribution will lose its asymmetry more slowly. Even with a very large number of consumer loans, the dispersion may not tend to zero because the general state of the economy is a common factor behind consumer credits. Indeed, many more defaults occur in a recession than in an expansion.

Institutions loosely attempt to achieve diversification by **concentration limits**. In other words, they limit the extent of exposure, say loans, to a particular industrial or geographical sector. The rationale behind this is that defaults are more highly correlated within sectors than across sectors. Conversely, **concentration risk** is the risk that too many defaults could occur at the same time.

FIGURE 18-3 Distribution of Credit Losses

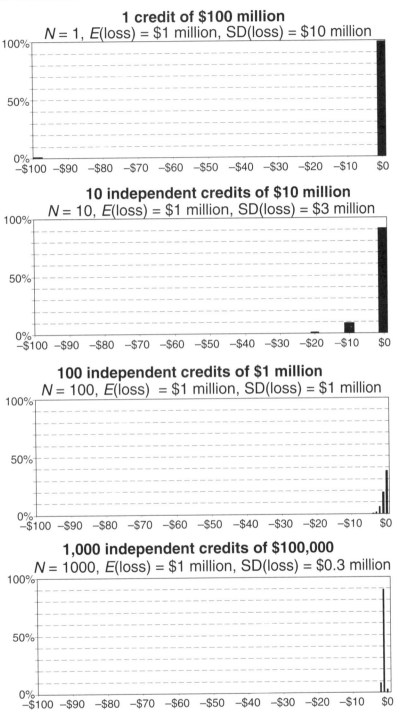

FIGURE 18-3 Distribution of Credit Losses (Continued)

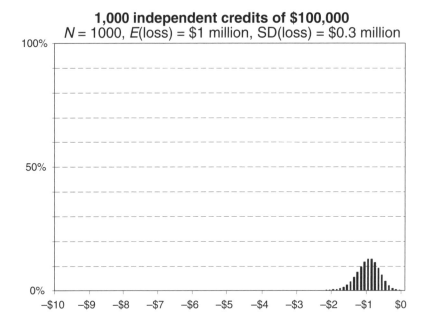

Example 18-9: FRM Exam 2002—Question 92

A portfolio consists of five bonds whose default correlation is zero. The one-year probabilities of default of the bonds are 1%, 2%, 5%, 10%, and 15%. What is the one-year probability of no default within the portfolio?

a) 71%

b) 67%

c) 85%

d) 99%

Example 18-10: FRM Exam 1997—Question 12

What is the probability of no defaults over the next year from a portfolio of 10 BBB-rated obligors? Assume that the one-year probability of default for a BBB-rated counterparty is 5% and assume zero correlation (independence) between the counterparty's and the obligor's probability of default.

a) 5.0%

b) 50.0%

c) 60.0%

d) 95.0%

Example 18-11: FRM Exam 2001—Question 5

What is the approximate probability of a particular bond defaulting, and none of the others, over the next year from a portfolio of 20 BBB-rated obligors? Assume the one-year probability of default for a BBB-rated counterparty to be 4% and obligor defaults to be independent from one another.

a) 2%

b) 4%

c) 45%

d) 96%

18.5   Answers to Chapter Examples

Example 18-1: FRM Exam 2000—Question 36

a) Settlement risk is due to the exchange of notional principal in different currencies at different points in time, which exposes one counterparty to default after it has made payment. There would be less risk with netted payments.

Example 18-2: FRM Exam 2000—Question 85

b) Answers c) and d) are both correct. Answers a) and b) are contradictory. A multilateral netting system concentrates the credit risk into one institution. This could potentially create much damage if this institution should fail.

Example 18-3: FRM Exam 2002—Question 130

a) The expected credit loss (ECL) is the notional amount times the probability of default times the loss given default. This is $\$50,000,000 \times 0.03 \times (1 - 70\%) = \$450,000$.

Example 18-4: FRM Exam 2000—Question 46

c) The expected loss is $\sum_i p_i \times CE_i \times (1 - f_i) = \$20,000,000 \times 0.02(1 - 0.60) + \$30,000,000 \times 0.04(1 - 0.40) = \$880,000$.

Example 18-5: FRM Exam 1998—Question 38

b) Since the subsidiary defaults when the parent defaults, the joint probability is simply that of the parent defaulting.

Example 18-6: FRM Exam 1998—Question 16

a) The fee must reflect the joint probability of default. As described in Equation (18.7), if defaults of A and B are highly correlated, the default of one implies a greater probability of a second default. Hence the fee must be higher.

Example 18-7: FRM Exam 1998—Question 42

c) The probability of losing money is driven by (1) a fall in the value of the collateral and (2) default by the Russian bank. If the two events are independent, the joint probability is $5\% \times 1\% = 0.05\%$. In contrast, if the value of securities always drops at the same time the Russian bank defaults, the probability is simply that of the Russian bank's default, or 5%.

Example 18-8: FRM Exam 2000—Question 51

a) The three loss events are

  (i) Default by the first alone, with probability $0.10 - 0.03 = 0.07$

 (ii) Default by the second, with probability $0.20 - 0.03 = 0.17$

(iii) Default by both, with probability 0.03

The respective losses are $£100 \times (1-0.4) \times 0.07 = 4.2$, $£100 \times (1-0.4) \times 0.17 = 10.2$, $£200 \times (1 - 0.4) \times 0.03 = 3.6$, for a total expected loss of £18 million.

Example 18-9: FRM Exam 2002—Question 92

a) Because the events are independent, the joint probability is given by the product $(1 - p_1)(1 - p_2)(1 - p_3)(1 - p_4)(1 - p_5) = (1 - 1\%)(1 - 2\%)(1 - 5\%)(1 - 10\%)(1 - 20\%) = 70.51\%$.

Example 18-10: FRM Exam 1997—Question 12

c) Since the probability of one default is 5%, that on a bond not defaulting is $100 - 5 = 95\%$. With independence, the joint probability of 10 nondefaults is $(1 - 5\%)^{10} = 60\%$.

Example 18-11: FRM Exam 2001—Question 5

a) This question asks the probability that a particular bond will default and 19 others will not. Assuming independence, this is $0.04(1 - 0.04)^{19} = 1.84\%$. Note that the probability that any bond will default and none of the others will is 20 times this, or 36.8%.

Chapter 19

Measuring Actuarial Default Risk

Default risk is the primary driver of credit risk. It is represented by the **probability of default** (PD). When default occurs, the actual loss is the combination of **exposure at default** (EAD) and **loss given default** (LGD).

Default risk can be measured using two approaches: (1) **actuarial methods**, which provide "objective" measures of default rates, usually based on historical default data; and (2) **market-price methods**, which infer from traded prices of debt, equity, or credit derivatives "risk-neutral" measures of default risk.

Risk-neutral measures were introduced earlier in relation to price options. They provide a useful shortcut for asset pricing. For *risk management* purposes, however, they are contaminated by the effect of risk premiums and often contain measures of loss given default. As a result, they do not directly measure default probabilities.

In contrast, objective measures describe the "actual" or "natural" probability of default. However, a major benefit of risk-neutral measures is that because they are based on current market prices, they are forward looking and responsive to the latest news.

Actuarial measures of default probabilities are provided by **credit rating agencies**, which classify borrowers by credit ratings that are supposed to quantify default risk. Such ratings are **external** to the firm. Similar techniques can be used to develop **internal** ratings.

Such measures can also be derived from **accounting variables models**. These models relate the occurrence of default to a list of firm characteristics, such as accounting variables. Statistical techniques such as discriminant analysis then examine how these variables are related to the occurrence or nonoccurrence of default. Presumably, rating agencies use similar procedures, augmented by additional data.

This chapter focuses on actuarial measures of default risk. Market-based measures of default risk will be examined in the next chapter. Section 19.1 examines the definition of a credit event. Section 19.2 then examines credit ratings, describing how historical default rates can be used to infer default probabilities. Recovery rates are discussed in Section 19.3. Section 19.4 presents an application to the construction and rating of a collateralized bond obligation. Finally, Section 19.5 broadly discusses the evaluation of corporate and sovereign credit risk.

19.1   Credit Event

A credit event is a discrete state. Either it happens or it does not. The issue is the definition of the event, which must be framed in legal terms.

One could say, for instance, that the definition of default for a bond obligation is quite narrow. Default on a bond occurs when payment on that bond is missed. The state of **default** is defined by **Standard & Poor's** (S&P), a credit rating agency, as

> *The first occurrence of a payment default on any financial obligation, rated or unrated, other than a financial obligation subject to a bona fide commercial dispute; an exception occurs when an interest payment missed on the due date is made within the grace period.*

Default on a bond, however, reflects the creditor's financial distress and is typically accompanied by default on other obligations. This is why rating agencies give a credit rating for the *issuer* in addition to a rating for specific bonds. The rating for specific bonds can be higher or lower than this issuer rating, depending on their relative priority.

This definition, however, needs to be defined more precisely for credit derivatives, whose payoffs are directly related to credit events. We will cover credit derivatives in Chapter 22. The definition of a **credit event** has been formalized by the **International Swaps and Derivatives Association** (ISDA), an industry group, which lists these events:

- **Bankruptcy**, which is a situation involving either
  —The *dissolution* of the obligor (other than by merger)
  —The obligor's *insolvency*, or inability to pay its debt
  —The *assignment* of claims

—The *institution of bankruptcy proceeding*

—The *appointment of receivership*

—The *attachment of substantially all assets by a third party*

■ **Failure to pay**, which means failure of the creditor to make due payment; this is usually triggered after an agreed-upon grace period and attainment of a certain threshold amount

■ **Obligation/cross-default**, which means the occurrence of a default (other than failure to make a payment) on any other, similar obligation

■ **Obligation/cross-acceleration**, which means the occurrence of a default (other than failure to make a payment) on any other, similar obligation, resulting in that obligation becoming due immediately

■ **Repudiation/moratorium**, which means that the counterparty is rejecting, or challenges, the validity of the obligation

■ **Restructuring**, which means a waiver, deferral, or rescheduling of the obligation with the effect that the terms are less favorable than before

Other events sometimes included are

■ **Downgrading**, which means the credit rating is lower than previously, or is withdrawn

■ **Currency inconvertibility**, which means the imposition of exchange controls or other currency restrictions by a governmental or associated authority

■ **Governmental action**, which means either (1) declarations or actions by a government or regulatory authority that impair the validity of the obligation, or (2) the occurrence of war or other armed conflict that impairs the functioning of the government or banking activities

Ideally, the industry should agree on a common set of factors defining a credit event, to minimize the possibility of disagreements and costly legal battles that create uncertainty for everybody. The ISDA definitions are designed to minimize **legal risk** by precisely wording the definition of credit event.

Even so, unforeseen situations sometimes develop. For example, there have been differences of opinion as to whether a bank debt restructuring constitutes a credit event, as in the recent cases of Conseco, Xerox, and Marconi.

Another notable situation is that of Argentina, which represents the largest sovereign default recorded so far, in terms of external debt. Argentina announced in November

2001 a restructuring of its local debt that was more favorable to itself. Some holders of credit default swaps argued that this was a "credit event," since the exchange was coerced, and that they were entitled to payment. Swap sellers disagreed. This became an unambiguous default, however, when Argentina announced in December that it would stop paying interest on its $135 billion foreign debt. Nonetheless, the situation was unresolved for holders of credit swaps that expired just before the official default.

Example 19-1: FRM Exam 1998—Question 5

Which of the following events is not a "credit event"?
a) Bankruptcy
b) Calling back a bond
c) Downgrading
d) Default on payments

Example 19-2: FRM Exam 1999—Question 128

Which of the following losses can be considered as resulting from an "event risk"?
  I. Losses on a diversified portfolio of stocks during the stock market decline and hedge fund crisis in the autumn of 1998.
 II. A U.S. investor bought a bond whose payments are in Japanese yen. The investor experienced a loss as the Japanese yen depreciated relative to the dollar.
III. A holding in RJR Nabisco corporate bonds sustained a loss in 1988 when RJR Nabisco was taken over for $25 billion via a leveraged buyout, which resulted in a reduction of its debt rating to non–investment grade.
IV. A municipal bond portfolio suffers a loss when municipal bonds are declared no longer tax exempt by the tax authority, with no compensation being paid to investors.
a) III only
b) All the above
c) I and IV
d) III and IV

19.2   Default Rates

19.2.1   Credit Ratings

A **credit rating** is an "evaluation of creditworthiness" issued by a rating agency. The major U.S. bond rating agencies are Moody's Investors Services, Standard & Poor's (S&P), and Fitch, Inc.

More technically, a credit rating has been defined by Moody's as an "opinion of the future ability, legal obligation, and willingness of a bond issuer or other obligor to make full and timely payments on principal and interest due to investors."

Table 19-1 presents the interpretation of various credit ratings issued by Moody's and S&P. These ratings correspond to long-term debt; other ratings apply to short-term debt. Generally, the two agencies provide similar ratings for the same issuer.

TABLE 19-1 Classification by Credit Ratings

	Standard & Poor's	Moody's Services
Investment grade		
Highest grade	AAA	Aaa
High grade	AA	Aa
Upper medium grade	A	A
Medium grade	BBB	Baa
Speculative grade		
Lower medium grade	BB	Ba
Speculative	B	B
Poor standing	CCC	Caa
Highly speculative	CC	Ca
Lowest quality, no interest	C	C
In default	D	

Modifiers: A+, A, A− and A1, A2, A3

Ratings are broadly divided into
- **Investment grade**, that is, at or above BBB for S&P and Baa for Moody's
- **Speculative grade**, or **below investment grade**, for the rest

This classification is sometimes used to define classes of investments allowable to some investors, such as pension funds.

These ratings represent objective (or actuarial) probabilities of default.[1] Indeed, the agencies have published studies that track the frequency of bond default in the United States, classified by initial ratings for different horizons. These frequencies can be used to convert ratings to default probabilities.

The agencies use a number of criteria to decide on the credit rating, including various accounting ratios. Table 19-2 presents median value for selected accounting

---

[1] In fact, the ratings measure the probability of default (PD) for S&P and the joint effect of PD×LGD for Moody's, where LGD is the proportional loss given default.

ratios for industrial corporations. The first column (under "leverage") shows that the ratio of total debt to total capital (debt plus book equity) varies systematically across ratings. Highly rated companies have low ratios, 23% for AAA firms. In contrast, BB-rated (just below investment grade) companies have a debt-to-capital (or debt-to-asset) ratio of 63%. This implies a capital-to-equity leverage ratio of 2.7 to 1.[2]

The right-hand panel (under "cash flow coverage") also shows systematic variations in a measure of free cash flow divided by interest payments. This represents the number of times the cash flow can cover interest payments. Focusing on earnings before interest and taxes (EBIT), AAA-rated companies have a safe cushion of 21.4, whereas BB-rated companies have coverage of only 2.1.

TABLE 19-2 S&P's Financial Ratios across Ratings

Rating	Leverage (Percent)		Cash Flow Coverage (Multiplier)	
	Total Debt/ Capital	LT Debt/ Capital	EBITDA/ Interest	EBIT/ Interest
AAA	23	13	26.5	21.4
AA	38	28	12.9	10.1
A	43	34	9.1	6.1
BBB	48	43	5.8	3.7
BB	63	57	3.4	2.1
B	75	70	1.8	0.8
CCC	88	69	1.3	0.1

Note: From S&P's *Corporate Ratings Criteria* (2002), based on median financial ratios over 1998 to 2000 for industrial corporations. EBITDA is defined as earnings before interest, taxes, depreciation, and amortization.

A related model for bankruptcy prediction is the **multiple discriminant analysis** (MDA), such as the **z-score** model developed by Altman.[3] MDA constructs a linear combination of accounting data that provides the best fit with the observed states of default and nondefault for the sample firms.

The variables used in the *z*-score are (1) working capital over total assets, (2) retained earnings over total assets, (3) EBIT over total assets, (4) market value of

---

[2]Defining D, E as debt and equity, the debt-to-asset ratio is $D/(D+E) = 63\%$. We then have an asset-to-equity ratio of $(D+E)/E = [D/E] + 1 = [D/(D+E)]/[E/(D+E)] + 1 = 63\%/(1 - 63\%) + 1 = 2.7$.

[3]Altman, E. (1968), Financial Ratios, Discriminant Analysis and the Prediction of Corporate Bankruptcy, *Journal of Finance* 23, 589–609.

equity over total liabilities, and (5) net sales over total assets. Lower scores indicate a higher likelihood of default. Each variable enters with a positive sign, meaning that an increase in each of these variables decreases the probability of bankruptcy.

Example 19-3: FRM Exam 2002—Question 110

If Moody's and S&P are equally good at rating bonds, the average default rate on BB bonds by S&P will be lower than the average default rate on bonds rated by Moody's as
a) Baa3
b) Ba1
c) Ba
d) Ba3

Example 19-4: FRM Exam 2002—Question 86

Limited to the following information, according to the Altman z-score model, which of the following counterparties would have the least credit risk?
a) A counterparty with earnings before interest and taxes (EBIT)/total assets (TA) value of 0.30 and a retained earnings (RE)/TA value of 0.20
b) A counterparty with a EBIT/TA value of 0.60 and a RE/TA value of 0.20
c) A counterparty with a EBIT/TA value of 0.30 and a RE/TA value of 0.40
d) A counterparty with a EBIT/TA value of 0.60 and a RE/TA value of 0.40

19.2.2   Historical Default Rates

Tables 19-3 and 19-4 display historical default rates as reported by Moody's and Standard & Poor's, respectively. These describe the proportion of firms that default, $\bar{X}$, which is a statistical estimate of the true default probability:

$$E(\bar{X}) = p \qquad (19.1)$$

For example, borrowers with an initial Moody's rating of Baa experienced an average default rate of 0.34% over the next year. Similar rates are obtained for S&P's BBB-rated credits, which experienced an average 0.36% default rate over the next year. On the other hand, A-rated firms experience a default rate around 0.08% over the next year. Firms at or below Caa have a default rate of 14.74%. Higher ratings are associated with lower default rates. As a result, this information could be used to derive estimates of default probability for an initial rating class.

In addition, the tables show that the default rate increases sharply with the horizon, for a given initial credit rating. The default rate for Baa firms increases from

0.34% over one year to 7.99% over the following 10 years. Because these are cumulative default rates, the number must increase with the horizon. For investment-grade credits, however, the increase is more than proportional with the horizon. The ratio is $7.99/0.34 = 23$ for Baa-rated credits, which is more than 10. In contrast, the ratio for B-rated credits is $36.10/4.79 = 8$. For speculative-grade credits, the increase is less than proportional with the horizon.

TABLE 19-3 Moody's Cumulative Default Rates (Percent), 1920–2002

Rating	Year									
	1	2	3	4	5	6	7	8	9	10
Aaa	0.00	0.00	0.02	0.09	0.19	0.29	0.41	0.59	0.78	1.02
Aa	0.07	0.22	0.36	0.54	0.85	1.21	1.60	2.01	2.37	2.78
A	0.08	0.27	0.57	0.92	1.28	1.67	2.09	2.48	2.93	3.42
Baa	0.34	0.99	1.79	2.69	3.59	4.51	5.39	6.25	7.16	7.99
Ba	1.42	3.43	5.60	7.89	10.16	12.28	14.14	15.99	17.63	19.42
B	4.79	10.31	15.59	20.14	23.99	27.12	30.00	32.36	34.37	36.10
Caa-C	14.74	23.95	30.57	35.32	38.83	41.94	44.23	46.44	48.42	50.19
Inv.	0.17	0.50	0.93	1.41	1.93	2.48	3.03	3.57	4.14	4.71
Spec.	3.83	7.75	11.41	14.69	17.58	20.09	22.28	24.30	26.05	27.80
All	1.50	3.09	4.62	6.02	7.28	8.41	9.43	10.38	11.27	12.14

Rating	Year									
	11	12	13	14	15	16	17	18	19	20
Aaa	1.24	1.40	1.61	1.70	1.75	1.85	1.96	2.02	2.14	2.20
Aa	3.24	3.77	4.29	4.82	5.23	5.51	5.75	5.98	6.30	6.54
A	3.95	4.47	4.94	5.40	5.88	6.35	6.63	6.94	7.23	7.54
Baa	8.81	9.62	10.41	11.12	11.74	12.33	12.95	13.49	13.93	14.39
Ba	21.06	22.65	24.23	25.61	26.83	27.96	29.13	30.24	31.14	32.05
B	37.79	39.37	40.85	42.33	43.62	44.94	45.91	46.68	47.32	47.60
Caa-C	52.30	54.4	56.24	58.22	60.08	61.78	63.27	64.81	66.25	67.59
Inv.	5.30	5.90	6.46	7.00	7.48	7.92	8.30	8.65	8.99	9.32
Spec.	29.47	31.08	32.64	34.07	35.36	36.58	37.72	38.78	39.67	40.46
All	13.01	13.85	14.66	15.40	16.07	16.69	17.24	17.75	18.21	18.64

TABLE 19-4 S&P's Cumulative Default Rates (Percent), 1981–2002

Rating	1	2	3	4	5	6	7	8	9	10	11	12	13	14	15
							Year								
AAA	0.00	0.00	0.03	0.07	0.11	0.20	0.30	0.47	0.54	0.61	0.61	0.61	0.61	0.75	0.92
AA	0.01	0.03	0.08	0.17	0.28	0.42	0.61	0.77	0.90	1.06	1.20	1.37	1.51	1.63	1.77
A	0.05	0.15	0.30	0.48	0.71	0.94	1.19	1.46	1.78	2.10	2.37	2.60	2.84	3.08	3.46
BBB	0.36	0.96	1.61	2.58	3.53	4.49	5.33	6.10	6.77	7.60	8.48	9.34	10.22	11.28	12.44
BB	1.47	4.49	8.18	11.69	14.77	17.99	20.43	22.63	24.85	26.61	28.47	29.76	30.98	31.70	32.56
B	6.72	14.99	22.19	27.83	31.99	35.37	38.56	41.25	42.90	44.59	45.84	46.92	47.71	48.68	49.57
CCC	30.95	40.35	46.43	51.25	56.77	58.74	59.46	59.85	61.57	62.92	63.41	63.41	63.41	64.25	64.25
Inv.	0.13	0.34	0.59	0.93	1.29	1.65	1.99	2.33	2.64	2.99	3.32	3.63	3.95	4.30	4.75
Spec.	5.56	11.39	16.86	21.43	25.12	28.35	31.02	33.32	35.24	36.94	38.40	39.48	40.40	41.24	42.05
All	1.73	3.51	5.12	6.48	7.57	8.52	9.33	10.04	10.66	11.27	11.81	12.28	12.71	13.17	13.69

Note: Static pool average cumulative default rates (adjusted for "not rated" borrowers).

One problem with such historical information, however, is the relative paucity of data. There are few defaults for highly rated firms over one year. In addition, the sample size decreases as the horizon lengthens. For instance, S&P reports default rates up to 15 years using data from 1981 to 2002. The one-year default rates represent 23 years of data, that is, 1981, 1982, and so on to 2002. There are, however, only eight years of data for the 15-year default period 1981–1995. The sample size is much shorter. The data are also overlapping and therefore not independent. So omitting or adding a few borrowers can drastically alter the reported default rate.

This can lead to inconsistencies in the tables. For instance, the default rate for CCC obligors is the same, 63.41%, from year 11 to 13. This implies that there is no further risk of default after 11 years, which is unrealistic. Also, when the categories are further broken down into modifiers, default rates sometimes do not decrease monotonically with the ratings, which is a small-sample effect.

We can try to assess the accuracy of these default rates by computing their standard error. Consider, for instance, the default rate over the first year for AA-rated credits, which averaged out to $\bar{X} = 0.01\%$ in this S&P sample. This was taken from a total of about $N = 8,000$ observations, which we assume to be independent. The variance of the average is, from the distribution of a binomial process,

$$V(\bar{X}) = \frac{p(1-p)}{N} \tag{19.2}$$

which gives a standard error of about 0.011%. This is on the same order as the average of 0.01%, indicating that there is substantial imprecision in this average default rate. So we could not really distinguish an AA credit from an AAA credit.

The problem is made worse with lower sample sizes, which is the case in non-U.S. markets or when the true p is changing over time. For instance, if we observe a 5% default rate among 100 observations, the standard error becomes 2.2%, which is very large. Therefore, a major issue with credit risk is that estimation of default rates for low-probability events can be very imprecise.

Example 19-5: FRM Exam 1997—Question 28

Based on historical data from S&P, what is the approximate historical one-year probability of default for a BB-rated obligor?

a) 0.05%

b) 0.20%

c) 1.0%

d) 5.0%

Example 19-6: FRM Exam 1998—Question 29

Based on historical evidence, a B-rated counterparty is approximately 16 times more likely to default over a 1-year time period than a BBB-rated counterparty. Over a 10-year time period, a B-rated counterparty is how many more times likely to default than a BBB-rated counterparty?

a) 5

b) 9

c) 16

d) 24

19.2.3 Cumulative and Marginal Default Rates

The default rates reported in Tables 19-3 and 19-4 are **cumulative default rates** for an initial credit rating; that is, measure the total frequency of default *at any time* between the starting date and year T. It is also informative to measure the **marginal default rate**, which is the frequency of default *during* year T.

The default process is illustrated in Figure 19-1. Here d_1 is the marginal default rate during year 1, and d_2 is the marginal default rate during year 2. To default during the second year, the firm must have survived the first year and defaulted in the second. Thus, the probability of defaulting in year 2 is given by $(1 - d_1)d_2$. The cumulative probability of defaulting up to year 2 is then $C_2 = d_1 + (1 - d_1)d_2$. Subtracting and adding 1, this is also $C_2 = 1 - (1 - d_1)(1 - d_2)$, which perhaps has a more intuitive interpretation, as this is 1 minus the probability of surviving the whole period. More formally,

- $m[t + N \mid R(t)]$ is the number of issuers rated R at the end of year t that default in year $T = t + N$

- $n[t + N \mid R(t)]$ is the number of issuers rated R at the end of year t that have not defaulted by the beginning of year $t + N$

Marginal Default Rate during Year T

This is the proportion of issuers initially rated R at initial time t that default in year T, relative to the number remaining at the beginning of the same year T:

$$d_N(R) = \frac{m[t + N \mid R(t)]}{n[t + N \mid R(t)]}$$

FIGURE 19-1 Sequential Default Process

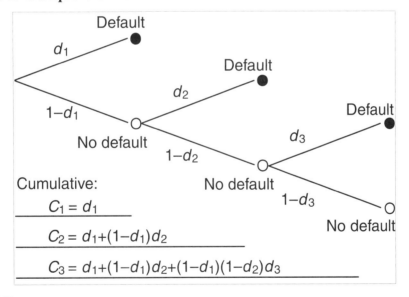

Survival Rate

This is the proportion of issuers initially rated R that will not have defaulted by T:

$$S_N(R) = \Pi_{i=1}^{N}(1 - d_i(R)) \tag{19.3}$$

Marginal Default Rate from Start to Year T

This is the proportion of issuers initially rated R that defaulted in year T, relative to the initial number in year t. For this to happen, the issuer will have survived until year $t + N - 1$, and then default the next year.

$$k_N(R) = S_{N-1}(R)d_N(R) \qquad (19.4)$$

Cumulative Default Rate

This is the proportion of issuers rated R that defaulted at any point until year T:

$$C_N(R) = k_1(R) + k_2(R) + \cdots + k_N(R) = 1 - S_N(R) \qquad (19.5)$$

Average Default Rate

We can express the total cumulative default rate as an average, per period default rate d, by setting

$$C_N = 1 - \Pi_{i=1}^{N}(1 - d_i) = 1 - (1 - d)^N \qquad (19.6)$$

As we move from annual to semiannual and ultimately continuous compounding, the average default rate becomes

$$C_N = 1 - (1 - d^a)^N = 1 - (1 - d^s/2)^{2N} \to 1 - e^{-d^c N} \qquad (19.7)$$

where d_a, d_s, d_c are default rates using annual, semiannual, and continuous compounding. This is exactly equivalent to various definitions for the compounding of interest.

Example: Computing cumulative default probabilities

Consider a B-rated firm that has default rates of $d_1 = 5\%$, $d_2 = 7\%$. Compute the cumulative default probabilities.

Answer

In the first year, $k_1 = d_1 = 5\%$. After one year, the survival rate is $S_1 = 0.95$. The probability of defaulting in year 2 is then $k_2 = S_1 \times d_2 = 0.95 \times 0.07 = 6.65\%$. After two years, the survival rate is $(1 - d_1)(1 - d_2) = 0.95 \times 0.93 = 0.8835$. Thus, the cumulative probability of defaulting in years 1 and 2 is $5\% + 6.65\% = 11.65\%$.

Based on this information, we can map these "forward," or marginal, default rates from cumulative default rates for various credit ratings. Figure 19-2 displays the cumulative default rates reported by Moody's in Table 19-3. The corresponding marginal default rates are plotted in Figure 19-3.

FIGURE 19-2 Moody's Cumulative Default Rates, 1920–2002

It is interesting to see that the marginal probability of default increases with maturity for initial high credit ratings, but decreases for initial low credit ratings. The increase is due to a mean reversion effect. The fortunes of an Aaa-rated firm can only stay the same at best, and often will deteriorate over time. In contrast, a B-rated firm that has survived the first few years must have a decreasing probability of defaulting as time goes by. This is a survival effect.

FIGURE 19-3 Moody's Marginal Default Rates, 1920–2002

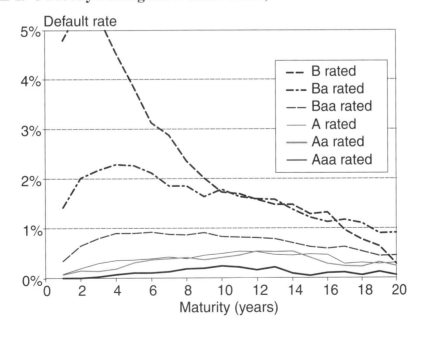

Example 19-7: FRM Exam 2002—Question 77

If the default probability for an A-rated company over a three-year period is
0.30%, then the most likely probability of default for this company over a
six-year period is

a) 0.30%

b) Between 0.30% and 0.60%

c) 0.60%

d) Greater than 0.60%

Example 19-8: FRM Exam 2000—Question 37

A company has a constant 30%-per-year probability of default. What is the
probability the company will be in default after three years?

a) 34%

b) 48%

c) 66%

d) 90%

Example 19-9: FRM Exam 2000—Question 31

According to Standard & Poor's, the five-year cumulative probability of default
for BB-rated debt is 15%. If the marginal probability of default for BB debt from
year 5 to year 6 (conditional on no prior default) is 10%, then what is the six-year
cumulative probability of default for BB-rated debt?

a) 25%

b) 16.55%

c) 15%

d) 23.50%

Example 19-10: FRM Exam 2000—Question 43

The marginal default rates (conditional on no previous default) for a BB-rated
firm during the first, second, and third years are 3%, 4%, and 5% respectively.
What is the cumulative probability of defaulting over the next three years?

a) 10.78%

b) 11.54%

c) 12.00%

d) 12.78%

Example 19-11: FRM Exam 2000—Question 34

What is the difference between the marginal default probability and the cumulative default probability?

a) The marginal default probability is the probability that a borrower will default in any given year, whereas the cumulative default probability covers a specified multi-year period.

b) The marginal default probability is the probability that a borrower will default due to a particular credit event, whereas the cumulative default probability is for all possible credit events.

c) The marginal default probability is the minimum probability that a borrower will default, whereas the cumulative default probability is the maximum probability.

d) Both (a) and (c) are correct.

19.2.4   Transition Probabilities

As we have seen, the measurement of long-term default rates can be problematic with small sample sizes. The computation of these default rates can be simplified by assuming a Markov process for the ratings migration, described by a transition matrix. **Migration** is a discrete process that consists of credit ratings changing from one period to the next.

The **transition matrix** gives the probability of moving to one rating conditional on the rating at the beginning of the period. The usual assumption is that these moves follow a **Markov process**, or that migrations across states are independent from one period to the next.[4] This type of process exhibits *no carry-over effect*. More formally, a **Markov chain** describes a stochastic process where the conditional distribution, given today's value, is constant over time. Only present values are relevant.

Table 19-5 gives an example of a simplified transition matrix for four states, A, B, C, D, where the last represents default. Consider a company in year 0 in the B category. The company could default

■ In year 1, with probability $D[t_1 \mid B(t_0)] = P(D_1 \mid B_0) = 3\%$

■ In year 2, after going from B to A in the first year, then A to D in the second; or from B to B, then to D; or from B to C, then to D. The default probability is
$$P(D_2 \mid A_1)P(A_1) + P(D_2 \mid B_1)P(B_1) + P(D_2 \mid C_1)P(C_1) = 0.00 \times 0.02 + 0.03 \times 0.93 + 0.23 \times 0.02 = 3.25\%.$$

---

[4]There is some empirical evidence, however, that credit downgrades are not independent over time but instead display a momentum effect.

The cumulative probability of default over the two years is then $3\% + 3.25\% = 6.25\%$. Figure 19-4 illustrates the various paths to default in years 1, 2, and 3.

TABLE 19-5 Credit Ratings Transition Probabilities

Starting State	Ending State				Total
	A	B	C	D	Prob.
A	0.97	0.03	0.00	0.00	1.00
B	0.02	0.93	0.02	0.03	1.00
C	0.01	0.12	0.64	0.23	1.00
D	0	0	0	1.00	1.00

The advantage of using this approach is that the resulting data are more robust and consistent. For instance, the 15-year cumulative default rate obtained this way will always be greater than the 14-year default rate.

FIGURE 19-4 Paths to Default

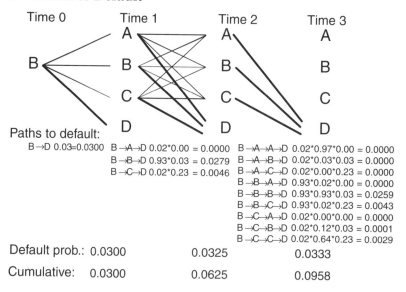

Paths to default:
B→D 0.03=0.0300   B→A→D 0.02*0.00 = 0.0000   B→A→A→D 0.02*0.97*0.00 = 0.0000
                  B→B→D 0.93*0.03 = 0.0279   B→A→B→D 0.02*0.03*0.03 = 0.0000
                  B→C→D 0.02*0.23 = 0.0046   B→A→C→D 0.02*0.00*0.23 = 0.0000
                                             B→B→A→D 0.93*0.02*0.00 = 0.0000
                                             B→B→B→D 0.93*0.93*0.03 = 0.0259
                                             B→B→C→D 0.93*0.02*0.23 = 0.0043
                                             B→C→A→D 0.02*0.00*0.00 = 0.0000
                                             B→C→B→D 0.02*0.12*0.03 = 0.0001
                                             B→C→C→D 0.02*0.64*0.23 = 0.0029

Default prob.: 0.0300   0.0325   0.0333
Cumulative: 0.0300   0.0625   0.0958

Example 19-12: FRM Exam 2000—Question 50

The transition matrix in credit risk measurement generally represents
a) Probabilities of migrating from one rating quality to another over the lifetime of the loan
b) Correlations among the transitions for the various rating quality assets within one year
c) Correlations of various market movements that impact rating quality for a 10-day holding period
d) Probabilities of migrating from one rating quality to another within one year

---

19.2.5   Time Variation in Default Probabilities

Defaults are also correlated with economic activity. Moody's, for example, has compared the annual default rate to the level of industrial production since 1920. Moody's reports a marked increase in the default rate in the 1930s at the time of the Great Depression and during the recent recessions. These default rates, however, do not control for structural shifts in the credit quality. In recent years, many issuers came to the market with a lower initial credit rating than in the past. This should lead to more defaults, even with a stable economic environment.

To control for this effect, Figure 19-5 plots the default rate for B credits as well as for investment-grade and speculative credits over the years 1981 to 2004. As expected, the default rate of investment-grade bonds is very low. More interestingly, however, it displays minimal variation through time. We do observe, however, significant variation in the default rate of B credits, which peaks during the recessions that started in 1981, 1990, and 2001. Thus, economic activity significantly affects credit risk, and the effect is most marked for speculative-grade bonds.

FIGURE 19-5 Time Variation in Defaults (from S&P)

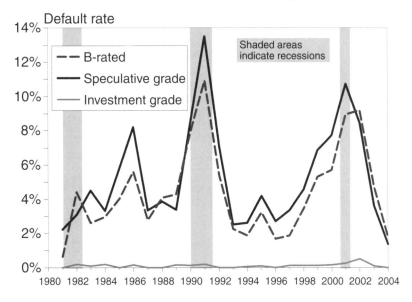

19.3   Recovery Rates

Credit risk also depends on the **loss given default** (LGD). This can be measured as 1 minus the **recovery rate**, or fraction recovered after default.

19.3.1 The Bankruptcy Process

Normally, default is a state that affects all obligations of an issuer equally, especially when accompanied by a bankruptcy filing. In most countries, a formal bankruptcy process provides a centralized forum for resolving all the claims against the corporation. The bankruptcy process creates a **pecking order** for a company's creditors. This spells out the order in which creditors are paid, thereby creating differences in the recovery rate across creditors. Within each class, however, creditors should be treated equally.

In the United States, firms that are unable to make required payments can file for either **Chapter 7** bankruptcy, which leads to the liquidation of the firm's assets, or **Chapter 11** bankruptcy, which leads to a reorganization of the firm, during which the firm continues to operate under court supervision.

Under Chapter 7, the proceeds from liquidation should be divided according to the **absolute priority rule**, which states that payments should be made first to claimants with the highest priority.

Table 19-6 describes the pecking order in bankruptcy proceedings. At the top of the list are **secured creditors**, who because of their property right are paid to the fullest extent of the value of the collateral. Then come **priority creditors**, which consist mainly of post-bankruptcy creditors. Finally, **general creditors** can be paid if funds remain after distribution to others.

TABLE 19-6 Pecking Order in U.S. Federal Bankruptcy Law

Seniority	Type of Creditor

Highest (paid first)	(1) Secured creditors
	     (up to the extent of secured collateral)
	 (2) Priority creditors
	     —Firms that lend money during bankruptcy period
	     —Providers of goods and services during bankruptcy period
	       (e.g., employees, lawyers, vendors)
	     —Taxes
	 (3) General creditors
	     —Unsecured creditors before bankruptcy

Lowest (paid last)	—Shareholders

Similar rules apply under Chapter 11. In this situation, the firm must submit a **reorganization plan**, which specifies new financial claims to the firm's assets. The absolute priority rule, however, is often violated in Chapter 11 settlements. Junior debt holders and stockholders often receive some proceeds even though senior share-holders are not paid in full. This is allowed in order to facilitate timely resolution of the bankruptcy and to avoid future lawsuits. Even so, there remain sharp differences in recovery across seniority.

19.3.2   Estimates of Recovery Rates

Credit rating agencies measure recovery rates using the value of the debt right after default. This is viewed as the market's best estimate of the future recovery and takes into account the value of the firm's assets, the estimated cost of the bankruptcy process, and various means of payment (e.g., using equity to pay bondholders), discounted to the present.

The recovery rate has been shown to depend on a number of factors:

- *The status or seniority of the debtor.* Claims with higher seniority have higher recovery rates. More generally, a greater **debt cushion**, or the percentage of total company debt below the instrument, also leads to higher recovery rates.

- *The state of the economy.* Recovery rates tend to be higher (lower) when the economy is in an expansion (recession).

- *The obligor's characteristics.* Recovery rates tend to be higher when the borrower's assets are tangible and when the previous rating was high. Utilities, for example, have more **tangible assets**, such as power-generating plants, than other industries and consequently have higher recovery rates. Also, companies with greater interest coverage, as measured by higher credit ratings, typically have higher recovery rates.

- *The type of default.* Distressed exchanges, as opposed to bankruptcy proceed-ings, usually lead to higher recovery rates. Unlike a bankruptcy proceeding, which causes all debts to go into default, a distressed exchange involves only the instru-ments that have defaulted.

Ratings can also include the loss given default. The same borrower may have various classes of debt, which may have different credit ratings due to the different levels of protection. If so, debt with lower seniority should carry a lower rating.

Recovery rates are commonly estimated from the market price of defaulted shortly after default, as a percentage of par. Table 19-7 displays recovery rates for corporate debt. Moody's estimates the average recovery rate for senior unsecured debt at $f = 37\%$. Derivative instruments rank as senior unsecured creditors and would be expected to have the same recovery rates as senior unsecured debt.

Bank loans are usually secured and therefore have higher recovery rates, typically around 60%. As expected, subordinated bonds have the lowest recovery rates, typically around 20% to 30%.

TABLE 19-7 Moody's Recovery Rates for Global Corporate Debt (Percent)

Priority	Count	Mean	S.D.	Min.	10th	Median	90th	Max.
All bank loans	310	61.6	23.4	5.0	25.0	67.0	90.0	98.0
Equipment trust	86	40.2	29.9	1.5	10.6	31.0	90.0	103.0
Sr. secured	238	53.1	26.9	2.5	10.0	34.0	82.0	125.0
Sr. unsecured	1,095	37.4	27.2	0.3	7.0	30.0	82.2	122.6
Sr. subordinated	450	32.0	24.0	0.5	5.0	27.0	66.5	123.0
Subordinated	477	30.4	21.3	0.5	5.0	27.1	60.0	102.5
Jr. subordinated	22	23.6	19.0	1.5	3.8	16.4	48.5	74.0
All bonds	2,368	36.8	26.3	0.3	7.5	30.0	80.0	125.0

Source: Adapted from Moody's, based on 1982–2002 defaulted bond prices

There is, however, much variation around the average recovery rates, as Table 19-7 shows. The table reports not only the average value but also the standard deviation, minimum, maximum, and 10th and 90th percentiles. Recovery rates vary widely. In addition, recovery rates are negatively related to default rates. During years with more bond defaults, prices after default are more depressed than usual. This correlation creates bigger losses, which extends the tail of the credit loss distribution. In practice, the distribution of recovery rates is often modeled with a beta distribution, which has an argument ranging from 0 to 1.

The legal environment is also a main driver of recovery rates. Differences across national jurisdictions will create differences among recovery rates. Table 19-8 compares mean recovery rates across Europe and North America. Recovery rates are significantly higher in the United States than in Europe.

TABLE 19-8 Moody's Mean Recovery Rates (Percent):
Europe and North America

Instrument	Europe	North America
Bank loans	47.6	61.7
Bonds		
Senior secured	52.2	52.7
Senior unsecured	25.6	37.5
Senior subordinated	24.3	32.1
Subordinated	13.9	31.3
Junior subordinated	NA	24.5
All bonds	28.4	35.3
Preferred stock	3.4	10.9
All instruments	27.6	35.9

Source: Adapted from Moody's, from 1982–2002 defaulted bond prices

Using trading prices of debt shortly after default as estimates of recovery is convenient and the most common approach. This is because the bankruptcy process can be slow, with an average of 12 to 18 months but sometimes taking many years. Computing the total value of payments to debtholders can also be complicated, and should take into account the time value of money.

The evidence, however, is that trading prices are significantly lower than the ultimate discounted recovery rate. Table 19-9 compares the two approaches and shows that the average recovery rate is systematically higher than the indication given by trading prices. This could be due to different clienteles for the two markets, or to a risk premium impounded in trading prices. This difference, however, also explains the hedge fund category called **distressed securities funds**. Such funds buy distressed debt right after default and then benefit from the increase in value.

TABLE 19-9 S&P's Recovery Rates for Corporate Debt (Percent)

Instrument	Trading Prices 15–45 Days	Discounted Recovery
Bank loans	58.0	81.6
Senior secured bonds	48.6	67.0
Senior unsecured bonds	34.5	46.0
Senior subordinated bonds	28.4	32.4
Subordinated bonds	28.9	31.2

Source: Adapted from S&P, from 1988–2002 defaulted debt

Example 19-13: FRM Exam 2000—Question 58

In measuring credit risk, for the same counterparty
a) A loan obligation is generally rated higher than a bond obligation.
b) A bond obligation is generally rated higher than a loan obligation.
c) A bond obligation is generally rated the same as a loan obligation.
d) Loans are never rated, so it's impossible to compare.

Example 19-14: FRM Exam 2002—Question 123

The recovery rate on credit instruments is defined as 1 minus the loss rate. The loss rate can be significantly influenced by the volatility of the value of a firm's assets before default. All other things being equal, in the event of a default, which type of company would we expect to have the highest recovery rate?
a) A trading company active in volatile markets
b) An Internet merchant of trendy consumer products
c) An asset-intensive manufacturing company
d) A highly leveraged hedge fund

19.4 Application to Portfolio Rating

Much of financial engineering is about repackaging financial instruments to make them more palatable to investors, creating value in the process. In the 1980s, **collateralized mortgage obligations** (CMOs) brought mortgage-backed securities to the masses by repackaging their cash flows into **tranches** with different characteristics. The same magic is performed with **collateralized debt obligations** (CDOs), which are securities backed by a pool of corporate bonds and loans. **Collateralized bond obligations** (CBOs) and **collateralized loan obligations** (CLOs) are backed by bonds and loans, respectively. Figure 19-6 illustrates a typical CDO structure.

The first step is to place a package of high-yield bonds in a **special-purpose vehicle** (SPV). The second step is to specify the **waterfall**, or priority of payments to the various tranches. Here, 69% of the capital structure is apportioned to tranche A, which has the highest credit rating, Aaa; it pays LIBOR + 45 bp. Other tranches have lower priority and rating; intermediate tranches are typically called *mezzanine*. At the bottom is the equity tranche, which is not rated. After payments to the other tranches and costs, the excess spread can be around 2.5% to 3%, which with a 10-to-1 leverage gives a yield of 25% to 30% to equity investors. In exchange, the equity is exposed to the first dollar loss in the portfolio. Thus, the rating enhancement for the senior classes is achieved through prioritizing the cash flows. Rating agencies have devel-

FIGURE 19-6 Collateralized Debt Obligation Structure

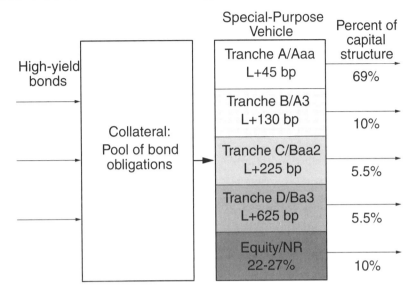

oped internal models to rate the senior tranches based on the probability of shortfalls due to defaults.

Whatever transformation is brought about, the resulting package must obey some basic laws of conservation. For the underlying and resulting securities, we must have the same cash flows at each point in time, apart from transaction costs. As a result, this implies (1) the same total market value and (2) the same risk profile, both for interest rate and default risk. The weighted duration of the final package must equal that of the underlying securities. The expected default rate, averaged by market values, must be the same. So, if some tranches are less risky, others must bear more risk. Like CMOs, CDOs are often structured so that most of the tranches have less risk. Inevitably, the remaining **residual** tranche is more risky. This is sometimes called "toxic waste." If this residual is cheap enough, however, some investors should be willing to buy it.

CDO transactions are typically classified as either balance sheet or arbitrage. The primary goal of **balance sheet CDOs** is to move loans off the balance sheet of commercial banks to lower regulatory capital requirements. In contrast, **arbitrage CDOs** are designed to capture the spread between the portfolio of underlying securities and that of highly rated, overlying tranches. Such CDOs exploit differences in the funding costs of assets and liabilities. The spreads on high-yield debt have historically more than compensated investors for their credit risk, which reflects a liquidity effect, or risk premium. Because CDO senior tranches create more liquid assets with automatic diversification, investors require a lower risk premium for these. The arbitrage profit then goes into the equity tranche (but also into management and investment banking fees).

The credit risk transfer can be achieved by cash flow or synthetic structures. The example in Figure 19-7 is typical of traditional, or *funded*, **cash-flow CDOs**. The physical assets are sold to an SPV and the underlying cash flows used to back payments to the issued notes. In contrast, the credit risk exposure of **synthetic CDOs** is achieved with credit derivatives, which will be covered in a later chapter.

Finally, CDOs differ in the management of the asset pool. In **static CDOs**, the asset pool is basically fixed. In contrast, with **managed CDOs**, a portfolio manager is allowed to trade actively the underlying assets. This allows him or her to unwind assets with decreasing credit quality or to reinvest redeemed issues.

Example 19-15: FRM Exam 2001—Question 12

A pool of high-yield bonds is placed in an SPV, and three tranches (including the equity tranche) of bonds are issued collateralized by the bonds to create a collateralized bond obligation (CBO). Which of the following is true?
a) At fair value the value of the issued bonds should be less than the collateral.
b) At fair value the total default probability, weighted by size of issue, of the issued bonds should equal the default probability of the collateral pool.
c) The equity tranche of the CBO has the least risk of default.
d) The yield on the low-risk tranche must be greater than the yield on the collateral pool.

Example 19-16: FRM Exam 1998—Question 8

In a typical collateralized bond obligation (CBO), a pool of high-yield bonds is posted as collateral, and the cash flows from the collateral are structured as several classes of securities (the offered securities) with different credit ratings and a residual piece (the equity), which absorbs most of the default risk. Comparing the market value–weighted average rating of the collateral and that of the offered securities, which of the following is *true*?
a) The market value–weighted average rating of the collateral is about the same as the offered securities.
b) The market value–weighted average rating of the collateral is higher than the offered securities.
c) The market value–weighted average rating of the collateral is lower than the offered securities.
d) The market value–weighted average rating of the collateral may be lower or higher than the offered securities.

Example 19-17: FRM Exam 2002—Question 32

A CBO (collateralized bond obligation) consists of several tranches of notes from a repackaging of corporate bonds, ranging from equity to super senior. Which of the following is generally true of these structures?

a) The total yield of all the CBO tranches is slightly less than the underlying repackaged bonds in order to allow the issuer to recover fees/costs/ profits.

b) The super senior tranche has an expected loss rate higher than that of the junior tranche.

c) The super senior tranche is typically rated below AAA and sold to bond investors.

d) The equity tranche does not absorb the first losses of the structure.

19.5   Assessing Corporate and Sovereign Rating

19.5.1   Corporate Default

One issue is whether these ratings are the best forecasts of default probability based on public information. A substantial academic literature has examined this question and has generally concluded that ratings can be reasonably predicted from accounting information. Indeed, the balance sheet and income statement provide important information about a firm's viability.

Analysts focus on the balance sheet **leverage**, often defined in terms of the debt-to-equity ratio, and the **debt coverage**, defined in terms of the ratio of income over debt payment. All else equal, companies with higher leverage and lower debt coverage are more likely to default. By nature, however, accounting information is backward looking. The economic prospects of a company are also crucial for assessing credit risk. These include growth potential, market competition, and exposure to financial risk factors.

The data presented so far have focused primarily on U.S. obligors. The next question is whether this historical experience applies to obligors in other countries. We would expect some difference in ratings because of a number of factors:

- *Differences in financial stability across countries.* Countries have differences in financial market structure, such as the strength of the banking system, and different government policies. The mishandling of economic policy can turn, for instance, what should be a minor devaluation into a major problem, leading to a recession.

■ *Differences in legal systems.* The protection accorded to creditors can vary widely across countries, some of which have not yet established a bankruptcy process.

■ *Differences in industrial structure.* There may be differences in default rates across countries simply due to different industrial structures. There is evidence that default rates vary across U.S. industries even with identical credit ratings.

Normally, ratings provided by credit rating agencies are supposed to be *consistent* across countries and industrial sectors. In other words, they should take into account such variations and represent the same probability of default.

19.5.2 Sovereign Default

Rating agencies have only recently started to rate sovereign bonds. In 1975, S&P rated only 7 countries, all of which were investment grade. By 1990, the pool had expanded to 31 countries, of which only 9 were from emerging markets. Now, S&P rates approximately 90 countries. The history of default is even more sparse, and it is difficult to generalize from a very small sample.

Assessing credit risk for sovereign nations is significantly more difficult than for corporates. When a corporate borrower defaults, legal action can be taken by the creditors. For instance, an unsecured creditor can file an action against a debtor and have the defendant's assets seized under a "writ of attachment." This creates a **lien** on these assets, or a claim on the assets as security for the payment of the debt. In contrast, it is impossible to attach the domestic assets of a sovereign nation. This implies that recovery rates on sovereign debt are usually lower rates than rates on corporate debt. Thus, sovereign credit evaluation involves not only **economic risk** (the ability to repay debts when due), but also **political risk** (the willingness to pay).

Sovereign credit ratings also differ depending on whether the debt is **local currency debt** or **foreign currency debt**. Table 19-10 displays the factors involved in local and foreign currency ratings.

TABLE 19-10 Credit Ratings Factors

Category	Local Currency	Foreign Currency
Political risk	X	X
Price stability	X	X
Income and economic structure	X	X
Economic growth prospects	X	X
Fiscal flexibility	X	X
Public debt burden	X	X
Balance of payment flexibility		X
External debt and liquidity		X

Political risk factors (e.g., degree of political consensus, integration in global trade and financial system, and internal or external security risk) play an important part in sovereign credit risk. Factors affecting *local currency debt* include economic, fiscal, and especially monetary risks. High rates of inflation typically reflect economic mismanagement and are associated with political instability. Countries rated AAA, for instance, have inflation rates from 0 to at most 10%; BB-rated countries have inflation rates ranging from 25% to 100%.

Important factors affecting *foreign currency debt* include the international investment position of a country (that is, public and private external debt), the stock of foreign currency reserves, and patterns in the balance of payment. In particular, the ratio of external interest payments to exports is closely watched.

In the case of the Asian crisis, rating agencies seem to have overlooked other important aspects of creditworthiness, such as the currency and maturity structure of national debt. Too many Asian creditors had borrowed short-term in dollars to invest in the local currency, which created a severe liquidity problem. Admittedly, the credit valuation process can be hindered by the reluctance of foreign nations to provide timely information. In the case of Argentina, most observers had anticipated a default. This was due to a combination of high external debt, slow economic growth, and unwillingness to make the necessary spending adjustments. Ultimately, the default was a political decision.

Because local currency debt is backed by the taxation power of the government, local-currency debt is considered to have less credit risk than foreign-currency debt. Table 19-11 displays local- and foreign-currency debt ratings for a sample of countries. Ratings for foreign-currency debt are the same, or one notch below, those for local-currency debt. Similarly, sovereign debt is typically rated higher than corporate debt in the same country. Governments can repay foreign-currency debt, for instance, by controlling capital flows or seizing foreign-currency reserves.

Overall, sovereign debt ratings are considered less reliable than corporate ratings. Indeed, bond spreads are greater for sovereigns than for corporate issuers. In 1999, for example, the average spread on dollar-denominated sovereign bonds rated BB was about 160 bp higher than for identically rated corporates. There are also greater differences in sovereign ratings across agencies than for corporates. The evaluation of sovereign credit risk seems to be a much more subjective process compared with corporate credit risk.

Example 19-18: FRM Exam 1999—Question 121

In assessing the sovereign credit, a number of criteria are considered. Which of the following is the more critical one?

a) Fiscal position of the government

b) Prospect for domestic output and demand

c) International asset position

d) Structure of the government's debt and debt service (external and internal)

Example 19-19: FRM Exam 2001—Question 2

(Requires knowledge of markets) Which of the following is the best-rated country according to the most important ratings agencies?

a) Argentina

b) Brazil

c) Mexico

d) Peru

Example 19-20: FRM Exam 1998—Question 36

What is the most significant difference to consider when assessing the creditworthiness of a country rather than a company?

a) The country's willingness and its ability to pay must be analyzed.

b) Financial data on a country are often available only with long lags.

c) It is more costly to do due diligence on a country than on a company.

d) A country is often unwilling to disclose sensitive financial information.

TABLE 19-11 S&P's Sovereign Credit Ratings, February 2005

Issuer	Local Currency	Foreign Currency
Argentina	SD	SD
Australia	AAA	AAA
Belgium	AA+	AA+
Brazil	BB	BB−
Canada	AAA	AAA
China	BBB+	BBB+
France	AAA	AAA
Germany	AAA	AAA
Hong Kong	AA−	A+
India	BB+	BB+
Italy	AA−	AA−
Japan	AA−	AA−
Korea	A+	A−
Mexico	A	BBB
Netherlands	AAA	AAA
Russia	BBB	BBB−
South Africa	A	BBB
Spain	AA+	AA+
Switzerland	AAA	AAA
Taiwan	AA−	AA−
Thailand	A	BBB
Turkey	BB	BB−
United Kingdom	AAA	AAA
United States	AAA	AAA

Note : Argentina is rated selective default (SD).

19.6   Answers to Chapter Examples

Example 19-1: FRM Exam 1998—Question 5

b) Calling back a bond occurs when the borrower wants to refinance its debt at a lower cost, which is not a credit event.

Example 19-2: FRM Exam 1999—Question 128

d) Losses I and II are due to market risk. Loss III is a credit event, due to restructuring. Loss IV is a tax event deriving from governmental action. So III and IV qualify as event risks.

Example 19-3: FRM Exam 2002—Question 110

d) The BB rating by S&P is similar to a Ba rating by Moody's. A BB bond will have lower default rate than a bond rated lower. Hence, the answer is the next lowest rating category by Moody's.

Example 19-4: FRM Exam 2002—Question 86

d) The least credit risk would be associated with the highest EBIT/TA and RE/TA ratios. Answer d) dominates all others for these two ratios.

Example 19-5: FRM Exam 1997—Question 28

c) This default rate is 1.47% from Table 19-4. Similarly, the Moody's default rate for Ba credits is 1.42%.

Example 19-6: FRM Exam 1998—Question 29

a) From Table 19-4, the ratio of B to BBB defaults for a 1-year horizon is 6.72/0.36 = 19, which is slightly higher than the ratio of 16 in the first part of the question. The numbers are different because of variances in sample periods. The ratio at 10-year horizon is 44.59/7.60 = 6, which is close to 5. Intuitively, the default rate on B credits should increase at a lower rate than that on BBB credits. The cumulative default rate on B credits starts with a high value but cannot go above 1.

Example 19-7: FRM Exam 2002—Question 77

d) The marginal default rate increases with maturity. So this could be, for example, 0.50% over the last three years of the six-year period. This gives a cumulative default probability greater than 0.60%.

Example 19-8: FRM Exam 2000—Question 37

c) The probability of surviving is $(1 - d)^3 = 0.343$; hence the probability of default at any point during the next three years is 66%.

Example 19-9: FRM Exam 2000—Question 31

d) The cumulative six-year default rate is given by $C_6(R) = C_5(R) + k_6 = C_5(R) + S_5 \times d_6 = 0.15 + (1 - 0.15) \times 0.10 = 0.235$.

Example 19-10: FRM Exam 2000—Question 43

b) This is 1 minus the survival rate over three years: $S_3(R) = (1-d_1)(1-d_2)(1-d_3) = (1-0.03)(1-0.04)(1-0.05) = 0.8856$. Hence, the cumulative default rate is 0.1154.

Example 19-11: FRM Exam 2000—Question 34

a) The marginal default rate is the probability of defaulting over the next year, conditional on having survived to the beginning of the year.

Example 19-12: FRM Exam 2000—Question 50

d) The transition matrix represents the conditional probability of moving from one rating to another over a fixed period, typically a year.

Example 19-13: FRM Exam 2000—Question 58

a) The recovery rate on loans is typically higher than that on bonds. Hence the credit rating, if it involves both probabilities of default and recovery, should be higher for loans than for bonds.

Example 19-14: FRM Exam 2002—Question 123

c) The recovery rate is higher when the assets of the firm in default consist of tangible assets that can be resold easily. More volatile assets mean that there is a greater probability of a fall in market value upon liquidation. So the tangible assets of a manufacturing company is the best answer.

Example 19-15: FRM Exam 2001—Question 15 b) The market values and weighted probability of default should be equal for the collateral and various tranches. So a) is wrong. The equity tranche has the highest risk of default, so c) is wrong. The yield on the low-risk tranche must be the lowest, so d) is wrong.

Example 19-16: FRM Exam 1998—Question 8

c) The rating of the collateral must be between that of the offered securities and the residual. Say the collateral is rated B, with 5% probability of default (PD); the offered securities represent 80% of the total market value. These are more highly rated than the collateral because the equity absorbs the default risk. If the offered securities are rated BB (with 1% PD), the equity must be such that $80\% \times 0.01 + 20\% \times x = 0.05$, which yields a PD of 21% for the equity, close to a CCC rating.

Example 19-17: FRM Exam 2002—Question 32

a) In the absence of transaction costs or fees, the yield on the underlying portfolio should be equal to the weighted average of the yields on the different tranches. With costs, however, the CBO yield will be slightly less. Otherwise, the senior tranche is typically rated AAA, has the lowest loss rate of all tranches, and absorbs the last loss on the structure.

Example 19-18: FRM Exam 1999—Question 121

d) Empirically, the ratio of debt to exports seems to be the most important factor driving sovereign ratings (see the *Handbook of Emerging Markets*, pp. 10–11).

Example 19-19: FRM Exam 2001—Question 2

c) Mexico is the most highly rated country of this group, according to the table of S&P ratings. Argentina has been in selective default (SD) since 2001. As of early 2005 Mexico is rated BBB and Brazil is rated BB−. Peru is not in the table but is rated BB.

Example 19-20: FRM Exam 1998—Question 36

a) Countries cannot be forced into bankruptcy. There is no enforcement mechanism for payment to creditors as for private companies. Recent history has shown that a country can simply decide to renege on its debt. So willingness to pay is a major factor.

Chapter 20

Measuring Default Risk
from Market Prices

The previous chapter discussed how to quantify credit risk from categorization into credit risk ratings. Based on these external ratings, we can forecast credit losses from historical default rates and recovery rates.

Credit risk can also be assessed from market prices of securities whose values are affected by default. These include corporate bonds, equities, and credit derivatives. In principle, these should provide more up-to-date and accurate measures of credit risk because financial markets have access to a very large amount of information. Agents also have very strong financial incentives to impound this information in trading prices. This chapter shows how to infer default risk from market prices.

Section 20.1 will show how to use information about the market prices of credit-sensitive bonds to infer default risk. In this chapter, we will call defaultable debt interchangeably credit-sensitive, corporate, and risky debt. Here *risky* refers to credit risk and not market risk. We show how to break down the yield on a corporate bond into a default probability, a recovery rate, and a risk-free yield.

Section 20.2 turns to equity prices. The advantage of using equity prices is that they are much more widely available and of much better quality than corporate bond prices. We show how equity can be viewed as a call option on the value of the firm and how a default probability can be inferred from the value of this option. This approach also explains why credit positions are akin to short positions in options and are characterized by distributions that are skewed to the left. Chapter 22 will discuss credit derivatives, which can also be used to infer default risk.

20.1   Corporate Bond Prices

To assess the credit risk of a transaction with a counterparty, consider **credit-sensitive** bonds issued by the same counterparty. We assume that default is a state that affects all obligations equally.

20.1.1   Spreads and Default Risk

Assume for simplicity that the bond makes only one payment of $100 in one period. We can compute a market-determined yield y^* from the price P^* as

$$P^* = \frac{\$100}{(1 + y^*)} \qquad (20.1)$$

This can be compared with the risk-free yield over the same period y.

The payoffs on the bond can be described by a simplified default process, which is illustrated in Figure 20-1. At maturity, the bond can be in default or not. Its value is $100 if there is no default and $f \times \$100$ if default occurs, where f is the fractional recovery. We define π as the default rate over the period. How can we value this bond?

FIGURE 20-1 A Simplified Bond Default Process

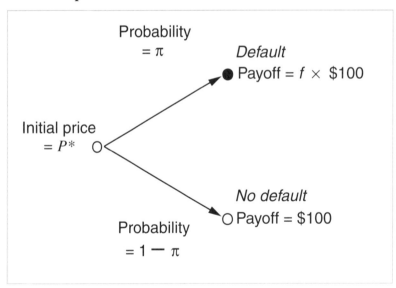

Using **risk-neutral pricing**, the current price must be the mathematical expectation of the values in the two states, discounting the payoffs at the risk-free rate. Hence,

$$P^* = \frac{\$100}{(1 + y^*)} = \left[\frac{\$100}{(1 + y)}\right] \times (1 - \pi) + \left[\frac{f \times \$100}{(1 + y)}\right] \times \pi \qquad (20.2)$$

Note that the discounting uses the risk-free rate y because there is no risk premium with risk-neutral valuation. After rearranging terms,

$$(1 + y) = (1 + y^*)[1 - \pi(1 - f)] \tag{20.3}$$

which implies a default probability of

$$\pi = \frac{1}{(1 - f)}\left[1 - \frac{(1 + y)}{(1 + y^*)}\right] \tag{20.4}$$

Dropping second-order terms, this simplifies to

$$y^* \approx y + \pi(1 - f) \tag{20.5}$$

This equation shows that the credit spread $y^* - y$ measures credit risk—more specifically, the probability of default, π, times the loss given default, $(1 - f)$. This makes sense because there is no credit risk either if the default probability is zero or if the loss given default is zero.

Let us now consider multiple periods, which number T. We compound interest rates and default rates over each period. In other words, π is now the *average* annual default rate. Assuming one payment only, the present value is

$$P^* = \frac{\$100}{(1 + y^*)^T} = \left[\frac{\$100}{(1 + y)^T}\right] \times (1 - \pi)^T + \left[\frac{f \times \$100}{(1 + y)^T}\right] \times [1 - (1 - \pi)^T] \tag{20.6}$$

which can be written as

$$(1 + y)^T = (1 + y^*)^T \{(1 - \pi)^T + f[1 - (1 - \pi)^T]\} \tag{20.7}$$

Unfortunately, this does not simplify further.

When we have risky bonds of various maturities, they can be used to compute default probabilities for different horizons. If we have two periods, for example, we could use Equation (20.3) to find the probability of defaulting over the first period, π_1, and Equation (20.7) to find the annualized, or average, probability of defaulting over the first two periods, π_2. As we saw in the previous chapter, the marginal probability of defaulting in the second period, d_2, is given by solving

$$(1 - \pi_2)^2 = (1 - \pi_1)(1 - d_2) \tag{20.8}$$

This enables us to recover a term structure of forward default probabilities from a sequence of zero-coupon bonds. In practice, if we have access to only coupon-paying bonds, the computation becomes more complicated because we need to consider the payments in each period with and without default.

20.1.2   Risk Premium

It is worth emphasizing that the preceding approach assumed risk-neutrality. As in the methodology for pricing options, we assumed that the value of any asset grows at the risk-free rate and can be discounted at the same risk-free rate. Thus the probability measure π is a risk-neutral measure, which is not necessarily equal to the objective, physical probability of default.

Defining this objective probability as π' and the discount rate as y', the current price can be also expressed in terms of the true expected value discounted at the risky rate y':

$$P^* = \frac{\$100}{(1+y^*)} = \left[\frac{\$100}{(1+y')}\right] \times (1 - \pi') + \left[\frac{f \times \$100}{(1+y')}\right] \times \pi' \qquad (20.9)$$

Equation (20.4) allows us to recover a risk-neutral default probability only. More generally, if investors require some compensation for bearing credit risk, the credit spread will include a risk premium, rp:

$$y^* \approx y + \pi'(1 - f) + \text{rp} \qquad (20.10)$$

To be meaningful, this risk premium must be tied to some measure of bond riskiness as well as investor risk aversion. In addition, this premium may incorporate a **liquidity premium** and tax effects.[1]

Key concept:
The yield spread between a corporate bond and an otherwise identical bond with no credit risk reflects the expected actuarial loss, or annual default rate times the loss given default, plus a risk premium.

Example: Deriving default probabilities

   We wish to compare a 10-year U.S. Treasury strip and a 10-year zero issued by International Business Machines (IBM), which is rated A by S&P and Moody's. The respective yields are 6% and 7%, using semiannual compounding. Assuming that the

---

[1]For a decomposition of the yield spread into risk premium effects, see Elton, E., M. Gruber, D. Agrawal, & C. Mann (2001), Explaining the Rate Spread on Corporate Bonds, *Journal of Finance* 56, 247–277. The authors find a high risk premium, which they relate to common risk factors from the stock market. Part of the risk premium is also due to tax effects. Because Treasury coupon payments are not taxable at the state level (for example, New York state), investors are willing to accept a lower yield on Treasury bonds, which artificially increases the corporate yield spread.

recovery rate is 45% of the face value, what does the credit spread imply for the probability of default?

Equation (20.3) shows that $\pi(1-f) = 1-(1+y/200)^{20}/(1+y^*/200)^{20} = 0.0923$. Hence, $\pi = 9.23\%/(1-45\%) = 16.8\%$. Therefore, the cumulative (risk-neutral) probability of defaulting during the next 10 years is 16.8%. This number is rather high compared with the historical record for this risk class. Table 19-3 shows that Moody's reports a historical 10-year default rate for A credits of 3.4% only.

If these historical default rates are used as the future probability of default, the implication is that a large part of the credit spread reflects a risk premium. For instance, assume that 80 basis points out of the 100-basis-point credit spread reflects a risk premium. We change the 7% yield to 6.2% and find a probability of default of 3.5%. This is more in line with the actual default experience of such issuers.

Example 20-1: FRM Exam 2002—Question 95

A one-year government bond yields 10% per annum while a one-year corporate bond yields 12%. Assuming a recovery rate of 50%, what is the best estimate of the implied default probability of the corporate bond?

a) 4%

b) 2%

c) 1%

d) 0.5%

Example 20-2: FRM Exam 2002—Question 96

A loan of $10 million is made to a counterparty whose expected default rate is 2% per annum and whose expected recovery rate is 40%. Assuming an all-in cost of funds of LIBOR for the lender, what would be the fair price for the loan?

a) LIBOR + 120 bp

b) LIBOR + 240 bp

c) LIBOR − 120 bp

d) LIBOR + 160 bp

20.1.3 The Cross-Section of Yield Spreads

We now turn to actual market data. Figure 20-2 illustrates a set of par yield curves for various credits as of December 1998. For reference, the spreads are listed in Table 20-1. The curves are sorted by credit rating, from AAA to B, using S&P's ratings.

These curves bear a striking resemblance to the cumulative default rate curves reported in the previous chapter. They increase with maturity and with lower credit quality.

FIGURE 20-2 Yield Curves for Different Credits

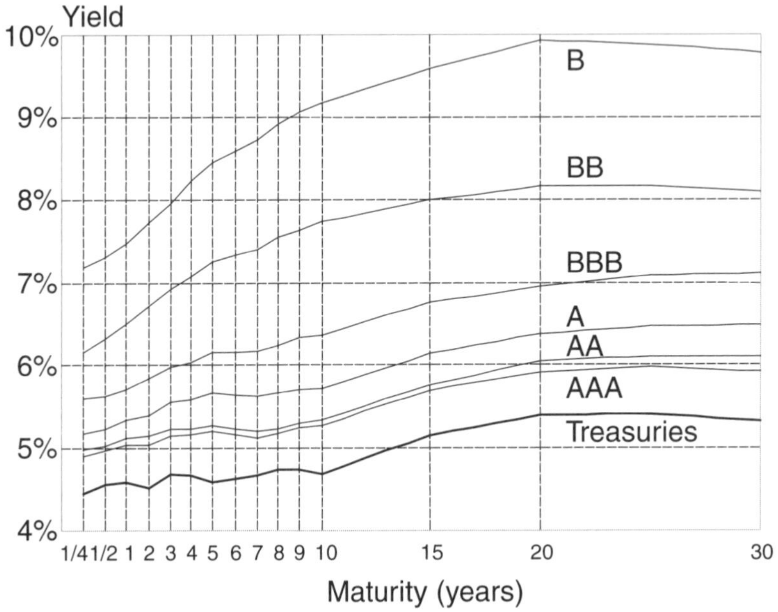

The lowest curve is the Treasury curve, which represents risk-free bonds. Spreads for AAA credits are low, starting at 46 bp at short maturities and increasing to 60 bp at longer maturities. Spreads for B credits are much wider; they also increase faster, from 275 to 450. Finally, note how close together the AAA and AA spreads are, in spite of the fact that default probabilities approximately double from AAA to AA. The transition from Treasuries to AAA credits most likely reflects other factors, such as liquidity and tax effects, rather than actuarial credit risk.

The previous sections showed that we could use information in corporate bond yields to make inferences about credit risk. Indeed, bond prices represent the best assessment of traders, or real "bets," on credit risk. Thus we would expect bond prices to be the best predictors of credit risk and to outperform credit ratings. To the extent that agencies use public information to form their credit ratings, this information should be subsumed into market prices. Bond prices are also revised more frequently than credit ratings. As a result, movements in corporate bond prices tend to *lead* changes in credit ratings.

TABLE 20-1 Credit Spreads

Maturity (Years)	AAA	AA	A	BBB	BB	B
3M	46	54	74	116	172	275
6M	40	46	67	106	177	275
1	45	53	74	112	191	289
2	51	62	88	133	220	321
3	47	55	87	130	225	328
4	50	57	92	138	241	358
5	61	68	108	157	266	387
6	53	61	102	154	270	397
7	45	53	95	150	274	407
8	45	50	94	152	282	420
9	51	56	98	161	291	435
10	59	66	104	169	306	450
15	55	61	99	161	285	445
20	52	66	99	156	278	455
30	60	78	117	179	278	447

Example 20-3: FRM Exam 2002—Question 81

Which of the following is true?

a) Changes in bond spreads tend to lead changes in credit ratings.

b) Changes in bond spreads tend to lag changes in credit ratings.

c) Changes in bond spreads tend to occur at the exact same time as changes in credit ratings.

d) There is absolutely no perceived general relationship in the timing of changes in bond spreads and changes in credit ratings.

Example 20-4: FRM Exam 1998—Question 11

What can be said about the spread between AAA and A credits (S1) and the spread between BBB and B credits (S2) in general?

a) S1 is equal to S2.

b) S1 $\geq$ S2.

c) S1 $\leq$ S2.

d) S1 may be less or more than S2.

Example 20-5: FRM Exam 1999—Question 136

Suppose XYZ Corp. has two bonds paying semiannually according to the following table:

Remaining Maturity	Coupon (sa 30/360)	Price	T-Bill Rate (Bank Discount)
6 months	8.0%	99	5.5%
1 year	9.0%	100	6.0%

The recovery rate for each in the event of default is 50%. For simplicity, assume that each bond will default only at the end of a coupon period. The market-implied risk-neutral probability of default for XYZ Corp. is

a) Greater in the first six-month period than in the second
b) Equal between the two coupon periods
c) Greater in the second six-month period than in the first
d) Cannot be determined from the information provided

20.1.4   Time Variation in Credit Spreads

Credit spreads reflect potential losses caused by default risk, and perhaps a risk premium. Some of this default risk is specific to the issuer and requires a detailed analysis of its prospective financial condition. Part of this risk, however, can be attributed to common credit risk factors. These common factors are particularly important, as they cannot be diversified away in a large portfolio of credit-sensitive bonds.

First among these factors are general economic conditions. Economic growth is negatively correlated with credit spreads. When the economy slows down, more companies are likely to have cash-flow problems and to default on their bonds. Indeed, Figure 11-6 shows that spreads widen during recessions.

Volatility is also a factor. In a more volatile environment, investors may require larger risk premiums, thus increasing credit spreads. When this happens, liquidity may also dry up. Investors may then require a greater credit spread in order to hold increasingly illiquid securities.

In addition, volatility can have an effect. Corporate bond indices include many callable bonds, unlike Treasury indices. As a result, credit spreads also reflect this option component. The buyer of a callable bond requires a higher yield in exchange for granting the call option. Because the value of this option increases with volatility, greater volatility should also increase the credit spread.

20.2 Equity Prices

The credit spread approach, unfortunately, is only useful when there is good bond market data. The problem is that this is rarely the case, for a number of reasons.

- Many countries do not have a well-developed corporate bond market. As Table 7-1 has shown, the United States has by far the largest corporate bond market. This means that other countries have much fewer outstanding bonds and a much less active market.
- The counterparty may not have an outstanding publicly traded bond or if so, the bond may contain other features such as a call.
- The bond may not trade actively and instead reported prices may simply be **matrix prices**, that is, interpolated from other, current yields.

An alternative is to turn to default risk models based on stock prices, because equity prices are available for a larger number of companies and because equities are more actively traded than corporate bonds. The Merton (1974) model views equity as akin to a call option on the assets of the firm, with an exercise price given by the face value of debt.

20.2.1 The Merton Model

To simplify to the extreme, consider a firm with total value V that has one bond due in one period with face value K. If the value of the firm exceeds the promised payment, the bond is repaid in full and stockholders receive the remainder. However, if V is less than K, the firm is in default and the bondholders receive V only. The value of equity goes to zero. We assume that there are no transaction costs and that the absolute-priority rule is followed. Hence, the value of the stock at expiration is

$$S_T = \text{Max}(V_T - K, 0) \tag{20.11}$$

Because the bond and equity add up to the firm value, the value of the bond must be

$$B_T = V_T - S_T = V_T - \text{Max}(V_T - K, 0) = \text{Min}(V_T, K) \tag{20.12}$$

The current stock price, therefore, embodies a forecast of default probability in the same way that an option embodies a forecast of being exercised. Figures 20-3 and 20-4 describe how the value of the firm can be split up into the bond and stock values.

FIGURE 20-3 Equity as an Option on the Value of the Firm

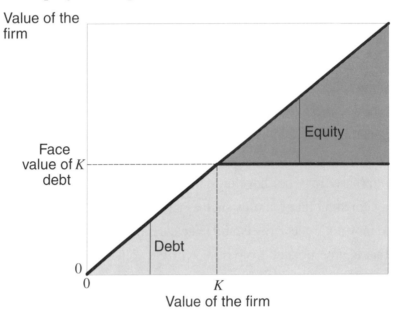

FIGURE 20-4 Components of the Value of the Firm

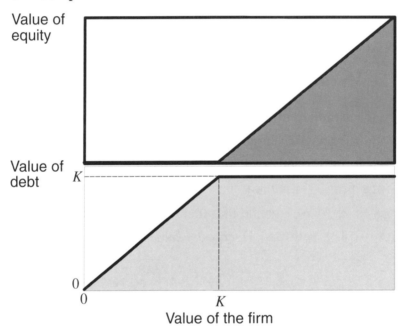

Note that the bond value can also be described as

$$B_T = K - \text{Max}(K - V_T, 0) \tag{20.13}$$

In other words, a long position in a risky bond is equivalent to a long position in a risk-free bond plus a short put option, which is really a credit derivative.

> **Key concept:**
> Equity can be viewed as a call option on the firm value with strike price equal to the face value of debt. Corporate debt can be viewed as risk-free debt minus a put option on the firm value.

This approach is particularly illuminating because it demonstrates that corporate debt has a payoff akin to a short position in an option, explaining the left skewness that is characteristic of credit losses. In contrast, equity is equivalent to a long position in an option due to its **limited-liability feature**; that is, investors can lose no more than their equity investment.

20.2.2 Pricing Equity and Debt

To illustrate, we proceed along the lines of the usual Black-Scholes (BS) framework, assuming that the firm value follows the geometric Brownian motion process:

$$dV = \mu V \, dt + \sigma V \, dz \tag{20.14}$$

If we assume that markets are frictionless and that there are no bankruptcy costs, the value of the firm is simply the sum of the firm's equity and debt: $V = B + S$.

To price a claim on the value of the firm, we need to solve a partial differential equation with appropriate boundary conditions. The corporate bond price is obtained as

$$B = F(V, t), \quad F(V, T) = \text{Min}[V, B_F] \tag{20.15}$$

where $B_F = K$ is the face value of the bond to be repaid at expiration, or the strike price.

Similarly, the equity value is

$$S = f(V, t), \qquad f(V, T) = \text{Max}[V - B_F, 0] \tag{20.16}$$

Stock Valuation

With no dividend, the value of the stock is given by the BS formula,

$$S = \text{Call} = V N(d_1) - K e^{-r\tau} N(d_2) \tag{20.17}$$

where $N(d)$ is the cumulative distribution function for the standard normal distribution, and

$$d_1 = \frac{\ln(V/Ke^{-r\tau})}{\sigma\sqrt{\tau}} + \frac{\sigma\sqrt{\tau}}{2}, \qquad d_2 = d_1 - \sigma\sqrt{\tau}$$

where $\tau = T - t$ is the time to expiration, r the risk-free interest rate, and σ the volatility of *asset* value. If we define $x = Ke^{-r\tau}/V$ as the debt/value ratio, the option value depends solely on x and $\sigma\sqrt{\tau}$.

Note that, in practice, this application is different from the BS model, where we plug in the value of V and of its volatility, $\sigma = \sigma_V$, and solve for the value of the call. Here we observe the market value of the firm S and the equity volatility σ_S and must infer the values of V and its volatility so that Equation (20.17) is satisfied. This can only be done iteratively. Defining Δ as the hedge ratio, we have

$$dS = \frac{\partial S}{\partial V}dV = \Delta dV \qquad (20.18)$$

Defining σ_S as the volatility of (dS/S), we have $(\sigma_S S) = \Delta(\sigma_V V)$ and

$$\sigma_V = \Delta \sigma_S (S/V) \qquad (20.19)$$

Bond Valuation

Next, the value of the bond is given by $B = V - S$, or

$$B = Ke^{-r\tau}N(d_2) + V[1 - N(d_1)] \qquad (20.20)$$

$$B/Ke^{-r\tau} = [N(d_2) + (V/Ke^{-r\tau})N(-d_1)] \qquad (20.21)$$

Risk-Neutral Dynamics of Default

In the Black-Scholes model, $N(d_2)$ is also the probability of exercising the call, or that the bond will not default. Conversely, $1 - N(d_2) = N(-d_2)$ is the risk-neutral probability of default.

Pricing Credit Risk

At maturity, the credit loss is the value of the risk-free bond minus the corporate bond, $CL = B_F - B_T$. At initiation, the expected credit loss (ECL) is

$$
\begin{aligned}
B_F e^{-r\tau} - B &= Ke^{-r\tau} - \{Ke^{-r\tau}N(d_2) + V[1 - N(d_1)]\} \\
&= Ke^{-r\tau}[1 - N(d_2)] - V[1 - N(d_1)] \\
&= Ke^{-r\tau}N(-d_2) - VN(-d_1) \\
&= N(-d_2)[Ke^{-r\tau} - VN(-d_1)/N(-d_2)]
\end{aligned}
$$

This decomposition is quite informative. Multiplying by the future value factor $e^{r\tau}$ shows that the ECL at maturity is

$$\text{ECL}_T = N(-d_2)[K - Ve^{r\tau}N(-d_1)/N(-d_2)] = p \times [\text{Exposure} \times \text{LGD}] \quad (20.22)$$

This involves two terms. The first is the probability of default, $N(-d_2)$. The second is the loss when there is default. This is obtained as the face value of the bond K minus the recovery value of the loan when in default, $Ve^{r\tau}N(-d_1)/N(-d_2)$, which is also the expected value of the firm in the state of default. Note that the recovery rate is endogenous here, as it depends on the value of the firm, time, and debt ratio.

Credit Option Valuation

This approach can also be used to value the put option component of the credit-sensitive bond. This option pays $K - B_T$ in case of default. A portfolio with the bond plus the put is equivalent to a risk-free bond $Ke^{-r\tau} = B + \text{Put}$. Hence, using Equation (20.20), the credit put should be worth

$$\text{Put} = Ke^{-r\tau} - \{Ke^{-r\tau}N(d_2) + V[1 - N(d_1)]\} = -V[N(-d_1)] + Ke^{-r\tau}[N(-d_2)]$$
$$(20.23)$$

This will be used later in the chapter on credit derivatives.

Example 20-6: FRM Exam 2001—Question 14

To what sort of option on the counterparty's assets can the current exposure of a credit-risky position better be compared?
a) A short call
b) A short put
c) A short knock-in call
d) A binary option

20.2.3   Applying the Merton Model

These valuation formulas can be used to recover, given the current value of equity and of nominal liabilities, the value of the firm and its probability of default. Figure 20-5 illustrates the evolution of the value of the firm. The firm defaults if this value falls below the liabilities at the horizon. We measure this risk-neutral probability by $N(-d_2)$.

FIGURE 20-5 Default in the Merton Model

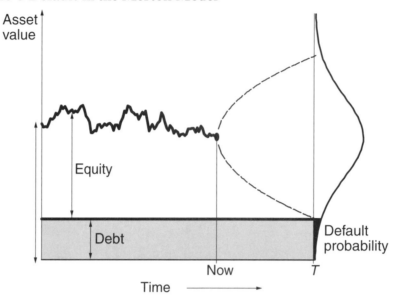

In practice, default is much more complex than depicted here. We would have to collect information about all the liabilities of the company, as well as their maturities. Default can also occur with coupon payments. So instead of default on a target date, we could measure default probability as a function of the distance relative to a moving floor that represents liabilities. This is essentially the approach undertaken by **KMV Corporation**, now part of Moody's, which sells **estimated default frequencies** (EDFs) for firms all over the world.

The Merton approach has many advantages. First, it relies on the prices of equities, which are more actively traded than bonds. Second, correlations between equity prices can generate correlations between defaults, which would be otherwise difficult to measure. Perhaps the most important advantage of this model is that it generates movements in EDFs that seem to *lead* changes in credit ratings.

Figure 20-6 displays movements in EDFs and credit rating for WorldCom, using the same vertical scale. WorldCom went bankrupt on July 21, 2002. With $104 billion in assets, this was America's largest bankruptcy ever. The agency rating was BBB until April 2002. It gave no warning of the impending default. In contrast, starting one year before the default, the EDF began to move up. In April, it reached 20%, presaging bankruptcy.

FIGURE 20-6 KMV's EDF and Credit Rating

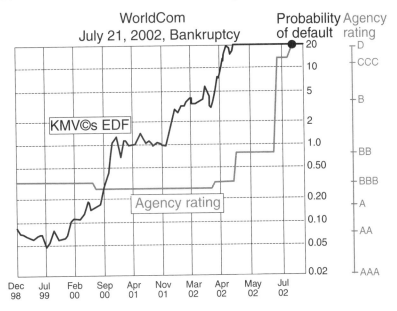

These models have disadvantages as well. The first limitation of the model is that it cannot be used to price sovereign credit risk, as countries obviously do not have a stock price. This is a problem for credit derivatives, where a large share of the market consists of sovereign risks.

A more fundamental drawback is that it relies on a static model of the firm's capital and risk structure. The debt level is assumed to be constant over the horizon. Also, the model needs to be expanded to a more realistic setting where debt matures at various points in time, which is not an obvious extension.

Another problem is that management could undertake new projects that increase not only the value of equity but also its volatility, thereby increasing the credit spread. This runs counter to the fundamental intuition of the Merton model, which is that, all else equal, a higher stock price reflects a lower probability of default and hence should be associated with a smaller credit spread.

Finally, this class of models fails to explain the magnitude of credit spreads we observe on credit-sensitive bonds. Recent work has attempted to add other sources of risk, such as interest rate risk, but still falls short of explaining these spreads. Thus these models are most useful in tracking *changes* in EDFs over time. Indeed, KMV calibrates the risk-neutral default probabilities to actual default data.

20.2.4   Example

It is instructive to work through a simplified example. Consider a firm with assets worth $V = \$100$ and with volatility $\sigma_V = 20\%$. In practice, one would have to start from the observed stock price and volatility and iterate to find σ_V.

The horizon is $\tau = 1$ year. The risk-free rate is $r = 10\%$ using continuous compounding. We assume a leverage $x = 0.9$, which implies a face value of $K = \$99.46$ and a risk-free current value of $Ke^{-r\tau} = \$90$.

Working through the Merton analysis, one finds that the current stock price should be $S = \$13.59$. Hence the current bond price is

$$B = V - S = \$100 - \$13.59 = \$86.41$$

which implies a yield of $\ln(K/B)/\tau = \ln(99.46/86.41) = 14.07\%$, or a yield spread of 4.07%. The current value of the credit put is then

$$P = Ke^{-r\tau} - B = \$90 - \$86.41 = \$3.59$$

The analysis also generates values for $N(d_2) = 0.6653$ and $N(d_1) = 0.7347$. Thus the *risk-neutral* probability of default is $\text{EDF} = N(-d_2) = 1 - N(d_2) = 33.47\%$. Note that this could differ from the *actual* or *objective* probability of default since the stock could very well grow at a rate that is greater than the risk-free rate of 10%.

Finally, let us decompose the expected loss at expiration from Equation (20.22), which gives

$$N(-d_2)[K - Ve^{r\tau}N(-d_1)/N(-d_2)] = 0.3347 \times [\$99.46 - \$110.56 \times 0.2653/0.3347]$$

$$= 0.3347 \times [\$11.85] = \$3.96$$

This combines the probability of default with the expected loss upon default, which is $\$11.85$. This future expected credit loss of $\$3.96$ must also be the future value of the credit put, or $\$3.59e^{r\tau} = \$3.96$.

Note that the model needs very high leverage, here $x = 90\%$, to generate a reasonable credit spread of 4.07%. This implies a debt-to-equity ratio of $0.9/0.1 = 900\%$, which is unrealistically high for this type of spread.

With lower leverage, say $x = 0.7$, the credit spread shrinks rapidly, to 0.36%. At $x = 50\%$ or below, the predicted spread goes to zero. As this leverage would be considered normal, the model fails to reproduce the size of observed credit spreads. Perhaps it is most useful for tracking time variation in estimated default frequencies.

Example 20-7: FRM Exam 2002—Question 97

Among the following variables, which one is the main driver of the probability of default in the KMV model?

a) Stock prices

b) Bond prices

c) Bond yield

d) Loan prices

Example 20-8: FRM Exam 1998—Question 22

Which of the following is used to estimate the probability of default in the KMV model?

a) Vector analysis

b) Total return analysis

c) Equity price volatility

d) None of the above

Example 20-9: FRM Exam 1999—Question 155

Having equity in a firm's capital structure adds to the creditworthiness of the firm. Which of the following statements support(s) this argument?

  I. Equity does not require payments that could lead to default.

 II. Equity capital does not mature, so it represents a permanent capital base.

III. Equity provides a cushion for debtholders in case of bankruptcy.

IV. The cost of equity is lower than the cost of debt.

a) I, II, and III

b) All of the above

c) I, II, and IV

d) III only

20.3   Answers to Chapter Examples

Example 20-1: FRM Exam 2002—Question 95

a) Using Equation (20.3), the risk-neutral default probability π is given by $y^* = y + \pi(1 - f)$, where y^* is the corporate yield, y is the Treasury yield, and f is the recovery rate. Thus, $\pi = (y^* - y)/(1 - f) = (12\% - 10\%)/(1 - 50\%) = 4\%$.

Example 20-2: FRM Exam 2002—Question 96

a) The credit spread should be $y^* - y = \pi(1 - f)$. Thus, $\pi(1 - f) = 2\%(1 - 40\%) = 1.2\%$. The spread over LIBOR should be 120 bp.

Example 20-3: FRM Exam 2002—Question 81

a) Changes in market prices, including bond spreads, tend to lead changes in credit ratings. This is because market prices reflect all publicly available information about a company.

Example 20-4: FRM Exam 1998—Question 11

c) Credit spreads widen considerably for lower-rated credits.

Example 20-5: FRM Exam 1999—Question 136

a) First, we compute the current yield on the six-month bond, which is selling at a discount. We solve for y^* such that $99 = 104/(1 + y^*/200)$ and find $y^* = 10.10\%$. Thus the yield spread for the first bond is $10.1 - 5.5 = 4.6\%$. The second bond is at par, so the yield is $y^* = 9\%$. The spread for the second bond is $9 - 6 = 3\%$. The default rate for the first period must be greater. The recovery rate is the same for the two periods, so it does not matter for this problem.

Example 20-6: FRM Exam 2001—Question 14

b) The lender is short a put option, since exposure exists only if the value of assets falls below the amount lent.

Example 20-7: FRM Exam 2002—Question 97

a) Stock prices are the main driver of KMV's estimated default frequency (EDF), because they drive the value of equity. These models also use the volatility of asset values and the value of liabilities.

Example 20-8: FRM Exam 1998—Question 22

c) The KMV model is based on the value of the equity and liabilities, the risk-free rate, and equity price volatility.

Example 20-9: FRM Exam 1999—Question 155

a) The cost of equity is generally higher than that of debt because it is riskier. Otherwise, all of the other arguments a), b), c) are true. Equity will not cause default. It does not mature and provides a cushion for debtholders, as stockholders should lose money before debtholders.

Chapter 21

Credit Exposure

Credit exposure is the amount at risk when default occurs. It is also called **exposure at default** (EAD). When banking simply consisted of making loans, exposure was essentially the face value of the loan. This is also a constant notional amount.

Since the development of the swap markets, the measurement of credit exposure has become much more sophisticated. This is because swaps, like most derivatives, have an up-front value that is much smaller than the notional amount. Indeed, the initial value of a swap is typically zero, which means that at the outset, there is no credit risk because there is nothing to lose.

As the swap contract matures, however, it can turn into a positive or negative value. The asymmetry of bankruptcy treatment is such that a credit loss can only occur if the instrument has positive value, or is a net liability owed by the defaulted counterparty. Thus, the credit exposure is the value of the asset if positive, like an option.

This chapter turns to the quantitative measurement of credit exposure. Section 21.1 describes the general features of credit exposure for various types of financial instruments, including loans or bonds, guarantees, credit commitments, repos, and derivatives. Section 21.2 shows how to compute the distribution of credit exposure and gives detailed examples of exposures of interest rate and currency swaps. Section 21.3 discusses exposure modifiers, or techniques that have been developed to reduce credit exposure. It shows how credit risk can be controlled by marking to market, margins, position limits, recouponing, and netting agreements. For completeness, Section 21.4 includes credit risk modifiers such as credit triggers and time puts, which also control default risk.

501

21.1   Credit Exposure by Instrument

The credit exposure is the positive part of the value of the asset. In particular, the **current exposure** is equal to the value of the asset at the current time V_t if positive:

$$\text{Exposure}_t = \text{Max}(V_t, 0) \tag{21.1}$$

The **potential exposure** represents the exposure on some future date, or sets of dates. Based on this definition, we can characterize the exposure of a variety of financial instruments. The measurement of current and potential exposure also motivates regulatory capital charges for credit risk, which are explained in Chapter 31.

Loans or Bonds

Loans or **bonds** are balance sheet assets whose current and potential exposure is the notional, which is the amount loaned or invested. In fact, this should be the market value of the asset given current interest rates, but, as we will show, this is not very far from the notional. The exposure is also the notional for **receivables** and **trade credits**, as the potential loss is the amount due.

Guarantees

These are off–balance sheet contracts whereby the bank has underwritten, or agrees to assume, the obligations of a third party. The exposure is the notional amount, because this will be fully drawn when default occurs. By nature, guarantees are **irrevocable**, that is, unconditional and binding, whatever happens.

An example of a **guarantee** is a contract whereby bank A makes a loan to client C only if it is guaranteed by bank B. Should C default, B is exposed to the full amount of the loan. Another example is an **acceptance**, whereby a bank agrees to pay the face value of a bill at maturity. Alternatively, **standby facilities**, or **financial letters of credit**, provide a guarantee to a third party of the making of a payment should the obligor default.

Commitments

These are off–balance sheet contracts whereby the bank commits to a future transaction that may result in creating a credit exposure at a *future* date. For instance, a bank may provide a **note issuance facility** whereby it promises a minimum price for notes regularly issued by a borrower. If the notes cannot be placed at the market at the minimum price, the bank commits to buy them at a fixed price. Such commitments have less risk than guarantees because it is not certain that the bank will have to provide backup support.

It is also useful to distinguish between **irrevocable commitments**, which are unconditional and binding on the bank, and **revocable commitments**, where the bank has the option to revoke the contract should the counterparty's credit quality deteriorate. This option substantially decreases the credit exposure.

Swaps or Forwards

These are off–balance sheet items that can be viewed as irrevocable commitments to purchase or sell some asset on prearranged terms. The current and potential exposure will vary from zero to a large amount depending on the movement in the driving risk factors. Similar arrangements are **sale-repurchase agreements** (repos), whereby a bank sells an asset to another in exchange for a promise to buy it back later.

Long Options

Options are also off–balance sheet items that may create credit exposure. The current and potential exposure also depends on movements in the driving risk factors. Here there is no possibility of negative values because options always have positive value, or zero value at worst: $V_t \geq 0$.

Short Options

Unlike long options, the current and potential exposure for short options is zero because the bank writing the option can incur only a negative cash flow, assuming the option premium has been fully paid.

Exposure also depends on the features of any embedded option. With an American option, for instance, the holder of an in-the-money swap may want to exercise early if the credit rating of its counterparty starts to deteriorate. This decreases the exposure relative to an equivalent European option.

Example 21-1: FRM Exam 2002—Question 93

Which transaction does not result in a long-term credit risk for party A?
a) Party A makes an unsecured loan to party B.
b) Party A is a fixed-price receiver in an interest rate swap from party B.
c) Party A buys a call option on September wheat from party B.
d) Party A sells a put option on the S&P 500 index to party B.

Example 21-2: FRM Exam 1999—Question 130

By selling a call option on the S&P 500 futures contract, which is cash settled, an organization is subject to

a) Market risk, but not credit risk

b) Credit risk, but not market risk

c) Both market risk and credit risk

d) Neither market risk nor credit risk

Example 21-3: FRM Exam 1999—Question 151

Trader A purchased an at-the-money one-year OTC put option on the DAX index for a cost of €10,000. What does trader A consider his maximum potential credit exposure to the counterparty over the term of the trade?

a) 0

b) Less than €8,000

c) Between €8,000 and €12,000

d) Greater than €12,000

Example 21-4: FRM Exam 2001—Question 84

If a counterparty defaults before maturity, which of the following situations will cause a credit loss?

a) You are short euros in a one-year euro/USD forward FX contract, and the euro has appreciated.

b) You are short euros in a one-year euro/USD forward FX contract, and the euro has depreciated.

c) You sold a one-year OTC euro call option, and the euro has appreciated.

d) You sold a one-year OTC euro call option, and the euro has depreciated.

21.2   Distribution of Credit Exposure

The credit exposure consists of the **current exposure**, which is readily observable, and the **potential exposure**, or future exposure, which is random. Define x as the potential value of the asset on the target date. We describe this variable by its probability density function $f(x)$. This is where market risk mingles with credit risk.

21.2.1   Expected and Worst Exposure

The **expected credit exposure** (ECE) is the expected value of the asset replacement value x, if positive, on a target date:

$$\text{Expected credit exposure} = \int_{-\infty}^{+\infty} \text{Max}(x, 0) f(x) dx \qquad (21.2)$$

The **worst credit exposure** (WCE) is the largest (worst) credit exposure at some level of confidence. It is implicitly defined as the value that is not exceeded at the given confidence level p:

$$1 - p = \int_{\text{WCE}}^{\infty} f(x)dx \tag{21.3}$$

To model the potential credit exposure, we need to (1) model the distribution of risk factors, and (2) evaluate the instrument given these risk factors. This process is identical to a market value-at-risk (VAR) computation except that the aggregation takes place first at the counterparty level and second at the portfolio level.

To simplify to the extreme, suppose that the payoff x is normally distributed with mean zero and volatility σ. The expected credit exposure is then

$$\text{ECE} = \frac{1}{2}E(x \mid x > 0) = \frac{1}{2}\sigma\sqrt{\frac{2}{\pi}} = \frac{\sigma}{\sqrt{2\pi}} \tag{21.4}$$

Note that we divided by 2 because there is a 50% probability that the value will be positive. The worst credit exposure at the 95% level is given by

$$\text{WCE} = 1.645\sigma \tag{21.5}$$

Figure 21-1 illustrates the measurement of ECE and WCE for a normal distribution. Note that negative values of x are not considered.

FIGURE 21-1 Expected and Worst Credit Exposures—Normal Distribution

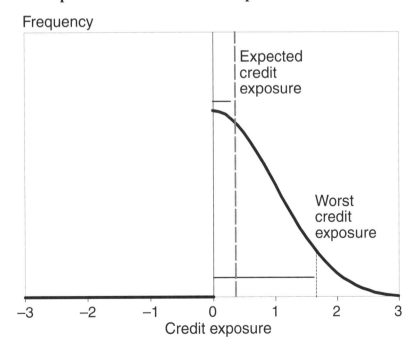

21.2.2   Time Profile

The distribution can be summarized by the expected and worst credit exposures at each point in time. To summarize even further, we can express the average credit exposure by taking a simple arithmetic average over the life of the instrument.

The **average expected credit exposure** (AECE) is the average of the expected credit exposure over time, from now to maturity T:

$$\text{AECE} = (1/T) \int_{t=0}^{T} \text{ECE}_t \, dt \tag{21.6}$$

The **average worst credit exposure** (AWCE) is defined similarly:

$$\text{AWCE} = (1/T) \int_{t=0}^{T} \text{WCE}_t \, dt \tag{21.7}$$

21.2.3   Exposure Profile for Interest Rate Swaps

We now consider the computation of the exposure profile for an interest rate swap. In general, we need to define (1) the market risk factors, (2) the function and parameters for the joint stochastic processes, and (3) the pricing model for the swap.

We start with a one-factor stochastic process for the interest rate, defining the movement in the rate r_t at time t as

$$dr_t = \kappa(\theta - r_t)dt + \sigma r_t^{\gamma} dz_t \tag{21.8}$$

as given in Chapter 4. The first term imposes **mean reversion**. When the current value of r_t is higher than the long-run value, the term in parentheses is negative, which creates a downward trend. More generally, the mean term could reflect the path implied in forward interest rates.

The second term defines the innovation, which can be given a normal distribution. An important issue is whether the volatility of the innovation should be constant or proportional to some power γ of the current value of the interest rate r_t. If the horizon is short, this issue is not so important because the current rate will be close to the initial rate.

When $\gamma = 0$, changes in yields are normally distributed, which is the Vasicek model (1977). As seen in a previous chapter, a typical volatility for *absolute* changes in yields is 1% per annum. A potential problem with this is that the volatility is the same whether the yield starts at 20% or 1%. As a result, the yield could turn negative, depending on the initial starting point and the strength of the mean reversion.

Another class of models is the lognormal model, which takes $\gamma = 1$. The model can then be rewritten in terms of $dr_t/r_t = d\ln(r_t)$. This specification ensures that the volatility shrinks as r gets close to zero, avoiding negative values. A typical volatility of *relative* changes in yields is 15% per annum, which is also the 1% value for changes in the level of rates divided by an initial rate of 6.7%.

For illustration purposes, we choose the normal process $\gamma = 0$ with mean reversion $\kappa = 0.02$ and volatility $\sigma = 0.25\%$ per month, which are realistic parameters based on recent U.S. data. The initial and long-run values of r are 6%. Typical simulation values are shown in Figure 21-2. Note how rates can deviate from their initial value but are pulled back to the long-term value of 6%.

FIGURE 21-2 Simulation Paths for the Interest Rate

This model is convenient because it leads to closed-form solutions. The distribution of future values for r is summarized in Figure 21-3 by its mean and two-tailed 90% confidence bands (called maximum and minimum values). The graph shows that the mean is 6%, which is also the long-run value. The confidence bands initially widen due to the increasing horizon, and then converge to a fixed value due to the mean reversion effect.

FIGURE 21-3 Distribution Profile for the Interest Rate

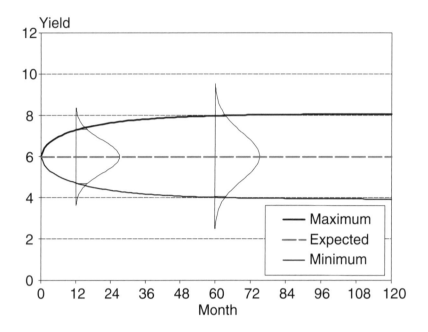

The next step is to value the swap. At each point in time, the current market value of the swap is the difference between the value of a fixed-coupon bond and a floating-rate note:

$$V_t = B(\$100, t, T, c, r_t) - B(\$100, \text{FRN}) \qquad (21.9)$$

Here c is the annualized *fixed* coupon rate, and T is the maturity date. The risk to the swap comes from the fact that the fixed leg has a coupon c that could differ from prevailing market rates. The principals are not exchanged.

Figure 21-4 illustrates the changes in cash flows that could arise from a drop in rates from 6% to 4% after five years. The receive-fixed party would then be owed every six months, for a semiannual pay swap, $\$100 \times (6 - 4)\% \times 0.5 = \$1$ million until the maturity of the swap. With 10 payments remaining, this adds up to a positive credit exposure of $10 million. Discounting over the life of the remaining payments gives $8.1 million as of the valuation date.

In what follows, we assume that the swap receives fixed payments that are paid at a continuous rate instead of semiannually, which simplifies the example. Otherwise, there would be discontinuities in cash-flow patterns, and we would have to consider

FIGURE 21-4 Net Cash Flows When Rates Fall to 4% after Five Years

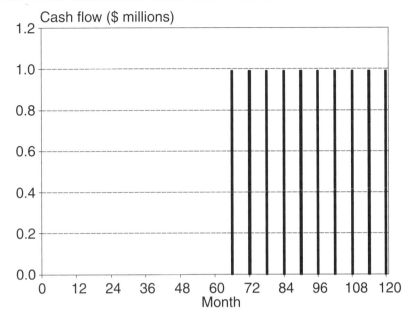

the risk of the floating leg as well. We also use continuous compounding. Defining N as the number of remaining years, the coupon bond value is

$$B(\$100, N, c, r) = \$100\frac{c}{r}[1 - e^{-rN}] + \$100e^{-rN} \qquad (21.10)$$

as seen in the appendix to Chapter 1. The first term is the present value of the fixed-coupon cash flows discounted at the current rate r. The second term is the repayment of principal. For the special case where the coupon rate is equal to the current market rate ($c = r$), the market value is indeed $100 for this par bond. The floating-rate note can be priced in the same way, but with a coupon rate that is always equal to the current rate. Hence, its value is always at par.

To understand the exposure profile of the coupon bond, we need to consider two opposing effects as time goes by:

- The **diffusion effect**, which increases the uncertainty in the interest rate
- The **amortization effect**, which decreases the bond's duration toward zero

The latter effect is described in Figure 21-5, which shows the bond's duration converging to zero. This explains why the bond's market value converges to the face value upon maturity, whatever happens to the current interest rate.

FIGURE 21-5 Duration Profile for a 10-Year Bond

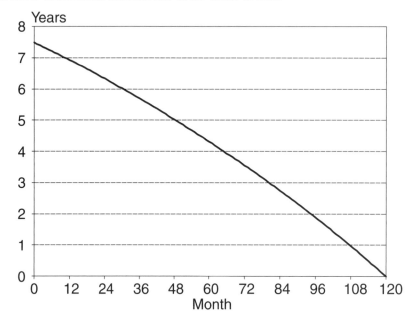

Because the bond is a strictly monotonous function of the current yield, we can compute the 90% confidence bands by valuing the bond using the extreme interest rates range at each point in time. We use Equation (21.10) at each point in time in Figure 21-3. This exposure profile is shown in Figure 21-6.

Initially, the market value of the bond is $100. After two or three years, the range of values is the greatest, from $87 to $115. Thereafter, the range converges to the face value of $100. But overall, the fluctuations as a *proportion* of the face value are relatively small. Considering other approximations in the measurement of credit risk, such as the imprecision in default probability and recovery rate, assuming a constant exposure for the bond is not a bad approximation.

This is not the case, however, for the interest rate swap. Its value can be found by subtracting $100 (the value of the floating-rate note) from the value of the coupon bond. Initially, its value is zero. Thereafter, it can take on positive or negative values. Credit exposure is the positive value only. Figure 21-7 presents the profile of the expected exposure and of the maximum (worst) exposure at the one-sided 95% level. It also shows the average maximum exposure over the whole life of the swap.

FIGURE 21-6 Exposure Profile for a 10-Year Bond

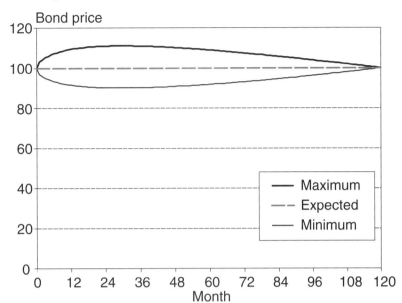

FIGURE 21-7 Exposure Profile for a 10-Year Interest Rate Swap

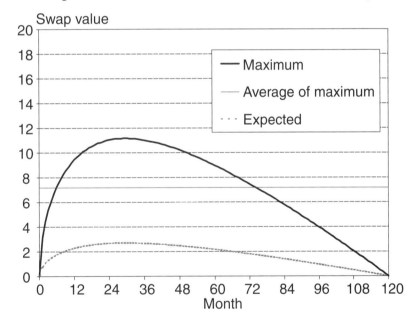

   Intuitively, the value of the swap is derived from the difference between the fixed and floating cash flows. Consider a swap with two remaining payments and a notional amount of $100. Its value is

$$V_t = \$100\left[\frac{c}{(1+r)} + \frac{c}{(1+r)^2} + \frac{1}{(1+r)^2}\right] - \$100\left[\frac{r}{(1+r)} + \frac{r}{(1+r)^2} + \frac{1}{(1+r)^2}\right] \tag{21.11}$$

$$= \$100\left[\frac{(c-r)}{(1+r)} + \frac{(c-r)}{(1+r)^2}\right]$$

Note how the principal payments cancel out and we are left with the discounted *net* difference between the fixed coupon and the prevailing rate $(c - r)$.

This information can be used to assess the expected exposure and worst exposure on a target date. The peak exposure occurs around the second year into the swap, or at about one-fourth of the swap's life. At that point, the expected exposure is about 3% to 4% of the notional, which is much less than that of the bond. The worst exposure peaks at about 10% to 15% of notional. In practice, these values depend on the particular stochastic process used, but the exposure profiles will be qualitatively similar.

To assess the potential variation in swap values, we can make some approximations based on duration. Consider first the very short-term exposure, for which mean reversion and changes in durations are not important. The volatility of changes in rates then simply increases with the square root of time. Given a 0.25% per month volatility and 7.5-year initial duration, we can approximate the volatility of the swap value over the next year as

$$\sigma(V) = \$100 \times 7.5 \times [0.25\%\sqrt{12}] = \$6.5 \text{ million}$$

Multiplying by 1.645, we get $10.7 million, which is close to the actual $9.4 million 95% worst exposure in a year reported in Figure 21-7.

The trade-off between declining duration and increasing risk can be formalized with a slightly more realistic example. Assume that the bond's (modified) duration is proportional to the remaining life, $D = k(T - t)$ at any date t. The volatility from 0 to time t can be written as $\sigma(r_t - r_0) = \sigma\sqrt{t}$. Hence, the swap volatility is

$$\sigma(V) = [k(T - t)]\sigma\sqrt{t} \tag{21.12}$$

To see where it reaches a maximum, we differentiate with respect to t:

$$\frac{d\sigma(V)}{dt} = [k(-1)]\sigma\sqrt{t} + [k(T - t)]\sigma\frac{1}{2\sqrt{t}}$$

Setting this to zero, we have

$$\sqrt{t} = (T - t)\frac{1}{2\sqrt{t}}$$

or

$$2t = (T - t)$$

or

$$t_{MAX} = (1/3)T \quad (21.13)$$

The maximum exposure occurs at one-third of the life of the swap. This occurs later than the one-fourth point reported previously because we assumed no mean reversion.

Further, we can check how this evolves with the maturity of the contract. At that point, the worst credit exposure will be

$$1.645 \, \sigma (V_{MAX}) = 1.645 \left[k(2/3)T\sigma \sqrt{T/3} \right] = \left[1.645k(2/3)\sigma \sqrt{1/3} \right] T^{3/2} \quad (21.14)$$

which shows that the WCE increases as $T^{3/2}$, which is faster than the maturity.

Figure 21-8 shows the exposure profile of a five-year swap. Here again, the peak exposure occurs at one-third of the swap's life. As expected, the magnitude is lower, with the peak expected exposure only about 1% of the notional.

FIGURE 21-8 Exposure Profile for a Five-Year Interest Rate Swap

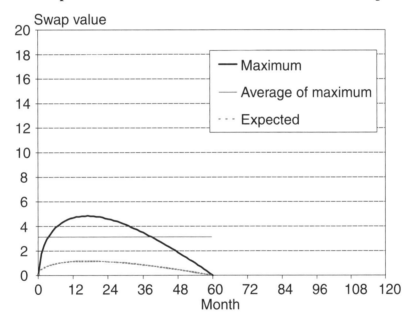

Finally, Figure 21-9 displays the exposure profile when the initial interest rate is at 5% with a coupon of 6%. The swap starts in-the-money, with a current value of $7.9 million. With a long-run rate of 6%, the total exposure profile starts from a positive value, reaches a maximum after about two years, then converges to zero.

FIGURE 21-9 Exposure Profile for a 10-Year in-the-Money Swap

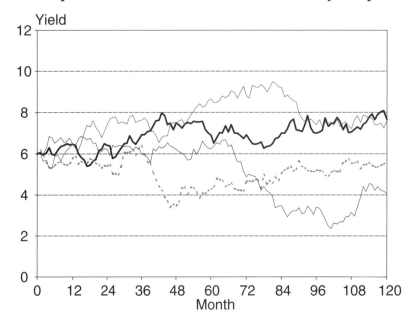

Example 21-5: FRM Exam 1999—Question 111

What is the primary difference between the default implications of loans versus those of interest rate swaps?

a) The principal in a swap is not at risk.

b) The cash flows in the loans are determined by the level of rates, not the difference in rates.

c) Default on a loan requires only that the firm be in financial distress; a swap also requires that the remaining value be positive to the dealer.

d) All of the above.

Example 21-6: FRM Exam 1999—Question 118

Assume that swap rates are identical for all swap tenors. A swap dealer entered into a plain-vanilla swap one year ago as the receive-fixed party, when the price of the swap was 7%. Today, this swap dealer will face credit risk exposure from this swap only if the value of the swap for the dealer is

a) Negative, which will occur if new swaps are being priced at 6%

b) Negative, which will occur if new swaps are being priced at 8%

c) Positive, which will occur if new swaps are being priced at 6%

d) Positive, which will occur if new swaps are being priced at 8%

Example 21-7: FRM Exam 1999—Question 148

Assume that the DV01 of an interest rate swap is proportional to its time to maturity (which at the initiation of the swap is equal to T). Also assume that the interest rate curve moves are parallel, stochastic with constant volatility, normally distributed, and independent. At what time will the maximum potential exposure be reached?

a) $T/4$

b) $T/3$

c) $T/2$

d) $3T/4$

Example 21-8: FRM Exam 2000—Question 29

Determine at what point in the future a derivatives portfolio will reach its maximum potential exposure. All the derivatives are on one underlying, which is assumed to move in a stochastic fashion (variance in the underlying's value increases linearly with time passage). The derivatives portfolio's sensitivity to the underlying is expected to drop off as $(T - t)^2$, where T is the time from today until the last contract in the portfolio rolls off, and t is the time from today.

a) $T/5$

b) $T/3$

c) $T/2$

d) None of the above

Example 21-9: FRM Exam 2002—Question 83

Assume that you have entered into a fixed-for-floating interest rate swap that starts today and ends in six years. Assume that the duration of your position is proportional to the time to maturity. Also assume that all changes in the yield curve are parallel shifts, and that the volatility of interest rates is proportional to the square root of time. When would the maximum potential exposure be reached?

a) In two months

b) In two years

c) In six years

d) In four years and five months

21.2.4   Exposure Profile for Currency Swaps

Exposure profiles are substantially different for other swaps. Consider, for instance, a currency swap where the notionals are 100 million U.S. dollars against 50 million British pounds (BP), set at an initial exchange rate of $S(\$/BP) = 2$.

The market value of a currency swap that receives foreign currency is

$$V_t = S_t(\$/BP)B^*(BP50, t, T, c^*, r^*) - B(\$100, t, T, c, r) \tag{21.15}$$

Following the usual conventions, asterisks refer to foreign-currency values.

In general, this swap is exposed to domestic as well as foreign interest rate risk. When we just have two remaining coupons, the value of the swap evolves according to

$$V = S \times 50 \left[\frac{c^*}{(1+r^*)} + \frac{c^*}{(1+r^*)^2} + \frac{1}{(1+r^*)^2} \right] - \$100 \left[\frac{c}{(1+r)} + \frac{c}{(1+r)^2} + \frac{1}{(1+r)^2} \right] \tag{21.16}$$

Note that, relative to Equation (21.11), the principals do not cancel each other since they are paid in different currencies.

In what follows, we will assume for simplicity that there is no interest rate risk, or that the value of the swap is dominated by currency risk. Further, we assume that the coupons are the same in the two currencies; otherwise there would be an asymmetrical accumulation of payments. As before, we have to choose a stochastic process for the spot rate. Say this is a lognormal process with constant variance and no trend:

$$dS_t = \sigma S_t \, dz_t \tag{21.17}$$

We choose $\sigma = 12\%$ annually, which is realistic, as seen in the chapter on market risk factors. This process ensures that the rate never turns negative.

Figure 21-10 presents the exposure profile of a 10-year currency swap. Here there is no amortization effect, and exposure increases continuously over time. The peak exposure occurs at the end of the life of the swap. At that point, the expected exposure is about 10% of the notional, which is much higher than for the interest rate swap. The worst exposure is commensurately high, at about 45% of notional.

Although these values depend on the particular stochastic process and parameters used, this example demonstrates that credit exposures for currency swaps is far greater than for interest rate swaps, even with identical maturities.

FIGURE 21-10 Exposure Profile for a 10-Year Currency Swap

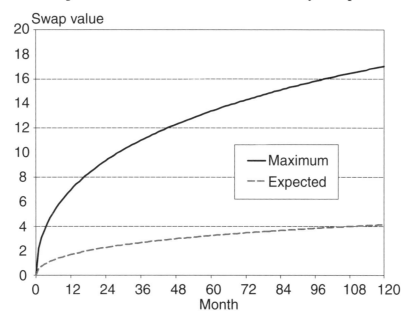

21.2.5   Exposure Profile for Different Coupons

So far, we have assumed a flat term structure and equal coupon payments in different currencies, which creates a symmetric situation for the exposure for the long and short parties. In reality, these conditions will not hold, and the exposure patterns will be asymmetric.

Consider, for instance, the interest rate swap in Equation (21.11). If the term structure slopes upward, the coupon rate is greater than the floating rate, $c > r$, and the fixed receiver receives a net payment in the near term. The value of the two-period swap can be analyzed by projecting floating payments at the forward rate:

$$V_t = \frac{(c - s_1)}{(1 + s_1)} + \frac{(c - f_{12})}{(1 + s_2)^2}$$

where s_1, s_2 are the one- and two-year spot rates, and f_{12} is the one- to two-year forward rate.

Example

Consider a \$100 million interest rate swap with two remaining payments. We have $s_1 = 5\%$, $s_2 = 6.03\%$ and hence, using $(1 + s_2)^2 = (1 + s_1)(1 + f_{12})$, we have $f_{12} = 7.07\%$. The coupon yield of $c = 6\%$ is such that the swap has zero initial value. The following table shows that the present value of the first payment (to the party receiving fixed) is positive and equal to $0.9524. The second payment then must be negative, and is equal to $-$0.9524. The two payments exactly offset each other because the swap has zero value.

Time	Expected Spot	Expected Payment	Discounted
1	5%	$6.00 - 5.00 = +1.00$	$+0.9524$
2	7.07%	$6.00 - 7.07 = -1.07$	-0.9524
Total			0.0000

This pattern of payments, however, creates more credit exposure to the fixed payer because it involves a payment in the first period offset by a receipt in the second. If the counterparty defaults shortly after the first payment is made, there could be a credit loss even if interest rates have not changed.

Key concept:
With a positively sloped term structure, the receiver of the floating rate (payer of the fixed rate) has greater credit exposure than the counterparty.

A similar issue arises with currency swaps when the two coupon rates differ. Low nominal interest rates imply a higher forward exchange rate. The party that receives payments in a low-coupon currency is expected to receive greater payments later during the exchange of principal. If the counterparty defaults, there could be a credit loss even if rates have not changed.

Key concept:
The receiver of a low-coupon currency has greater credit exposure than the counterparty.

Example 21-10: FRM Exam 2000—Question 47
Which one of the following deals would have the greatest credit exposure for a $1,000,000 deal size (assume the counterparty in each deal is an AAA-rated bank and has no settlement risk)?
a) Pay fixed in an Australian dollar (AUD) interest rate swap for one year.
b) Sell USD against AUD in a one-year forward foreign exchange contract.
c) Sell a one-year AUD cap.
d) Purchase a one-year certificate of deposit.

Example 21-11: FRM Exam 2001—Question 8
Which of the following 10-year swaps has the highest potential credit exposure?
a) A cross-currency swap *after* 2 years
b) A cross-currency swap *after* 9 years
c) An interest rate swap *after* 2 years
d) An interest rate swap *after* 9 years

Example 21-12: FRM Exam 1998—Question 33
The amount of potential exposure arising from being long an over-the-counter
USD/euro forward contract will be a function of the
a) Credit quality of the counterparty
b) Credit quality of the counterparty and the tenor of the contract
c) Volatility of the USD/euro exchange rate and the tenor of the contract
d) Volatility of the USD/DEM exchange rate and the credit quality of the
counterparty

21.3   Exposure Modifiers

In a continuing attempt to decrease credit exposures, the industry has developed a
number of methods to limit exposures. This section analyzes marking to market, margins and collateral, exposure limits, recouponing, and netting arrangements.

21.3.1   Marking to Market

The ultimate form of reducing credit exposure is marking to market (MTM). **Marking
to market** involves settling the variation in the contract value on a regular basis (e.g.,
daily). For OTC contracts, counterparties can agree to longer periods (e.g., monthly
or quarterly). If the MTM treatment is symmetrical across the two counterparties, it is
called **two-way marking to market**. Otherwise, if one party settles losses only, it is
called **one-way marking to market**.

   Marking to market has long been used by organized exchanges to deal with credit
risk. The reason is that exchanges are accessible to a wide variety of investors, including retail speculators, who are more likely to default than others. On OTC markets,
in contrast, institutions interacting with each other typically have an ongoing relationship. As one observer put it,

> *Futures markets are designed to permit trading among strangers, as against
> other markets which permit only trading among friends.*

With daily marking to market, the *current* exposure is reduced to zero. There is still, however, *potential* exposure because the value of the contract could change before the next settlement. Potential exposure arises from (1) the time interval between MTM periods and (2) the time required for liquidating the contract when the counterparty defaults.

In the case of a retail client, the broker can generally liquidate the position fairly quickly, within a day. When positions are very large, as in the case of brokers dealing with Long-Term Capital Management (LTCM), however, the liquidation period could be much longer. Indeed, LTCM's bailout was motivated by the potential disruption to financial markets had brokers attempted to liquidate their contracts with LTCM at the same time.

Marking to market introduces other types of risks, however:

- **Operational risk**, which is due to the need to keep track of contract values and to make or receive payments daily
- **Liquidity risk**, because the institution now needs to keep enough cash to absorb variations in contract values

Margins

Potential exposure is covered by margin requirements. **Margins** represent cash or securities that must be advanced in order to open a position. The purpose of these funds is to provide a buffer against potential exposure.

Exchanges, for instance, require a customer to post an **initial margin** when establishing a new position. This margin serves as a performance bond to offset possible future losses should the customer default. Contract gains and losses are then added to the posted margin in the **equity account**. Whenever the value of this equity account falls below a threshold, set at a **maintenance margin**, new funds must be provided.

Margins are set in relation to price volatility and to the type of position, speculative or hedging. Margins increase for more volatile contracts. Margins are typically lower for hedgers because a loss on the futures position can be offset by a gain on the physical, assuming no basis risk. Some exchanges set margins at a level that covers the 99th percentile of worst daily price changes, which is a daily VAR system for credit risk.

Collateral

Over-the-counter markets may allow posting securities as **collateral** instead of cash.

This collateral protects against current and potential exposure. Typically, the amount of the collateral will exceed the funds owed by an amount known as the **haircut**.

The haircut reflects both default risk and market risk. Safe counterparties will in general have lower haircuts. This also depends, however, on the downside risk of the asset. For instance, cash can have a haircut of zero, which means that there is full protection against current exposure. Government securities can require a haircut of 1%, 3%, and 8% for short-term, medium-term, and longer-term maturities, respectively. With greater price volatility, there is an increasing chance of losses if the counterparty defaults and the collateral loses value, which explains the increasing haircuts.

21.3.2 Exposure Limits

Credit exposure can also be managed by setting **position limits** on the exposure to a counterparty. Ideally, these should be evaluated in a portfolio context, taking into account all the contracts between an institution and a counterparty.

To enforce limits, information on transactions must be centralized in middle-office systems. This generates an *exposure profile* for each counterparty, which can be used to manage credit line usage for several maturity buckets. Proposed new trades with the same counterparty should then be examined for their incremental effect.

These limits can be also set at the instrument level. In the case of a swap, for instance, an **exposure cap** requires a payment to be made whenever the value of the contract exceeds some amount. Figure 21-11 shows the effect of a $5 million cap on our 10-year swap. If, after 2 years, say, the contract suddenly moves into a positive value of $11 million, the counterparty would be required to make a payment of $6 million to bring the swap's outstanding value back to $5 million. This limits the worst exposure to $5 million and also lowers the average exposure.

21.3.3 Recouponing

Another method for controlling exposure at the instrument level is recouponing. **Recouponing** refers to a clause in the contract requiring the contract to be marked to market at some fixed date. This involves (1) exchanging cash to bring the MTM value to zero and (2) resetting the coupon or the exchange rate to prevailing market values.

Figure 21-12 shows the effect of 5-year recouponing on our 100-year swap. The exposure is truncated to zero after 5 years. Thereafter, the exposure profile is that of a swap with a remaining 5-year maturity.

FIGURE 21-11 Effect of Exposure Cap

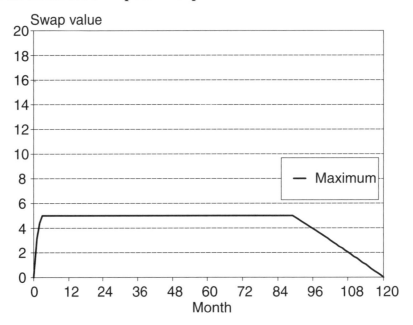

FIGURE 21-12 Effect of Recouponing After Five Years

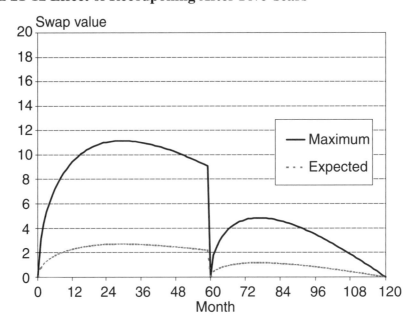

21.3.4   Netting Arrangements

Perhaps the most powerful mechanism for controlling exposures are **netting agreements**. These are now a common feature of standardized **master swap agreements** such as the one established in 1992 by the **International Swaps and Derivatives Association** (ISDA).

The purpose of these agreements is to provide for the **netting** of payments across a set of contracts. In case of default, a counterparty cannot stop payments on contracts that have negative value while demanding payment on positive-value contracts. As a result, this system reduces the exposure to the net payment for all the contracts covered by the netting agreement.

Table 21-1 gives an example with four contracts. Without a netting agreement, the exposure of the first two contracts is the sum of the positive part of each, or $100 million. In contrast, if the first two fall under a netting agreement, their value would offset each other, resulting in a net exposure of $100 − $60 = $40 million. If contracts 3 and 4 do not fall under the netting agreement, the exposure is then increased to $40 + $25 = $65 million.

TABLE 21-1 Comparison of Exposure with and without Netting

Contract	Contract Value	Exposure	
		No Netting	With Netting for 1 and 2
	Under netting agreement		
1	+$100	+$100	
2	−$60	+$0	
Total, 1 and 2	+$40	+$100	+$40
	No netting agreement		
3	+$25	+$25	
4	−$15	+$0	
Grand total, 1 to 4	+$50	+$125	+$65

To summarize, the **net exposure** with netting is

$$\text{Net exposure} = \text{Max}(V, 0) = \text{Max}\left(\sum_{i=1}^{N} V_i, 0\right) \tag{21.18}$$

Without netting agreement, the **gross exposure** is the sum of all positive-value contracts:

$$\text{Gross exposure} = \sum_{i=1}^{N} \text{Max}(V_i, 0) \qquad (21.19)$$

This is always greater than, or equal to, the exposure under the netting agreement.

The benefit from netting depends on the number of contracts N and the extent to which contract values covary. The larger the value of N and the lower the correlation, the greater the benefit from netting. It is easy to verify from Table 21-1 that if all contracts move into positive value at the same time, or have high correlation, there will be no benefit from netting.

Figures 21-13 and 21-14 illustrate the effect of netting on a portfolio of two swaps with the same counterparty. In each case, interest rates could increase or decrease with the same probability.

In Figure 21-13, the bank is long both a 10-year and 5-year swap. The top panel describes the worst exposure when rates fall. In this case there is positive exposure for both contracts, which we add to get the total portfolio exposure. Whether there is netting or not does not matter, because the two positions are positive at the same time. The bottom panel describes the worst exposure when rates increase. Both positions as well as the portfolio have zero exposure.

In Figure 21-14, the bank is long the 10-year and short the 5-year swap. When rates fall, the first swap has positive value and the second has negative value. With netting, the worst exposure profile is reduced. In contrast, with no netting the exposure is that of the 10-year swap. Conversely, when rates increase, the swap value is negative for the first and positive for the second. With netting, the exposure profile is zero, whereas without netting it is the same as that of the 5-year swap. This shows that netting is more effective with diversified positions.

Banks provide some information in their annual report about the benefit of netting for their current exposure. Without netting agreements or collateral, the **gross replacement value** (GRV) is reported as the sum of the worst-case exposures if all counterparties K default at the same time:

$$\text{GRV} = \sum_{k=1}^{K} (\text{Gross exposure})_k = \sum_{k=1}^{K} \left[\sum_{i=1}^{N_k} \text{Max}(V_i, 0) \right] \qquad (21.20)$$

With netting agreements and collateral, the resulting exposure is defined as the **net replacement value** (NRV). This is the sum, over all counterparties, of the net positive exposure minus any collateral held:

$$\text{NRV} = \sum_{k=1}^{K} (\text{Net exposure})_k = \sum_{k=1}^{K} \left[\text{Max}\left(\sum_{i=1}^{N_k} V_i, 0 \right) - \text{Collateral}_k \right] \quad (21.21)$$

FIGURE 21-13 Netting with Two Long Positions

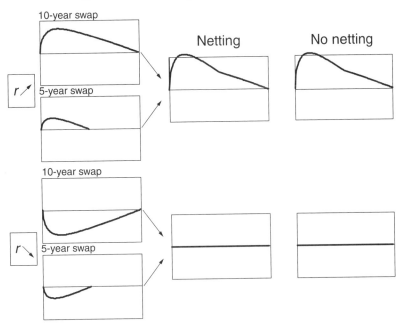

FIGURE 21-14 Netting with a Long and a Short Position

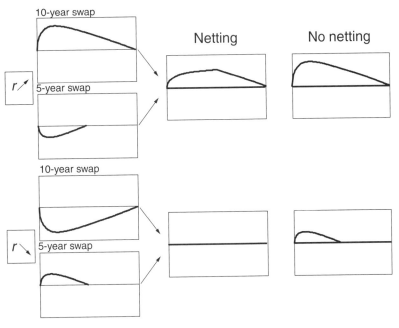

Example 21-13: FRM Exam 2002—Question 89

If we assume that the VAR for the portfolio of trades with a given counterparty can be viewed as a measure of potential credit exposure, which of the following could *not* be used to decrease this credit exposure?

a) A netting agreement

b) Collateral

c) A credit derivative that pays out if the counterparty defaults

d) An offsetting trade with a different counterparty

Example 21-14: FRM Exam 1999—Question 131

To reduce credit risk, a company can

a) Expose itself to many different counterparties

b) Take on a variety of positions

c) Set up netting agreements with all of its approved trading partners

d) All of the above

Example 21-15: FRM Exam 1999—Question 154

A diversified portfolio of OTC derivatives with a single counterparty currently has a net mark-to-market value of USD 20,000,000 and a gross absolute mark-to-market value (the sum of the value of all positive-value positions minus the value of all negative-value positions) of USD 80,000,000. Assuming there are no netting agreements in place with the counterparty, determine the current credit exposure to the counterparty.

a) Less than or equal to USD 19,000,000

b) Greater than USD 19,000,000 but less than or equal to USD 40,000,000

c) Greater than USD 40,000,000 but less than USD 60,000,000

d) Greater than USD 60,000,000

Example 21-16: FRM Exam 1998—Question 34

A diversified portfolio of OTC derivatives with a single counterparty currently has a net mark-to-market value of $20 million. Assuming that there are no netting agreements in place with the counterparty, determine the current credit exposure to the counterparty.

a) Less than $20 million

b) Exactly $20 million

c) Greater than $20 million

d) Unable to be determined

Example 21-17: FRM Exam 1999—Question 123

An equity repo is a repo in which common stock is used as collateral in place of the more usual fixed-income instrument. The mechanics of equity repos are effectively the same as for fixed-income repos, except that the haircut

a) Is smaller because equities are more liquid than for fixed-income instruments

b) Is larger because equity prices are more volatile than those of fixed-income instruments

c) About the same for both equity and fixed-income deals because the counterparty credit risk is the same

d) Cannot be determined in advance because equity prices, in contrast to fixed-income instrument prices, are not martingales

---

Example 21-18: FRM Exam 2002—Question 73

Consider the following information. You have purchased 10,000 barrels of oil for delivery in one year at a price of $25/barrel. The rate of change of the price of oil is assumed to be normally distributed with zero mean and annual volatility of 30%. Margin is to be paid within two days if the credit exposure becomes greater than $50,000. There are 252 business days in the year. Assuming enforceability of the margin agreement, which of the following is the closest number to the 95% one-year credit risk of this deal governed under the margining agreement?

a) $50,000

b) $58,000

c) $61,000

d) $123,000

21.4   Credit Risk Modifiers

Credit risk modifiers operate on credit exposure, default risk, or a combination of the two. For completeness, this section discusses modifiers that affect default risk.

21.4.1   Credit Triggers

Credit triggers specify that if either counterparty's credit rating falls below a specified level, the other party has the right to have the swap cash settled. These are not exposure modifiers, but rather attempt to reduce the probability of default on that contract. For instance, if all outstanding swaps can be terminated when the counterparty rating falls below A, the probability of default is lowered to the probability that a counterparty will default when rated A or higher.

These triggers are useful when the credit rating of a firm deteriorates slowly, because few firms directly jump from investment-grade into bankruptcy. The increased protection can be estimated by analyzing transition probabilities, as discussed in a previous chapter. For example, say a transaction with an AA-rated borrower has a cumulative probability of default of 0.81% over 10 years. If the contract can be terminated whenever the rating falls to BB or below, this probability falls to 0.23%.

21.4.2   Time Puts

Time puts, or **mutual termination options**, permit either counterparty to terminate unconditionally the transaction on one or more dates in the contract. This feature decreases both the default risk and the exposure. It allows one counterparty to terminate the contract if the exposure is large and the other party's rating starts to slip.

Triggers and puts, which are types of **contingent requirements**, can cause serious trouble, however. They create calls on liquidity precisely in states of the world where the company is faring badly, putting further pressure on the company's liquidity. Indeed, triggers in some of Enron's securities forced the company to make large cash payments and propelled it into bankruptcy. Rather than offering protection, these clauses can trigger bankruptcy, affecting all creditors adversely.

21.5   Answers to Chapter Examples

Example 21-1: FRM Exam 2002—Question 93

d) Selling an option does not create credit exposures, because the premium has been received up front and the option can only create a future liability.

Example 21-2: FRM Exam 1999—Question 130

a) There is no credit risk from selling options if the premium is received up front.

Example 21-3: FRM Exam 1999—Question 151

d) The maximum exposure is potentially very large because this is a *long* position in an option, certainly larger than the initial premium. At a minimum, the exposure is the current exposure of €10,000.

Example 21-4: FRM Exam 2001—Question 84

b) Being short an option creates no credit exposure, so answers c) and d) are false. With the short forward contract, a gain will be realized if the euro has depreciated.

Example 21-5: FRM Exam 1999—Question 111

d) For a loan, the principal is at risk, and the payments depend on the level of rates; the swap needs to be in-the-money for a credit loss to occur.

Example 21-6: FRM Exam 1999—Question 118

c) The value of the swap must be positive to the dealer to have some exposure. This will happen if current rates are less than the fixed coupon.

Example 21-7: FRM Exam 1999—Question 148

b) See Equation (21.14).

Example 21-8: FRM Exam 2000—Question 29

a) This question alters the variance profile in Equation (21.12). Taking now the variance instead of the volatility, we have $\sigma^2 = k(T - t)^4 \times t$, where k is a constant. Differentiating with respect to t,

$$\frac{d\sigma^2}{dt} = k[(-1)4(T - t)^3]t + k[(T - t)^4] = k(T - t)^3[-4t + T - t]$$

Setting this to zero, we have $t = T/5$. Intuitively, because the exposure profile drops off faster than in Equation (21.12), we must have earlier peak exposure than $T/3$.

Example 21-9: FRM Exam 2002—Question 83

b) Exposure is a function of duration, which decreases with time, and interest rate volatility, which increases with the square root of time. Define T as the original maturity and k as a constant. This give $\sigma(V_t) = k(T - t)\sqrt{t}$. Taking the derivative with respect to t gives a maximum at $t = (T/3)$. This gives $t = (6/3) = 2$ years.

Example 21-10: FRM Exam 2000—Question 47

d) The CD has the whole notional at risk. Otherwise, the next greatest exposure is for the forward currency contract and the interest rate swap. The short cap position has no exposure if the premium has been collected. Note that the question eliminates settlement risk for the forward contract.

Example 21-11: FRM Exam 2001—Question 8

a) The question asks about potential exposure for various swaps during their life. Interest rate swaps generally have lower exposure than currency swaps because there is no market risk on the principals. Currency swaps with longer remaining maturities have greater potential exposure. This is the case for the 10-year currency swap, which after 2 years has 8 years remaining to maturity.

Example 21-12: FRM Exam 1998—Question 33

c) The credit quality is not involved in the calculation of the potential exposure. It is taken into account only for the computation of the Basel risk weights, or for the distribution of credit losses.

Example 21-13: FRM Exam 2002—Question 89

d) An offsetting trade with a different party will provide no credit protection. If the first party defaults while the contract is in-the-money, there will be a credit loss.

Example 21-14: FRM Exam 1999—Question 131

d) Credit risk will be decreased with netting, more positions, and more counterparties.

Example 21-15: FRM Exam 1999—Question 154

c) Define X and Y as the absolute values of the positive and negative positions. The net value is $X - Y = 20$ million. The absolute gross value is $X + Y = 80$. Solving, we get $X = 50$ million. This is the positive part of the positions, or exposure.

Example 21-16: FRM Exam 1998—Question 34

d) Without additional information and no netting agreement, it is not possible to determine the exposure from the net amount only. The portfolio could have two swaps with values of $100 million and −$80 million, which gives an exposure of $100 million without netting. Or the portfolio could have one swap with a value of $20 million, in which case the exposure is also $20 million.

Example 21-17: FRM Exam 1999—Question 123

b) The haircut on equity repos is greater due to the greater price volatility of the collateral.

Example 21-18: FRM Exam 2002—Question 73

c) The worst credit exposure is the $50,000 plus the worst move over two days at the 95% level. The worst potential move is $\alpha\sigma\sqrt{T} = 1.645 \times 30\% \times \sqrt{(2/252)} = 4.40\%$. Applied to the position worth $250,000, this gives a worst move of $10,991. Adding this to $50,000 gives $60,991.

Chapter 22

Credit Derivatives

Credit derivatives are the latest tool in the management of portfolio credit risk. From 1996 to 2004, the market is estimated to have grown from about $40 billion to more than $6,000 billion. The market has doubled in each of these years.

Credit derivatives are contracts that pass credit risk from one counterparty to another. They allow credit risk to be stripped from loans and bonds and placed in a different market. Their performance is based on a credit spread, a credit rating, or default status. Like other derivatives, they can be traded on a stand-alone basis or embedded in some other instrument, such as a credit-linked note.

Section 22.1 presents the rationale for credit derivatives. Section 22.2 describes credit default swaps, total return swaps, credit spread forward and option contracts, and credit-linked notes. Section 22.3 then provides a brief introduction to the pricing and hedging of credit derivatives. Finally, Section 22.4 discusses the pros and cons of credit derivatives.

22.1 Introduction

Credit derivatives have grown so quickly because they provide an efficient mechanism for exchanging credit risk. While modern banking is built on the sensible notion that a portfolio of loans is less risky than single loans, banks still tend to be too concentrated in geographic or industrial sectors. This is because their comparative advantage is "relationship banking," which is usually limited to a clientele that the banks know best. So far, it has been difficult to lay off this credit exposure, as there is only a limited market for secondary loans. In addition, borrowers may not like to see their bank selling their loans to another party, even for diversification reasons.

In fact, credit derivatives are not totally new. **Bond insurance** is a contract between a bond issuer and a guarantor (a bank or insurer) to provide additional payment should the issuer fail to make full and timely payment. A **letter of credit** is a guarantee by a bank to provide a payment to a third party should the primary credit fail on its obligations. The **call feature** in corporate bonds involves an option on the risk-free interest rate as well as the credit spread. Indeed, the borrower can also call back the bond should its credit rating improve. At an even more basic level, a long position in a **corporate bond** is equivalent to a long position in a risk-free bond plus a short position in a credit default swap (CDS).

Thus, many existing instruments embed some form of credit derivative. What is new is the transparency and trading made possible by credit derivatives. Corporate bonds, notably, are difficult to short. This position can be replicated easily, however, by the purchase of a CDS. Thus, credit derivatives open new possibilities for investors, hedgers, and speculators.

Example 22-1: FRM Exam 1998—Question 44

All of the following can be accomplished with the use of a credit derivative *except*

a) Reducing credit concentration risk
b) Allowing a fund to invest in corporate loans
c) Preventing the bankruptcy of a loan counterparty
d) Leveraging credit risk

22.2   Types of Credit Derivatives

Credit derivatives are over-the-counter contracts that allow credit risk to be exchanged across counterparties. They can be classified in terms of

• *The underlying credit*, which can be either a single entity or a group of entities
• *The exercise conditions*, which can be a credit event (such as default or a rating downgrade, or an increase in credit spreads)
• *The payoff function*, which can be a fixed amount or a variable amount with a linear or nonlinear payoff

Table 22-1 provides a breakdown of the credit derivatives market by instruments, which will be defined later. The largest share of the market consists of plain-vanilla credit default swaps, typically with five-year maturities. The next segment consists of **synthetic securitization**, or collateralized debt obligations (CDOs), where the special-purpose vehicle gains exposure to a specified portfolio of credit risk via credit derivatives, and the payoffs are redistributed across different tranches. We now define each category in turn.

TABLE 22-1 Credit Derivatives by Type:

Percentage of Total Notionals

Type	Percent
Credit default swaps	73%
Synthetic securitization	22%
Credit-linked notes	3%
Total return swaps	1%
Credit spread options	1%
Total	100%

Source: *Risk* (February 2003).

22.2.1 Credit Default Swaps

In a **credit default swap** contract, a protection buyer (say A) pays a premium to the protection seller (say B) in exchange for payment if a credit event occurs. The **premium payment** can be a lump sum or periodic. The **contingent payment** is triggered by a credit event (CE) on the underlying credit. The structure of this swap is described in Figure 22-1.

FIGURE 22-1 Credit Default Swap

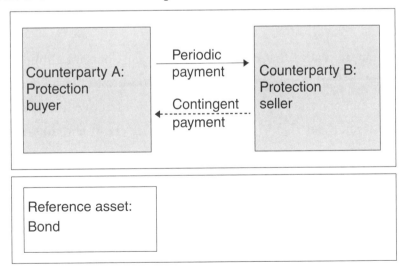

These contracts represent the purest form of credit derivatives, as they are not affected by fluctuations in market values as long as the credit event does not occur. In the next chapter, we will define this approach as "default mode" marking to market (MTM). Also, these contracts are really options, not swaps. The main difference from a regular option is that the cost of the option is paid in installments instead of up front. When the premium is paid up front, these contracts are called *default put options*.[1]

Example

The protection buyer, call it A, enters a 1-year credit default swap on a notional of $100 million worth of 10-year bonds issued by XYZ. The swap entails an annual payment of 50 bp. The bond is called the *reference credit asset*.

At the beginning of the year, A pays $500,000 to the protection seller. Say that at the end of the year, company XYZ defaults on this bond, which now trades at 40 cents on the dollar. The counterparty then has to pay $60 million to A. If A holds this bond in its portfolio, the credit default swap provides protection against credit loss due to default.

Default swaps are embedded in many financial products: Investing in a risky (credit-sensitive) bond is equivalent to investing in a risk-free bond plus selling a credit default swap.

Say, for instance, that the risky bond sells at $90 and promises to pay $100 in one year. The risk-free bond sells at $95. Buying the risky bond is then equivalent to buying the risk-free bond at $95 and selling a credit default swap worth $5 now. The up-front cost is the same, $90. If the company defaults, the final payoff will be the same.

It is important to realize that entering a credit swap does not eliminate credit risk entirely. Instead, the protection buyer decreases exposure to the reference credit but assumes new credit exposure to the CDS seller. To be effective, there has to be a low correlation between the default risk of the underlying credit and that of the counterparty.

Table 22-2 illustrates the effect of the counterparty on the pricing of the CDS. If the counterparty is default free, the CDS spread on this BBB credit should be 194 bp. The spread depends on the default risk for the counterparty as well as the correlation with the reference credit. In the worst case in the table, with a BBB rating for the

---

[1] Default swaps and default options are not totally identical instruments, however, because a default swap requires premium payments only until a triggering default event occurs.

counterparty and correlation of 0.8, protection is less effective, and the CDS is worth only 134 bp.

TABLE 22-2 CDS Spreads for Different Counterparties (Reference Obligation Is Five-Year Bond Rated BBB)

Correlation	Counterparty Credit Rating			
	AAA	AA	A	BBB
0.0	194	194	194	194
0.2	191	190	189	186
0.4	187	185	181	175
0.6	182	178	171	159
0.8	177	171	157	134

Source: Adapted from Hull, J., and A. White (2001), Valuing Credit Default Swaps II: Modeling Default Correlations, *Journal of Derivatives* 8, 12–21.

Credit events must be subject to precise definitions. Chapter 19 provided such a list, drawn from the ISDA's master netting agreement. Ideally, there should be no uncertainty about the interpretation of a credit event. Otherwise, credit derivative transactions can create legal risks.

The payment on default reflects the loss to the holders of the reference asset when the credit event occurs. Define Q as this payment per unit of notional. It can take a number of forms:

- **Cash settlement**, or a payment equal to the strike minus the prevailing market value of the underlying bond.
- **Physical delivery** of the defaulted obligation in exchange for a fixed payment.
- A **lump sum**, or a fixed amount based on some agreed-upon recovery rate. For instance, if the CE occurs, the recovery rate is set at 40%, leading to a payment of 60% of the notional.

The payoff on a credit default swap is

$$\text{Payment} = \text{Notional} \times Q \times I(\text{CE}) \tag{22.1}$$

where the indicator function $I(\text{CE})$ is 1 if the credit event has occurred and 0 otherwise.

These default swaps have several variants. For instance, the **first-of-basket-to-default swap** gives the protection buyer the right to deliver *one and only one* defaulted security out of a basket of selected securities. Because the protection buyer has more choices among a basket instead of just one reference credit, this type of protection will be more expensive than a single credit swap, all else kept equal. The price of protection also depends on the correlation between credit events. The lower the correlation, the more expensive the swap.

Example 22-2: FRM Exam 2002—Question 88

A credit default swap is an instrument that can be best characterized as

a) Any swap that has one or more parties in default

b) A swap that can only be valued against non–investment grade debt securities

c) An option to sell defaulted securities at par value to a third party in exchange for a series of fixed cash flows

d) Any swap that defaults to a third-party guarantor should a party to the swap file for bankruptcy protection

---

Example 22-3: FRM Exam 1999—Question 122

A portfolio manager holds a default swap to hedge an AA corporate bond position. If the counterparty to the default swap is acquired by the bond issuer, then the default swap

a) Increases in value

b) Decreases in value

c) Decreases in value only if the corporate bond is downgraded

d) Is unchanged in value

Example 22-4: FRM Exam 2000—Question 39

A portfolio consists of one (long) $100 million asset and a default protection contract on this asset. The probability of default over the next year is 10% for the asset and 20% for the counterparty that wrote the default protection. The joint probability of default for the asset and the contract counterparty is 3%. Estimate the expected loss on this portfolio due to credit defaults over the next year, with a 40% recovery rate on the asset and a 0% recovery rate for the counterparty.

a) $3.0 million

b) $2.2 million

c) $1.8 million

d) None of the above

22.2.2 Total-Return Swaps

A **total-return swap** (TRS) is a contract where one party, called the protection buyer, makes a series of payments linked to the total return on a reference asset. Such swaps are also called **asset swaps**. In exchange, the protection seller makes a series of payments tied to a reference rate, such as the yield on an equivalent Treasury issue (or LIBOR) plus a spread. If the price of the asset goes down, the protection buyer receives a payment from the counterparty; if the price goes up, a payment is due in the other direction. The structure of this swap is described in Figure 22-2.

This type of swap is tied to changes in the market value of the underlying asset and provides protection against credit risk in a mark-to-market (MTM) framework. The TRS removes all the economic risk of the underlying asset without selling it.

FIGURE 22-2 Total Return Swap

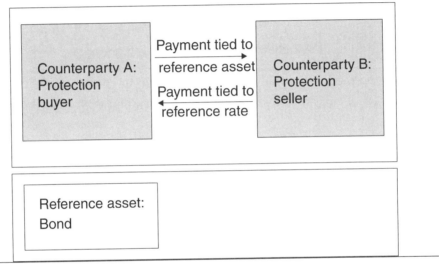

Example

Suppose that a bank, call it bank A, has made a $100 million loan to company XYZ at a fixed rate of 10%. The bank can hedge its exposure by entering a TRS with counterparty B, whereby it promises to pay the interest on the loan plus the change in the market value of the loan in exchange for LIBOR plus 50 bp. If the market value of the loan increases, the bank has to make a greater payment. Otherwise, its payment will decrease, possibly becoming negative.

Say that LIBOR is currently at 9% and that after one year, the value of the loan drops from $100 to $95 million. The *net* obligation from bank A is the sum of

- Outflow of $10\% \times \$100 = \$10$ million, for the loan's interest payment
- Inflow of $9.5\% \times \$100 = \$9.5$ million, for the reference payment
- Outflow of $\frac{(95-100)}{100}\% \times \$100 = -\$5$ million, for the movement in the loan's value

This sums to a net receipt of $-10 + 9.5 - (-5) = \$4.5$ million. Bank A has been able to offset the change in the economic value of this loan by a gain on the TRS.

22.2.3 Credit Spread Forwards and Options

These instruments are derivatives whose value is tied to an underlying credit spread between a risky and a risk-free bond.

In a **credit spread forward contract**, the buyer receives the difference between the credit spread at maturity and an agreed-upon spread, if positive. Conversely, a payment is made if the difference is negative. An example of the formula for the cash payment is

$$\text{Payment} = (S - F) \times \text{MD} \times \text{Notional} \qquad (22.2)$$

where MD is the modified duration, S is the prevailing spread, and F is the agreed-upon spread. Alternatively, this could be expressed in terms of prices:

$$\text{Payment} = [P(y + F, \tau) - P(y + S, \tau)] \times \text{Notional} \qquad (22.3)$$

where y is the yield to maturity of an equivalent Treasury, and $P(y + S, \tau)$ is the present value of the security with τ years to expiration, discounted at y plus a spread. Note that if $S > F$, the payment will be positive, as in the previous expression.

In a **credit spread option contract**, the buyer pays a premium in exchange for the right to "put" any increase in the spread to the option seller at a predefined maturity:

$$\text{Payment} = \text{Max}(S - K, 0) \times \text{MD} \times \text{Notional} \qquad (22.4)$$

where K is the predefined spread. The purchaser of the option buys credit protection, or the right to put the bond to the seller if it falls in value. The payout formula could also be expressed directly in terms of prices, as in Equation (22.3).

Example

A credit spread option has a notional of \$100 million with a maturity of 1 year. The underlying security is an 8% 10-year bond issued by the corporation XYZ. The current spread is 150 bp against 10-year Treasuries. The option is European type with a strike of 160 bp.

Assume that, at expiration, Treasury yields have moved from 6.5% to 6% and the credit spread has widened to 180 bp. The price of an 8% coupon, 9-year semiannual bond discounted at $y + S = 6 + 1.8 = 7.8\%$ is \$101.276. The price of the same bond discounted at $y + K = 6 + 1.6 = 7.6\%$ is \$102.574. Using the notional amount, the payout is $(102.574 - 101.276)/100 \times \$100,000,000 = \$1,297,237$.

22.2.4   Credit-Linked Notes

Credit-linked notes are not stand-alone derivatives contracts but rather combine a regular coupon-paying note with some credit risk feature. The goal is generally to increase the yield paid to the investor in exchange for the investor taking some credit risk. The simplest form is a corporate, or credit-sensitive, bond.

A general example is provided in Figure 22-3. The investor makes an up-front payment that represents the par value of the credit-linked note. A trustee then invests the funds in a top-rated investment and takes a short position in a credit default swap. The investment could be an AAA-rated Fannie Mae agency note, for instance, that pays LIBOR plus a spread of Y bp. The credit default swap is sold by a provider—for example, a bank—for an additional annual receipt of X bp. The total regular payment to the investor is then LIBOR $+ Y + X$. In return for this higher yield, the investor must be willing to lose some of the principal should a default event occur.

FIGURE 22-3 Credit-Linked Note

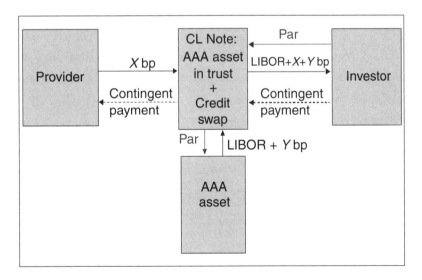

More generally, credit-linked notes can have exposure to one or more credit risks and increase the yield through leverage. The downside risk may be limited through the features described in Table 22-3.

These structures offer various trade-offs between risk and return. "Asset-backed securities" could lose up to the whole initial investment. The payoffs on "compound credit" notes are linked to various credits and can lose only the amount corresponding to the first credit's default. "Principal protection" notes have their principal guaranteed. "Enhanced asset return" notes have a predetermined maximum loss.

TABLE 22-3 Types of Credit-Linked Notes

Type	Maximum Loss
Asset-backed	Initial investment
Compound credit	Amount from first note's default
Principal protection	None on the principal
Enhanced asset return	Predetermined

Example 22-5: FRM Exam 1999—Question 144

Which of the following is a type of credit derivative?
 I. A put option on a corporate bond
 II. A total return swap on a loan portfolio
III. A note that pays an enhanced yield in the case of a bond downgrade
IV. A put option on an off-the-run Treasury bond
a) I, II, and III
b) II and III only
c) II only
d) All of the above

Example 22-6: FRM Exam 1998—Question 26

The BIS considers all of the following products to be credit derivatives *except*
a) Credit-linked notes
b) Total-return swaps
c) Credit spread options
d) Callable floating-rate notes

Example 22-7: FRM Exam 2000—Question 33

Which one of the following statements is *most* correct?
a) Payment in a total-return swap is contingent upon a future credit event.
b) Investing in a risky (credit-sensitive) bond is similar to investing in a risk-free bond plus selling a credit default swap.
c) In the first-to-default swap, the default event is a default on two or more assets in the basket.
d) Payment in a credit swap is contingent only upon the bankruptcy of the counterparty.

Example 22-8: FRM Exam 1999—Question 114

In the first-to-default swap, the default event is a default on

a) Any one of the assets in the basket

b) All of the assets in the basket

c) Two or more assets in the basket

d) None of the above

Example 22-9: FRM Exam 1998—Question 46

Company A and company B enter into a trade agreement in which company A will periodically pay all cash flows and capital gains arising from bond X to company B. On the same dates company B will pay company A LIBOR + 50 bp plus any decrease in the market value of bond X. What type of trade is this?

a) A total-return swap

b) A fixed-income-linked swap

c) An inverse floater

d) An interest rate swap

Example 22-10: FRM Exam 2000—Question 61

(*Complex—use the valuation formula with prices*) A credit spread option has a notional amount of $50 million with a maturity of 1 year. The underlying security is a 10-year, semiannual bond with a 7% coupon and a $1,000 face value. The current spread is 120 bp against 10-year Treasuries. The option is a European option with a strike of 130 bp. If at expiration, Treasury yields have moved from 6% to 6.3% and the credit spread has widened to 150 bp, what will be the payout to the buyer of this credit spread option?

a) $587,352

b) $611,893

c) $622,426

d) $639,023

Example 22-11: FRM Exam 2000—Question 62

Bank One has made a $200 million loan to a software company at a fixed rate of 12%. The bank wants to hedge its exposure by entering into a total-return swap with a counterparty, Interloan Co., in which Bank One promises to pay the interest on the loan plus the change in the market value of the loan in exchange for LIBOR plus 40 bp. If after one year the market value of the loan has decreased by 3% and LIBOR is 11%, what will be the net obligation of Bank One?

a) Net receipt of $4.8 million

b) Net payment of $4.8 million

c) Net receipt of $5.2 million

d) Net payment of $5.2 million

22.3 Pricing and Hedging Credit Derivatives

We have developed tools to price and hedge credit risk, and these can be extended to credit derivatives. Credit derivatives, however, are complex instruments, as they combine market risk and the joint credit risk of the reference credit and of the counterparty. In general, we need a long list of variables to price these derivatives, including the term structure of risk-free rates, of the reference credit, and of the counterparty credit, as well as the joint distribution of default and recoveries. Practitioners use shortcuts that typically ignore the default risk of the counterparty.

22.3.1 Methods

The first approach is the *actuarial approach*, which uses historical default rates to infer the objective expected loss on the credit derivative. For instance, we could use a transition matrix and estimates of recovery rates to assess the actuarial expected loss. This process, however, does not rely on a risk-neutral approach and will not lead to a *fair* price, which includes a risk premium. Neither does it provide a method to hedge the exposure. It only helps to build up a reserve that, in large samples, should be sufficient to absorb the average loss.

The second approach relies on *bond credit spreads* and requires a full yield curve of liquid bonds for the underlying credit. This approach allows us to derive a fair price for the credit derivative, as well as a hedging mechanism, which uses traded bonds for the underlying credit.

The third approach relies on *equity prices* and requires a liquid market for the common stock for the underlying credit as well as information about the structure of liabilities. The Merton model, for instance, allows us to derive a fair price for the credit derivative, as well as a hedging mechanism, which uses the common stock of the underlying credit.

22.3.2 Example: Credit Default Swap

We are asked to value a credit default swap on a $10 million two-year agreement, whereby A (the protection buyer) agrees to pay B (the guarantor, or protection seller) a fixed annual fee in exchange for protection against default of two-year bonds XYZ. The payout will be the notional times $(100 - P_B)$, where P_B is the price of the bond at expiration, if the credit event occurs. Currently, XYZ bonds are rated A and trade at 6.60%. The two-year T-note trades at 6.00%.

Actuarial Method

This method computes the credit exposure from the current credit rating and the probability that the company XYZ will default. We use a simplified transition matrix, shown in Table 22-4.

TABLE 22-4 Credit Ratings Transition Probabilities

Starting State	Ending State				Total
	A	B	C	D	
A	0.90	0.07	0.02	0.01	1.00
B	0.05	0.90	0.03	0.02	1.00
C	0	0.10	0.85	0.05	1.00
D	0	0	0	1.00	1.00

Starting from an A rating, the company could default

- In year 1, with a probability of $P(D_1 \mid A_0) = 1\%$
- In year 2, with a probability of $P(D_2 \mid A_1)P(A_1) + P(D_2 \mid B_1)P(B_1) + P(D_2 \mid C_1)P(C_1) = 0.01 \times 0.90 + 0.02 \times 0.07 + 0.05 \times 0.02 = 1.14\%$

If the recovery rate is 60%, the expected cost is, for the first year, $1\%(1 - 60\%)$, and $1.14\%(1 - 60\%)$ in the second year. Ignoring discounting, the average annual cost is

$$\text{Annual cost} = \$10,000,000 \times (1\% + 1.14\%)/2 \times (1 - 60\%) = \$42,800$$

This approach assumes that the credit rating is appropriate and that the transition probabilities and recovery rates are accurately measured.

Credit Spread Method

Here we compare the yield on the XYZ bond with that on a default-free asset, such as the T-note. If all bonds are treated equally, the bonds must have the same term as the maturity of the option. The annual cost of protection is then

$$\text{Annual cost} = \$10,000,000 \times (6.60\% - 6.00\%) = \$60,000$$

This is higher than the cost from the actuarial approach. The difference can be ascribed to a risk premium, or to liquidity or tax effects.

To hedge the CDS, the protection seller would go short the corporate bond and go long the equivalent Treasury. Any loss on the default swap because of a credit event would be offset by a gain on the hedge. If the company defaults, the protection buyer could deliver the bond to the protection seller, who could in turn deliver the bond to close out the short sale.

Equity Price Method

This method is more involved. We require a measure of the stock market capitalization of XYZ, of the total value of liabilities, and of the volatility of equity prices.

Using the notations of the chapter describing the Merton model, the fair value of the put is

$$\text{Put} = -V[N(-d_1)] + Ke^{-r\tau}[N(-d_2)] \tag{22.5}$$

where d_1 and d_2 depend on V, K, r, σ_V, and the tenor of the put, τ. We could, for example, have a "fair" put option value of \$120,000, which, again ignoring discounting, translates into an annual cost of \$60,000.

To hedge, the protection seller would go short the stock, in the amount of

$$\frac{\partial \text{Put}}{\partial V} \times \frac{\partial V}{\partial S} = -[N(-d_1)] \times \frac{1}{N(d_1)} = -[1 - N(d_1)] \times \frac{1}{N(d_1)} = 1 - \frac{1}{N(d_1)} \tag{22.6}$$

which indeed is negative, plus an appropriate position in the risk-free bond.

Example 22-12: FRM Exam 2002—Question 131

Which of the following transactions could be entered into to decrease credit risk with a specific counterparty?

a) Buy a call option on the counterparty's common stock.
b) Sell a put option on the counterparty's common stock.
c) Go long shares of the counterparty's common stock.
d) Go short shares of the counterparty's common stock.

Example 22-13: FRM Exam 1999—Question 147

Which of the following are needed to value a credit swap?

I. Correlation structure for the default and recovery rates of the swap counter-party and reference credit

II. The swap or treasury yield curve

III. Reference credit spread curve over swap or treasury rates

IV. Swap counterparty credit spread curve over swap or treasury rates

a) II, III, and IV

b) I, III, and IV

c) II and III

d) All of the above

Example 22-14: FRM Exam 1999—Question 135

The Widget Company has outstanding debt of three different maturities as outlined in the table.

	Widget Company Bonds		Corresponding U.S. Treasury Bonds	
Maturity	Price	Coupon (sa 30/360)	Price	Coupon (sa 30/360)
1 year	100	7.00%	100	6.00%
5 years	100	8.50%	100	6.50%
10 years	100	9.50%	100	7.00%

All Widget Co. debt ranks pari passu, all its debt contains cross-default provisions, and the recovery value for each bond is 20. The correct price for a 1-year credit default swap (sa 30/360) with the Widget Co., with a 9.5% 10-year bond as a reference asset, is

a) 1.0% per annum

b) 2.0% per annum

c) 2.5% per annum

d) 3.5% per annum

22.4   Pros and Cons of Credit Derivatives

The rapid growth of the credit derivatives market is the best testimony of their use-fulness. These instruments are superior risk management tools, allowing the *transfer of risks* to those who can bear them best. Many observers, including bank regula-tors, have stated that credit risk diversification using credit derivatives helped banks to weather the recession of 2001 and its accompanying increase in defaults, without apparent major problems. This period witnessed the largest corporate bankruptcies ever (WorldCom and Enron) and sovereign default (Argentina), with barely a ripple in global financial markets. The losses have been spread widely, saving the major U.S. banks from the catastrophic failures typical of previous downturns. In the case of Enron, for instance, exposures amounting to around $2.7 billion were transferred by credit derivatives.

This is confirmed by a 2003 survey by the British Bankers's Association (BBA). The survey reveals that the banking sector accounts for 51% of protection buyers but only 38% of protection sellers. In contrast, insurance companies account for only 1% of protection buyers versus 20% of protection sellers. Hedge funds and securities firms, on the other hand, are fairly balanced, each with about 16% of protection buyers and sellers. These statistics indicate that credit risk has been moved from the banking sector toward the insurance industry.

Credit derivatives have another useful function, which is *price discovery*. By creating or extending a market for credit risk, this new market gives market observers a better measure of the cost of credit risk.

Credit derivatives also allow *transactional efficiency*, because they have lower transaction costs than in the cash markets. Counterparties can also take advantage of disparities in the pricing of loans and bonds, making both markets more efficient.

On the downside, this market may be relatively *illiquid*. This is because, unlike interest rate swaps, there is no standardization of the reference credit. By definition, credit risk is specific.

Also, the market still uses *various valuation methods*. This is due to the short supply of data on essential parameters, such as default probabilities and recovery rates. As a result, there is less agreement on the fair valuation of credit derivatives compared with other derivatives instruments.

Credit derivatives also introduce a new element of risk, which is *legal risk*. Indeed, parties can sometimes squabble over the definition of a credit event. Such disagreement occurred during the Russian default as well as in notable debt restructurings and demergers. No doubt this explains why bank regulators are watching the growth of this market with some concern. The question is whether these contracts will be fully effective with widespread defaults.

This is especially important because this market has evolved from *regulatory arbitrage*, that is, attempts to defeat onerous capital requirements mandated by bank regulators. Commercial banks have systematically lowered their capital requirements by laying off loan credit risk through credit derivatives. This can be advantageous if an economically equivalent credit exposure has lower capital requirements (we will discuss regulatory capital requirements in a later chapter). Whether this is a benefit or drawback depends on one's perspective.

Example 22-15: FRM Exam 2000—Question 30

Which one of the following statements is *not* an application of credit derivatives for banks?
a) Reduction in economic and regulatory capital usage
b) Reduction in counterparty concentrations
c) Management of the risk profile of the loan portfolio
d) Credit protection of private banking deposits

22.5 Answers to Chapter Examples

Example 22-1: FRM Exam 1998—Question 44

c) Credit derivatives certainly do not prevent the credit events from happening.

Example 22-2: FRM Exam 2002—Question 88

c) A CDS is an option to exchange securities at par value even if their market value is less, due to a credit event.

Example 22-3: FRM Exam 1999—Question 122

b) This is an interesting question demonstrating that the credit risk of the underlying asset is exchanged for that of the swap counterparty. The swap is now worthless; if the underlying credit defaults, the counterparty will default as well (since it is the same).

Example 22-4: FRM Exam 2000—Question 39

c) The only state of the world with a loss is a default on the asset jointly with a default of the guarantor. This has a probability of 3%. The expected loss is $100,000,000 \times 0.03 \times (1 - 40\%) = \$1.8$ million.

Example 22-5: FRM Exam 1999—Question 144

a) Parts I, II, and III are correct. An option on a T-bond has no credit component.

Example 22-6: FRM Exam 1998—Question 26

d) The first three instruments have a major credit component. Callable FRNs are not considered credit derivatives. The call option is primarily an interest rate option.

Example 22-7: FRM Exam 2000—Question 33

b) Answer a) is not correct because payment is simply a function of market variables (this is not a credit default swap). Answer c) is incorrect because the default event in this case is the first default. Answer d) is incorrect because a credit event is more general than simple bankruptcy. Answer b) says that a risky bond is the sum of a risk-free bond plus a short position in a credit default swap.

Example 22-8: FRM Exam 1999—Question 114

a) The default event is triggered when there is a first default on *any* of the assets in the basket.

Example 22-9: FRM Exam 1998—Question 46

a) The payments are linked to the total return on bond X.

Example 22-10: FRM Exam 2000—Question 61

c) We need to value the bond with remaining semiannual payments for nine years using two yields, $y + S = 6.30 + 1.50 = 7.80\%$ and $y + K = 6.30 + 1.30 = 7.60\%$. This gives $948.95 and $961.40, respectively. The total payout is then $50,000,000 \times$ [$961.40 - $948.95]/$1000 = $622,424.

Example 22-11: FRM Exam 2000—Question 62

a) The net payment is an outflow of $12\% - 3\%$ minus inflow of $11\% + 0.4\%$, which is a net receipt of -2.4%. Applied to the notional of $200 million, this gives a receipt of $4.8 million.

Example 22-12: FRM Exam 2002—Question 131

d) Selling the shares of the counterparty's equity would provide a gain if the counterparty defaults, because the stock price would then drop, creating a profit on the short sale.

Example 22-13: FRM Exam 1999—Question 147

d) As a first approximation, the reference credit spread curve may be enough. To be complete, however, we also need information about the credit risk of the swap counterparty, the treasury curve (for discounting), and correlations. The correlation structure enters the pricing through the expectation of the product of the default and loss given default.

Example 22-14: FRM Exam 1999—Question 135

a) Because all bonds rank equally, all default occur at the same time and have the same loss given default. Therefore, the cash flow on the one-year credit swap can be replicated (including any risk premium) by going long the one-year Widget bond and short the one-year T-bond.

Example 22-15: FRM Exam 2000—Question 30

d) Credit derivatives are used to reduce regulatory capital usage and counterparty concentrations and to manage the risk profile of the loan portfolio. Private banking deposits are bank liabilities, not assets.

Chapter 23

Managing Credit Risk

Previous chapters have explained how to estimate default probabilities, credit exposures, and recovery rates for individual credits. We now turn to the measurement and management of credit risk for the overall portfolio.

In the past, credit risk was measured on a stand-alone basis, in terms of a "yes" or "no" decision by a credit officer. Some consideration was given to portfolio effects through very crude credit limits at the overall level. Portfolio theory, however, teaches us that risk should be viewed in the context of the contribution to the total risk of a portfolio, not in isolation. Diversification creates what is perhaps the only "free lunch" in finance: The pricing of risk is markedly lower when portfolio effects are considered.

The revolution in risk management is now spreading from the portfolio measurement of market risk to credit risk. This is a result of a number of developments. At the top of the list are technological advances that now enable us to aggregate financial risk in close to real time. Second, the market has witnessed an exponential growth in new products, such as credit derivatives, which allow better management of credit risk. Finally, developments in government policies and financial markets are leading to greater emphasis on credit risk. With the European Monetary Union (EMU), exchange rate risk has disappeared within the Eurozone. This has transformed currency risk into credit risk for European government bonds.[1] Thus, French government debt now carries credit risk, like debt issued by the state of California. Correspondingly,

---

[1]In the past there was very little credit risk on European government debt. Although governments could have defaulted on their national-currency–denominated debt, it was easier to create inflation to expropriate bondholders. Some have done so with a vengeance, such as Italy. Governments do not have this option any more, as the value of the new currency, the euro, is now in the hands of the European Central Bank. Indeed, Chapter 19 showed that the credit rating of countries is lower when the debt is denominated in foreign currency rather than in the local currency.

the increasing depth and liquidity of EMU corporate bond markets is leading to a rapid expansion of this market.

Section 23.1 introduces the distribution of credit losses. This has two major features. The first is the expected credit loss, which is essential information for pricing and reserving purposes, as explained in Section 23.2. The second component is the unexpected credit loss, or worst deviation from the expected loss at some confidence level. Section 23.3 shows how this credit value at risk (CVAR), like market VAR, can be used to determine the amount of capital necessary to support a position. The pricing of loans should cover not only expected losses, but also the remuneration of the economic capital set aside to cover the unexpected loss. Finally, Section 23.4 provides an overview of recently developed credit risk models, including CreditMetrics, CreditRisk+, the KMV model, and Credit Portfolio View.

23.1 Measuring the Distribution of Credit Losses

The previous chapters provided a detailed analysis of default probabilities, credit exposures, and recovery rates. We can now pool this information to measure the distribution of losses due to credit risk. For simplicity, we consider only losses in **default mode** (DM), that is, losses due to defaults instead of changes in market values.

For one instrument, the potential credit loss is

$$\text{Credit loss} = b \times \text{Credit exposure} \times \text{LGD} \qquad (23.1)$$

which involves the random variable b that takes on the value of 1 with probability of default (PD) p, when the discrete state of default occurs; the credit exposure, also called exposure at default (EAD); and the loss given default (LGD).

For a portfolio of N counterparties, the loss is

$$\text{Credit loss} = \sum_{i=1}^{N} b_i \times \text{CE}_i \times \text{LGD}_i \qquad (23.2)$$

where CE_i is now the total credit exposure to counterparty i, across all contracts and taking into account netting agreements.

The distribution of credit loss is quite complex. Typically, information about credit risk is described by the **net replacement value** (NRV), which is

$$\text{NRV} = \sum_{i=1}^{N} \text{CE}_i \qquad (23.3)$$

evaluated at the current time. This is the most that could be lost if all parties defaulted at the same time and if there was no recovery. This is not very informative, however. The NRV, which is often disclosed in annual reports, is equivalent to using notionals to describe the risks of derivatives portfolios. It does not take into account the probability of default or correlations across defaults and exposures.

Chapter 18 gave an example of a loss distribution for a simple portfolio with three counterparties. This example was tractable, as we could enumerate all possible states. In general, we need to consider many more credit events. We also need to account for movements and co-movements in risk factors, which drive exposures, uncertain recovery rates, and correlations among defaults. This can be done only with the help of *Monte Carlo simulations*. Once this is performed for the whole portfolio, we obtain a distribution of credit losses on a target date. Figure 23-1 describes a typical distribution.

FIGURE 23-1 Distribution of Credit Losses

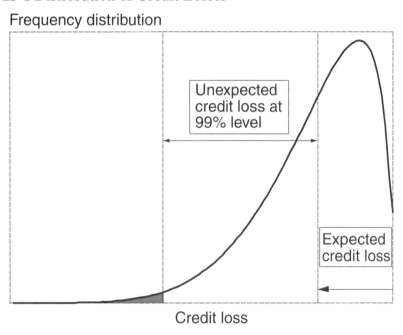

This leads to a number of fundamental observations.

■ **Distribution.** The distribution of credit losses is *highly skewed to the left,* in contrast to that of market risk factors, which is in general roughly symmetrical. This credit distribution is similar to a short position in an option, as explained in the

Merton model, which equates a risky bond to a risk-free bond plus a short position in an option.

■ **Expected credit loss (ECL).** The **expected credit loss** represents the average credit loss. The *pricing* of the portfolio should be such that it covers the expected loss. In other words, the price should be advantageous enough to offset average credit losses. In the case of a bond, the price should be low enough, or the yield high enough, to compensate for expected losses. In the case of a derivative, the bank that takes on the credit risk should factor the expected loss into the pricing of its product. Loan loss reserves should be accumulated as a **credit provision** against expected losses.

■ **Worst credit loss (WCL).** The **worst credit loss** represents the loss that will not be exceeded at some level of confidence. Like a VAR figure, the unexpected credit loss (UCL) is the deviation from the expected loss. The institution should have enough capital to cover the unexpected loss. As we have seen before, the UCL depends on the distribution of joint default rates, among other factors. Notably, the dispersion in the distribution narrows as the number of credits increases and when correlations among defaults decrease.

■ **Marginal contribution to risk.** The distribution of credit losses can also be used to analyze the incremental effect of a proposed trade on the total portfolio risk. As in the case of market risk, individual credits should be evaluated on the basis not only of their stand-alone risk, but also of their contribution to the portfolio risk. For the same expected return, a trade that lowers risk should be preferable over one that adds to the portfolio risk. Such trade-offs can be made only with a formal measurement of portfolio credit risk.

■ **Remuneration of capital.** The measure of worst credit loss is also important for the pricing of credit-sensitive instruments. Say the distribution has an ECL of $1 billion and UCL of $5 billion. The bank then needs to set aside $5 billion just to cover deviations from expected credit losses. This equity capital, however, will require remuneration. So, the pricing of loans should cover not only expected losses, but also the remuneration of this economic capital. This is what we call a *risk premium* and explains why observed credit spreads are larger than necessary simply to cover actuarial losses.

Example 23-1: FRM Exam 1998—Question 41

Credit provisions should be taken to cover all of the following *except*

a) Nonperforming loans

b) The expected loss of a loan portfolio

c) An amount equal to the VAR of the credit portfolio

d) Excess credit profits earned during below-average-loss years

---

23.2   Measuring Expected Credit Loss

23.2.1   Expected Loss over a Target Horizon

For pricing purposes, we need to measure the expected credit loss, which is

$$E[\text{CL}] = \int f(b, \text{CE}, \text{LGD})(b \times \text{CE} \times \text{LGD}) \, db \, d\text{CE} \, d\text{LGD} \qquad (23.4)$$

If the random variables are independent, the joint density reduces to the product of densities. We have

$$E[\text{CL}] = \left[\int f(b)(b) \, db\right] \left[\int f(\text{CE})(\text{CE}) \, d\text{CE}\right] \left[\int f(\text{LGD})(\text{LGD}) \, d\text{LGD}\right]$$
$$(23.5)$$

which is the product of the expected values. In other words,

$$\text{Expected credit loss} = \text{Prob[default]} \times E[\text{Credit exposure}] \times E[\text{LGD}] \qquad (23.6)$$

As an example, the expected credit loss on a BBB-rated $100 million five-year bond with 47% recovery rate is $2.28\% \times \$100,000,000 \times (1 - 47\%) = \$1.2$ million. Note that this expected loss is the same whether the bank has one $100 million exposure or one hundred exposures worth $1 million each. The distributions, however, will be very different with more credits.

Example 23-2: FRM Exam 1998—Question 39

Calculate the one-year expected loss of a $100 million portfolio comprising 10 B-rated issuers. Assume that the one-year probability of default for each issuer is 6% and the average recovery value for each issuer is 40%.

a) $2.4 million

b) $3.6 million

c) $24 million

d) $36 million

Example 23-3: FRM Exam 1999—Question 120

Which loan is more risky? Assume that the obligors are rated the same, are from the same industry, and have more or less the same-sized idiosyncratic risk.
a) $1,000,000 with 50% recovery rate
b) $1,000,000 with no collateral
c) $4,000,000 with 40% recovery rate
d) $4,000,000 with 60% recovery rate

23.2.2 The Time Profile of Expected Loss

So far, we have focused on a fixed horizon, say a year. For pricing purposes, however, we need to consider the total credit loss over the life of the asset. This should involve the time profile of the exposure, the probability of default, and the discounting factor. Define PV_t as the present value of a dollar paid at time t.

The **present value of expected credit losses** (PVECL) is obtained as the sum of the discounted expected credit losses:

$$\text{PVECL} = \sum_t E[\text{CL}_t] \times \text{PV}_t = \sum_t [k_t \times \text{ECE}_t \times (1 - f)] \times \text{PV}_t \qquad (23.7)$$

where the probability of default is $k_t = S_{t-1}\, d_t$, or the probability of defaulting at time t, conditional on not having defaulted before.

Alternatively, we could simplify by using the average default probability and average exposure over the life of the asset:

$$\text{PVECL}_A = \text{Ave}[k_t] \times \text{Ave}[\text{ECE}_t] \times (1 - f) \times \left[\sum_t \text{PV}_t\right] \qquad (23.8)$$

This approach, however, may not be as good an approximation when default risk and exposure profile are correlated over time. For example, currency swaps with highly rated counterparties have an exposure and a default probability that increase with time. Due to this correlation, taking the product of the averages understates credit risk. In other cases, it could overstate credit risk.

An even simpler approach, when ECE is constant, considers the final maturity T only, using the cumulative default rate c_T and the discount factor PV_T:

$$\text{PVECL}_F = c_T \times \text{ECE} \times (1 - f) \times \text{PV}_T \qquad (23.9)$$

Table 23-1 shows how to compute the PVECL. We consider a five-year interest rate swap with a counterparty initially rated BBB and a notional of $100 million. The discount factor is 6% and the recovery rate 45%. We also assume that default can occur only at the end of each year.

TABLE 23-1 Computation of Expected Credit Loss for a Swap

Year	P(default) (%)			Exposure	LGD	Discount	Total
t	c_t	d_t	k_t	ECE_t	$(1 - f)$	PV_t	$PVECL_t$
1	0.22	0.220	0.220	$1,660,000	0.55	0.9434	$1,895
2	0.54	0.321	0.320	$1,497,000	0.55	0.8900	$2,345
3	0.88	0.342	0.340	$1,069,000	0.55	0.8396	$1,678
4	1.55	0.676	0.670	$554,000	0.55	0.7921	$1,617
5	2.28	0.741	0.730	$0	0.55	0.7473	$0
Total			2.280			4.2124	$7,535
Average			0.456	$956,000			
$PVECL_A$			0.456	×$956,000	×0.55	×4.2124	= $10,100

In the first column, we have the cumulative default probability, c_t, for a BBB-rated credit from years 1 to 5, expressed as a percentage. The second column shows the marginal probability of defaulting during that year, d_t, and the third column shows the probability of defaulting in each year, conditional on not having defaulted before, $k_t = S_{t-1}d_t$. The fourth column reports the end-of-year expected credit exposure, ECE_t. The fifth column shows the constant LGD. The sixth column displays the present value factor, PV_t.

The final column gives the product $[k_t ECE_t (1 - f)PV_t]$. The first entry, for example is 0.220% × $1,660,000 × 0.55 × 0.9434 = $1,895. Summing across years gives $7,535 on a swap with notional of $100 million, or 0.007% of principal. This is very small, less than 1 basis point. So the expected credit loss on an interest rate swap is minuscule. Basically, the expected credit loss is very low due to the small exposure profile. For a regular bond or currency swap, the expected loss is much greater.

The last line shows a shortcut to the measurement of expected credit losses based on averages, from Equation (23.8). The average annual default probability is 0.456. Multiplying by the average exposure, $956,000, the LGD, and the sum of the discount rates gives $10,100. This is on the same order of magnitude as the exact calculation.

Table 23-2 details the computation for a bond assuming a constant exposure of $100 million. The expected credit loss is $1.020 million, about a hundred times larger than for the swap. This is because the exposure is also about a hundred times larger.

As in the previous table, the next line shows results based on averages. Here the expected credit loss is $1.056 million, very close to the exact number, as there is no variation in credit exposures over time.

We could also take the usual shortcut and simply compute an expected credit loss given by the cumulative five-year default rate times $100 million times the loss given default, which is $1.254 million. Discounting to the present, we get $0.937 million, close to the previous result.

TABLE 23-2 Computation of Expected Credit Loss for a Bond

Year	P(default) (%)			Exposure	LGD	Discount	Total
t	c_t	d_t	k_t	ECE_t	$(1-f)$	PV_t	$PVECL_t$
1	0.22	0.220	0.220	$100,000,000	0.55	0.9434	$114,151
2	0.54	0.321	0.320	$100,000,000	0.55	0.8900	$156,639
3	0.88	0.342	0.340	$100,000,000	0.55	0.8396	$157,009
4	1.55	0.676	0.670	$100,000,000	0.55	0.7921	$291,887
5	2.28	0.741	0.730	$100,000,000	0.55	0.7473	$300,024
Total			2.280			4.2124	$1,019,710
Average			0.456	$100,000,000			
$PVECL_A$			0.456	×$100,000,000	×0.55	×4.2124	= $1,056,461
$PVECL_F$	2.280			×$100,000,000	×0.55	×0.7473	= $ 937,062

23.3   Measuring Credit VAR

The other feature of the credit loss distribution is the **credit VAR**, defined as the unexpected credit loss at some confidence level. Using the measure of credit loss in Equation (23.1), we construct a distribution of the credit loss $f(CL)$ over a target horizon. At a given confidence c, the worst credit loss (WCL) is defined such that

$$1 - c = \int_{WCL}^{\infty} f(x)dx. \tag{23.10}$$

The credit VAR is then measured as the deviation from ECL

$$CVAR = WCL - ECL. \tag{23.11}$$

This CVAR number should be viewed as the economic capital to be held as a buffer against *unexpected* losses. Its application is fundamentally different from the *expected* credit loss, which is additive across obligors and can be aggregated over time.

Instead, the CVAR is measured over a target horizon, say one year, which is deemed sufficient for the bank to take corrective actions should credit problems start to develop. Corrective action can take the form of exposure reduction or adjustment of economic capital, all of which take considerably longer than the typical horizon for market risk.

Once credit VAR is measured, it can be managed. The portfolio manager can examine the trades that contribute most to CVAR. If these trades are not particularly profitable, they should be eliminated.

The portfolio approach can also reveal correlations between different types of risk. For example, **wrong-way trades** are positions where the exposure is negatively correlated with the probability of default. Before the Asian crisis, for instance, many U.S. banks had lent to Asian companies in dollars, or entered equivalent swaps. Many of these Asian companies did not have dollar revenues but instead were speculating, reinvesting the funds in the local currency. When currencies devalued, the positions were in-the-money for the U.S. banks, but could not be collected because the counterparties had defaulted.

Conversely, **right-way trades** are those where increasing exposure is associated with a lower probability of counterparty default. This occurs when the transaction is a *hedge* for the counterparty—for instance, when a loss on its side of the trade offsets an operating gain.

Example 23-4: FRM Exam 2002—Question 74

Following is a set of identical transactions. Assuming all counterparties have the same credit rating, which transaction should preferably be executed?
a) Buying gas from a trading firm
b) Buying gas from a gas producer
c) Buying gas from a distributor
d) Indifferent between a), b), and c).

Example 23-5: FRM Exam 1998—Question 13

A risk analyst is trying to estimate the credit VAR (CVAR) for a risky bond. CVAR is defined as the maximum unexpected loss at a confidence level of 99.9% over a one-month horizon. Assume that the bond is valued at $1,000,000 one month forward, and the one-year cumulative default probability is 2% for this bond. What is the best estimate of the CVAR for the bond, assuming no recovery?
a) $20,000
b) $1,682
c) $998,318
d) $0

Example 23-6: FRM Exam 1998—Question 10

A risk analyst is trying to estimate the credit VAR for a portfolio of two risky bonds. The credit VAR is defined as the maximum unexpected loss at a confidence level of 99.9% over a one-month horizon. Assume that each bond is valued at $500,000 one month forward, and the one-year cumulative default probability is 2% for each of these bonds. What is the best estimate of the credit VAR for this portfolio, assuming no default correlation and no recovery?

a) $841
b) $1,682
c) $998,318
d) $498,318

23.4 Portfolio Credit Risk Models

23.4.1 Approaches to Portfolio Credit Risk Models

Portfolio credit risk models can be classified according to their approaches.

Top-down versus Bottom-up Models

Top-down models group credit risks using single statistics. They aggregate many sources of risk viewed as *homogeneous* into an overall portfolio risk, without going into the details of individual transactions. This approach is appropriate for retail portfolios with large numbers of credits, but less so for corporate or sovereign loans. Even within retail portfolios, top-down models may hide specific risks, by industry or geographic location.

 Bottom-up models account for features of each instrument. This approach is most similar to the structural decomposition of positions that characterizes market VAR systems. It is appropriate for corporate and capital market portfolios. Bottom-up models are also most useful for taking corrective action, because the risk structure can be reverse-engineered to modify the risk profile.

Risk Definitions

Default-mode models consider only outright default as a credit event. Hence any movement in the market value of the bond or in the credit rating is irrelevant.

 Mark-to-market models consider changes in market values and ratings changes, including defaults. These fair market value models provide a better assessment of risk, which is consistent with the holding period defined in terms of the liquidation period.

Conditional versus Unconditional Models of Default Probability

Conditional models incorporate changing macroeconomic factors into the default probability through a functional relationship. Notably, we observe that the rate of default increases in a recession.

Unconditional models have fixed default probabilities and tend to focus on borrower- or factor-specific information. Some changes in the environment, however, can be allowed by manually changing the input parameters.

Structural versus Reduced-Form Models of Default Correlations

Structural models explain correlations by the joint movements of assets, for example, stock prices. For each obligor, this price is the random variable that represents movements in default probabilities.

Reduced-form models explain correlations by assuming a particular functional relationship between the default probability and "background factors." For example, the correlation between defaults across obligors can be modeled by the loadings on common risk factors, say, industrial and country.

Table 23-3 summarizes the essential features of portfolio credit risk models in the industry. The four models are described next.

TABLE 23-3 Comparison of Credit Risk Models

	CreditMetrics	CreditRisk+	KMV	CreditPf.View
Originator	J.P. Morgan	Credit Suisse	KMV	McKinsey
Model type	Bottom-up	Bottom-up	Bottom-up	Top-down
Risk definition	Market value (MTM)	Default losses (DM)	Default losses (MTM/DM)	Market value (MTM)
Risk drivers	Asset values	Default rates	Asset values	Macro factors
Credit events	Rating change/ default	Default	Continuous default prob.	Rating change/ default
Probability	Unconditional	Unconditional	Conditional	Conditional
Volatility	Constant	Variable	Variable	Variable
Correlation	From equities (structural)	Default process (reduced-form)	From equities (structural)	From macro factors
Recovery rates	Random	Constant within band	Random	Random
Solution	Simulation/ analytic	Analytic	Analytic	Simulation

23.4.2   CreditMetrics

CreditMetrics, published in April 1997 by J.P. Morgan, was one of the first models to measure portfolio credit risk. The system is a "bottom-up" approach where credit risk is driven by movements in bond ratings. The components of the system are described in Figure 23-2.

(1) Measurement of exposure by instrument

This starts from the user's portfolio, decomposing all instruments by their exposure and assessing the effect of market volatility on expected exposures on the target date. The range of covered instruments includes bonds and loans, swaps, receivables, commitments, and letters of credit.

FIGURE 23-2 Structure of CreditMetrics

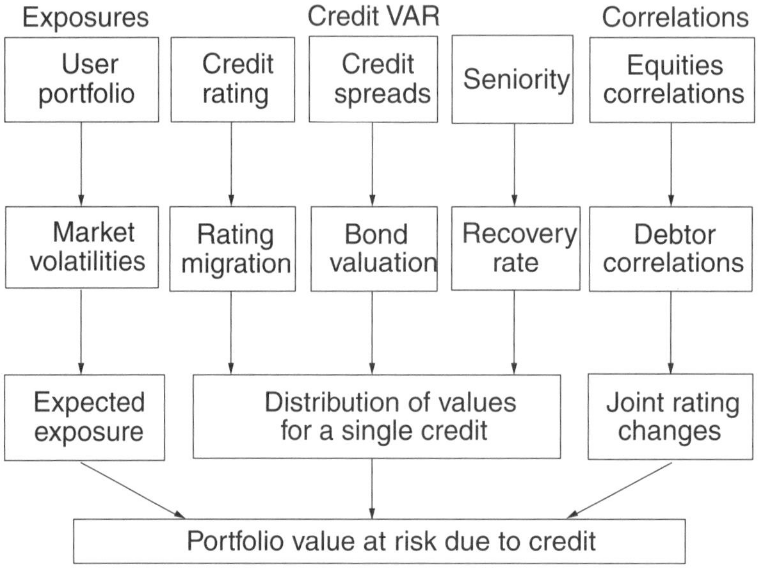

Source: CreditMetrics

(2) Distribution of individual default risk

This step starts with assigning each instrument to a particular credit rating. Credit events are then defined by rating migrations, which include default, through a matrix of migration probabilities. Thus movements in default probabilities are discrete. After the credit event, the instrument is valued using credit spreads for each rating class. In the case of default, the distributions of recovery rates are used from historical data for various seniority classes.

This is illustrated in Figure 23-3. We start from a bond or credit instrument with an initial rating of BBB. Over the horizon, the rating can jump to eight new values, including default. For each rating, the value of the instrument is recomputed—for example, to $109.37 if the rating goes to AAA, or to the recovery value of $51.13 in case of default. Given the state probabilities and associated values, we can compute an expected bond value, which is $107.09, and a standard deviation of $2.99.

FIGURE 23-3 Building the Distribution of Bond Values

		Probability (p_i)	Value (V_i)	Exp. $\Sigma(p_iV_i)$	Var. $\Sigma p_i(V_i - m)^2$
	AAA	0.02%	$109.37	0.02	0.00
	AAA	0.33%	$109.19	0.36	0.01
	AAA	5.95%	$108.66	6.47	0.15
BBB	BBB	86.93%	$107.55	93.49	0.19
	BB	5.30%	$102.02	5.41	1.36
	B	1.17%	$98.10	1.15	0.95
	CCC	0.12%	$83.64	0.10	0.66
	Default	0.18%	$51.13	0.09	5.64

Sum = 100.00% m = $107.09 σ^2 = 8.95
SD = $2.99

(3) Correlations among defaults

Correlations among defaults are inferred from correlations between asset prices. Each obligor is assigned to an industry and a geographical sector, using a factor decomposition. Correlations are inferred from the co-movements of the common risk factors, using a database with some 152 country-industry indices, 28 country indices, and 19 worldwide industry indices.

As an example, company 1 may be such that 90% of its volatility comes from the U.S. chemical industry. Using standardized returns, we can write

$$r_1 = 0.90r_{US,Ch} + k_1\epsilon_1$$

where the residual ϵ is uncorrelated with other variables. Next, company 2 has a 74% weight on the German insurance index and 15% on the German banking index:

$$r_2 = 0.74r_{GE,In} + 0.15r_{GE,Ba} + k_2\epsilon_2$$

The correlation between asset values for the two companies is

$$\rho(r_1, r_2) = (0.90 \times 0.74)\rho(r_{US,Ch}, r_{GE,In}) + (0.90 \times 0.15)\rho(r_{US,Ch}, r_{GE,Ba}) = 0.11$$

CreditMetrics then uses simulations of the joint asset values, assuming a multivariate normal distribution. Each asset value has a standard normal distribution with cutoff points selected to represent the probabilities of changes in credit ratings.

Table 23-4 illustrates the computations for our BBB credit. From Figure 23-3, there is a 0.18% probability of going from BBB into the state of default. We choose z_1 such that the area to its left is $N(z_1) = 0.18\%$. This gives $z_1 = -2.91$. Next, we need to choose z_2 so that the probability of falling between z_1 and z_2 is 0.12%, or that the total left-tail probability is $N(z_2) = 0.18\% + 0.12\% = 0.30\%$. This gives $z_2 = -2.75$, and so on.

TABLE 23-4 Cutoff Values for Simulations

Rating i	Prob. p_i	Cum. Prob. $N(z_i)$	Cutoff z_i
AAA	0.02%	100.00%	
AA	0.33%	99.98%	3.54
A	5.95%	99.65%	2.70
BBB	86.93%	93.70%	1.53
BB	5.30%	6.77%	-1.49
B	1.17%	1.47%	-2.18
CCC	0.12%	0.30%	-2.75
Default	0.18%	0.18%	-2.91

The simulation generates joint assets values that have a multivariate standard normal distribution with the prespecified correlations. Each realization is mapped to a credit rating and a bond value for each obligor. This gives a total value for the portfolio and a distribution of credit losses over an annual horizon.

These simulations can also be used to compute correlations among default events. Because defaults are much less common than rating changes, the correlation is typically much less than the correlation between asset values. CreditMetrics reports that asset correlations in the range of 40% to 60% will typically translate into default correlations of 2% to 4%.[2]

Another drawback of this approach is that it does not integrate credit and market risk. Losses are generated only by changes in credit states, not by market movements. There is no uncertainty over market exposures. For swaps, for instance, the exposure on the target date is taken from the expected exposure. Bonds are revalued using

---

[2]This result, however, is driven by the joint normality assumption, which is not totally realistic. Other distributions can generate a greater likelihood of simultaneous defaults.

today's forward rate and current credit spreads, applied to the credit rating on the horizon. So there is no interest rate risk.

23.4.3   CreditRisk+

CreditRisk+ was made public by Credit Suisse in October 1997. The approach is drastically different from CreditMetrics. It is based on a purely actuarial approach derived from the property insurance literature.

CreditRisk+ is a default mode (DM) model rather than a mark-to-market (MTM) model. Only two states of the world are considered—default and no-default. Another difference is that the default intensity is time-varying, as it can be modeled as a function of factors that change over time.

When defaults are independent, the distribution of default probabilities resembles a Poisson distribution. The system also allows for some correlation by dividing the portfolio into homogeneous sectors within which obligors share the same systematic risk factors.

The other component of the approach is the severity of losses. This is roughly modeled by sorting assets by severity bands, say loans around $20,000 for the first band, $40,000 for the second band, and so on. A distribution of losses is then obtained for each band. These distributions are combined across bands to generate an overall distribution of default losses.

The method provides a quick analytical solution to the distribution of credit losses with minimal data inputs. As with CreditMetrics, however, there is no uncertainty over market exposures.

23.4.4   Moody's KMV

Moody's KMV provides forecasts of estimated default frequencies (EDFs) for approximately 30,000 public firms globally.[3] Much of its technology is considered proprietary and is unpublished.

The basic idea, however, is an application of the Merton approach to credit risk.

---

[3]KMV was founded by S. Kealhofer, J. McQuown, and O. Vasicek (hence the abbreviation KMV) to provide credit risk services. KMV started as a private firm based in San Francisco in 1989 and was acquired by Moody's in April 2002.

The value of equity is viewed as a call option on the value of the firm's assets,

$$S = c(A, K, r, \sigma_A, \tau) \qquad (23.12)$$

where K is the value of liabilities, taken as the value of all short-term liabilities (one year and under) plus half the book value of all long-term debt. This equation has to be iteratively estimated from observable variables, in particular the stock market value S and its volatility σ_S. This model generates an estimated default frequency based on the distance between the current value of assets and the boundary point. Suppose, for instance, that $A = \$100$ million, $K = \$80$ million, and $\sigma_A = \$10$ million. The normalized distance from default is then

$$z = \frac{A - K}{\sigma_A} = \frac{\$100 - \$80}{\$10} = 2 \qquad (23.13)$$

If we assume normally distributed returns, the probability of a standard normal variate z falling below -2 is about 2.3%. Hence the default frequency is EDF $= 0.023$. In practice, these are calibrated to actual default data to get objective (as opposed to risk-neutral) probabilities of default.

The strength of this approach is that it relies on what is perhaps the best market data for a company—its stock price. KMV claims that this model predicts defaults much better than credit ratings. The recovery rate and correlations across default are also automatically generated by the model.

23.4.5   Credit Portfolio View

The last model we consider is **Credit Portfolio View** (CPV), published by the consulting firm McKinsey in 1997. The focus of this top-down model is on the effect of macroeconomic factors on portfolio credit risk.

This approach models loss distributions from the number and size of credits in subportfolios, typically consisting of customer segments. Instead of considering fixed transition probabilities, this model conditions the default probability on the state of the economy, allowing increases in defaults during recessions. The default probability p_t at time t is driven by a set of macroeconomic variables x^k for various countries and industries through a linear combination called y_t. The functional relationship to y_t, called the *logit model*, ensures that the probability is always between 0 and 1:

$$p_t = 1/[1 + \exp(y_t)], \qquad y_t = \alpha + \sum \beta^k x_t^k \qquad (23.14)$$

Using a multifactor model, each debtor is assigned to a country, industry, and rating segment. Uncertainty in recovery rates is also factored in. The model uses numerical simulations to construct the distribution of default losses for the portfolio. While useful for modeling default probabilities conditioned on the state of the economy, this approach is mainly top-down and does not generate sufficient detail of credit risk for corporate portfolios.

23.4.6   Comparison

The International Swaps and Derivatives Association (ISDA) recently conducted a comparative survey of credit risk models. The empirical study consisted of three portfolios of one-year loans with a total notional of $66.3 billion each.

A. High-credit-quality, diversified portfolio (500 names)

B. High-credit-quality, concentrated portfolio (100 names)

C. Low-credit-quality, diversified portfolio (500 names)

The models are listed in Table 23-5 and include CreditMetrics, CreditRisk+, and two internal models, all with a one-year horizon and 99% confidence level. Also reported are the charges from the Basel I "standard" rules, which will be detailed in a later chapter. Suffice it to say that these rules make no allowance for variation in credit quality or diversification effects. Instead, the capital charge is based on 8% of the loan notional.

The top of the table examines the case of zero correlations. The Basel rules yield the same capital charge, irrespective of quality or diversification effects. The charge is also uniformly higher than most others, at $5,304 million, which is 8% of the notional.

Generally, the four credit portfolio models show remarkable consistency in capital charges. Portfolios A and B have the same credit quality, but B is more concentrated. Portfolio A has indeed lower CVAR, approximately $800 million against $2,000 million for B. This reflects the benefit from greater diversification. Portfolios A and C have the same number of names, but C has lower credit quality. This increases CVAR from around $800 million to $2,000 million.

TABLE 23-5 Capital Charges from Various Credit Risk Models

	Assuming Zero Correlation		
	Portfolio A	Portfolio B	Portfolio C
CreditMetrics	777	2,093	1,989
CreditRisk+	789	2,020	2,074
Internal model 1	767	1,967	1,907
Internal model 2	724	1,906	1,756
Basel I rules	5,304	5,304	5,304
	Assessing Correlations		
	Portfolio A	Portfolio B	Portfolio C
CreditMetrics	2,264	2,941	11,436
CreditRisk+	1,638	2,574	10,000
Internal model 1	1,373	2,366	9,654
Basel I rules	5,304	5,304	5,304

The bottom panel assesses empirical correlations, which are typically positive. The Basel charges are unchanged, as expected because they do not account for correlations. Internal models show capital charges to be systematically higher than in the previous case. There is also more dispersion in results across models, however. It is interesting to see, in particular, that the economic capital charge for portfolio C, with low credit quality, is typically twice the Basel charge. Such results demonstrate that the Basel rules can lead to inappropriate credit risk charges. As a result, banks subject to these capital requirements may shift the risk profile to lower-rated credits until their economic capital is in line with regulatory capital. This shift to lower credit quality was certainly not an objective of the Basel rules.

Example 23-7: FRM Exam 2001—Question 27

What can be said about default correlations in CreditMetrics?
a) Default correlations can be estimated by ratings changes.
b) Firm-specific aspects are more important than correlation.
c) Past history is insufficient to judge default correlations.
d) Default correlations can be estimated by equity valuation.

Example 23-8: FRM Exam 2001—Question 23

What is the central assumption made by CreditMetrics?
a) An asset or portfolio should be thought of in terms of its diversification.
b) An asset or portfolio should be thought of in terms of the likelihood of default.
c) An asset or portfolio should be thought of in terms of the likelihood of default and in terms of changes in credit quality over time.
d) An asset or portfolio should be thought of in terms of changes in credit quality over time.

Example 23-9: FRM Exam 2002—Question 129

A bank computes the distribution of its loan portfolio marked-to-market value one year from now using the CreditMetrics approach of computing values for rating transition outcomes using (a) a rating agency transition matrix, (b) current forward curves, and (c) correlations among rating transition outcomes derived from stock returns of the obligors. In computing firm-wide risk using this distribution of its loan portfolio, the bank is most likely to understate its risk because it ignores

a) The term structure of interest rates

b) Rating drift

c) Spread risk

d) The negative correlation between the Treasury rates and credit spreads

---

Example 23-10: FRM Exam 1999—Question 146

Which of the following is used to estimate the probability of default for a firm in the KMV model?

I. Historical probability of default based on the credit rating of the firm (KMV has a method to assign a rating to the firm if unrated)

II. Stock price volatility

III. The book value of the firm's equity

IV. The market value of the firm's equity

V. The book value of the firm's debt

VI. The market value of the firm's debt

a) I only

b) II, IV, and V

c) II, III, and VI

d) VI only

Example 23-11: FRM Exam 2002—Question 109

KMV measures the normalized distance from default. How is this defined?

a) (Expected assets − Weighted debt) / (Volatility of assets)

b) Equity/ (Volatility of equity)

c) Probability of stock price falling below a threshold

d) Leverage times stock price volatility

Example 23-12: FRM Exam 2000—Question 60

The KMV credit risk model generates an estimated default frequency (EDF) based on the distance between the current value of assets and the book value of liabilities. Suppose that the current value of a firm's assets and the book value of its liabilities are $500 million and $300 million, respectively. Assume that the standard deviation of returns on the assets is $100 million, and that the returns on the assets are normally distributed. Assuming a standard Merton model, what is the approximate default frequency (EDF) for this firm?

a) 0.010

b) 0.015

c) 0.020

d) 0.030

Example 23-13: FRM Exam 2000—Question 44

Which one of the following statements regarding credit risk models is *most* correct?

a) The CreditRisk+ model decomposes all the instruments by their exposure and assesses the effect of movements in risk factors on the distribution of potential exposure.

b) The CreditMetrics model provides a quick analytical solution to the distribution of credit losses with minimal data input.

c) The KMV model requires the historical probability of default based on the credit rating of the firm.

d) The Credit Portfolio View (McKinsey) model conditions the default rate on the state of the economy.

23.5   Answers to Chapter Examples

Example 23-1: FRM Exam 1998—Question 41

c) Credit provisions should be made for actual and expected losses. Capital, however, is supposed to provide a cushion against unexpected losses based on CVAR.

Example 23-2: FRM Exam 1998—Question 39

b) The expected loss is $100,000,000 \times 0.06 \times (1 - 0.4) = \$3.6$ million. Note that correlation across obligors does not matter for expected credit loss.

Example 23-3: FRM Exam 1999—Question 120

c) The exposure times the loss given default is, respectively, $500,000, $1,000,000, $2,400,000, and $1,600,000. Loan c) has the most to lose.

Example 23-4: FRM Exam 2002—Question 74

b) This is an example of right-way trade. To have lower credit risk, you would prefer a trade where there is a lower probability of a default by the counterparty when the contract is in-the-money. This will happen if the counterparty enters a transaction to hedge an operating exposure. For instance, a gas producer has a natural operating exposure to gas. If the producer sells gas at a fixed price, the swap will lose money if the market price of gas goes up. In this situation, however, there is little risk of default because the producer is sitting on an inventory of gas anyway. A trading firm or distributor could go bankrupt if the transaction loses money.

Example 23-5: FRM Exam 1998—Question 13

c) First, we have to transform the annual default probability into a monthly probability. Using $(1 - 2\%) = (1 - d)^{12}$, we find $d = 0.00168$, which assumes a constant probability of default during the year. Next, we compute the expected credit loss, which is $d \times \$1,000,000 = \$1,682$. Finally, we calculate the WCL at the 99.9% confidence level, which is the lowest number CL_i such that $P(CL \leq CL_i) \geq 99.9\%$. We have $P(CL = 0) = 99.83\%$; $P(CL \leq 1,000,000) = 100.00\%$. Therefore, the WCL is \$1,000,000, and the CVAR is $\$1,000,000 - \$1,682 = \$998,318$.

Example 23-6: FRM Exam 1998—Question 10

d) As in the previous question, the monthly default probability is 0.0168. The following table shows the distribution of credit losses.

Default	Probability (p_i)	Loss L_i	$p_i L_i$	$1 - \sum p_i$
2 bonds	$d^2 = 0.00000282$	\$1,000,000	\$2.8	100.00000%
1 bond	$2d(1 - d) = 0.00335862$	\$500,000	\$1,679.3	99.99972%
0 bonds	$(1 - d)^2 = 0.99663854$	\$0	\$0.0	99.66385%
Total	1.00000000		\$1,682.1	

This gives an expected loss of \$1,682, the same as before. Next, \$500,000 is the WCL at a minimum 99.9% confidence level because the total probability of observing a number equal to or lower than this is greater than 99.9%. The CVAR is then $\$500,000 - \$1,682 = \$498,318$.

Example 23-7: FRM Exam 2001—Question 27

a) Correlations are important drivers of portfolio risk, so b) is wrong. In CreditMetrics, correlations in asset values drive correlations in ratings change, which drive default correlations. Answer d) is not correct, as it refers to the Merton model, where default probabilities are inferred from equity valuation, liabilities, and volatilities.

Example 23-8: FRM Exam 2001—Question 23

c) The central assumption in CreditMetrics is that asset values are driven by changes in their credit ratings, including default. So this is more general than b) and d).

Example 23-9: FRM Exam 2002—Question 129

c) CreditMetrics ignores spread risk. It does account for ratings drift and the term structure of interest rates, albeit not their volatility.

Example 23-10: FRM Exam 1999—Question 146

b) KMV uses information about the market value of the stock plus the book value of debt.

Example 23-11: FRM Exam 2002—Question 109

a) The distance-to-default measure is a standardized variable that measures how much the value of firm assets exceeds the liabilities.

Example 23-12: FRM Exam 2000—Question 60

c) The distance between the current value of assets and that of liabilities is $200 million, which corresponds to twice the standard deviation of $100 million. Hence the probability of default is $N(-2.0) = 2.3\%$, or about 0.020.

Example 23-13: FRM Exam 2000—Question 44

d) Answer d) is most correct. Answer a) is wrong because CreditRisk+ assumes fixed exposures. Answer b) is also wrong because CreditMetrics is a simulation, not an analytical model. Finally, KMV uses the current stock price and not the historical default rate.

Operational and Integrated Risk Management

Chapter 24

Operational Risk

The financial industry has developed standard methods to measure and manage market and credit risks. The industry is turning next to operational risk, which has proved to be an important cause of financial losses. Indeed, most financial disasters can be attributed to a combination of market and credit risk along with some failure of controls, which is a form of operational risk.

As in the case of market and credit risk, the financial industry is being pushed in the direction of better control of operational risk by bank regulators. For the first time, the Basel Committee will establish capital charges for operational risk, in exchange for lowering them on market and credit risk. This new charge, which would constitute approximately 12% of the total capital requirement, is forcing the banking industry to pay close attention to operational risk.

As with market and credit risk, the management of operational risk follows a sequence of logical steps: (1) identification, (2) assessment, (3) monitoring, and (4) control or mitigation.[1]

Historically, operational risk has been managed by internal control mechanisms within business lines, supplemented by the audit function. The industry is now starting to use specific structures and control processes specifically tailored to operational risk.

To introduce operational risk, Section 24.1 summarizes lessons from well-known financial disasters. Given this information, Section 24.2 turns to definitions of operational risk. Various measurement approaches are discussed in Section 24.3. Finally, Section 24.4 shows how to use the distribution of operational losses to manage this risk better and offers some concluding comments.

---

[1] See Basel Committee on Banking Supervision (2003), *Sound Practices for the Management and Supervision of Operational Risk*, BIS.

24.1   The Importance of Operational Risk

The Basel Committee recently reported that "[a]n informal survey ... highlights the growing realization of the significance of risks other than credit and market risks, such as operational risk, which have been at the heart of some important banking problems in recent years." These problems are described in case histories next.

24.1.1   Case Histories

- *February 2002—Allied Irish Bank ($691 million loss):* A rogue trader, John Rusnack, hides three years of losing trades on the yen/dollar exchange rate at the U.S. subsidiary. The bank's reputation is damaged.

- *March 1997—NatWest ($127 million loss):* A swaption trader, Kyriacos Papouis, deliberately covers up losses by mispricing and overvaluing option contracts. The bank's reputation is damaged. NatWest is eventually taken over by the Royal Bank of Scotland.

- *September 1996—Morgan Grenfell Asset Management ($720 million loss):* A fund manager, Peter Young, exceeds his guidelines, leading to a large loss. Deutsche Bank, the German owner of MGAM, agrees to compensate the investors in the fund.

- *June 1996—Sumitomo ($2.6 billion loss):* A copper trader amasses unreported losses over three years. Yasuo Hamanaka, known as "Mr. Five Percent," after the proportion of the copper market he controlled, is sentenced to prison for forgery and fraud. The bank's reputation is severely damaged.

- *September 1995—Daiwa ($1.1 billion loss):* A bond trader, Toshihide Igushi, amasses unreported losses over 11 years at the U.S. subsidiary. The bank is declared insolvent.

- *February 1995—Barings ($1.3 billion loss):* Nick Leeson, a derivatives trader, amasses unreported losses over two years. Barings goes bankrupt.

- *October 1994—Bankers Trust ($150 million loss):* The bank becomes embroiled in a high-profile lawsuit with a customer that accuses it of improper selling practices. Bankers settles, but its reputation is badly damaged. It is later bought out by Deutsche Bank.

The largest of these spectacular failures can be traced to a **rogue trader**, or a case of internal fraud. These failures involve a mix of market risk and operational risk (failure to supervise). It should be noted that the cost of these events has been quite high. They led to large direct monetary losses, sometimes even to bankruptcy. In addition to these direct costs, banks often suffered large indirect losses due to reputational damage.

24.1.2 Business Lines

These failures have occurred across a variety of business lines. Some are more exposed than others to market risk or credit risk. All have some exposure to operational risk.

Commercial banking is exposed mainly to credit risk, less so to operational risk, and least to market risk. Investment banking, trading, and treasury management have greater exposure to market risk. On the other hand, business lines such as retail brokerage and asset management are exposed primarily to operational risk. Asset managers, for instance, take no market risk since they act as agents for the investors. If they act in breach of guidelines, however, they may be liable to clients for their losses, which represents operational risk.

Table 24-1 presents a partial list of risks for market banks that are primarily involved in trading, and credit banks that specialize in lending activities. The table shows that different lines of business are characterized by very different exposures to the listed risks. Credit banks deal with relatively standard products, such as mortgages, with little trading. Hence they have medium operations risk and low operations settlement risk. This is in contrast with trading banks, with constantly changing products and large trading volume, for which both risks are high. Trading banks also have high model risk, because of the complexity of products, and high fraud risk, because of the autonomy given to traders. In contrast, these two risks are low for credit banks.

For trading banks that deal with so-called sophisticated investors, misselling risk has low probability but high value; hence it is a medium risk. A good example is Merrill Lynch settling with Orange County for about $400 million following allegations that the broker had sold the county unsuitable investments. For credit banks that deal with retail investors, this risk has higher probability but lower value: hence it is a medium risk. Legal risks are high for market banks and medium for credit banks due to the more litigious environment of corporations relative to retail investors.

TABLE 24-1 Examples of Operational Risks

Type of Risk	Definition	Market Bank	Credit Bank
Operations risk	Losses due to complex systems and processes	High risk	Medium risk
Ops. settlement risk	Lost interest/fines due to failed settlements	High risk	Low risk
Model risk	Losses due to imperfect model or data	High risk	Low risk
Fraud risk	Reputational/financial damage due to fraud	High risk	Low risk
Misselling risk	Losses due to unsuitable sales	Medium risk	Medium risk
Legal risk	Reputational/financial damage due to fraud	High risk	Medium risk

Source: Financial Services Authority (1999), "Allocating Regulatory Capital for Operational Risk," FSA: London.

24.2   Identifying Operational Risk

One could argue that operational risk has no clear-cut definition, unlike market risk and credit risk. There is still debate as to the proper definition of operational risk, or even whether it makes sense to attempt to measure it.

After much industry consultation, the Basel Committee has settled on a definition that is becoming an industry standard. Operational risk is defined as

> *the risk of loss resulting from inadequate or failed internal processes,*
> *people and systems, or from external events*

This excludes business risk but includes external events such as external fraud, security breaches, regulatory effects, or natural disasters. It includes legal risk, which arises when a transaction proves unenforceable in law, but excludes strategic and reputational risk.

The British Bankers' Association provides further detail for this definition. Table 24-2 breaks down operational risk into categories of **people risk**, **process risk**,

system risk, and **external risk**. Among these, a notable risk for complex products is **model risk**, which is due to the use of wrong models for valuing and hedging assets. This is an internal risk that combines lack of knowledge (people) with product complexity/valuation errors (process) and perhaps programming errors (technology).

TABLE 24-2 Operational Risk Classification

Internal Risks		
People	Processes	Systems
Employee collusion/fraud	Accounting error	Data quality
Employee error	Capacity risk	Programming errors
Employee misdeed	Contract risk	Security breach
Employer liability	Misselling/suitability	Strategic risks
Employment law	Product complexity	(platform/suppliers)
Health and safety	Project risk	System capacity
Industrial action	Reporting error	System compatibility
Lack of knowledge/skills	Settlement/payment error	System delivery
Loss of key personnel	Transaction error	System failure
	Valuation error	System suitability

External Risks	
External	Physical
Legal	Fire
Money laundering	Natural disaster
Outsourcing	Physical security
Political	Terrorism
Regulatory	Theft
Supplier risk	
Tax	

Source: British Bankers' Association survey.

Example 24-1: FRM Exam 2001—Question 48

Which of the following best reflects an operational risk faced by a bank?

a) A counterparty invokes force majeure on a swap contract.

b) The Federal Reserve unexpectedly cuts interest rates by 100 bps.

c) A power outage shuts down the trading floor indefinitely with no back-up facility.

d) The rating agencies downgrade the sovereign debt of the bank's sovereign counterparty.

Example 24-2: FRM Exam 2002—Question 133

Which one of the following cases or events can be considered as resulting from operational risk?

a) A bank reports losses on a diversified portfolio of stocks during the stock market decline.

b) The bank becomes embroiled in a high-profile lawsuit with a customer that accuses it of improper selling practices.

c) The bank reports the loss of $1.5 billion due to rises in interest rates.

d) A U.S. investor makes a loss as the Japanese yen depreciates relative to the dollar.

Example 24-3: FRM Exam 2002—Question 104

Which of the following risks is *not* a process risk?

a) Model error

b) Booking error

c) Rogue trader risk

d) Documentation risk

Example 24-4: FRM Exam 1998—Question 3

Which of the following risks are *not* related to operational risk?

a) Errors in trade entry

b) Fluctuation in market prices

c) Errors in preparing a master agreement

d) Late confirmation

Example 24-5: FRM Exam 1997—Question 32

Which of the following is *not* an example of model risk in the context of VAR measurement models?

a) Model assumptions are adjusted on an annual basis regardless of market and political conditions.

b) The model is developed by a small group of quantitative professionals who are the only personnel who understand its strengths and limitations.

c) Models are validated by an independent risk professional employed by the institution, but who works in another division.

d) Risk managers who use the models are not familiar with underlying model assumptions.

Example 24-6: FRM Exam 1998—Question 6

Which of the following steps should be done first during a risk management process?

a) Risk measurement

b) Risk control

c) Risk identification

d) Limit setting

24.3   Assessing Operational Risk

Once identified, operational risk should be measured, or assessed if it is less amenable to precise quantification than market or credit risk. Various approaches can be broadly classified into top-down models and bottom-up models.

24.3.1   Comparison of Approaches

Top-down models attempt to measure operational risk at the broadest level, that is, using firm-wide or industry-wide data. Results are then used to determine the amount of capital that needs to be set aside as a buffer against this risk. This capital is allocated to business units.

Bottom-up models start at the individual business unit or process level. The results are then aggregated to determine the risk profile of the institution. The main benefit of such approaches is that they lead to a better understanding of the causes of operational losses.

Tools used to manage operational risk can be classified into six categories:

■ **Audit oversight**, which consists of reviews of business processes by an external audit department.

■ **Critical self-assessment**, where each business unit identifies the nature and degree of operational risk. These *subjective* evaluations include expected frequency and severity of losses, as well as a description of how risk is controlled. The tools used for this type of process include checklists, questionnaires, and facilitated workshops. The results are then aggregated, in a bottom-up approach.

■ **Key risk indicators**, which consist of simple measures that provide an indication of whether risks are changing over time. These *early warning signs* can include audit scores, staff turnover, trade volumes, and so on. The assumption is that operational risk events are more likely to occur when these indicators increase. These *objective* measures allow the risk manager to forecast losses through the application of regression techniques, for example.

- **Earnings volatility** can be used, after stripping the effect of market and credit risk, to assess operational risk. The approach consists of taking a time series of earnings and computing its volatility. This measure is simple to use but has numerous problems. This risk measure also includes fluctuations due to business and macroeconomic risks, which fall outside of operational risk. Also, such a measure is backward-looking and does not account for improvement or degradation in the quality of controls.

- **Causal networks** describe how losses can occur from a cascade of different causes. Causes and effects are linked through conditional probabilities. This process is explained in the appendix. Simulations are then run on the network, generating a distribution of losses. Such bottom-up models improve the understanding of losses since they focus on drivers of risk.

- **Actuarial models** combine the distribution of frequency of losses with their severity distribution to produce an *objective* distribution of losses due to operational risk. These can be either bottom-up or top-down models.

24.3.2   Actuarial Models

Actuarial models estimate the objective distribution of losses from historical data and are widely used in the insurance industry. Such models combine two distributions, loss frequencies and loss severities. The **loss frequency distribution** describes the number of loss events over a fixed interval of time. The **loss severity distribution** describes the size of the loss once it occurs.

Loss severities can be tabulated from historical data—for instance, measures of the loss severity y_k, at time k. These measures can be adjusted for inflation and some measure of current business activity. Define P_k as the consumer price index at time k and V_k as a business activity measure such as the number of trades. We could assume that the severity is proportional to the volume of business V and to the price level.

The *scaled* loss is measured as of time t as

$$x_t = y_k \times \frac{P_t}{P_k} \times \frac{V_t}{V_k} \tag{24.1}$$

Next, define the loss frequency distribution by the variable n, which represents the number of occurrences of losses over the period. The density function is

$$\text{p.d.f. of loss frequency} = f(n), \quad n = 0, 1, 2, \ldots \tag{24.2}$$

If x (or X) is the loss severity when a loss occurs, its density is

$$\text{p.d.f. of loss severity} = g(x \mid n = 1), \quad x \geq 0 \tag{24.3}$$

Finally, the total loss over the period is given by the sum of individual losses over a random number of occurrences:

$$S_n = \sum_{i=1}^{n} X_i \tag{24.4}$$

Table 24-3 provides a simple example of two such distributions. Our task is now to combine these two distributions into one, that of total losses over the period.

TABLE 24-3 Sample Loss Frequency and Severity Distributions

Frequency Distribution		Severity Distribution	
Probability	Frequency	Probability	Severity
0.6	0	0.5	$1,000
0.3	1	0.3	$10,000
0.1	2	0.2	$100,000
Expectation	0.5	Expectation	$23,500

Assuming that the frequency and severity of losses are independent, the two distributions can be combined into a distribution of aggregate loss through a process known as convolution. **Convolution** can be implemented, for instance, through tabulation. **Tabulation** consists of systematically recording all possible combinations with their associated probabilities and is illustrated in Table 24-4. Generally, convolution must be implemented by numerical methods, as there are too many combinations of variables for a systematic tabulation.

TABLE 24-4 Tabulation of Loss Distribution

Number of Losses	First Loss	Second Loss	Total Loss	Probability
0	$ 0	$ 0	$ 0	0.6
1	1,000	0	1,000	0.15
1	10,000	0	10,000	0.09
1	100,000	0	100,000	0.06
2	1,000	1,000	2,000	0.025
2	1,000	10,000	11,000	0.015
2	1,000	100,000	101,000	0.010
2	10,000	1,000	11,000	0.015
2	10,000	10,000	20,000	0.009
2	10,000	100,000	110,000	0.006
2	100,000	1,000	101,000	0.010
2	100,000	10,000	110,000	0.006
2	100,000	100,000	200,000	0.004
Expectation			11,750	

We start with the obvious case, no loss, which has probability 0.6. Next, we go through all possible realizations of one loss only. From Table 24-3, we see that a loss of $1,000 can occur with total probability of $P(n = 1) \times P(x = \$1,000) = 0.3 \times 0.5 = 0.15$. Similarly, for one-time losses of $10,000 and $100,000, the probabilities are 0.09 and 0.06, respectively. We then go through all occurrences of two losses, which can result from many different combinations. For instance, a loss of $1,000 can occur twice, for a total of $2,000, with a probability of $0.1 \times 0.5 \times 0.5 = 0.025$. We can have a loss of $1,000 and $10,000, for a total of $11,000, with probability $0.1 \times 0.5 \times 0.3 = 0.015$. And so on until we exhaust all combinations.

The resulting distribution is displayed in Figure 24-1, where losses are recorded as positive values. It is interesting to note that the very simple distributions in Table 24-3, with only three realizations, create a complex distribution. We can compute the expected loss, which is simply the product of expected values for the two distributions, or $E[S] = E[N] \times E[X] = 0.5 \times \$23,500 = \$11,750$. The risk manager can also report the lowest number such that the probability is greater than 95%. This is $100,000, with a probability of 96.4%. Hence the unexpected loss, or **operational VAR**, is $100,000 − $11,750 = $88,250.

FIGURE 24-1 Construction of the Loss Distribution

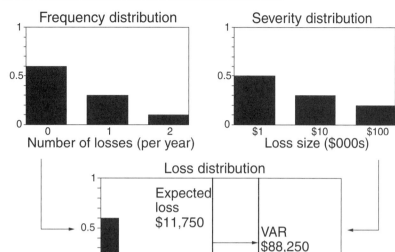

Example 24-7: FRM Exam 2000—Question 64

Which statement about operational risk is *true*?

a) Measuring operational risk requires estimating both the probability of an operational loss event and the potential size of the loss.

b) Measurement of operational risk is well developed, given the general agreement among institutions about the definition of this risk.

c) The operational risk manager has the primary responsibility for management of operational risk.

d) Operational risks are clearly separate from other risks, such as credit and market.

Example 24-8: FRM Exam 1999—Question 166

In measuring operational risk, the complete distribution of potential losses for each risk type is formed using

a) An insurance-based volatility distribution

b) Back-office distributions of transaction size and number of transactions per day

c) An operational and catastrophic distribution

d) A frequency and severity distribution

Example 24-9: FRM Exam 1999—Question 167

A particular operational risk event is estimated to occur once in 200 years for an institution. The loss for this type of event is expected to be between HKD 25 million and HKD 100 million, with equal probability of loss in that range (and zero probability outside that range). Based on this information, determine the fair price of insurance to protect the institution against a loss of over HKD 80 million for this particular operational risk.

a) HKD 133,333
b) HKD 90,000
c) HKD 120,000
d) HKD 106,667

Example 24-10: FRM Exam 1999—Question 169

The measurement of exposure to operational risk should be based on the assessment of

I. The probability of an operational failure
II. The extent of insurance coverage
III. The probability distribution of losses in case of failure

a) I only
b) II only
c) I and III only
d) I, II, and III

24.4   Managing Operational Risk

24.4.1   Capital Allocation and Insurance

Like market VAR, the distribution of operational losses can be used to estimate expected losses as well as the amount of capital required to support this financial risk. Figure 24-2 highlights important attributes of a distribution of losses due to operational risk.

The **expected loss** represents the size of operational losses that should be expected to occur. Typically, this represents high-frequency, low-severity events. This type of loss is generally absorbed as an ongoing cost and managed through internal controls. Such losses are rarely disclosed.

The **unexpected loss** represents the deviation between the quantile loss at some confidence level and the expected loss. Typically, this represents lower-frequency, higher-severity events. This type of loss is generally offset against capital reserves or transferred to an outside insurance company, when available. Such losses are sometimes disclosed publicly but often with little detail.

FIGURE 24-2 Distribution of Operational Losses

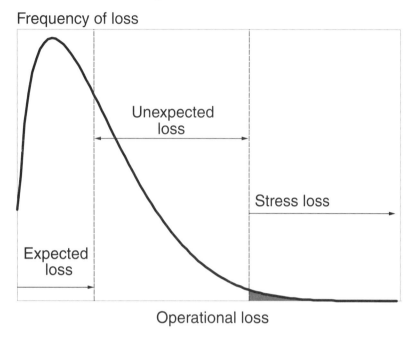

The **stress loss** represents a loss in excess of the unexpected loss. By definition, such losses are very infrequent but extremely damaging to the institution. The Barings bankruptcy can be attributed, for instance, in large part to operational risk. This type of loss cannot be easily offset through capital allocation, as it would require too much capital. Ideally, it should be transferred to an insurance company. Due to their severity, such losses are disclosed publicly.

However, purchasing insurance is no panacea. The insurance payment would have to be made very quickly and in full. The bank could fail while waiting for payment or arguing over the size of compensation. In addition, the premium may be very high. This is because once the insurance is acquired, the purchaser has less incentive to control losses. This problem is called **moral hazard**. The insurer will be aware of this and will increase the premium accordingly. The premium may also be high because of the **adverse selection** problem. This describes a situation where banks vary in the quality of their controls. Banks with poor controls are more likely to purchase insurance than banks with good controls. Because the insurance company does not know what type of bank it is dealing with, it will increase the average premium.

Example 24-11: FRM Exam 2002—Question 102

Capital is used to protect the bank from which of the following risks?

a) Risks with an extreme financial impact

b) High-frequency low-loss events

c) Low-frequency risks with significant financial impact

d) High-frequency uncorrelated events

Example 24-12: FRM Exam 2001—Question 49

Which of the terms below is used in the insurance industry to refer to the effect of a reduction in the control of losses by an individual who is insured because of the protection provided by insurance?

a) Control trap

b) Moral hazard

c) Adverse selection

d) Control hazard

Example 24-13: FRM Exam 2001—Question 51

Which of the terms below refers to the situation where the various buyers of insurance have different expected losses, but the insurer (or the capital market, as the seller of insurance) is unable to distinguish between the different types of hedge buyer and is therefore unable to charge differentiated premiums?

a) Moral hazard

b) Average insurance

c) Adverse selection

d) Control hazard

24.4.2 Mitigating Operational Risk

The approach so far has been to take operational risk as given. Such measures are extremely useful because they highlight the size of losses due to operational risk. Armed with this information, the institution can then decide whether it is worth spending resources on decreasing operational risk.

Say that a bank is wondering whether to install a **straight-through processing** system, which automatically captures trades in the front office and transmits them to the back office. Such a system eliminates manual intervention and the potential for human errors, thereby decreasing losses due to operational risk. The bank should purchase the system if its cost is less than its operational risk benefit.

More generally, reduction of operational risk can occur in terms of the frequency of losses and/or the size of losses when they occur. Operational risk is also contained by a firm-wide risk management framework. In a later chapter, we will discuss *best practices* in risk management, which are designed to provide some protection against operational risk.

Consider, for instance, a transaction in a plain-vanilla, five-year interest rate swap. This simple instrument generates a large number of cash flows, each of which has the potential for errors. At initiation, the trade needs to be booked and confirmed with the counterparty. It must be valued so that a P&L can be attributed to the trading unit. With biannual payments, the swap will generate 10 cash flows along with 10 rate resets and net payment computations. These payments need to be computed with absolute accuracy, that is, to the last cent. Errors can range from minor issues, such as paying a day late, to major problems, such as failure to hedge or fraudulent valuation by the trader.

The swap will also create some market risk, which may need to be hedged. The position needs to be transmitted to the market risk management system, which will monitor the total position and risk of the trader and of the institution as a whole. In addition, the current and potential credit exposure must be regularly measured and added to all other trades with the same counterparty. Errors in this risk measurement process can lead to excessive exposure to market and/or credit risk.

Operational risk can be minimized in a number of ways.[2] Internal control methods consist of

- *Separation of functions*: Individuals responsible for committing transactions should not perform clearance and accounting functions.

- *Dual entries*: Entries (inputs) should be matched from two different sources, that is, the trade ticket and the confirmation by the back office.

- *Reconciliations*: Results (outputs) should be matched from different sources—for instance, the trader's profit estimate and the computation by the middle office.

- *Tickler systems*: Important dates for a transaction (e.g., settlement and exercise dates) should be entered into a calendar system that automatically generates a message before the due date.

---

[2]See Brewer (1997), Minimizing Operations Risk, in R. Schwartz & C. Smith (eds.), *Derivatives Handbook*, New York: Wiley.

■ *Controls over amendments*: Any amendment to original deal tickets should be subject to the same strict controls as original trade tickets.

External control methods consist of

■ *Confirmations*: Trade tickets need to be confirmed with the counterparty, which provides an independent check on the transaction.

■ *Verification of prices*: To value positions, prices should be obtained from external sources. This implies that an institution should have the capability of valuing a transaction in-house before entering it.

■ *Authorization*: The counterparty should be provided with a list of personnel authorized to trade, as well as a list of allowed transactions.

■ *Settlement*: The payment process itself can indicate if some of the terms of the transaction have been incorrectly recorded—for instance, if the first cash payments on a swap are not matched across counterparties.

■ *Internal/external audits*: These examinations provide useful information on potential weakness areas in the organizational structure or business process.

24.4.3 Conceptual Issues

The management of operational risk is beset by conceptual problems. First, unlike market and credit risk, operational risk is largely internal to financial institutions. This makes it difficult to collect data on operational losses because institutions are understandably reluctant to advertise their mistakes. Another problem is that losses may not be directly applicable to another institution, as they were incurred under possibly different business profiles and internal controls.

Second, market and credit risk can be conceptually separated into exposures and risk factors. Exposures can be easily measured and controlled. In contrast, the link between risk factors and the likelihood and size of operational losses is not so easy to establish. Here, the line of causation runs through internal controls.

Third, very large operational losses, which can threaten the stability of an institution, are relatively rare (thankfully so). This leads to a very small number of observations in the tails. This "thin tails" problem makes it very difficult to come up with a robust "value for operational risk" (VOR) at a high confidence level. As a result, there is still some skepticism as to whether operational risk can be subject to the same quantification as market and credit risks.

Example 24-14: FRM Exam 1998—Question 4

What can be said about the impact of operational risk on both market risk and credit risk?

a) Operational risk has no impact on market risk and credit risk.

b) Operational risk has no impact on market risk but has impact on credit risk.

c) Operational risk has an impact on market risk but no impact on credit risk.

d) Operational risk has an impact on market risk and credit risk.

24.5   Answers to Chapter Examples

Example 24-1: FRM Exam 2001—Question 48

c) A power outage is an example of system failure, which is part of the operational risk definition. Answer d) is a case of credit risk. Answer b) is a case of market risk. Answer a) is a mix of credit and legal risk.

Example 24-2: FRM Exam 2002—Question 133

b) Answers a), c), and d) correspond to the market risk of stocks, fixed-income securities, and currencies, respectively. Lawsuits, on the other hand, are part of operational risk.

Example 24-3: FRM Exam 2002—Question 104

c) Rogue trader risk is related not to trade processing, but to people risk.

Example 24-4: FRM Exam 1998—Question 3

b) Fluctuations in market prices reflect market risk.

Example 24-5: FRM Exam 1997—Question 32

c) Model risk includes model assumptions that are too rigid, a), that are understood only by a small group of people, b) or that are not understood by risk managers, d). Having the models validated by independent reviewers decreases model risk.

Example 24-6: FRM Exam 1998—Question 6

c) We need to identify risks before measuring, controlling, and managing them.

Example 24-7: FRM Exam 2000—Question 64

a) Constructing the operational loss requires the probability, or frequency, of the event as well as estimates of potential loss sizes. Answer b) is wrong as measurement of operational risk is still developing. Answer c) is wrong as the business unit is also responsible for controlling operational risk. Answer d) is wrong as losses can occur due to a combination of operational and market or credit risks.

Example 24-8: FRM Exam 1999—Question 166

d) The distribution of losses due to operational risk results from the combination of loss frequencies and loss severities.

Example 24-9: FRM Exam 1999—Question 167

c) The expected loss severity is, with a uniform distribution from 80 to 100 million, 90 million. The frequency of this happening would be once every 200 years times the ratio of the [80, 100] range to the total [25, 100] range, which is $(20/75)/200 = 0.001333$. The expected loss is $90,000,000 \times 0.00133 = \text{HKD } 120,000$.

Example 24-10: FRM Exam 1999—Question 169

c) The distribution of losses due to operational risk is derived from the loss frequency (I) and loss severity (III) distributions.

Example 24-11: FRM Exam 2002—Question 102

c) Capital is supposed to absorb risks that have significant financial impact on the firm. Risks with extreme financial impact, such as systemic risk, cannot be absorbed by capital alone, so answer a) is wrong. Low-loss events are unimportant, so b) is wrong. Uncorrelated events tend to diversify, so d) is wrong.

Example 24-12: FRM Exam 2001—Question 49

b) Moral hazard arises when insured individuals have no incentive to control their losses because they are insured.

Example 24-13: FRM Exam 2001—Question 51

c) Adverse selection refers to the fact that individuals buy insurance knowing that they have greater risk than average, but the insurer charges the same premium to all.

Example 24-14: FRM Exam 1998—Question 4

d) As seen in the example on the effect of a failure to record the terms of the swap correctly, operational risk can create both market and credit risk.

Appendix: Causal Networks

Causal networks explain losses in terms of a sequence of random variables. Each variable itself can be due to a combination of other variables. For instance, settlement losses can be viewed as caused by a combination of (1) exposure and (2) time delay. In turn, exposure depends on (a) the value of the transaction and (b) whether it is a buy or a sell. Next, the causal factor for time delay can be chosen as (a) the exchange, (b) the domicile, (c) the counterparty, (d) the product, and (e) daily volume.

These links are displayed through graphical models based on process work flows. One approach is the **Bayesian network**. Here each node represents a random variable and each arrow represents a causal link.

Causes and effects are related through conditional probabilities, an application of Bayes' theorem. For instance, suppose we want to predict the probability of a settlement failure, or *fail*. Set $y = 1$ if there is a failure and $y = 0$ otherwise. The causal factor is, say, the quality of the back-office team, which can be either good or bad. Set $x = 1$ if the team is bad. Assume there is a 20% probability that the team is bad. If the team is good, the conditional probability of a fail is $P(y = 1 \mid x = 0) = 0.1$. If the team is bad, this probability is higher, $P(y = 1 \mid x = 1) = 0.7$. We can now construct the unconditional probability of a fail, which is

$$P(y = 1) = P(y = 1 \mid x = 0)P(x = 0) + P(y = 1 \mid x = 1)P(x = 1) \quad (24.5)$$

which is here $P(y = 1) = 0.1 \times (1 - 0.20) + 0.7 \times 0.20 = 0.22$. Armed with this information, we can now evaluate the benefit of changing the team from bad to good through training, for example, or through new hires. Or we could assess the probability that the team is bad given that a fail has occurred. Using Bayes' rule, this is

$$P(x = 1 \mid y = 1) = \frac{P(y = 1, x = 1)}{P(y = 1)} = \frac{P(y = 1 \mid x = 1)P(x = 1)}{P(y = 1)} \quad (24.6)$$

which is here $P(x = 1 \mid y = 1) = \frac{0.7 \times 0.20}{0.22} = 0.64$. In other words, the probability that the team is bad has increased from 20% to 64% based on the observed fail. Such an observation is useful for process diagnostics.

Once all initial nodes have been assigned probabilities, the Bayesian network is complete. The bank can now perform Monte Carlo simulations over the network, starting from the initial variables and continuing to the operational loss, to derive a distribution of losses.

Chapter 25

Risk Capital and RAROC

The methodologies described so far have covered market, credit, and operational risk. In each case, the distribution of profits and losses reveals a number of essential insights. First, the expected loss is a measure of the reserves necessary to guard against future losses. At the very least, the pricing of products should provide a buffer against expected losses. Second, the unexpected loss is a measure of the amount of economic capital required to support the bank's financial risk. This capital, also called **risk capital**, is basically a value-at-risk (VAR) measure.

Armed with this information, institutions can make better-informed decisions about business lines. Each activity should provide sufficient profit to compensate for the risks involved. Thus, product pricing should account not only for expected losses but also for the remuneration of risk capital.

Some activities may require large amounts of risk capital, which in turn requires higher returns. This is the essence of **risk-adjusted return on capital (RAROC)** measures. The central objective is to establish benchmarks to evaluate the economic return of business activities. This includes transactions, products, customer trades, and business lines, as well as the entire business.

RAROC is also related to concepts such as shareholder value analysis and economic value added. In the past, performance was measured by yardsticks such as **return on assets (ROA)**, which adjusts profits for the associated book value of assets, or **return on equity (ROE)**, which adjusts profits for the associated book value of equity. None of these measures is satisfactory for evaluating the performance of business lines, however, as they ignore risks.

Section 25.1 introduces RAROC measures for performance evaluation. This section also demonstrates the link between RAROC and other concepts, such as shareholder value analysis and economic value added. Section 25.2 shows how to use risk-adjusted returns to evaluate products and business lines.

25.1   RAROC

RAROC was developed by Bankers Trust in the late 1970s. The bank was faced with the problem of evaluating traders involved in activities with different risk profiles.

25.1.1   Risk Capital

RAROC is part of the family of **risk-adjusted performance measures (RAPM)**. Consider, for instance, two traders that each returned a profit of $10 million over the last year. The first is a foreign currency trader, the second a bond trader. The question is, How do we compare their performance? This is important in providing appropriate compensation as well as deciding which line of activity to expand.

Assume the FX and bond traders have notional amount and volatility as described in Table 25-1. The bond trader deals in larger amounts, $200 million, but in a market with lower volatility, at 4% per annum, against $100 million and 12% for the FX trader. The **risk capital** (RC) can be computed as a VAR measure, say at the 99% level over a year, as Bankers Trust did. Assuming normal distributions, this translates into a risk capital of

$$RC = VAR = \$100,000,000 \times 0.12 \times 2.33 = \$28 \text{ million}$$

for the FX trader and $19 million for the bond trader. More precisely, Bankers Trust computes risk capital from a weekly standard deviation σ_w as

$$RC = 2.33 \times \sigma_w \times \sqrt{52} \times (1 - \text{Tax rate}) \times \text{Notional} \qquad (25.1)$$

which includes a tax factor that determines the amount required on an after-tax basis.

TABLE 25-1 Computing RAPM

	Profit	Notional	Volatility	VAR	RAPM
FX trader	$10	$100	12%	$28	36%
Bond trader	$10	$200	4%	$19	54%

The risk-adjusted performance is then measured as the dollar profit divided by the risk capital,

$$\text{RAPM} = \frac{\text{Profit}}{\text{RC}} \tag{25.2}$$

and is shown in the last column. Thus the bond trader is actually performing better than the FX trader, as the activity requires less risk capital. More generally, risk capital should account for credit risk, operational risk, and any interaction.

It should be noted that this approach views risk on a stand-alone basis, that is, using each product's volatility. In theory, for capital allocation purposes, risk should be viewed in the context of the bank's whole portfolio and measured in terms of its marginal contribution to the bank's overall risk. In practice, however, it is best to charge traders for risks under their control, which means the volatility of their portfolios.

25.1.2   RAROC Methodology

The RAROC methodology proceeds in three steps.

■ *Risk measurement.* This requires the measurement of portfolio exposure, of the volatility and correlations of the risk factors.

■ *Capital allocation.* This requires the choice of a confidence level and horizon for the VAR measure, which translates into an economic capital. The transaction may also require a regulatory capital charge.

■ *Performance measurement.* This requires the adjustment of performance for the risk capital.

Performance measurement can be based on an RAPM method or one of its variants. For instance, **economic value added (EVA)** focuses on the creation of value during a particular period in excess of the required return on capital. EVA measures residual economic profits as

$$\text{EVA} = \text{Profit} - (\text{Capital} \times k) \tag{25.3}$$

where profits are adjusted for the cost of economic capital, with k defined as a discount rate. Assuming the whole worth is captured by the EVA, the higher the EVA, the better the project or product.

RAROC is formally defined as

$$RAROC = \frac{Profit - (Capital \times k)}{Capital} \tag{25.4}$$

This is a *rate of return*, obtained by dividing the dollar EVA return by the dollar amount of capital.[1]

Another popular performance measure is **shareholder value analysis (SVA)**, whose purpose is to maximize the total value to shareholders. The framework is that of a net present value (NPV) analysis, where the worth of a project is computed by taking the present value of future cash flows, discounted at the appropriate interest rate k, minus the up-front capital. A project that has positive NPV creates positive shareholder value.

Although SVA is a prospective multiperiod measure whereas EVA is a one-period measure, EVA and SVA are consistent with each other provided the same inputs are used. Consider, for instance, a one-period model where capital is fully invested or excess capital has zero return. The next-period payoff is then the profit plus the initial capital. We discount this payoff at the cost of capital and subtract the initial capital. We seek to maximize the NPV (or SVA), which is

$$NPV = \frac{Profit + Capital}{1 + k} - Capital = \frac{Profit - Capital \times k}{1 + k} \tag{25.5}$$

which is equivalent to maximizing the numerator, or EVA.

If the risk capital can be invested at the rate r, the final payoff must account for the return on capital. The numerator is then modified to

$$EVA = Profit - Capital \times (k - r) \tag{25.6}$$

25.1.3 Application to Compensation

This system allows the trader's compensation to be adjusted for the risk of the activities. The goal is not to decrease total compensation, however. This is illustrated in Table 25-2. Under the old bonus system, the bonus is 20% of the profit, or $2 million for the FX trader. We assume that the FX trader has control over the average volatility and want to encourage him or her to lower risk.

---

[1]This measure is sometimes called RARORAC, or risk-adjusted return on risk-adjusted capital. Some definitions of RAROC use regulatory capital in the denominator. Another measure is RORAC, or return on risk-adjusted capital, which omits the adjustment in the denominator.

The benchmark, or target risk, is set at $20 million and described in the last row. The new bonus scheme pays a percentage of the EVA using a cost of capital of 15%. Thus for the FX trader, the EVA is $10 − 15% × $28 = $5.8 million. We now calibrate the multiplier so that a target RC of $20 million would result in a bonus of $2 million. Hence, the total compensation is still the same if the risk capital is equal to the benchmark. This yields a multiplier of 29%. Note that the benchmark compensation is the same under the old and the new system.

Table 25-2 shows that the new bonus system would result in a payment of 29% × $5.8 = $1.7 million to the FX trader. This is less than under the old system due to the fact that the risk capital was higher than the benchmark. Such a system will immediately capture the attention of the trader, who will now focus on risk as well as profits. The other trader, with the same profit but lower capital, has a higher bonus than under the old system, at $2.1 million instead of $2 million.

TABLE 25-2 Risk-Adjusted Compensation ($ Millions)

	Profit (1)	Capital (VAR) (2)	Bonus (old) (3) 20% × (1)	Capital Charge (4) 15% × (2)	EVA (5) (1) − (4)	Bonus (new) (6) 29% × (5)
FX trader	$10	$28	$2.0	$4.2	$5.8	$1.7
Bond trader	$10	$19	$2.0	$2.8	$7.2	$2.1
Benchmark	$10	$20	$2.0	$3.0	$7.0	$2.0

Example 25-1: FRM Exam 2000—Question 70

A bond trader deals in $100 million in a market with very high volatility of 20% per annum. He yields $10 million profit. The risk capital (RC) is computed as a value-at-risk (VAR) measure at the 99% level over a year. Assuming a normal distribution of returns, calculate the risk-adjusted performance measure (RAPM).

a) 15.35%
b) 19.13%
c) 21.46%
d) 25.02%

Example 25-2: FRM Exam 1999—Question 159

To calculate risk-adjusted return on capital, what information is required?

a) One-year holding period, 99% confidence interval loss for the portfolio

b) Tax rate

c) Both a) and b)

d) None of the above

25.2   Performance Evaluation and Pricing

We now give an example of the analysis of the risk-adjusted return for an interest rate swap. All revenue and cost items should be attributed to the product.

■ *Gross revenue* consists of the present value of the bid-ask spread plus any fees.

■ *Hedging costs* can be traced to the need to hedge out market risk, as incurred.

■ *Expected credit costs* measure the statistically expected losses due to credit risk (also known as **credit provision**) and operational risk.

■ *Operating costs* reflect direct, indirect, and overhead expenses.

■ *Tax costs* measure tax expenses.

The sum of revenues minus all costs can be called the *expected net income*. It still does not account for the remuneration of risk capital. This is the purpose of EVA, as in Equation (25.3). EVA and RAROC allow the institution to evaluate an existing product or business line.

This application is still passive. The same methodology can be inverted to make **pricing decisions**, that is, to determine the minimum revenue required for a transaction to be viable. Consider the EVA formula, Equation (25.3). This can also be viewed as the minimum amount of revenues that covers costs and the cost of risk capital:

$$\text{Revenue} = \text{Costs} + [\text{Capital} \times (k - r)] \qquad (25.7)$$

As an example, we illustrate the pricing of a five-year interest rate swap for various credit counterparties, which is shown in Table 25-3.[2] Assuming there is only credit

---

[2] See also Lam (1997), Firmwide Risk Management, in R. Schwartz and C. Smith (eds.), *Derivatives Handbook*, New York: Wiley.

risk or that the swap is hedged against market risk, we can compute various costs expressed in basis points (bp) of the notional, including the expected credit loss. This corresponds to the actuarial estimate of credit loss, from the combination of credit exposure, probability of default, and loss given default. For the Aaa credit, for example, this amounts to 0.29 bp of principal, which is very low, reflecting the low probability of default.[3]

The next step is to compute the amount of risk capital required to support the transaction. This can be derived from the unexpected loss, or credit VAR. For the Aaa credit, this is 4.00 bp. Assume that the cost of capital is 15% but that capital is invested at 8%, which yields a net cost of capital of 7%. The required net income is then 7% of 4.00 bp, or 0.28 bp.

The rest of the table works backward, starting with a tax of 40%, which requires a pretax net income of $0.28/(1 - 40\%) = 0.47$ bp. To this we add operating costs, the credit provision, and hedging costs, for a total of 2.25 bp in required revenues. For a Baa credit counterparty, the required revenue would be higher, at 8.50 bp, due to higher credit provisions and a higher risk capital.

TABLE 25-3 Pricing a Swap (Basis Points)

	Aaa	Aa	A	Baa
Capital at risk	4.00	8.00	15.00	25.00
Cost of capital (7%)				
Required net income	0.28	0.56	1.05	1.75
Tax (40%)	0.19	0.37	0.70	1.17
Pretax net income	0.47	0.93	1.75	2.92
Operating costs	1.00	1.50	2.00	2.50
Credit provision	0.29	0.56	1.05	2.58
Hedging costs	0.50	0.50	0.50	0.50
Required revenue	2.25	3.50	5.30	8.50

---

[3]This should be obtained using the methodology presented in Chapter 23 for computing the PVECL. For instance, with a five-year cumulative default rate of 0.29%, average credit exposure of 1% of notional, 100% loss given default, and no discounting, we get a PVECL of exactly 29 bp.

25.3   Answers to Chapter Examples

Example 25-1: FRM Exam 2000—Question 70

c) VAR is $100,000,000 \times 0.2 \times 2.33 = \$46,600,000$; hence RAPM is $10/$46 = 21.46\%$.

Example 25-2: FRM Exam 1999—Question 159

c) Bankers RAROC computes the risk capital using the quantitative parameters in a) plus a tax factor. So, the answer is both a) and b).

Chapter 26

Best Practices Reports

Best practices in the industry have evolved from the lessons of financial disasters. Some well-publicized losses in the early 1990s led to the threat of regulatory action against derivatives. Indeed, a warning shot was fired on January 1992 by Gerald Corrigan, then president of the New York Federal Reserve Bank:

> *High-tech banking and finance has its place, but it's not all it's cracked up to be. I hope this sounds like a warning, because it is.*

Financial institutions then realized that it was in their best interests to promote a set of best practices to forestall regulatory action. This led to the Group of Thirty (G-30) report, which was issued in July 1993.

The 1995 Barings failure was followed by an in-depth report from the Bank of England in July. Similarly, the 1998 near-failure of Long-Term Capital Management (LTCM) was analyzed in a report produced by the Counterparty Risk Management Policy Group (CRMPG) in June 1999. These reports added to the collective wisdom about best practices.

This chapter reviews the lessons from reports that have shaped the risk management profession. Section 26.1 summarizes the G-30 report, Section 26.2 the Bank of England report, and Section 26.3 the CRMPG report.

26.1   The G-30 Report

The Group of Thirty (G-30) is a private, nonprofit associations, consisting of senior representatives of the private and public sectors and academia. In the wake of the derivatives disasters of the early 1990s, the G-30 issued a report in 1993 that has become a milestone document for risk management.[1] The report provides a set of 24 sound management practices. The most important ones are summarized here.

- **Role of senior management**

  Dealers and end-users should use derivatives in a manner consistent with the overall risk management and capital policies approved by their boards of directors. ... Policies governing derivatives use should be clearly defined, including the purposes for which these transactions are to be undertaken. Senior management should approve procedures and controls to implement these policies, and management at all levels should enforce them.

In other words, derivatives policies should be set by top management.

- **Marking to market**

  Dealers should mark their derivatives positions to market, on at least a daily basis, for risk management purposes.

In other words, marking to market is the most appropriate valuation technique. Countless mistakes have resulted when institutions valued instruments using a historical, accrual method.

- **Measuring market risk**

  Dealers should use a consistent measure to calculate daily the market risk of their derivatives positions and compare it with market risk limits. Market risk is best measured as "value at risk" using probability analysis based on a common confidence interval (e.g., two standard deviations) and time horizon (e.g., a one-day exposure).

This recommendation endorsed VAR as the "best" measure of market risk.

- **Stress simulations**

  Dealers should regularly perform simulations to determine how their portfolios would perform under stress conditions.

- **Investing and funding forecasts**

  Dealers should periodically forecast the cash investing and funding requirements arising from their derivatives portfolios.

- **Independent market risk management**

  Dealers should have a market risk management function, with clear independence and authority, to ensure that the following responsibilities are carried out:

  - *Risk limits (recommendation 5)*

---

[1]Group of Thirty (1993), *Derivatives: Practices and Principles*, New York: Group of Thirty.

- *Stress tests (recommendation 6)*
- *Revenue reports (recommendations 4 and 5)*
- *Back-testing VAR*
- *Review of pricing models and reconciliation procedures*

This recommendation stresses the need for a market risk management function with "clear independence and authority" (of the trading function).

- **Measuring credit exposure**

  Dealers and end-users should measure credit exposure on derivatives in two ways:

  - *Current exposure, which is the replacement cost of derivatives transactions, that is, their market value*
  - *Potential exposure, which is an estimate of the future replacement cost of derivatives transactions*

Credit exposure is a function of the current market value of the asset and of potential further increases.

- **Independent credit risk management**

  Dealers and end-users should have a credit risk management function with clear independence and authority, . . . responsible for:

  - *Approving credit exposure measurement standards*
  - *Setting credit limits and monitoring their use*
  - *Reviewing credits and concentrations of credit risk*
  - *Reviewing and monitoring risk reduction arrangements*

This also endorses the need for a credit risk management function. Here again, the emphasis is on "clear independence."

Perhaps the most important principle behind these recommendations is the separation of the risk management functions from those of trading.

Example 26-1: FRM Exam 1997—Question 4

What did the Group of 30 develop?

a) A set of risk management principles
b) A regulatory framework for the Federal Reserve and the BIS
c) A manual for derivatives users
d) A set of recommendations for international futures exchanges

---

26.2   The Bank of England Report on Barings

Violation of the fundamental principle of separation of functions was the primary cause of the Barings failure. Nick Leeson had control over both the front office and the back office. This organizational structure allowed him to falsify trading entries, hiding losses in a special account.

But new lessons were also described in the main report on Barings, produced by the Bank of England (BoE).[2] The report mentioned for the first time "reputational risk." **Reputational risk** is the risk of indirect losses to earnings arising from negative public opinion. These losses are distinct from the direct monetary loss ascribed to an event.

As an example, Bankers Trust became embroiled in a dispute with Procter & Gamble, a U.S. consumer product company, over losses in a swap contract. This feud damaged the reputation of Bankers Trust and caused indirect reputational losses over and above the amount that the bank eventually paid.

The BoE report listed several lessons from this disaster.

- **Duty to understand:** Management teams have a duty to understand fully the businesses they manage. Senior Barings management later claimed they did not fully understand the nature of their business (which is equivalent to claiming financial insanity, or that one is not responsible for financial losses due to a lack of understanding).

- **Clear responsibility:** Responsibility for each business activity must be clearly established. Barings had a *matrix* structure, with responsibilities assigned by product and region, which made it harder to assign responsibility to one person.

- **Relevant internal controls:** Internal controls, including clear segregation of duties, is fundamental to any effective risk control system.

- **Quick resolution of weaknesses:** Any weakness identified by an internal or external audit must be addressed quickly. In the Barings case, an internal audit report in the summer of 1994 had identified the lack of segregation of duties as a significant weakness. Yet this was not addressed by Barings top management.

---

[2]Bank of England (1995), *Report of the Board of Banking Supervision Inquiry into the Circumstances of the Collapse of Barings*, London: HMSO Publications.

26.3 The CRMPG Report on LTCM

The near-failure of the hedge fund Long-Term Capital Management (LTCM) also led to useful lessons for the industry. The Counterparty Risk Management Policy Group (CRMPG) was established in the wake of the LTCM setback to strengthen practices related to the management of financial risks.

The CRMPG consists of senior-level practitioners from the financial industry, including many banks that provided funding to LTCM. The industry came under criticism for allowing LTCM to build up so much leverage. Apparently, loans to LTCM were fully collateralized as to their current, but not potential, exposure. In fact, it was fear of the disruption of markets and the potential for large losses that led the New York Federal Reserve Bank to orchestrate a bailout of LTCM.

In response, the CRMPG report provides a set of recommendations, which are summarized here.[3]

- **Information sharing**: Financial institutions should obtain more information from their counterparties, especially when significant credit exposures are involved. This includes the capital condition and market risk of the counterparty.

- **Confidentiality**: As some of this information is considered confidential, institutions should safeguard the use of proprietary information.

- **Leverage, market risk, and liquidity**: Financial risk managers should monitor the risks of large counterparties better, focusing on the interactions between leverage, liquidity, and market risk.

- **Risk management expertise**: Financial institutions should ensure that risk managers have the appropriate level of experience and skills.

- **Liquidation-based estimates of exposure**: When exposures are large, information on exposures based on marked-to-market values should be supplemented by liquidation-based values. This should include current and potential exposures.

- **Stress testing**: Institutions should stress-test their market and credit exposure, taking into account the concentration risk to groups of counterparties and the risk that liquidating positions could move the markets.

- **Collateralization**: Loans to highly leveraged institutions should require appropriate collateral, taking into account liquidation costs.

---

[3]Counterparty Risk Management Policy Group (1999), *Improving Counterparty Risk Management Practices,* New York: CRMPG.

- **Valuation and exposure management**: Institutions should recognize the cost of credit risk in capital charges and continuously monitor their exposures using, if possible, external valuation services.

- **Management responsibilities**: Senior management should convey clearly its tolerance for risk, expressed in terms of potential losses. The function of risk managers is then to design a reporting system that enables senior management to monitor the risk profile.

- **Large exposure/risk reporting**: Senior management should receive regular reports on large exposures.

- **Concentration analysis**: Senior management should be informed about concentrations of market and credit risk due to positive correlations between the firm's own principal positions and counterparties' positions.

- **Contextual information**: Senior management should be able to assess key assumptions behind the analysis.

The report makes a number of other recommendations related to market practices and conventions, as well as regulatory reporting. In particular, the report identifies areas for improvements in standard industry documents, which should help to ensure that netting arrangements are carried out in a timely fashion.

Perhaps the most important lesson from LTCM for lenders is the relationship between market risk and credit risk. The G-30 report recommends the establishment of market and credit risk functions but does not discuss integration of these functions. When LTCM was about to fail, lenders realized that they had no protection for potential exposure and that many of their positions were similar to those of LTCM. Had LTCM defaulted (a credit event), they could have lost billions of dollars due to market risk.

The second lesson from LTCM is the need for risk managers to make adjustments for large or illiquid positions. The third lesson from LTCM is that institutions should perform systematic stress tests, because VAR models based on recent history can fail to capture the extent of losses in a disrupted market. This seems obvious, as VAR purports to give only a first-order magnitude of the size of losses in a normal market environment.

26.4   Answer to Chapter Example

Example 26-1: FRM Exam 1997—Question 4

a) The G-30 developed best-practices risk management principles.

Chapter 27

Firm-Wide Risk Management

This chapter turns to best practices for firm-wide management of financial risks. The financial industry has come to realize that risk management should be implemented on a global basis, across business lines and types of risk. This is due to a number of factors, including (1) increased exposures to more global sources of risk as institutions expand their operations, (2) interactions between risk factors, and (3) linkages in products across types of market risks as well as types of financial risks. These linkages make it important to consider correlations among risks and products.

Interactions between types of risk bear emphasis, as they are too often ignored. The industry has made great strides in recent years in the measurement of market and credit risk. Once measured, risk can be penalized, as with a RAROC measure. The danger is that this creates an incentive to move risk to areas where it is not well measured or controlled.

The industry has also recognized that for diversification effects to produce benefits, various risks have to be measured and compared. This explains the trend toward integrated, or firm-wide, risk management. **Integrated risk management** provides a consistent and global picture of risk across the whole institution. This requires measuring risk across all business units and all risk factors, using consistent methodologies, systems, and data.

Section 27.1 reviews different types of financial risks. Section 27.2 discusses the three pillars of global risk management: best-practices policies, methods, and infrastructure. Section 27.3 then turns to a description of organizational structures that are consistent with these best practices. Finally, Section 27.4 shows how traders can be controlled through compensation adjustment and limits.

27.1 Integrated Risk Management

27.1.1 Types of Risk

We first briefly review various types of financial risks.

- **Market risk** is the risk of loss due to movements in the level or volatility of market prices.

- **Liquidity risk** takes two forms, asset liquidity risk and funding liquidity risk. **Asset liquidity risk**, also known as **market/product liquidity risk**, arises when a transaction cannot be conducted at prevailing market prices due to the size of the position relative to normal trading lots. **Funding liquidity risk**, also known as **cash-flow risk**, refers to the inability to meet payment obligations. Asset liquidity risk generally falls under the market risk management function.

- **Credit risk** is the risk of loss due to the fact that counterparties may be unwilling or unable to fulfill their contractual obligations.

- **Operational risk** is generally defined as the risk of loss resulting from failed or inadequate internal processes, systems, and people, or from external events.

27.1.2 Risk Interactions

Risk categories do not fit into neat, separate silos. Operational risk can create market and credit risk, and vice versa. For instance, collateral payments in swaps decrease credit risk by marking to market on a regular basis but create a greater need for cash flow management, which increases operational and liquidity risk. The reverse can also occur as an operational failure, such as incorrect confirmation of a trade, can lead to inappropriate hedging or greater market risk. Incorrect data entry of swap terms can create incorrect market risk measurement as well as incorrect credit exposures.

Another important example is the interaction between market risk and credit risk. **Wrong-way trades** are those where market risk amplifies credit risk. Consider, for example, a swap between a bank and a speculator. If the bank loses money on the swap, credit risk is not an issue. On the other hand, if the bank makes a large profit on the swap, this must be at the expense of the speculator. If the loss to the other party is sufficiently large, the speculator could default precisely because of the swap. Therefore, such trades are inherently more dangerous than those where the counterparty is a hedger. For a hedger, the loss on the swap should be offset by a gain on the hedged position. As a result, such trades are safer for the bank.

As discussed in the previous chapter, many banks were not aware of their exposure to LTCM due to the separation of their credit risk and market risk functions. This is why it is essential to view financial risks on a firm-wide basis.

This is easier said than done, however. In theory, interactions between different types of risk should be taken into account. In practice, banks that now report VAR estimates for market, credit, and operational risk simply add up the three risk measures to get an estimate of the bank's total risk. This consolidation, however, overstates the risk because it assumes that the worst loss will occur simultaneously across the three risk categories.

Example 27-1: FRM Exam 1998—Question 10

What are the driving forces of integrated risk management?
  I. The increasing complexity of products
 II. Linkages between markets
III. The potential benefits offered by portfolio effects
a) I only
b) II only
c) II and III only
d) I, II, and III

Example 27-2: FRM Exam 2001—Question 130

Liquidity risk is the risk that
  I. The markets become less active, making it difficult to exit
 II. The offices get flooded
III. It becomes difficult to borrow money
IV. The process for settlement becomes less smooth
a) I and II
b) II and III
c) I and III
d) I and IV

Example 27-3: FRM Exam 1999—Question 160

The risk that one of the parties will fail to meet its obligation to make payments in a swap agreement is called
a) Counterparty risk
b) Operational risk
c) Market risk
d) Notional risk

Example 27-4: FRM Exam 2002—Question 74

Following is a set of identical transactions. Assuming all counterparties have the same credit rating, which transaction would it be preferable to execute?

a) Buying gas from a trading firm
b) Buying gas from a gas producer
c) Buying gas from a distributor
d) Indifferent between a), b), and c)

Example 27-5: FRM Exam 2002—Question 103

Consider a bank that wants to have an amount of capital so that it can absorb unexpected losses corresponding to a firm-wide VAR at the 1% level. It measures firm-wide VAR by adding up the VARs for market risk, operational risk, and credit risk. There is a risk that the bank has too little capital because

a) It does not take into account the correlations among risks.
b) It ignores risks that are not market, operational, or credit risks.
c) It mistakenly uses VAR to measure operational risk because operational risks that matter are rare events.
d) It is meaningless to add VARs.

27.2 Three-Pillar Framework

Firm-wide risk management is best viewed as resting on three pillars, all equally important. These pillars include policies, methodologies, and infrastructure.

27.2.1 Best-Practices Policies

Best-practices policies should reflect the mission statement of the corporation. In many cases, this is framed in terms of increasing shareholder value, which is equivalent to providing a return that is consistent with the risks assumed. Thus, strategic decisions to enter or exit a business should be made after appropriate consideration of expected returns as well as risks involved.

In practice, the institution also needs to specify the extent of the risks that it feels comfortable taking. This can be translated into a target credit rating, for instance. The resulting risk tolerance will provide the philosophy for firm-wide risk policies.

These policies need to be established at the highest level of the organization, that is, the board of directors and senior management. Policies must set limits on market risk—for instance, through a worst loss expressed in terms of VAR or stress testing analysis. Similarly, these policies need to be translated into credit and operational risk VAR measures, along with internal risk controls.

27.2.2   Best-Practices Methodologies

Best-practices policies could not be implemented without appropriate analytical methods to measure, control, and manage financial risks. State-of-the-art techniques are needed to value portfolios and to measure their risks. Clearly, risk needs to be measured and priced at the portfolio level, using the most appropriate method.

Risk measurement methodologies also provide tools to set and monitor risk-based limits for traders and business units, as well as to adjust profits and losses for the relevant cost of risk capital.

27.2.3   Best-Practices Infrastructure

Best-practices policies and methodologies can be implemented only with the appropriate infrastructure. This includes an organizational design that reflects a firm-wide risk management philosophy: people with the requisite training, expertise, and compensation; and systems that can support risk management decisions.

Example 27-6: FRM Exam 1998—Question 11

The best-practices risk management approach is a three-pillar framework. The three pillars are best-practices policy, best-practices infrastructure, and best-practices methodologies. Which of the following aspects of a financial institution are highly dependent on the *best-practices* policies?

  I. Business strategies

 II. Risk tolerance

III. Disclosure

a) I only

b) I and II only

c) II and III only

d) I, II, and III

27.3   Organizational Structure

To be effective, the organizational structure must be designed to reflect the policy of effective firm-wide risk management. Figure 27-1 reflects a typical organizational structure of an old-style commercial bank.

FIGURE 27-1 Old-Style Organizational Structure

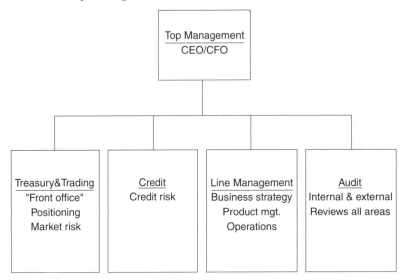

Here risk is monitored mainly by the business lines. The risk manager approves transactions, sets exposure limits, and monitors the exposure limits as well as the counterparty's financial health. Treasury and trading implement proprietary trading and hedging. At the same time, this unit measures and monitors position and perhaps VAR limits. Line management deals with business and product strategy. It also controls operations. Finally, the audit function, external or internal, provides an independent review of business processes.

There are numerous problems with such a structure. Perhaps the main one is that market risk management reports to trading, which violates the principle of independence of risk management. In addition, the decentralization of risk management among separate lines leads to a lack of coordination and failure to capture correlations between different types of risk. The credit risk manager, for instance, will prefer an instrument that transforms credit risk into operational risk, which is under another manager's watch. Situations where credit risk and market risk exacerbate each other (as in the case of LTCM) will also be missed. Finally, models and databases may be inconsistent across lines.

To maintain independence, risk managers should report not to traders but directly to top management. Ideally, the risk management function should be a firm-wide function, covering market, credit, and operational risks. Such a structure will avoid situations where risks are pushed from one area, where they are well measured, toward other areas. Firm-wide risk management should also be able to capture interactions between different types of risks.

The philosophy of separation of functions and independence of risk management must be embodied in the organizational structure of the institution. Figure 27-2 describes one such implementation. The most important aspect of this flowchart is that the risk management unit is independent of the trading unit.

FIGURE 27-2 Modern Organizational Structure

The **front office** is concerned with positioning and perhaps some local hedging, subject to position and VAR limits established by risk management. The **back office** deals with trade processing and reconciliation as well as cash management. The **middle office** has expanded functions, which include risk measurement and control.

The **chief risk officer** is responsible for

- Establishing risk management policies, methodologies, and procedures consistent with firm-wide policies

- Reviewing and approving models used for pricing and risk measurement

- Measuring risk on a global basis as well as monitoring exposures and movements in risk factors

- Enforcing risk limits with traders

- Communicating risk management results to senior management

Figure 27-3 describes the centralization of the risk management function under an executive vice president or chief risk officer. The figure shows the units reporting to this new function. To this officer report *market risk management*, which monitors risk in the trading book; *credit risk management*, which monitors risk in the banking and trading books; *operational risk management*, which monitors operational risks; and systems. The latter unit deals with *risk management information systems (MIS)*, which include hardware, software, and data capture; *analytics*, which develops and tests risk management methodologies; and RAROC, which ensures that economic capital is allocated according to risk.

FIGURE 27-3 Risk Management Organizational Structure

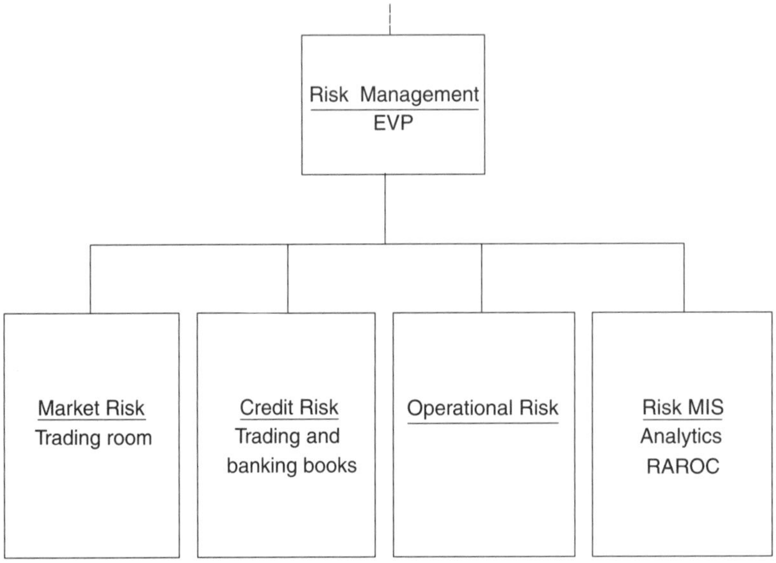

Example 27-7: FRM Exam 1997—Question 3

To ensure an effective risk management function within a large financial institution, the head of risk management should report to whom?

a) The head of trading
b) The head of IT
c) The board of directors
d) Depends on the institution

Example 27-8: FRM Exam 1999—Question 164

When would it be prudent for a trader to direct accounting entries?
a) Never
b) When senior management of the firm and the board of directors are aware and have approved the practice on an exception basis
c) When audit controls are such that the entries are reviewed on a regular basis to ensure detection of irregularities
d) Solely during such times as staffing turnover requires the trader to back-fill until additional personnel can be hired and trained

---

Example 27-9: FRM Exam 1998—Question 7

Independent credit risk management should be responsible for
 I. Approving credit exposure measurement standards
 II. Setting credit limits and monitoring adherence to such limits
 III. Reviewing counterparty creditworthiness and concentration of credit risk
a) I only
b) II only
c) I and II only
d) I, II, and III

Example 27-10: FRM Exam 1998—Question 9

The members of the board of directors should have which of the following responsibilities related to risk management?
 I. The board must approve the firm's risk management policies and procedures.
 II. The board must be able to evaluate the performance of risk management activities.
 III. The board must maintain oversight of risk management activities.
a) I and II only
b) II and III only
c) I and III only
d) I, II, and III

Example 27-11: FRM Exam 2000—Question 63

Which one of the following statements about operations risk is *not* correct?

a) The operations unit for derivatives activities, consistent with other trading and investment activities, should report to an independent unit and should be managed independently of the business unit.

b) It is essential that operational units be able to capture all relevant details of transactions, identify errors, and process payments or move assets quickly and accurately.

c) Because the business unit is responsible for the profitability of a derivatives function, it should be responsible for ensuring proper reconciliation of front- and back-office databases on a regular basis.

d) Institutions should establish a process through which documentation exceptions are monitored, resolved, and appropriately reviewed by senior management and legal counsel.

27.4   Controlling Traders

27.4.1   Trader Compensation

The compensation structure for traders should also be given due thought. Usually, traders are paid a bonus that is directly related to their performance—for instance, 20% of profits—when positive. Note that the design of this compensation contract is asymmetric, like that of an option. If the trader is successful, he or she can become a millionaire at a very young age. If the trader loses money, he or she is simply fired. In many cases, the trader will find another employer since he or she now has experience.

Such a contract is designed to attract the very best talents into trading. The downside is that the trader, who is now long an option, has an incentive to increase the value of this option by increasing the risk of the positions. This, however, may not be in the best interests of the company.

Such a tendency for risk taking can be controlled in a variety of fashions:

- By modifying the structure of the compensation contract to better align the interests of the trader and the company (e.g., by paying with company stock or tying compensation to longer-term performance)

- By subtracting a risk-based capital charge from trading profits, as in a RAROC-type system

- By appointing an independent risk manager

To be effective, it is essential that the compensation structure for *risk managers* be independent of how well traders perform. The compensation for risk managers needs to be attractive enough to draw talented individuals, however.

27.4.2 Trader Limits

To some extent, trading risk can be managed by appropriately altering the incentives of traders. Alternatively, this risk can be controlled by imposing limits. These can be separated into backward-looking and forward-looking limits. The former consist of stop-loss limits. The latter consist of exposure or VAR limits.

Stop-loss limits are restrictions on traders' positions that are imposed after a trader has accumulated losses. Because their design is backward-looking, they cannot prevent losses from occurring. What they do prevent, however, are attempts by traders who lose money to recover their losses by "doubling their bets," that is, taking bigger bets in the hope that a future gain will be sufficient to wipe out a string of previous losses. These limits may also be useful if markets are trending, as losses would then be amplified if positions were not changed.

Exposure limits are systematically imposed on traders as a means to control losses before they occur. These are defined in terms of notional principal. For example, the maximum position for a yen trader could be set at the equivalent of $10 million. These limits are typically set by considering the worst loss a unit could absorb, combined with an extreme move in the risk factor.

The problem with such limits is that they do not account for diversification or movements in market risks. Also, complex products for which the notional does not represent the worst loss lend themselves to a form of limit "arbitrage," where the trader abides by the limit guideline but not its spirit. For instance, a trader may have a $10 million limit on notes with maturities up to 5 years. Typically, such notes will have duration of, say, 4 years. The spirit of the limit is to cap the interest rate exposure. The trader, however, may circumvent the spirit of the limit by investing in inverse floaters with a duration of 12 years.

VAR limits are becoming a more common addition to conventional limits. These account for diversification and time variation in risk. For example, the VAR limit for a business unit may be less than the sum of the VAR limits for individual desks due to diversification. In practice, VAR limits are also susceptible to arbitrage, so they are used together with exposure limits.

A potential drawback of VAR limits is that their effect may be highly influenced by the volatility of underlying risk factors. Consider, for instance, a bond trader with a $10 million position with a duration of 10 years. If the daily volatility of the 10-year zero is 0.41%, the 95% confidence VAR is about $10,000,000 × 0.41% × 1.65 = $67,000. Say the VAR limit is set at $70,000. The next day, markets become more volatile and the forecast volatility, using an EWMA model, jumps to 0.60%. The position's VAR now becomes $99,000, which is in excess of the VAR limit by $29,000. Without an increase in the limit, the trader has to cut down the position in order to satisfy the VAR requirement.

While such a system usefully anticipates a forward-looking increase in volatility, it is worth making a number of points. The first is that the estimate of increased volatility is not perfectly measured. A GARCH model may produce slightly different results, say, an increase in volatility to 0.50 instead of 0.60. If the statistical models cannot be distinguished from each other, who is to say that the correct number is 0.60? Also, the higher VAR may be offset by an increased return. Indeed, periods of high volatility often reflect falling asset prices due to a higher risk premium. In other words, future expected returns may be higher. One has to be careful about systematically allowing traders to invoke this interpretation, though. Finally, cutting down positions may not be feasible or acceptable in the face of large liquidation costs.

Example 27-12: FRM Exam 2002—Question 132

The following is *not* a problem of having one employee perform trading functions and back-office functions.

a) The employee gets paid more because she performs two functions.
b) The employee can hide trading mistakes when processing the trades.
c) The employee can hide the size of her book.
d) The employee's firm may not know its true exposure.

Example 27-13: FRM Exam 1999—Question 165

All of the following would strengthen the internal controls for sales personnel *except*

a) Tape-recording of incoming and outgoing calls
b) Prompt confirmation of trades and acquisition of completed legal agreements
c) Compensation schemes directly linked to calendar-year revenues
d) Independent credit department personnel reviewing and approving, as deemed appropriate, all over-line requests

---

Example 27-14: FRM Exam 1999—Question 162

The best example of an effective risk control function is a unit that

a) Uncovers numerous control exceptions, violations of law, and procedural errors while maintaining a noncontroversial relationship with risk-taking personnel

b) Is staffed by competent personnel who report to the head of the trading department while maintaining independence from front-office personnel

c) Conveys issues regarding control mechanisms, risk levels, and the quality of managerial governance; achieves timely and constructive action by responsible personnel; and thereby has few repeat criticisms

d) Efficiently skews review coverage toward areas experiencing high losses or mediocre performance, thereby reducing resource requirements

---

Example 27-15: FRM Exam 1998—Question 13

Which of the following roles should *not* reside within an independent global risk management function?

a) Establishing risk management policies and procedures

b) Reviewing and approving risk management methodologies and models, in particular those used for pricing and valuation

c) Executing trading strategies to hedge out global market risk

d) Communicating risk management results to executive management and the board of directors, as well as investors, rating agencies, stock analysts, and regulators

---

Example 27-16: FRM Exam 2000—Question 69

Which of the following strategies can contribute to minimizing operational risk?

  I. Individuals responsible for committing to transactions should perform clearance and accounting functions.

 II. To value current positions, price information should be obtained from external sources.

III. Compensation schemes for traders should be directly linked to calendar revenues.

IV. Trade tickets need to be confirmed with the counterparty.

a) I and II

b) II and IV

c) III and IV

d) I, II, and III

27.5   Answers to Chapter Examples

Example 27-1: FRM Exam 1998—Question 10

d) Integrated risk management is driven by linkages between products and markets, as well as correlations.

Example 27-2: FRM Exam 2001—Question 130

c) Liquidity risk arises as asset liquidity risk, when transactions cannot be conducted at prevailing market prices (exiting positions is difficult, i.e., costly, to liquidate), and as funding liquidity risk, when losses cannot be funded easily by borrowing.

Example 27-3: FRM Exam 1999—Question 160

a) This also belongs to the credit risk category.

Example 27-4: FRM Exam 2002—Question 74

b) To have lower credit risk, one would prefer a trade where there is a lower probability of a default by the counterparty when the contract is in-the-money. This will happen if the counterparty enters a transaction to hedge an operating exposure. For instance, a gas producer has a natural operating exposure to gas. If the producer sells gas at a fixed price, the swap will lose money if the market price of gas goes up. In this situation, however, there is little risk of default because the producer is sitting on an inventory of gas anyway. A trading firm or distributor could go bankrupt if the transaction loses money.

Example 27-5: FRM Exam 2002—Question 103

b) VAR can be added across different types of risk, but this will provide a conservative estimate of capital as diversification effects are ignored. So answer a) would be for *too much* capital. Answer c) is not correct because rare events can be factored into operational VAR. Most likely, the bank may have too little capital for other types of risk than those measured by these three categories.

Example 27-6: FRM Exam 1998—Question 11

d) Policies are derived from business strategies and include risk tolerance and disclosure.

Example 27-7: FRM Exam 1997—Question 3

c) The G-30 recommends an independent risk control function for market and credit risk. As a result, the head of risk management should report directly to the board of directors, or senior management, but certainly *not* to the head of trading.

Example 27-8: FRM Exam 1999—Question 164

a) As one risk manager has said, this is one of the few instances where *never* means *absolutely never*. Allowing traders to tabulate their profits and losses is a recipe for disaster.

Example 27-9: FRM Exam 1998—Question 7

d) The credit risk manager goes through all the steps in the risk management process; he participates in approving standards, and he sets and monitors risk limits.

Example 27-10: FRM Exam 1998—Question 9

d) The board must approve policies, and be able to evaluate and maintain oversight of risk management.

Example 27-11: FRM Exam 2000—Question 63

c) Answers a), b), and d) are all reasonable. Answer c) violates the principle of separation of trading and back-office functions.

Example 27-12: FRM Exam 2002—Question 132

a) Answers b), c), and d) all can lead to a situation where the trader loses money and hides the losses. Answer a) is not a problem per se.

Example 27-13: FRM Exam 1999—Question 165

c) Linking compensation to revenues provides incentives for better performance but, unfortunately, for avoiding controls as well.

Example 27-14: FRM Exam 1999—Question 162

c) Having too many exceptions indicates that the control function is not working properly, so a) is wrong. Risk managers cannot report to the head of trading, so b) is wrong. Reducing personnel requirements is not an end in itself, so d) is wrong. The goal is to create an environment that is conducive to controlled risk taking.

Example 27-15: FRM Exam 1998—Question 13

c) Risk management cannot implement any trading activity due to the potential conflict of interest, even for hedging.

Example 27-16: FRM Exam 2000—Question 69

b) Answer I violates the principle of separation of functions. Answer III may create problems of traders taking too much risk. Answer II advises the use of external sources for valuing positions, as traders may affect internal price data.

seven

Legal, Accounting, and Tax Risk Management

Chapter 28

Legal Issues

We now turn to legal, accounting, and tax issues in risk management.[1] **Legal risk** can be defined as the risk that a contract is not legally enforceable or documented correctly. More generally, this is "the risk that a transaction cannot be consummated because of some legal barrier, such as inadequate documentation, a regulatory prohibition on a specific counterparty, and non-enforceability of bilateral and multilateral close-out netting and collateral arrangements in bankruptcy." This includes changes in law, mistakes, liabilities of agents, and political risks.

Legal risk invariably arises when the counterparty lost money on a transaction. Legal risk is also intimately related to credit risk, as situations of default require enforcement of contracts, which creates legal uncertainty.

This chapter will focus on legal risk for derivatives, although many of the concepts developed here also apply to legal risks for other financial instruments, such as loans or bonds. This chapter is structured as follows. Section 28.1 briefly reviews the history of legal risks in the derivatives markets. Section 28.2 discusses netting, an important feature of swaps that has been developed to control market, credit, and legal risk. Section 28.3 summarizes the master netting agreement established by the **International Swaps and Derivatives Association (ISDA)** in 1992. Readers, however, should also read the full text of the agreement.

The legal environment has drastically changed in the wake of corporate scandals such as Enron and WorldCom. This has led to new regulations that apply to all public companies listed on U.S. exchanges. Section 28.4 presents the main provisions

---

[1]The topics described in this part are important for risk managers and have been covered in previous FRM examinations. The reader should be aware, however, that the list of required FRM topics is subject to change.

of the Sarbanes-Oxley Act, which aims at strengthening firm-wide risk management practices. Finally, Section 28.5 contains a glossary of useful legal terms.

28.1   Legal Risks with Derivatives

While legal risks have always existed in derivatives contracts, they became more significant with the inception of the swap markets. Unlike exchange-traded futures, which are standardized, the essence of the over-the-counter market is to *tailor* contracts to the counterparty. This, however, requires not only customizing financial terms (prices, quantities, maturities) but also the legal documentation to the counterparty, which creates additional risk.

Legal risks are also intermingled with market and credit risks. When a counterparty loses a large amount of money on a transaction, reflecting market risk, there may be a tendency to resort to legal action as a means to recover some of the losses. For example, when Procter & Gamble lost $157 million on swaps arranged by Bankers Trust, the company sued the bank and recovered its losses.

Another famous example of legal risk is the case of **Hammersmith & Fulham**. This concerned a series of interest rate swaps entered into by city councils in Britain. The municipalities had taken large positions in interest rate swaps that turned out to produce major losses as British interest rates almost doubled from 1988 to 1989.

The swaps were later ruled invalid by the British High Court. The court decreed that the city councils did not have the authority to enter these transactions, which were found to be **ultra vires** (or "beyond the power" of the cities to enter). All the contracts were deemed void and hence the cities were not responsible for the losses. As a result, losses of $178 million had to be absorbed by their counterparty banks.

After this experience, banks have tried to control their legal risks by verifying that the counterparty indeed has the right to enter into a transaction. Even so, this is not always easy to assess. Before the Hammersmith verdict, for instance, many lawyers were convinced that the swaps in question would withstand legal scrutiny.

Until recently, the Hammersmith loss was the greatest single credit loss in the swap markets. For instance, a study by the ISDA noted that total losses amounted to only $358 million by the end of 1991. About 50% of this sum was due to the Hammersmith case.

Even so, these losses are relatively small compared with the size of the market. The total of $358 million represents only 0.012% of the notional amount of $4.3 trillion. As we have learned, however, notionals provide an exaggerated measure of the size of derivatives markets. A more relevant measure is the credit exposure, which is the maximum amount that can be lost. Current exposure is measured by mark-to-market values, which amounted to $77.5 billion in 1991. Compared with this number, the loss percentage is still very small, only 0.46%.

For more recent data, we can turn to information provided by the **Office of the Comptroller of the Currency (OCC)** for U.S. commercial banks.[2] The OCC provides quarterly reports on the charge-offs from derivatives (or credit losses). Figure 28-1 presents quarterly charge-offs since 1996. By the end of the period sampled, these losses had accumulated to approximately $2,200 million.

FIGURE 28-1 Charge-offs on Derivatives: U.S. Commercial Banks

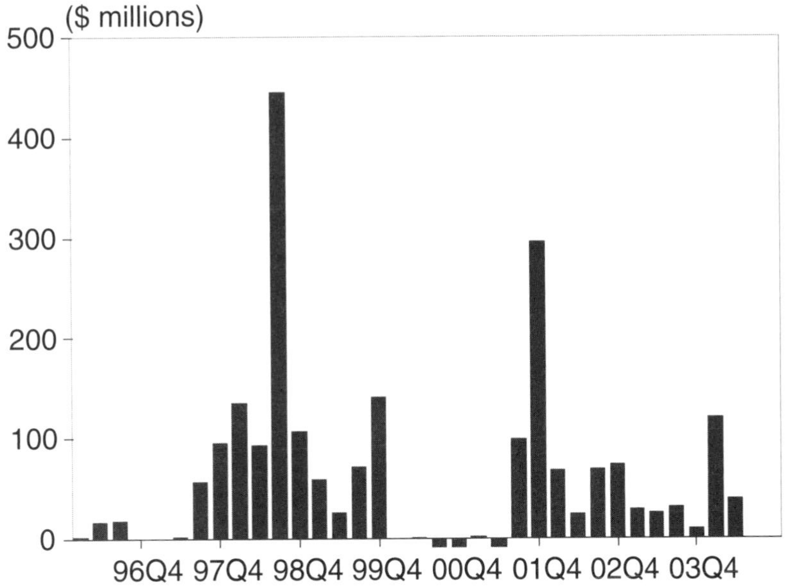

Source: Office of the Comptroller of the Currency Bank Derivatives Reports.

The peak quarterly losses occurred in the third quarter of 1998, as a result of the Asian financial crisis and the Russian default. Even this number, $445 million, represents only 0.0014% of the total notional of $33 trillion, or 0.11% of the total credit exposure at that time. Another perspective would be to compare this peak number with the charge-offs on loans, which was 0.49% in the same quarter. Overall, deriva-

---

[2]The OCC is an agency overseeing U.S. commercial banks. A subsequent chapter will present an overview of bank regulators.

tives credit losses are very small relative to the size of these markets. More often than not, these involve litigation, however.

Legal risks can arise from a number of sources.

■ *A failure in contracting.* This can happen if the contract is not properly authorized or executed, as in the Hammersmith case. Even in the United States, there was some uncertainty as to the legal status of swaps until recently. The Commodity Exchange Act did not make it clear that swaps are legally distinct from futures contracts. If swaps had been ruled to be futures contract, they could have been found illegal and thus void. This changed only with the passage of the **Commodity Futures Modernization Act** of 2000, which secured legal certainty for OTC derivatives transactions.

■ *A failure in contract documentation.* Mistakes can arise in contract documentation, such as incorrect number entries.

■ *Bankruptcy risks.* By nature, the bankruptcy process is fraught with uncertainties. For instance, the bankruptcy court could "cherry pick" the contracts, or choose to honor the contracts having the greatest value for the defaulting party only, to the detriment of counterparties.

Special protection is accorded, however, for the set-off of margin payments and liquidation of collateral under securities contracts and commodities contracts. In the United States, close-out netting agreements (to be defined in the next section) are specifically exempted from the automatic stay provision that applies upon the filing of a bankruptcy petition. This protection was adopted by the **Financial Institutions Reform Recovery and Enforcement Act (FIRREA)** of 1989, which also confirmed the right to access the collateral posted by the defaulting counterparty.

Even so, there is often uncertainty in the application of these laws. The case of Long-Term Capital Management (LTCM) is a good example, because LTCM was chartered in the Cayman Islands. Had LTCM declared bankruptcy in the Cayman Islands, there would have been legal uncertainty as to whether counterparty banks would have the right to liquidate their collateral under the U.S. Bankruptcy Code. This uncertainty is reportedly one reason why the same banks wanted to avoid a messy bankruptcy scenario and agreed to bail out LTCM.

■ *Changes in laws and regulations*. Contracts may contain clauses protecting, for instance, one party against changes in tax or regulatory treatments. For instance, coupons on Eurobonds are exempt from withholding taxes. If the country of the bond issuer suddenly imposes new taxes, the issuer may be subject to a so-called **gross-up clause** that requires it to pay the investor additional money to make up for the new tax.[3] Changes in the regulatory environment may also lead to changes in the value of contracts.

Example 28-1: FRM Exam 2002—Question 60

Lawsuits involving derivatives to major corporations are most likely to involve which of the following issues?
a) The type of derivative
b) Broker size
c) Breach of fiduciary duty
d) Enforceability of contract

28.2 Netting

As we have seen in analyzing credit risk, netting has developed over time as a powerful mechanism to reduce credit exposure. The purpose of **netting** is to offset transactions between two parties, with settlement of the *net* difference in cash flows across all contracts covered by a netting agreement. In the case of bankruptcy, however, netting is fully beneficial only when enforced by the courts.

ISDA keeps track of countries that have adopted or are considering changes in legislation to allow netting. It has obtained legal opinions that netting would be upheld in most leading jurisdictions. Similarly, the Bank for International Settlements has issued a report concluding that bilateral netting is likely to be effective in G-10 countries.[4]

---

[3] Additional complications may arise if the issuer has the right to redeem the bond at par. If the bond is trading at a premium, this provides a windfall profit for the issuer.

[4] Bank for International Settlements (1990), *Report of the Committee on Interbank Netting Schemes of the Central Banks of the Group of Ten Countries (Lamfalussy Report)*, available at http://www.bis.org/publ/cpss04.pdf.

28.2.1 Netting under the Basel Accord

In 1995 the Basel Committee on Banking Supervision (BCBS) lowered capital charges to recognize, and encourage, netting agreements.[5] The BCBS recognizes netting under **novation**, which substitutes outstanding debt payments for new ones that provide for *net* payment obligations. Under novation, any obligation between a bank and its counterparty to deliver a given currency on a given value date is automatically amalgamated with all other obligations for the same currency and value date, legally substituting one single amount for the previous gross obligations.

Another form is the **close-out netting agreement**, which is a bilateral contract specifying that upon default, the non-defaulting party nets gains and losses with the defaulting counterparty to a single payment for all covered transactions.

The ability to **terminate** financial market contracts upon an event of default is central to the effective management of financial risk. Without a close-out or termination clause, counterparties would helplessly watch their contracts fluctuate in value during the bankruptcy process, which could take years.

The Basel Accord recognizes netting, as long as the bank can assure its national supervisor that it has

(1) A netting contract or agreement with the counterparty which creates a single legal obligation, covering all included transactions, such that the bank would have either a claim to receive or obligation to pay only the net sum of the positive and negative mark-to-market values of included individual transactions in the event a counterparty fails to perform due to any of the following: default, bankruptcy, liquidation or similar circumstances

(2) Written and reasoned legal opinions that, in the event of a legal challenge, the relevant courts and administrative authorities would find the bank's exposure to be such a net amount under

—the law of the jurisdiction in which the counterparty is chartered and, if the foreign branch of a counterparty is involved, then also under the law of the jurisdiction in which the branch is located;

—the law that governs the individual transactions; and

—the law that governs any contract or agreement necessary to effect the netting.

The national supervisor, after consultation when necessary with other relevant super-

---

[5]See BCBS (1995), *Basel Capital Accord: Treatment of Potential Exposure for Off-Balance-Sheet Items.* Available at http://www.bis.org/publ/bcbs18.pdf .

visors, must be satisfied that the netting is enforceable under the laws of each of the relevant jurisdictions

(3) Procedures in place to ensure that the legal characteristics of netting arrangements are kept under review in the light of possible changes in relevant law

28.2.2   Walk-Away Clauses

Netting, however, attracts a favorable capital treatment only for contracts without **walk-away clauses**. These clauses, also known as **limited two-way payment provisions**, allow both parties to walk away from the contract in case of default.

Consider, for example, the collapse in 1990 of the Drexel Burnham Lambert Group (DBL Group), which placed its swap subsidiary, DBL Products, in default. Some swaps were out-of-the-money for DBL Products, in which case counterparties had a claim against DBL Products. This placed them in the same position as other unsecured senior creditors, which seems normal.

Other swaps, however, were in-the-money for DBL Products, which means that counterparties owed money. In theory, the walk-away clause would have permitted them to reap a windfall profit, randomly benefiting from the misfortune of others, which seems questionable.

Even so, nearly all in-the-money contracts were fully paid. Counterparties settled to avoid expensive litigation over the enforceability of these contracts. Financial institutions also recognized that walk-away clauses create uncertainty for financial markets. Contracts have now evolved to contain a **full two-way payment provision**, which provides for full payment to the counterparty, subject to a bankruptcy distribution rule.

The final nail in the coffin for the walk-away clause was the ruling by the Basel Committee that such contracts are not provided any regulatory relief in terms of lower capital requirement.

28.2.3   Netting and Exchange Margins

Netting also applies to the credit risk that futures traders face from their brokers. Clients deposit margins with their brokers. Assuming the broker is a clearing member, the broker in turn deposits margins with the clearinghouse.

If a broker goes bankrupt, clients could lose the part of their margins held by the broker. In the United States, two clearinghouses (CME and NYMEX) collect *gross margins*, that is, a separate margin for all client positions. Others collect *net margins*, allowing the broker to offset long and short positions by different customers. This netting decreases the margin held by the clearinghouse. In theory, a gross margin system is safer for the client because a greater fraction of the margin is held by the clearinghouse. The risk of a net margin system is lessened, however, if the broker properly *segregates* client accounts by holding them separately from its own accounts.

Example 28-2: FRM Exam 2002—Question 117

You are an investment manager trying to decide whether the Chicago Mercantile Exchange, the Chicago Board of Trade, or the OTC marketplace is where you will place part of your portfolio hedge. You will have to make an OTC transaction with your broker in any case. You also are considering a direct OTC deal with your broker for the whole hedge. You want to carry out the transaction that will result in the lowest possible exposure to your broker. Assuming that the size of the OTC hedge if you use an exchange is the same regardless of the exchange and that the effectiveness of the hedge is the same absent counterparty risks, how would you hedge?

a) Hedge on the Chicago Mercantile Exchange and with your broker.
b) Hedge on the Chicago Board of Trade and with your broker.
c) It doesn't matter, as the broker exposure is the same for each exchange.
d) Hedge your portfolio with a series of over-the-counter transactions, with your broker as counterparty.

28.3   ISDA Master Netting Agreement

At the beginning of the 1980s, swaps were tailor-made financial contracts that required documentation to be drafted on a case-by-case basis. This was very time-consuming and costly, and it introduced a time lag between the commercial agreement and the signing of the legally binding contract.

In response, the industry developed standardized terms for swaps. As with futures, this made it easier to offset the contracts, increasing liquidity and decreasing legal uncertainty. Out of this effort came the **master netting agreement** established by the ISDA in 1987 and revised in 1992. This form establishes a template for a standardized contract, which is supplemented by a **schedule to the master agreement** and the actual **confirmation of contract**. Parties have the flexibility to select parts of the agreement or to amend the base document through the schedule. The more specific clauses (e.g., confirmation) override more general clauses.

The ISDA master agreement contains the following provisions, as does any contract for payment.

- A list of *obligations*, detailing the mechanics of payment conditions (section 2 in the ISDA agreement), including the netting of obligations.

- A list of *credit provisions*, which describe events of default and termination (section 5), early termination (section 6), and credit support provisions (e.g., the system of collateral payments). The event of default includes

    —Failure to pay

    —Breach of agreement

    —Credit support default (e.g., failure to provide collateral when due)

    —Misrepresentation

    —Default under a specified transaction

    —Cross-default, which is optional

    —Acts pertaining to bankruptcy or liquidation

    —Mergers without the successor assuming the obligation to perform under the swap

    Termination includes

    —An illegality in which a party is unable to perform due to a change in law or regulation

    —A tax event such as a change in tax law that causes a party to make an additional payment (called gross-up)

    —A tax event upon merger

    —A credit event upon merger where the creditworthiness of the successor is materially weaker than the original entity

- A list of contractual *boilerplate statements*, including representations (section 3), agreements (section 4), transfer provisions (section 7), governing law (section 13), and so on.

Although the ISDA forms attempt to provide comprehensive and standardized coverage of swap events, they cannot anticipate every eventuality. When Russia defaulted on its domestic-currency debt on August 17, 1998, it imposed a moratorium on foreign-currency debt payments as well as a 90-day freeze on forward foreign exchange contracts. It has maintained payment on its foreign debt, however. Whether this constitutes a credit event on the foreign debt was not clearly defined by the swap agreements in place. This has created considerable disagreement over the interpretation of standard contracts. By 1999, the ISDA had published a revised set of definitions for credit derivatives that considers both sovereign and non-sovereign entities. This list is provided in the credit derivatives chapter.

Example 28-3: FRM Exam 2001—Question 124

Most credit derivatives contracts
a) Are based on English law
b) Are written on a one-off basis
c) Have a clause about restructuring
d) Are based on the ISDA agreement

Example 28-4: FRM Exam 1999—Question 175

The ISDA master agreement and other, similar agreements for derivative contracts address primarily
a) Legal and credit risk
b) Market and legal risk
c) Legal and operational risk
d) Liquidity and legal risk

Example 28-5: FRM Exam 1999—Question 176

The framework in which the ISDA master agreement is used includes the master agreement, schedule, and confirmation. What is the order of precedence of these if any clauses conflict?
a) Master agreement, schedule, confirmation
b) Schedule, master agreement, confirmation
c) Master agreement, confirmation, schedule
d) Confirmation, schedule, master agreement

Example 28-6: FRM Exam 2000—Question 22

A typical master netting agreement as established by the ISDA will contain all of the following *except* a list of
a) Obligations
b) Historical market prices
c) Credit provisions
d) Contractual boilerplate statements

Example 28-7: FRM Exam 1999—Question 179

Which of the following are considered termination events by the ISDA master agreement?

  I. An illegality in which a party is unable to perform based on changes in law or regulation

 II. A tax event that causes a party to make an additional payment (gross-up) or to have an amount withheld from a payment because of a change in the tax law

III. A credit event upon merger in which the creditworthiness of the merged entity becomes materially weaker than that of the original entity

a) I and II

b) I and III

c) II and III

d) All of the above

Example 28-8: FRM Exam 1999—Question 180

In 1998, many credit derivatives contracts dependent on Russian credits faced legal problems because

a) Netting was unenforceable with Russian counterparties.

b) Collateral posted by a Russian counterparty and held in Russia could not be kept if the counterparty defaulted.

c) There were disputes over whether credit events had occurred or not, because the definitions of credit events were not sufficiently rigorous in credit derivatives contracts.

d) A Russian court ruled that it was illegal to enter a credit derivatives contract.

Example 28-9: FRM Exam 1998—Question 24

If a bank executes a derivatives contract with a client for whom the transaction is not appropriate, the bank has

a) Booked an illegal transaction

b) Placed the bank's reputation at risk due to potential litigation and credit risks

c) An obligation to reverse the trade

d) To closely monitor the market value to ensure that pre-settlement risk does not exceed the customer's internal credit limit

---

28.4 The 2002 Sarbanes-Oxley Act

The U.S. Congress passed the **Sarbanes-Oxley Act** in the wake of Enron, WorldCom, and Global Crossing, the three largest bankruptcies in recent corporate history.[6] The

---

[6]The act, sometimes called SOX, is named after Senator Paul Sarbanes and Congressman Michael Oxley.

act is an attempt to restore investor confidence in public corporations by improving their corporate governance and control.[7] This legislation applies to all companies with a public listing in the United States and contains these key provisions:

- *Creation of a new regulator:* The **Public Company Accounting Oversight Board (PCAOB)** now registers and oversees public accounting firms. PCAOB is under the supervision of the **Securities and Exchange Commission**. PCAOB has resources and muscles: It is well funded and can impose penalties. Previously, the industry was self-regulated, which critics claimed led to lax controls.

- *Certification by CEOs and CFOs:* This provision requires CEOs and CFOs to sign off on the company's financial statements and internal controls. Penalties for false statements include fines or jail time. This should improve the quality of financial statements. Another result is that top management is now likely to require middle managers to certify that the information they provide is accurate. This should give middle management a strong incentive to resist pressures from above to cook the books.

- *Ban on non-audit consulting services:* The company's auditor is barred from performing several kinds of additional services due to perceived conflicts of interest. In the case of **Enron**, for instance, the consulting services provided by Arthur Andersen were so profitable that it became lax in auditing its client. In 2000, Andersen earned $25 million from audit services and $27 million from consulting services to Enron alone.

- *Independence of audit committee:* This requires that all audit committee members be *outside* directors, who are not employed by the company. The audit committee, which is part of the board of directors, appoints and supervises outside accounting firms. At least one member of this committee must be a *financial expert*. This provision should minimize management influence over the audit process.

A major goal of the act is to minimize the possibility of harmful conflicts of interest, such as those that led to false disclosures for Enron and WorldCom. The spirit

---

[7]One definition of **corporate governance** is the process of high-level control of an organization. It involves the combination of board of directors, management, and controls that guide the firm.

of the act is actually very much in line with best practices for risk management, delineated in a previous chapter. Separation of duties and independent oversight are essential for effective governance.

On the downside, the act will create more paperwork and rising audit fees. There may be greater reluctance for qualified individuals to serve on corporate boards due to the perception of increased legal liabilities. Another issue is that the act applies to foreign companies listed on U.S. exchanges. This can create conflicts with foreign laws, such as those concerning board composition in some countries. In response, the SEC has exempted foreign companies from some of the provisions of the Sarbanes-Oxley Act.

28.5   Glossary

28.5.1   General Legal Terms

Civil law: (1) Legal system whose law is centered around a comprehensive legislative code (e.g., such as that established by Napoléon in France). (2) In the United States, law under which a person (the plaintiff) may sue another person (the defendant) to obtain redress for a wrong committed by the defendant—for example, a breach of contract. This is in contrast with criminal law.

Common law: System of law derived from the English system of laws "common to the population," produced primarily by a group of judges to harmonize their decisions with those in other parts of the country. It was introduced after the Norman conquest of England as a means of unifying the country. Common law builds on precedents. This is in contrast to the French-type system of civil law.

Criminal law: Law that defines public offenses against the state or government and prescribes their punishment. This is a part of public law, which also includes constitutional and administrative law.

28.5.2   Bankruptcy Terms

Absolute priority rule (APR): Hierarchical rule for the distribution of a firm's assets: Payments go first to secured creditors, then to priority creditors (e.g., to cover taxes and bankruptcy costs), then to unsecured creditors (such as bondholders and bank depositors), then to subordinated-debt holders, and finally to stockholders. (See also the credit derivatives chapter.)

Automatic stay: In bankruptcy, the suspension of legal actions (other than the bankruptcy proceeding itself) until the bankruptcy case is over.

Bankruptcy: A legal process under which (1) a financially troubled debtor is declared to be insolvent, or incapable of meeting debt payments; (2) the assets of the debtor are distributed to creditors according to bankruptcy law; and (3) the debtor, if honest, is discharged from liability for remaining unpaid debt.

The word *bankruptcy* comes from the Italian *banca rotta*, or "broken bench." The tradition was that when a medieval trader failed to pay his creditors, his trading bench was broken.

Liquidating proceeding: A bankruptcy proceeding in which the debtor's assets are converted to cash and distributed to creditors. In the United States, liquidation is covered under Chapter 7 of the U.S. Bankruptcy Code.

Reorganization proceeding: A bankruptcy proceeding in which the troubled firm may stay in business as it reorganizes in a process of financial rehabilitation. In the United States, reorganization is covered under Chapter 11 of the U.S. Bankruptcy Code. A majority of creditors and equity holders must approve the plan; otherwise liquidation proceeds under Chapter 7.

28.5.3   Contract Terms

Acceleration clause: A provision in a promissory note permitting the debtor to make, or the creditor to receive, payment before the due date.

Close-out or termination clause: A provision that gives the right to terminate a contract upon certain specified events and to calculate a termination amount due to, or due from, the defaulting party.

Covenant: A contractual provision whereby one party promises to take certain specific actions (positive covenant) or to refrain from taking certain actions (negative covenant). Bond covenants contain clauses prohibiting, for instance, the creditor from selling major assets or paying too large a dividend to stockholders.

Cross-default clause: A contractual provision whereby default on a contract occurs whenever the counterparty defaults on *any* other obligation.

Negative pledge clause: A provision that prevents the subordination of a contract to secured creditors, by pledging assets for new debt, for instance.

Netting: A provision that gives the right to *set off*, or net, claims or payment obligations between two or more parties, with the goal of arriving at a single net payment.

Novation: The extinguishment of a party's obligation (e.g., the debt of the obligee) through an agreement between the old obligor, a new obligor, and the obligee to substitute the old obligor for a new one.

Pari passu: Equal ranking (from Latin), meaning that all creditors within the same class will be treated equally. This term often used in bankruptcy proceedings where creditors are paid pro rata in accordance with the amount of their claims.

Secured transaction: An arrangement such that the creditor is provided with a backup source of payment if the debtor defaults.

Security agreement: An agreement between a debtor and a creditor whereby the creditor receives security interest, or property, to secure debt payments.

Ultra vires: Outside the power of a person or corporation (from Latin). This is in contrast to *intra vires*.

28.6   Answers to Chapter Examples

Example 28-1: FRM Exam 2002—Question 60

d) Most derivatives lawsuits arise from interpretation of the provisions of the contract. There is generally no fiduciary duty issue, as most contracts are with major corporations, which are supposed to be more informed than individual investors.

Example 28-2: FRM Exam 2002—Question 117

a) The CME clearinghouse (along with the NYMEX) collects gross margins, that is, separate margins for all clients. Other exchanges collect net margins, that is, allow the broker to mingle client positions. The gross margin system is safer for the client.

Example 28-3: FRM Exam 2001—Question 124

d) Most derivatives contracts are based on the standard form provided by the ISDA, which ensures uniformity in contracts and reduces legal uncertainty.

Example 28-4: FRM Exam 1999—Question 175

a) The master agreement deals primarily with legal issues in case of default.

Example 28-5: FRM Exam 1999—Question 176

d) The general principle is that specific amendments overrule general contract terms. So the order of precedence is from specific to general.

Example 28-6: FRM Exam 2000—Question 22

b) A master agreement will contain a list of obligations, credit provisions, and boiler-plate statements. There is no reason to have historical market prices.

Example 28-7: FRM Exam 1999—Question 179

d) All of these satisfy the definition of a termination event. For precise definitions, see the ISDA master agreement.

Example 28-8: FRM Exam 1999—Question 180

c) The ISDA form did not cover events from sovereign entities such as a moratorium. Russia had defaulted on its ruble-denominated debt, but continued to make payment on its foreign-currency debt.

Example 28-9: FRM Exam 1998—Question 24

b) The transaction may not be appropriate but in general will be legal. This places the bank's reputation at risk, but there is no obligation to reverse the trade. Nor does the bank know the customer's credit limit.

Chapter 29

Accounting and Tax Issues

We now turn to general issues related to reporting, or accounting. This includes **internal reporting**, which is essential for performance evaluation and attribution, as well as **external reporting**, which is required for shareholders and for tax purposes.[1]

While risk management is essentially a forward-looking process, accounting focuses on past performance and current positions. Obviously, reporting remains a fundamental component of doing business, as it provide a measure of performance. It also drives the compensation of business units and strategic decisions to enter or exit markets. Bonuses are distributed based on the performance of business units. Likewise, decisions to allocate capital and resources to various units are generally driven by an extrapolation of their past performance. Hence, it is essential that reporting rules provide transparent, reliable, and comparable measures of performance.

Accounting risk arises when inappropriate accounting methods could cause losses. This risk is subsumed within operational risk. It is also related to **tax risk**, which is the risk of loss due to inappropriate tax computations, or changes in tax regulations. As in the previous chapter, we place particular emphasis on derivatives, given their importance and recent changes in regulatory requirements.

Section 29.1 reviews the organizing principles of accounting for financial assets with a view toward internal reporting. Section 29.2 discusses two major issues in reporting, the valuation of positions and the choice of hedge accounting method. We then discuss external financial reporting, or disclosure rules, for derivatives. Section 29.3 focuses on pronouncements by the **Financial Accounting Standards Board (FASB)**, which is an independent agency responsible for developing **generally**

---

[1] The reader interested in the FRM examination should check whether all the materials in this chapter are still among the FRM required topics.

accepted accounting principles (GAAP) for U.S. corporations. The accounting treatment of special-purpose entities (SPEs) is also examined because of their importance in the Enron debacle. This topic is also important because it explains why Fannie Mae, a U.S. government agency, has recently run into trouble for failing to adhere to the FASB reporting standards for derivatives.

Section 29.4 discusses required disclosures by the **International Accounting Standards Board (IASB)**, which develops *international* accounting standards. Section 29.5 then briefly summarizes relevant tax issues. Finally, Section 29.6 provides some concluding comments. Given the complexity of these topics, the purpose of this chapter is only to provide a summary of the issues.

29.1   Internal Reporting

Internal reporting was discussed in the chapter on risk-adjusted return on capital (RAROC). The central objective of RAROC measures is to evaluate the economic return of business activities, specifically focusing on the return to risk-adjusted capital.

29.1.1   Purpose of Internal Reporting

At an even more basic level, however, the purpose of internal accounting is to measure the raw performance of various business units. This may involve conflicts between the business units, which will argue in favor of showing large profits, and the accounting unit, which should strive for objectivity, transparency, and conservativeness. In practice, this translates into an asymmetry in the potential for accounting errors. Profits are usually not understated, as traders have a strong incentive to scrutinize their performance numbers and will complain if profits appear too low. More often than not, errors end up producing *overstatements* of profits that must be corrected later, if caught.

Reporting rules can have an effect on real decisions and create or aggravate real financial losses. A good example is that of two Japanese trading companies, Showa Shell and Kashima Oil, that lost more than $1 billion each in the currency markets in 1993 and 1994. Apparently, some employees entered forward contracts to purchase large amounts of dollars, in excess of the company's limit. The problem was compounded by Japanese accounting rules, which allowed traders to roll over their forward contracts into new ones without having to realize losses (no marking to market). As the dollar started to depreciate, the losses were not visible and were allowed to balloon to huge amounts.

Ideally, the *accounting* treatment of transactions and positions should reflect their *economic* substance. Sometimes this is defined as a "true and fair view." This is easier said than done, however.

29.1.2 Comparison of Methods

Consider first the problem of valuing outstanding assets and liabilities at a point in time. Many, if not most, items on balance sheets are recorded at historical cost, that is, at their original purchase price with some adjustments, such as depreciation. This is the **historical cost method**.

For other items, economic values can be assessed from **market prices**, which are widely viewed as providing fair value. Indeed, the FASB formally defines **fair value** as the "amount at which an asset could be bought or sold in a current transaction between willing parties, that is, other than in a forced or liquidation sale." This is also called the **mark-to-market method (MTM)**. The main advantage of this method is its *transparency*.

Various methods also exist for dealing with profits and losses over a time period. The **cash method** recognizes profits and losses when the actual cash flow occurs. This is simple but does not reflect economic reality. Another method is the **accrual method**, which recognizes revenues when earned and expenses when incurred. From an economic standpoint, this is more precise but raises other issues.

As soon as a contract is signed, the business unit could book the current value of the future stream of profits. Some valuations, however, often involve judgment calls that may create conflicts within the company. Typically, traders will want to book the profits as early as possible, in order to get a bonus early. From the viewpoint of the company, however, the full capture of the cash flow occurs at the end only. The danger is that early recognition could fail to account for other costs or uncertainties. For instance, there may be unexpected operational expenses or credit losses during the term of the contract.

Assume, for instance, that an energy trader enters a contract with a utility to deliver natural gas at the price of $5/MMBTU for the next 10 years at a specific location. The contract could be valued by marking to market with a forward price curve for natural gas. The issue, however, is that there may not be reliable quotes for deliveries several years into the future.

29.2   Major Issues in Reporting

We now turn to two major issues in internal and external reporting. The first is the valuation of positions. The second is the choice of reporting method for hedging instruments.

29.2.1   Valuation Issues

The **valuation** problem affects all financial institutions. The most important aspect of valuation is to ensure that prices are truly *objective*, that is, not affected by the trader whose position is being evaluated. This is not as easy as it seems for exotic deals. There have been many instances of traders manipulating market prices in order to inflate their profits artificially.

Choice of Prices
Following is a hierarchy of sources and methods for determining the value of an instrument, going from most to least preferred.

- *Public exchange markets.* These provide the most reliable and transparent measure of value, provided there is sufficient trading activity. In our example, this would be represented by quotations on natural gas futures contracts going up to 10 years.

- *Dealer markets.* Dealers provide bid-ask quotes for a variety of financial instruments. Generally, these quotes can be trusted to represent objective, although perhaps noisy, measures of value. The quality of the data can be improved by polling several dealers and taking the average of their quotes. In our case, this would be represented by dealer quotes for natural gas contracts going up to 10 years.

  Even so, we have to decide whether to use **bid or ask prices**. To be conservative, we could use bid (lower) prices for all long positions and ask (higher) prices for all short positions. For a dealer bank, however, many of these positions may be *crossed* across desks and will not involve a separate transaction. In this case, one could use mid-market quotes with perhaps a provision for the spread.

■ *External pricing services.* Specialist firms can provide valuation models and price forecasts. Normally, these services provide objective or unbiased measures of value, although the dispersion in values can be high. In our case, this pricing service would be performed by an external consultant.

■ *Market comparables.* This method consists of using market prices for similar instruments and then making an adjustment for the specific features of the contract. In our case, this would be represented by using natural gas futures for delivery at some other location and then applying a *basis* to derive long-dated forward prices for this particular contract.

■ *Internal pricing services.* The company could develop its own pricing model, which is called **marking to model**. This approach, however, is likely to be most biased to make the trade look favorable, unless the pricing methodology is under the control of a totally independent unit.

David Askin, for instance, used his proprietary valuation models to value his $600 million CMO portfolio. When the mortgage market dropped in February 1994, he initially reported a loss of 2% that was later revised to 28%. As a result, he was sanctioned by the Securities and Exchange Commission for misrepresentation.

Nonsimultaneous Quotes

The fact that markets around the world close at different times imparts additional noise to the MTM value of hedged portfolios. Suppose that a trading desk is long a futures contract in London and short a contract with the same specifications in Chicago. Eventually, the contracts will converge to the same value, capturing arbitrage profits. Marking to market using London and Chicago closing times will create artificial volatility. This can be handled by recording market prices at the same time (e.g., London at 4 P.M. and Chicago at 9 A.M., both local times) or by using some price interpolation (e.g., forecasting the London price at 4 P.M. Chicago time).

This issue of **stale prices** was at the root of the recent mutual fund scandal in that U.S. Mutual funds investing in foreign assets allow trading based on their net asset value (NAV) up to the close of the U.S. trading day. These NAVs, however, reflect prices quoted much earlier during the day (e.g., at the close of Japanese markets), and in the meantime, markets may have moved. If, for instance, the S&P 500 index goes up by 5% during the day, there is a high likelihood that Japanese stocks will go up the next day.

Some unscrupulous investors took advantage of this, buying at the current NAV and reselling the next day, with the blessing of the mutual fund. Of course, this comes at the expense of other investors, who are not actively timing their funds but still have to pay for the transaction costs and resulting loss of value. Such **market timing** is not illegal but often violates fund rules. Another practice is executing orders after NAVs are priced at the 4 P.M. close of the market. This is called **late trading**, which is illegal.

In December 2003, the hedge fund Canary Partners was accused of market timing and settled for $40 million. Over the following year, a number of mutual funds accused of facilitating these practices settled for a total of $2.3 billion. These penalties can be classified as "operational risk."

29.2.2 Reporting Method for Derivatives

We now turn to the choice of the **reporting method for derivatives**. It is widely recognized that marking to market imposes a powerful discipline and should be used whenever possible. This general principle, however, is tempered by the fact that some items in financial statements are valued using historical cost data, or with cash flows amortized using the **accrual method**.

If so, the accounting method for the derivative should be *consistent* with that of the hedged item. Otherwise, marking to market one side of the hedge only will produce an artificial impression of volatility that does not reflect the economic reality of the hedge.

In fact, much of the discussion of the appropriate accounting method for derivatives centers on this issue of excess volatility. Corporations apparently strive to smooth out their earnings by active management of their accounting numbers. Marking to market financial instruments on the balance sheet does introduce some additional volatility, which is typically shunned by financial officers. The counterargument is that this volatility represents fluctuations in actual economic value.

Figure 29-1 describes general principles for choosing an accounting method for derivatives. The crucial factor is management *intent* in holding the derivative. The issue is, is it held for trading or hedging purposes?

FIGURE 29-1 Accrual versus Mark-to-Market Accounting

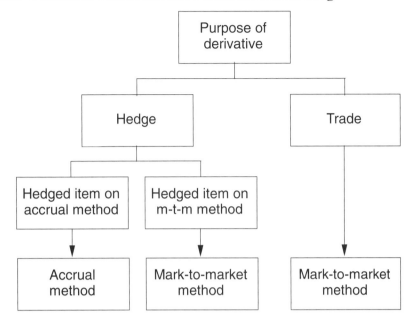

In trading portfolios where financial assets are valued using MTM prices, derivatives should be valued using the MTM method as well. In contrast, when the derivative is used as a hedge, the appropriate method depends on the accounting method used for the hedged item. In the ideal case, the hedged item is marked to market, in which case the derivative should be marked to market also. With an effective hedge, market fluctuations should cancel out.

The problem is that most often the hedged item (say a foreign-currency–denominated debt) is booked on an accrual basis. It then makes little sense to use MTM valuation for the derivative (say a currency swap designed to take out currency risk), as this would create artificial volatility. Instead, the derivative should be booked using the same accrual basis. This is still not ideal, because the hedge could be imperfect, creating residual volatility that remains hidden.

Example 29-1: FRM Exam 1998—Question 8

Which of the following price sources for derivative transactions is the most prudent for financial reporting purposes?
a) Trader marks
b) Valuation models
c) Directly observable market prices
d) Broker quotes

Example 29-2: FRM Exam 2000—Question 25

Marking to market on a futures contract that is long in London and short in Chicago can be handled by which of the following?

  I. Recording the close price in both locations

 II. Recording market prices at the same instant, regardless of time zones

III. Recording market prices at the same local time in both locations

IV. Forecasting the London price at 4 P.M. Chicago time

a) I or II

b) II or IV

c) I, II or IV

d) I, II, III or IV

29.3 External Reporting: FASB

For a long time, derivatives were off–balance sheet items that did not appear in the financial statements, except perhaps in footnotes. This may have been acceptable when derivatives were marginal items. Over time, however, the market for derivatives has grown to enormous amounts, over 100 trillion dollars. For most financial institutions, derivatives now dwarf balance sheet items. The notional amount of derivatives held by U.S. commercial banks, for instance, is now more than 10 times the size of their assets. Even nonfinancial corporations have become heavy users of derivatives. As a result, it has become increasingly important to reflect derivatives in financial statements.

29.3.1 FAS 133

The Financial Accounting Standards Board (FASB) has long struggled to set standards for the disclosure and accounting treatment of derivatives. The FASB's view is that derivatives are, in effect, assets or liabilities, like other balance sheet items. Keeping them off balance sheet can conceal their risk.

In June 1998 the FASB passed a new set of standards, No. 133, *Accounting for Derivative Instruments and Hedging Activities*, which unifies derivatives accounting, hedge accounting, and disclosure in a single statement. **FAS 133** represents a radical change in the accounting of derivatives and supersedes a hodgepodge of previous rules.

Effective June 15, 2000, it basically requires derivatives to be recorded on the balance sheet at *fair value*, that is, at market prices. For the first time, changes in the market value of derivatives must be reported in earnings. A major exception remains, however, for derivatives used (and designated) as a hedge. In this situation, FAS 133 allows the gain or loss to be recognized in earnings at the same time as the hedged item. FAS 133 has been amended by FAS 137, 138, and 149. The following discussion incorporates these amendments.

29.3.2 Definition of Derivative

FAS 133 provides a formal and complete definition of a **derivative instrument**. This is defined as a contract with all three of the following characteristics.

(i) It has one or more *underlyings* and one or more *notional amounts*. The underlying is that from which the contract derives its value (e.g., an asset price, reference rate, or index—such as a stock, bond, currency, or commodity). The underlying is a market-related characteristic that gives rise to changes in value. As an example, the value of a futures contract for oil will change as the price of oil changes; the underlying is the price of oil, not oil itself. The notional amount is a number of currency units, shares, or other physical units specified in the contract. The payoff on the derivative instrument is a function of the notional and the underlying. For instance, a NYMEX oil futures contract has a notional of 1,000 barrels. The dollar payment is the change in price per barrel times the notional.

(ii) It requires an *initial investment* of zero, or "smaller" than would be required for an equivalent position that has the same response to market factors. For instance, the initial investment in a forward currency contract is generally zero, even though the contract is economically equivalent to a leveraged spot position in the foreign currency. For an option, the initial investment is the premium, which is much less than the cost of taking a delta-equivalent position in the underlying.

(iii) Its terms require or permit *net settlement* (e.g., for interest rate swaps, the payment is the net of the fixed and floating amounts). Alternatively, there is a market mechanism for net settlement (e.g., liquidating a futures contract by going back to the exchange), or the asset to be delivered is readily convertible to cash or is itself a derivative instrument (e.g., an option on futures).

Notwithstanding these conditions, the following contracts do not fall in this category:

(a) Regular-way securities trades (e.g., a transaction to purchase a stock to be settled in the normal three-day period)

(b) Normal purchases and sales (of nonfinancial instruments, such as machinery, in the course of normal business)

(c) Traditional insurance contracts (such as life insurance or property and casualty insurance, where the payoff is the result of an identifiable event instead of a change in the underlying)

(d) Certain financial guarantee contracts (where the payoff is a credit event instead of a change in the underlying, but only when the buyer of the guarantee is exposed to a loss on the underlying asset)

(e) Certain over-the-counter contracts, such as weather derivatives, options on real estate, and capital goods (which are not readily convertible to cash)

(f) Derivatives that serve as an impediment to sales accounting

(g) Investments in life insurance

(h) Certain investment contracts, such as pension plans

(i) Loan commitments

In addition, FAS 133 excludes (j1) contracts indexed to an entity's own stock, (j2) executive stock options, and (j3) contracts issued as a contingent consideration from a business combination (such as the acquisition of another company).

29.3.3 Embedded Derivative

Another provision of FAS 133 deals with the treatment of **embedded derivatives**. These are derivatives that are included in the provisions of other contracts. An example is a structured note where the payoff is a function of the return on the S&P index. Under FAS 133, such a hybrid instrument should be split between the host contract and the embedded derivative if and only if these conditions are met.

(1) The economic characteristics of the contract and embedded derivative are not "clearly and closely related."[2]

(2) The fair market value for the hybrid contract would not otherwise be reported on the balance sheet.

---

[2]Embedded derivatives that depend on an interest rate in an interest-bearing host contract are considered related, unless (1) the embedded derivative can lead to a near-total loss of the investment or (2) there is substantial leverage. Interest-only and principal-only strips are generally exempt from FAS 133.

(3) The embedded derivative would meet the definition of a derivative on a stand-
alone basis.

When the split occurs, the embedded derivative component is subject to FAS 133
rules. A few examples illustrate these rules. Hybrid securities held in the trading portfolio do not need to be separated because they are marked to market anyway. Condition (2) is not satisfied.

In other situations, one has to interpret the term *clearly and closely related*. Consider a corporate callable bond. Conditions (2) and (3) are satisfied. Condition (1),
however, is not satisfied because the host contract and derivative are closely related.
The call option to the issuer involves an underlying (the interest rate) that also drives
the value of the host contract. So there is no need to separate the components.

Consider next a convertible bond. Conditions (2) and (3) are satisfied. The option
feature is driven by the stock price, which is not related to the interest rate in the host
bond contract. As a result, condition (1) is satisfied. FAS 133 thus requires an investor
in a convertible bond to separate the option feature from the host contract. On the
other hand, this does not apply to the issuer of a convertible bond, since the derivative
is indexed to the entity's own stock (condition (3) is not satisfied due to the additional
exclusion (j1)).

29.3.4   Disclosure Rules

Under FAS 133, the **disclosure** method depends on the purpose of the derivative and
is classified as one of four methods, which are described in Figure 29-2.

a. *No hedging designation.* The gain or loss on the derivative should flow into *earnings*.

b. *Cash-flow hedge.* This category involves the risk of an uncertain *cash flow*, such
as the future purchase of an asset or an interest rate exposure. For this category to
apply, the derivative must be designated and qualify as a hedge. In this case, the
gain or loss on the derivative should go into **other comprehensive income (OCI)**,
an account outside earnings. Later this is reclassified as *earnings* at the same time
that the hedged transaction affects earnings.

More precisely, the company must determine the component in the hedge result
that is **effective** and **ineffective**. The effective component indeed flows through
OCI, but the ineffective component must be realized in earnings.

c. *Fair-value hedge.* This category applies when the derivative is used to hedge changes in the value of a recognized asset or liability or of an unrecognized firm commitment. These represent hedges of existing or anticipated *positions*. For this category to apply, the derivative must be designated and qualify as a hedge. The gain or loss on the derivative then goes into *earnings*. Simultaneously, the underlying exposure due to the risk being hedged must be marked to market and recorded in earnings as well.

d. *Foreign currency hedge.* This category applies when the derivative is used to hedge the foreign currency exposure of

—*An unrecognized firm commitment* (using the fair-value method)

—*An available-for-sale security* (using the fair-value method)

—*A forecast transaction* (using the cash-flow method)

—*A net investment in a foreign operation* (using a translation adjustment in an equity account)

The last case applies when the company must translate into dollars the foreign-currency value of its balance sheet assets and liabilities. Derivatives and non-derivatives (such as foreign-currency debt) can be designated as hedges. As before, effective results are treated the same way as translation adjustments; ineffective hedges must flow into earnings.

FIGURE 29-2 Choice of Accounting Method for Derivatives

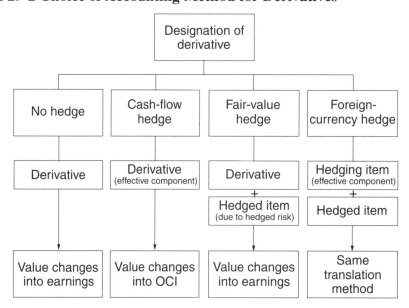

29.3.5   Hedge Effectiveness

To obtain hedge treatment, the derivative should be designated as a hedge at inception. Users are required to create documentation that supports the business purpose and effectiveness of the hedge **at inception**. Further, the hedge must be monitored regularly, **on an ongoing basis**, at least quarterly, in line with the financial reporting cycle. If, after initially qualifying for hedge status, the criteria are no longer satisfied, the reporting requirements then change to the "no hedging" category.

To qualify for hedge accounting, the company must expect the hedge relationship to be *highly effective* in offsetting changes in fair value or cash flows. FAS 133 does not prescribe a particular method for measuring hedging effectiveness, however.[3]

As described in Figure 29-3, this must be done using a *prospective evaluation* (forward looking), where the user must be able to justify that the hedge *will be* effective, and a *retrospective evaluation* (backward looking), where the user must assess whether the hedge *has been* effective. Evaluations can be done by comparing the changes in the values of the hedged position and of the hedge, or using a regression analysis.

Hedge effectiveness may be assumed to be perfect when either (1) the hedging instrument is a forward contract that perfectly matches the hedged item and has initial market value of zero, or (2) the hedging instrument is an interest rate swap that perfectly matches the hedged item. This is called the *short-cut* method.

As an example, consider the case of a company with an inventory of 1,000 barrels of oil that is hedged using a forward sale. The current spot price is $13 per barrel. The company designates the derivative as a "fair-value hedge" of the oil. In this case, the company expects no ineffectiveness because the notional amount of the derivative matches the amount of the hedged inventory, and the underlying of the derivative is the price of the same grade and location as the inventory.

Assume that after three months the price of oil falls from $13 to $10 per barrel. Ignoring time effects, the value of the short derivative position should increase by $3. We would then have an entry into earnings that reflects a loss of $3,000 in the inventory and is offset by a gain of $3,000 on the derivative. This is a "perfect" hedge.

Let us say now that the terms of the derivative do not exactly match those of the

---

[3]See the Derivatives Implementation Group (2000), *Statement 133 Implementation Issue No. E7: Hedging–General: Methodologies to Assess Effectiveness of Fair Value and Cash Flow Hedges*, Norwalk, CT: FASB, available at http://www.fasb.org.

FIGURE 29-3 Effectiveness Assessment

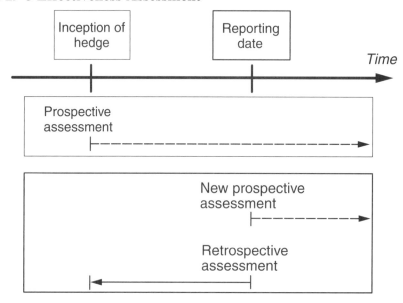

inventory and that the derivative position increases in value by only $1 per barrel. The entries in earnings would then reflect a loss of $3,000 in the inventory and a gain of $1,000 on the derivative, for a net loss of $2,000. The $2,000 amount, or difference between the value of the hedged position and the hedging instrument, is the "hedge ineffectiveness." This difference reflects a true economic loss.

29.3.6   General Evaluation of FAS 133

FAS 133 is widely viewed as a complex set of standards. The initial rules were published in a 245-page document, which is comparable to a course textbook. Later amendments are also very long. When the standards were initially proposed, there was some opposition, in part due to the complexity of the rules but also from banks fearing that derivatives usage would be aversely affected. Far from it, however, derivatives have continued their unabated growth.

Another source of concern was that FAS 133 would increase the volatility of reported earnings. This is not always the case, however. With construction of effective hedges, adding derivatives has a minimal impact on earnings volatility. FAS 133, however, does penalize **macro hedges**, which are hedges applied at the portfolio level as opposed to the individual transaction level. Macro hedges reduce the number and volume of hedging transactions but do not benefit from hedge treatment.

As an example, consider a car manufacturer that has a yen exposure not because it exports to Japan but because its competitors are Japanese. The firm has no yen transactions on its books, but would reduce its risk by hedging its yen exposure. Such a hedge does not qualify for hedge accounting. Derivatives profits and losses have to be shown in earnings. However, the hedge should offset movements in operating cash flows. When the yen depreciates, domestic sales and profits should suffer, but at the same time gains should accrue on the hedges. So there should be some economic offsets in earnings.

29.3.7   Accounting Treatment of SPEs

The **Enron** failure has highlighted deficiencies in the application of U.S. financial reporting standards. Enron made extensive use of **special-purpose entities (SPEs)**, which are financial vehicles used to convert income-producing assets, such as loans, bonds, credit card receivables, or pipelines to cash. In a clean securitization process, a company transfers assets to an SPE in return for cash, accounting for the deal as a sale, thus removing the assets from the balance sheet.

In the case of Enron, however, the company kept an equity stake in the SPE. Even so, Enron was not required to *consolidate*, that is, include its interests in the SPE on its balance sheet. This was because the SPE was structured to have *sufficient independent economic substance,* defined as a situation where outside investors have an equity stake of at least 3% of the SPE's capital. Enron had to show only *equity in the SPE affiliate* on its balance sheet. The end result was that Enron was able to move assets and debt out of its balance sheet, artificially lowering its leverage. This increased Enron's credit rating and made its stock look more desirable than it really was.

The problem was that Enron gave outside investors guarantees of the SPE's performance. In most cases, such support operations are optional. Problems arise with explicit guarantees, however. Some SPEs carried guarantees that effectively placed all the risk on Enron itself, without being reflected on Enron's balance sheet. When the SPEs began to perform poorly, Enron was obligated to prop them up with cash or its own shares. As the size of those liabilities became clear, Enron's stock collapsed and the company was forced into bankruptcy. Compounding the scandal were conflicts of interest created by some Enron executives' personal holdings in the SPEs.

The FASB has revised its rules to make it harder for companies to keep SPEs off the books. The new guidance, called interpretation 46, is based on two provisions.

First, to qualify for off–balance sheet treatment, a SPE must contain at least 10% outside equity, up from the current 3%. Second, the outside equity should be at risk, and as such cannot be protected by side agreements with the parent company.

Example 29-3: FRM Exam 2002—Question 58

A key principle of FAS 133 is that

a) Fair value is most appropriate for derivative instruments.

b) The book value of derivative instruments is used to prepare financial statements.

c) Derivative instruments are off–balance sheet items.

d) Derivative instrument value is used for tax reporting only.

Example 29-4: FRM Exam 1998—Question 10

All of the following instruments are considered to be derivatives under FAS 133 *except*

a) Futures contracts

b) Total return swaps

c) Credit default swaps

d) Option contracts

Example 29-5: FRM Exam 2002—Question 61

Under FAS 133, a derivative that currently has positive value

a) Must be marked to market on a daily basis

b) Necessarily affects the balance sheet and may affect earnings

c) Remains off balance sheet if it had no value at inception

d) Is marked to market if its current marked-to-market value is below its cost

---

Example 29-6: FRM Exam 2000—Question 24

According to a provision in FAS 133, under which of the following conditions should embedded derivatives be split between the host contract and the embedded derivative?

  I. The economic characteristics of the contract and embedded derivative are not "clearly and closely related."

 II. The fair market value for the hybrid contract otherwise would not be reported on the balance sheet.

III. The embedded derivative would meet the definition of a derivative on a stand-alone basis.

IV. The payoff is not a function of the return on a linked instrument.

a) I and II

b) II and III

c) I, II, and III

d) I, II, III, and IV

Example 29-7: FRM Exam 1998—Question 11

Under FAS 133, which of the following instruments would require bifurcation of the cash instrument and the embedded derivative instrument?

a) Inverse floater

b) Inflation-indexed bond

c) Indexed amortizing notes

d) Callable debt

Example 29-8: FRM Exam 1998—Question 12

Which type of derivative contract is least appropriate for a manufacturing company trying to hedge a rise in the cost of its raw materials?

a) Long futures

b) Long call option

c) Short put option

d) Floating-price payer on commodity swap

Example 29-9: FRM Sample Question

Which of the following approaches for measuring the effectiveness of hedges are permissible under FAS 133 hedge accounting rules?

a) Statistical techniques

b) Cash-flow analysis

c) Dollar offset

d) Any of the above

29.4 External Reporting: IASB

The **International Accounting Standards Committee (IASC)** was set up in 1973 to champion global accounting standards. IASC was superseded by the **International Accounting Standards Board (IASB)** in 2001. International securities regulators gave IASB a mandate to devise common reporting standards acceptable for listing on any stock exchange. In particular, the European Union will require all EU companies to comply with IASB standards by January 1, 2005. This applies to more than 7,000 listed companies.

IASB publishes its standards in a series of pronouncements called International Financial Reporting Standards (IFRS). It has also adopted the body of standards issued by the IASC. Those pronouncements continue to be designated **International Accounting Standards (IAS)**.

The FASB is not bound to adopt IASB's standards, although each body has agreed to try to converge to the highest-quality accounting treatment. Their goal is to achieve convergence by 2007–2008, removing the need for reconciliation between U.S. accounting principles and international ones.

There are also differences of opinion with respect to the philosophy of accounting standards. Should they be guided by *principles* or by *detailed rules*? Both approaches have strengths and weaknesses. U.S. regulators tend to emphasize detailed rules, which may, however, encourage companies to exploit loopholes in the system. Indeed, Enron devoted much effort to game its financial reporting system. Enron may have followed the letter, but certainly not the spirit, of the system. However, guiding principles may allow too much leeway in interpretation. A proper balance between the two approaches is required.

29.4.1   IAS 39

An important standard for risk managers is **IAS 39**, *Financial Instruments: Recognition and Measurement*, which was issued in December 1998 and went in force after January 2001. The standard has been amended several times since then.

IAS 39 deals with these financial instruments: cash; demand and time deposits; commercial paper; accounts, notes, and loans receivable and payable; debt and equity securities; asset-backed securities, such as collateralized mortgage obligations and repurchase agreements; derivatives; and leases, rights, and obligations of insurance contracts and pension contracts. **Financial instruments** are defined as contracts that give rise to a financial asset of one entity and a financial liability or equity instrument of another entity. IAS 39 defines derivatives similarly to FAS 133 and includes provisions for the treatment of embedded derivatives.

The key principle behind IAS 39 is that all financial instruments must be recognized on the balance sheet. Note that this is broader than FAS 133, which applies only to derivatives.

Financial assets must fall in one of the following categories:

- *Financial assets at fair value through profits or loss*

- *Available-for-sale financial assets*, measured at fair value on the balance sheet but with changes recognized in an equity account

- *Loans and receivables*, measured at amortized cost

- *Held-to-maturity investments*, also measured at amortized cost

Financial liabilities must fall in one of the following categories:

- *Financial liabilities at fair value through profits or loss*

- *Other financial liabilities*, measured at amortized cost

For derivatives, changes in value must flow into earnings, except for hedges. To qualify for **hedge accounting**, the company must designate a derivative financial instrument as either a **fair-value hedge**, a **cash-flow hedge**, or a **foreign-operation hedge**. The designation must be in writing, up front, and be consistent with an established risk management strategy.

Like FAS 133, IAS 39 requires hedge effectiveness to be assessed both prospectively and retrospectively. In addition, the retrospective results must be within the range of 80% to 125%. To measure effectiveness, define the change in the value of the hedged item as y_t and the change in the value of the hedging instrument as x_t. Results can then be measured by the ratio of y_t over x_t. Alternatively, results can be defined in terms of the slope b of the regression

$$y_t = bx_t + \epsilon_t \tag{29.1}$$

A hedge is effective if $0.8 < b < 1.25$. In practice, this rule is also broadly used in the United States for testing effectiveness under FAS 133.

In March 2004, IASB amended IAS 39 for **macro hedges**. Fair-value hedge accounting treatment is permissible for a *portfolio* hedge of assets or liabilities exposed to interest rate risk.

The body of international accounting standards had to be adopted by the European Commission (EC) to be transformed into EU law. The EC has approved 33 standards in full. The remaining standard, IAS 39, was approved by the EC in November 2004, albeit with two *carve-outs* (exceptions).[4]

---

[4]The first carve-out concerns the option to designate any financial asset or liability as one to be measured at *fair value*, with gains and losses recognized in profit or loss. The EC does not allow fair valuation for a company's own liabilities. The second carve-out concerns *certain hedge accounting provisions* dealing with portfolio hedging of core deposits, which have been criticized by European banks as likely to produce unwarranted volatility. The EC allows, but does not require, EU companies to apply these provisions.

29.5 Tax Considerations

The taxation of financial instruments is a complex topic that evolves over time, differs across jurisdictions, and is often not consistent across economically equivalent assets.

In fact, financial innovations are often viewed as a response to changes in the *tax code* and *regulation*. One example is the differential treatment of capital gains and ordinary income, which can lead to arbitrage opportunities. For instance, zero-coupon bonds were initially created to take advantage of the fact that their returns were viewed entirely as capital gains, which are taxed at a lower rate than income. Since then, tax authorities have changed the tax code to bring in line the taxation of zeros and coupon-paying bonds.

Even though their tax advantages have faded, however, zeros are still widely used as they provide effective hedges for investors with fixed liabilities. The continued growth of derivatives is explained by the fact that they make markets more complete by increasing opportunities for *risk sharing* among investors. Even so, avoidance of taxes and regulation often have provided the impetus for the creation of new financial instruments.

Generally, key issues in taxation are

■ The *nature* or *character* of taxable gains and losses (i.e., capital or ordinary income)

■ The *timing* of their recognition (i.e., at inception, during the life of, or at expiration of the transaction)

■ The *source* of revenues, which determines whether income will bear tax (i.e., U.S. income of non-U.S. persons attracts a U.S. withholding tax, and foreign-source income of U.S. persons is subject to U.S. federal income tax)

Consider, for instance, U.S. tax rules. The character issue is more important for noncorporate taxpayers, who face lower tax rates on capital gains than on ordinary income. For corporate taxpayers, in contrast, capital gains and income are taxed at the same rate.

Futures contracts fall under Section s1256 of the Internal Revenue Code. Positions in futures are marked to market and treated as if they are closed out on the last day of the tax year. Gains and losses are of a *capital* nature, except for foreign exchange gains and losses, which are treated as ordinary income, falling under Section s988.

Hedging transactions, however, are treated differently. These are defined as transactions entered into for one of these reasons:

To reduce the risk of price changes with respect to assets held or to be held for the purpose of producing ordinary income

To reduce the risk of price changes (e.g., interest rate changes or currency fluctuations) with respect to borrowings

Hedging transactions are taxed as *ordinary income*, with recognition of gains or losses matching the recognition of that of the hedged item. Note that the definition of hedge transaction for tax purposes differs from that for accounting purposes, requiring a different set of books.

Example 29-10: FRM Exam 2000—Question 21

Hedging transactions are taxed as

a) Capital gains

b) Dividend income

c) Ordinary income

d) Interest income

29.6   Answers to Chapter Examples

Example 29-1: FRM Exam 1998—Question 8

c) Directly observable market quotes are least susceptible to price manipulation.

Example 29-2: FRM Exam 2000—Question 25

b) The prices should be recorded at the same time using actual quotes or, possibly, forecasting the price of the closed market based on information from the other market.

Example 29-3: FRM Exam 2002—Question 58

a) The key principle of FAS 133 is that derivatives are off–balance sheet items but must be reported at fair market value.

Example 29-4: FRM Exam 1998—Question 10

c) Credit default swaps do not necessarily satisfy the third condition, which is to allow net settlements.

Example 29-5: FRM Exam 2002—Question 61

b) A derivative that has any nonzero value must appear on the balance sheet as an asset or liability, and the change in value will affect earnings, except under hedge accounting.

Example 29-6: FRM Exam 2000—Question 24

c) Answers I, II, and III are correct. The derivative should have a payoff that does depend on an underlying.

Example 29-7: FRM Exam 1998—Question 11

a) The inverse floater is a fixed-rate bond plus a long position in a receive-fixed swap. Thus it is a hybrid instrument. We need to check whether the three conditions for separation are satisfied. The swap is not closely related to the host contract and hence satisfies condition (1). The inverse floater is not marked to market on the balance sheet, which satisfies condition (2). Finally, the swap is a derivative and hence satisfies condition (3). Answer b) is incorrect because the coupon payments and the inflation index are clearly and closely related. Same for answers c) and d). Indexed amortizing notes repay the principal according to a schedule that depends on the value of a reference index.

Example 29-8: FRM Exam 1998—Question 12

d) The company has a natural *short* position in the product. Price increases can be hedged by taking a long futures or long call position, so answers a) and b) are appropriate hedges. Selling a put does not provide a hedge against price increases but offsets the benefit of falling prices. This is not a hedge but is consistent with the natural short position. Finally, paying the floating price on the swap means that the company will have to pay *more* if the commodity price increases. This is the opposite of what the company should do to hedge.

Example 29-9: FRM Sample Question

d) Any of the methods is permissible. The approach should be chosen at inception, however, and should not vary during the hedging period.

Example 29-10: FRM Exam 2000—Question 21

c) As stated in the text, hedging transactions are taxed as ordinary income.

eight

Regulation and Compliance

Chapter 30

Regulation of Financial Institutions

We now tackle the last part of this manual, which deals with regulatory capital. Banks and securities houses must now comply with risk-based capital requirements. These regulatory capital requirements have been the catalyst for the revolution in risk management of the last decade. They have spurred the industry into better understanding and management of their risks. In turn, regulators are now forced to upgrade their regulatory requirements to keep up with modern developments in risk management. Analyzing the rationale behind these regulations yields interesting insights into broader issues that we have not addressed yet, such as systemic risk.

This chapter is structured as follows. Section 30.1 provides a broad classification of financial institutions subject to regulation. Section 30.2 discusses systemic risk, which is as a major rationale for regulation of financial institutions. Next, Sections 30.3 and 30.4 describe the regulation of commercial banks and securities houses, respectively. Section 30.5 concludes with a summary of the tools and objectives of financial regulation.

30.1   Definition of Financial Institutions

Financial institutions are fundamentally different from other corporations. When an industrial corporation goes bankrupt, shareholders, bondholders, and other creditors suffer financial losses. The overall effects of the failure, however, are limited to direct stakeholders.

In contrast, the failure of a financial institution can be potentially much more harmful. Financial institutions include

- **Commercial banks**, whose primary function is to hold customer deposits and to extend credit to businesses, households, or governments.[1]

- **Securities houses**, whose primary function is to intermediate in securities markets. These include **investment banks**, which specialize in the initial sale of securities in the primary markets,[2] and **broker-dealers**, whose primary function is to assist in the trading of securities in the secondary markets.[3]

- **Insurance companies**, which provide property and casualty (P&C) or life insurance coverage.

In some countries, the first two types are separated and subject to different regulators. This was the case in the United States until the recent repeal of the Glass-Steagall Act, which separated banking and securities functions. This is an example of **asset restrictions** on financial institutions. In other countries with a so-called **universal bank** model, a bank can engage in traditional banking and securities activities.

Financial institutions also include other intermediaries that constitute the "buy side" of Wall Street, in contrast with banks and brokers, the "sell side" that intermediates in financial markets. The buy side consists of professional (as opposed to private) investors, called **institutional investors**, which include insurance companies, pension and endowment funds, investment companies (e.g., mutual and closed-end funds), and hedge funds. These are subject to different regulatory requirements from banks and securities houses.

At the outset, we should ask the question of whether regulation of financial institutions is at all necessary. After all, other industries are not regulated (except for antitrust-related reasons, i.e., to avoid monopolies, as in the recent Microsoft case). Private corporations already have their own governance mechanism, which is shareholder supervision. Shouldn't shareholders decide on the appropriate risk-return profile for the company in which they have invested their own funds? Why should governments intervene in free markets? Why do we need regulators?

---

[1]Similar intermediaries are **savings institutions**, which specialize in residential mortgages, and **credit unions**, which extend mortgage and consumer credit. These are generally local and relatively small institutions whose failure is unlikely to destabilize financial markets.

[2]The term *bank* in *investment bank* is a misnomer, since these institutions do not extend credit as commercial banks do.

[3]Brokers act as pure intermediaries and simply match buyers with sellers. As a result, they take no market risk. In contrast, dealers stand ready to buy and sell securities at given prices. Therefore, they must maintain an inventory of securities and are exposed to market risk.

30.2 Systemic Risk

Unlike other entities, banks and securities houses play a special role of intermediation. They facilitate payment flows across customers and maintain markets for financial instruments. This very role, however, can make bank failures much more disruptive to the economy than the failure of other entities. The threat is systemic risk.

Systemic risk can be defined as the risk of a sudden shock that would damage the financial system to such an extent that the whole economy would suffer.

Systemic risk involves the contagious transmission of a shock due to the actual or suspected exposure to a failing bank. This is usually accompanied by a **flight to quality**, which reflects an increased demand for government securities, pushing up the relative cost of capital for the corporate sector. If prolonged, this can lead to a fall in investment spending and can dampen consumption.

Indeed, failures in the domestic banking system have been particularly damaging. Among emerging markets, domestic financial collapses have often cost more than 10% of a country's gross domestic product. In each case, the government (or rather, the taxpayer) has covered the cost of the failure based on the principle that this would be less costly than letting a domestic banking failure spread to the rest of the economy.

Systemic risk can come from two sources:

■ *Panicky behavior of depositors or investors.* This can arise from the failure of an institution or a political shock. In a **bank run**, depositors become worried about the stability of their bank (when there is no deposit insurance) and demand immediate return of their funds, which may lead to failure of the bank. Similarly, a sudden drop in securities prices may lead to margin calls, forcing leveraged investors to liquidate their positions, which puts further pressure on prices. Some institutions may fail, resulting in a loss of liquidity and a credit crunch.

■ *Interruptions in the payment system.* This can arise from the failure of an institution or from a technological breakdown in the payment system. Banks and securities houses are central to the payment system by which transactions for goods, services, and assets are cleared and settled. When an institution cannot pay, it may expose the payment system to a breakdown.

30.3 Regulation of Commercial Banks

Our experience with systemic risk is profoundly marked by the banking crisis of the 1930s in the United States. The banking system was subject to bank runs, when depositors lost faith in the ability of their deposit bank to make full payment and "ran to the bank" to withdraw their funds.

The problem is that the bank may be perfectly solvent, that is, have assets (e.g., loans, real estate) whose value exceeds its liabilities (e.g., demand deposits). Because such assets are illiquid, however, the bank may not be able to meet redemptions immediately, leading to default. Indeed, during the U.S. banking crisis of the 1930s, one bank in three failed, causing a severe contraction of credit.

In response, the United States established federal **deposit insurance** in 1933. The insurance fund protects investors if their bank fails, thereby eliminating the need for a bank run. This scheme has been widely credited for stopping bank runs. By now, most countries have developed a compulsory deposit insurance program.

The problem with deposit insurance, however, is that some of the financial risk is passed on to the deposit insurance fund (i.e., ultimately the government or taxpayer). This creates a need for regulation of insured institutions.

Turning next to the other source of systemic risk, the prime example of a breakdown in the payment system was the June 1974 failure of Bankhaus Herstatt, a small German bank active in the foreign exchange market. The bank was shut down by noon, U.S. time, after having received payments in German marks. In exchange, the counterparty banks were due to receive payment the same afternoon in U.S. dollars. These payments never came, however, creating substantial losses and a serious liquidity squeeze for counterparties. This event caused severe disruption in the payment system and was perhaps the most extreme shock experienced in the foreign exchange market. What has become known as **Herstatt risk** has led to a concerted effort by bank regulators to avoid such situations, which ultimately gave birth to the **Basel Committee on Banking Supervision (BCBS)**.

The BCBS consists of central bankers from the Group of Ten (G-10) countries.[4] Its primary objective is to promote the **safety and soundness** of the global financial

---

[4]The Basel Committee's members are senior officials from the G-10 (Belgium, Canada, France, Germany, Italy, Japan, the Netherlands, Sweden, United Kingdom, and the United States, plus Luxembourg and Switzerland), who meet four times a year, usually in Basel, under the aegis of the Bank for International Settlements. Its Web site is http://www.bis.org.

system, that is, to try to control systemic risk. Another objective is to create a system that ensures a **level playing field** for global financial institutions.[5]

The Basel Committee has established minimum risk-based capital standards that apply to so-called **core institutions**. These represent internationally active *commercial* banks, which are major players in large-value payment systems. The capital adequacy rules are described in a series of documents known as the **Basel Accord**, which will be analyzed in the following chapters.

It should be emphasized that core institutions are ultimately regulated by their domestic banking regulators. Although pronouncements of the Basel Committee are not legally binding, member countries have implemented them. Even countries that are not part of the Basel Committee often feel obligated to abide by the regulations. By now, over 100 countries have adopted the framework of the Basel Accord. De facto, the accord applies to all internationally active commercial banks.

In the United States, for instance, commercial banks are regulated by the **Board of Governors of the Federal Reserve System** ("the Fed"),[6] the **Office of the Comptroller of the Currency** (OCC),[7] and the **Federal Deposit Insurance Corporation (FDIC)**.[8] This fragmentation of supervision is somewhat puzzling but is common among U.S. agencies.

In the United Kingdom, the regulatory framework is more logical, with only one regulator for banks, securities markets, and insurance firms: the **Financial Services Authority** (FSA).[9] This all-powerful regulator was created in October 1997, taking over banking supervision from the Bank of England.

In Japan, supervision of financial markets, including banking, securities business, and insurance, rests with the **Financial Services Agency** (FSA), established in July 2000. This responsibility is shared with the central bank, or **Bank of Japan**, which

---

[5]One concern was that Japanese banks were expanding into global markets and were able to undercut their competitors due to more lenient Japanese regulations.

[6]The Federal Reserve supervises all bank holding companies and state-chartered banks that are members of the Federal Reserve System. Its Web site is http://www.federalreserve.gov.

[7]The principal function of the OCC is to supervise U.S. national banks and branches and agencies of foreign banks in the United States. National banks are defined as those chartered by the federal government, as opposed to state banks. The OCC is a bureau of the Treasury Department. Its Web site is http://www.occ.treas.gov.

[8]The FDIC is a U.S. government agency whose mission is to maintain the stability of and public confidence in the nation's financial system. It has provided deposit insurance since 1933. Its Web site is http://www.fdic.gov.

[9]Its Web site is http://www.fsa.gov.uk.

conducts monetary policy and ensures the stability of the financial system by monitoring financial institutions.[10]

Banks in the **European Union** (EU) are subject to minimum standards, which are binding over all member countries.[11] The **Solvency Ratio Directive** was published in December 1989 and implements the 1988 Basel rules for credit risk. To this was added the **Capital Adequacy Directive (CAD)** in March 1993, which implements the building-block approach to market risk. This was updated in 1998 to allow the use of internal models. France and Germany have different regulators for retail and wholesale markets. In France, this responsibility is split up between the Commission des Operations de Bourse and the Commission Bancaire (Banque de France).[12] In Germany, the agencies are the Federal Securities Supervisory Office, formally Bundesaufsichtsamt für den Wertpapierhandel (BAWe), and the Federal Banking Supervisory Office, formally Bundesaufsichtsamt für das Kreditwesen (BAKred).[13] There is now discussion of having a single pan-European regulator to achieve a truly integrated financial market.

The Basel Accord (to be examined in detail in the next chapter) sets *minimum* risk-based levels of capital for core institutions. National authorities, however, are free to adopt arrangements that set higher levels or other criteria. The Federal Reserve board, for example, has an additional requirement based on the bank's **leverage ratio**.[14] This places a constraint on the degree to which a banking organization can leverage its equity capital base.

Failure to meet the capital adequacy requirements triggers regulatory action, affecting the types of activities in which institutions can engage and requiring **prompt corrective action** (PCA), including the possible appointment of a receiver.

To summarize, the regulation of commercial banks is motivated by two objectives:

■ *Minimizing systemic risk*

■ *Protecting the deposit insurance fund*

---

[10]The Web sites for the FSA and the Bank of Japan are http://www.fsa.go.jp and http://www.boj.or.jp.

[11]The EU includes Austria, Belgium, Denmark, Finland, France, Germany, Greece, Ireland, Italy, Luxembourg, the Netherlands, Portugal, Spain, Sweden, and the United Kingdom, among others. This covers all countries in Western Europe except for Switzerland and Norway.

[12]The Web sites are http://www.cob.fr and http://www.banque-france.fr.

[13]The Web sites are http://www.bwade.de and http://www.bakred.de.

[14]The ratio of (tier 1) capital to total consolidated assets must be greater than 3% plus an additional cushion of 100 to 200 basis points. Tier 1 capital will be defined in Chapter 31.

30.4   Regulation of Securities Houses

The regulation of securities houses differs substantially from that of commercial banks. Broker-dealers hold securities on the asset and liability sides (usually called long and short sides) of their balance sheets. Because securities are much more liquid than bank loans, there is no rationale for bank runs.

The objectives of regulation for securities houses are

- *Protecting the customer.* One goal is to protect the firm's customers against a default of their broker-dealer. The rationale here is that small investors (e.g., the traditional "widows and orphans") are less capable of informed investment decisions. Another goal is to protect consumers against excessive prices or opportunistic behavior by financial intermediaries.

- *Ensuring the integrity of markets.* The goal is to ensure that failure by one institution does not destabilize financial markets, causing systemic risk.

Let us first examine the consumer protection argument. First, it must be emphasized that investors are risk takers by definition. As Philip McBride Johnson, former chairman of the Commodities Futures Trading Commission, has put it,

> *Regulation is not meant to insulate investors from the consequences of free economic forces, or from their own poor judgment, but rather from abuses perpetrated by other persons.*

Regulation, however, is generally considered necessary when the market fails in two respects, through either **excessive prices** or **opportunistic behavior**.

In a free market with informed customers, prices can be excessive only if sellers collude to maintain high prices. This is why there is a need for **antitrust legislation** to prevent collusion among financial intermediaries.

Opportunistic behavior can arise if sellers have more information than buyers because, for instance, of access to inside information. This justifies laws against trading on **inside information**. Or brokers may have **conflicts of interest** that push them to give bad advice to their clients for the brokers' personal profit. Likewise, accounting standards and **disclosure rules** help to reduce asymmetries of information in financial markets, which is ultimately socially beneficial as it increases participation in financial markets.

Finally, brokers are subject to **suitability standards**. Broker-dealers are obligated, when making recommendations to clients, to recommend only transactions that are suitable to the client's financial situation, investment objectives, and sophistication. Unsuitable recommendations may constitute fraud, which is punishable by law.

Securities regulators require a prudent capital reserve to achieve the goals of protecting consumers and markets. The purpose of this capital is to ensure an orderly *liquidation* of the institution, in contrast to banks, for which capital is measured on an ongoing basis. These minimum reserves are calculated using different methods that consider the total amount of debt, the total amount of money owed customers, and, more recently, measures of market risk based on VAR.

As with commercial banks, securities regulators meet in a global forum, the **International Organization of Securities Commissions (IOSCO)**, based in Montréal.[15] Its Technical Committee addresses regulatory problems related to international securities transactions. The IOSCO and the Basel Committee collaborate on common regulatory issues. Likewise, regulatory authority rests with a domestic supervisor, for example, the **Securities and Exchange Commission** (SEC) in the United States.[16]

Securities regulation is based on either the "comprehensive approach" or the "simplified approach." The **comprehensive approach** is a system of capital charges detailed by the regulator. In contrast, the **simplified approach** uses a VAR model.

In the United States, the SEC uses the comprehensive approach with its **net capital rule**, Rule 15c3-1 under the Securities Exchange Act of 1934. A broker-dealer must satisfy a minimum capital ratio based on the calculated ratio of capital to debt or receivables. This ratio is 6.67% of aggregate debt, or 2% of the total amount of money owed by customers. To compute net capital, only liquid assets are considered, minus **haircuts**, which provide a further margin of safety in case of default and reflect market risk, liquidity risk, and counterparty risk.

The SEC's net capital rule, however, is widely viewed as quite conservative. As a result, it has become too expensive to operate derivatives activities under these rules.

---

[15]Its Web site is http://www.iosco.org.

[16]The SEC is a U.S. federal agency that has wide authority to oversee the nation's security markets. Among other responsibilities, it regulates the financial reporting practices of public corporations. To make information reporting more transparent, the SEC now requires registrants to disclose quantitative information on market risks using one of three possible alternatives: (1) a tabular presentation of expected cash flows and contract terms summarized by risk category, (2) a sensitivity analysis expressing possible losses for hypothetical changes in market prices, and (3) a VAR measure. Its Web site is http://www.sec.gov.

In January 1999, the SEC issued a ruling that created a class of **OTC derivatives dealers**, which are dealers active in OTC derivative markets. To bring their regulatory requirements in line with foreign firms and U.S. banks, the SEC created risk-based capital rules based on internal VAR models, which parallel the Basel rules.

30.5   Tools and Objectives of Regulation

Table 30-1 provides a summary of the tools and objectives of financial regulation. Systemic risk is controlled through capital adequacy rules, asset restrictions, and disclosure standards. Consumer protection is achieved through capital standards, disclosure rules, and conflict-of-interest rules.

TABLE 30-1 Tools and Objectives of Financial Regulation

Tools	Objectives	
	Systemic Risk	Consumer Protection
Capital standards	√	√
Disclosure standards	√	√
Asset restrictions	√	
Antitrust enforcement		√
Conflict-of-interest rules		√

Source: Herring and Litan (1995), *Financial Regulation in the Global Economy*, Washington, DC: Brookings Institution.

Capital adequacy and disclosure rules can help to achieve both objectives. Disclosure reduces asymmetries in capital markets, protecting consumers. In addition, more disclosure can stabilize capital markets. Firms that fail to reveal much information about their activities may be susceptible to market rumors, possibly resulting in loss of business or funding difficulties. Indeed, the turmoil that surrounded the near-failure of Long-Term Capital Management illustrates the panic behavior of banks that suspect that a financial institution with large positions similar to theirs may fail.

The Basel Committee has stated that disclosure

can reinforce the efforts of supervisors to foster financial market stability in an environment of rapid innovation and growing complexity. If provided with meaningful information, investors, depositors, creditors and counterparties can impose strong market discipline on financial institutions to manage their trading and derivatives activities in a prudent fashion and in line with their stated business objectives.

Example 30-1: FRM Exam 1999—Question 187/Regulation

The Basel (Basle) Capital Accord applies to these entities:

a) National banks chartered in the United States
b) All internationally active commercial banks
c) All banks and securities firms in the G-10 countries plus Luxembourg
d) Banks regulated by the Swiss banking regulatory authorities

---

Example 30-2: FRM Exam 1999—Question 186/Regulation

Which statement best defines "suitability" as it relates to a dealer's recommendation of a security transaction to a customer?

a) Customer suitability requires that a securities dealer run stress test simulations against a customer's portfolio, before recommending a particular transaction.
b) Customer suitability suggests that a securities dealer should verify that a proposed financial transaction is suitable for a customer's stated cash resources objectives.
c) Customer suitability requires that a securities dealer have reasonable grounds for believing that its recommendations are suitable based on customer information regarding the customer's securities holdings, financial status, and needs.
d) Customer suitability suggests that a securities dealer should make a quantitative assessment of the customer's level of sophistication.

Example 30-3: FRM Exam 1999—Question 188/Regulation

Which of the following financial institutions needs to comply with the provisions of CAD, the Capital Adequacy Directive? This question concerns the main home-country operations of these banks, not certain overseas subsidiaries or branches.

a) J. P. Morgan (an American Bank)
b) Credit Suisse First Boston (a Swiss Bank)
c) Deutsche Bank (a German Bank)
d) Sumitomo Bank (a Japanese Bank)

Example 30-4: FRM Exam 2000—Question 129/Regulation

The Bank of Japan

a) Is the primary Japanese bank authorized to review risk management practices of foreign investment banks and brokers in Japan

b) Shares its bank supervisory and audit role with the FSA

c) Has no supervisory or audit responsibilities with regard to financial institutions

d) Is authorized to supervise broker-dealer entities only

30.6   Answers to Chapter Examples

Example 30-1: FRM Exam 1999—Question 187/Regulation

b) The capital accord applies to commercial banks with international activities.

Example 30-2: FRM Exam 1999—Question 186/Regulation

c) Customer suitability does not require specific actions, such as running a stress test, verifying cash balances, or computing quantitative measures. Rather, the dealer must reasonably believe that the transaction is well suited to the objectives of the customer.

Example 30-3: FRM Exam 1999—Question 188/Regulation

c) The Capital Adequacy Directive applies to banks within the European Union. Of the four countries listed, only Germany belongs to the EU.

Example 30-4: FRM Exam 2000—Question 129/Regulation

b) The BOJ is a central bank that has responsibility over stability of financial markets and regulates commercial banks. This responsibility is shared with the Financial Services Agency (FSA).

Chapter 31

The Basel Accord

The **Basel Capital Accord**, concluded on July 15, 1988, represents a landmark financial agreement for the regulation of internationally active commercial banks. It instituted for the first time minimum levels of capital to be held by international banks against financial risks.

Initially, the capital charges were based on a set of standard, rigid rules defined by the Basel Committee on Banking Supervision (BCBS). These risk-based capital adequacy requirements evolved over time, first covering credit risk and then market risks. The latest rules by the Basel Committee, called Basel II and finalized in June 2004, represent an extensive revision of the capital charges that creates more risk-sensitive capital requirements. The new rules also add a charge against operational risks. Overall, Basel II represents a quantum leap in the measurement of risk and endorses risk management practices recently developed by the industry.

The Basel Accord was approved by all members of the committee and is endorsed by the Central Bank Governors and Heads of Banking Supervision of the G-10 countries. Although, strictly speaking, it applies only to internationally active banks within the G-10, these minimum capital requirements have been applied to banks in more than 100 countries. U.S. regulators intend to apply Basel II to top U.S. banks only, perhaps 10. In contrast, the European Union (EU) intends to write the Basel II rules into EU law, and they would then apply to all banks within the Union.

This chapter is structured as follows. Section 31.1 provides a broad overview of the Basel Accord. Section 31.2 details the original Basel capital requirements, with particular emphasis on credit risk. Market risk is a complex subject in itself and will be developed in the next chapter. Section 31.3 illustrates the application of capital adequacy ratios for Citigroup. Finally, Section 31.4 discusses major drawbacks of the original Basel Accord and describes the main components of the New Accord.

31.1   Steps in the Basel Accord

31.1.1   The Basel I Accord

The original goal of the 1988 Basel Accord, which came into force in 1992, was to provide a set of minimum capital requirements for commercial banks. Its primary objective was to promote the safety and soundness of the global financial system and to create a level playing field for internationally active banks. The **risk-based capital charges** were roughly intended to create a greater penalty for riskier assets.

Initially, the 1988 Basel Accord covered only credit risk. The Accord set a minimum level of capital expressed as a ratio of the total risk-weighted (RW) assets, which include on–balance sheet and off–balance sheet items. Banks have to hold capital that covers at least 8% of their risk-weighted assets. The purpose of this capital is to serve as a buffer against unexpected financial losses, thereby protecting depositors and financial markets.

31.1.2   The 1996 Amendment

In 1996 the Basel Committee amended the Capital Accord to incorporate market risks. This amendment, which came into force at the end of 1997, added a capital charge for market risk. Banks are allowed to use either a standardized model or an **internal models approach** (IMA), based on their own risk management system.

The amendment separates the bank's assets into two categories, the trading book and banking book. The **trading book** represents the bank portfolio with financial instruments that are intentionally held for short-term resale and typically marked to market. The **banking book** consists of other instruments, mainly loans, that are held to maturity and typically valued on a historical-cost basis.

The 1996 amendment adds a capital charge for (1) the market risk of the trading book and (2) the currency and commodity risk of the banking book. In exchange, the credit risk charge excludes debt and equity securities in the trading book and positions in commodities. As before, it includes all OTC derivatives, whether in the trading or banking book.

31.1.3   The Basel II Accord

Capital markets have undergone enormous changes since the initial Capital Accord of 1988. Increasingly, these credit risk charges have appeared outdated and, even worse, may be promoting unsound behavior by some banks.

In June 2004 the Basel Committee finalized a comprehensive revision to the Basel Accord. The implementation date has been set at year-end 2006 to allow for domestic rule-making processes and time to prepare for the new rules. The most advanced credit risk and operational risk approaches, however, are currently planned to take effect one year later, at year-end 2007.

The new framework is based on **three pillars**, viewed as mutually reinforcing:

- *Pillar 1: Minimum capital requirement.* These are meant to cover credit, market, and operational risk. Relative to the 1988 Accord, banks have a wider choice of models for computing their risk charges. The BCBS, however, tried to keep constant the total level of capital in the global banking system, at 8% of risk-weighted assets.

- *Pillar 2: Supervisory review process.* Relative to the previous framework, supervisors are given an expanded role. Supervisors need to ensure that
  —Banks have in place a process for assessing their capital in relation to risks.
  —Banks indeed operate above the minimum regulatory capital ratios.
  —Corrective action is taken as soon as possible when problems develop.

- *Pillar 3: Market discipline.* The New Accord emphasizes the importance of risk disclosures in financial statements. Such disclosures enable market participants to evaluate banks' risk profile and the adequacy of their capital positions. The new framework sets out disclosure requirements and recommendations. Banks that fail to meet disclosure requirements will not qualify for using internal models. As internal models generally lead to lower capital charges, this provides a strong incentive to comply with disclosure requirements. In essence, the trade-off for greater reliance on a bank's own models is greater transparency.

The New Accord provides for finer measurement of credit risk, which will generally lead to lower capital requirements. To maintain the overall level of bank capital, however, new capital charges are set against **operational risk**. Capital adequacy will be measured as follows:

$$\frac{\text{Total capital}}{\text{Credit risk} + \text{Market risk} + \text{Operational risk}} = \text{Bank's capital ratio} > 8\% \quad (31.1)$$

As before, credit risk in the denominator is measured by the sum of risk-weighted assets for credit risk. The other items are measured from the multiplication of the **market risk charge** (MRC) and **operational risk charge** (ORC) by $(1/8\%) = 12.5$. For instance, if a bank has \$875 in risk-weighted assets and MRC = \$10 and ORC = \$20, the denominator would be computed as $\$875 + [(\$10 + \$20) \times 12.5] = \$1,250$. The bank then has to hold at least $8\% \times \$1,250 = \$100$ in capital to satisfy the minimum requirement. This is equivalent to saying that the total charge must be at least $8\% \times \$875 + \$10 + \$20 = \$70 + \$10 + \$20 = \$100$.

Figure 31-1 summarizes the coverage of credit, market, and operational risk charges for the banking and trading books. Banks will also have access to a menu of methods to compute their risk charges. These are described in Table 31-1.

FIGURE 31-1 Summary of Basel II Risk Charges

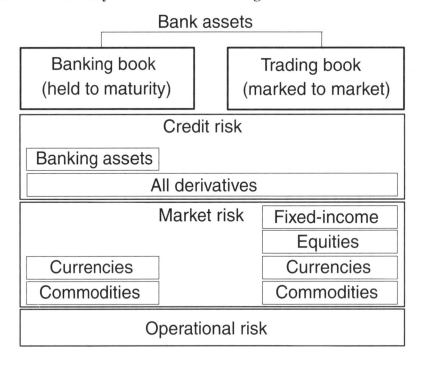

TABLE 31-1 Menu of Approaches to Measure Risk

Risk Category	Allowed Approach
Credit	Standardized approach (based on the 1988 Accord)
	Foundation internal ratings–based approach
	Advanced internal ratings–based approach
Market	Standardized approach
	Internal models approach
Operational	Basic indicator approach
	Standardized approach
	Advanced measurement approach

Example 31-1: FRM Exam 1997—Question 17

For regulatory capital calculation purposes, what market risks must be incorporated into a bank's VAR estimate?

a) Risks in the trading account relating to interest rate risk and equity risk

b) Risks in the trading account relating to interest rate risk and equity risk, and risks throughout the bank related to foreign exchange risk and commodity risk

c) Risk throughout the bank related to interest rate risk, equity risk, foreign exchange risk, and commodity risk

d) Interest rate risk, equity risk, foreign exchange risk, and commodity risk in the trading account only

---

31.2   The 1988 Basel Accord

31.2.1   Risk Capital

The 1988 capital adequacy rules require any **internationally active bank** to carry capital of at least 8% of its total risk-weighted assets. This applies to commercial banks on a consolidated basis. So, for instance, holding companies that are parents of banking groups have to satisfy the capital adequacy requirements.

In the Basel Accord, "capital" has a broader interpretation than the book value of equity. The key purpose of capital is its ability to absorb losses, providing some protection to creditors and depositors. Hence, to be effective, capital must be permanent, cannot impose mandatory fixed charges against earnings, and must allow for legal subordination to the rights of creditors and depositors.

The Basel Accord recognizes three forms of capital.

(1) Tier 1 capital, or "core" capital

Tier 1 capital includes equity capital and disclosed reserves, most notably after-tax retained earnings. Such capital is regarded as a buffer of the highest quality.

- **Equity capital** consists of issued and fully paid common stock and nonredeemable, noncumulative preference shares (also called preferred stock).

- **Disclosed reserves** correspond to share premiums, retained profits, and general reserves.

(2) Tier 2 capital, or "supplementary" capital

Tier 2 capital includes components of the balance sheet that provide some protection but ultimately must be redeemed or contain a mandatory charge against future income. These include

- **Undisclosed reserves**, or hidden reserves that are allowed by the accounting standards of some countries. These are reserves that passed through the earnings statement but remain unpublished. Due to this lack of transparency, as well as the fact that many countries refuse to recognize undisclosed reserves, undisclosed reserves are not part of core capital.

- **Asset revaluation reserves**, which arise, for instance, from long-term holdings of equity securities that are valued at historical acquisition costs. Such capital could be used to absorb losses on a going-concern basis, subject to some discount to reflect market volatility and future taxes in case of sales.

- **General provisions/loan loss reserves**, which are held against future unidentified losses. These are the result of **loan loss allowances**, which are deductions taken against interest income in anticipation of probable credit losses. These deductions reduce retained profits in tier 1 capital but may qualify as tier 2 capital to the extent that they do not reflect a known deterioration in particular assets (in which case they are "specific").[1] General provisions will play a special role under Basel II.

- **Hybrid debt capital instruments**, which combine some characteristics of equity and of debt. When they are unsecured, subordinated, and fully paid up, they are

---

[1]As credit losses occur, they are charged against this reserve instead of profits, which helps to smooth out earnings.

allowed into supplementary capital. These include, for instance, **cumulative preference shares**.

■ **Subordinated term debt**, with a minimum original maturity of five years and subject to a discount of 20% during the last five years. Subordinated debt would be junior in right of payment to all other indebtedness in the event of liquidation.

(3) Tier 3 capital, for market risk only

Tier 3 capital consists of short-term subordinated debt with a maturity of at least two years. This is eligible only for covering market risk.

There are additional restrictions on the relative amounts of various categories. Of the 8% capital charge for credit risk, at least 50% must be covered by tier 1 capital. Next, the amount of tier 3 capital is limited to 250% of tier 1 capital allocated to support market risks (tier 2 capital can be substituted for tier 3 capital if needed). Other restrictions apply to various elements of the three tiers.

Finally, some items are deducted from the capital base, including goodwill and investments in financial entities. The latter is motivated by the need to discourage cross-holding and double-counting of capital.

For credit risk, the eligible capital must exceed the regulatory capital, or

$$\text{Eligible tier 1 capital for CR} + \text{Allowed tier 2 capital} \geq \text{CRC} \qquad (31.2)$$

A similar constraint applies to market risk capital:

$$\text{Eligible tier 1 capital for MR} + \text{Allowed tier 3 (or 2) capital} \geq \text{MRC} \qquad (31.3)$$

A worked-out example will be given later. Next, we look at the construction of risk charges.

Example 31-2: FRM Exam 2002—Question 71

What is the best definition of tier 1 regulatory capital?
a) Equity capital, retained earnings, disclosed reserves
b) Subordinated debt, undisclosed reserves
d) Equity capital, subordinated debt with a maturity greater than five years
d) Long-term debt, revaluation reserves

Example 31-3: FRM Exam 2000—Question 139

Tier 1 capital includes all of the following *except*

a) Asset revaluation reserves

b) Common stock

c) Noncumulative preferred shares

d) Disclosed reserves

Example 31-4: FRM Exam 1999—Question 189

Banks are required to maintain a percentage of their assets as tier 1 capital. Which of the following count toward this capital requirement?

  I. Shareholder's equity

  II. Sovereign debt held in the trading book

 III. Common stock of other banks

 IV. Subordinated debt issued by the bank in question (subject to certain qualifying rules)

a) I, II, and IV

b) II and III

c) I and IV

d) I only

31.2.2   On–Balance Sheet Risk Charges

We first examine on–balance sheet assets, which consist principally of loans for most credit institutions. Ideally, the capital charges should recognize differences in asset credit quality.

Indeed, the 1988 Basel Accord applies to the notional of each asset a **risk capital weight** taken from four categories, as described in Table 31-2. Each dollar of risk-weighted notional exposure must be covered by 8% capital.

These categories provide an extremely rough classification of credit risk. For instance, claims on Organization for Economic Cooperation and Development (OECD) central governments, such as holdings of U.S. Treasuries, are assigned a weight of zero since these assets presumably have no default risk.[2] Cash held is also assigned a zero weight. At the other extreme, claims on corporations, including loans, bonds, and equities, receive a 100% weight, whatever the risk of default or maturity of the loan.

---

[2]The OCED currently consists of Austria, Belgium, Canada, Denmark, France, Germany, Greece, Iceland, Ireland, Italy, Luxembourg, the Netherlands, Norway, Portugal, Spain, Sweden, Switzerland, Turkey, the United Kingdom, the United States, Japan, Finland, Australia, New Zealand, Mexico, the Czech Republic, Hungary, Korea, and Poland, in order of accession.

TABLE 31-2 Risk Capital Weights by Asset Class

Weight	Asset Type
0%	Cash held
	Claims on OECD central governments
	Claims on central governments in national currency
20%	Cash to be received
	Claims on OECD banks and regulated securities firms
	Claims on non-OECD banks below 1 year
	Claims on multilateral development banks
	Claims on foreign OECD public-sector entities
50%	Residential mortgage loans
100%	Claims on the private sector (corporate debt, equity, etc.)
	Claims on non-OECD banks above 1 year
	Real estate
	Plant and equipment

The **credit risk charge** (CRC) is then defined for balance sheet (BS) items as

$$\text{CRC(BS)} = 8\% \times (\text{Risk} - \text{Weighted assets}) = 8\% \times \left(\sum_i w_i \times \text{Notional}_i \right) \quad (31.4)$$

where w_i is the risk weight attached to asset i.

Example 31-5: FRM Exam 2001—Question 38

A bank subject to the Basel I Accord makes a loan of \$100m to a firm with a risk weighting of 50%. What is the basic on–balance sheet credit risk charge?

a) \$8m

b) \$4m

c) \$2m

d) \$1m

31.2.3 Off–Balance Sheet Risk Charges

By the late 1980s, focusing on balance sheet items only led to neglect of an important component of credit risk of the banking system, the exposure to swaps. The first swaps were transacted in 1981. By 1990, the outstanding notional of open positions had grown to \$3,500 billion, which seems enormous. Some allowance had to be made for the credit risk of swaps. Unlike the case for loans, however, the notional amount does not represent the maximum loss.

To account for such **off–balance sheet** (OBS) items, the Basel Accord computes a "credit exposure" that is equivalent to the notional for a loan, through **credit conversion factors** (CCFs). The Accord identifies five broad categories:

- Instruments that substitute for loans (e.g., guarantees, bankers' acceptances, and standby letters of credit serving as guarantees for loans and securities) carry the full 100% weight (or credit conversion factor). The rationale is that the exposure is no different from a loan. Take a **financial letter of credit** (LC), for instance, which provides irrevocable access to bank funds for a client. When the client approaches credit distress, it will almost assuredly draw down the letter of credit. Like a loan, the full notional is at risk. This category also includes asset sales with recourse, where the credit risk remains with the bank, and forward asset purchases.

- Transaction-related contingencies (e.g., performance bonds or **commercial letters of credit** related to particular transactions) carry a 50% factor. The rationale is that a performance letter of credit is typically secured by some income stream and has lower risk than a general financial LC.

- Short-term, self-liquidating trade-related liabilities (e.g., documentary credits collateralized by the underlying shipments) carry a 20% factor.

- Commitments with maturity greater than a year (such as credit lines), as well as note issuance facilities (NIFs), carry a 50% credit conversion factor. Shorter-term commitments or revocable commitments have a zero weight. Note that this applies to the unfunded portion of commitments only, as the funded portion is an outstanding loan and appears on the balance sheet. Under Basel II, shorter-term commitments now receive a CCF of 20%.

- Other derivatives, such as swaps, forwards and options on currency, interest rate, equity, and commodity products are allowed special treatment given the complexity of their exposures.

For the first four categories, the position is replaced by a credit equivalent, computed as

$$\text{Credit equivalent} = \text{Credit conversion factor} \times \text{Notional} \qquad (31.5)$$

For the last category (derivatives), the credit exposure is computed as the sum of the current, **net replacement value** (NRV) plus an **add-on** that is intended to capture future or **potential exposure**:

$$\text{Credit exposure} = \text{NRV} + \text{Add-on}$$

(31.6)

$$\text{Add-on} = \text{Notional} \times \text{Add-on factor} \times (0.4 + 0.6 \times \text{NGR})$$

Here the add-on factor depends on the **tenor** (maturity) and type of contract, as listed in Table 31-3 (NGR will be defined later). It roughly accounts for the maximum credit exposure, which, as we have seen before, depends on the volatility of the risk factor and the maturity. Volatility is highest for commodities, then equity, then currencies, then fixed-income instruments. This explains why the add-on factor is greater for currency, equity, and commodity swaps than for interest rate instruments, and also increases with maturity.

TABLE 31-3 Add-on Factors for Potential Credit Exposure
(Percent of Notional)

Residual Maturity (Tenor)	Contract				
	Interest Rate	Exchange Rate, Gold	Equity	Precious Metals	Other Commodities
<1 year	0.0	1.0	6.0	7.0	10.0
1–5 year	0.5	5.0	8.0	7.0	12.0
>5 year	1.5	7.5	10.0	8.0	15.0

More precisely, the numbers have been obtained from simulation experiments (such as those in Chapter 21) that measure the 80th percentile worst loss over the life of a matched pair of swaps. The matching of pairs reflects the hedging practice of swap dealers and effectively divides the exposure in two, since only one swap can be in-the-money. Take, for instance, a currency swap with five-year initial maturity. Assuming exchange rates are normally distributed and ignoring interest rate risk, the maximum credit exposure as a fraction of the notional should be

$$\text{WCE} = \frac{1}{2} \times 0.842 \times \sigma \sqrt{5}$$

(31.7)

where the $\frac{1}{2}$ factor reflects swap matching and the 0.842 factor corresponds to a one-sided 80% confidence level. Assuming a 10% annual volatility, this gives WCE = 9.4%. This is in line with the add-on of 7.5% in Table 31-3.

Further simulations by the Bank of England and the New York Fed have shown that these numbers also roughly correspond to a 95th percentile loss over a six-month horizon. In the case of a new five-year interest rate swap, for instance, the worst exposure over the life at the 80th percentile level is 1.49%; the worst exposure over six months at the 95th percentile level is 1.58%. This is in line with the add-on of 1.5% for this category.

The NGR factor in Equation (31.6) represents the **net-to-gross ratio**, or ratio of current net market value to gross market value, which is always between 0 and 1. The purpose of this factor is to reduce the capital requirement for contracts that fall under a legally valid netting agreement. Without netting agreements in place (i.e., with NGR = 1), the multiplier $(0.4 + 0.6 \times \text{NGR})$ is equal to 1. There is no reduction in the add-on.

Alternatively, take the situation where a bank has two swaps with the same counterparty currently valued at +100 and at −60. The gross replacement value is the sum of positive values, which is 100. The net value is 40, creating an NGR ratio of 0.4. The multiplier $(0.4 + 0.6 \times \text{NGR})$ is equal to 0.64.

At the other extreme, if all contracts currently net out to zero, NGR = 0, and the multiplier $(0.4 + 0.6 \times \text{NGR})$ is equal to 0.4. The purpose of this minimum of 0.4 is to provide protection against *potential movements* in the NGR, which, even if currently zero, could change over time.

The computation of risk-weighted assets is obtained by applying counterparty risk weights to the credit exposure in Equation (31.6). Since most counterparties for such transactions tend to be associated with excellent credit, the risk weights from Table 31-3 are multiplied by 50%. The **credit risk charge** for OBS items is defined as

$$\text{CRC(OBS)} = 8\% \times \left(\sum_i w_i \times 50\% \times \text{Credit exposure}_i \right) \qquad (31.8)$$

Example: The credit charge for a swap

Consider a $100 million interest rate swap with a domestic corporation. Assume a residual maturity of four years and a current market value of $1 million. What is the credit risk charge?

Answer

Since there is no netting, the factor $(0.4 + 0.6 \times \text{NGR}) = 1$. From Table 31-3, we find an add-on factor of 0.5. The credit exposure is then CE = $1,000,000 + $100,000,000 × 0.5% × 1 = $1,500,000. This number must be multiplied by the counterparty-specific risk weight and one-half of 8% to derive the minimum level of capital needed to support the swap. This gives $60,000.

Example 31-6: FRM Exam 2001—Question 45

The Basel Accord computes the credit exposure of derivatives using both replacement cost and an "add-on" to cover potential future exposure. Which of the following is the correct credit risk charge for a purchased seven year OTC equity index option of $50m notional with a current mark to market of $15m, no netting, and a counterparty weighting of 100%?

a) $1.6m
b) $1.2m
c) $150,000
d) $1m

Example 31-7: FRM Exam 2000—Question 134

The BIS capital requirement for an unfunded, short-term (under one year) credit commitment is

a) 0%
b) 4%
c) 8%
d) 100%

Example 31-8: FRM Exam 2000—Question 137

The BIS requirement for capital charge of an unfunded commitment of original maturity greater than one year, as compared with an equivalent funded commitment (or loan), is

a) The same
b) Half
c) A quarter
d) Zero

Example 31-9: FRM Exam 2000—Question 135

As of November 2000, which one of the following will generally receive an 8% BIS capital charge (100% asset weight)?

a) Investment in a publicly traded stock for trading purposes
b) Investment in a U.S. government bond
c) Investment in a venture capital fund for speculation purposes
d) None of the above

31.2.4 Total Risk Charge

Finally, the total risk charge is computed as the sum of the credit risk charges, both for balance sheet and off–balance sheet items, plus the market risk charge. Define MRC as the market risk charge, which will be detailed in the next chapter.

To translate all numbers into similar risk-adjusted assets, the MRC is transformed into a risk-adjusted asset equivalent by dividing the MRC by 8%. For instance, if MRC is computed as $1,832 million, the risk-adjusted asset number would be $22.9 billion, which is taken as equivalent to the notional of loans.

We can then simply sum the risk-adjusted assets across all risk categories to find the total risk charge (TRC):

$$\text{TRC} = \text{CRC} + \text{MRC} = 8\% \times (\text{Total risk} - \text{Adjusted assets}) \tag{31.9}$$

subject to various restrictions on the use of different tiers. The New Accord adds an operational risk charge to this.

Table 31-4 gives an example.[3] The total risk-adjusted assets for credit risk are 7,500. The market risk charge is 350, which translates into 350/8% = 4,375 in risk assets. The credit risk charge is 8% of 7,500, or 600. Of this, no more than 50% can be accounted by tier 2 capital. So we could have 300 in tier 1 capital plus 300 in tier 2 capital covering credit risk. For market risk, we know the maximum ratio of tier 3 to tier 1 capital is 250 to 100. Hence, with a 350 market risk charge, we can have a maximum allocation of 250 for tier 3 for every 100 of tier 1.

The next step is to match these numbers with the available capital. Assume the bank has available capital of 700, 100, and 600 in tiers 1, 2, and 3, respectively. For credit risk, we have only 100 in tier 2 capital, so the remaining 500 must be in the form of tier 1 capital. For market risk, we apply the maximum of 250 in tier 3 capital, so that the remainder of 100 comes from tier 1 capital.

This leaves a buffer of excess capital. We can compute the capital ratio using all eligible capital. All tier 1 capital is eligible, plus 100 in tier 2, plus 250 in tier 3. This sums to 1,050, which translates into an "eligible" capital ratio of 1,050/11,875 = 8.8%. The bank has also 600 − 250 = 350 in unused tier 3 capital.

---

[3]This expands on the BCBS publication (January 1996), page 50.

TABLE 31-4 Computation of Capital Requirements

Category	Risk Assets	Capital Charge (8%)	Miminum Capital, Required	Available Capital	Minimum Capital, Actual	Eligible Capital
Credit risk	7,500	600	Tier 1: 300		Tier 1: 500	
			Tier 2: 300		Tier 2: 100	
Market risk	4,375	350	Tier 1: 100		Tier 1: 100	
			Tier 3: 250		Tier 3: 250	
Tier 1				700		700
Tier 2				100		100
Tier 3				600		250
Total	11,875	950		1,400	950	1,050
Capital ratio						8.8%

Example 31-10: FRM Exam 1999—Question 134

A risk analyst is asked to prepare a Basel I credit risk report based on accounting data. She receives a report that shows the mark-to-market value of the following instruments by client: interest rate caps bought, interest rate caps sold, interest rate swaps. The analyst's system contains the following additional information:

  I. The time to maturity of the instruments

 II. The presence or absence of a netting agreement

III. The amount of "add-on"(for each instrument)

IV. The credit rating of the client

Which items does the analyst need to create the report?

a) I and IV only

b) II and III only

c) II and III and IV

d) All the above

31.3   Illustration

As an illustration, let us examine the capital adequacy requirements for Citigroup, which is the biggest global bank.

Table 31-5 summarizes on–balance sheet and off–balance sheet items as of December 2002. The bank has total assets of $1,097 billion, consisting of cash equivalents, securities, loans, trading assets, and other assets. The notional for each asset is assigned to one of the four risk weight categories, ranging from 0% to 100%. For example, out of the $301.9 billion in securities, $161.3 have a zero risk weight (e.g., because they represent positions in OECD government bonds). Of the remainder, $73 billion have a 20% weight, $5.1 billion have a 50% weight, and $56.9 have a 100% weight. Most of the loans carry a risk weight of 100%. Trading assets are excluded from this computation because they carry a market risk charge only.

TABLE 31-5 Citigroup's Risk-Weighted Assets

On–Balance Sheet Assets ($ Billions)							
Item	Notional	Not Covered		Risk Weight Category			
				0%	20%	50%	100%
Cash and due	33.7	0.0		12.6	20.4	0.0	2.0
Securities	301.9	5.6		161.3	73.0	5.1	56.9
Loans and leases	465.8	−12.8		8.7	33.5	97.6	338.9
Trading assets	155.2	155.2		0.0	0.0	0.0	0.0
All other assets	140.6	34.5		25.3	9.7	2.4	68.7
Total on-BS	1,097.2	182.4		208.0	136.6	105.1	466.4
Off–Balance Sheet Items ($ Billions)							
Item	Notional	Conv. Factor	Credit Equiv.	Risk Weight Category			
				0%	20%	50%	100%
Financial standby LC	32.5	1.00	32.5	10.0	3.2	0.3	19.0
Performance standby LC	7.3	0.50	3.7	0.2	0.3	0.0	3.1
Commercial LC	5.0	0.20	1.0	0.1	0.2	0.0	0.7
Securities lent	38.0	1.00	38.0	37.9	0.1	0.0	0.0
Other credit substitutes	3.0	12.50	26.5	0.0	0.0	0.0	26.5
Other off–balance sheet	1.7	—	2.4	0.0	0.1	0.6	1.7
Unused commit. > 1 yr	82.1	0.50	41.0	0.9	1.3	1.1	37.7
Derivative contracts	2,380.9		96.2	8.5	41.3	46.4	0.0
Total off-BS	2,550.4		241.2	57.5	46.5	48.4	88.8

The lower panel of the table displays off–balance sheet information. The second column displays the notional, the third the conversion factor, and the fourth the credit equivalent, which is the product of the previous two. As described in the previous section, the conversion factors are 1.00 for financial LCs and securities lent, 0.50 for performance LCs and unused commitments greater than one year, and 0.20 for commercial LCs.[4]

---

[4]The category "credit substitutes" represent residual interests, such as the equity tranche from securitizations of assets, which are subject to a dollar-for-dollar capital requirement. This implies a credit conversion factor of $(1/8\%) = 12.50$. U.S. regulators have imposed this high capital requirement to reflect the higher risk of such residual interests, whose value can be wiped out easily in case of losses on the underlying assets.

Finally, note the huge size of the notional derivatives position. At $2,381 billion, it is more than twice Citigroup's total assets of $1,097 billion and dwarfs its equity of $87 billion. The notional amounts, however, give no indication of the risk. The credit equivalent amount, which consists of net replacement value plus the add-on, is $96.2 billion, a much lower number.

From this information, we can compute the total risk-weighted assets and capital adequacy ratios. These are shown in Table 31-6. The first line adds up on–balance sheet and off–balance sheet items for each category. Multiplication by the risk weights gives the second line. The total RW assets for credit risk are $668.6 billion, which consists of $546.3 billion for on-BS items and $122.3 billion for off-BS items. To this we add the RW assets for market risk, or $30.6 billion. Thus, most of Citigroup's regulatory risk capital covers credit risk. Market risk represents only 4% of the total.

TABLE 31-6 Citigroup's Capital Requirements

Risk-Weighted Assets ($ Billions)					
	Risk Weight Category				
Item	0%	20%	50%	100%	Total
On-BS and off-BS items	265.4	183.1	153.5	555.2	
Credit RW assets	0.0	36.6	76.8	555.2	668.6
Market RW assets					30.6
Others					−2.8
Total RW assets					696.3

Capital	Amount ($ Billions)	Ratio (Percent)
Tier 1	59.0	8.5
Tier 2	19.3	2.8
Total	78.3	11.2

The total RW assets add up to $696.3 billion. Applying the 8% ratio, we find a minimum regulatory capital of $55.7 billion. In fact, the available risk capital adds up to $78.3 billion, which represents an 11.2% ratio, comfortably above the regulatory minimum. The ratio for a **well-capitalized bank** would be 10%. Apparently, the regulatory constraint is not binding.

The bank could decide itself on the optimal capital ratio, based on a careful consideration of the trade-off between increasing expected returns and increasing risks. If the current capital ratio is viewed as too high, the bank could shrink its capital base through dividend payments or share repurchases. Like other major banks, Citigroup has decided to hold more capital than the minimum regulatory standard of 8%.

31.4   The New Basel Accord

The Basel Accord has been widely viewed as successful in raising banking capital ratios. As a result of the Accord, the aggregate tier 1 ratio increased from $840 to $1,500 billion from 1990 to 1998 for the 1,000 largest banks. Indeed, the banking system now seems to have enough capital to weather most storms, including the Asian crisis of 1997 and the recession of 2001–2002.

31.4.1   Issues with the 1988 Basel Accord

Over time, however, these regulations have shown their age. The system has led to **regulatory arbitrage**, which can be broadly defined as bank activities aimed at getting around these regulations. Lending patterns have been transformed, generally in the direction of taking on more credit risk to drive the economic capital up to the level of regulatory capital.

To illustrate, consider a situation where a bank can make a loan of $100 million to an investment-grade company rated AAA or to a speculative-grade company rated CCC. The bank is forced to hold regulatory capital of $8 million, so it has to borrow $92 million. Suppose the rate of return on the AAA loan is 6%, after expenses. The cost of borrowing is close, at 5.7%. The dollar return to shareholders is then $100,000,000 × 6% − $92,000,000 × 5.7% = $756,000. Compared with a capital base of $8 million, this represents a rate of return of 9.5% only, which may be insufficient for shareholders. The bank could support this loan with a much smaller capital base. For instance, a capital base of $2 million would require borrowing $98 million and would yield a return of $100,000,000 × 6% − $98,000,000 × 5.7% = $414,000, assuming the cost of debt remains the same. This translates into a rate of return of 20.7%, which is much more acceptable. The bank, however, is unable to lower its capital due to the binding regulatory requirement.

Suppose now the rate of return on the CCC loan is 7%, after expenses and expected credit losses. The dollar return to shareholders is now $1.756 million, which represents a 22.0% rate of return. In this situation, the bank has an incentive to increase the risk of its loan in order to bring the economic capital more in line with its regulatory capital. This simple example has shown that regulation may perversely induce banks to shift lending to lower-rated borrowers.

In addition to inadequate differentiation of credit risk, the 1988 Accord did not recognize credit mitigation techniques or diversification effects for credit risk. Some of these drawbacks have been corrected with Basel II.

Example 31-11: FRM Exam 1998—Question 3

A bank that funds itself at LIBOR − 5 bp purchases an A+-rated corporate floating-coupon loan paying LIBOR + 15 bp. Based on the Basel I minimum capital requirements, what is the annualized return on regulatory capital for this loan?

a) 2.5%
b) 5.0%
c) 11%
d) None of the above

31.4.2 Definition of Capital

The new Basel Accord, dubbed **Basel II**, was finalized in June 2004. It gives banks a choice between a standardized approach, which is a simple extension of the Basel I rules, and a more complex internal ratings–based (IRB) approach.

For the former, capital is defined as before. However, **general provisions** or **loan loss reserves** can be included in tier 2 only, subject to a limit of 1.25% of risk-weighted assets.

For the IRB approach, in contrast, the new Accord distinguishes between expected loss (EL) and unexpected loss (UL). Capital is supposed to absorb unexpected losses, which means that it cannot support expected losses as well. Banks typically fund accounts called general provisions, or loan loss reserves, to absorb expected credit losses.

Hence, Basel II withdraws general provisions from tier 2 capital. If total expected losses are less than eligible provisions, however, the difference may be recognized in tier 2 capital, up to a maximum of 0.6% of risk-weighted assets. If total expected losses exceed eligible provisions, the bank must deduct the difference from capital (50% from tier 1 and 50% from tier 2).

31.4.3 The Credit Risk Charge

For the credit risk charges, banks now have a choice of three approaches.

(1) Standardized Approach

This is an extension of the 1988 Accord, but with a finer classification of categories for credit risk, based on external credit ratings, provided by **external credit assessment institutions**. Table 31-7 describes the new weights, which now fall into five categories for banks and sovereigns, and four categories for corporates. For sovereigns, OECD membership is no longer given preferential status. For banks, two options are available. The first assigns a risk weight one notch below that of the sovereign; the other uses an external credit assessment. The new Accord also removes the 50% risk weight cap on derivatives.

TABLE 31-7 Risk Weights: Standardized Approach

Claim	Credit Rating					
	AAA/ AA−	A+/ A−	BBB+/ BBB−	BB+/ B−	Below B−	Unrated
Sovereign	0%	20%	50%	100%	150%	100%
Banks—option 1	20%	50%	100%	100%	150%	100%
Banks—option 2	20%	50%	50%	100%	150%	50%
Short-term	20%	20%	20%	50%	150%	20%
Claim	AAA/ AA−	A+/ A−	BBB+/ BB−		Below BB−	Unrated
Corporates	20%	50%	100%		150%	100%

Note: Under option 1, the bank rating is based on the sovereign country in which it is incorporated. Under option 2, the bank rating is based on an external credit assessment. Short-term claims are defined as having an original maturity less than three months.

(2) Foundation Internal Ratings–Based Approach (FIRB)

Under the **internal ratings–based approach** (IRB), banks are allowed to use their internal estimate of creditworthiness, subject to regulatory standards. Under the foundation approach, banks estimate the **probability of default** (PD) and supervisors supply other inputs, which carry over from the standardized approach. Table 31-8 illustrates the link between PD and the risk weights for various asset classes.[5] For instance, a corporate loan with a 1.00% probability of default would be assigned a risk weight of 92.32%, which is close to the standard risk weight of 100% from Basel I. Note that

---

[5]For more detail, see the BCBS documents.

retail loans have much lower risk weights than the other categories, reflecting their greater diversification.

TABLE 31-8 IRB Risk Weights

Probability of Default	Corporate	Residential Mortgage	Other Retail
0.03%	14.44%	4.15%	4.45%
0.10%	29.65%	10.69%	11.16%
0.25%	49.47%	21.30%	21.15%
0.50%	69.61%	35.08%	32.36%
0.75%	82.78%	46.46%	40.10%
1.00%	92.32%	56.40%	45.77%
2.00%	114.86%	87.94%	57.99%
3.00%	128.44%	111.99%	62.79%
4.00%	139.58%	131.63%	65.01%
5.00%	149.86%	148.22%	66.42%
10.00%	193.09%	204.41%	75.54%
20.00%	238.23%	253.12%	100.28%

Note: Illustrative weights for LGD = 45%, maturity of 2.5 years, and large corporate exposures (firms with turnover greater than 50 million euros).

(3) Advanced Internal Ratings–Based Approach (AIRB)

Under the advanced approach, banks can supply other inputs as well. These include **loss given default** (LGD) and **exposure at default** (EAD). The combination of PDs and LGDs for all applicable exposures are then mapped to regulatory risk weights. The capital charge is obtained by multiplying the risk weight by EAD by 8%. The advanced IRB approach applies only to sovereign, bank, and corporate exposures and not to retail portfolios.

The capital charges are calibrated to correspond to the amount of capital required to support a 99.9% confidence level over a one-year horizon.

The New Accord also recognizes **credit risk mitigation** (CRM) techniques, such as collateralization, third-party guarantees, credit derivatives, and netting. **Collateralized credit exposures** are those where the borrower has posted assets as collateral. Recognition is given only to cash, gold, listed equities, investment-grade debt, sovereign securities rated BB− or better, or mutual funds investing in the same assets.

Under the standardized approach, two treatments are possible. In the simple approach, the risk of the collateral is simply substituted for that of the counterparty, generally subject to a 20% floor. In contrast, the comprehensive approach is more accurate and will lead to lower capital charges.

Even if the exposure is exactly matched by the collateral, there is some credit risk due to the volatility of values during a default. In the worst case, the value of the exposure could go up and that of the collateralized assets could go down. This volatility effect is measured by a **haircut** parameter (H) that is instrument-specific and approximates the 99% VAR over a 10-day period. For equities, for example, $H = 25\%$. For cash, this is zero.

The exposure after risk mitigation is then

$$E^* = E \times (1 + H_e) - C \times (1 - H_c - H_{fx}) \tag{31.10}$$

if positive, where E is the value of the uncollateralized exposure, C is the current market value of the collateral held, H_e is the haircut appropriate to the exposure, H_c is the haircut appropriate to the collateral, and H_{fx} is the haircut appropriate for a currency mismatch between the two.

Other forms of CRM are **guarantees** and **credit derivatives**, which are a form of protection against obligor default provided by a third party, called the guarantor. Capital relief, however, is granted only if there is no uncertainty as to the quality of the guarantee. Protection must be direct, explicit, irrevocable, and unconditional. In such a situation, one can apply the principle of **substitution**. In other words, if bank A buys credit protection against a default of company B from bank C, it may substitute C's credit risk for B's risk. It will do so if the credit rating of bank C is better than that of B.

No allowance is made, however, for **double default**. In order for bank A to incur a credit loss, both B and C must default. The likelihood of such a double-default occurrence is generally very low. For instance, if defaults are independent, the probability of a credit loss is given by the *product* of the two default probabilities. The current framework, however, does not recognize the additional risk mitigation feature due to the nonperfect correlation of defaults. This issue remains a high priority for the financial services industry.

Finally, the New Accord also deals explicitly with **securitization**, which involves the economic or legal transfer of assets to a third party, typically called a **special-purpose vehicle** (SPV). Examples are asset-backed securities such as collateralized loan obligations, where the underlying asset is a pool of bank loans. Because of the high regulatory cost of keeping loans on their balance sheets, banks are now routinely transforming loans into tradable securities.

A bank can remove these assets from its balance sheet only after a **true sale**, which is defined using **clean break** criteria. These are satisfied if a number of conditions are all met: (1) Significant credit risk must be transferred to third parties, (2) the seller does not maintain effective or indirect control over the assets,[6] (3) the securities are not an obligation of the seller, and (4) the holders of the SPV have the right to pledge or exchange those interests. Two other technical conditions are also involved.

If these conditions are all met, then the bank can remove the assets from its balance sheet and becomes subject to new risk weights for securitization tranches. These are described in Table 31-9 under the standardized approach. For example, the risk weight for a BBB-rated tranche is 100%. For the lowest-rated tranches, the bank must hold capital equal to the notional amount, which implies a risk weight of $(1/8\%) = 1250\%$.

TABLE 31-9 Risk Weights for Securitizations: Standardized Approach

	AAA/ AA−	A+/ A−	BBB+/ BBB−	BB+/ BB−	B+ and Below (or Unrated)
Tranche	20%	50%	100%	350%	1250% (deduction)

Example 31-12: FRM Exam 2002—Question 14

Under the new Basel Accord, credit risk charges may be calculated using the internal ratings–based approach. Which of the following is the best description of this approach?

a) Banks estimate default probabilities of counterparties using their own methods. subject to regulatory standards, which then are used with modified standardized inputs that come from the standardized approach.

b) Banks use their own models to generate their own credit risk calculation using their own proprietary methods, which are not divulged to third parties.

c) Banks use the ratings of credit-rating agencies to calculate loss given default.

d) Banks hire their own ratings analysts, who supply data to the firm's trading teams so that they can better judge value in their trading.

---

[6] In particular, the transferred assets must be legally separated from the seller so that it does not have additional obligations in case the SPV goes bankrupt. Also, the seller cannot maintain effective control either by being able to repurchase the assets at a profit or by being obligated to retain the risk of the transferred assets.

Example 31-13: FRM Exam 2002—Question 69

The latest proposal of the Basel Committee on Banking Supervision (BCBS, Basel II) for the New Basel Accord introduces the advanced internal rating approach for credit risk. Banks will input their own

a) EDF

b) LGD

c) EDF and LGD

d) None of the above

31.4.4 The Operational Risk Charge

One of the most significant, and controversial, additions to the New Accord is the operational risk charge (ORC). The Basel Committee expects that the ORC will represent on average 12% of the total capital charge.

The new rules give three alternative methods. The simplest is called the **basic indicator approach**. This is based on an aggregate measure of business activity. The capital charge equals a fixed percentage, called the **alpha factor**, of the exposure indicator defined as gross income (GI)[7]:

$$\text{ORC}^{BIA} = \alpha \times \text{GI} \tag{31.11}$$

where α has been set at 15%. The advantage of this method is that it is simple, transparent, and uses readily available data. The problem is that it does not account for the quality of controls. As a result, this approach is expected to be used mainly by nonsophisticated banks.

The second method is the **standardized approach**. Here a bank's activities are divided into eight **business lines** (BLs). Within each business line, gross income is taken as an indicator of the scale of activity. The capital charge is then obtained by multiplying gross income by a fixed percentage, called the **beta factor**, and summing across business lines:

$$\text{ORC}^{SA} = \sum_{i=1}^{8} \beta_i \times \text{GI}_i \tag{31.12}$$

The beta factors are described in Table 31-10. This approach is still simple but better reflects varying risks across business lines.[8] It can be used only if the bank demonstrates effective management and control of operational risk.

---

[7]This is taken as the average of positive gross income numbers over the last three years. Negative values are excluded.

[8]The formula is actually more complex and allows offsets for some negative GI numbers in a year

The third method is the **advanced measurement approach** (AMA). This allows banks to use their own internal models in the estimation of required capital using quantitative and qualitative criteria set by the Accord.

The qualitative criteria are similar to those for the use of internal market VAR systems.[9] Once these are satisfied, the risk charge is obtained from the unexpected loss (UL), or VAR at the 99.9% confidence level over a one-year horizon,

$$\text{ORC}^{AMA} = \text{UL}(1 - \text{year}, \ 99.9\% \ \text{confidence}) \tag{31.13}$$

provided the expected loss is accounted for.

TABLE 31-10 Beta Factors

Business Line	Beta Factor
Corporate finance	18%
Trading and sales	18%
Retail banking	12%
Commercial banking	15%
Payment, settlement	18%
Agency services	15%
Asset management	12%
Retail brokerage	12%

Other quantitative criteria are as follows: (1) Banks must track internal loss data measured over a minimum period of five years, (2) banks must use external data, (3) banks must use scenario analysis to evaluate its exposure to high-severity events, and (4) banks must take into account the business environment and internal control factors. Finally, insurance can be used to offset up to 20% of the operational risk charge.

This approach offers the most refined measurement of operational risk and is expected to be used by more sophisticated institutions.

31.4.5 Evaluation

The BCBS has organized a large-scale analysis of the effect of the new capital requirements on the banking system. Table 31-11 report the results for 188 banks in the G-10

---

with positive numbers in other business lines, up to a limit of zero. The exact formula is $\text{ORC}^{SA} = \{\sum_{t=1}^{3} \text{Max}[\sum_{i=1}^{8}(\beta_i \times \text{GI}_i), 0]\}/3$.

[9] Specifically, (a) the bank must have an independent operational risk function, (b) the system must be integrated in day-to-day management, (c) there must be regular reporting, (d) documentation must exist, (e) auditors must perform regular reviews, and (f) there must be external validation.

countries. The table shows that the new capital charge will affect banks differentially. Smaller banks, with more retail exposures, will have much lower capital requirements than before. Retail risks are indeed more diversified than other types.

For larger banks, more advanced methods lead to lower capital requirements. For instance, large banks will suffer a higher capital charge (by 11%) under the standardized approach, which is primarily due to the addition of the operational risk charge. Under the AIRB approach, however, the credit risk charge drops by 13%, which leads to a net decrease in capital requirements of 2%.

Because the Basel Committee wants to keep the total level of global banking capital unchanged, the new framework introduces the idea of a **scaling factor**, which applies to the credit capital requirements under the IRB approach. The BCBS states that it "may apply" this scaling factor, which could be greater than or less than 1, and is currently set at 1.06.

TABLE 31-11 Percentage Changes in Capital Requirements
(Banks in G-10 Countries)

	Larger Banks			Smaller Banks	
	Method			Method	
Portfolio	Standardized	FIRB	AIRB	Standardized	FIRB
Corporate	1%	−2%	−4%	−1%	−4%
Sovereign	0%	2%	1%	0%	0%
Bank	2%	2%	0%	0%	−1%
Retail	−5%	−9%	−9%	−10%	−17%
SME	−1%	−2%	−3%	−2%	−4%
Securitized	1%	0%	0%	0%	−1%
General provisions	0%	−1%	−2%	0%	−2%
Other	2%	4%	2%	1%	3%
Overall credit risk	0%	−7%	−13%	−11%	−27%
Operational risk	10%	10%	11%	15%	7%
Overall change	11%	3%	−2%	3%	−19%

Source: QIS3 study conducted by the BCBS (2003).

31.5   Conclusions

The Basel II Accord represents an enormous step forward for the measurement and management of banking risks. It creates more risk-sensitive capital charges for credit risk and, for the first time, attempts to measure operational risk.

Among winners will be firms that invest wisely in risk management, banks with large retail portfolios and with high-grade corporate credits. All of these indeed have lower credit risk than the rest of the industry.

This new framework is certainly not perfect, however. Like any set of formal rules, it leaves open some possibilities of regulatory arbitrage, due to discrepancies between economic and regulatory capital for some assets. In addition, the Basel II rules incorporate "typical" correlations in the construction of the credit risk charge. Institutions that have greater diversification than typical banks cannot enjoy lower capital charges.

More generally, there is still no acceptance of internal **portfolio credit risk models**, developed at great cost by advanced banking organization. Perhaps this is because these models are still not fully developed, rely on incomplete data, and seem to generate different economic capital numbers.

Regulators, however, recognize that in the long term, a new framework, called Basel III, could be developed so that firms will indeed be allowed to use their internal models. In the meantime, the application of Basel II will create an accumulation of data that should improve our understanding of financial risks.

Example 31-14: FRM Exam 2002—Question 72

Under the New Basel Accord, which of the following best defines the overall minimum capital ratio?

a) (Total capital) / (Credit risk + Market risk + Operational risk) = Capital ratio > 8%

b) (Total capital) / (Credit risk+ Market risk + Operational risk) = Capital ratio < 8%

c) (Total capital) / (Credit risk + Market risk) = 8%

d) (Tier 1 capital) / (Market risk + Operational risk) = 8%

31.6   Answers to Chapter Examples

Example 31-1: FRM Exam 1997—Question 17

b) In addition to all the risks in the trading book (interest rate, equity, forex, commodity), the market capital charges also include forex and commodity risks in the banking book.

Example 31-2: FRM Exam 2002—Question 71

a) Tier 1 capital includes equity capital, disclosed reserves, and retained earnings. Tier

2 capital includes undisclosed reserves, hybrid debt, and subordinated debt.

Example 31-3: FRM Exam 2000—Question 139

a) Tier 1 capital includes common stock, disclosed reserves, and noncumulative preferred shares.

Example 31-4: FRM Exam 1999—Question 189

d) Allowable tier 1 capital includes equity (book equity) and disclosed reserves only. Subordinated debt with maturity greater than five years is only for tier 2.

Example 31-5: FRM Exam 2001—Question 38

b) Under the Basel I rules, the charge is $100 \times 50\% \times 8\% = \$4$ million.

Example 31-6: FRM Exam 2001—Question 45

a) From Table 31-3, the add-on factor is 10%. This gives a credit exposure of $\$15 + \$50 \times 10\% = \$20$ million, and a credit risk charge of $\$20 \times 8\% = \$1.6$ million.

Example 31-7: FRM Exam 2000—Question 134

a) Unfunded commitments are off–balance sheet items (unlike funded commitments, which are loans). Below a year, the credit conversion factor is zero, which means zero BIS weight.

Example 31-8: FRM Exam 2000—Question 137

b) Unfunded commitments with maturities greater than a year (and irrevocable) have a 50% conversion factor, or 4% BIS weight instead of the usual 8%.

Example 31-9: FRM Exam 2000—Question 135

c) The capital charges for the trading portfolio do not follow the 8% credit risk charges, so a) does not apply. A U.S. government bond held in the banking book has a zero weight, so b) is false. An investment in a venture capital fund, however, is typically not marked to market and as a result will be classified into the banking book with the usual 8% risk charge.

Example 31-10: FRM Exam 1999—Question 134

b) The BIS method does not take into account the credit rating of the counterparty. The add-on already incorporates the type of instrument and maturity. The analyst needs only items II and III.

Example 31-11: FRM Exam 1998—Question 3

a) An 8% capital charge applies to this bond. We buy $100 worth of the bond, which is funded at the bank rate, for a net dollar return of $\$100[(L+0.15\%) - (L-0.05\%)] = \$0.20$. We need to keep \$8 in capital, which we assume is not invested. The rate of return is then $\$0.20/\$8 = 2.5\%$. (Also note that the capital adequacy rules are from the Basel Committee on Banking Supervision, not the BIS.)

Example 31-12: FRM Exam 2002—Question 14

a) Under the IRB approach, banks compute PDs, which are then entered into a Basel function to derive capital charges. Internal models are still not allowed, so b) is false. Also, c) is not correct because this is the standardized approach. Finally, d) is false because the credit charge is not related to trading.

Example 31-13: FRM Exam 2002—Question 69

c) Banks will provide their estimates of EDF and LGD, which will be entered into a risk weight function.

Example 31-14: FRM Exam 2002—Question 72

a) The ratio of capital to total risk must be greater than 8%.

Chapter 32

The Basel Market Risk Charges

After the credit risk charges were instituted in 1988, regulators turned their attention to market risk in response to the increased proprietary trading activities of commercial banks. The Capital Accord was amended in 1996 to include a capital charge for market risk, to be implemented by January 1, 1998, at the latest. The capital charge can be computed using two methods. The first is based on a "standardized" method, similar to the credit risk system with add-ons determined by the Basel rules. Because diversification effects are not fully recognized, this method generates a high market risk charge.

The second method is called the **internal models approach** (IMA) and is based on the banks' own risk management systems, which are more precise and adaptable than the rigid set of standardized rules. This approach must be viewed as a breakthrough in financial regulation. For the first time, regulators relied on the banks' own VAR systems to determine the capital charge. Since banks may have an incentive to understate their market risk, however, the internal models approach also includes a strong system of verification, based on backtesting.

This chapter discusses the implementation of capital charges for market risk. Section 32.1 summarizes the standardized method. The application of the internal models approach is described in Section 32.2. Section 32.3 then turns to stress testing. Finally, the framework for backtesting is presented in Section 32.4.

32.1 The Standardized Method

The objective of the market risk amendment was "to provide an explicit capital cushion for the price risk to which banks are exposed." This was viewed as important in further strengthening the soundness and stability of the international banking system and of financial markets. The original proposal was issued in April 1993 and was based on a prespecified **building-block approach**. Essentially, this consists of attaching add-ons to all positions, which are added up across the portfolio.

The bank's market risk is first computed for portfolios exposed to interest rate risk (IR), equity risk (EQ), foreign-currency risk (FX), commodity risk (CO), and option risk (OP), using specific guidelines. The bank's total risk is then obtained from the summation of risks across the four categories. Because the construction of the risk charge follows a prespecified process, this approach is sometimes called the **standardized method**.[1]

The bank's total risk is obtained from the summation of risks across different types of risks, j, on each day, t:

$$\text{MRC}_t^{\text{STD}} = \sum_{j=1}^{5} \text{MRC}_t^j = \text{MRC}_t^{\text{IR}} + \text{MRC}_t^{\text{EQ}} + \text{MRC}_t^{\text{FX}} + \text{MRC}_t^{\text{CO}} + \text{MRC}_t^{\text{OP}} \quad (32.1)$$

The standardized model is relatively easy to implement. It is also robust to model misspecification. The building-block approach, however, has been criticized on several grounds. First, the risk classification is arbitrary. For instance, a capital charge of 8% is applied uniformly to equities and currencies without regard for their actual return volatilities. Different currencies have different volatilities relative to the dollar that also can change over time.

Second, the approach leads to high capital requirements because risk charges are systematically added up across different sources of risk, which ignores diversification. For instance, fixed-income charges are computed for each currency separately, then added up across markets. Implicitly, this approach is a worst-case scenario that assumes that the worst loss will occur at the same time across all sources of risk. In practice, these markets are not perfectly correlated, which means that the worst loss will be less than the sum of individual worst losses. Thus the standardized model fails to recognize the benefits of diversification, which gives no incentive for banks to diversify prudently. Recognition of these problems has led to another, more flexible approach based on internal models.

---

[1] For more detail, see BCBS (1996), *Amendment to the Basel Capital Accord to Incorporate Market Risk*.

32.2   The Internal Models Approach

In contrast to the simplistic standardized approach, the **internal models approach** (IMA) relies on internal risk management systems developed by banks themselves as the basis for the market risk charge.

This approach must be considered a watershed in financial regulation. For the first time, regulators implicitly recognized that banks had developed sophisticated risk management systems, far more precise than simple standardized rules. Indeed, the complexity and speed of development of innovations in financial markets is such that rigid rules can be easily skirted with new products. The other motivation for the IMA is that because this approach leads to lower capital charges, banks will have an incentive to develop sound risk management systems.

Regulators, however, have not totally given up their authority. A bank can use internal models only after it has been explicitly approved by the supervisory authority. The bank must satisfy qualitative requirements first. Second, the output is subject to a rigorous backtesting process.

32.2.1   Qualitative Requirements

Not any bank can use internal models, though. Regulators first must have some general reassurance that the bank's risk management system is sound. As a result, banks have to satisfy various **qualitative standards**:

- *Independent risk control unit.* The bank must have a risk control unit that is independent of trading and reports to senior management. This structure minimizes potential conflicts of interest.
- *Backtesting.* The bank must conduct a regular backtesting program, which provides essential feedback on the accuracy of internal VAR models.
- *Involvement.* Senior management and the board need to be involved in the risk control process and devote sufficient resources to risk management.
- *Integration.* The bank's internal risk model must be integrated with day-to-day management. This is to avoid situations where a bank could compute its VAR simply for regulatory purposes and otherwise ignore it.
- *Use of limits.* The bank should use its risk measurement systems to set internal trading and exposure limits.

- *Stress testing.* The bank should conduct stress tests on a regular basis. Stress tests results should be reviewed by senior management and be reflected in policies and limits set by management and the board of directors.

- *Compliance.* The bank should ensure compliance with a documented set of policies.

- *Independent review.* An independent review of the trading units and of the risk control unit should be performed regularly, at least once a year. This includes verification with backtesting.

32.2.2   The Market Risk Charge

In addition to the preceding requirements, the bank's risk model must contain a sufficient number of risk factors, where the definition of *sufficient* depends on the extent and complexity of trading activities.

For material exposures to interest rates, there should be at least six factors for yield curve risk plus separate factors to model spread risk. For equity risk, the model should at least involve beta mapping on an index; a more detailed approach would have industry and even individual risk factor modeling. For active trading in commodities, the risk model should account for movements in spot rates plus convenience yields. Banks should also capture the nonlinear price characteristics of option positions, including vega risk. Correlations *within* broad risk categories are recognized explicitly. Regulators can also recognize correlations *across* risk categories provided the model is sound.

Once these requirements are satisfied, the market risk charge is computed according to these rules:

■ *Quantitative parameters.* The computation of daily VAR shall be based on a set of uniform quantitative inputs:

—A horizon of 10 trading days, or two calendar weeks; banks can, however, scale their daily VAR by the square root of time.

—A 99% confidence interval.

—An observation period based on at least a year of historical data or, if a non-equal weighting scheme is used, an average time lag of at least six months.[2]

---

[2]This is similar to a duration computation. For instance, with equal weights over the last 250 trading days, this average time lag is $\sum_{t=1}^{N} t(1/N) = N(N+1)/2 \ (1/N) = (N+1)/2 = 125.5$ days, or six months. Note that this rules out models such as the GARCH process if the weight on more recent

—Updating at least quarterly, or whenever prices are subject to material changes (so that sudden increases in risk can be picked up).

■ *Market risk charge.* The general market capital charge shall be set at the higher of the previous day's VAR, or the average VAR over the last 60 business days, times a "multiplicative" factor k. The exact value of this **multiplicative factor** is to be determined by local regulators, subject to an absolute floor of 3.

The purpose of this factor is twofold. Without this risk factor, a bank would be expected to have losses that exceed its capital in one 10-day period out of a hundred, or about once in four years. This does not seem prudent. Second, the factor serves as a buffer against model misspecifications—for instance, assuming a normal distribution when the distribution really has fatter tails.

■ *Plus factor.* A penalty component, called the **plus factor**, shall be added to the multiplicative factor, k, if verification of the VAR forecasts reveals that the bank systematically underestimates its risks. We will discuss this further in the context of backtesting.

The purpose of this factor is to penalize a bank that provides an overly optimistic projection of its market risk. It provides a feedback mechanism that rewards truthful internal monitoring and should provide incentives to build sound risk management systems.

In summary, the market risk charge on any day t is

$$\text{MRC}_t^{\text{IMA}} = \text{Max}\left(k\frac{1}{60} \sum_{i=1}^{60} \text{VAR}_{t-i},\ \text{VAR}_{t-1} \right) + \text{SRC}_t \qquad (32.2)$$

where VAR_{t-i} is the bank's VAR over a 10-day horizon at the 99% level of confidence. Here the factor k reflects both the multiplicative and plus factors.

The first term consists of a multiplier k times the average VAR over the last 60 days. The second term uses solely yesterday's VAR, and will be binding only if the positions change dramatically. In practice, this second term is rarely binding.

Finally, SRC represents the **specific risk charge**, which represents a buffer against idiosyncratic factors, including default and event risk, related to individual bond and equity issuers. Banks that use internal models can incorporate specific risk in their

---

observations is too high.

VAR as long as they (i) satisfy additional criteria and (ii) can demonstrate that they can deal with event and default risk.[3]

32.2.3   Combination of Approaches

The banks' market risk capital requirement will be either (a) the risk charge obtained by the standardized methodology, obtained from an arithmetic summation across the five risk categories, or (b) the risk charge obtained by the internal models approach, or (c) a mixture of (a) and (b) summed arithmetically.

Example 32-1: FRM Exam 2002—Question 10

Banks have to meet a number of qualitative criteria before they are permitted to use a models-based approach. The qualitative criteria include:

a) The bank should have an independent risk control unit that is responsible for the design and implementation of the bank's risk management system; the unit should conduct a regular backtesting program.

b) The board of directors and senior management should be actively involved in the risk control process; the bank's internal risk measurement model must be closely integrated into the day-to-day risk management process of the bank; an independent review of the risk management system should be carried out regularly; the risk measurement system should be used in conjunction with internal trading and exposure limits.

c) a) and b) together.

d) a) and b), except that the risk measurement system does not have to be used in conjunction with exposure limits.

Example 32-2: FRM Exam 1999—Question 190

The Amendment to the Capital Accord requires that internal models

a) Utilize at least six months of historical data

b) Utilize at least one year of equally weighted historical data

c) Utilize enough historical data so that the weighted average age of the data is at least six months

d) Utilize two years of historical data, unequally weighted

---

[3]The difficulty with event and default risk is that it is typically not reflected in historical data. When a bank cannot satisfy (ii), a prudential surcharge is applied to the measure of specific risk. (This is detailed in the September 1997 modification of the Market Risk Amendment, available at www.bis.org/publ/bcbs24a.pdf.)

Example 32-3: FRM Exam 2001—Question 42

Which of the following best describes the quantitative parameters of the internal models approach?

a) 10-day trading horizon, 99% confidence interval, minimum one year of data, minimum quarterly updates

b) 1-day trading horizon, 95% confidence interval, five years of data, updated weekly

c) 1-day trading horizon, 99% confidence interval, minimum one year of data, updated monthly

d) 10-day trading horizon, 97.5% confidence interval, minimum five years of data, updated daily

---

Example 32-4: FRM Exam 1999—Question 184

The RiskMetrics VAR for a portfolio is $1,000,000. What is the approximate Basel Committee VAR?

a) $4,450,000

b) $225,000

c) $1,000,000

d) $1,412,121

Example 32-5: FRM Exam 1999—Question 196

Under the Amendment to the Capital Accord to Incorporate Market Risks, VAR

a) Must be calculated using a 99th-percentile one-tailed confidence interval and a 10-day holding period

b) Must be calculated using a 99th-percentile one-tailed confidence interval, but may use a shorter holding period and a square-root-of-time scaling

c) May use any percentile (e.g., 95th, as used in RiskMetrics) scale to the 99th percentile using normal distribution assumptions; may use a shorter or longer holding period than 10 days, and scale using the square root of time

d) May use any percentile or holding period as long as backtesting results are satisfactory

---

Example 32-6: FRM Exam 1999—Question 197

The capital requirement specified in the Amendment to the Capital Accord to Incorporate Market Risks is

a) The previous day's VAR number multiplied by a multiplication factor

b) The greater of (i) the previous day's VAR number multiplied by a multiplication factor or (ii) the average of the daily VAR over the last 60 business days multiplied by a multiplication factor

c) The greater of (i) the previous day's VAR risk number or (ii) the average of the daily VAR over the last 60 business days multiplied by a multiplication factor

d) The greater of (i) the previous day's VAR number multiplied by a factor or (ii) the maximum of the daily VAR over the last 60 business days

---

Example 32-7: FRM Exam 1999—Question 194

According to the current version of the Amendment to the Capital Accord to Incorporate Market Risks, a specific risk method must meet certain criteria if a bank is to be allowed to use it for calculating capital requirements. Which of the following statements are *true*?

  I. If the method does not meet the criteria, the capital figure produced for specific risk is subject to a lower limit of 50% of the capital figure under the standardized methodology.

 II. If the method does not meet the criteria, the bank must use the figure produced by the standardized methodology instead.

III. If the method does meet the criteria, but the bank has no methodologies in place that adequately capture event and default risk for its traded debt and equity positions, the specific risk capital charge is subject to a prudential surcharge.

IV. The specific risk charge is not affected by any methodologies the bank may have for measuring default or event risk, as these risks are currently covered by credit risk capital charges.

a) I and IV

b) I and III

c) II and IV

d) II and III

Example 32-8: FRM Exam 1998—Question 18

What would be the market risk capital requirement for a bank with a one-day VAR of $100 and a specific risk surcharge of $30, based on the current BIS minimum capital requirements?

a) $300

b) $316

c) $949

d) $979

Example 32-9: FRM Exam 1998—Question 19

Which one of the following statements is *false* regarding the calculation of the specific risk charge for the market risk capital rule?

a) If the bank can demonstrate that its specific risk modeling captures all aspects of specific risk, a surcharge will not be required.

b) If a bank's model captures idiosyncratic variation in its debt and equity portfolios, but does not measure default and event risk, a model calculated surcharge should be added to the capital charge.

c) Specific risk includes default and event risk but not idiosyncratic variation.

d) If a bank's model does not measure specific risk, the surcharge for specific risk should be 100% of the standardized specific risk charge.

32.3 Stress Testing

Stress testing is one of the qualitative requirements for a bank to use internal models. The purpose of stress testing is to identify events that could greatly impact the bank but are not captured in VAR measures. A major goal of stress testing is to "evaluate the capacity of the bank's capital to absorb large potential losses."

Stress testing can be described as a process to identify and manage situations that could cause extraordinary losses. This can be done with a set of tools, including (i) scenario analysis; (ii) stressing models, volatilities, and correlations; and (iii) policy responses.

Scenario analysis consists of evaluating the portfolio under various states of the world. Stress testing also involves evaluating the effect of changes in valuation models, as well as in inputs such as volatilities and correlations. Policy responses consist of identifying steps the bank can take to reduce its risk and conserve capital.

Stress tests fall into three categories:

- *Scenarios requiring no simulation.* These consist of analyzing large past losses over a recent reporting period to gain a better understanding of the vulnerabilities of the bank. While providing useful information, this approach is backward looking and does not account for changes in portfolio composition.

- *Scenarios requiring a simulation.* These consist of running simulations of the current portfolio subject to large historical shocks—for example, the stock market crash of 1987, the ERM crisis of September 1992, the bond market rout of 1994, and so on.

■ *Bank-specific scenarios.* These scenarios would be driven by the current position of the bank, instead of historical experience. For instance, a strategy of going long the off-the-run bond while shorting the equivalent on-the-run bond may appear safe based on recent historical patterns of high correlations between these two bonds. With high correlations, a loss on one position will be offset by a gain on the other. This may not be the case, however, if correlations break down. So the institution should evaluate the effect of a correlation breakdown in this particular example.

The assessment of stress testing is essential to evaluating the risk profile of institutions. Results should be reported routinely to senior management and periodically to the board of directors. When stress test results reveal a particular vulnerability, corrective action should be taken, by reducing or hedging the position.

In practice, stress testing is much more subjective than VAR measures. The Basel guidelines are suitably vague. First, there is no systematic method to identify scenarios of interest. Second, the process assigns no probability to the extraordinary loss that has been identified. As a result, it is often difficult to know how to follow up on stress test results. In particular, it would be impractical to guard against every single potential disaster. Overall, however, the most useful aspect of stress testing is that it can help to identify potential weaknesses in the bank's portfolio.

Example 32-10: FRM Exam 1999—Question 195

According to the current version of the Amendment to the Capital Accord to Incorporate Market Risks in relation to stress testing, which of the following statements is *true*?

  I. Stress testing results should be communicated to traders.
  II. Stress testing results should be communicated to senior management.
III. Stress testing results should be communicated to the bank's board of directors.
IV. Limits should be set on the loss indicated by stress tests.
  V. The levels of limits (e.g., VAR limits) should reflect the results of stress testing.
a) I, II, III, and IV
b) I, II, and V
c) II, III, and V
d) II, III, and IV

Example 32-11: FRM Exam 1998—Question 20

Value at risk (VAR) measures should be supplemented by portfolio stress testing because

a) VAR does not indicate how large the losses will be beyond the specified confidence level.

b) Stress testing provides a precise maximum loss level.

c) VAR measures are correct only 95% of the time.

d) Stress testing scenarios incorporate reasonably probable events.

Example 32-12: FRM Exam 1997—Question 15

Which one of the following is *not* an explicitly permitted VAR modeling technique of the Amendment to the Capital Accord to Incorporate Market Risk?

a) Historical simulation

b) Variance/covariance matrices

c) Monte Carlo simulation

d) Scenario analysis

32.4   Backtesting

Internal models were allowed by the Basel Committee in large part because they are amenable to verification. **Verification** is the general process of checking whether the model is adequate. This can be made with a set of tools, including backtesting, stress testing, and independent review and oversight. This section focuses on backtesting techniques for verifying the accuracy of VAR models. **Backtesting** is a statistical testing framework that consists of checking whether actual trading losses are in line with VAR forecasts. Each exceedance is called an **exception**.

32.4.1   Measuring Exceptions

First, we have to define the **trading outcome**. One definition is the actual profit or loss over the next day. This return, however, does not exactly correspond to the previous day's VAR. All VAR measures assume a *frozen* portfolio from the close of one trading day to the next, and ignore fee income. In practice, trading portfolios do change. Intraday trading will generally increase risk. Fee income is more stable and decreases risk. Although these effects may offset each other, the actual portfolio may have more or less volatility than implied by VAR.

This is why it is recommended to construct **hypothetical portfolios**, which are constructed to match the VAR measure exactly. Their returns are obtained from fixed positions applied to the actual price changes on all securities, measured from close to close.

The Basel framework recommends using both hypothetical and actual trading outcomes in backtests. The two approaches are likely to provide complementary information on the quality of the risk management system.

32.4.2 Statistical Decision Rules

The Basel backtesting framework consists of recording *daily* exceptions of the 99% VAR over the last year. Note that even though capital requirements are based on a 10-day period, backtesting uses a daily interval, which entails more observations. On average, we would expect 1% of 250, or 2.5, instances of exceptions over the last year. Too many exceptions indicate that either the model is understating VAR or the bank is unlucky. How do we decide which explanation is most likely?

Such statistical testing framework must account for two types of error:

■ **Type 1 errors**, which describe the probability of rejecting a correct model, due to bad luck

■ **Type 2 errors**, which describe the probability of not rejecting a model that is false

Ideally, one would want to structure a test that has low type 1 and type 2 error rates. In practice, one has to trade off one type of error against the other. Most statistical tests fix the type 1 error rate, say at 5%, and structure the test to minimize the type 2 error rate, or to maximize its power. The **power of a test** is 1 minus the type 2 error rate.

Define x as the number of exceptions, n as the total number of observations, and p as the confidence level. The random variable x then has a binomial distribution. Armed with this information, we can find the cutoff point for a type 1 error rate.

32.4.3 The Penalty Zones

The Basel Committee has decided that up to four exceptions is acceptable, which defines a "green" zone. If the number of exceptions is five or more, the bank falls into a "yellow" or "red" zone and incurs a progressive penalty where the multiplicative factor, k, is increased from 3 to 4. The "plus factor" is described in Table 32-1.

An incursion into the red zone generates an *automatic*, nondiscretionary penalty. This is because it would be extremely unlikely to observe more than 10 exceptions if the model was indeed correct.

TABLE 32-1 The Basel Penalty Zones

Zone	Number of Exceptions	Potential Increase in k
Green	0 to 4	0.00
Yellow	5	0.40
	6	0.50
	7	0.65
	8	0.75
	9	0.85
Red	≥ 10	1.00

If the number of exceptions falls within the yellow zone, the supervisor has discretion to apply a penalty, depending on the causes for the exceptions. The Basel Committee uses these categories:

- *Basic integrity of the model:* The deviation occurred because the positions were incorrectly reported or because of an error in the program code. This is a very serious flaw. In this case, a penalty "should" apply and corrective action should be taken.

- *Deficient model accuracy:* The deviation occurred because the model does not measure risk with enough precision (e.g., does not have enough risk factors). This is a serious flaw, too. A penalty "should" apply and the model should be reviewed.

- *Intraday trading:* Positions changed during the day. Here, a penalty "should be considered." If the exception disappears with the hypothetical return, the problem is not in the bank's VAR model.

- *Bad luck:* Markets were particularly volatile or correlations changed. These exceptions "should be expected to occur at least some of the time" and may not suggest a deficiency of the model but, rather, bad luck.

Example 32-13: FRM Exam 2002—Question 20

Which of the following procedures is essential in validating the VAR estimates?
a) Stress testing
b) Scenario analysis
c) Backtesting
d) Once approved by regulators, no further validation is required.

Example 32-14: FRM Exam 1999—Question 192

The Amendment to the Capital Accord recommends that backtesting compare VAR to

a) Actual P&L

b) Hypothetical P&L (i.e., P&L based on end-of-day positions)

c) Both actual and hypothetical P&L

d) Does not specify a choice

Example 32-15: FRM Exam 1999—Question 193

The Amendment to the Capital Accord defines the "yellow zone" as the following range of exceptions out of 250 observations:

a) 3 to 7

b) 5 to 9

c) 6 to 9

d) 6 to 10

Example 32-16: FRM Exam 1999—Question 191

For purposes of backtesting a VAR internal model, the Amendment to the Capital Accord requires

a) Comparing one year of daily P&L to a 99% one-tail confidence 1-day VAR with an exception produced whenever $P\&L < -VAR$

b) Comparing one year of daily P&L to a 98% two-tail confidence 1-day VAR with an exception produced whenever P&L is outside the interval $(-VAR, +VAR)$

c) Comparing one year of rolling 10-day P&L to a 99% one-tail confidence 10-day VAR with an exception produced whenever $P\&L < -VAR$

d) Comparing one year of rolling 10-day P&L to a 99% one-tail confidence 10-day VAR with an exception produced whenever $P\&L < -3VAR$

Example 32-17: FRM Exam 2002—Question 23

Backtesting routinely compares daily profits and losses with model-generated risk measures to gauge the quality and accuracy of risk measurement systems. The 1996 Market Risk Amendment describes the backtesting framework that is to accompany the internal models capital requirement. This backtesting framework involves

  I. The size of outliers

  II. The use of risk measure calibrated to a 1-day holding period

III. The size of outliers for a risk measure calibrated to a 10-day holding period

IV. Number of outliers

a) II and III

b) II only

c) I and II

d) II and IV

32.5   Answers to Chapter Examples

Example 32-1: FRM Exam 2002—Question 10

c) The qualitative criteria include those in a), independent risk control and backtesting, as well as those in b), involvement, integration, independent review, and use of limits.

Example 32-2: FRM Exam 1999—Question 190

c) Answer b) is correct if the bank uses fixed weights only. Otherwise, the average time lag of the observations cannot be less than six months.

Example 32-3: FRM Exam 2001—Question 42

a) The IMA is based on a 10-day horizon, 99% confidence level, and one year of data, with at least quarterly updates.

Example 32-4: FRM Exam 1999—Question 184

a) Assuming normally and independently distributed returns, the RM VAR needs to be adjusted from 95% to 99% confidence and from 1 day to 10 days. This gives $1,000,000 \times (2.326/1.645) \times \sqrt{10} = \$4.5$ million.

Example 32-5: FRM Exam 1999—Question 196

b) Under the IMA, VAR must be computed at the 99% confidence level, either over a 10-day period or over a 1-day period with appropriate time scaling.

Example 32-6: FRM Exam 1999—Question 197

c) See Equation (32.2).

Example 32-7: FRM Exam 1999—Question 194

d) Banks can use their internal models if they satisfy a list of criteria; otherwise, they have to use the standardized approach. Even so, if they do not account for default and event risk, a prudential surcharge applies.

Example 32-8: FRM Exam 1998—Question 18

d) The total MRC is $3 \times \$100 \times \sqrt{10} + \$30 = \$949 + \$30 = \$979$.

Example 32-9: FRM Exam 1998—Question 19

c) Specific risk includes (i) idiosyncratic risk plus (ii) default/event risk.

Example 32-10: FRM Exam 1999—Question 195

c) Stress test results should be reported to senior management and the board, who have control over traders. So II and III are correct. V is also correct, because it describes a situation where the stress test exercise leads to a reduction in the position. IV is wrong. The loss indicated by stress tests is too large to establish stop-loss limits; it would then be too late to save the bank.

Example 32-11: FRM Exam 1998—Question 20

a) VAR only gives an indication of the worst loss under normal conditions (e.g., 95% confidence). It does not address the behavior in the tails. Stress test results are certainly not precise.

Example 32-12: FRM Exam 1997—Question 15

d) Scenario analysis is not a probabilistic description of potential losses, unlike the covariance matrix approach or historical or Monte Carlo simulations.

Example 32-13: FRM Exam 2002—Question 20

c) VAR estimates need to be compared with actual P&L results to be validated, which is called backtesting.

Example 32-14: FRM Exam 1999—Question 192

c) Both measures are informative.

Example 32-15: FRM Exam 1999—Question 193

b) See Table 32-1.

Example 32-16: FRM Exam 1999—Question 191

a) Backtesting is based on daily data at the one-tail 99% level.

Example 32-17: FRM Exam 2002—Question 23

d) The backtesting framework in the IMA counts only the number of times a daily exception occurs (i.e., a loss worse than VAR). So this involves the number of outliers and the daily VAR measure.

About the CD-ROM

Introduction

This appendix provides you with information on the contents of the CD that accompanies this book. For the latest and greatest information, please refer to the ReadMe file located at the root of the CD.

System Requirements

- A computer with a processor running at 120 Mhz or faster
- At least 32 MB of total RAM installed on your computer; for best performance, we recommend at least 64 MB
- A CD-ROM drive

Using the CD with Windows

To install the items from the CD to your hard drive, follow these steps:

1. Insert the CD into your computer's CD-ROM drive.
2. The CD-ROM interface will appear. The interface provides a simple point-and-click way to explore the contents of the CD.

If the opening screen of the CD-ROM does not appear automatically, follow these steps to access the CD:

1. Click the Start button on the left end of the taskbar and then choose Run from the menu that pops up.
2. In the dialog box that appears, type d:\setup.exe. (If your CD-ROM drive is not drive d, fill in the appropriate letter in place of d.) This brings up the CD Interface described in the preceding set of steps.

Using the CD with a MAC

1. Insert the CD into your computer's CD-ROM drive.
2. The CD-ROM icon appears on your desktop, double-click the icon.
3. Double-click the Start icon.
4. The CD-ROM interface will appear. The interface provides a simple point-and-click way to explore the contents of the CD.

What's on the CD

The following sections provide a summary of the software and other materials you'll find on the CD.

Content

The *Financial Risk Manager Sample Review Test* CD-ROM is a preparatory review for anyone studying for the FRM(Exam and for risk professionals interested in self-study to review and improve their knowledge of market, credit, and operational risk management. This interactive CD-ROM contains hundreds of multiple-choice questions from the 2000, 2001 and 2002 FRM exams, with answers and solutions provided.

Customer Care

If you have trouble with the CD-ROM, please call the Wiley Product Technical Support phone number at (800) 762-2974. Outside the United States, call 1(317) 572-3994. You can also contact Wiley Product Technical Support at http://www.wiley.com/techsupport. John Wiley & Sons will provide technical support only for installation and other general quality control items. For technical support on the applications themselves, consult the program's vendor or author.

To place additional orders or to request information about other Wiley products, please call (877) 762-2974.

Index